T0342566

STRANGERS WITHIN

Strangers Within

THE RISE AND FALL OF
THE NEW CHRISTIAN
TRADING ELITE

Francisco Bethencourt

PRINCETON UNIVERSITY PRESS
PRINCETON & OXFORD

Published by Princeton University Press
41 William Street, Princeton, New Jersey 08540
99 Banbury Road, Oxford OX2 6JX

press.princeton.edu

All Rights Reserved

Library of Congress Cataloging-in-Publication Data

Names: Bethencourt, Francisco, author.
Title: Strangers within : the rise and fall of the New Christian trading
    elite / Francisco Bethencourt.
Other titles: Rise and fall of the New Christian trading elite
Description: Princeton : Princeton University Press, [2024] | Includes
    bibliographical references and index.
Identifiers: LCCN 2023018699 (print) | LCCN 2023018700 (ebook) | ISBN
    9780691209913 (hardback) | ISBN 9780691256801 (ebook)
Subjects: LCSH: Crypto-Jews—Iberian Peninsula—Economic conditions. |
    Crypto-Jews—Iberian Peninsula—Commerce. | Jewish merchants—Social
    conditions. | Religion—Economic aspects. | Commerce—History. |
    Economic history—16th century. | Economic history—1600–1750.
Classification: LCC DS135.S7 B52 2024 (print) | LCC DS135.S7 (ebook) |
    DDC 946/.004924009031—dc23/eng/20230630
LC record available at https://lccn.loc.gov/2023018699
LC ebook record available at https://lccn.loc.gov/2023018700

British Library Cataloging-in-Publication Data is available

Editorial: Ben Tate, Josh Drake
Production Editorial: Elizabeth Byrd
Jacket: Katie Osborne
Production: Danielle Amatucci
Publicity: William Pagdatoon, Charlotte Coyne

Jacket Credit: Anthonis van Dyck, Filips Godines, around 1630,
Bavarian State Painting Collections - Alte Pinakothek Munich

This book has been composed in Miller

Printed on acid-free paper. ∞

Printed in the United States of America

10 9 8 7 6 5 4 3 2 1

For João and Sophie

TABLE OF CONTENTS

ILLUSTRATIONS

MAPS AND GENEALOGIES

NOTES ON INDIVIDUALS AND LOCATIONS

IN THE EARLY modern period, the spelling of personal names varied significantly between languages and places, sometimes even within the same document. I decided to modernise the spelling in most common personal names, indicating some variations. I respected, as much as possible, divergent accentuation of the same names in Spain and Portugal (such as Núñez and Nunes). I have left names written consistently in the original untouched, such as the feminine name Gracia. I have used the English translation for the names of primary kings and popes. I also used the English denomination of the main cities, but I have left distinguishable cases such as Livorno. Fidelity to my sources made me use Constantinople rather than Istanbul, Salonika rather than Thessaloniki, Aleppo rather than Haleb, and Ragusa rather than Dubrovnik.

ABBREVIATIONS

ACDF   Archivio della Congregazzione per la Dottrina della Fede (Vatican)

AGI   Archivo General de Indias (Seville)

AGN   Archivo General de la Nación (Lima)

AGS   Archivo General de Simancas (Simancas)

AHN   Archivo Histórico Nacional (Madrid)

AIPSA   Arquivo do Instituto Português de Santo António (Rome)

ANTT   Arquivo Nacional da Torre do Tombo (Lisbon)

ASBI   Archivio Storico della Banca d'Italia

ASC   Archivio Storico Capitolino (Rome)

ASF   Archivio di Stato di Firenze (Florence)

ASR   Archivio di Stato di Roma (Rome)

BINE   Biblioteca de la Iglesia Nacional de España (Rome)

BL   British Library (London)

BNE   Biblioteca Nacional de España (Madrid)

BNP   Biblioteca Nacional de Portugal (Lisbon)

CDP   *Corpo Diplomático Portuguez*, 15 vols. (Lisbon: Imprensa Nacional, 1862–1936)

NA   National Archives for the UK government, England, and Wales (London)

RA-B   Rijksarchief Antwerpen-Beveren (Antwerp)

STRANGERS WITHIN

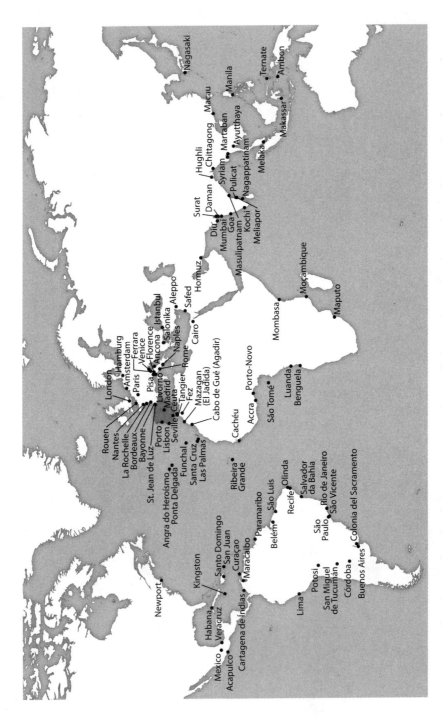

MAP 1. New Christians and Sephardic communities in the world during the sixteenth to eighteenth centuries. The map only indicates the main towns with New Christians and, in some cases, Sephardic Jews. The concentration of New Christians in Iberia is highlighted.

Introduction

WHY DID NEW CHRISTIAN MERCHANTS, descendants of Jews forced to convert to Christianity in Iberia between 1391 and 1497, rise to play a pivotal role in intercontinental trade in the following two centuries only to decline and virtually disappear as an ethnic elite by the mid-eighteenth century? This question guides this book and links to issues of identity, religious allegiance, economic and social opportunities, political negotiation, and cultural innovation. It is a global study, since this New Christian elite moved between the kingdoms of Castile, Aragon, and Portugal and between the Iberian empires; from Western Europe to Africa and the Ottoman Empire; from the Portuguese Atlantic to the Indian Ocean and East Asia; from Spanish America to Asia; and from Iberia to Italy, France, Flanders, the Netherlands, Germany, England, and Dutch and English America.

1. Object and Argument

One way into this world is the case of Duarte de Paz, and his son Tomé Pegado de Paz, who was born in the Portuguese city of Porto, allegedly around 1536. In 1552, Duarte, who had taken refuge in Constantinople, asked for Tomé to be sent to him. The boy's uncle, Diogo de Paz, a well-known New Christian merchant and farmer of the king's rents, organised the journey to Constantinople.[1] Tomé went first to Venice, where arrangements were made for him to travel with the mission of the new French Ambassador to the Ottoman Empire, Michel de Codignac.[2] The father had had a complicated life: having achieved the status of a wealthy merchant, contractor for royal rents, and member of the military order of Christ, he compromised this high financial and social position to become a New Christian agent (or procurator) in Rome, where he tried to block the negotiations of the Portuguese king for the establishment of the Inquisition.

Duarte de Paz had some initial success in Rome but was then subjected to a murder attempt in which he was stabbed fifteen times on the street, probably by agents of the Portuguese king, John III. His efforts were eventually defeated by the financial and political power of John III, who in 1536 obtained the creation of the tribunal of faith. Protected by the pope but isolated from his New Christian sponsors, who accused him both of duplicity concerning the king and ludicrous promises to the papal curia, Duarte finally escaped to Constantinople via Venice. In Constantinople, he first converted to Judaism, and then became a Muslim, according to the testimony of his son before the Inquisition.[3] For the rest of his life, Duarte de Paz tried to revive his relationship with the Portuguese king by providing intelligence concerning Jewish and New Christian involvement in Ottoman policies, particularly in the Indian Ocean.

After the death of his father, Tomé Pegado de Paz served the celebrated Duke of Naxos, João Micas, who had become openly Jewish and changed his name to Joseph Nasi when he arrived at Constantinople in 1554. Tomé declared that the Duke of Naxos ordered his circumcision, following which he had married a Jewish young woman.[4] The relationship between Tomé and the Duke of Naxos broke down after an initially successful trip to France to collect 150,000 écus owed by the French king to the Nasi family ended with a disastrous shipwreck. Tomé was saved, but the money disappeared. Later, he was detained in Aleppo and accused of owing more than 1,400 cruzados to the Duke of Naxos.[5] He was released in return for converting to Islam, and finally decided to travel to Portugal to claim the money his father had left to the family in Porto.

Tomé started the journey as a Muslim, then dressed as a Jew, then as a Greek, and finally as a Catholic, in a telling reversal of his previous religious journey. During the trip, he asked for, and obtained, absolution from the archbishop of Ragusa (Dubrovnik) and from the Jesuit Baltasar de Sousa in Rome.[6] In Naples, he was received by the viceroy, who temporarily detained him following accusation from several Christians, former slaves of the Turks.[7] In 1578, he was detained on the coast of Andalusia and brought to Lisbon, where he was interrogated by a secular judge who sent him to the Inquisition. He was liberated in May 1579, after denouncing a significant number of important Jews and New Christians in different parts of the Mediterranean.[8]

This story from the archives reveals the extraordinary reach of a New Christian family in sixteenth-century Europe: the international networks family members built, the different religious allegiances they assumed, and the wide range of places where they could carry on their business activities (Tomé was also in Cyprus, Algiers, and Marseille). It is astonishing how many people recognised Tomé in Naples, having met him in Algiers or Constantinople, and how many people, called to testify before the Inquisition in Lisbon, had interacted with him in various Mediterranean locations. One of them had even been a captive in the same Ottoman galley that had been shipwrecked with Tomé on board. The trial of Tomé Pegado de Paz gives us a vision of the Mediterranean world as highly interconnected. This story offers a glimpse of the world of the New Christian merchant elite whose history has never been comprehensively written.

The history of the New Christians begins in Spain towards the end of the fourteenth century. Massive conversions of Jews into Christians occurred in 1391 in the wake of an anti-Jewish riot in Seville that spread through the urban networks of Castile and Aragon. Converting was the only way for these Jews to save their lives. The following decades saw renewed conflicts between Christians and Jews, with the remaining Jewish communities forced to attend sessions of Catholic preaching targeted at them. Over time, more Jews converted due to the oppressive atmosphere, and Jewish communities shrank, although the two ethnicities kept their ties. From the very beginning, converted Jews were targeted as strangers and as people who were only simulating conversion, and they were soon labelled as *conversos*, *marranos*, or *cristãos novos*. In 1449, an anti-New Christian riot in Toledo sealed the transfer of hatred of Jews to those who had been violently converted. The statutes of blood purity, which excluded New Christians from public offices, were then experimented with for the first time but were opposed by the king and the pope on the grounds that they violated the universalism of the Christian Church.

The Spanish Inquisition was established in 1478. This led to the massive persecution of New Christians, who were accused of returning to practicing Judaism in secrecy. These accusations reinforced the racial divide and contributed to the eventual acceptance of blood purity statutes by the pope and the king. The decision to expel Jewish communities from Spain in 1492 was justified by their supposed contamination of New Christians; many fled to Portugal, following in the steps of previous generations since 1391. In 1496, this decision to expel Jews was replicated and extended to Muslims by the Portuguese king, Manuel. The expulsion of the Jews was not really implemented; rather, they were forced to convert. The establishment of the Inquisition in Portugal in 1536 replicated the institutionalisation of persecution of New Christians in Spain. These harsh decisions completed a long process of exclusion; the segregation of Jewish people was replaced by discrimination against New Christians and their descendants. This new racial divide within Christianity, based on blood purity rules, would define Iberian societies in Europe for the early modern period.

By the end of the fifteenth century, many New Christian families had relatives in the three kingdoms, whilst those who sought to keep their Jewish allegiance migrated to North Africa and the Ottoman Empire. Family relationships were maintained in many cases, even between those who lived as Christians and those who returned to their Jewish faith, migrating to Sephardic communities. This is, by its nature, a connected and international history.

The size of the New Christian ethnicity was very large by the end of the fifteenth century: at least 260,000 people in Iberia in a population estimated from 5 to 5.5 million, which means around 5 percent of the total population.[9] But the members of this ethnicity were overwhelmingly located in urban areas, which in 1500 were home to around 400,000 to 440,000 people.[10] The New Christians would have represented 60 to 65 percent of this urban population and would certainly have been very visible in that dynamic setting. This demographic approach, curiously absent from most of the literature, should be extended to intermarriage, for the stereotype of endogamous New Christians needs to be scrutinised. Robert Rowland estimated 20 percent of intermarriage between Old and New Christians in each generation in the region of Lisbon based on sources from the 1630s.[11] Even if this intermarriage rate varied from region to region and time to time, it is obvious that the number of New Christians grew much faster than the rest of the population due to the rule of defining as New Christian anyone having one Jewish ancestor in several generations. This estimate exposes the fiction of blood purity.

The New Christian merchant elite must be studied taking into consideration this demographic background. They came out of this large ethnic group, mainly from small towns in the interior of Castile and Portugal. They maintained relationships with their places of origin, partly due to the patronage system ties that defined extended families. Rendering assistance to poor family members was an informal obligation, while a large kinship solved practical needs to renew families that did not have direct issue with heirs who could receive an inheritance.

A study of the New Christian merchant elite will need to include these relations, but also the ties this elite established both with Old Christians, in some cases even titled nobility, and Sephardic Jewish communities. This large set of relationships allows us to better understand their role as major players in intercontinental trade and finance, as bankers and lenders to kings, cardinals, bishops, and noblemen. This gave them the economic power to become involved (and interfere) with royal and papal policies, while some obtained aristocratic status as knights of military orders. But we also need to be attentive to the constraints this merchant elite suffered, mainly from inquisitorial persecution and permanent extortion by the royal and papal powers.

The argument of this book is necessarily complex, since it comprehends the rise and fall of the New Christian merchant elite. I summarise it here. The expansion of this elite was related to the inheritance of Jewish economic positions and to a radical enlargement of business opportunities during the late fifteenth and sixteenth centuries. New Christians obtained royal contracts, such as those for tax farming and money lending, and expanded their dealings with the nobility and the dignitaries of the Church; and they combined these activities with investment in new intercontinental trade and distribution circuits in Europe, Asia, Africa, and the Americas. The constant flow of migration to the Mediterranean, Northern Europe, and beyond, which partly absorbed the impact of inquisitorial persecution, the success of New Christians in education, liberal professions, and ecclesiastical careers, and the deft alliances made with Old Christians at all levels, contributed to this expansion. The precarious status of this merchant elite, positioned between royal and papal extortion for support on the one hand, and inquisitorial pressure on the other, stimulated the creation of multiple identities, including those that bypassed blood purity rules and claimed to be Old Christians. This status also triggered innovative behaviour in spiritual and religious quests, artistic and literary expression, and in legal and social thought. The decline of New Christians as a recognisable ethnicity between the mid-seventeenth and the mid-eighteenth centuries resulted from growing inquisitorial persecution, the backlash that followed the pope's suspension of the Portuguese Inquisition from 1674 to 1681, the War of Succession in Spain, and structural changes in international trade. The abolition of discrimination against New Christians in Portugal in 1773, legally implemented, preceded Spanish abolition by almost one century. It was not the cause of the disappearance of New Christians as a distinct ethnicity; it just accelerated a process of decline, while in Spain discrimination was pursued at the local level.

2. Conceptual Framework

New Christians were shaped by labelling processes, inquisitorial prosecution, and blood purity statutes. Instead of integration after their forced conversion, they were confronted with new hurdles that imposed permanent suspicion, enquiries, and persecution. Even for those who managed to pass the barrier of blood purity through bribery or social alliances, their acquired status of Old Christian could be challenged at any time. It is a typical case of racism, understood as prejudices concerning ethnic descent coupled with discriminatory action.[12] Anti-Judaism can be interpreted as a useful fantasy that facilitated the construction of identity among the aggressors, but it had dire consequences for the people who were victims of the process.[13] The notions of lineage and blood in Iberia played a major role of identification and recognition. The Jewish community, politically subordinated and targeted at times of upheaval, became racialized as sharing the same blood and supposed attributes (or stereotypes) from generation to generation. The supposed attributes included dealing in falsehoods, dissimulation, greed, and destructive hate against Christians.[14] This racialisation, which included the fear of retribution by the persecutors, was then projected onto their descendants who were forced to convert to Christianity. They were accused of carrying with them the beliefs of their ancestors, transmitted by the same blood and mother's milk, another important lineage marker.[15]

This social construction of New Christians by dominant social groups to exclude them from competition for resources had a decisive impact: for the first time there was a division, eventually accepted by the Iberian kings and the Church, against the universalist tradition of the Christian Church. The creation of a new ethnicity of religious origin within Christianity by political interests raises problems of analysis and conceptualisation. It is difficult to talk about community, "a body of people who live in the same place, usually sharing a common cultural or ethnic identity."[16] New Christians can be defined instead by diaspora, frequent changes to their place of residence, and a split in (or multiple) cultural and ethnic identities.[17] On the other hand, New Christians retained family ties across borders and religions, sharing a certain nostalgia for the lost past under duress.[18] They were more defined by others than by themselves, which complicates the analysis. Because of this reflection I decided to use the notion of ethnicity as a fluid set of features that contribute to identifying a social group with shared ancestry.[19] In this case, the New Christians were first labelled and aggregated by their competitors in the context of power relations within Iberian societies. Yet they developed internal dynamics of desire for affiliation and belonging, together with their own historical memory and perceptions of kinship.[20]

The focus of this book on the New Christian merchant elite requires understanding this background and the specific conceptual framework related to this group. The noun *elite* was part of the French early modern lexicon, but it only entered the English language in the late eighteenth century, with its meaning of the best, the selected members, of a group.[21] It did not enter the Portuguese and Spanish languages until the nineteenth century. The inquisitors never used it, even if they were well aware of the distinctive economic power of the main merchants, financiers, and bankers. The involvement of this elite in intercontinental trade helps us to think about the meaning of globalization, conceived of here as a phenomenon that goes beyond cumulative or interdependent national histories.[22] The notion of a network to identify interconnected systems of trade may be useful in this case if applied with caution;[23] most New Christian commerce was based on temporary partnerships, although the accumulation of associates and long-distance trade circuits may have configured intersecting lines. Study of the New Christian diaspora stimulates new reflection on the relationships between trading networks, access to capital, state formation, imperial practices, regulation of markets, and merchant cultures in different parts of the world.[24]

The opposition between the established and the outsiders, pointed out by Norbert Elias and John Scotson in their study of internal migration in post-war England, when tensions arose in specific communities outside the centre of Leicester, may be applied to situations of racial divide.[25] New Christians were perceived by many Old Christians as outsiders, whose newly acquired equal rights following forced conversion enabled them to compete for positions within the hierarchies of State and Church. Old Christian resentment forced many New Christians to migrate to other regions of Iberia, which meant they were perceived as outsiders in a double way—as former Jews and as migrants.

The issue of values, as principles or moral standards held by a social group or by good part of the society, must be taken on board. New Christians contributed to merchant culture with its values of competence, merit, trust, saving for investment, and seriousness in fulfilling a contract; but they were also attracted by the aristocratic values of lineage, status, and conspicuous consumption. They occupied a liminal situation at different levels. In Iberia there was more: blood purity functioned as the cornerstone of a value system created from the mid-fifteenth century onwards.[26] The extreme disruption produced by blood purity statutes has been well studied, but the long-term impact needs further analysis. Blood purity is considered by several historians to be one among several criteria of social hierarchy, the others being a noble or *hidalgo* background versus that of *pecheros* (taxed plebeians), clean hands versus manual work, and legitimate versus illegitimate birth.[27] It is possible to establish a hierarchy among these criteria in which *limpieza de sangre* does not come at the top. However, blood purity is a specifically Iberian criterion in early modern Europe, imposing a blurred caste divide across the three orders.[28]

The difficulty here is to understand the exchange, transfer, or equivalence between the notion of religious purification, which developed in different parts of the world to protect communities from supposed impurity, and the notion of pure descent, which defined both external and internal social boundaries. Roberto Calasso showed how the notion of impurity pervaded Hindu tradition, explaining rituals of sacrifice, in which blood was overwhelmingly present, as a metonymy of life and atonement of the soul that guaranteed purification.[29] Mary Douglas called attention to the perception of impurity or pollution as matter out of place in different cultures. Contamination was a threat to life that linked to transitional states and interstitial positions.[30] This notion was internalised in Iberia to redefine hierarchies. The statutes of blood purity can be considered as rites of institution, which defined access to the main organisations.[31] The main issue was the rejection of mixed-race people, who were identified with degradation due to contamination by supposedly lower races. The notion of pure descent, by contrast, promoted even poor Old Christians.

The liminal condition of New Christians needs to be better conceptualised here. *Liminal* is understood as something transitional or intermediate between two states, on a boundary or threshold. New Christians were positioned as outsiders coming from inside, what Georg Simmel would call "the stranger within."[32] Even if the majority accepted a normative behaviour as Christian—and many managed to pass the barrier to be considered Old

Christians—their ancestry, which became an increasingly long shadow simply due to demographics, was a permanent threat. Liminality raised interesting identification, labelling, and self-perception problems. It meant permanent fear and abuse, but it could also open new venues for social and intellectual experiment. In my view, this condition does not fit the approach of rites of passage linked to a life cycle, as was suggested by van Gennep, because all New Christians were by default perpetually marginalised. Closer to the idea of subversive possibilities created by a liminal experience highlighted by Victor Turner, the New Christians' social and religious status offers new possibilities for theoretical development.[33]

The notion of identity is also important. It emerged in the sixteenth century from the Latin *idem*, meaning "the same," and the late Latin *identitas*. It indicates the quality of sameness, the possibility of attributing to a person or a thing continuous and unchanging properties.[34] In the social sciences, the notion of identity was extended to sets of features (ideas, values, perceptions, behaviour) that define individuals, social groups, or political parties. Lévi-Strauss was sceptical about this notion, fearing it as a functionalist tool that would homogenise societies and erase differences and diversity.[35] Michel Foucault derided the imposing of historical identities as pretentious.[36] However, Foucault acknowledged that individual identity was the result of power relations exercised on bodies, multiplicities, movements, desires, and wills.[37] Judith Butler's sharp criticism of the top-down approach followed by Foucault in *Surveiller et punir* is relevant for our argument. Butler highlights the possibility of resistance being fuelled by the subconscious under constraint, which supports the idea of agency among the different individuals and groups involved, generating opposition and alternative behaviour.[38]

Henri Tajfel's focus on the relationship between the individual and the social group stressed the complexity of individuals' emotional feelings and attachment to the reference group. Tajfel showed that the dynamics of opposed perceptions are part of the definition of social hierarchies, which fuel discriminatory behaviour, show hostility towards other groups, and protect members of one's own group. Relationships of power are thus part of the processes of creating identity, processes that include defining the enemy, establishing forms of discrimination between and within groups, and ensuring the internalisation of upper-class values by the lower classes.[39]

Pierre Bourdieu considered that social identity was defined by and through difference. In his view, the mobilisation of values, religious allegiance, political participation, scholarly titles, and professional standing was always relational and played on antagonism and imitation to define an identity that was never static or singular but rather hung in the balance.[40] However, this vision is not entirely adequate for use with early modern Iberia, an area subject to situations of extreme violence in which members of minorities were under constant threat of detention and torture. New Christians struggled both with perceptions imposed on them and with self-perceptions, classifications, and identity crises, which partly explains the permanent flow of migration and reorganisation of life abroad within Sephardic communities.[41]

To sum up, identities can change. They are ever fluid and unstable: they involve a desire for affiliation and recognition and a feeling of belonging, but at the same time there are split identities and multiple identities.[42] Identification as both a process of nomination and a process of constitution through power relationships is a related notion that addresses the fluidity of belonging.[43] This set of observations, which refuses any essentialised vision of identity, can serve for the analysis of diversity among New Christians in time and space. *Agency*, meaning the actions and intentions of specific agents or groups of agents that reveal their positions, goals, and self-perceptions, is a part of these processes of identity formation and identification that need to be approached from below.[44] The formative role of events, suggested by Erik Erikson, can be relevant from a collective point of view, underlining the usefulness of this category in historical analysis.[45] Finally, the notion of acts of identity, suggested by Erving Goffman, contributes to defining individual and collective positions in everyday life.[46] This notion can be useful to our argument, because the transformative power of circumventing the blood purity barrier, meaning discretely changing status from New to Old Christian, was a common practice that provided some protection but did not prevent further enquiries down the line, even within the same generation.

3. Semantics

The field of semantics offers an insight into the historically pervasive labelling created by dominant social groups to undermine converted Jews and their descendants. This labelling has been used by historians with varying degrees of reflection on its origins. Take, for example, the use of the word *marrano(a)*, widely used to denigrate New Christians in fifteenth- and sixteenth-century Iberia. Its origin is the Arab noun *muḥarram*, which meant "declared anathema."[47] In Castilian, marrano(a) was used to designate a converted Jew, all of whom were presumed to be persisting in their old religion. By extension, it also signified "damned," "dirty," "impure," and "rough." Furthermore, it was used as a synonym for *pig*, which represented a double insult to converted Jews, as both a filthy animal and a requirement to confront the traditional food interdictions of Judaism.[48] In France, marrano or *marani* was used as an insult against Spaniards in general, but it was also used to designate those of Jewish or Muslim origin who were pretending to be Christians.[49] New Christians rarely used this adjective to designate themselves.

By the mid-eighteenth century, the adjective marrano(a) had been modified to form the noun *marranism*, which signified the outward profession of Christianity by Jews under threat. The noun was adopted by many historians during the 1950s and 1960s and beyond, particularly by Benzion Netanyahu, I. S. Révah, and Jonathan Israel. It also appeared in encyclopaedias of Judaism, although in recent decades it has been less used. I find this acceptance of historical linguistic contamination by the politics of racialisation problematic, even if the use of marrano(a) and marranism became qualified and evolved over time.

The nouns *converso(a)* (converted) and *cristã(o) novo(a)* (New Christian) certainly served to underline recent conversion and define a caste of stigmatised outsiders with "stained blood," in contrast to the established Old Christians, who were supposed to have pure blood. These nouns ended up being used by the converted Jews themselves under constraint, but though they were used with derogatory intention, they were less offensive than marrano(a).[50] Because of the absence of other useful and identifiable linguistic taxonomy, I shall use the terms *New Christians* or *conversos* to indicate the population of converted Jews and their descendants.

It is difficult to find a balance, in historical research, between labels of identification thrust on minorities by dominant social groups, which certainly contributed to creating those minorities, and the self-perceptions of these minorities. In the case of New Christians, their designation as Jews was pervasive and used as a label to enforce a racial divide through the idea of perpetual religious beliefs maintained after conversion, which could lead to a formal accusation of apostasy. This labelling carried with it an explicit physical threat. The double accusation of *judío judaizante* (Judaizing Jew) that we find in so many trials meant that the accused were racially (or ethnically) Jews and had returned to their ancestral religion. But Jews they were in any case, produced by an historical fight for supremacy by Old Christians. It is this trap of repeating historical labels that historians, right up to the present day, have been unable to avoid in a consistent way. Even more difficult is to reconstitute self-perceptions among New Christians, although we find permanent protest to the king and pope against being labelled marranos or Jews.

Nation, as a noun applied to New Christians, is also problematic.[51] It was used in late medieval and early modern Europe to convey the idea of a shared, collective, inherited language and culture located in a precise territory.[52] New Christians were designated as a nation without having a distinct language (few of them retained any acquaintance with Hebrew) or being located in a specific territory. Portugal functioned as a main reference location after 1497 because of the massive forced conversion at that one date and in that one place, but larger communities existed in Castile, while New Christians eventually became scattered around the world. Historical memory, networks of kinship, and transfer of prejudices might explain the identification. The difficulty is increased because the noun *nation* could designate either New Christians or Portuguese, and often both together.[53]

Northern Europeans, especially in the seventeenth century, equated Portuguese with Jews. In doing so, they ironically confounded Old Christians and New Christians, persecutors and persecuted, blurring the dividing line fuelled by many Old Christians, while accepting inquisitorial propaganda that New Christians were Jews. Historiography has not yet solved this difficulty.[54] We shall try to keep the waters clear and focus on the New Christians, but sometimes identification is not easy. New Christians intersected with Old Christians as merchants, but they also intersected with Jews and New Jews, as Yosef Kaplan named the Sephardic communities created in Northern Europe by New Christians.[55]

4. Method

Biographies of New Christian businessmen have been drawn on by Caro Baroja, Domínguez Ortiz, I. S. Révah, James Boyajian, Carmen Sanz Ayán, Jonathan Israel, Herman Salomon, Claude Stuczynski, Fernanda Olival, and many other authors.[56] I have selected diversified and representative cases to overcome an essentialist approach based on the assumption that all New Christians were crypto-Jews. Because I am working across three centuries in different countries and continents, a key strategy is to reconstitute the story of several generations of the same family, or particular cases that help us understand changes at specific historical conjunctures or the conditions offered by specific locations. The cases must be relevant for the study of group assertion, external and internal rivalry, and exchange and interdependence with both Old Christians and Jewish communities.

Economic, political, and social significance are not the only criteria for the selection of cases; some cases have been chosen for their relevance to the study of gender, kinship, and strategies of reproduction. Forced conversion changed the gender dynamics within families, while the Iberian tradition of equitable inheritance had an impact on Sephardic communities, but these features must be better studied. Inequality within New Christian extended families also needs to be tackled if we are to understand mutual assistance and pooling of resources in cases of infertility. Relationships between New Christians and the Catholic Church also need to be addressed through the pursuit of spiritual search; participation in confraternities; membership of third orders and convents; access to ecclesiastical benefices and ecclesiastical career paths; and pious bequests and chapel endowments. These Church dealings are important if we are to understand the clusters of social positions achieved by New Christians. By the same token, relationships between New Christians and Jewish communities in different parts of the world must be taken on board.

The trials of the Inquisition are important sources in this research, because they give us information on kinship, business relations, property, behaviour, and decision-making. I am more interested in genealogical enquiries, inventories of property, testimonies, and declarations of the accused than in sentences. This information needs to be weighed against that from other sources, particularly wills, inventories of property established after death to enable partition among heirs, contracts, royal records of tax farming, *asientos* (royal contracts), attribution of pensions, and investment in state bonds. Records of access to noble status, military orders, knighthood, or *hidalguia* promoted by the king, religious orders, cathedral chapters, or benefices are also significant for understanding social mobility.

Material culture has naturally been included in the study of New Christians merchants, but more can be done to reconstitute their lifestyle. The involvement of this group with long-distance trade meant familiarity with luxury commodities from different continents. The development of a sharp eye to recognise the quality of gem stones or gold and silver; a tactile sensitivity for Asian textiles; a capacity to discern the scent of perfumes, woods, and dyes; and a subtle recognition of new flavours would arguably inform a refined cosmopolitan taste. I shall pay attention to the clothing, food habits, and interior decor enjoyed by major New Christian merchants, as revealed by inventories of their property, which included maps, paintings, tapestries, exotic furniture, cutlery, glass, linen, textiles, and porcelain. What is at stake here is the shaping of taste by intercontinental trade, in which New Christians directly participated as a result of time spent in Asia, Africa, and the New World as young partners and merchant associates.[57]

Paintings and literary texts have been studied on their own, but these cultural products can be better integrated into historical analysis. Literary and artistic sources are specific, defined by genre and tradition, but they can shed new light when placed in context and set against other historical sources. The purpose is to use these sources to catch New Christians (and New Jews) in the act of reflecting on exile, or the liminal situation in which they had been placed. These sources can illuminate the cultural environment of New Christian merchants, the sensibility this created, and how it reflected these merchants' social condition.

Understanding the legal and economic cultures in which New Christian merchants operated is crucial to analysing the context of their activities. The early modern period stimulated a notable production of treatises on contracts, exchange, and usury that reflected extensively on the practices of trade and shaped, to a certain degree, the legal framework. The most significant treatises are analysed in this book. Commercial culture, as exemplified in contracts, bills of exchange, business correspondence, documents granting powers of agent, accounting books and other records involving merchant associations, joint investment groups, temporary companies, customs houses, and the royal courts, is also important, and sources produced by this environment are used. The context of financial fluctuations over time and in various locations is important, because royal bankruptcies, for instance, could mean either losses or opportunities for New Christians.[58]

Political action through legislation, consultation, petitions, regulation of the markets, and royal contracts will be scrutinised. *Arbítrios*, or written pieces of advice to kings—many of them in manuscript but also in printed form—are relevant if we are to understand the political debate in certain periods, mainly in the first half of the seventeenth century.[59] Through arbítrios, we can see how New Christian agency and Old Christian opposition worked, but we need to complement this source with pamphlets from the period to grasp the decisive moments of intense public debate on political, social, and economic reform.

5. *Scope*

The defining features of this book are its focus on the New Christian merchant elite, its long-term approach, and its intercontinental scope. It spans a period from the fifteenth century, when the New Christian merchants emerged from massive, forced conversion in Iberia, to the decline of this ethnicity in the eighteenth century. It includes the intersection between New Christians and Jewish communities, as well as integration, persecution, and resistance within the Christian world. The research encompasses Spain, Portugal, Italy, Northern Europe, North Africa, West Africa, the Americas, the Middle East, South Asia, and East Asia, since the New Christian merchants were a global elite. The analysis is based on the extensive and excellent bibliography available and on intensive research in eighteen archives and manuscript sections of public and private libraries in Portugal, Spain, the Vatican, Italy, the United Kingdom, Belgium, and Peru.

The book is structured both in a chronological and a thematic way. The purpose of this is to understand distinctive features in certain periods of time, particularly royal policies, business patterns, destinations for migration, and cultural and religious expression. There are bridges between these parts, and these are provided either by focusing on continuities in policies or by looking at successive generations of the same families. Temporal divisions are always arbitrary, so I have tried to find clusters of events that can function as markers rather than turning points, because there are always continuities and discontinuities, although new economic, political, and social configurations can be identified.

Part I is titled "Transitions" because I am seeking to understand transfers of capital and kinship between Jewish and New Christian elites in the fifteenth century and first half of the sixteenth century. Continuities in royal advisers and royal contracts are visible, while the arrival of New Christians in municipal and ecclesiastic offices was a novelty and arguably unleashed retribution from Old Christian elites. The impact of Jewish expulsion and inquisitorial prosecution of New Christians is analysed. The activity of New Christian merchants from Castile and Aragon is integrated into our story, while information from new archival research on Portuguese merchants is introduced. Continuities of overseas trade leading to new business developments in the Atlantic, the Indian, and the Pacific Ocean is contrasted with breaks in continuity related to racial division and political events that created disruptions and encouraged emigration, primarily to Italy, North Africa, the Ottoman Empire, and Antwerp. Patterns of behaviour are followed through precise case studies. Important events with consequences, such as the riot of Toledo in 1449, the first wave of inquisitorial persecution in Spain, the Lisbon riot of 1506, and the voyage of David Reubeni to Portugal, are analysed. Part I is completed by a consideration of creativity, which includes a look at New Christian engagement with literary and artistic expression, and this is followed by an examination of the power struggle for the establishment of the Inquisition in Portugal, with a renewal of arguments from the fifteenth-century Castilian debate in favour and against New Christians.

Part II addresses the expansion of New Christian merchant networks in the Iberian world and in other parts of Europe, the Ottoman Empire, South Asia, and East Asia from the mid-sixteenth century to the 1600s, which includes consideration of the impact of the Iberian Union of Crowns in 1580. I start with a case study of contraband trade with Morocco in the mid-sixteenth century, followed by selected cases of the banker Simón Ruiz's associates, to understand interregional links and those operations of New Christian entangled with the interests of Old Christian merchants and financiers. New Christian migration, particularly to Northern Europe (Amsterdam and Hamburg), triggered by a new wave of inquisitorial persecution and new international conditions of acceptance of Jewish communities, is studied in its complexity. The different strategies of investment and social mobility, including noble status, pursued by New Christians are analysed in the chapter on property, which reflects on local conditions. Merchant cultures, literary and spiritual searches, and the debate around blood purity are analysed in the chapter on values, a notion comprising moral standards and social beliefs that is seldom used in historical analysis but is crucial to an understanding of conflicted views. This part concludes with the general pardon obtained by New Christian financiers in 1604–1605, an important historical event that had consequences.

Part III covers the period from the 1600s to the mid-seventeenth century, a period in which New Christian merchants asserted their presence as bankers in Madrid, created and developed Sephardic communities in Northern Europe, expanded their interests in the Spanish Empire and in Asia, and saw an exemption from property confiscation imposed by King John IV on the Inquisition in Portugal in 1649. "Resistance" is an obvious title for this part, which opens with a chapter on conflict exacerbated by the Inquisition, which required negotiation by the New Christian elite both in Madrid and in Rome. Periods of political transition, defined by the accession of new kings and new popes, unleashed requests from both sides of the dispute. The chapter on politics tackles a larger picture in which international war, Dutch competition in the Atlantic and the Indian Oceans, the decline of the Spanish Crown, and the disruption of New Christian networks provoked by the restoration of the independence of Portugal in 1640 are addressed. The business strategies of New Christians in different parts of the world are analysed region by region, including the major issue of the slave trade in the Atlantic, the reinforcement of links to foreign merchants, and the backlash from Old Christian merchants installed as familiars of the Inquisition. This part is completed by a chapter on identities that tackles religious and political allegiances but also literary and artistic forms of expression.

Part IV spans a long period, from the 1650s to the 1770s, which moved from renewed persecution by the Portuguese Inquisition, leading to the tribunal's suspension by the pope from 1674 to 1681, successive conflicts in Spain, and the abolition of the distinction between New and Old Christians by the government of Pombal in 1773. The decline and disappearance of the New Christians as a recognisable ethnic group is the subject of this part. The new heights of inquisitorial persecution and their impact on merchants in the Iberian world and beyond are analysed through precise case studies, which show the development of strategies of evasion but also of ennoblement, both in Iberia and abroad. At the core of this part is the suspension of the Portuguese Inquisition, which played a major role in this story. The New Christian merchants, who had been heavily persecuted during the late 1650s, 1660s, and early 1670s, were confronted with the restoration of the tribunal without any breathing space being conceded. The Portuguese king's change of attitude concerning contracts and privileges is included in this analysis. The consequences for emigration are tackled by the chapter on the breakdown of the New Christian merchant families, largely pushed by relentless inquisitorial persecution both in Spain and Portugal from the 1700s to the 1740s, while foreign merchants became favoured by the Iberian kings. The decline of Sephardic communities in Northern Europe occurred at the same time as the assimilation of New Christians in Italy, while the assumption of Jewish status emerged in France. The last chapter addresses the persistence of some level of New Christian identity until the mid-eighteenth century, but the main phenomenon is this group's immersion in global society, followed by the ideological turn against blood purity, surprisingly more successful in Portugal than in Spain, favoured by a decisive shift in the state's assertion of its political and jurisdictional powers.

6. Historiography

In 1817, Juan Antonio Llorente, the first historian of the Spanish Inquisition, considered that the economic and social success of the New Christians had transferred to them the hatred previously directed against the Jews. In his view, the Inquisition had been created for political and financial reasons and was driven by a desire for extortion. Formal accusations of Judaism targeted Jewish food and hygiene habits, not just religious beliefs.[60] Llorente was a former secretary of the Inquisition of Madrid who had extensive access to the archives, served the French government, and went into exile with the restoration of the Spanish monarchy. His arguments resonated with the thinking of the time. One generation later, Alexandre Herculano thoroughly researched the establishment of the Inquisition in Portugal, focusing on the negotiations in Rome on behalf of the Portuguese king, John III, which the New Christians opposed. The wealth of material Herculano uncovered remains fundamental; he proved there had been pervasive corruption in the Eternal City that led to an increased use of extortion against New Christians.[61]

In the early twentieth century, Henry Charles Lea agreed, in general, with Llorente and Herculano, but his method was different: whereas the previous historians had analysed the main inquisitorial decisions in their social and political context, and the diplomatic clashes of the different interests at play, Lea engaged with individual trials. Rich detail emerged, but limited analysis reproduced the tribunal's racial prejudices that underlined the accusation of Judaism against New Christian victims.[62] In the early 1920s, João Lúcio de Azevedo offered a comprehensive history of the New Christians in Portugal, from the late fifteenth to the mid-eighteenth century. Despite anti-Jewish prejudices, this history suggested a critical vision of the Inquisition and established a solid institutional and historical narrative based on archival research. It was weakened by the virtual absence of life stories, but the analysis of the main events, including the suspension of the Portuguese Inquisition in 1674–1681, set an excellent basis for future research.[63]

The subsequent decades saw new approaches that enlarged understanding of New Christians as a minority with their own agency. In 1937, Marcel Bataillon published an important book on Erasmus and Spain, a model of carefully nuanced religious and intellectual history in which he showed the overwhelming presence of New Christians among Erasmians, mystics, and early spiritual movements—namely, the *alumbrados* (literally, the "enlightened"), who sought direct contact with God.[64] The information he collected on the participation of New Christians in the first generations of Jesuits was, in due course, extended.[65] More recently, this line of research inspired another important book by Stefania Pastore, who analysed the complexity of fluid and innovative spiritual quest among New Christians, whose ideas cannot be neatly mapped onto specific religious movements.[66]

Bataillon's study was the first to integrate the story of discrimination against converted people of Jewish descent into the mainstream of Spanish history. The second historiographical move in this direction came in the 1940s and 1950s, from Américo Castro, who departed from the traditional view that Hispanic culture was characterised by a purely Christian background. Instead, he included Jewish and Muslim contributions.[67] Although Castro considered New Christians to be crypto-Jews, he opened an exciting area of research concerning the literary developments of this ethnicity, a line pursued later by other scholars, particularly Stephen Gilman and Francisco Márquez Villanueva.[68] This perspective was reinforced by a powerful parallel vein of research done by the historian Antonio Domínguez Ortiz, who contributed to recognition of the historical importance of conversos as a social group. This historian's work addressed the economic and financial New Christian intervention in Spain, particularly during the reign of Philip IV, but he also included an investigation of the literary output of these people.[69]

Julio Caro Baroja contributed work of the highest quality to this field with his substantial research on Jews in Spain from the late Middle Ages to the nineteenth century. It was marred by its title, which suggests that the author subscribed to the idea that all New Christians were crypto-Jews. However, Caro Baroja made an extraordinary effort to integrate both the Spanish and the Portuguese sides of this story, to engage with life stories, and to use a wide variety of archival sources, mainly trials. His is probably the most comprehensive history of New Christians in the Iberian world.[70]

It should be said that Caro Baroja's problematic equating of New Christians with Jews was shared by most historians from the 1930s onwards, particularly by Cecil Roth, Yitzhak Baer, and Haim Beinart.[71] More recently, Jonathan Israel unveiled an extraordinary set of case studies in Iberia, Northern Europe, Italy, and Iberian America relating New Christians to Sephardic communities, although accepting a New Christian plural religious identity.[72] The flourishing of studies on Sephardic communities in the past fifty years, for example, those by Aron de Leone Leoni, Cristina Galasso, Yosef Kaplan, Miriam Bodian, Daniel Swetschinski, Michael Studemund-Halevy, Jorun Poettering, Edgar Samuel, Gérard Nahon, Evelyne Oliel-Grausz, Lionel Levy, José Alberto Tavim, Hugo Martins, and Francesca Trivellato, is crucial not only for Jewish history but also for the history of New Christians.[73]

The convergence of Catholic and Jewish historiographies concerning the idea of New Christians as crypto-Jews was challenged in the 1950s and 1960s by António José Saraiva and Benzion Netanyahu.[74] These two historians shared the view that the Inquisition fabricated Jews, an idea that replicated a plausible argument originally formulated by the New Christians themselves. However, Saraiva considered the Inquisition to have been an instrument of feudal social retribution against the New Christians as an emergent bourgeoisie, a hardly convincing Marxist approach belied by the fact that common interests between merchants or bankers and noblemen are easy to prove. Although Saraiva's refusal to work with the inquisitorial sources is unacceptable, his critique of a positivist reading of the trials that had been accepted at face value must be taken on board.

Benzion Netanyahu approached the subject from an entirely different angle: he too rejected the idea of a continuing Jewish allegiance among New Christians, considering them as true Christians, who in many cases decided on conversion without constraint. Netanyahu's theory of racism as an explanation for the persecution suffered by the New Christians became more convincing in time, due to the progress of historical studies on that issue; however, the idea of pure Christians, many of them converted of their own will, based on Jewish sources, is problematic. Criticism of exclusive use of Jewish sources related to inheritance and divorce matters lodged outside Iberia has already been levelled at Netanyahu's ideas. The argument of racism is sustainable, but it needs to be better explained in its variable historical context.

I. S. Révah rightly rejected António José Saraiva's denial of the religious dimension of New Christian history.[75] The two had a lively debate, in which Révah did not convincingly address Saraiva's criticism of a positivist approach to the sources, but he acknowledged plural identities among New Christians.[76] This line of research was developed by Nathan Wachtel, who systematically studied whole inquisitorial trials in context. Wachtel contributed to the creation of a much more nuanced image of New Christians, who were certainly constrained by the Catholic Church but could end up choosing a variety of religious behaviour, from orthodox to heterodox: at the margins of heresy, engaged in innovative spiritual quest, returning to Judaism, or even, at times, experimenting with Protestantism. Nathan Wachtel talked about a faith of remembrance, about efforts to retrieve lost doctrine and ritual, obscured by an inquisitorial focus on food habits and hygienic customs.[77] This important approach stimulated a new reflection on conditions and consequences of conversion.[78]

A critique of the imaginary Jewish underground religion created by the Inquisition has been developed by David Graizbord, who points to the traditional absence of separation between the secular and religious spheres and between individual duties and a collective stance among Jews. By the same token, inquisitorial expressions such as the "religion of Moses" or "individual salvation under Judaism," which were integrated into daily life, need to be scrutinised.[79] This critique feeds into an old question: What were the possibilities of recovering Judaism within a strict Christian society, without rabbis or the Talmud? Graizbord focuses on split and problematic New Christian identities, showing constant processes of change from one religion to the other, hesitations, returns, and doubts that verged on agnosticism or atheism. This approach calls our attention to a much more flexible early modern world than we might envisage—a flexibility in which religious allegiance was not always set for life, manifested in a community submitted to forced conversion.

A legal and institutional framework based on blood purity defined boundaries, but it would be a colossal misjudgment to build an interpretation based on norms during the early modern period. How did the New Christians deal with rules of exclusion? How did they circumvent these adverse conditions? Under what circumstances could these norms be infringed? The work of

Enrique Soria and Ruth Pike, among other authors, has called attention to the significant number of New Christians bribing genealogists and subverting the testimonies of the enquiries into blood purity so that they could become Old Christians.[80] We also know, from the *libros verdes* of malicious genealogy, that many noble families were accused of being "contaminated" by Jewish blood. It is exactly this New Christian elite capacity for social promotion that needs to be properly assessed. But we cannot forget the opposite possible outcomes: failure to gain acceptance, fear of the consequences of exposure, loss of reputation, and ejection from previous positions in this atmosphere of systematic downgrading.

New Christian migration, mainly to the Mediterranean, the Atlantic, South Asia, and East Asia, has been one of the main issues tackled by historiography.[81] The major periods of migration are becoming more clear, and although the number of people involved is still difficult to estimate, we have some overall figures for those who settled. The impact of New Christian migration on the creation and development of Sephardic communities is probably the most productive area, as I indicated earlier. Although there is significant work on the relationships between New Christians and Jewish communities, this topic needs to be better addressed for the eighteenth century. It is important to better understand this relationship, because common decline might be explained by common causes.

Finally, the merchant and financial activities of New Christians have been under scrutiny since the 1950s, with much of this study based on the correspondence of the banker Simón Ruiz.[82] There is also good information on New Christian merchants in monographs on district tribunals and national histories of the Inquisition.[83] The importance of partnerships between New Christians and Old Christians has already been pointed out by David Grant Smith in the case of Brazil, and this kind of approach has been extended.[84] The crucial role of New Christian merchants in Asia has been studied by James Boyajian, who has reconstituted the links back to Lisbon and Madrid.[85] The financial investments of New Christians in Spain and Portugal have also been researched, as well as the communities' commercial activities in specific periods of time.[86] Relationships of New Christians with foreign merchants have been tackled, but it is an area that requires more research.[87] The excellent work by Francesca Trivellato on the cross-cultural trade of the Sephardic community in Livorno should inspire new research on New Christians.[88] Trivellato refused, for instance, the automatic vision of intra-ethnic exclusive trust, calling attention to internal conflict and external links.

In general, it is necessary to draw together all these threads, including the important contexts of legal and economic thought, social and political practice, and intellectual and artistic expression, to build a more comprehensive history of the New Christian merchant elite, its rise, and its fall.

PART I

Transitions
(1490s–1540s)

RIOTS AGAINST JEWISH communities in Castile and Aragon started in 1391, in Seville, and quickly spread to more than ninety towns and villages in Castile, Catalonia, Aragon, and Valencia.[1] Massacres forced the conversion to Christianity of many Jews. This violent process was followed by forced attendance at sermons instigated by the Dominican St. Vincent Ferrer, which multiplied baptism in Jewish communities.[2] Estimates for societies in prestatistical times are risky, but most authors agree that more than half of Castilian and Aragonese Jews, over 100,000 people located in the urban network, were forced to convert between the 1390s and the 1410s. In the early 1490s, there were probably fewer than 75,000 Jews in Castile, 12,000 in Aragon, and 1,500 in Navarra.[3] The expulsion of Jews from Castile and Aragon on March 31, 1492, with the justification that they were corrupting converted people and their descendants, led to a new wave of conversions and departures to Portugal, the Ottoman Empire, North Africa, and Italy.[4]

Dispossession of communitarian beliefs and loss of collective identity were the consequences of the assault on Jewish communities for those forced to convert. The descendants of this generation of Jews who escaped murder and resisted forced conversion were finally expelled. The impulse to abuse and annihilate Jewish people, considered the predecessors of Christianity who refused to accept Jesus as the Messiah, was followed by the impulse to eradicate their religion. The violence of this bottom-up movement created a division that had social and political consequences in the former Jewish communities: converted people (theoretically) had access to all the positions and honours available in Christian society, including ecclesiastical careers. Because of their educated backgrounds, they quickly became extremely successful in this, being appointed counsellors of kings, members of municipal councils, and dignitaries of the Church; they also enrolled in universities, where they excelled in medicine, law, and theology.[5]

Swift integration unleashed resentment, a powerful factor in history.[6] The political tensions in a conflicted fifteenth-century Castile did not facilitate the process: in 1449, a riot in Toledo, led by the governor (*alcalde mayor*) and member of the council of Castile, Pedro Sarmiento, accused New Christians (labelled, *conversos*) of keeping their old faith, which meant being apostates; following this claim, they were massacred and robbed, then stripped of municipal offices. The main political issue was the supposed New Christian support for King John II and the constable, Álvaro de Luna, who imposed new taxes for the war with Aragon. The removal of municipal jobs was the purpose of the first published blood purity statute. An immediate reaction by the pope and the king against a division of Christendom restored the status quo ante; but new riots in the following decades in different towns kept the new political issue of blood purity on the table. Eventually, in 1495, Pope Alexander VI accepted the blood purity statutes for the Jeronimites, which opened the door for other statutes. Segregation of another religion was thus followed by discrimination against people forced to convert and their descendants, although it took a century of social and political struggle to reach this outcome.[7] However, the upper groups of New Christians, primarily the elite courtiers close to the king, managed to negotiate their economic and social survival.[8]

Portugal was not immune to this movement, although it did not have a similar impact there, particularly as regarded conversions: riots occurred in the early 1390s but were swiftly controlled, while a constant flow of refugees arrived from Castile. There were also riots in 1449, but again without the same consequences as they had in Castile, owing to a more stable political framework.[9] The turning point occurred in 1492 with the expulsion of all Jews from Castile and Aragon. An estimate of Jewish communities in Portugal indicates 30,000 people before 1492, a number which doubled with the arrivals from other regions of Iberia at that date.[10] The refugees were accepted, although under harsh conditions imposed by the Portuguese king, John II. King Manuel, who succeeded John in 1495, alleviated those conditions; but he decided to replicate the Spanish expulsion on December 4, 1496, during the negotiations for his marriage to Isabel, Princess of Aragon.[11] He included Muslims in the decree of expulsion, the first time this had ever been tried in Iberia. The expulsion of Muslims was implemented, but the expulsion of Jews was obstructed by the king, who resorted to such vicious tactics as abducting their children and making it impossible to obtain maritime transport to leave the country. Thus he succeeded in imposing mass forced conversion, which was, however, implemented with a promise of twenty years free of enquiry into the religious beliefs of those converted.[12] This top-down process packed into less than a year what had taken more than a century of socially complex and largely decentralised political struggle in Castile and Aragon.

The blood purity statutes took time to be adopted across Castile and Aragon, and they only entered Portugal in the 1550s.[13] A gap of 60 years also occurred between the arrival of the Inquisition in the two countries: it was created in 1478 in Spain, and implemented in 1480–1481 in Castile and in 1484–1485 in Aragon; but in Portugal it was only created in 1536, becoming fully established in 1547. In all cases, the purpose was to target New Christians of Jewish origin. Racialisation of the converted Jews, to whom was attributed a supposed infidelity inherited from their religious past, a deviousness, and a talent for simulation, started in Castile and was transmitted to Portugal along with forced conversion. The same pattern of violent integration followed by discrimination occurred. The Portuguese case included bottom-up conflicts fuelled by Old Christians and expressed in the major riot of Lisbon in 1506, but a higher degree of political centralisation prevented the diffusion of chaotic massacres. The division of Christendom was slowly imposed through institutional mechanisms controlled by the king.

There were at least 260,000 New Christians in all Iberia by the end of the fifteenth century, mainly concentrated in Castile (4–5 percent of the total population, between 4 and 4.5 million) and Portugal (6–7 percent of the total population, slightly more than 1 million).[14] It is a matter of dispute how many Jews who refused to convert managed to emigrate from Iberia, particularly to the Ottoman Empire, to Morocco, and also to Italy where, in some states, they could keep their identity.[15] While Judaism was formally eradicated from Iberia, although not from all Iberian overseas territories, particularly in North Africa and South Asia, there was to be a constant flow of New Christians escaping the peninsula in the face of continuing constraints, reaching high numbers at specific moments of persecution.[16] Despite the violent first wave of inquisitorial repression in Castile and Aragon, there are solid indications that the New Christian merchant elite there resisted annihilation and managed to play an important economic role, both as merchants involved in international trade and as financiers.

This is the historical framework for the first part of the book. Within it we shall follow the story of the New Christian merchant elite, particularly from 1497, the final moment of exclusion for Jewish communities in Iberia, to the end of the 1540s. The terminus ad quem was defined by the new blood purity statutes promoted in Toledo by Archbishop Juan Martínez Silíceo in 1547, the papal assertion of the Portuguese Inquisition the same year, and the attempt to repress the New Christian community of Antwerp by Charles V in 1549. During this period, the New Christians had to deal with the trauma of being cut off from their ancestral community coupled, for a significant number, with the loss of their place of residence because of expulsion. Reconstitution of a religious identity proved to be a complicated process because of the divisive idea of blood purity that emerged among Old Christians. However, New Christians in Spain obtained a significant degree of integration despite heavy inquisitorial persecution, while the first signs of racialisation and conflict occurred in Portugal.[17] We shall try to shift the focus from the institutional framework to the agency of the New Christian merchants, as they sought to mobilise support for their permanent power struggle, including making representations to the Pope.

This part will therefore be guided by the following questions: What was the commercial, financial, and political position of the Jews in Iberia before the expulsions? Were there continuities between Jewish and converted trading families? How did New Christian merchants develop their activities in different parts of Iberia and the world in the first half of the sixteenth century? What alliances did they establish with Old Christians, and how diversified were their activities? What was the impact of the Inquisition on New Christians from different regions of Iberia? What was the role of the state in both the protection and the persecution of New Christians? How did the New Christian merchants react to division and discrimination? This part will thus explore the background of Jewish expulsion and the persecution of New Christians, the continuities from Jewish to New Christian trade, the disruptions provoked by particular events, and the different family strategies. It will include creative reactions against discrimination, the context of the political struggle, and the spiritual quests and literary innovation triggered by the liminal position imposed on the New Christian elite.

CHAPTER ONE

Background

THE POSITION ASSUMED by the New Christian merchant and financial elite in Iberia needs to be compared with the role that Jewish people had hitherto played in trade and finance. The impact of the expulsion of the Jews, and the realities of inquisitorial prosecution against New Christians, will complete the chapter.

1. Jewish Elite

The development of state finances in Iberia in the fourteenth and fifteenth centuries favoured a significant role, first for Jewish and then for New Christian merchants. The traditional involvement of Jewish people in agriculture declined in Castile due to two laws, passed in 1282 and 1293, which required the selling of Jewish hereditary property.[1] After the passing of these laws, the development of arts and crafts, including the production of textiles and the silk industry, trade and financial operations became the obvious paths for Jewish economic activity. However, there are indications of later investment by Jews in rural real estate.[2] In Portugal, nothing similar occurred. On the contrary, the Portuguese king, Dinis (r. 1279–1325), insisted that the rich Jews of Bragança should acquire rural property, while we know that in many other places they owned vineyards, orchards, and olive groves, growing produce for the market. In some cases, they even had restricted access to Christian workers. However, the dependent status of Jews, who were protected by the king but whose wealth was considered part of the royal treasure, was common to the two Iberian kingdoms, which exercised an enormous fiscal pressure on these communities.[3]

In the thirteenth and fourteenth centuries, the vast majority of members of Jewish communities worked in the arts and crafts, whilst the Jewish elite was involved in trade and authorised to create entailed properties. In these pursuits—and in privileges such as the owning of horses and arms—they mirrored the top layer of urban Christians, but they were barred from many professions. They were also involved in finance, benefitting from a prohibition on usury that (theoretically) banned Christians from lending money at interest. However, this possibility would also expose Jewish lenders to social unrest. The prohibition proved problematic because of the absence, in Iberia, of any version of the charitable Christian institution, the *Monti di Pietà*, which was created in Italy in the fifteenth century to lend money at a low interest rate, although the Portuguese confraternities sponsored by the royal family, which were called *misericórdias*, played some role in lending and transferring inherited property.[4]

In the meantime, successive layers of taxation extending from local to central level, particularly customs duties on the circulation of goods and taxes on transactions, as well as overseas expansion, which carried with it royal monopolies on trade that were farmed through private concessions, exposed the administrative incapacity of the emerging Iberian states to guarantee direct and regular collection of their revenues. Royal imposition of special taxation, particularly on Jewish communities, and requests for loans approved by the parliaments were the usual means of dealing with the extreme burdens of royal weddings and wars. However, there was a market for credit in Iberia to which kings, noblemen, municipalities, and private people turned in their need.[5] The fact is that public debt rocketed in the fifteenth and sixteenth centuries due to successive loans for wars, protection costs for overseas trade, and an expansion of colonial administration from North Africa to the Indian Ocean and the New World. This meant that loans had to be repaid with interest, and current expenses had to be set against specific income and farmed if governments were to keep their growing commitments under control.

The farming of royal rents and taxes, and of royal expenses, became a significant business, involving Christian and Jewish bankers and merchants. Those offering credit needed to arrange guarantors and securities for collateral damage in case of breach of contract, so only merchants with a strong background in trade and with access to credit and liquidity could bid. Even so, there were many cases of bankruptcy, of contractors accused of smuggling and compelled to pay significant penalties, and of lenders suffering from adverse economic and political conditions, which justified the renegotiation of the terms of contracts, in some cases leading to royal pardons due to proven losses. Studies are available on the farming of royal rents at the local level, as in the case of the *almoxarifado* (customs) of Guarda, a significant area in Beira Alta, Portugal, close to the frontier with Castile. In the years 1431–1436, Christians won 96 contracts worth 129,878,929.5 *libras*, while Jews won 46 contracts worth 84,856,491 libras. There were also contracts involving partnerships between Christians and Jews, although the main contracts in Lisbon and Porto seem to have been controlled by Jewish merchants.[6]

Jews became treasurers and accountants to the Iberian kings, as well as managers for noblemen's estates, municipal councils, and even convents, military orders, and bishoprics, although the Portuguese king, John II (r. 1477/81– 1495), forbade the latter practice, which was specifically excluded by canon law.[7] In fifteenth century Portugal, the highest group of Jewish courtiers, which included representatives of the communities (particularly the *arrabi mor* or chief rabbi in Portugal, equivalent to the *rab de la corte* in Castile), as well as physicians, financiers, and main merchants with strong links to Christians, including foreign (particularly, Italian) merchants, consolidated their position. In Castile and Aragon, in spite of a general decline (with regional differences) due to the impact of mass conversions, the highest segment of Jews at the royal courts managed to keep a significant number of their positions until the expulsion. The links between court Jews and local communities have been reevaluated in specific cases.[8]

Jewish money significantly contributed to the Christian conquest of Iberia: the battle of Navas de Tolosa in 1212, for example, was partly funded by Joseph ben Salomon ben Shoshan. In Aragon, in 1260, Yehuda ben Levi de la Caballería was collector of rents for the kingdom. In the 1380s, in Zaragoza, the powerful family of the Benveniste de la Caballería were bankers and collectors of rents for the archbishopric and the military order of San Juan.[9] Following the family's conversion, one of their descendants, Alfonso de la Caballería, would be vice-chancellor to King Ferdinand, the Catholic Monarch of Aragon. Judah Abravanel, from Seville, was treasurer and tax collector under Sancho IV (1284–1295) and Fernando IV (1295–1312).[10] Between 1355 and 1357, Samuel ha-Levi Abulafia, chamberlain and treasurer to King Pedro I of Castile, built the beautiful synagogue of El Transito in Toledo, and he also owned the palace now known as Casa Museo del Greco.[11]

In 1391, the widespread anti-Jewish riots that forced massive conversions had an impact on all Iberia. Navarra and Portugal, which were largely untroubled by violence, received a significant number of refugees. However, there were still Jewish communities surviving in Castile and Aragon during the fifteenth century. In Aragon, a new credit market based on *censal* (long-term loans) and *violari* (loans limited in time) was dominated by Christians, who extended loans to the Crown, the municipalities, the Jewish *aljamas* (or self-governed communities), the Church, and noblemen and their domains, replacing the previous predominance of credit provided by Jews, while a more balanced royal fiscal system taxed Jewish communities in a regular and moderate way, liberating them from being too great a burden on their Christian creditors. This explains why some Jewish communities thrived in fifteenth century Aragon, for example, that of Morvedre, near Valencia.[12]

In Castile, although the New Christians, as we shall see, assumed more and more important financial positions, Jews kept some control of royal rents and tax farming, holding around 20 percent of the contracts during the fifteenth century.[13] Even the Catholic monarchs were surrounded by Jews until the latter's expulsion in 1492, with the most significant case probably being that of Abraham Seneor, the rab de la corte of Castile, who lent money to the Crown in the early period, managed the *Santa Hermandad*, and became royal treasurer. On June 15, 1492, Seneor, together with his relatives, underwent baptism at the monastery of Guadalupe, with the Catholic kings as godparents, and changed his name to Fernán Núñez Coronel. He was nominated *regidor* of Segovia, a member of the royal council and the main accountant to Prince Juan.[14]

The Jewish elite in Portugal had to reorganise themselves in 1391 due to the arrival of families who had escaped from Castile and Aragon, mainly the Abravanel, but probably also the Palaçano and the Latam, who joined forces with established local Jewish merchants such as the Negro family, becoming bankers to the king. Together they controlled a part of public and private credit, the main international merchant routes, and royal rents and tax farming during most of the fifteenth century, until they were forced to convert. In 1478, Isaac Abravanel and Guedelha Palaçano guaranteed a loan of over 4 million reais to King Afonso V. Isaac Abravanel, who owned important rural properties, participated in another massive loan of 12 million reais to the king in 1480, after the wars in Castile. However, in 1483 he was accused by the king, John II, of direct involvement in the conspiracy of the Duke of Bragança, to whom his family allegedly had made available about 1 million reais.[15] He escaped to Castile with most of his family and in 1492 moved to Naples. Isaac Abravanel, who died in 1508 in Venice, was not only a successful financier but also a recognised intellectual figure of his time.[16]

In the final decades of the fifteenth century, several Jewish merchants, particularly the Abravanel, joined forces with Italian merchants, mainly the Lomelino and the Marchione, to control royal rents on Madeira's sugar, which was traded to Flanders. Guedelha Palaçano was involved with trade in North Africa, providing food, arms, and munitions for the Portuguese forts and paying the salaries of those stationed there. Jewish families were also involved in trade along the rivers of Guinea between Senegal and Sierra Leone, the rents from this area being known as the *vintena* (the one twentieth or 5 percent) *da Guiné*. These rents derived from licenses issued and taxes paid for trade in ivory and slaves, both of which involved obtaining licenses for import and export in Lisbon. Isaac Abeacar, Moses Benafaçam, David Negro, and Bento Sapaio farmed royal rents and expenses, such as salaries and daily allowances to royal judges, officers, and knights, including the *moradias do rei*, which were salaries for noblemen registered in the royal books as receiving rewards for services to the king, and that were transformed into interest for the recipients' heirs.[17] These activities triggered protests in the Portuguese *cortes* or parliament, in which the royal monopoly of trade was criticised, as was the control of maritime trade by Jews and foreigners; but those protests had no effect on royal policies.

2. New Christian Elite

In spite of Jewish resistance in Castile and Aragon during the fifteenth century, the significant number of conversions there meant that New Christians assumed most positions as financiers and farmers of the kings' rents, while Jewish relatives managed to maintain a significant position. In the ecclesiastical sphere, some became distinguished members of religious orders, canons of cathedrals, and bishops. Pablo de Santa Maria, for example, born Solomon ha-Levi (1352–1435), converted around 1390 and became a significant scholar and polemicist against Judaism, being nominated bishop of Cartagena, bishop of Burgos, and Chancellor of Castile. Alfonso de Cartagena (1386–1456), his second son, became a man of letters and a diplomat, and in 1435 succeeded his father as bishop of Burgos. Gonzalo de Santa Maria (1379–1448), another son of Pablo, was also a diplomat and bishop of Astorga, Plasencia, and Siguenza. The Cardinal Juan de Torquemada (1388–1468), a Dominican and uncle of Tomás de Torquemada (1420–1498), the first general inquisitor, had relatives of Jewish descent. Hernando de Talavera (c. 1430–1507), Jeronymite bishop of Ávila and then archbishop of Granada, and confessor to Queen Isabel, was also of Jewish descent.[18]

In civil society there were several cases of New Christians serving as *contadores mayores*, or major accountants for the royal treasury, particularly under the kings Juan I (r. 1379–1390), Enrique III (r. 1390–1406), Juan II (r. 1406–1454), and Enrique IV (r. 1454–1474), and some served as members of municipal councils. Samuel Abravanel, the grandfather of Isaac Abravanel, the leading rabbi of Portugal and Castile, had converted and taken the name of Juan Sánchez before the riots of 1391. He was treasurer of Seville in 1388, becoming treasurer to Queen Catherine of Lancaster in 1397. His descendants were involved with the noble houses of Araujo, Porras, Valdez, Anaya, Campo, Monroy, Solis de Sosa, Villa-Quirán, and Bobadilla.[19] Diego Arias (d. 1466), accountant and treasurer to Enrique IV, is another significant case, being succeeded by his son Pedro de Arias, who created an aristocratic lineage leading to the counts of Puñonrostro.[20] Juan Arias Davila (1436–1497), another son of Diego Arias, followed an ecclesiastic career to become a protonotary apostolic, bishop of Segovia, and a member of the royal council under Enrique IV and the Catholic monarchs. These positions did not prevent the Inquisition, in 1490, launching a trial against his parents and maternal grandmother. Juan Arias decided to go to Rome, where he obtained absolution for the accused. Prudently, he had brought their bones with him to avoid having them unearthed and burnt by order of the inquisitors.[21] Queen Isabel of Castile appointed Hernando del Pulgar, who had already served King Henry IV, chronicler of the kingdom, in which role he became critical of the establishment of the Inquisition and the persecution it unleashed.

Continuities between the activities of Jews and those of New Christian merchants and financiers after conversion have been well studied by Maria Pilar Rábade Obradó. She points to the fact that New Christians contracted to handle all types of rents from the king, the municipalities, the noble landlords, and the Church in different parts of Spain. The importance of financiers is obvious, but they included among their associates wealthy merchants and artisans who saw the possibilities of investment. Some of these New Christians managed to obtain the noble status of *hidalgo*. Other contractors for rents were detained by the Inquisition or decided to escape the first wave of persecution, thus losing their positions. However, the highest-ranking New Christian contractors operated in the king's immediate circle. These were people such as Fernán Pérez Coronel and Fernán Núñez Coronel, converted in 1492, who accumulated rents from Segovia, Medina del Campo, Zamora, Toro, and other territories totalling 91 million maravedíes; they were also involved with the royal *receptoría y pagaduría* (literally, receivership and payment), managing 90 percent of the royal income at the peak of their activities (which had declined by the turn of the century). These high-ranking New Christians were not subjected to investigation by the Inquisition.[22]

The presence of New Christians in local government is well known since the riot of Toledo in 1449 targeted them as tax collectors and as alleged allies to the king. As we have seen, this riot produced the first attempt at implementing statutes of blood purity, which were devised to exclude New Christians from municipal office, and fifteen New Christians immediately lost their jobs in Toledo. The king resisted this local initiative, and in doing so he had the support of the pope, who saw the threat of a division in Christendom.[23] The integration of new converts to Christianity became collectively contested against the universalist vision of Paul of Tarsus. Further anti–New Christian riots in 1465 in Seville, in 1467 again in Toledo, in 1473 in Córdoba, and in 1474 in Ciudad Real, to mention only the most important, kept on the table the issue of discriminating against New Christians, showing how racism was manipulated by groups of Old Christians in their struggle for a monopoly of resources. The struggle reached its climax in 1495, when Pope Alexander VI accepted the statute of blood purity requested by the important Castilian order of St. Jerome.[24]

The long-term presence of New Christians in local government and administration (*regidores, alcaldes, alguaziles, escribanos*) is well attested by successive petitions presented to the monarchs against the actions of the Inquisition—the most notorious led to the investigation and removal of the inquisitor Lucero in Córdoba—which targeted many officers appointed by the king or locally elected. These petitions fuelled parallel protests voiced by representatives of the third estate at the cortes (parliament) until the 1520s. This institutional support to the New Christians in Castile contrasted with relative silence or even animosity from municipal councils against New Christians in Portugal.

This vocal local power was apparently curbed after the revolt of the *comuneros* in Castile. However, the fifteenth century entrenchment of New Christians in Toledo (the Cota, Núñez, Arroyo, Illescas, González, Rodriguez, Ortiz, Rojas, and Díaz families), Seville (the Fernández and Sánchez), Córdoba (the Mena, Ayora, and Baeza), Granada, Jerez (the Alemán and Carmona), Ciudad Real (the Álvarez Pintado and González Pintado), Segovia (the Cabrera and Arias), Burgos (the Torre), Talavera (the Rojas), Toro (the Deza), Cuenca (the Valdés), Burgos (the Santa María, Maluenda, and Cartagena), Guadalajara, Mérida, Medina del Campo, Zaragoza, Lérida, and Teruel, deepened in the following centuries.[25] It is true that we cannot see these New Christian groups as consistently engaged in factional conflict: sometimes they were on both sides of local divisions.

Blood purity became a major ideological point of reference in Iberia, having been appropriated by Old Christian groups as a weapon to undermine rival social groups.[26] Old Christians used blood purity as a guarantee of loyalty to the monarchy and to the basic principle of collective identity, although this strategy was not shared by all: counsellors of the monarchs, bishops, landlords, and members of local elites opposed the translation into law of such a divisive notion. The diffusion of blood purity rules to block *conversos'* (and Moriscos') access to cathedral chapters, religious orders, military orders, colleges, and municipal councils cannot be defined as a linear process. There were many instances of resistance, petitions against these rules, and setbacks, including some caused by papal intervention, while individual cases of promotion led to vicious instances of factional fighting fuelled by these statutes.[27] The blood purity rules were drawn up by the mid-fifteenth century and were in widespread use in Castile by the second half of the sixteenth century, but without complete coverage of the territory. In Portugal they were introduced much later, in the 1550s, having received a boost during the Iberian Union of Crowns.[28]

The blood purity statutes filtered access to economic resources. This is very obvious with regard to access to chapters of cathedrals, which managed significant rents from the dioceses; to military orders, which controlled significant properties whose rents were attributed to the knights; and to university colleges, which educated future judges, lawyers, physicians, and dignitaries of the Church. Municipal offices could be important, dealing as they did with the regulation of the market and the control of notaries and records related to property. However, there was another important issue in Castile: blood purity was used to justify exemption from the royal taxes on plebeians, *pecherías*, exemption claimed as a customary right during the fourteenth and fifteenth century; but in fact this was illegal, as the inspections carried out between 1525 and 1540 revealed. Radical differences between lands controlled by the king and those controlled by landlords emerged, the former paying much more in taxes. What matters for us here is that the exclusion of New Christians from municipal offices was related to illegal exemptions and the management of clienteles.[29] Again, it was a matter of money, not only prestige.

In any case, blood purity as a huge impediment to integration started to gain traction in this early period. The way people turned these rules to their advantage is another interesting issue. The grandfather of Saint Teresa of Ávila, Juan Sánchez, was a wool and silk merchant, a converso, who was accused of Judaism and abjured his apostasy at the Inquisition of Toledo in 1485. He was then rehabilitated, having made a significant contribution to the cost of the War of Granada, and moved to Ávila. His son, Alonso de Cepeda, a rich wool merchant, took Beatrice de Ahumada as his second wife. She was a noblewoman from an Old Christian family who was famed for her piety, and it was she who raised their daughter, Teresa, as a deeply pious girl. In 1519 the three Cepeda brothers refused to pay tribute and brought a case to prove their *hidalguia*, supported by the noble families into which they had married. Despite several ambiguous testimonies, they finally won their case, with their hidalguia being recognised at local level. However, they bribed the officers who were to issue the resulting certificates, with the result that these documents were phrased in the same way as the certificates generally issued to the hidalguia.[30]

3. Expulsions

The background presented in this chapter has focused on Castile, Aragon, and Portugal, where most of the action recounted in this book took place; but we shall also look at events in Europe and other continents that intruded on New Christian and Jewish history. First, we need to have a broader comparative view of expulsions and the creation of Jewish and New Christian communities outside Iberia, which was so important for these peoples' interaction, and ultimately for their resistance and for their long-term development, with the latter's impact on intercontinental trade. The expulsions of Jewish communities from England (1290) and France (1306–1394) preceded the Iberian deportations.[31] The Black Death triggered another wave of massacres and expulsions, mainly in Germany, although there were cases of returns and new expulsions during the first half of the fifteenth century, particularly in the Ruhr area, Bavaria, and Austria.[32] The situation of Jewish communities in Italy, paradoxically, was not disrupted by the Black Death, but the 1480s and 1490s saw expulsions and massacres in Perugia, Vicenza, Parma, Milan, Lucca, Ravenna, and Florence, the last case following the expulsion of the Medici from the city in 1494.[33]

In 1492, expulsions in Spain were replicated in Sicily and Sardinia, while the French king expelled Jewish communities from Provence in 1498 after a period of riots and massacres against them. Expulsions from Germany and Switzerland reached another peak in those years (Geneva, Mecklenburg,

Pomerania, Halle, Magdeburg, Nuremberg, Ulm, Styria and Carinthia, Würt-temberg, Salzburg), followed by expulsions from Brandenburg in 1510 and Regensburg in 1519.[34] German Jews received some protection from Charles V, while Luther inspired the decision to expel Jews from Saxony in 1537, and this was followed by another wave of expulsions from Germany from the 1540s to the 1570s. In 1541, in the Kingdom of Naples, the Jews were finally expelled after several decades of resistance.[35] In the papal states, Venice, Mantova, Ferrara, Tuscany, and Urbino, the protection traditionally granted to Jews started to be challenged with the election of the Inquisitor Gian Pietro Carafa as Pope Paul IV (r. 1555–1559) and the latter's decision to root out all New Christians who might have returned to Judaism. The Jewish community invited to Ancona after the expulsion from Naples was devastated in 1555. In 1569, Pius V, another inquisitor who had been elected pope, reduced in size all Jewish communities in the papal states except Ancona, Rome, Avignon, and Carpentras.[36] These expulsions had consequences for the New Christian diaspora, since they were accused of aiming at a return to Judaism. They were temporarily expelled or restricted in their movements in Venice, Urbino, Tuscany, and Ferrara.

The result of all these expulsions was to evacuate most Jewish people from Western Europe to Eastern Europe (Poland and Lithuania), while a part of the Iberian and Italian Jewish populations emigrated to North Africa and the Eastern Mediterranean, mainly to the Ottoman Empire. This period of near eradication from Western Europe, according to Jonathan Israel, lasted until 1570 (I would say earlier), when mercantilist policies started to place reason of state above religious reason. This would explain the new policy, particularly in Flanders, France, and Italy, of turning a blind eye on the real faith of New Christians that began in the first half of the sixteenth century. The return of Jewish communities in Germany, where they had not entirely disappeared, Austria, the Netherlands, and finally England would occur later, from the 1570s to the 1650s.

The settlement of Jewish communities in the eastern Mediterranean increased after the expulsion from Spain and was later fed by the New Christian diaspora. It is estimated that 12,000 families, or 60,000 people, moved from Iberia to the Ottoman Empire between 1492 and the mid-sixteenth century.[37] Portuguese and Spanish synagogues were created in Salonika and Constantinople, Safed, Jerusalem, Hebron, Gaza, and Tiberiades. By 1545, the Jewish community in Constantinople had over 8,000 families, around 40,000 individuals, while in 1519, in Salonika, there were about 3,150 households, which would have been nearly 16,000 individuals, and in Safed, in the 1560s, there was a concentration of 5,000 Jews.[38]

These communities, which had doubled or tripled in a few decades, remained key as possible destinies in case of new surges of persecution, while they created new possibilities for extensive trade across the Mediterranean.[39]

A preference for Jewish communities, rather than New Christian, in the Ottoman Empire was only mirrored during the seventeenth century in the Protestant Netherlands, in Hamburg, and in England, since Jewish communities posed fewer problems for the constitutional and religious environment there. These northern European Jewish communities boosted the northern European share of international commercial profits, an outcome that involved economic competition against the Spanish and Portuguese empires in the Atlantic, Indian, and Pacific Oceans. The seeds of these international networks were planted from the end of the fifteenth to the end of the sixteenth centuries.

4. Prosecution

The relationship between Jewish communities and New Christians was an important issue after the process of forced conversion. Separation between them was constantly predicated. The expulsion from Castile and Aragon meant a brutal removal from ancestral lands, creating a trauma that triggered a unique moment of Jewish historiography, as Yerushalmi rightly pointed out, contrasting the historicity of the sacred texts to the virtual absence of Jewish historiography in the Middle Ages and the early modern period.[40] Many, mainly children, pregnant women, and old people, died during their deportation due to disease and harsh conditions of travel, while those expelled also experienced suffering on account of those left behind, such as New Christian relatives and the dead, buried in cemeteries that were subject to desecration.

The establishment of the Inquisition in Castile and Aragon in the 1480s preceded the expulsion of Jewish communities. Instead of contributing to the separation of Jews and New Christians, harsh persecution reinforced ethnic solidarity while promoting the political idea of a single religion under the Catholic monarchs. Jews and New Christians were united by deep suffering from expulsion and vicious persecution. These shared experiences would explain the constant communication and mutual assistance between Portugal, Spain, Italy, France, Flanders, North Africa, and the Ottoman Empire in this period from the 1490s to the 1540s that would sow the seeds for further exchange in later periods. Divergent religious choices, very much based on political constraints and different ways of life, did not prevent the nurturing and even extension of previous ties.

The first decades of persecution of supposedly Judaizing New Christians—the 1480s and 1490s, arguably extended to the 1520s—were probably the busiest of 350 years of inquisitorial activity in Spain, including the highest levels of executions ever. Thousands of accused were detained, subjected to swift trials, and presented to the public in massive autos da fé reported to have each published the sentences of hundreds of condemned. The terror launched in this first inquisitorial wave must be set against the massacres produced by the urban riots one century before. The expulsion of all Jews from Castile and Aragon in 1492 and forced collective conversion in 1497 in Portugal complete this intensive period of dispossession, humiliation and subordination, which involved many thousands of deaths, mostly due to displacement. Expulsion of Jews cannot be detached from institutionalised discrimination and persecution of New Christians, which in turn led to plural identities.

The inquisitors started operating in Seville, where they targeted all groups of conversos, including the richest and the holders of ecclesiastic and public office.[41] The decision of the Catholic monarchs was political: Seville had been the stage, as had all lower Andalucía, of a recent civil war between the Duke of Medina Sidonia and the Marquis of Cadiz in which the Catholic monarchs had been ignored; New Christians were powerful throughout the region, particularly in Seville, where they held high office both in the municipality and in the Church. The Catholic kings saw an opportunity to assert their jurisdiction and political clout through exemplary repression in a territory charged with symbolism.

Noblemen, in particular the Duke of Medina Sidonia and the Marquis of Cadiz, who had received thousands of refugees on their estates, were summoned to present the lists of those conversos and requested to deliver the accused under threat of excommunication, confiscation of property, and loss of privileges.[42] By this one act, the inquisitors asserted their authority and made clear that their jurisdiction would be imposed over all other jurisdictions, including the vast seigneurial domains. It was the first fully centralised institution in Castile and Aragon. Although an ecclesiastic court created by the pope, the Inquisition was backed by the state and became part of the institutional framework of Iberian monarchies. It was the kings who suggested the name of the general inquisitor to the pope, and the Council of the Inquisition had the status of a royal council.[43]

The impact of this initial activity, which was quickly extended to most parts of Castile and Aragon, was twofold. First, it concentrated on urban areas, where it disrupted New Christian networks and delivered thousands of excommunicated people to the secular arm (the civil authorities) to be executed, while their wealth was confiscated. The implementation of terror deprived many families of their basic livelihood, leading to another enormous outflow of refugees and remaining capital. Many escaped to Portugal and Italy, where they filed complaints and petitions to the pope, even offering money to suppress the Inquisition—an activity that would later be replicated by the New Christians of Portugal.[44] Depopulation of towns, reduction of trade, and a fall in Crown rents immediately ensued.[45] Moreover, inquisitorial action legitimised accusations of apostasy levelled against New Christians by competing groups of urban Old Christians who resented the huge social success of converted Jews and their descendants. The blood purity statutes promoted by those groups of Old Christians only started to be accepted after

FIGURE 1.1. Cristóbal de Morales, Paintings of the chapel de
las Doncellas, cathedral of Seville, ca. 1534 (baroque retable
added) endowed by García de Gibraleón. Courtesy Cabildo
de la Catedral de Sevilla. Photo courtesy of José Manuel Díaz
Blanco.

the establishment of the Inquisition.[46] These statutes were extended to the
cathedral of Badajoz in 1511 by Alonso Manrique (future general inquisitor)
and the cathedral of Seville in 1515 by Diego de Deza (former general inquisitor).[47] The tribunal coupled persecution with discrimination, with the descendants of those excommunicated being excluded from access to universities and

FIGURE 1.2. Cristóbal de Morales, Portrait of Micer García de Gibraleón, chapel de las Doncellas, cathedral of Seville, ca. 1534. Courtesy Cabildo de la Catedral de Sevilla. Photo courtesy of José Manuel Díaz Blanco.

public positions by royal decree in 1488 and 1501. Other interdictions for New Christians included a ban on travel to the Indies and exclusion from dressing in silk.[48]

In this early period of institutional terror the New Christians also faced extortion from the king, who was happy to habilitate New Christians reconciled by the Inquisition (and their descendants) to public jobs, authorise the return from self-imposed exile, prevent confiscation of property, or even authorise trade with the Indies against significant payments. These collective agreements, called *composiciones*, were in place by the 1480s and 1490s, and were extended to the 1510s and then probably to the 1520s. The value of these composiciones reached, in the case of Seville alone, 20,000 ducados in 1508, 40,000 in 1509, and 80,000 in 1511. But there was also extensive negotiation of individual agreements, which makes it difficult to evaluate how many New Christians were involved.[49]

While many New Christians emigrated, the majority blended into Old Christian society. There are indications that some wealthy New Christians who avoided confiscation of property married into the nobility, thus becoming relatively protected from inquisitorial enquiry. In the late sixteenth and seventeenth centuries, the so-called *libros verdes* were written (and censored), providing genealogies that cast a slur on many noble houses with supposed Jewish backgrounds.[50] We also know that New Christians were not entirely excluded as counsellors to the Catholic monarchs, while they kept a strong presence as contractors for royal taxes and rents, financiers to the kings, and merchants with important interests in the Indies.[51] Up until the 1520s, they maintained a clear political visibility, being targeted for special financial contributions to the Crown, as in 1510, and playing some part in the revolt of the comuneros in

FIGURE 1.3. Tomb of D. Baltasar del Rio, bishop of Scalas, at the cathedral of Seville (ca. 1541) under the chapel of Nuestra Señora de la Consolación he endowed. Courtesy Cabildo de la Catedral de Sevilla. Photo courtesy of José Manuel Díaz Blanco.

1520–1521. However, their capacity for petitioning the king as a pressure group does not appear to have lasted beyond that period.[52]

The wealthy New Christians who decided to avoid emigration did their best to integrate into Christian society. They became members of religious orders, invested in the ecclesiastic career, played a double role in Rome as agents of New Christian interests but also as representatives of cathedral chapters, joined or even created confraternities, and entered into contracts for the establishment of chapels for family burial in cathedrals, convents, and parish churches. In 1515, Micer García de Gibraleón, for example, protonotary apostolic in Rome and son of Pedro Fernández Benadeva, excommunicated by the Inquisition and burnt, founded the chapel of the Annunciation (or de las Doncellas) at the cathedral of Seville and a brotherhood to endow poor maidens with dowries (his descendants managed the brotherhood and the chapel where the family would be buried). Cristóbal de Morales celebrated the foundation of the confraternity and the endowment with a portrait of García de Gibraleón.[53] Baltasar del Rio, another son of an excommunicated and burnt New Christian, made a brilliant career in Rome, became bishop of Scala and in 1532 created the chapel and brotherhood of the Consolation (or de Escalas) at the cathedral of Seville, where his tomb can be seen.[54] In 1552, Diego Caballero, mariscal (marshall) of the island of Hispaniola and major accountant of the cardinal Loaísa, endowed the chapel of Purificación (or of the mariscal) at the same cathedral of Seville, which included an extraordinary investment in a lavish retable by Pedro de Campaña.[55]

The Inquisition was only established in Portugal in 1536, and the crucial issue of confiscation of property was postponed for almost 30 years due to permanent negotiation by New Christians in Rome. The latter obtained suc-

FIGURE 1.4. Pedro de Campaña (born Pieter Kampeneer), Retable of the chapel de la Purificación, cathedral of Seville, 1556, endowed by Diego Caballero. Courtesy Cabildo de la Catedral de Sevilla. Photo courtesy of José Manuel Díaz Blanco.

cessive exemptions from confiscation for periods of ten years, starting in 1536 and continuing until the last one was published by the regent, D. Catarina, in 1558, with the support of the pope. This exemption was revoked by the new regent (and general inquisitor), Cardinal Henry, in 1563. In 1577, King Sebastian reinstated the exemption of confiscation to the New Christians due to a

FIGURE 1.5. Pedro de Campaña, Portrait of Diego Caballero and male members of his family, chapel de la Purificación, cathedral of Seville, 1556. Courtesy Cabildo de la Catedral de Sevilla. Photo courtesy of José Manuel Díaz Blanco.

contract to finance war in Morocco, which was again cancelled in 1579 by the pope under pressure from King Henry, the former general inquisitor.[56]

In 1497, King Manuel had ruled out enquiring into the religion of converted Jews for twenty years, a policy reinforced in 1512 for another sixteen years. However, in 1515, he asked the pope to permit the establishment of the Inquisition, a request renewed by his successor, King John III, in 1525.[57] In 1519, King Manuel wrote to the municipality of Goa instructing the authorities there that New Christians should be excluded from being members of the council, although exceptions defined by special provisions could be made.[58]

In the meantime, royal policies for promotion and access to honours for New Christians were put in place, a move downplayed in accounts written much later, which are echoed by Jonathan Israel.[59] For example, on May 6, 1499, King Manuel granted to Nicolau Coronel, royal physician, and all his descendants, the privilege of being considered a *fidalgo de solar*, literally, the son of someone owning a manor, meaning an old noblemen, in this case cleansed of any stain of birth.[60] This period of relative integration in Portugal, from the late 1490s to the late 1520s, if we except the major anti–New Christian

FIGURE 1.6. Pedro de Campaña, Portrait of D. Leonor Caballero and female members of her family, chapel de la Purificación, cathedral of Seville, 1556. Courtesy Cabildo de la Catedral de Sevilla. Photo courtesy of José Manuel Díaz Blanco.

riot in Lisbon in 1506, which will be analysed later, created some rootedness in converted people and their descendants, which made possible the formation of an identity—a process that had a historical parallel in Castile and Aragon from the 1390s to the 1440s.

In this early period, the persecution of New Christians accused of Judaism in Portugal was weak due to the late establishment of the Inquisition and the constraints imposed by the pope, who acted on the prompting of New Christians agents. Besides exemption from confiscation of property, in 1544 the pope temporarily suspended the conclusion of trials that were then ongoing. In the period 1536 to 1548 there were 245 trials for Judaism in Lisbon (then the main tribunal) in a total of 372, or 66 percent.[61] In Castile and Aragon, the persecution of New Christians of Jewish origin became relatively insignificant from 1540 to 1559 (a total of fifty-seven trials, less than 3 percent of the total).[62]

We need to retain here the initial terror of inquisitorial activity in Castile and Aragon, followed by a relatively low level of prosecution of New Christians, although there were periods of renewed activity against Judaism in the late sixteenth century, from the 1630s to the 1650s, and from the late 1710s to the 1730s. In Portugal, by contrast, there was a long and steady inquisitorial persecution of New Christians, and this represented from 68 percent to more than 80 percent of the total trials in different tribunals from the 1540s to the 1740s.[63] This long and steady inquisitorial repression in Portugal, paradoxically, reinforced a New Christian identity. A major indicator of this identity can be found in New Christian elite political activity in relation to the king and the pope. The last petitions to either of these authorities by Castilian New Christians occurred in the 1520s, while Portuguese New Christians were active petitioners on a regular basis throughout the sixteenth and the seventeenth centuries.

{~~~~~~~~}

Forced conversion led to difficult transitions from Jewish to Christian status in Castile, Aragon, and Portugal. Riots and violent integration were followed, after many decades of struggle, by blood purity statutes, promoted by the establishment of the Inquisition, which legitimised claims of collective apostasy, while reinforcing unprecedented forms of discrimination within Christianity based on racial divide. Expulsion of Jewish people and massive persecution of New Christians implied deep traumas of dispossession, humiliation, and widespread death imposed by the state, resulting not in separation of the two groups but in shared ethnic solidarity bridging religious divergence. This extremely harsh background did not prevent New Christians from achieving surprising social mobility at different levels, becoming counsellors, treasurers, and accountants to kings; members of local government, often entrenched in municipal councils (in Castile, not in Portugal); successful scholars at universities; and members of religious orders and cathedral chapters, and even bishops. It is against this background that we shall endeavour to understand the position of New Christian merchants in Iberia and beyond.

CHAPTER TWO

Continuities

IN THIS CHAPTER, the position of leading New Christian merchants in this period, mainly in Portugal, because the situation in Spain has been better analysed, will be addressed. A certain lack of balance still exists between archival research and the possibilities for such research in different parts of Iberia in this early period. Individuals and their families will be analysed to provide a representative number of case studies among the merchant elite.

1. João Rodrigues Mascarenhas

On the night of April 17, 1506, a magistrate and some constables broke into a New Christian house in Lisbon where there was a gathering to celebrate the Passover seder (a feast that involved eating unleavened bread that was held in Jewish homes to commemorate the exodus from Egypt). Sixteen people were arrested, but liberated two days later, probably as a result of the decree by King Manuel in 1497 that prohibited enquiries into New Christian faith for twenty years. That liberation aroused indignation. The memory of a previous collective punishment administered to around forty Old Christians who were detained and flogged for offending New Christians in the Rua Nova (April 25, 1504) must not have been forgotten; and the riot against New Christians in Évora that same year, which led to the destruction of the old synagogue, must have also been well known in Lisbon. Duties and taxes paid in Lisbon had been reformed in 1506, which increased the financial pressure on the population. In addition, the city had been hit by plague, prompting the evacuation of the royal family, noblemen, and wealthy people.

On a Sunday, when those New Christians accused of celebrating the Passover seder were liberated, there was an alleged miracle at the chapel of Jesus in the Church of Saint Dominic: the crucifix seemed to shine. A New Christian present gave a worldly explanation involving a reflection from a candle (reports diverge here). Accused of impiety and mockery, the New Christian was taken out of the church, killed, and burnt. Dominican monks carrying a cross called for a riot and promised salvation in return for the extermination of Jews, by which they clearly meant New Christians. For over a week, the city witnessed a savage plunder of houses and persecution of New Christians, which led several eyewitnesses to estimate the number of murders at between 1,000 and 3,000. The high point of the persecution, on which all accounts agree, was the pursuit of João Rodrigues Mascarenhas, a very wealthy contractor of the king's rents and expenditure. On Monday, April 20, the mob finally found him trying to escape from the city and murdered him on the spot.

It took more than two weeks for royal forces to regain control of the city. The two leading Dominicans were arrested and taken to Évora, where the king had stayed during the events. They were defrocked and burnt. It is estimated that around forty people were hanged for their role during the riot. King Manuel took one month to issue a general punishment: those directly involved would have their entire property confiscated; those who did not oppose the riot would have one-fifth of their property confiscated; the House of Twenty-Four, which represented the city's artisans, would lose its four elected members on the municipal council; the feudal right of *aposentadoria*, or the requisitioning of burghers' houses by royal officials and noblemen, was reinstated; and the city lost its title of "loyal."[1]

What was at stake here was the crime of lèse-majesté committed by the people of Lisbon: there was no compensation for the mass murder and plunder perpetrated against the New Christians. It took less than two years for these punishments to be forgotten and the "loyal" title reinstated, and in 1512 King Manuel forbade further prosecutions for participation in the massacre. In the meantime, the policies of forced integration instituted in 1499, such as the prohibition of emigration without royal licence, the prohibition of immigration to New Christians accused of heresy, the interdiction on selling real estate, and trading in bills of exchange by New Christians, were interrupted. In 1507, King Manuel allowed New Christians to emigrate, sell their property, and take with them all the money they wanted. At the same time, they were recognised as having the same rights as Old Christians. In 1512, the prohibition on enquiry into New Christians' beliefs was extended for another 16 years, while King Manuel included one New Christian among the four representatives of artisans on the municipal council of Lisbon (a decision later rescinded). In the following year, he instituted penalties for those who sought to offend New Christians by calling them *marranos*.[2]

Between 1506 and 1528 there were no more riots against New Christians in Portugal, but in 1515 a campaign of offensive posters and graffiti was launched against New Christians, and in the same year, King Manuel secretly asked the pope to establish the Inquisition. There was permanent Castilian pressure on the Portuguese king to persecute New Christian refugees from Castile. In 1513 the Dominican Juan Hurtado de Mendonza, the order's visitor in the province, asked D. Manuel to collaborate with the Castilian Inquisition to return condemned and accused New Christians who had escaped to Portugal. Hurtado de Mendonza also advised the Portuguese king to obtain the pope's approval for a tribunal of the Inquisition on the Castilian model, an idea that must have been floated in Portugal before.[3] We do not have data for the quantity of people who migrated from Castile, taking advantage of the weak position in which the riot of 1506 had left the Portuguese king, but we know that there were major New Christian merchants and financers who decided to stay.

The story of João Rodrigues Mascarenhas, the main target of the 1506 Lisbon riot, will guide us as to the adaptation of the wealthiest New Christian merchants after forced conversion in Portugal. On July 20, 1499, King Manuel made João Rodrigues Mascarenhas a squire of his house.[4] Nine days later another royal letter made him a citizen of Lisbon.[5] He was to enjoy the right to residence, and the privileges, honours, and freedoms of a squire and citizen of Lisbon, and to be exempted from municipal ballots and offices, an exemption requested by other citizens. He must already have been a significant merchant whom the king wanted to honour and place under his protection to help him develop his business, and he must have been able to bid for the farming of royal rents and expenditure. Those involved in tax or rent farming needed a royal mandate to implement the collection of taxes and to mobilise constables in extreme cases of refusal. This is the clue to why so many New Christians were made squires and knights of the royal house. This promotion occurred two years after the merchant's forced conversion. Unfortunately, we do not know the former Hebrew name of João Rodrigues Mascarenhas.

In 1500 in Castile, João Rodrigues Mascarenhas received 500,000 maravedis (about 1,333 cruzados) from Pero de Andrade, knight of the king, who had been ordered to distribute between several merchants a large sum of 12,192,308 maravedis (32,513 cruzados) paid to the king by the Duke of Bragança.[6] João Rodrigues Mascarenhas was probably representing the king at the Medina del Campo fair, one of the most important European fairs for contracts and future contracts on wool and other commodities, and also for the clearance of bills of exchange. In that same year of 1500, João Rodrigues Mascarenhas already had the contract for paying the royal *moradias*. A royal quittance from May 27, 1502, declares that João Rodrigues Mascarenhas used 29,112,577 reais (then about 75,617 cruzados, an enormous sum) for the payment of moradias in the years 1500 and 1501, and that the money came from the customs revenues of Lisbon, Aveiro, Porto, and Viana, the various taxes levied in Setúbal and Lisbon on wood, wine, and textiles, and the revenues of the houses controlling trade with Guinea and East Indies.[7] Another royal quittance, from March 3, 1503, declares that João Rodrigues Mascarenhas satisfied a contract for the two previous years relating to the rents on trade along the rivers of Guinea but was exempted from payment for the third year due to losses incurred in trade, and compensated for losses on payment of the moradias with more money levied on the *sisa* of wine in Lisbon. The contract for trade on the rivers of Guinea at that time represented 3,259,331 reais (8,466 cruzados) for three years.[8]

Documents of quittance passed to his heirs in 1509 declare that João Rodrigues de Mascarenhas died in 1506, and that his heirs have fulfilled his contracts. One document, dated July 6, 1509, concerns the *vintena* on trade along the rivers of Guinea, the value of which had increased to 4,600,000 reais through the period 1505, 1506, and 1507; although the quittance only concerns the period up to February 5, 1506, which produced 1,109,157 reais.[9] Another document, dated June 27, 1509, concerns the rents owed to the royal chancellery, under contract, by João Rodrigues Mascarenhas: a sum of 5,860,000 reais (15,220 cruzados) for the years 1504, 1505, and 1506, which was made good by the heirs.[10] There are also two contracts with João Rodrigues Mascarenhas concerning royal rents on sugar from Madeira, and the documents indicate that the heirs made good a payment of 1,800,000 reais for 6,000 arrobas of sugar bought in 1505.[11] Finally, there are receipts issued by João Serrão, the royal judicial clerk, who in 1501 received 1,800 reais of maintenance from João Rodrigues Mascarenhas, as the person responsible for payments to the *desembargadores do Paço* (royal high court judges).[12]

Careful checking of all the original documents in the *Livros de Chancelaria* (registry of the royal administration) to find marginalia, where the names of Mascarenhas's heirs could have been written, has produced nothing. Such names could have belonged to children or even the deceased's wife, since, according to Portuguese inheritance law, wives (or husbands) received half of the deceased's property, besides the dowry, plus a possible payment of an extra third at the discretion of the deceased, while the remainder was divided equally among the children, male and female.[13] There are many João Rodrigues, even among contemporaries of João Rodrigues Mascarenhas, and in 1524 one of them was receiver for the rents owing to the royal chancellery for 1524–1525.[14]

A more likely heir, however, is António Rodrigues Mascarenhas, who in 1510 won the right to farm for three years the rents and the tenth taxation on the Cape Verde islands of Santiago (where he was a neighbour), Fogo, and Maio, together with the quarts and vintenas on Guinea, which together were worth 900,000 reais each year.[15] The duties on cotton, cattle, hides, and slaves were at stake. António Rodrigues Mascarenhas could involve up to four partners, and he had to pay his rents in the form of slaves. Another document from 1514 shows that António Rodrigues Mascarenhas, associated with Nicolau Rodrigues (probably a brother or relative), in 1511–1513, paid rents on hides from the Cape Verde islands of Santiago, Fogo, and Maio to Gonçalo Lopes, royal factor in the islands and *almoxarife* (royal customs agent) for slaves and the vintena on Guinea.[16] António Rodrigues Mascarenhas is otherwise mentioned as receiver and farmer of rents for the chancellery in 1527.[17] It is possible that he had already been working in his father's business before 1506, alone or with relatives.

Whatever the identity of the heirs of João Rodrigues Mascarenhas, this story shows how West Africa was already an important economic area, frequented by New Christians who had adapted to local religious traditions, plural lineages, and relatively open trade.[18] The logic of my search on Mascarenhas is based on a steady legal and practical organizational framework followed by the Portuguese kings. If they were satisfied with the work of their contractors, they would tend to renew contracts after the latter's death with their heirs or relatives. Even when financiers betrayed the trust of the king and had their property expropriated, more reliable relatives or partners could benefit from the redistribution of the miscreant's property, as happened with Lourenço Vasques (formerly, Isaac Latam, son of Moisés Latam), who received houses expropriated from Isaac Abravanel in 1483.[19]

The fact is that João Rodrigues Mascarenhas was a magnate who farmed the significant expenditure of the royal moradias, the payments to royal judges and judicial officers, the rents of the royal chancellery, the rents on trade in the area along the rivers of Guinea, and the contracts for royal sugar in Madeira. He was also, most probably, an agent of the king at the fairs of Castile. These positions had been controlled in the last decades of the fifteenth century by the rich Jewish Abravanel and Palaçano families, and by the Abeacar, Benafaçam, Negro, and Sapaio families. It is possible that João Rodrigues Mascarenhas had links with one of those houses. However, the 1490s had seen the arrival of wealthy families from Castile—namely, the Nasi from Soria and the Benveniste from Calahorra and Soria—and these new families would become important financiers under King Manuel. The problem is that we know very little about the transfer of names, since it was the Christian names that were used for the purposes of administration, although in some cases the Jewish names were added, as in the cases of Jorge Fernandes Bixorda, Afonso Lopes Sapaio, Henrique Fernandes Abravanel, Duarte Fernandes Palaçano, Tristão Palaçano, Duarte Rodrigues Zaboca, and Gonçalo Fernandes Gordilha.[20]

2. Loronha, Pimentel, Tristão, and Negro

Besides the Rodrigues Mascarenhas, we can identify the following New Christians and their families among the most active merchants and financiers in early sixteenth century Portugal: Master João de Paz, whose son Duarte, as we saw in the Introduction to this book, would play an important role as the New Christian agent in Rome against the establishment of the Inquisition in Portugal; the brothers Francisco, Diogo, and Gonçalo Mendes, from the Benveniste family, associated with the Nasi family; Luís Vaz de Negro and other members of the Negro family; Henrique Fernandes Abravanel, associated with Duarte Tristão; Jorge Lopes Bixorda; and Fernão de Loronha, associated with Álvaro

Pimentel and Duarte Tristão (both here identified as New Christians). Fernão de Loronha (also written Noronha) is an unusual case, since he was of English Jewish, not Iberian Jewish, origin. He had obtained a coat of arms in England, which King Manuel, in 1506, authorised to be used in Portugal; and in 1532, King John III gave him the status of *fidalgo* and a new coat of arms.[21]

Fernão de Loronha, in association with Álvaro Pimentel, had the contract for the royal moradias from 1494 to 1496. Both men were then knights of the royal house, and the letter of quittance for that contract, dated 1498, indicates that the king owed them money for the *Casa da Mina* (the agency in Lisbon for the fort built in the Gulf of Guinea to import gold). Fernão de Loronha was made a citizen of Lisbon in that same year. In that period, he was involved in the contract for sugar from Madeira, while he was also trading in West Africa,[22] and he was later responsible, among other entrepreneurs, for taking sugar cane cultivation from Madeira and São Tomé to Brazil. For the years 1502 to 1505, he took on the contract for the rent on *pau-brasil* (wood used for dyeing cloth which gave its name to Brazil) at four thousand ducados a year. In the same years, he also had the contract for the exploration of the coast of Brazil, in association with other merchants. In 1504, King Manuel presented him with the archipelago of São João, 354 kilometres from the northeast tip of the coast of Brazil, which became known as the Archipelago of Fernando de Noronha.

In the meantime, Fernão de Loronha invested in ships fitted out for voyages to India and Brazil, which he used regularly in the first decades of the sixteenth century for his own trade in pepper and hired out to carry freight needed by the king and other merchants. He also traded in *malagueta* (a small, fiery red pepper) from West Africa. We know that he owned several ships in association with other merchants, such as the famous *nau Bretoa*, co-owned with Bartolomeo Marchione, Benedetto Morelli, and Francisco Martins. A certificate from the *Casa da Índia* dated July 28, 1522, stated that the contractors for *pau-brasil* (brazilwood), Fernão de Loronha, Jorge Lopes (Bixorda?), and Duarte Tristão, had paid 2,337,795 reais (5,844 cruzados) from a total debt of 9,838,339 reais (24,596 cruzados).[23] The scope of these merchants' activities is staggering, ranging from West Africa to Brazil and South Asia. Fernão de Loronha, who died around 1547, was a major financial player in the first half of the sixteenth century.

Álvaro Pimentel was an associate of Fernão de Loronha in the latter's first contracts. Although Loronha undertook many partnerships with Old Christians and foreigners, his first contracts were mentioned in a letter by Pietro Rondinelli from Seville, in 1502, as being with New Christians.[24] As we know, the designation New Christian (or *converso*) was not used in documents at that time, with a few exceptions, which particularly included the trials of the Inquisition; even in that case it only became the norm in specific accusations of Judaism. It is difficult to ascertain, in many cases, whether a merchant is a

New Christian or an Old Christian, especially in the period before the establishment of the Inquisition. However, the case of Álvaro Pimentel, although not fully proven, seems quite safe. He was, without any doubt, one of the major merchant bankers of the first two decades of the sixteenth century.

In the years 1509 to 1511, Álvaro Pimentel had the biggest contract for pepper, valued at 10,530,000 reais. When this was added to his contracts for sugar (12,000 arrobas), the total value reached 24,580,000 reais (63,844 cruzados). In the period 1510 to 1512, he entered into two contracts for pepper, plus contracts for other spices, and these contracts together totalled 64,300,000 reais, or 21,433,333 reais a year.[25] He was a contractor for royal pensions (tenças, used as a reward for services), royal purchases, and the maintenance of the royal guard, all of which were itemized in the contract. The two quittances for that contract, dated November 19, 1510, and covering 1508 and 1509, indicate the annual staggering sum of 24,580,000 reais involved.[26] Pimentel was associated with Fernão Gomes for the business of shipping freight on the *carreira da Índia*, for which he could be paid in pepper, as happened in 1511, when the king acknowledged a total debt of 10,640,000 reais (27,636 cruzados), from which he ordered the payment of 1,238,000 in pepper, calculated at 22 cruzados per *quintal*.[27] In the same year the partners received another 3,900,000 reais in pepper as partial payment for fitting out three new ships and refurbishing two old ships.[28]

In 1508, several payments ordered by the king indicate that huge debts to contractors were the norm: the receiver for fish and wood taxation in Lisbon was ordered to pay Pimentel 470,000 reais out of 16 million reais due.[29] In the same year, the almoxarife of *quartos* (taxation) in Madeira was ordered to give Pimentel 3,000 arrobas of sugar, at 360 reais per arroba, as part of 12,000 arrobas due. This order was subcontracted by Álvaro Pimentel's son, Garcia, to other merchants, probably to settle accounts for other transactions. In this document, Álvaro Pimentel was identified as a contractor for royal pensions and weddings, which meant big business.[30] In 1508, the king ordered the payment of 250,000 reais on account from a total of 16 million reais owed to Álvaro Pimentel, with a similar amount payable in 1509, and more—235,500 reais plus 100,000 reais—in 1510.[31] In this same year the king ordered the payment of 100,000 reais to Álvaro Pimentel from the sisa on wheat in Lisbon.[32] In 1509, the receiver for the taxes on textiles was ordered to pay Pimentel 253,500 réis.[33]

In 1508, Álvaro Pimentel imported from Lille, then part of the Habsburg territories, significant quantities of rich textiles for the royal household.[34] He was involved as well in the malagueta (red pepper) trade from West Africa, valued at 31,299 *libras* in 1508.[35] In 1511, he invested in spices from the king, 20,000 cruzados and 10,000 *in specie* before the departure of the carreira da Índia.[36] There are receipts for tenças paid in 1509 and 1510.[37] In 1516, he received 130,138 reais from the receiver for textile taxes in Alentejo.[38] Finally, he was negotiating a delivery of arms from Biscay to the king when he died, around 1520.[39] In the aforementioned details, we can see not only the diversity of trades for which there were royal contracts but also the deeply rooted system of permanent debt managed by the royal house and everyone else. In 1511, King Manuel even took the opportunity to use the pepper left by Álvaro Pimentel at the Casa da Índia, valued at 180,000 réis, to pay the dowry he offered to Duarte Galvão's daughter, a famous courtier who represented him in Ethiopia.[40] The document states that Pimentel would be compensated, but permanent royal debt seems to have been the norm.

Duarte Tristão had a similar profile. In the years 1509 to 1511, he had the second highest contract for pepper among the Portuguese investors, valued at 6,240,000 reais.[41] In 1512, he was given the privileges of a citizen of Lisbon by King Manuel.[42] From 1514, he invested in ships and freight for the carreira da Índia: in 1514, he received 546,679 reais for a specific cargo shipped to the royal agents in Cochim and Cananor;[43] in 1523, he received 2,000 cruzados for a royal cargo from India;[44] and in 1525, King John III ordered the payment to him of 152,500 reais, levied on money for work on the cathedral of Évora, for another freight from India.[45] In 1516, King Manuel ordered the almoxarife for textile taxes in Lisbon to pay Duarte Tristão 106,980 reais, which were due to him on account of pepper delivered.[46] He traded in malagueta from West Africa, as revealed in royal documents dated from 1517 to 1529.[47] Between 1518 and 1528, he delivered more than 634 marcos of silver to the *Casa da Moeda* (the Mint), although this was a mid-sized rather than a major delivery.[48] In 1519, a royal document shows that he was trading in coral, sent to the royal agent in Cochin (five boxes with 13 quintais, 1 arroba, and 13 arráteis).[49]

In 1520, Duarte Tristão was released, for 11,816,995 reais (29,542 cruzados), from two years of a contract as the receiver for taxes on textiles in Lisbon.[50] In 1524, he received maintenance for the passengers on his ship, the *São Miguel*, on their way back to Portugal from India.[51] In 1536, he received a significant loan of two million reais from the treasurer of the Casa da Índia.[52] In 1537, Tristão's ships on the carreira da Índia, the *São Miguel* and the *Santa Maria da Graça*, were fitted out by the House of India.[53] I have not mentioned here Duarte Tristão's partnership with Fernão de Loronha in a contract for brazilwood. Duarte Tristão was thus involved in the main overseas trades carried on in the first three decades of the sixteenth century, although he also invested in a significant contract for the taxation of textiles imported into Lisbon. While in other cases the highest-ranking merchants were invited to invest in royal bonds and lend money to the king, Duarte Tristão received a significant loan, showing that the financial relationship could go either way. However, we do not know the level of royal debt that his contracts involved.

Luís Vaz de Negro was the head of a traditional Jewish family, the ibn Yahya, who had lived in Portugal for several centuries before being forced to convert in 1497. Unfortunately, documentation concerning him is not as extensive as might be expected. In the early 1510s, he was receiver for the royal tenth payable on the islands of the Azores and farmer for the royal rent on wheat produced there, wheat he traded to the island of Madeira.[54] In 1510, he used his brother, Pedro Álvares de Negro, as his agent for the collection of a royal payment of 53,350 reais at the *almoxarifado* of Ponte de Lima.[55] The next year, he gave a warrant to Diogo de Paz for the same purpose, subcontracted to Diogo de Soure, and this brought in 200,000 reais.[56] In 1524, he held contracts for the royal rents on sugar on the island of Madeira: in one case this was for the selling of 1,000 arrobas, in association with Jorge Rodrigues; in another case he passed on a warrant to his son, Gabriel de Negro, to receive 666 arrobas.[57] In 1527, he received some royal reimbursement of a loan imposed on the New Christians, to which he had contributed 120,000 reais; 60,000 reais were assigned to him on the dry ports of Trás-os-Montes.[58]

The practice of irregular lending imposed by the king on the New Christians emerges quite early in this story. We should keep in mind that King John III was already requesting that the pope establish the Inquisition in Portugal. The activities of Luís Vaz de Negro were concentrated on the Atlantic islands, a solid platform for trade, and were based on royal rents, but we do not have information on other forms of private trade used by him or on his participation in other royal monopolies. In 1524 his son, Gabriel de Negro, was in Venice, from where he kept communication with the Portuguese king; it seems that the Portuguese consul there could not leave his house due to the size of his debts.[59] Gabriel de Negro lived in Antwerp later, then in Venice again, and finally in Salonika.[60]

3. Abravanel, Bixorda, Paz, and Mendes

Information on Henrique Fernandes Abravanel is scarce. He was a receiver for textile taxes in Lisbon, in association with Duarte Tristão, during the years 1515, 1516, and 1517, and the two men had 150,000 reais of losses written off by the king in 1520.[61] In 1517, Henrique Fernandes received confirmation from the king that he could keep the contract for rented houses in Lisbon that were part of the royal warehouses on the street known as *Poço da Fotea*. He had inherited the position as tenant of these houses from his aunt, Leonor Fernandes, who had received them from Abraham Beacar, who had acquired the contract from Isaac Abete.[62] Previously, in 1504, Abravanel had received confirmation of the *aforamento* (long-term contract) for three-storied houses and farms around Lisbon, also inherited from Leonor Fernandes, who had passed away and made her niece, Inês Fernandes, Abravanel's wife, her heir.[63] In 1512, he received 400,000 reais from the king, part of a debt of 1,540,404 reais owed to his uncle, Judas Abravanel, on the contract for moradias and the vintena on trade along the rivers of Guinea in 1482 and 1483.[64] There are indications that

Henrique Fernandes Abravanel had a connection with the main Portuguese banker, Francisco Mendes, but documents concerning this are scarce.

Jorge Lopes Bixorda was considered a major financier in this period. Vitorino Magalhães Godinho observes that he was involved in all overseas trade and regularly delivered silver to the Casa da Moeda in Lisbon, supplying a total of more than 8,495 marcos between 1520 and 1530, the fourth-largest quantity supplied in the years from 1517 to 1556.[65] He was a pepper buyer at the Casa da Índia in the years 1509 to 1511 and belonged to the consortium for pepper trading, in which he had the third largest contract among the Portuguese investors—for 5,850,000 reais (15,194 cruzados).[66] Documents show that he controlled the contracts for royal sugar in Madeira between 1522 and 1531, and these documents are very specific concerning the prices and weights and agents involved, including for direct trade to Flanders.[67] There are records of a Jorge Lopes involved in buying wheat from Luís Vaz de Negro in 1512 and trading in sealing wax and textiles with Morocco in 1515 as an agent of the Jew Yusuf Cofem in Fez.[68] However this may have been someone else with the same name. More interesting is a long document issued by King Manuel on August 25, 1517, in which he declares that Jorge Lopes Bixorda, knight of the royal house, and his descendants, can sell, exchange, and create an entailed property (*morgado*) in their domain near the beach of Santos (Lisbon), notwithstanding the *lei mental* (meaning the protection of royal property; there was indeed a royal palace nearby). He was allowed to build houses and develop the property, including extending it to the sea, a rare privilege.[69] This document reveals the high social position achieved by Jorge Lopes Bixorda.

Master João de Paz was the founder of the extraordinary Paz family, who lived in Guimarães, Porto, and Lisbon from the late fifteenth to the eighteenth century. He came to Portugal with three brothers and one sister. Within two generations, the family included physicians, surgeons, clergymen, academics, judges, lawyers, merchants, farmers of royal rents, and tax collectors. Master João de Paz, declared by King Manuel to be "our physician and surgeon," asked for a letter of confirmation of his status as surgeon, and this was issued on August 8, 1499. The letter declares that he was examined for his profession seventeen years earlier, which means that he was already in Portugal in 1482.[70] He had seven children: Duarte, the New Christians' agent in Rome in the 1530s; Isidro, Fernando, and Diogo, who received minor religious orders; Brites, who married Vasco Leite, a member of an important Old Christian family from Porto; Maria, who married Manuel Figueiredo; and Tomás, who went to Cochin when the Inquisition was established in Portugal.

Master João de Paz was a tax collector in various towns of the region and responsible for the customs of Porto and the district of Entre-Douro e Minho, extending his activities to Trás-os-Montes and Beiras. He also traded with Flanders. He endowed a chapel at the monastery of São Francisco in Porto and was buried there, next to two Old Christian families (the Brandão and the

Carneiro), which shows an impressive sociability in death. He had been associated with a significant number of merchants, both New Christians (Miguel
Gomes Bravo, Duarte Manrique, Dinis Eanes, and Miguel Fernandes Pina) and
Old Christians (Paio Rodrigues, Gonçalo Rocha, Fernão Gonçalves, Pero Anes,
and Afonso Francês, this last a partner in ship investment whose ethnic status
needs to be better researched). He also had social relations with the nobility,
not only the Duke of Bragança, but also the Mesquita, Noronha, Brandão, and
Leite families.[71] His son, Diogo de Paz, was receiver for customs duties in Porto
in 1516, 1517, and 1518; and a letter of quittance dated April 14, 1520, records
him collecting 14,747,462 reais (36,869 cruzados) of duties.[72]

Duarte de Paz, João's eldest son, was involved in the conquest of Azem-
mour, in 1513, which was led by the Duke of Bragança. He was made a knight
at the end of that campaign and later received the habit of the military order of
Christ.[73] On June 8, 1525, Duarte de Paz was nominated receiver for customs
duties in the dry ports of the Beiras district.[74] On July 23, 1529, Duarte de
Paz, knight of the royal house, was made customs administrator of Porto.[75] On
February 23, 1534, Duarte de Paz, collector of silk taxes from Castile, received
a letter of quittance after collecting 40,055,579 reais in money and 155,579
reais in fabrics (in total, 100,528 cruzados).[76] Duarte de Paz's position as New
Christian agent in Rome after 1532 led to a temporary interruption in the relationship between his family and King John III (see chapter 4). That the family
not only survived this serious upset but also survived in the long term was
certainly due to its policy of intermarrying and maintaining steady relations
with the nobility and traditional local elites.

The case of the Mendes family is even better known. After the death of
Francisco Mendes, his widow, Beatriz Luna, became head of the family and
moved to Antwerp, Venice, Ferrara, and finally Constantinople, where she
assumed the Jewish name Gracia Nasi and played a crucial role in the Jewish community.[77] This family followed an opposite strategy to that chosen by
the Paz family: close marriages among tightly linked families related to the
Benveniste family of Calahorra and Soria, which was where the family originated from. Francisco Mendes Benveniste, probably born in the 1470s, was
associated all his life with his younger brother Diogo, who moved to Antwerp
in 1512, while Francisco stayed in Lisbon, where he lived on the street known
as *Poço da Fotea* (next to Henrique Fernandes Abravanel), in the former Jewish ghetto. He married Beatriz Luna, probably in the late 1520s, and had one
daughter, Ana (later Reina), before he died in 1535.

Francisco Mendes was deeply involved in the pepper business and the carreira da Índia from the 1500s on, in association with the Italian merchant
Giovanni Battista Affaitati.[78] In 1499, it seems that Francisco Mendes acted as
guarantor, with Duarte Rodrigues, for João Rodrigues Mascarenhas's bid for
the farming of royal rents in Lisbon.[79] In 1502, Francisco Rebelo and Francisco Mendes, both knights of the royal house, with João Vaz and Gomes

Anes, squires of the royal house, were nominated brokers of horses, mules, and slaves [*sic*] to the court.[80] Surviving royal documents make various references to Francisco Mendes, including mention of payments he received for the pepper he imported from India: in 1514 and 1516 payments from the almoxarifado of Viseu and from the tenth in Trás-os-Montes, around 740,000 reais;[81] on July 20, 1530, King John III granted him the same privileges that German merchants enjoyed;[82] and on August 4, 1534, King John III ordered the payment of 10,000 reais to him, to redeem an unspecified debt.[83]

Francisco Mendes was also a private banker and pawnbroker. Many other documents that refer to him concern the payment of debts due on loans taken out by private individuals, some of them noblemen and noblewomen, using royal pensions: between 1511 and 1515, we find references to loans taken out by D. Branca Coutinho; Fernão de Ferreira, fidalgo of the royal house; Henrique de Melo; D. Beatriz Cabral; and Gabriel de Brito, fidalgo of the royal house.[84] In operating his business, Francisco Mendes naturally received and issued bills of exchange, some of them with Manuel Cirne, the royal factor in Andalusia, which may indicate that he was involved in providing food and arms to the Portuguese forts in North Africa.[85] Also interesting is an order issued by King Manuel, on August 28, 1511, to the Casa da Índia to pay 202,800 reais in ginger to Francisco Mendes, who had just delivered 490 quintais of sulphur to the House of Powder.[86] The most significant indicator of Francisco Mendes's extreme wealth is given by the quantity of silver he delivered to the Casa da Moeda between 1517 and 1534: an extraordinary total of more than 17,845 marcos, making him the highest of all the suppliers on the list compiled by Vitorino Magalhães Godinho.[87]

Francisco Mendes had a special relationship with the kings, particularly John III, who supported him until Mendes's death in 1535. John III accepted Francisco Mendes's claims that merchandise had been stolen at sea by the French and wrote to the French king. In one piece of information, we learn that spices valued at 640,000 reais carried by one ship in 1522 were captured by a French admiral. In the same year, another ship with a cargo of 740,000 reais worth of spices was captured off the coast of Brittany on its way to Flanders. In 1527, a cargo of Flemish textiles shipped by Diogo Mendes from Antwerp in the name of Francisco's father-in-law, Álvaro de Luna, was captured near the coast of Portugal.[88] When Diogo Mendes was detained in Antwerp in 1531, and again in 1532, accused of monopoly, manipulation of prices, and Judaism, King John III was prompted by Francisco Mendes to write to the Emperor Charles V, in August 1532, asking for his release.[89] John III was certainly directly interested, because he had long-term business with the two brothers: Diogo Mendes guaranteed the spice trade in northern Europe, from which the king benefitted, while he constantly helped to keep the royal agent in Antwerp afloat financially. We shall see how the death of Francisco Mendes precipitated a realignment of religious allegiance in his family, which came under extraordinary pressure both in Lisbon and in Antwerp, while the New Christian negotiations in Rome, which he appears to have supported, received a major blow.

4. In Castile and Beyond

New Christian traders in Castile were arguably then more important than their relatives in Portugal because of their strong attachments to municipalities and the royal court, despite massive early inquisitorial persecution. In the early sixteenth century, the farming of royal rents was controlled by New Christians in Seville, Segovia, Arjona, Toledo, Baeza, Malaga, and Almagro.[90] The powerful financier Pedro del Alcázar, a *jurado* (citizen responsible for the administration of justice) from Seville who had been reconciled and whose sequestered property had been returned to him by the Inquisition, was a prominent member of a group of farmers of royal rents. This group of farmers included Juan López and Alvar Sánchez, sons of another jurado, Alonso Fernández, who had also been reconciled by the Inquisition, as well as Juan de Palma and Rodrigo de Córdoba (again with relatives who had been reconciled or condemned by the Inquisition).[91]

The New Christians in Seville not only controlled the taxation contracts in the late fifteenth and first decades of the sixteenth century but also monopolised the production and trade of fabrics, mainly the silk industry, through the rich families Cisbón, the Baeza, the Córdoba, and the Herrera, who all had interests in different economic activities. Rodrigo de Loro and his family controlled the important dye industry, which involved imports from the Atlantic, partly based on pastel. The hide industry, extended in time to the Caribbean, was controlled in the first decades of the sixteenth century by Pedro López Gavilán and his family. The use of hides in shoemaking, wallpaper, and upholstery was extensive. Trade with the West Indies eventually involved most of these families from Seville, particularly the Cisbón, the Córdoba, the Alfaro, the Illescas, the Caballero, the Fernández, the Alemán, the Barrera, and the Jerez. Some of them were involved with Hernando Cortés and other conquistadores. They associated with Portuguese New Christians for the slave trade. And the Segura, the Medina, and the Fernández, linked to the Maldonado, the Jerez and the Bastidas, farmed taxation in the Caribbean from the 1520s to the 1540s.[92]

Francisco Hernández Coronel, a well-known New Christian from Segovia, controlled the royal *alcabalas* (equivalent to the Portuguese sisas, taxes on transactions) in Medina del Campo (1506–1508) and was *repartidor general* for the royal rents in the districts of Palencia, Trasmiera, and La Rioja (1511–1516), which were worth a total of 36 million maravedis. In the following years, he extended his farming of royal rents to Burgos, Logroño, Madrid, Sigüenza, and Las Alpujarras, which, in 1519, brought the total to 57 million maravedis. He was also associated with other families in this business, mainly the Santa Cruz family, New Christians from Aranda de Duero.[93]

Pedro de Baeza was another major New Christian financier, who controlled the rents of the military order of Calatrava in Andalusia, being also involved in the farming of royal rents in Jaén and Granada with Luis Núñez de Andújar, Hernando de Córdoba, Juan Lobo, and Martin Yánes de Ávila (all with the reputation of being *conversos*). In 1519, an exceptional need for funds in the royal treasury forced Charles V to auction all the Castilian royal rents for the next six years (in general, the contracts would run for two to three years), obtaining for him close to 1 million ducados, an extraordinary sum. The resulting agreement with the major financiers, known as the *postura general* of Barcelona, reveals the prominent position of New Christians in this period: Fernando de Cuenca, a leading farmer who had controlled the rents of Galicia in previous years, was reputed to be a New Christian, as were Pedro del Alcázar, who controlled most of the rents of Seville; Pedro de Santa Cruz and Francisco Hernández Coronel, who controlled the rents of Burgos, Palencia, Trasmiera, Toro, Soria, and parts of Seville; Rodrigo Álvarez de Madrid, who controlled the rents of Jaén, part of Córdoba, and Calatrava de Andalusia, and also Merida and Llerena; Marcos de Madrid, who controlled the rents of Toledo, Madrid, and Campo de Calatrava; and Luis Núñez de Andújar and Hernando de Cordoba, who controlled the rents of the kingdom of Granada.[94]

Carretero Zamora, who has provided the best studies on New Christian financiers in early sixteenth century Castile, attributes the success of Pedro del Alcázar to his capacity for establishing partnerships with other financiers, particularly Diego de Alarcón, Francisco de Mena, Lope de Urueña, Francisco Ortiz, Francisco de Alcocer, and Juan de Almansa. Alcocer and Almansa were New Christians as identified by Juan Gil.[95] It is likely that the others were Old Christians, which would have increased Alcázar's room for negotiation and given him some protection from inquisitorial investigation. The most successful relationships he established were with Charles V's general treasurer, Francisco de Vargas, and the royal secretary, Francisco de los Cobos, and these officials would have helped him to develop his position as repartidor general for royal rents in Andalusia. He had already participated in the forced New Christian contribution to the royal finances in 1510, the *Composición* (agreement), in which he had made one of the highest payments, 800 ducados.[96]

This Composición has helped scholars identify New Christian families involved in other financial developments, particularly the sequestration of goods being privately traded from the Indies from the beginning of 1534 to the early months of 1535 to underwrite the military expedition to Tunis in 1535.[97] The commodities involved in the sequestration were inventoried as a mandatory loan to be returned to the owners with a low 5 percent interest. The operation alone provided Charles V with 60,000 ducados. In any case, the study by Carretero Zamora shows the inclusion of the main New Christian families in this sequestration, which means that they were heavily involved in trade with the Indies, despite the prohibitions in place at the beginning, but alleviated after 1504. Records show that the Núñez, Jerez, Caballero, Jaén, Illescas, Martínez, Tarifa, Palma, Torres, Plasencia, and Carrión families, among others, recorded high total values for their transactions, having relatives acting as agents in the Americas.[98]

The identification of the primary New Christian merchants, through the contracts they had with the Iberian kings and the main economic developments they were engaged in, as far as available studies and documentation allow us to go, underlines continuities in economic and social patterns before and after the forced conversion of 1492 to 1497. The number of New Christian families involved increased after 1492, but there were decisions to abandon Iberia in order to live openly in the Jewish faith, which meant the reorganisation of the New Christian merchant elite.[99] In the meantime, the development of the Castilian and also the Portuguese overseas empires received a major boost with the discovery of the Americas and the maritime route to India around the Cape of Good Hope, while trade with North Africa, West Africa, Caribbean, Brazil, New Spain, and Peru boomed.[100]

The networks of trade between Portugal, Castile, Flanders, and Italy were similarly expanded. The early move to Antwerp of one of the most important New Christian bankers, Diogo Mendes, is a sign that this was a period in which Portuguese merchants were still at the top of their game when it came to distribution of overseas commodities in northern Europe. Castilian New Christians were already in Antwerp, constituting an important community until the end of the sixteenth century. Foreign merchants and bankers, such as the Italians but also the Germans, had a major role in all these trades. They were associated in many cases with Iberian merchants but did not manage to displace New Christians among the main merchants. They were a minority; this was the case even for the German merchants, who were so important in the early sixteenth century for the import of silver from central Europe, and who received successive grants of trade privileges from the Portuguese and Castilian kings, and, naturally, from Charles V, who had well-known, important connections to the bankers Fugger and Welser.[101]

To consider the Portuguese case, particularly the contracts for pepper issued between 1509 and 1511, New Christians were at the top of the list of Portuguese investors, but foreign merchants had a significant share: 31,182,824 reais of a total of 66,934,893 reais, or 47 percent. Marcos de Cimarmão (certainly, the German Markus Zimmerman), then an agent for the Fugger interests, controlled the second highest contract (9,750,000 reais), and the Germans Johann, Gabriel, and Philip Rem controlled the third highest contract (total of 9,370,391 reais). The Castilian Cristóbal de Haro had the sixth highest contract (4,646,705 reais), followed by two other important Spanish merchants, whereas the first Italian, Sernigi, had only the thirteenth highest contract (1,029,600 reais).[102] The lists of merchants delivering silver and gold to the Casa da Moeda in the period 1517–1556 is more evenly balanced, with a larger number of foreign merchants involved, mainly concerned with silver; the Portuguese merchants, however, still predominated.[103] A comparison of wealth between Portuguese and foreign merchants in Lisbon at the end of the seventeenth century would reveal a reversal of this balance.

It is undeniable that in the booming overseas economy of the Iberian world in the first half of the sixteenth century, New Christian merchants controlled a significant amount of capital and were major participants, in many cases, in association with Old Christians and foreign merchants. They also benefitted from the diaspora of Jews and New Christians to North Africa, Italy, the Ottoman Empire, and northern Europe, and that of New Christians to the East Indies and West Indies. This meant that an extraordinary intercontinental network was in place by the mid-sixteenth century. German bankers and merchants played an important role in this period, while the Genoese already had a strong foothold in both Castile and Portugal, but only later, under Philip II, would they control the royal finances in Castile. Shared cultural and ethnic identities contributed to New Christian trading networks, which survived divergent or plural religious allegiances, although they were not exclusive. Forced conversion to Christianity left a deep scar in these communities but created new possibilities for business owing to the wider access to royal and ecclesiastic positions and contracts that was available to those who survived inquisitorial persecution. We shall see how these networks—understood here in the low-key form of extensive practice of temporary partnerships, which benefitted from the system of correspondence and association between merchants in different countries and continents—reacted to disruptions and resisted political and religious challenges.

CHAPTER THREE

Disruptions

ANTI-*CONVERSO* RIOTS BETWEEN 1449 and 1474, which triggered and supported the struggle to impose blood purity statutes, the implementation of the Inquisition in the 1480s, and the expulsion of Jews in 1492, were direct or indirect major blows to the Castilian and Aragonese New Christian merchant elite. However, we find New Christians acting as royal bankers and contractors, as well as being prominent merchants involved with the *carrera de Indias*, during the first half of the sixteenth century. Many resisted exclusion from municipal councils and cathedral chapters, and some found their way into the lower—and even titled—nobility, in spite of inquisitorial terror. By contrast, the Portuguese New Christian merchant elite, who were also royal bankers and prominent merchants involved in overseas contracts, were only confronted with a really challenging period from the late 1520s to the 1540s, if we exclude the riots in 1504 in Évora and 1506 in Lisbon. This period of change was triggered by negotiations to establish the Inquisition in Portugal, the messianic movement inspired by David Reubeni, and the new anti-converso stance of the Habsburg authorities in Antwerp.

Therefore, the periods of antagonism, integration, and segregation experienced by Jews and New Christians occurred at different times, as did the policies that affected the two groups, according to whether they were in Castile and Aragon or in Portugal. We need to acknowledge this absence of synchronism, which had consequences for migration and identity dynamics. The European context is also important. From the 1520s to the 1540s, rulers across the continent took the initiative in directing religious adherence among their populations. Major events and political processes occurred in this period, such as the attempt by the Holy Roman emperor to control Protestant dissidence in his territories, the rejection of papal authority by Henry VIII in Britain, the creation of the Roman Congregation of the Inquisition in 1542, and the confessionalisation of most states of Europe.[1]

The division between Christians formally imposed by the blood purity statutes created in Castile needs to be better analysed because it had long-term consequences. We also need to understand the debate that this divide immediately triggered, because the arguments on both sides would create the basis for renewed discussions during the sixteenth and seventeenth centuries.[2] This chapter will then tackle a major event that arguably played a significant role in the establishment of the Inquisition in Portugal: the visit of David Reubeni, a Jew allegedly from Arabia who proposed an alliance to fight the Muslims. The consequences of the formal and informal divide between New and Old Christians will then be addressed through the stories of two families of international merchants and financiers who ended up outside Christianity. They are introduced here as representative of many other members of the Iberian population who chose to withdraw from living under constant threat, whilst maintaining an ambiguous relationship with their countries of origin for economic, social, and sentimental reasons.

1. Division

The anti–New Christian riot in Toledo in 1449 has been identified as the point at which a situation of relative integration for this massive group of people turned into one of discrimination, introducing a division that became rooted in the subsequent centuries. If this picture is accepted, there are nuances to be introduced. First, it seems that there had been attempts to stir up racial feeling against New Christians at a local level well before 1449, particularly during the mass conversions of 1391 to 1416. There are several letters from kings reassuring New Christians that they will be treated equally; there is a decree from Queen Maria of Aragon, issued in 1433, forbidding the exclusion of New Christians from positions in Barcelona, another attempt at which was made three years later; there is a record of a plot, exposed in Seville in 1434, to murder and rob New Christians, which led to the detention and exile of the conspirators; there is evidence of an attempt, in 1437, to impose a rule that only those whose families had been "natural Christians" for four generations could have access to the office of exchange broker in Lérida; and in this same year, the Archbishop Diego de Anaya, who had founded the college of St. Bartholomew in Salamanca, added a blood purity clause to the statutes of the college.[3] There are also appeals made to the pope by large communities of New Christians, for example, by those of Aragon, who complained about constant discrimination and who obtained support from Pope Eugenius IV through a bull issued on January 31, 1437.[4] David Nirenberg highlights the social earthquake that the drastic reduction of Jews represented, a reduction that meant less fiscal income and the loss of ready scapegoats, while the continuing inter-religious kinship and relations between Jews and converted people produced an anxiety about identifying the two groups, because traditional barriers, particularly sexual ones, were seen as threatened.[5] Segregation of Jews followed at the local level, as well as suspicion of conversos' religious behaviour.

The early stages of the integration of New Christians were therefore a permanent struggle for survival and recognition that required a significant amount of energy, resources, and diplomatic skills. That many New Christians reached high positions as Church dignitaries and royal and urban administrators must be considered a major achievement in a time of instability, constant threat, envy, and duress. Toledo's riot was unique in the way the following circumstances coincided: growing conflict between Castile and Aragon that would lead to war; a request for a significant financial contribution (a loan of 1 million *maravedis*) to the city by the king, John II, perceived by the city as a violation of traditional privileges; civil war between the king and Prince Henry, to whom the city declared allegiance; and fury against New Christians, such as Alfonso Cota, a royal tax collector.[6]

The riot started on January 27, immediately after a request to be exempted from the aforementioned loan was refused by the *condestable* (constable), Álvaro de Luna: New Christians were killed, their houses attacked and plundered, and those who survived and had jobs at the cathedral chapter or the municipality were forced to escape. The rioters held fraudulent trials of New Christians, who were forced to confess to apostasy and then burnt. On June 5, they published a sentence-statute excluding all conversos from holding local office, particularly as *escribanías* (clerks), and fourteen were named and dismissed on the spot, accused of abusing their office and destroying the city. The riot lasted more than a year. The pope issued three bulls on September 24 condemning this case of opposition to the universalism of the Church and to the equal rights of believers, although he encouraged the prosecution of suspected heretics. The condemnation of the riot by the pope forced a compromise between the king and the prince. They detained two senior canons of the cathedral, who had launched illegal investigations of New Christians, since no powers to do so had been delegated to them by the archbishop, and they executed two jurists who had offered legal justification for the revolt. The main nobleman who had supported the riot, Pero Sarmiento, was excommunicated by the pope and forced into exile, but after one year he obtained pardon from both the king and the pope. The city received a royal interdict as punishment for its crime of lèse-majesté. The New Christians received neither compensation for, nor the return of, their property and offices.[7]

This riot was quelled, but it sowed the seeds for further riots and the eventual proclamation of the blood purity statutes. What matters here is to understand both sides of the argument. The blood purity sentence-statute already existed in its main arguments, having appeared in both Visigoth and medieval law: New Christians were accused of continuing in their old faith, celebrating their traditional rituals, and dishonouring Christianity; they would take advantage of achieving public office to oppress good Old Christians and depopulate the city; "all descendants of the perverse lineage of Jews . . . due to their heresies and other offences, insults, seditions and crimes . . . will be considered . . . infamous, incapable, unfit and unworthy for any office and public or private benefice in this city of Toledo and its jurisdiction." In addition to all this, New Christians were excluded as public notaries and as witnesses, and they were denied any office or benefice they had previously had in the city. The explicit purpose was to avoid damaging the status of Old Christians and to further favour these excellent Old Christians (*cristianos viejos lindos*).[8] Briefly, New Christians were stripped of their rights as citizens, and the promise of equal rights achieved through baptism became void. Marcos García de Mora, one of the jurists involved in the riot, fomented further argument when the condemnations of both the pope and the king were proclaimed to the city. In a petition titled *Apelaçión y suplicaçión* addressed to the pope and the world, he declared the documents of condemnation null and without effect, because they had been influenced by an unfaithful congregation of "beasts at the synagogue" [*sic*] led by the tyrant Álvaro de Luna and by Mose Hamomo, the purported Hebrew name of the converso Fernán Díaz de Toledo, royal secretary and *relator* (rapporteur). Fernán Díaz was the main target, considered by Marcos García to be a man of particularly evil lineage and filthy customs, and thus condemned as a heretic, a true Jew, and a false Christian. The jurist considered New Christians to be a fourth order or estate, bad by nature and fraudulently converted, labelled as damned and of bastard lineage, children of incredulity and infidelity, fathers of all greed, disseminators of intrigue and division, malicious and perverse, ungrateful to God, deniers of the commandments, cast out from eternal glory, and perpetually condemned for their perfidy to the punishment of hell. Assuming the role of avenger of the dishonouring of God, Marcos García declared the exclusion of New Christians from all offices to be a virtuous action and insisted that attacking, robbing, hanging, and burning these people was not a crime but justice meted out for betrayal and deception. His only regret was that more of their property had not been plundered, but that could be remedied in the future. Marcos García was so blinded by his presumption that he attacked the only person who could save him, Prince Henry, for not respecting his pact with the city of Toledo, stating that not even the false bishop of Jewish lineage (not named) could absolve him.[9]

This torrent of unbridled hate and delirious pretension defined a framework within which an unhinged mind justified plunder, murder, and exclusion by attributing the worst motives to the persecuted in a typical reversal of roles, the victims being presented as perpetrators. It offered a template for diatribes of extermination that denied human status to the victims. Such extreme violence of language defined an attitude of complete hatred and contempt for a racialised and persecuted minority; we would recognise the equivalent in different periods of time. Béatrice Perez wrote an interesting article calling attention to the humanist (I would prefer "scholarly") background of some quotes used by Marcos García, which is correct, but the real novelty, in my view, is the definition of New Christians as a fourth estate, to whom is transferred the traditional hatred of Jews, here pushed beyond its usual limits.[10] This frame of mind would be normalised by the institutional prosecutors appointed in the early 1480s, the inquisitors, who would pursue it with efficiency on a much larger scale.

Several major jurists and ecclesiastics intervened in this debate with some fundamental counterarguments in favour of New Christians. Fernán Díaz de Toledo underlined the Jewish background of Jesus Christ and suggested that it would be completely unacceptable if the Saviour's own lineage was to be excluded from offices, benefices, honours, liberties, and dignities. The second major argument, one that would become a template for future debate, concerned the efficacy of baptism as a sacrament that cleansed and regenerated a person, freeing them of all crime, guilt, and sin. Denial of baptism efficacy was considered by Fernán Díaz a heresy. He considered that it was a mistake to draw on Visigoth sources exclusively related to converted people returning to Judaism, while he pointed out the friendly and charitable attitude displayed to attract Jews promoted by the *Partidas* (compilation of norms) of King Alfonso X the Wise. He also mentioned the resolution of the Council of Basel on September 7, 1434, which recommended the charitable integration of converted people with full enjoyment of all the "privileges, liberties and immunities of the cities and localities in which they are regenerated by holy baptism."[11]

However, the most innovative part of the opinion written by Fernán Díaz de Toledo, and a part that certainly had an impact, concerned the reasoning that most of the population of Iberia, including noble and titled families in Castile, Aragon, Portugal, and Navarra, right up to the royal families, had Jewish ancestors. The argument is made citing precise names: Mendoza, Sarabia, Solis, Miranda, Osorio, Hurtado de Mendoza, Fernández de Córdoba, Sánchez, Araujo, Porres, Valdés, Anaya, Ocampo, Monroy, Sosa, Villaquirán, Bobadilla, Fernández Marmolejo, Álvarez, Carrillo, Sottomayor, Ayala, Guzmán, Enrique, Luna, Portocarrero, Rojas, Osorio, Aguilar, Manrique, Herrera, Tobar, Quiñones, Pimentel, Suñiga, and Arellano.[12]

This text circulated among the other supporters of the New Christians, particularly the jurist Alfonso Díaz de Montalvo, the Dominican Lope de Barrientos, bishop of Cuenca, Alfonso de Cartagena, son of the famous Pablo de Santa Maria (Salomón Ha Levi), whom he succeeded as bishop of Burgos, and Cardinal Juan de Torquemada. They all wrote important texts against the sentence-statute of Toledo, some of them based on this model.[13] In the case of Lope de Barrientos, he blasted dissenters within Christianity for creating a divide and went as far as praising the two contributions to double descent (original Christian and Jewish) as fitting and reinforcing each other.[14] Alfonso

García de Santa Maria, also known as Alfonso de Cartagena, published a better structured text asserting the idea of the unity of the Christian Church and labelling the divisive ideas and practices of Pero Sarmiento and García de Mora as heretic.[15] This reasoning was developed by Juan de Torquemada, who objected to discrimination against New Christians as contrary to the unity of the Church and the teachings of St. Paul about one God, one faith, and one baptism. He condemned the persecutors and murderers of those newly reborn in the Christian faith as impious followers of Herod, known for his Massacre of Innocents.[16] Alonso de Oropesa's *Lumen ad revelationem gentium*, completed in 1464, reflected the change of political atmosphere: he reiterated that conversos who apostatised should be punished, but he opposed collective discrimination as contrary to the unity of the Church. Oropesa rejected the idea of a Judaizing nature of the conversos and denounced their persecutors as promoting dissent within the Church motivated by envy and self-interest.[17]

There is a hint concerning the social background of this riot that can be useful to retain. Pero Sarmiento was a member of the royal council, who had inherited from his father the office of royal *repostero mayor* (responsible for the personal objects of the king). He had been nominated *alcalde mayor* (equivalent to president) of Toledo and commander of all its forts, but there was a reallocation of some of these privileges to the condestable, Álvaro de Luna, general commander of the royal troops and master of the order of Santiago, a reallocation that Sarmiento used to justify the clash. The community of Old Christian artisans, shopkeepers, and merchants felt aggrieved at the imposed loan, which arguably negatively affected their *fuero* (royal charter of the city). Only two members of the cathedral chapter sided with the revolt; the others fled. The most vocal jurist, Marcos García de Mora, who ended up being executed, was targeted by Fernán Díaz de Toledo as a *Marquillos*, a villain from a village peasant family. The derision of villainous Old Christians, which resonated in literature up to Cervantes, started at the time of the assault on conversos. It targeted an alliance of interests and competition among a local population that was used against New Christians caught in a political upheaval that ended in assault, murder, and robbery.

The actions taken by the king and the pope to condemn divisiveness and support the unity of the Church were less decisive than we might think because pardon was at hand for high nobility and compromise for Old Christian citizens, and surveillance of the practices of New Christians was reinforced, even being recommended in the papal bulls issued to quell the riot. Instead of meeting swift opposition as a dangerous precedent, Toledo's riot became an example used by other riots, which unleashed new forms of extortion, massacre, and exclusion on New Christians, recipients of all the hate previously concentrated on Jewish people. Moreover, the arguments against the New Christians as collective judaizers who kept their traditional ceremonies and rejected Christ, undermining the Church from within, were accepted by the

Franciscan Alonso de Espina in *Fortalitium fidei*, a text written between 1458 and 1464, which was printed in Strasbourg in 1471, reprinted eight times, and translated into French and German. Espina advocated the exclusion of conversos from office and the establishment of the Inquisition.[18]

Unsettling shifts between integration and exclusion prevailed until the first blood purity statute (promoted by the Jeronimites) was approved by the pope in 1495, opening the way for the support of exclusion by the monarchs, but the process was slow. New Christian resistance is visible in this struggle that carried on to the mid-sixteenth century: the statutes of the cathedral of Toledo, imposed in 1547 by Archbishop Silíceo, did not define an endgame, since other cathedral chapters refused them, but represented an important step towards institutionalising a discrimination based on blood (or a racial divide) previously condemned as heresy. In the first decades of the sixteenth century the situation in Portugal was relatively benign for New Christians, but it deteriorated fast in the late 1520s, until in the 1550s the first blood purity rules were introduced.[19]

The intervention of the Inquisition in Castile and Aragon in the last decades of the fifteenth century contributed powerfully to the assertion of the requirement for blood purity at a time when the struggle was still undecided. The first phase of terror confirmed the idea that all New Christians were apostates, penalising many thousands and sending many hundreds to execution.[20] The Inquisition immediately started to draw up lists of New Christians, an activity that contributed to singling them out. The edicts of grace, which promised to absolve people who presented themselves and confessed within a certain time period, were a trap: confession could only be accepted with denunciations. Basically, the inquisitors launched these edicts of grace to create or complete lists of relatives for both immediate and future prosecution, as was well demonstrated in the case of Valencia.[21] The lists of those condemned by the Inquisition were handy to identify ancestors. Because Canon Law rejected New Christians from positions in the Church, and the Catholic monarchs excluded descendants (through two generations) from public office (in 1488) and also the universities (in 1501), these lists became black lists of *inhabilitados* (those excluded from public jobs and universities), which had a multiple effect.[22] They could be used by the monarchs to negotiate rehabilitation against payments en bloc or to impose levies—in short, to exercise regular extortion with devastating effect.[23]

Institutional racial division was thus swiftly implemented in Castile and Aragon with immediate life-and-death consequences for New Christians. Many took refuge in Portugal, before and after the expulsion of Jews. In their new country, top-down forced conversion compressed one hundred years of a complicated process into a far shorter period, but without immediate discrimination, if we exclude the major riots and massacres in 1504 in Évora and in 1506 in Lisbon. The 1510s registered a relative appeasement, although not an exemption from local conflicts and ambiguous royal policies. However, the threat of a racial divide became evident in the 1520s, with several significant conflicts and a new request to Rome for the creation of an inquisition, while the 1530s represented a turning point with the creation of the tribunal in Portugal. We have chosen to highlight three moments of growing conflict taken from the viewpoint of New Christians: first, the arrival in Portugal of David Reubeni, which had a clear impact; then events in the lives of two sets of top merchants and bankers, the Mendes/Nasi and the Henriques/Nunes families, who were forced to migrate at different times and in different situations.

2. David Reubeni

David Reubeni arrived in Europe in 1524 claiming to be the brother of the Jewish king, Yosef of Habur, and to have been the commander of his brother's troops. He declared repeatedly that he had been sent to negotiate with the pope a military alliance to defeat the Turks and recover the territory of Israel.[24] He managed to mobilise some of the Jewish communities in Italy, who financed him, clothed him, and supported him. In his account, Reubeni expressed his gratitude to Signora Benvenida, wife of Samuel Abravanel, financier in Naples, who sent him a banner of fine silk with the Ten Commandments embroidered in two columns in gold thread, a Turkish gown of gold brocade, and money, three times, while he was in Rome.[25] The banker David da Pisa, head of the Jewish community in Rome, who helped him in his audiences with Cardinal Egido da Viterbo and Pope Clement VII, left this portrait: "He comes from afar . . . his appearance is dark, short, lean; his language is a mixture of Arabic and some Hebrew. He is a man of merit and fasts daily. . . . He is great of spirit, stout-hearted and fearless in the face of multitudes."[26] In his report of his conversations with the pope, Reubeni showed that he was aware of the legend of Prester John, and he suggested including this legendary figure in the military alliance between the Jews and the Christian princes. Reubeni managed to get a letter of recommendation to the Portuguese king, John III, from the pope.

In 1525, Reubeni entered Portugal through the small port of Tavira in the Algarve and travelled by land to meet the king in Almeirim, where the latter had taken refuge from the plague that afflicted Lisbon. If we are to believe his account, Reubeni had an overwhelming reception from the New Christians in each town he visited: he always lodged with one of them, and many would come from afar to kiss his hand. The king, who received him well, became sensitive to the stir David Reubeni's presence caused among the New Christians, particularly because they would kiss Reubeni's hand. John III then accused Reubeni of having a synagogue in his lodgings and of persuading New Christians to return to Judaism. The scandalous case of Diogo Pires, a New Christian clerk of the royal tribunal, the *Casa da Suplicação*, who circumcised himself and declared himself to be a Jew, was also raised by the king in one of their conversations. Reubeni denied any intervention in these matters, but he lost the king's trust, and the account describes the uncomfortable vigilance exercised on Reubeni in the final months while he was waiting for transport in the Algarve. However, he was not molested.[27]

Reubeni returned to Rome with letters from King John III to the pope. In the meantime, his disciple Diogo Pires, who had become Shlomo Molkho, escaped from Portugal and travelled to Salonika, where he studied the Kabbalah and Jewish mysticism with Yoseph Taitazak. He became involved in apocalyptic prophecy and apparently claimed to be the messiah. This is a claim Reubeni never made. In his account, he denied being a messiah, although the fervour he inspired fanned expectations among communities that had been systematically assaulted, murdered, forced to convert, and persecuted. Lenowitz rightly considers these two figures as providing a bridge linking the medieval period of militarist Jewish messiahs from the Islamic world with the later Jewish messiahs, who were driven by cosmic goals and apocalyptic mysticism.[28] The two can be also considered as the Janus face of these two types of Jewish messiah—the militarist leader and the mystic leader.

Shlomo Molkho also went to Italy, but his reception by the Jewish communities there was not enthusiastic. In Rome, he was put through an inquisitorial trial and only avoided execution because of the pope's intervention. Eventually, he teamed up with David Reubeni and both went to meet the Emperor Charles V in Regensburg around 1532.[29] The idea was to insist on their plan for a military alliance against the Ottoman Empire, but the presence of a New Christian turned Jew who tried to convert the emperor did not go down well. They were detained and sent to Italy in chains by the emperor. In Mantova, Shlomo Molkho was tried by the Inquisition, excommunicated, and given to the secular arm for execution.[30]

David Reubeni seems to have been sent to the tribunal of the Inquisition in Llerena, in Extremadura. References to the trial have yet to be found, but one record of *sambenitos* (penitential dress) hung in the main church of Badajoz attests that he was delivered to the secular arm and executed in 1538.[31] The last description we have of Reubeni, written by a well-known man of letters, Giambattista Ramusio, who interviewed him in Venice and made a report to the Senate, represents him as an adventurer and offers a sharp verdict in Ramusio's usual style: "He is an Arab, for his build and colour show that he is not from one of our lands. He is thin and very spare, like the Jews of Prester John. His appearance bears witness that he is quite wealthy: he is clothed in silks and accompanied by five respectable servants, one of whom is Portuguese, intelligent and clever."[32]

Dates are crucial in this story. As we shall see later, the Portuguese king, John III, had sent a new request to the pope for the establishment of the Inquisition in 1525. The request was submitted before the arrival of David

Reubeni in Portugal, but the emotion Reubeni's presence raised among the Portuguese New Christians did not go unnoticed. In 1525, the third estate of the *cortes* (Portuguese parliament) deplored the speculation in cereals by New Christians. It was a period of droughts and bad crops, which raised the usual accusations against Jews, this time turned against New Christians.[33] Regular epidemics were the normal consequence of famine and inflation. The early 1530s, which saw the arrest of Reubeni and Molkho in Regensburg, should be considered alongside events in Antwerp, where the replacement of Margaret of Austria by Mary of Hungary in 1530 was followed by intermittent persecution of New Christians, who were accused of returning to Judaism and protecting a network facilitating clandestine migration to the Ottoman Empire through Italy. It is this story that we need to address now, since it had consequences for the development of the New Christian merchant elite.

3. The Mendes/Nasi

In the 1520s, Charles V issued several safe conducts for Portuguese New Christians who sought to establish residence in Antwerp. He thus followed in the footsteps of his grandfather, the Emperor Maximilian, who in 1488 promoted the transfer of international merchants from Bruges to that city, which offered better conditions for access to the sea. For most of the sixteenth century, Antwerp became the centre of a world economy fuelled by the riches of Iberian America and Asian spices, textiles, and porcelain.[34] Communities from southern Europe—Italians, Castilians, and Portuguese—established themselves in the city, which also attracted German bankers and English merchants, becoming a crossing point for traffic between northern and southern Europe, the Baltic Sea and the Mediterranean, and Europe and the other continents. The early 1530s saw a surge of New Christian migration from Portugal as a result of the first papal bull (1531) to establish a tribunal of the Inquisition there. This migration fuelled tension between a desire for the financial benefits these communities offered Charles V, in which bankers and financiers played a major role, and a growing suspicion about their religious behaviour.

In 1532, an unexpected confession to Charles V's confessor in Bruges confirmed what the emperor's spies had been suggesting for some time: there was a network in place that assisted the escape of New Christians from Portugal through Antwerp to Italy and the Ottoman Empire. The confession was made by the estranged son of a woman who had escaped from Portugal, and from her husband, with her children, in 1521. In Antwerp, she obtained support from the major Portuguese New Christian financiers (Gabriel de Negro, Manuel Serrão, Luís Peres, and Diogo Mendes) for her passage to Italy and thence to the Ottoman Empire.[35] This confession—not so uncommon because inquisitorial tribunals in various countries obtained information from a significant number of disaffected people who decided to return to the Christian faith—triggered an enquiry into the activities of these merchants. The enquiry concluded that they had connections in different parts of the Mediterranean, including the Ottoman Empire.

Diogo Mendes was a particularly difficult case for the authorities to take on, because he had contributed significantly to a major loan to Charles V in 1527 (30,000 livres), controlled a significant share of the Asian spice trade via Lisbon, had a major presence at the Bourse, and had recently guaranteed a loan of 200,000 florins promised by the king of Portugal to Charles V for a war against the Turks. It was estimated that he managed between 300,000 and 400,000 ducados of capital invested in trade on his own account and another 50,000 ducados for other people.[36] Mendes was accused of returning to Judaism, favouring the return to Judaism of other people, monopolising trade, and trading with Salonika. The attorney general in Brabant detained him, triggering protests by the authorities in Antwerp, who considered that the attorney was violating their jurisdiction and the privileges given to their merchants.

The direct intervention of the Portuguese king, John III, with the emperor in August 1532, less than two months after the aforementioned detention, showed the importance of the case and the impact the imprisonment of Diogo Mendes would have on royal finances and Portuguese trade in general. The Portuguese royal factor in Antwerp joined his voice to that of the Portuguese authorities, and a Portuguese delegation, including the humanist Damião de Góis, presented the case to the emperor. The damage to the Portuguese king, to Portuguese trade, and to the central position of the city was demonstrated. Diogo Mendes also defended himself well, and most of the accusations were quickly dropped. He was released in September against a deposit of 50,000 ducados, an enormous amount of money, guaranteed by Italian and German bankers. It was agreed he should present himself when called and provide information about New Christian finances. Apparently, he was finally cleared by a payment of 44,000 florins carolus.[37]

This investigation and its outcome became a template for future judicial action in the Low Countries; that is, opportunities to squeeze money from the accused were taken, but there was restraint concerning spectacular new arrests because this case and the following case of António Fernandes (Mendes's partner in business) were concluded in their favour. King John III also intervened on January 1, 1534, with the governor of the Low Countries, Queen Mary of Hungary, in favour of António Fernandes, brother of Gabriel Fernandes, merchant of Lisbon, both of them major merchants of the kingdom (says the royal letter), merchants at the Casa da Índia, and owing the king some money. John III claimed that António Fernandes had been detained in possession of the king's safe conduct and asked for the merchant to be set free.[38] Just to show the range of business involved, there is a warrant dated April 17, 1539, given to Diogo Jorge by Diogo Mendes, António Fernandes, and Luís Fernandes, for him to operate in France and give quittance to their agents there.[39]

Portuguese New Christians, whose rate of arrival fluctuated according to the waves of inquisitorial action in Portugal, were kept under surveillance. In 1540, one hundred artisans who arrived in Zeeland were detained but then released. We are talking about hundreds, not thousands, of people—it is sufficient to consider the size of the Portuguese colony in Antwerp, which grew from a few dozen to around one hundred households. However, arrivals may have peaked in the 1540s, when the colony reached a significant number, around 900, and it is true that many passed through on the way to Italy and thence to the Ottoman Empire.[40]

In 1537, the emperor reaffirmed the privileges of merchants and welcomed faithful New Christians, and it was the passage to the Ottoman Empire through Italy that was clearly targeted. Nevertheless, in 1544, the Inquisition in the Low Countries prosecuted New Christians, which led to a significant number of executions before the release of the remaining Portuguese detainees (including Diogo Fernandes Neto, former agent of the New Christians in Rome) was negotiated by João Micas, the future Duke of Naxos in the Ottoman Empire.[41] To make a long story short, on July 17, 1549, the emperor expelled all Portuguese New Christians who had emigrated to the Netherlands after 1543. The decree was rescinded after the intervention of Antwerp's authorities, but the precariousness of the New Christians' situation became even more clear.

We need to go back to the Mendes family to better understand the extension of the disruption of New Christian networks outside Portugal and the ambiguities of state intervention. Francisco Mendes had discreetly supported the New Christian negotiations in Rome to prevent the establishment of the Inquisition in Portugal.[42] At the same time, cautious as he was, he procured for himself and his family (including children not yet born) a papal brief of protection against eventual accusations of heresy, dated December 11, 1531. These briefs were part of the regular activity of the papal chancery in those days, as a papal pardon issued to António Fernandes (and his family) on May 11, 1536, while he was detained in Antwerp, demonstrates.[43] Wealthy New Christians were thus regularly threatened and financially squeezed not only by the Habsburgs and the Portuguese kings but also by the popes.

The death of Francisco Mendes in 1535 dramatically changed the situation of his family. King John III, aware of the massive wealth at stake, jumped at the opportunity to ask for an immediate inventory of property, a process generally conducted by a certified judge. Beatriz de Luna resisted on the pretext that her husband's will had forbidden the division of his property, but in the end an inventory was taken. The documents have not yet been found, but the outcome may be guessed, because Portuguese law assigned half of the deceased's estate to the living spouse (wife or husband), plus one-third to be disposed of at the discretion of the deceased, and the rest to be divided by the children, in this case one small daughter, who was most probably left by Francisco Mendes in the guardianship of Beatriz de Luna. The target was the child, whom João III wanted to join the household of the Queen. Moreover, there were rumours that the king would have liked to marry the child into one of the big noble houses, possibly into the family of Conde de Castanheira, the royal treasurer.[44] Pressure provoked the opposite outcome.

In 1537, Beatriz de Luna managed to emigrate to Antwerp via London with her daughter Ana, her sister Brianda, and her nephews Bernardo and João Micas, the sons of Dr. Agostinho Henriques Micas.[45] Letters from Henry VIII guaranteed her safe passage, prompted by Diogo Mendes, but we do not know on what grounds Beatriz de Luna, also called Beatriz Mendes, managed to obtain authorisation for the trip in Lisbon or who intervened to obtain that authorisation. In 1539, in Antwerp, Diogo Mendes married Brianda de Luna and the following year they had a child named Beatriz. When Diogo Mendes died, around August 1543, he left a will declaring Beatriz de Luna the overall manager of his estate, assisted by Guilherme Fernandes and João Micas.[46] The exclusion of his wife Brianda from this arrangement would trigger a significant feud between the two sisters, with judicial consequences.

The death of Diogo Mendes happened to come just after a major inquisitorial action against the New Christians in Antwerp, and it set Beatriz de Luna on the move again. This time, it was the emperor's protégé and rumoured illegitimate son, Don Francisco de Aragon, who showed an interest in a marriage with Ana Mendes, which produced the same effect as before. First Beatriz de Luna asked for a safe conduct from the pope to go to Rome, which was given, but she waited until 1545 to travel to Venice with her sister, their daughters, and their retinue. Probably it was the illness of Gonçalo Mendes, the younger brother of Francisco, that kept her from leaving. He died in 1545, leaving half of his fortune to her and half to his widow, Ana Fernandes. Beatriz de Luna left in Antwerp and in Aachen a significant number of boxes that she was unable to carry with her. These were sequestered, and it took João Micas a great deal of negotiation and bribery to get them back.[47]

Having established herself in Venice, Beatriz de Luna also lived temporarily in Ferrara, from where she responded to the legal proceedings initiated by her sister over her brother-in-law's estate.[48] In both Venice and Ferrara, Beatriz de Luna supported the arts and helped many New Christians and Jews. Finally, in 1552, she reached a financial settlement with her sister and left Venice for Constantinople, where she began to live openly as a Jew under the name Gracia Nasi. The fortune of the family was kept more-or-less undivided from then on using a clever stratagem. In 1553, João Micas staged the kidnap of Beatriz, the daughter of Brianda, from Venice, and organized a sham marriage in Ravenna to avoid likely moves to marry the girl into the Venetian aristocracy. It was João Micas's brother, Bernardo, later Samuel Nasi, who came from Constantinople to conclude a real marriage with Beatriz, in Ferrara, in 1557, after the death of her mother, and take her to her extended family in the Ottoman Empire. João Micas himself, who in Constantinople became Yosef

Nasi and Duke of Naxos, married Beatriz de Luna's daughter Ana, then named Reina.[49]

This family maintained the tightest imaginable endogamy. The wives of Francisco and Diogo Mendes, Beatriz and Brianda, were their nieces, born to Filipa, Francisco and Diogo's sister, who was married to Álvaro de Luna. Another sister of Francisco and Diogo Mendes married Agostinho Henriques Micas, and their children, Bernardo and João Micas, were the nephews of Francisco, Diogo, and cousins of Beatriz and Brianda , marrying the offspring of these close relatives.[50] The desire to keep their inheritance as undivided as possible explains not only the restricted choice of spouses but also the late age at which the men married: Francisco was probably 48 years old, and Diogo 54.

The lowering of the age gap in the next generation—Bernardo (then Samuel Nasi) married at the age of thirty-seven, and João Micas (then Yosef Nasi) probably married at thirty-four—can be explained by the more advanced ages of, and competition for, their cousins. This strategy can also be explained by the desire to accumulate enough capital to live according to their faith in Italy or the Ottoman Empire later in life. It is a strategy of secrecy and loyalty to the faith of their ancestors, which can explain cases of systematic refusal of marriage until the parties were in their late 30s and 40s, probably because adults had been promised in marriage to children who were still growing up elsewhere. What is fascinating about this case is how the will of an extraordinary woman, Gracia Nasi, contributed to overcoming a succession of difficult situations. She even managed to obtain an authorisation from the pope to remove the bones of her husband from Lisbon under pretext of burying them in Venice.

4. The Henriques/Nunes

The other branch of the Benveniste family, the Henriques, had very little formal interaction with the Mendes, but their story followed a similar trajectory, although it included serious and open conflict with the Portuguese king. The children of Henrique de Santa Fé and Leonor Henriques—Nuno Henriques, Henrique Nunes, and Violante Henriques—all born after 1475, together formed a family unit that first migrated from Lisbon to Antwerp, between the early 1520s and the 1540s, and then moved to Ferrara, Venice, and Salonika. They all returned to Judaism. Nuno Henriques, who died in Venice in 1549, married Violante Henriques (the same name as her sister-in-law), and they had eleven children, ten of whom survived into adulthood, a remarkable achievement in those days. Henrique Nunes waited to marry one of these children, his niece Marquesa Henriques, who became Reina Benveniste, and they had two sons. Henrique Nunes ended his days in the Ottoman Empire after periods in Ferrara and Venice. His sister, Violante Henriques, married the aforementioned Gabriel de Negro, who was from a traditional Jewish family that had been rooted in Portugal for centuries. Gabriel lived in Antwerp from a very early age, probably from the late 1510s, after the arrival of Diogo Mendes, and played a major role in the Portuguese community there. He was a cautious man who escaped to Germany every time there was a rumour of repression. Their son, David de Negro, born in 1528, is also mentioned in commercial documentation.[51]

Nuno Henriques and Henrique Nunes were merchants dealing with North Africa and São Tomé who had contracts with the Casa da Índia.[52] They also lent money.[53] Nuno Henriques fell out with King John III, and although the cause is unknown, it may have concerned financial support given to New Christian agents in Rome. A certificate dated December 1, 1540, attests that, by order of Dr. Diogo Gonçalves, royal judge and vicar-general of the diocese of Lisbon, Nuno Henriques and Tomé Serrão were expelled from the city of Lisbon. The two merchants had declared to the vicar-general that they wanted to comply with the decision and avoid a public scandal. Tomé Serrão went to Nossa Senhora da Luz and Nuno Henriques to Alvalade, both places near Lisbon.[54] The charges are not indicated on the certificate.

In mid-1542, the judge responsible for the town of Arronches brought letters from Flanders to the king that he had intercepted, probably under royal orders. A bundle of ciphered letters was addressed to Nuno Henriques. They were interpreted as being written by Cardinal D. Miguel da Silva, who had been banished by the king after escaping to Italy, where he was made cardinal against the wishes of the Portuguese royal court, a major case to which we will return next chapter. According to testimonies given in an inquisitorial trial, Nuno Henriques had been detained that year and released on a bail of 33,000 ducados.[55] Either in the bundle of letters from Flanders or in a search made at Nuno Henriques's house, a letter was found that had been sent by Gonzalo de la Caballería to Nuno Henriques that same year of 1542, informing him that the property of his brother-in-law, Gabriel de Negro, had been sequestered in Antwerp. A sum of 80,000 ducados from Nuno Henriques was at stake, and Gonzalo de la Caballería advised him how to recover the money.[56]

Among Nuno Henriques's papers, the royal officers also found a letter to New Christian agents in Rome, dated December 1540. It is a long letter containing some extraordinary information, including financial details about bills of exchange sent by the Giraldi brothers to the banker Cavalcanti in Rome for the New Christian agents, many comments about the diplomats sent by the Portuguese king, bulls obtained from the pope but never published or implemented in Lisbon, and comments on the precise activities of the Inquisition.[57] This letter would have been sufficient to trigger the ire of the king, because it profusely documents parallel and unauthorised diplomatic activity directed towards the pope against royal policy.

We do not know how (or when) Nuno Henriques escaped to Antwerp, but on June 24, 1542, a royal order was already promising 2,000 cruzados to anyone who would denounce him, plus a reduction of their penalty if they were prisoners or freedom if they were captives. The document also threatened a range of penalties from execution to exile to Brazil for those who lodged or protected Nuno Henriques, his factor Manuel Pires, Henrique Nunes, or Master Jorge Leão. The protectors would have their property confiscated, and half would be given to those who had denounced them.[58] These are almost the terms of a proclamation concerning the crime of lèse-majesté, which is rare. But there is more. In April 1543, the royal judge responsible for the case tried to extend the threat of punishment to territories outside Portugal, suggesting that the king should order his factor in Flanders to execute the sentence there, a difficult matter, because the royal agent obviously did not have jurisdiction in that country, and the property of those accused had already been sequestered by the emperor's officials.[59]

King John III must have been frustrated to find that all the members of the Henriques family not only managed to escape to Antwerp, but ended up in Salonika, as Jews, after a long itinerary that included Venice and Ferrara. It was a good lesson on the limits of royal power and the precariousness of the patronage system nurtured by the king. In the 1530s, John III was willing to support the main Portuguese New Christian merchants in Antwerp, by no coincidence his contractors and agents, even though this apparently contradicted his request to Rome for the establishment of the Inquisition in Portugal. However, the disruptions brought about by Charles V in Antwerp and Milan from 1540 to 1544, with inquisitorial action against New Christians, and the emperor's interference in Milan with the New Christians' passage to Venice, including detention and search and seizure of property, seem to have contributed to a harsher stance that was reflected in the search for, and banishment of, the Henriques family in Lisbon.

⟨⟩

The anti-converso riot of Toledo launched the first attempt to institutionalise the racial divide between Old and New Christians. It is striking that the main arguments in favour and against that division were produced immediately, during and after the conflict. They structured the debate on conversos in the years to come. New riots and the final acceptance of the blood purity statutes, first by the pope, then by the Catholic kings, reversed power relationships and meant that arguments against New Christians became dominant. The involvement of different dignitaries of the Catholic Church, some of them of Jewish origin, supported by a significant number of Old Christians, defined a time period in which the supporters of the statutes had not managed to corner the opposition as "lovers of Jews." These opponents were placed in a difficult position, because they rejected the stereotypical accusation that all conversos were apostates but at the same time had to accept rigorous enquiry into individual accusations. The first generations of inquisitors, even at the highest level, themselves had several conversos or converso relatives.

The case of David Reubeni was introduced here to indicate the impact of a Jew suggesting a possible alliance against the Muslims and obtaining access to the Portuguese royal court. Reubeni stirred an extraordinary commotion among New Christians. Many greeted, supported, and even revered Reubeni as a messenger from a Jewish community with whom they could renew links. This excitement did not escape King John III's notice, and he sent Reubeni back to Italy on bad terms. Although the secret request for an Inquisition made by King John III to the pope had been sent before Reubeni's visit, the impact of this visit played a role in the political battle. The later detention of Reubeni by the Emperor Charles V, followed by excommunication at the Inquisition and execution, provides a revealing background for the establishment of the Inquisition in Portugal.

The two cases of top merchant and banker families analysed here, the Mendes/Nasi and the Henriques/Nunes, represent the most extreme disruption in three decades of religious and social relative integration of New Christians in Portugal. However, they did not trigger massive migration of other significant commercial houses. Part II will show how they were replaced by other New Christians in Lisbon in their functions. Racial division, which began to be seriously rooted in Castile and Aragon by the mid-fifteenth century, took an equivalent time to create a similar institutional framework in Portugal. The harsh control exerted over New Christians in Antwerp, and over their passage to Italy (and from there to the Ottoman Empire) imposed by Charles V in the 1540s, also had an impact on their circulation in Europe. It is not a coincidence that the Portuguese lost most, if not all, of the trade between Portugal and Northern Europe in the second half of the sixteenth century. In the meantime, the Spanish community in Antwerp, which included a significant number of New Christians, was not targeted by imperial enquiries into religion. They kept a low profile, but as was shown with the case of Gonzalo de la Caballería, they maintained family ties and assisted the Portuguese New Christians. Interestingly, the Portuguese king did not change his policy with the closure of the royal factory in Antwerp, partly owing to the persecution of New Christians, and by the mid-sixteenth century the Inquisition was well established, and its ideology prevailed.

CHAPTER FOUR

Creativity

NONCONFORMISM AMONG *CONVERSOS* has been researched in the last decades with stimulating results.[1] It is true that the majority of New Christians did not question the foundations of the religion they were forced to adopt, but many kept their traditional rituals and ceremonies, while others engaged in legal and political fight over their status, and some others even pursued a spiritual search for a new relationship with God. They suffered trauma from a loss of collective identity, and forced relocation imposed (for many) a simultaneous break with the past. Soon the conversos were placed in a liminal position because of the blood purity statutes, and they faced the permanent threat of new enquiries even when they managed to be accepted as Old Christians. This liminal position, resulting from racial division, opened up new experiences and new possibilities of action. We can talk about innovation and creativity because we are looking at behaviour and ideas that did not have clear roots in the past and were not part of the mainstream but had an impact and left a cultural imprint. I will first address the New Christian fight against the establishment of the Inquisition in Castile, Aragon, and Portugal as a decisive experience that would last almost two centuries. I will consider both actions and arguments. Then I will address the spiritual search, which allowed the expression of a vivid sensibility and development of the self. Finally, I will include experiments in art and literature that arguably indicate detachment, critical reasoning, self-reflection or even strategies of integration. There were direct or indirect links to New Christian merchants in all these cases.

1. Power Struggle

The establishment of the Inquisition and the acceptance of the blood purity statutes institutionalised a racial divide in Castile and Aragon. New Christians of Jewish origin were the main target at the beginning, followed later by Moriscos, and then Old Christians accused of heretical propositions subject to minor penalties. Acceptance of the blood purity statutes progressed slowly and faced strong resistance in Castile and Aragon until they were adopted by the cathedral of Toledo, being pronounced by the archbishop (later cardinal) Silíceo in 1547, accepted by Pope Paul III in 1548, and eventually supported by Philip II in 1556, thus creating a new dynamic of diffusion. Opposition, however, was not eradicated. These statutes were used as a weapon against both the New Christian elite in Toledo and the new college of the Jesuits, who had ties with converso families and refused, for several decades, to adopt blood purity statutes for themselves.[2] In Portugal the blood purity statutes only started to be introduced in the 1550s, and an increased intensity in their diffusion only came decades later, under the Iberian Union of Crowns. In the meantime, the ideology of blood purity was supported not only by political and institutional actions but also by treatises against the Judaism of New Christians.[3]

The classification of anti-Judaism by mainstream historiography as simple religious rivalry, already dubious, does not stand up to scrutiny in the case of New Christians, because forced conversion consecrated by baptism radically changed the status of Jewish populations. Descendants of converted people were living as Christians from birth to death, without any access to Jewish scriptures. They could replicate traditional practices but without any institutional framework or proper spiritual guidance. Moreover, Silíceo's use of the blood purity statutes to both discriminate against conversos and undermine the Society of Jesus as an emerging power within the Church showed that religious issues were not the major concern; rather, it was the monopolisation of resources at different levels. Prejudices against ethnic descent coupled with discriminatory action, in this case and many others, proved to be a powerful tool for religious and political struggle.

Racialisation of Jewish populations was thus transferred to those forced to convert and their descendants, and racial division and hatred was introduced within the Christian Church and supported by institutions that played a major role in state building. We could consider that the emerging early modern state in Castile, Aragon, and Portugal was a racial state, which discriminated against minorities whose former religions had been racialised and which promoted a population of Old Christians.[4] However, the situation was much more complex, with constant resistance against blood purity in the three countries and surprising political action that brought with it a reversal of alliances and a temporary disappearance of New Christians from the public space.

Other divisions were at play in Iberia beyond the projection of ethnic prejudices against conversos. We will focus briefly on a significant political event that had consequences at different levels, including on the status and visibility of the New Christians. Discontent in Castile, which supported most of the expenses of the Catholic kings, reached a new height with the election of Charles V as emperor of the Holy Roman Empire in 1519. That Charles

had assumed the Crown of Castile, with a significant retinue of Flemish secretaries, consultants, and courtiers, had not gone down well, but the idea that
Castile would need to pay for the German election and the distant political
manoeuvring of the king exasperated the political mood. The revolt of the
comuneros, involving the main urban communities of Castile, erupted in
the spring of 1520, anticipating and following the departure of Charles V to
Germany. The revolt turned against noble interests, which had long had divergent goals. Whether or not New Christians were deeply involved in this revolt
is still a matter of debate, but there is no doubt that they played some kind of
role. Just to give one example, Juan Bravo, one of the three leaders of the revolt
and commander of the troops that were defeated by the royalists in the decisive
battle of Villalar, had married Maria Coronel, granddaughter of the converso
Abraham Seneor.[5]

The apparent breakdown of the usual alliance between New Christians
and the king is an interesting development that needs to be linked to the racial
divide eventually supported and promoted by the Crown. On the other hand,
the supposed engagement of New Christians with urban Old Christians seems
at odds with the previous divide that looked so significant in the fifteenth
century. The hypothesis is that New Christians rooted in municipalities, expe-
riencing relatively low levels of animosity, and even support, in the *cortés* in
the first half of the sixteenth century, managed to establish bridges with Old
Christians. In any case, Charles V's amnesty to almost all *communeros* and
the promotion of Castilians into the government helped to repair the wounds.
After inquisitorial terror, migration, and civil war, the New Christians kept a
low profile in Castile, but their presence in religious orders, ecclesiastic struc-
tures, and spiritual movements, along with their rootedness in business and
trade, suggest a permanent negotiation with local, institutional, and central
authorities.

The situation in Portugal evolved under constant pressure from the Spanish Inquisition concerning the flow of New Christians who escaped to this
neighbouring country. The idea of establishing a similar tribunal had been
floated, but the New Christians still had powerful allies at the royal court and
in the Church. In the 1510s, Fernando Coutinho, bishop of Algarve, and Diogo
Pinheiro, bishop of Madeira, did not accept forced baptisms as valid and
refused accusations against New Christians.[6] However, the situation started
to shift. King Manuel, who had twice guaranteed that he would not prosecute
New Christians for heresy and had authorised them to leave the country, asked
the pope in 1515 to establish the tribunal in Portugal. His successor, John III,
repeated the same guarantees in 1522 and 1524, but changed tack in the latter year. He ordered an enquiry into the New Christians' faith and religious
behaviour in Lisbon and hired a well-known New Christian spy, Henrique
Nunes, nicknamed "Firme Fé," who had worked with the Spanish Inquisition, particularly with the infamous inquisitor, Lucero, in Córdoba. This spy,

who had obtained information on New Christians in Lisbon, Santarém, and Évora, was murdered on his way to Olivença. The murderers were detained and executed on information collected and sent by the inquisitor, Selaya, of the tribunal of Llerena, who had also complained about the escape of New Christians and suggested the establishment of a tribunal in Portugal.[7]

The change of attitude by the Portuguese Crown must have leaked out, coupled with the commotion provoked by the voyage of David Reubeni in 1525, and the renewed request to the pope, this time by King John III, to establish the Inquisition. In 1528, riots against New Christians erupted in Lamego and Gouveia. New Christians started to be seen as fair game, owing to waning royal protection. The events in Gouveia ended in three New Christians being accused of desecration of an image of the Virgin Mary and being burnt in Lisbon, even whilst claiming to be Christians. The two major promoters of the riot had a falling out, with one accusing the other of breaking the image and deliberately provoking accusations against the New Christians. These Old Christians were detained and sent to Lisbon, where they managed to escape, conveniently, because the case would have undermined assumptions against the New Christians as apostates.[8] In any case, the riots do not seem to have been widespread.

King John III's obsession with establishing the Inquisition must be related to his political strategy to push for the naturalisation of the Church in Portugal, placing under his supervision the nomination of bishops and cardinals, as well as the attribution of rents and benefices from monasteries.[9] The Inquisition was seen as another tool in this arsenal of state centralisation, this time at the expense of New Christians; obviously, the strategy of racial division had conquered the royal court.

Papal resistance was based on an evaluation of the risk of the Portuguese royal court using the Inquisition to extort money from New Christians through property confiscation, the appropriation by the king of a jurisdiction that belonged to the pope, and potential abuses by inquisitors who lacked proper supervision from Rome.[10] Jurisdiction was the main issue, but other issues were involved, the most important of all being money. The pope was reluctant to lose a revenue source because the Portuguese New Christians were knocking at his door, as their relatives in Castile and Aragon had done, offering money to avoid the establishment of the tribunal. This would be a crucial issue during the negotiations for the creation of a Holy Office in Portugal from 1531 to 1547.

The history of the establishment of the Inquisition in Portugal was reconstituted very well by Alexandre Herculano, who pointed out the main chronology and the financial interests involved. The pope backtracked on his concessions to the king several times until the Inquisition became institutionalised between 1536 and 1547. The king forbade New Christians to leave the country, sell property or bonds, or send bills of exchange abroad without guaranteeing to import merchandise of identical value. He also provided the Inquisition with rents. Conversely, the pope issued general pardons concerning the crime of Judaism, exempted New Christians from property confiscation, and even suspended sentences and autos da fé. This contrary papal policy, produced by pressure from New Christian agents in Rome, explains the absence of a major wave of repression immediately after the Inquisition was established, as had happened in Spain.

In the meantime, King John III kept up a strong relationship with the primary New Christian bankers. Moreover, from the 1520s to the 1550s he did not interrupt the selective promotion of New Christians. For example, on October 2, 1532, the New Christian Diogo de Crasto was made a *fidalgo* of the royal house. In 1533 and 1552 he received other letters of privilege and financial rewards for his extensive activities in Asia and support to the *Estado da Índia*.[11] In another case, that of the New Christian Gaspar Pacheco (knight of the Order of Christ, knight of the royal house, and administrator of the kingdom's rents), his wife, Guiomar Rodrigues, and his sister Mor Pacheca, wife of Diogo Fernandes das Póvoas, who was also a knight of the royal house and general manager of the kingdom's customs, had their blood cleansed by a royal letter dated November 24, 1542.[12]

There is not necessarily any contradiction between the request for the Inquisition and the support given to individual New Christians by the Portuguese king; indeed, the same thing occurred in Castile. The prevailing *ancien régime* ideology would have considered that added pressure put on the New Christian ethnicity would make individuals more amenable and submissive to the king. The honouring of New Christians particularly loyal to the king— "loyal" meaning able to lend him enormous amounts of money in moments of crisis at very low, or even no, interest—was guided by an accepted patronage pattern.

We still need to analyse the prohibitions on New Christians leaving the country and restrictions on their investments and financial activities, which had an impact on international trade.[13] The purpose might have been to obtain money for exemptions, a typical feature of the ancien régime's legal system. However, a significant number of New Christians decided to leave the country, while the wealthy ones who decided to stay concentrated a significant part of their resources in Rome.[14] This would have been considered a betrayal of loyalty and a disruption of the patronage system patiently constructed by successive kings. Resources obtained through royal contracts and trade promoted by the Portuguese Empire were channeled to the pope, a competing source of authority. Royal feeling is revealed by a sneering comment made by Cardinal Afonso, brother of the king and archbishop of Lisbon: "In case of another riot against you [New Christians], you can go to the pope for protection."[15]

In 1547, a process of negotiation that lasted sixteen years was concluded. The pope had been visibly pulled in different directions, under constant pressure from the ambassador and envoys of the king, against the agents of the New Christians. The battle had been engaged with powerful amounts of money mobilised on both sides, although John III had the upper hand because he controlled the ecclesiastical rents coveted by the cardinals in Rome. The change of mood in Rome must be related to the creation in 1542 of the congregation of cardinals in charge of the Roman Inquisition. The presence of Cardinal Carafa, the driving force behind the establishment of the congregation, who became Pope Paul IV in 1555, created a different balance of power in Rome.[16]

In contrast to the Spanish Inquisition, there was no initial terror in Portugal. The number of New Christians prosecuted in these first decades was relatively limited because of papal surveillance through active nuncios and the exemption from property confiscation. The social profile of the New Christians detained in this period does not seem to be particularly elevated—they were mostly artisans, servants of the royal court, and merchants. Wealthy merchants and bankers seemed to be protected in this initial period.[17] One of the few high-profile cases concerned the couple Gil Vaz Bugalho and Beatriz Vaz, both Old Christians who had converted to Judaism and triggered a major scandal in Lisbon because he was a senior judge of the royal tribunal of appeal, the *Desembargo do Paço*, and a member of the Order of Christ.[18]

2. *Arguments*

The battle to establish the Inquisition in Spain defined a template that was followed in Portugal, although with some features specific to that country. There are arguably more documents on the second case, inspired by the experience of the first. This explains our focus, because the structure of the arguments from both sides did not change significantly. The Portuguese king and his agents claimed there were continual cases of apostasy by New Christians more than thirty years after their conversion; that soft strategies would not solve the problem; that permanent offence was being given to the people because of the daily violation of the sacraments, which meant a risk of riots; and that special agents were necessary because the bishops were unwilling to act or lacked the means to undertake major enquiries. Those arguing against the Inquisition, on the other hand, pointed out that the violence of the forced conversions of 1497 was against canon law, which should have invalidated them; the royal policy protecting New Christians from enquiries into their faith and property confiscation had been reinstated as recently as 1524; evidence of widespread apostasy was weak; the constant accusations against New Christians were suspect and some had been proven false, though the culprits had not been prosecuted; and the goal of confiscating the property of New Christians represented extortion.[19]

The Roman curia was clearly impressed by New Christians arguments, because the cardinals and the pope had no clear idea of either the violence of the conversions or the steady policy of protecting and integrating New Christians developed by King Manuel and King John III. In the papal documents, particularly the bull *Sempiterno regi* of April 7, 1533, in which the pope gave a general pardon to the New Christians after suspending the Inquisition, the legitimacy of violent conversions was clearly refuted.[20] The religious status of a considerable section of the Portuguese population, then probably greater than 7 percent of the total, was thus clearly questioned. This position was in line with canon law. The collection compiled by Gratian in 1140, and the *Decretales*, compiled under Gregory IX in 1234, both integrated the decision of the Fourth Council of Toledo, held in 633, that Jews should not be forced to convert. Thomas Aquinas, who considered the Jews to be perpetual slaves protected by kings, followed the same line, refusing forced conversion, although accepting the consequences.[21]

Mass forced conversion thus triggered criticism, and even refusal of its legitimacy, by New Christians—a refusal shared at times by the Roman curia as a political tool and implicitly by Catholic chroniclers of the reign of Manuel, such as Damião de Góis and Jerónimo Osório. The royal answer to this claim of illegitimacy, which could derail all attempts to create the Inquisition, was twofold: the (surviving) converted Jews had lived for more than thirty years as Christians, receiving all the sacraments, and could not be told to return to their previous beliefs; nor could the new generation, which had willingly received baptism (through the will of their parents because it was compulsory for Christians to baptise their children), be excluded from the Church.[22] These arguments were in line with the traditional Christian practices of condemning the act of violent conversion but accepting its consequences.

The first documented New Christian agent in Rome, from late 1531 or early 1532 to 1538, Duarte de Paz (ca. 1490–ca.1553), played a major role in this process. As we have seen, he was a New Christian holding royal contracts and privileges and was an active international merchant who owned a ship trading between West Africa and Flanders.[23] Why Duarte de Paz decided to stray from the path of ambition and risk political and financial ruin to engage in an uneven battle in favour of his ethnicity is anyone's guess, but his case shows once more that decisions are triggered by feelings and emotions, not always by reason. He was extremely successful in his first years in Rome. He distributed copies of important royal documents, defined the main arguments, and influenced all the papal decisions in favour of the New Christians. He even obtained a brief of exemption from the Portuguese Inquisition for himself and his family, two days before the issue of the bull *Cum ad nil magis*, in 1536.[24]

In 1535, Duarte de Paz's fortunes changed because of two factors: the inevitable failure to reverse the establishment of the Inquisition; and the conflict in Portugal between the papal nuncio, Marco della Rovere, and the representatives of the New Christians, who refused to pay the large sum (20,000 ducati) promised by Duarte de Paz for the brief of pardon.[25] Dissension among New Christians arose, and Duarte de Paz was accused of mismanagement. As his position weakened, he became vulnerable to threats as clearly suggested in the correspondence between the king and the royal ambassadors in Rome.

In 1536, Duarte de Paz survived a murderous attack in Rome, and he was cared for in the Castel Sant'Angelo by the pope's doctors. In 1538, his position had been substantially eroded. He received a safe-conduct from the pope to go to Antwerp, where the Regent of the Low Countries, Queen Mary of Hungary, had sequestered his trade, valued at 20,000 ducados.[26] The first section of his itinerary followed the normal route, through Ferrara and Venice, but then he diverted to the Ottoman Empire, where he converted first to Judaism and finally to Islam, before dying in 1553.[27] He probably received information that he would not be welcomed by the New Christian community in Antwerp or that he would be detained by the authorities. In 1542, the pope revoked the privileges given to Duarte de Paz and his family.

The fall of Duarte de Paz reveals the enormous constraints he was facing, even with all his obvious social skills. While he genuinely promoted New Christian interests in Rome, he tried to keep his ties with King John III. He played a double game between his ethnicity and the king: he denounced New Christians who had become Jews or had fled to the Ottoman Empire, and he suggested the king use a cipher for their correspondence. Even after settling in the Ottoman Empire, Duarte de Paz tried to renew his relationship with the Portuguese king, offering his services as a spy in return for permission to return to Portugal. It is unsurprising that the New Christians and then the Jewish community in Constantinople kept a suspicious eye on him and then decided to cut their ties with him.

Duarte de Paz's dual allegiance explains why, at least until 1534, he kept his contracts with the king and duly acquitted his financial duties, particularly that of farming the taxation on silk from Castile.[28] He might have visited Portugal as late as 1635, if we believe his son Tomé's declaration of birth in 1536. Duarte de Paz's life story is an emotional cry of distress at the impossible situation in which the New Christian merchant elite was placed even before the creation of the Inquisition. That he decided to become a Jew and eventually a Muslim reveals neither a well-laid plan nor strong convictions, but rather the succession of reduced options that took him first away from Rome and then to the Ottoman Empire. The impact of his fall was felt by his extended family in Portugal, who had to fight (successfully) a ban from the king in 1542. The social environment and his broken ties explain his dramatic choices. He ended up isolated from the royal court, from his ethnicity, and from part of his family.

The case of Miguel da Silva (ca. 1480–1556), an Old Christian, known as the courtier to whom Baldassare Castiglione dedicated his book *Il cortegiano*, in 1528, is a parallel story curiously entangled with the struggle to establish the

Inquisition, which has not been sufficiently studied. Miguel da Silva studied in Paris and Siena, and from 1515 to 1525 he was Portuguese ambassador to Rome, where he reinforced his ties with the Medici family and with the main men of letters, painters, and architects. His allegiances soon shifted from the Portuguese king to the pope. He supported Clement VII's pro-French alliance in January 1525 against the interests of Charles V, which probably triggered his recall to Lisbon. His betrayal of the interests of the Habsburgs, then entangled with the Portuguese Avis dynasty through the marriages of siblings on both sides, would never be forgotten in his lifetime.[29]

In Lisbon, Miguel da Silva accumulated honours and riches as bishop of Viseu and governor of wealthy monasteries, while he was appointed *escrivão da puridade* (main secretary) to King John III. The king tried to woo him as a valuable insider in Roman intrigues, but he was viewed with suspicion by the royal court. The election of Paul III did not change Miguel da Silva's allegiances. The new pope was also an old friend, and they kept up a regular correspondence. Moreover, there were extraordinary gifts and loans by the bishop of Viseu to the pope. The convergence of political and personal interests, but also an affinity in their artistic and literary tastes, played a role in this story.[30] The access of Miguel da Silva to both the royal and the papal archives allowed him to obtain secret information on delicate matters, such as the inadequacy of the dispensation granted for the marriage of King Manuel with Queen Maria, which could raise problems of legitimacy for the Avis dynasty. He passed this information on to Charles V, thus burning his bridges with both Iberian kings.[31]

In 1540, the death of Cardinal-Infante Afonso, archbishop of Lisbon and brother of King John III, triggered a sequence of fatal events. Miguel da Silva immediately sent a special courier to alert Pope Paul III in Rome, who seized the occasion to nominate his grandson, Cardinal Alessandro Farnese, to the governorship of the extremely wealthy monastery of Alcobaça, left vacant by the death of Cardinal-Infante Afonso. King John III flew into a fury because he had lined up his other brother, Henrique, already archbishop of Braga and inquisitor general, as successor to Afonso in his dignities and benefices, including as a future cardinal.

Meanwhile, Miguel da Silva had been called to Rome for the preparation of the council. His trip was forbidden by the king, who was suspicious that he was aiming to be nominated cardinal himself against his sovereign's wishes. Miguel da Silva decided to escape to Italy, taking temporary residence in Venice. In 1541, he was in fact nominated cardinal, and in 1542 King John III banned him and sequestered all his ecclesiastic rents. From being a wealthy client and sponsor, Miguel da Silva became dependent on papal generosity. With few options left, he supported the New Christian interests in Rome. His case was eventually used by King John III both to settle the vexing issue of sequestered ecclesiastic rents and to finally establish the Inquisition in

Portugal. In 1547, the king made an agreement with the pope: the rents of the diocese of Viseu would be administered by Cardinal Farnese, and in the same year the bull *Meditatio cordis* was issued to establish the Inquisition according to a configuration proposed by the Portuguese king.[32]

These two stories show different possibilities and different ambitions. Duarte de Paz did not have to act as a New Christian agent in Rome; his involvement in the negotiations in Rome revealed a commitment to his ethnicity that was at odds with his personal financial interests. When he tried to reconcile both feelings and interests, becoming a double agent, he lost the support of his ethnicity and never managed to recover the trust of the king. Miguel da Silva could have shifted his allegiance to the Portuguese king, but he would never have obtained the status of cardinal. It seems that he never doubted where his interests lay. He accumulated wealth, invested in architectural and artistic projects, and kept alive his prestige in Rome, but he eventually placed status above wealth. The game was extremely risky, because he might have lost everything. The pope, who had designated him cardinal *in pectore* (reserved) in 1539, might have withdrawn the nomination following Miguel da Silva's flight from Portugal. However, it was during that window of opportunity between 1540 and 1541, while King John III was trying to lure him back to Portugal and was refraining from publicly dismissing him, that the nomination came.

It is striking that both cases are linked to the establishment of the Inquisition. Duarte de Paz tried to prevent it, while Miguel da Silva's sequestered wealth was used by the king to obtain the definitive bull that created it. Both men incurred royal rage, having broken the rules of the patronage system, which meant impeccable loyalty, or better still, submission, to the king. Miguel da Silva was able to play with two centres of power and managed to obtain the high position he coveted in Rome. Duarte de Paz depended on his ethnicity for support, but his ethnicity, which was vulnerable to internal rifts and conflicts of interest, did not have political power, despite having financial strength. In this struggle to establish the Inquisition, it was political power that prevailed, as it had in the case of Castile and Aragon.

3. Spiritual Search

In Jewish communities, sacredness was a distinct quality defined by ritual and moral acts. The idea of salvation was linked with messianic redemption, meaning deliverance from oppression and exile, while the righteous would access the kingdom of heaven at the end of all time. In Jewish communities, individual responsibility was not separated from collective solidarity—understood in a synchronic and also in a diachronic way—from generation to generation.[33] The disruption of this framework by forced conversion imposed a redefinition of religious identity. This identity could assume many different aspects, including the adaptation or refusal of old rituals and ways of doing everyday things; endorsement or restraint concerning new prayers, new rituals, and a new doctrine based on the notion of Jesus Christ as Messiah; the Trinity as the unity of three persons (Father, Son, and Holy Spirit) in one God; a world of saints, mediations, and miracles; and the idea of individual salvation. The liminal position in which New Christians were placed by the blood purity statutes arguably facilitated a more personal search for a relationship with God, for a seeking out of spiritual comfort within and without an institutional framework.

The movement of the *alumbrados* (literally, the enlightened) started very early in Castile, in the 1500s. The label, produced by the Spanish Inquisition in an edict of faith issued in 1525, aggregated several different sensibilities. However, this loose movement can be defined by the rejection of (or at most, the lacklustre practice of) religious ceremonies, rituals, and the liturgy; criticism of nonreformed religious communities, which were considered corrupt; and detachment from formally declared Christian belief where there was no corresponding faith or spiritual commitment. A real spiritual life in Christ was actively sought and discussed in small circles where religious and lay people, men and women, gathered together. Silent prayer and meditation could lead to direct communication with God, and possibly to ecstasy and revelation, although most alumbrados were ascetics who refused to make gestures or publicly manifest any change in their mental state, deeming these demonstrations suspicious and ostentatious. The idea was to develop an interior contemplation of Christ that could free the self from the oppressive ties of daily life, opening it up to divine grace, as a result of intense personal experience guided by joy and spiritual happiness.[34]

The modalities of this spiritual search could be expressed as *dejamiento* (abandonment) or *recojimiento* (withdrawal). In both cases, the search involved austerity and control of earthly deployment of the senses, a discipline of the soul that would clear the heart and prepare it for the love of God. The alumbrados did not favour an extreme version of quietism; rather, there was always an active search that involved exchange and communication with others. Although there were points in common with the late fourteenth- and fifteenth-century movement for religious reform known as the *Devotio Moderna*, expressed, for example, by Thomas à Kempis in *De Imitatione Christi*—points such as contempt for the world, humility, refusal of vanity, and submission to God—the dual nature of Christ was less accentuated, as were the importance of communion and the elevated position of the priest.[35] The alumbrados strongly believed in equality between lay and religious people, and women could be highly regarded for their knowledge of the Scriptures and experience of spiritual progress.

Marcel Bataillon correctly highlighted the three main features of this movement: a high participation of New Christians (nearly all known alumbrados accused before the Inquisition were New Christians), a degree of participation by women that was unusual for the time, and the involvement of merchant families.[36] When Fr. Melchor, from a converso family in Burgos, created a stir in 1512 Castile with his messianic prophecies and proposals of reform to religious orders, all of them considered corrupt, he had connections with Fr. Juan de Cazalla, chaplain of Cisneros and future bishop; Sor Maria de Santo Domingo, a well know *beata* (blessed) of the Dominican third order; Francisca de Salamanca; and Madre Marta in Toledo, a Benedictine nun visited by the royal family and prelates.[37] Already active in those days were the beata Isabel de la Cruz, from the third order of the Franciscans, and the layman Pedro Ruiz de Alcaraz, who advocated complete abandonment in God (dejamiento). They inspired a significant number of disciples who spread this spiritual model in the 1520s and 1530s. The cautious position of Fr. Francisco Ortiz, Fr. Cristóbal de Tendilla, and Fr. Francisco de Osuna, who wrote extremely influential guides for meditation, starting with the *Tercer Abecedario* in 1527, made the recojimiento (withdrawal) advocated less exposed to prosecution.[38]

Women *alumbradas* had the reputation of being enlightened by the Holy Spirit, having accumulated a significant knowledge of the Scriptures, even without being instructed in Latin or theology, and of being able to teach about the love of Christ in an accessible way.[39] These servants of God attracted friars, mostly Franciscans and Dominicans, and exercised spiritual influence: the beata Francisca Hernández, first in Salamanca and then in Valladolid, was visited by Bernardino Tovar, Antonio de Medrano, and Fr. Gil López; she lived in the houses of Bernardino and then of Pedro Cazalla. Isabel de la Cruz left a disciple in Pastrana, Fr. Diego de Barreda, and influenced Maria de Cazalla, sister of the bishop Fr. Juan Cazalla, who also knew Francisca Hernández.[40] Maria, married to an important notable of Guadalajara, Lope de Rueda, favoured intimate preaching and played a major role in the diffusion of the movement in the region, including in Pastrana, where she had access to the palaces of noble women.[41] However, having confessed in 1525, taking advantage of the edict of grace for alumbrados issued that year, she ended up being detained by the Inquisition in 1532. She was an extraordinary character, who behaved in a controlled and convincing way, resisting torture; she was finally released in 1534 with a verdict of mild suspicion of heresy owing to lack of proof.[42]

If the involvement of New Christian merchants with the alumbrados is well known, so also is the involvement of titled nobility. The link between the two groups was direct, because many conversos were administrators, majordomos, and secretaries to noblemen. The Cazalla family had relatives working for the count of Palma, and the Ortiz family served the Ambassador Rojas and his brother, the Admiral of Castile, Fadrique Enríquez. Alcaraz, already mentioned, served as an accountant for the Marquis of Priego and was then hired for spiritual services by the Marquis of Villena, Diego López Pacheco, who lived in the Ducal Palace of Escalona. The Mendozas, Dukes of Infantado in Guadalajara, were receptive to the spiritual services of Maria de Cazalla and Petronilla de Lucena, another alumbrada. The Admiral of Castile even invited and funded a mission of alumbrados on his estates in 1525.[43]

It seems impossible to separate the alumbrados from other spiritual movements of the early sixteenth century, particularly Erasmism. Bataillon pointed out the exchanges that would have naturally taken place between the two movements, with close reading of Erasmus's texts by the main alumbrados. More recently Stefania Pastore demonstrated how the movement of New Christians between different spiritual and religious movements cannot be treated in a compartmentalised way.[44] Many of those accused rejected the label *alumbrado*, while the definition of a consistent system of thought among members of this loose movement, attempted by Antonio Márquez, was somehow imposed on a variety of testimonies, texts, and depositions.[45]

The edict listing the main heretical propositions attributed to the alumbrados, signed by the general inquisitor, Alonso Manrique, after a sequence of meetings with theologians, assembled a disparate set of phrases, including these: there is no hell; the Host is a little piece of dough; confession is not divine but positive law; abandonment to God is all, works are useless; humility is in the heart, gestures are body playing; worship of statues is idolatry; married people are more united to God; the soul should be free from excommunication, fast, abstinence; there is no need for papal bulls or prayers for the souls in purgatory; it is useless to swear an oath; and there is no need for mediators with God.[46]

This list is a typical case of accusations produced to please the inquisitors that would give a Lutheran flavour to the spiritual purpose of the alumbrados. The accusations were collected, taken out of context, and standardised by the secretaries of different tribunals and then by the secretary of the Suprema, as shown by many formularies for interrogatories related to specific crimes. The interesting thing, as Stefania Pastore rightly highlights, is that Judaism is nowhere to be seen among the accusations.[47] The New Christian spiritual search, in this case, had completely departed from the Jewish tradition, turning on its head the usual slander on ritualistic Jews. In this search, they also departed from the ritualistic Catholic tradition of lukewarm religious practice.

It is true that many of the accusations against the alumbrados were related to a long medieval tradition of spirituality and criticism of a pompous and wealthy Church, detached from the needs of the population, which had been updated and enlarged by Erasmus with some crucial texts, such as *Stultitiae Laus* or *Moriae Encomium* (*The Praise of Folly*) published in 1511, although the search by New Christians had specific features, as we mentioned earlier. The impact of Erasmus in Spain is well documented for the years from the 1500s to the 1520s. The *Enchiridion* was translated into Castilian and published in

1526, obtaining an immediate success. In 1527, Erasmus's work was publicly discussed and supported by Emperor Charles V.[48] It was only in the 1530s that reaction against his criticism of an absence of spirituality in nonreformed monasticism, the secular interests of the Catholic Church, including papal wars, and the ecclesiastic elite's wealth, started to gain traction among the main institutions, including the Inquisition.

Although Erasmus would never be classified as a heretic by the Catholic Church (in which he died having engaged in polemic against Luther and other Protestant thinkers, particularly owing to his defence of free will and his refusal to break away from Rome), some of his texts were censored from the 1550s onwards. Therefore, the accusation of Erasmism could not be formally levelled by the Inquisition: alumbrados were accused of contempt for the Church and the established rituals, deprecation of the Inquisition, and false sanctity.

The accusation of Lutheranism was more damning because Luther had been condemned by the pope as a heretic in 1520. Protestant texts circulated in Castile, although the first trial for Lutheranism was only launched in 1528, against Diego de Uceda, and resulted from ambiguous declarations.[49] Some of the heretical propositions attributed to the alumbrados did have points of contact with Luther's teachings, particularly those concerning the existence of purgatory, the validity of works, and the legitimacy of confession. The inquisitors were unable to prove accusations of Lutheranism against the alumbrados, but there were New Christians among the famous Protestants sentenced at the autos da fé of Valladolid and Seville in 1559, particularly members of another branch of the Cazalla family.[50] In the early years, however, Protestants were mainly foreigners, particularly in Portugal.

The case of Miguel Servet (ca. 1511–1553) was unusual. Servet, a New Christian on his mother's side and a polymath who enjoyed a meteoric career as a lawyer and a physician, published anti-Trinitarian opinions from the 1530s on and finally was condemned by the Catholic Church and burnt by the Calvinists in Geneva.[51] The heterodoxy of conversos, represented by Juan del Castillo, Juan López de Celain, Juan de Valdés, Juan Gil, and Constantino Ponce de la Fuente, which has been so well studied by Stefania Pastore, can be defined not only by the certainty of divine grace bestowed on people enlightened by the faith and engaged in a life of interior Christianity alien to rituals and ceremonies but also by opposition to the Inquisition and discrimination against minorities.[52]

Repression by the Inquisition curbed the spread of this spiritual search. However, the phenomenon did not completely disappear, emerging here and there, including in Portugal.[53] The links of this New Christian sensibility with Erasmism, analysed by Bataillon in the works left by Juan de Valdés, Alfonso de Valdés, and many other authors, proved to be deep and productive, leaving traces in literature, despite a new repressive push in the last years of the 1550s.

In the meantime, new religious experiences emerged from this atmosphere of spiritual search. Ignatius of Loyola, inspired by the reformist movement Devotio Moderna, studied at the university of Alcalá, where Erasmians and the alumbrados were influential, in the 1530s. He moved on to the University of Paris, where he met the companions who would create with him the Society of Jesus, which was recognised by the pope in 1540. The new atmosphere in Rome led to the middle way chosen by Loyola; that is, the way between the old monasticism and religious reform that launched a new form of congregation, one certainly based on spiritual activity but strongly directed towards apostolic action guaranteed by complete loyalty to the pope. The interesting point is that Loyola, an Old Christian of Basque origin, was surrounded by New Christians. He protected them and resisted pressure in Castile to implement rules of blood purity against them. In Part II it will be shown how the engagement of New Christians with the Society of Jesus had consequences, particularly for the debate around blood purity, but it is sufficient to acknowledge that the Society provided a new platform for a sincere spiritual search combined with missionary activity.[54]

The spiritual search engaged in by New Christians did not by any means involve most of them, who led a normal life in their parishes and performed the sacraments without further seeking for a better relationship with God. Many were accused of continuing to follow old Jewish practices that had been transmitted from generation to generation, including food taboos. The findings about New Christian engagement with the alumbrados and Erasmians highlight the possibilities created by the liminal situation they found themselves in when uprooted from their previous religion. Forced conversion did not equate with immediate integration even though promises had been made by the political powers. Finally, the involvement of merchants in these spiritual and religious experiments is well demonstrated: either direct involvement through renunciation and the engagement of their family members or indirect involvement through sponsorship. The idea of participation by self-interested merchants more usually defined by activities such as savings, investment, and risk calculation, needs to be enlarged on, particularly with reference to their disrupted traditions, and their need for cultural, religious, and spiritual search.

I will complete this section with a case that lies between spiritual search, theological enquiry, and power struggle. It concerns an entirely different matter—the Iberian expansion and the relationship between colonisers and Native Americans. Although many New Christians were involved with the slave trade and slavery, it was a converso, the Dominican Bartolomé de las Casas (1484–1566), who eloquently denounced the revolting atrocities perpetrated by his compatriots during the process of conquest in the Americas. Las Casas is perhaps the most famous converso in this period, although his genealogy has only recently been established.[55] He rejected the application of the Aristotelian idea of natural slavery to Native Americans, defended them from being enslaved, advocated their right to property and self-government, denounced the usurpation of land, contested the idea that waging war against them was fair, and protested against the imposition of forced labour under the control of the *conquistadores* (*encomiendas*).[56] His ethical stance may have been informed by the suffering of several family members at the hands of the Inquisition. Las Casas's perseverance obtained surprising support from Charles V, although the legislation designed to protect the Indians and curtail the tyranny of the colonisers was not consistently implemented. In any case, Las Casas's strong lifelong commitment in favour of the Indians influenced the "school of Salamanca," particularly the Dominicans Francisco de Vitoria, Domingo de Soto, and Melchor Cano, who shaped the ideas of a second generation of Jesuits—namely, Luís de Molina and Francisco Suárez.

4. Art and Literature

The impact of New Christians on art is arguably limited in their early years as a new ethnicity, because there was no tradition of figurative painting in Jewish communities. However, the main fifteenth century Spanish artist, Bartolomé de Cardenas was probably a New Christian. He was better known as Bartolomé Bermejo (ca. 1440–ca. 1501) and was apparently born in Córdoba, but he worked in Valencia, Zaragoza, and Barcelona.[57] His wife, Gracia de Palaciano, was accused of Judaism and prosecuted by the Inquisition. In this case, we are confronted with an extraordinary painter, who not only absorbed Flemish techniques of oil painting to create a daring set of original and extremely detailed images with unique landscapes but also engaged with biblical subjects to reflect the interests of a clientele that included New Christian merchants, such as Juan de Loperuelo in Daroca, in the kingdom of Aragon.

Bermejo's paintings show a consistent interest in the figure of Christ, particularly his descent to limbo, where the just, who had died in a state of grace, were finally admitted into the presence of God.[58] This was a crucial issue for the conversos and their descendants, who wondered what would happen to their ancestors regarding redemption by Jesus. The rescue of Jewish people (the just), who were supposed to have paid all the debt of their sins and finally saw God with the descent of Christ into limbo, represented a comforting solution. In another painting, the representation of the just on both sides of the ascension of Christ is even more original, not directly related to biblical texts.[59] The imprint of Christ's feet on the ground before ascension, matching his feet up in the air, is another pictorial note which underlines both physical and spiritual presence. The representation of the Virgin Mary, particularly the protective Virgin of the mantle, is part of a set of paintings by Bermejo

FIGURE 4.1. Bartolomé Bermejo, *Descent of Christ into Limbo*, ca. 1474–1479, oil and gold on pine panel, 89.5 × 69.5 cm, inv. nr. 015872, purchased 1914. © Museu Nacional d'Art de Catalunya, Barcelona.

and offers a response to anxieties related to the main Christian narrative of redemption and protection.[60]

Bermejo's compositions depart from previous forms, particularly as regards the ascension of Christ, and the content could be seen as addressing conversos' anxieties concerning their ancestors and the link between generations after life on earth. Bermejo sets the tone for further enquiries, offering a firm Christological stance structured around redemption and the mediation of saints, particularly highlighting the Virgin Mary's role in protecting sinners. It is interesting that, in this case, the main subjects are in total conformity with the Christian doctrine: Christ as the redeemer, his dual nature, and the

FIGURE 4.2. Bartolomé Bermejo, *Ascension of Christ*, ca.
1474–1479, oil and gold on pine panel, 104.5×69 cm, inv. nr.
251908. Fundació Privada Institut Amatller d'Art Hispànic,
in long-term loan at Museu Nacional d'Art de Catalunya,
2018. © Museu Nacional d'Art de Catalunya, Barcelona.

importance of the saints' intercession. New Christian concerns may be seen as
being present in depictions of ancestors as the just in limbo. Artistic expressions of Old Testament topics would only be introduced later. It was clearly
not in the New Christian interest to develop them at this stage.

The important contribution of New Christians to literature has been
acknowledged since the 1940s and 1950s by the work of Américo Castro, Antonio Domínguez Ortiz, and Marcel Bataillon, followed by that of other scholars,
particularly Stephen Gilman and Francisco Márquez Villanueva.[61] There is
still some debate about the attribution of ethnic descent to authors without
a clear genealogical record, but content analysis and social and intellectual
context have helped to establish common ground. However, the innovative

dimensions developed by New Christians, such as new forms in genre and structure or suggestions of new content, are difficult to distinguish from similar efforts by Old Christians.

Juan Álvarez Gato (ca. 1450–ca. 1510), an official of New Christian origin who held positions in the administration at the royal courts, produced a significant number of poems on courtly love and prose related to morals and politics. Close to the spiritual circle of the archbishop of Granada, Hernando de Talavera, he developed a religious piety influenced by the inner spirituality and austerity of the Devotio Moderna religious reform movement. When he lamented the humiliation of honourable people and criticised the attribution of distinction to lineage as stemming from the arrogance of earthly life, he was probably reacting against the trial of Hernando de Talavera and the New Christian condition.[62]

There is some debate around the identity of Diego de San Pedro, who lived in the second half of the fifteenth century. He served the second count of Urueña and wrote extraordinary novels and poems.[63] The three main texts in prose, the Sermón, Arnalte y Lucenda, and Cárcel del amor, placed within the courtly love literary tradition, include descriptions, dialogues, correspondence, and debates, particularly debates in defence of women.[64] The allegory is pushed to the limits to reflect the crucial tension between the states of liberty and imprisonment in love, particularly in Cárcel del amor, but one wonders whether this tension is not a double metaphor for the human condition and for the lives of New Christians, permanently under threat as they were.[65]

The voyage of the narrator in the Cárcel del amor is a reversal of Dante's descent into hell; the common theme is that there is no hope in that high tower on top of the mountain. The story develops with intrigues, the confinement of Laureola by her father, battles, the final release of Laureola, and the death of her lover, Leriano, inspired by the model of chivalric novels. However, the intervention of a cardinal against the harsh justice of the king—"Don't be an executioner of your own blood," "Don't let vicious advice push you into blaming innocence,"—and his praise of moderation and exposure of political intrigue can have a double meaning.[66]

Another case of ambiguous converso descent is Fernando de Rojas (?-1541), who spectacularly overturns the medieval tradition of love, coming up with a mess of urban intrigue and low interests in which desire is pushed around by many mediators and dragged down without any scruple to reveal the repulsive guts of society.[67] The Tragicomedia de Calisto y Melibea (ca. 1499) depicts the corrosive power of carnal love manipulated by an old procuress, Celestina, the main character, who argues about natural inclinations created by God and her role as a straightforward professional negotiator required by all parties, loathed but at the same time respected by those who seek her services.[68] In a story plagued by murder and suicide, punishment could be seen as moral retribution, but the final lament of Melibea's father denounces society as a permanent carnival of deception and false proprieties; a labyrinth of errors; a desert of wild animals; a game with humans; and a sea of miseries, fruitless work, vain hope, and true pain.[69]

The logic of the market pervades the articulate discourse of Celestina, who praises herself as a broker who buys and sells (bodies) to all types of people, particularly noblemen and clergymen, the latter including abbots and bishops.[70] But *La Celestina*, as the text is justly known, has more to offer. When Celestina defends a friend who has been punished as a witch, she praises the blessed who were persecuted on earth to reach heaven and argues that false confession can easily be extracted through false testimonies and harsh torture.[71] Critique of the common practice of the Inquisition is here explicit. Another comment on lineage is less risky: "Bad is the one who considers herself bad. Works produce lineage, since we are all children of Adam and Eve. Each person should search to be good by himself; there is no need to search for virtue from our ancestors."[72]

The literary influence of *La Celestina* on *La lozana andaluza*, published by Francisco Delicado (ca. 1480–c.1550) in Venice in 1530, has been studied.[73] This content analysis only adds new evidence: between 1528 and 1534, Delicado, a priest, organised the reissue of the *Tragicomedia de Calisto y Melibea* and the *Cárcel de amor*, besides that of several chivalric novels. *La lozana*, which means witty, fresh, spirited, is built around the life of Aldonza, a woman born in Cordoba who ends up in Rome, where she becomes a prostitute, procuress, sorceress, healer, manager, and helper of all people in need of sex or suffering from love. The picaresque atmosphere suggested by *Celestina* is taken further: papal Rome is depicted as a city of vice, in which money from all those celibates—priests, abbots, bishops, monsignors, managers of the Penitenziaria, and other crucial Roman institutions—flows to courtesans and prostitutes. Contrary to *Celestina*, there is no punishment, and Aldonza retires to the island of Lipari with her servant/protector Rampín with the capital she has accumulated, thereby avoiding the harsh retribution usually meted out to old and impoverished whores.

The main protagonists of the novel are conversos, and they live comfortably in a New Christian environment, enjoying close relations with Jewish people.[74] Although the novel has been considered by some scholars, such as Ángel Chiclana, quite straightforward, just a humorous play on sexual practices and carnal pleasures, hidden meanings have been looked for, with some convincing findings. The constant mockery of the Trinity and the Annunciation has been studied thoroughly by Manuel da Costa Fontes, who looks at the background of Jewish theological debate on these issues.[75] Francisco Márquez Villanueva insists the novel offers political justification for the sack of Rome in 1527 by the troops of Charles V as a punishment for complete debauchery, a hypothesis already suggested by Menéndez Pelayo.[76] I will limit my analysis to the mockery of corrupt ecclesiastic Rome and blood purity.

Noble and religious clients of the prostitutes are present in all parts of the book, but heavy irony is reserved for the enforcers of Christian ethics. After a reference to the procurator of a monastery who used to roam the city at night in a wig, Lozana comments, "There is nothing more delightful than to eat the alms."[77] When Lozana's servant is detained, she mobilises an archbishop, an abbot, a captain, and a senator, who obtain his quick release.[78] Lozana knows the value of each office in Rome, so when an officer of the Penitenziaria asks how much would be adequate to maintain a certain lover on exclusive terms, she replies half of his salary.[79] Lozana equates the legion of whores in Rome (estimated as 30,000) with old Roman soldiers, because they fight daily to keep the spirit of the city alive.[80] The ironic treatment of lineage in the novel is no less corrosive. The legion of prostitutes in Rome is defined as a most noble confraternity, since they include all the good lineages of the world.[81] The best joke is reserved for the comparison between Lozana and another prostitute, Çelidonia. Lozana declares that she might be at a disadvantage as to money and wealth, but not in lineage and blood. The reply from her interlocutor demolishes the logic of blood purity: "You are probably right, but to know for sure it is necessary to bleed both of you, to see who has the best blood."[82]

This very limited number of cases of art and literature reveal how the new system of values based on blood purity, pushed by local groups of Old Christians and reinforced by the Inquisition, was contested in a clever way, even if not successfully. Humour and derision are always the best arms of the oppressed. Art absorbed the Christological lesson, while the Jewish ancestors were depicted as the just in limbo. The main arguments against blood purity were formulated very early and passed on in a spirited way through literature. This area expressed the main examples of nonconformism and resistance, daring to depict the debauchery of Christian society and Rome as a centre of all vices. The majority of New Christians most probably kept to a low-key behaviour within the orthodox Catholic framework and grafted traditional customs onto this behaviour. But the examples provided here constitute a useful window into the margins and possibilities of the New Christian merchant elite's intellectual context.

Among New Christians, the blood purity rules encouraged a reflection about their origins and their place in Christianity. Pride in their lineage and in their carefully thought-out theological contributions inspired a new search and a new language that justified their position under threat. The way in which Spanish and then Portuguese rulers opted for racial division among their subjects created new constraints in an uneven battle for discrimination against inclusion. The claim of belonging to the lineage of the Virgin Mary and Christ, even if ignored, left a long-lasting imprint that would explain later developments. The insistence on the merits of the sacrament of baptism in purging previous sins and alleged defects of birth, although defeated, had created a powerful background that could be waived but not entirely forgotten because it was part of the Christian doctrine. The legal reasoning against discrimination towards Christians by Christians, also defeated, left traces that were developed by New Christians for more than two centuries.

A spiritual quest was visible in the movement of the alumbrados, who circumvented institutional mediation to establish a direct relationship with God through renunciation, withdrawal, and meditation. The prioritising of faith over ritual was inspired by previous developments such as Devotio Moderna and by the contemporary criticism of misplaced ceremony articulated by Desiderius Erasmus. However, the alumbrados presented specific features concerning equality between lay and religious people and between men and women. Respect for knowledge of the Scriptures and the spiritual experience of women indicated the new role these were assuming among New Christians. The participation of conversos in new religious experiments was extended to the foundation of the Society of Jesus, in which they played an important role. There were also individual experiments with Protestantism and even fringe anti-Trinitarian positions condemned both by Catholics and Protestants. Although the majority of New Christians conformed to normative Catholic institutions and practices, their liminal position favoured a certain openness to experiments at different levels. It is also noted that the most vocal defender of Native Americans, Bartolomé de las Casas, had a converso origin.

The rules of medieval courtly love were ideal for the expression of a collective sense of nostalgia, but soon the reversal of these rules allowed engagement with the sinful side of Christian society, not only in Spain but also at the heart of Christianity—Rome. Prostitution, meddling in affairs of the heart, sorcery, and ribaldry were placed centre stage, certainly not for the first time, but with a new wealth of detail and the adoption of everyday dialogue as the preferred format. The classical tradition of satire and mockery was renewed in this context, creating a new literary dynamic that would lead to the picaresque novel. The impact of New Christians in art is less visible, but the extraordinary Bartolomé Bermejo, working in Valencia and Aragon in the late fifteenth century, expressed New Christian sensitivity concerning the Christological lesson, which would distinguish them from Jewish people, and also expressed a hope for the redemption of their ancestors as represented in the descent of Christ into limbo and his ascent into heaven.

Conclusions to Part I

THE NEW CHRISTIAN trading elite was at the forefront of an exceptional struggle between integration and exclusion within Christianity after mass forced conversion of Jewish people. The issue of racial division can be followed from the very beginning, showing how its implementation resulted from a long-term deliberately instigated struggle that involved the main powers in Iberia and Rome. The refusal by king and pope of a division that went against the universalism of Christianity was overwhelmed by successive riots and protests until the establishment of the Inquisition, the expulsion of Jewish communities, and the acceptance of blood purity rules became part of the process of confessionalisation and centralisation of the Castilian and Aragonese states under the Catholic monarchs. Arguments and policies of division, first labelled as heretic, triumphed after a century of permanent fight and negotiation, but the arguments of the New Christian elite against discrimination and their insistence on equality among all believers, the efficacy of the sacrament of baptism, and a distinguished lineage connected to the Virgin Mary and Jesus Christ were reproduced over time, particularly in Portugal, where their proponents' capacity for collective organisation resisted for two centuries.

Bottom-up mass conversion followed by discriminatory action imposed through blood purity rules defined a complex and long-term process in Castile and Aragon that contrasted with the top-down forced conversion, under the threat of expulsion, condensed into one year by the Portuguese king, Manuel, who wanted to reconcile his matrimonial alliance with the Castilian royal family with the maintenance of converted Jews as an important financial and economic asset. Blood purity rules took time to put in place, both in Castile and then in Portugal. Although there were chronological gaps between Castile and Portugal concerning forced conversion and discrimination, there was clearly an ongoing exchange that justifies a parallel history. The fate of New Christians with branches of the same family reaching across borders was entangled. The particularities of the negotiations to establish the Inquisition by the Portuguese king in the 1530s, opposed in Rome by the New Christian agents, reveal the vast canvas across which political power eventually condemned the converted to defeat. It was the continuous resistance of the New Christians that imposed a much less aggressive start to the Inquisition in Portugal than in Spain; that is, there was no initial terror, owing to careful surveillance and to an exemption from property confiscation until the 1560s.

In the meantime, the New Christian merchant elite managed to occupy a central position, both in Castile and Portugal, in tax farming and royal contracts, including loans to the king. They participated in intercontinental trade, first with North Africa, the Atlantic islands, and West Africa, then with the New World and with Asia via the Cape of Good Hope. The case studies presented in this chapter have highlighted the extraordinary presence of New Christian merchants in the Atlantic, who traded in sugar from Madeira and then from São Tomé; brasil wood, which gave its name to Brazil; gold from West Africa; enslaved people from Africa, infamously transported to Iberia and then to the Americas; spices, textiles, and porcelain from Asia; and hides, gold and silver, indigo, and cochineal from the New World. New Christians developed their financial capacity in Seville, Lisbon, Medina del Campo, Rome, Goa, Mexico, and Antwerp, then the centre of a world economy fed by the Iberian expansion. They did not invent intercontinental trade, but they were at the forefront of new connections between different markets. They mobilised capital from different sources, found trading partners and local associates, and used means of transport to very long-distance forms of export and import.

A focus on the New Christian merchant elite has shown that it was this elite that provided the financial resources for the fight against discrimination, first at the royal courts and then in Rome. It is through the vast trail of documents left by this elite that we understand continuities between Jews and New Christian merchants, and commercially and socially disruptive decisions to emigrate as a reaction to continual threats, as happened with the Mendes and Nunes families. Finally, creativity within segments of the New Christian elite has been studied in its expression in political and legal discourse, spiritual quests, and literature and art. Representatives of this group were directly or indirectly involved as artists, authors, advisers, and sponsors in all these fields; thereby they contributed to new literary forms, topics, and genres; artistic reflection on Christology and the fate of Jewish ancestors; and religious and spiritual enquiry. Political arguments against discriminatory action highlighted the way it affected access to offices, benefices, and universities, while discussion of legal procedure concerning how trials were conducted drew attention to the unequal treatment of a minority that would have a long-term impact.

PART II

Expansion
(1550s–1600s)

THE NEW CHRISTIAN trading elite expanded in the second half of the sixteenth century owing to the enlargement of the Iberian world and the development of intercontinental trade. Disruptions produced by the establishment of the Inquisition were absorbed by emigration, which created new possibilities for international trade, while new bankers and financiers emerged from the ranks of the multitude of merchants fed by overseas exploration. In this section, I will present two case studies related to North Africa and to the financial hub of Simón Ruiz in Medina del Campo that will reveal forms of investment; partnerships; relations between *conversos* and Old Christians; and relations between conversos and royal power.

The Portuguese enlarged their presence in Asia, Africa, and Brazil. In the 1540s, the Portuguese (among them, New Christians Francisco and Diogo Zeimoto) reached Japan, and in the 1550s a settlement was created in Macau.[1] Portuguese merchants asserted themselves in various enclaves in West Africa, expanded to Central West Africa in the 1570s, and in the same period, sugar production in Brazil became significant because of the slave trade from Africa.[2] It is arguable that mobility within an expansive, relatively open, and fragmentary empire, opposed to the future controlled model of the English and Dutch companies, created favourable conditions for New Christian merchants.

In the meantime, the Spanish Empire extended its reach to the Pacific, with the colonisation of the west coast of Mexico and Peru from the 1530s, and the Philippines from the 1560s, while the occupation of the Americas intensified with the discovery of silver mines and the exploration of peripheral areas.[3] The two empires became interdependent because of the Portuguese need for silver and the Spanish need for slaves. This created an Atlantic geographical and historical complex, based on busy trading routes from West and Central West Africa to Rio de la Plata, Bahia, Cartagena de Indias, Habana, and Vera Cruz, complemented by a Pacific route from Acapulco to Manila that linked both empires in the Far East through Macau.[4] It is true that Castilian royal control of *carrera de Indias* through the *consulado* of Seville contrasted with the Portuguese model of relatively open trade in the Atlantic. Despite several prohibitions of conversos' participation in trade overseas, they were present from the very beginning.

However, Portuguese control of trade between Lisbon and Northern Europe started to be affected by Charles V's and John III's religious intolerance. Later, the decline of Antwerp, combined with the emergence of Amsterdam that resulted from the Dutch revolt against the Habsburg dominion, shifted economic and political power relationships. Dutch and then English maritime transport became more and more efficient. The Iberian Union of Crowns in 1580 followed the military defeat and death of the Portuguese king, Sebastian, in North Africa in 1578; the short reign of his successor as king, Cardinal Henry; and the invasion of Portugal by Philip II, who asserted his rights to the succession. The Union of Crowns stirred up Spanish rivals to compete with the Portuguese empire, but it also reinvigorated ties between New Christian families across borders that had never been lost and an economic expansion of this ethnicity in Iberia and the Iberian empires.[5]

The emigration of New Christians under pressure from the Inquisition provided a continuous flow that can be identified by several indicators but not rigorously quantified. The pull factor of Italian states eager to attract Jewish communities increased in this period, while the French authorities decided to turn a blind eye to the religious practices of thriving New Christian communities in their South West and West territories. The religious divide within Christianity also played a role: New Christians were attracted to Protestant northern Germany (Hamburg), while the revolt of the Netherlands opened the way for the establishment of a Jewish community there by the turn of the seventeenth century. These were all factors that further enhanced the impact of the Portuguese Inquisition on New Christian emigration. Religious enquiry into the faith of New Christians, which had initially spared major merchants and bankers, became more and more pervasive by the last decades of the sixteenth century. This explains the negotiations that pursued a general pardon from the late 1590s on, negotiations that were finally successful in 1604–1605, the *terminus ad quem* of Part II of this book.

As the New Christian merchant elite grew, new concerns arose about political and economic relations with Old Christians that went beyond the necessary management of monarchs and popes. What to do with accumulated wealth became a major issue. Transfer it to the Ottoman Empire or the tolerant Italian cities (or later Northern Europe) and live openly as Jews in one of these locations? Invest it in real estate? Create entailed property? Donate to convents and found chapels as places of burial, so as to live and die a Christian and guarantee family succession for several generations?

The conditions for royal contracts in Iberia and the Iberian world would favour local investment, but growing inquisitorial enquiry into merchants created an unbalanced situation. For those who wanted to keep strong ties with Iberia and were not ready to break away from Christianity, the alternative of a peaceful life in Italy, Western France, or Antwerp were attractive, because they would not face the same racial prejudices and social discrimination in these places. They would be relatively protected from the Inquisition, even in Italy, although we are talking here about the wealthy stratum. The refuge in Northern Europe, which opened in the late sixteenth century in Amsterdam and Hamburg, would mean a return to the Jewish norm, partly attributable to local religious constraints. From there it was possible to keep ties with Iberia, enlarging the access to northern European markets of New Christian communities, although the risk of inquisitorial prosecution for the latter increased.

Economic issues were obviously entangled with ethnic, religious, political, and cultural ones. The complexity of New Christian decision-making was not limited to geographic and religious choices between Christianity and Judaism. Their liminal position implied a reflection on inherited Jewish traditions, Christian patterns of behaviour, and values in general. A search for new religious experiences, including a quest for a direct relationship with God, as was shown in Part I, was favoured by the New Christians' environment of forced conversion and the difficulty of achieving full integration into Iberian Christian society. Multiple religious experiences within Christianity cannot be omitted from our research because they express a quest for identity in which the merchant elite played an important role. As for political and social issues, it is the challenging of values of blood over merit and blood purity statutes by the end of the sixteenth century that needs to be considered.

CHAPTER FIVE

Networks

IN THIS PERIOD, New Christian international merchants and bankers reinforced their position as a segment—albeit a subordinate one—of the political and institutional elite in Castile and Portugal, despite the risk of being targeted by the Inquisition. It is precisely this dual status that explains their alertness, exploration of financial and commercial possibilities, and constant adaptation to different economic, religious, and political conditions. Overseas expansion was important to create networks that would span the Mediterranean, the Atlantic, the Indian Ocean, and the Pacific. In this chapter I shall first explore the importance of North Africa as a growing market that linked East and West, an issue that has been overlooked by the available historiography on New Christians.[1] I shall then look at the New Christian intervention in financial deals organised around the famous banker Simón Ruiz, who was based in the Castilian town of Medina del Campo.[2] These reveal the growing trade between southern and northern Europe, East and West, Mediterranean and Atlantic. The involvement of different powers and different ethnic backgrounds will be at issue in both cases.

I need to qualify my understanding of networks. The activity of New Christian merchants in this period was based on temporary partnerships, which was then the usual pattern of business among the vast majority of merchants. We have found many temporary partnerships among New Christians, but there were also some that involved Old Christians. The idea of partnerships exclusively based on ethnic trust has been rightly questioned by Francesca Trivellato.[3] It is arguable that growing inquisitorial pressure in the seventeenth century might have tempted New Christians to reduce external links, but even in that period we find persistent partnerships with Old Christians and foreign merchants. The notion of a network is used here not as an ethnically exclusive configuration but as an interconnected system of trade in which the New Christians participated. Although international and intercontinental trade was largely based on temporary partnerships, the accumulation of correspondents and long-distance trade circuits configured intersecting lines.

1. North Africa

Rootedness of Jewish communities in North Africa before and after the forced conversion in Portugal in 1497 facilitated the New Christian presence in that environment.[4] The string of Portuguese forts along the coast of Morocco that had been built over a century needed constant provisioning and acted as a midpoint for long-distance trade with the main markets in the hinterland. Portuguese defeat and withdrawal from most of these ports in the 1530s and 1540s led to an enquiry concerning trade with Muslims, which was forbidden. The Inquisition stepped in and prosecuted a significant number of cases of illegal trading with Morocco in 1550–1554. These trials reveal a flourishing trade, against all odds, in which New Christians were involved as well as Old Christians and various layers of Portuguese society. The exceptionally comprehensive information available allows us to study a significant case of cooperation and interdependence between merchants from different ethnic and religious backgrounds.

The economic crisis of the Portuguese empire in 1545–1552 coincided with the centralization of power in Morocco in 1549 by the new Saadi dynasty.[5] If trade between Christians and Muslims had survived military defeat and the withdrawal of the Portuguese, this new political situation offered a market for South Asian products.[6] However, the pope had placed an embargo on trade with Muslim countries in the period of the crusades that was still in place. The supply of strategic commodities, such as iron, arms, timber, and other materials for naval construction was explicitly forbidden by canon 24 of the Third Lateran Council, held in 1179. The *Decretals* of Gregory IX extended the embargo to all trade in time of war. Clement V defined the absolution of those caught illegally trading as a papal prerogative.[7] These prohibitions were included in the bull *In cœna domini*, which was published irregularly but repeatedly during the sixteenth century.[8]

In the 1540s, the Portuguese king, John III, asked Charles V to block trade between Andalusia and North Africa, a trade that was arguably favouring the military power of Morocco.[9] The target was probably sugar production in the southern Moroccan region of Souss, which attracted Castilian, Genoese, English, and French ships in a trade that competed with the interests of the island of Madeira, one of the world's biggest centres of sugar production by the end of the fifteenth century.[10] Charles V finally forbade all kinds of trade in 1549, just before the conquest of Fez by the Sharif of Souss created a new dynasty.[11] It is interesting to note that it was from June to July 1550 that the first secular enquiry on illegal trade with Morocco was launched in Portugal, although the accused were acquitted.[12] However, the policy of the Portuguese kings was never straightforward, not even when they were dealing with Muslim powers. As will be shown, the royal family was involved in trade with North Africa at the highest level, which inevitably meant contracts with the authorities in Fez.

It is difficult to explain why the Portuguese Inquisition claimed jurisdiction over trade with North Africa when this had not been included in the papal documents setting up the Inquisition. On September 25, 1550, after the failure of the enquiry into contraband trade with Morocco launched by secular tribunals, Cardinal Henry, the general inquisitor, brother of King John III, published an edict according to which all believers must denounce and confess trade with Muslims involving metals, arms, materials for naval construction, and food. He invoked canon law and the bull *In cœna domini* to justify this new jurisdiction of the Portuguese Holy Office.[13] It seems that he alone took the decision to extend the limits of his jurisdiction, only later asking for official recognition by the king. This recognition came in February 1552 and was confirmed in January 1553 and in April 1553.[14]

However, in July 1554, when the investigation reached the upper levels of the royal administration, threatening to incriminate the main bankers to the king and the royal family itself, John III ordered the trial of Bento Rodrigues to be shelved.[15] This decision terminated, for all practical purposes, the inquisitorial jurisdiction over contraband trade with Morocco. There are no indications that the Inquisition ever again sought to exercise this particular jurisdiction, with one exception in 1575, when it acted in response to a request from the Spanish Inquisition.[16] This four-year window of enquiry, between the Inquisition's edict and the shelving of Bento Rodrigues's trial, produced twenty-nine specific trials and many more denunciations, which I will explore here. In this unusual and temporary jurisdiction of the Inquisition, there were no sessions dealing with genealogy, and accusations of heresy or murder produced during the enquiry were not pursued. The ambiguity of this jurisdiction—more secular than ecclesiastical—did not go unnoticed.

The wealthy accused—Bento Rodrigues, Duarte Álvares, and João de Campos, all New Christians, plus Lucas Giraldo, an important Florentine banker, and Cristóvão Cerqueira, most probably an Old Christian, agent of the Duke of Aveiro—confronted the inquisitors. They argued that customary law allowed trade between Portugal and Africa; royal legislation only forbade the trade of arms and food in time of war, and any other trade, such as textiles and sealing wax, was allowed; in 1509, the convention of Sintra had permitted Portuguese and Spanish trade with infidels in nonforbidden commodities as long as taxes were paid in the nearest Christian ports; civil jurisdictions had already absolved several merchants of blame for trading in Africa; the appropriateness of trade with Muslims should be judged by civil tribunals, not ecclesiastical tribunals; and the rights of the accused as private citizens should be respected.[17] Duarte Álvares refused to provide the primary undertakings required of him, saying that they belonged to the forum of conscience, not the judicial forum; and he did not recognise the inquisitor as his judge, because he was not an ecclesiastic.[18] He soon received his retribution. When he presented a papal brief from the *Penitenzieria Apostolica* absolving him of the crime of trade with Muslims, it was rejected by the inquisitors with the argument that he had been absolved in the forum of conscience but not in the judicial forum.[19]

There were various groups of people directly or indirectly involved in the proscribed trade. First, there were the king and queen, who pursued their own commercial interests. King John III had negotiated a contract with the king of Fez whereby he had the monopoly on importing wheat;[20] he also had a contract with the Sharif of Tarudant for the import of copper;[21] and he was involved in the export to North Africa of spices, textiles, and sealing wax brought from India. He had his own factors in North Africa, but the protection he gave to Bento Rodrigues (and Duarte Álvares) revealed other links. The king had signed a contract with them that was extended to include João de Campos and Belchior Rodrigues (also New Christians), whereby 1,000 *quintais* of sealing wax (58,800 kgs) was to be sold in North Africa.[22] The queen, D. Catarina, was also heavily involved in trade in textiles and sealing wax from India. Vicente Lourenço (an Old Christian) and João de Campos, two major merchants, were her agents.[23] In 1552, 1553, and 1555, both the king and the queen obtained specific declarations of absolution from the pope regarding their trade with Muslims.[24]

Then, there was the Duke of Aveiro, who traded in sealing wax through his representative, Cristóvão Cerqueira. With the sealing wax, the duke simply provided the commodity, but he also intervened to release a cargo of sugar that had been seized in 1552 as it was being brought from Cabo de Gué by a caravel owned by João Salvado.[25] From 1546 to 1547, the Count of Castanheira, then *vedor da fazenda* (royal secretary for finances), contracted with Bento Rodrigues and João de Campos to sell 200 quintais of sealing wax, roughly equivalent to 11,760 kgs.[26] Rui Lourenço de Távora (an Old Christian aristocrat), knight of the king's house and ambassador to Emperor Charles V in the 1540s, had a licence to trade textiles and sealing wax from India in Morocco. He was associated in this commerce with Lucas Giraldo, the Florentine banker who became a knight of the king's house and received a donatary captaincy in Brazil. Rui Lourenço de Távora paid customs duties in Mazagan, a major Portuguese fort on the Morocco coast. The Inquisition opened an investigation into his affairs, but the file contains only denunciations, and Giraldo was not even interrogated. Rui Lourenço de Távora had partnerships with Bento Rodrigues, João de Campos, Pedro Martins, and Vicente Reinel (all New Christians), and they had a factor in Cabo de Gué.[27] This aristocrat is a good example of the ideal type of knight-merchant well-defined by the Portuguese historian Magalhães Godinho. However, the reversed type of the ennobled merchant is also part of the new social formation cutting across status and blood hierarchies.

The next group of people are the factors and merchants who benefitted as trade grew, some of them taking on the role of bankers and some even reaching the status of minor aristocrats. The size of the bail fees imposed by the Inquisition indicates their importance: 3,000 cruzados (roughly equivalent to ducados) on Bento Rodrigues, and 2,000 cruzados on Duarte Álvares, João de Campos, Cristóvão Pais (probably an Old Christian), and Vicente Lourenço (also presumably an Old Christian).[28] Consider that the wages of unskilled and specialised workers varied in those years from 25 to 45 cruzados a year, whereas court clerks could earn 160 cruzados a year and royal judges more.[29] These figures underline the amount of wealth accumulated in trade.

Bento Rodrigues was one of the wealthiest New Christians of his time. We know nothing of his origins, but the first document related to him produced by the royal chancery is crucial to understanding the position he achieved: on September 12, 1545, King John III decided that Bento Rodrigues, then squire of his royal house, would manage the affairs of Nuno Henriques and Henrique Nunes, both banished, and while doing so he would enjoy the same privileges as had been given by King Manuel to the German merchants; that is, he would not pay for commodities despatched through the custom house, up to the value of 8,000 réis each year.[30] This previously unknown document establishes a link between the first and second generation of bankers. Bento Rodrigues had probably been associated with the Henriques/Nunes brothers but he must have remained loyal to the king, being rewarded with the management of contracts and property confiscated from the banished brothers, since the dates coincide. This case confirms previous indications (see part I) that royal institutions did not have the capacity to deal with asset confiscation. The administration of these was sent back to New Christians who knew the specific business, had highly specialised knowledge, and could guarantee liquidity requirements.

The privileges of Bento Rodrigues grew over time: the annual rent (*foro*) of 22,000 réis he was paying to the king for houses in the Rua Nova (a wealthy street known for trade) in Lisbon was reduced to 12,000 réis on November 19, 1548, then to 8,000 réis on March 15, 1549, until the foro was waived for the rest of his life on August 8, 1555.[31] By that time, Bento Rodrigues was already mentioned as a *cavaleiro fidalgo* (knight of aristocratic origin), which meant that his blood had been cleansed by royal fiat. On July 4, 1555, Bento Rodrigues received a *tença* (or annual payment) for life of 20,000 réis in recognition of his services to the king in the fairs of Castile. The king ordered the royal treasurer to advance Bento Rodrigues 10,000 réis immediately, a rare gesture that hints at Bento Rodrigues having provided the king with major financial backing.[32] One significant letter from Bento Rodrigues to the king, sent from Medina del Campo on December 30, 1553, shows the scope of the information he supplied, from discussion of financial problems to the latest commercial and political news from Turin and the Ottoman Empire.[33] But the service rendered by Bento Rodrigues, and mentioned in royal documents, was not confined to the king: on December 18, 1551, he guaranteed a credit of 5,000 cruzados to Francisco Carneiro, merchant of the queen, Catarina, in Flanders (the real amount mobilised was more than 6,100 cruzados).[34] Again, in 1553, Bento Rodrigues rendered service to the queen in France, for which activity he received significant payments.[35]

According to the investigations of the Inquisition, Bento Rodrigues traded in North Africa from 1546 to 1553, dealing especially in sealing wax for the king and for the Count of Castanheira, but also in textiles from India. He partnered with João de Campos and Lucas Giraldo. Bento Rodrigues's son-in-law, Manuel Caldeira, was the object of several denunciations concerning contraband trade with Morocco, but these were not pursued.[36] Royal documents indicate other aspects of the partnership between Bento Rodrigues and his son-in-law related to North Africa: on May 27, 1553, Manuel Caldeira, with a warrant from his father-in-law, entered into a three-year contract with the king to deliver to Mazagan each year 1,300 *moios* of wheat, at a price of 80 réis per *alqueire*.[37] There is much more information on the dealings of this family, but I shall return to this later, to avoid losing our thread concerning contraband trade with Morocco.

Duarte Álvares, who was identified by the Inquisition as a close associate of Bento Rodrigues, and who apparently benefitted from a royal order to shelve the latter's trial, was also a knight of the king's house. He had been a tax receiver for the dry ports in Alentejo in the late 1520s.[38] Even more important, he had been the *almoxarife* for taxes on textiles in the municipality of Lisbon in the 1530s and 1540s, handling more than 5 million reais a year of business, and in some years more than 9 million.[39] Duarte Álvares also partnered with Fernão Rodrigues da Loja, another wealthy New Christian, for trading commodities from Flanders to Cabo de Gué, where they had a factor.[40] These examples show the extent of trading networks to northern Europe, while in other cases the pattern of relationships spanned Andalusia and the Mediterranean.

João de Campos, knight of the king's house, lived in Tangier and had a network of brothers in Tetouan, Marrakesh, Fez, and Cadiz who were involved in trade with Morocco, mainly importing sealing wax, Indian clothing, and spices and exporting sugar and hides. A landowner in Tangier and a broker of ransoms for Christian captives in Morocco, João de Campos had been a captive of the Muslim authorities in North Africa, and it was perhaps this experience that gave him the skill to fulfil this role. At one point he had a partnership with Bento Rodrigues and Duarte Álvares. Despite the explicit support given by the Captain of Tangier at his trial by the Inquisition, João de Campos received a penalty of 100 cruzados.[41]

Pedro Pardo, a New Christian from Burgos and resident of Lisbon since the 1530s, was a knight of the Order of Christ. He traded with Morocco and had a factor in Cabo de Gué. He was also in partnership with his relatives Jeronimo Pardo and Álvaro Pardo, residents of Burgos and well-known New Christians, and with Guillaume le Gras, chairman of the city council of Paris, which demonstrates the international dimensions of trade between Europe and Morocco in those days. The partners were trading in arms from the Basque Country and textiles from Rouen. Pedro Pardo was a friend of Vicente Lourenço, who advised him to leave Portugal.[42] This case and the following one reveal the constant flow of New Christians between Castile and Portugal in the first decades of the sixteenth century.

Pedro Martins, a New Christian merchant from Castile and knight of the king's house, took up residence in Lisbon in the 1520s. He dealt in currency on the Lisbon exchange and possessed houses in Asilah. He traded for twenty years between Asilah and Fez but also with Taroudant. One of his sons, Diogo Martins, was based in Andalusia, while the other, Henrique Martins, was based in Morocco. According to one witness, Martins had been a goldsmith to the king of Fez.[43] If this is true, it is an interesting case of a top artisan, a jeweller, who moved from this function, traditionally linked with trade in gold and silver, to international trade, reaching the status of minor aristocracy. One of his associates was Juan Inguez, a merchant from Elorrio in the Basque Country, who traded in spears in Lisbon. Inguez was also investigated by the Inquisition, which reveals the importance of the Basque community in Lisbon.[44]

There was a wide range of ship owners, middle merchants, ships' pilots, masters, and sailors involved in trade with Morocco. In some cases, it is difficult to assess their economic standing owing to the vicissitudes of trade. The New Christians Miguel Dias, André Dias, and Jorge Fernandes, who appear on the list of Portuguese natives established in Antwerp in 1522, also had a significant role in trade between Flanders and Morocco.[45] Tristão Borges, a New Christian from Guarda in Portugal, partnered with Pedro Cardoso, Pedro Martins, and Cristóvão Pais for trade in North Africa, which involved investment in ships. He managed freights for other merchants, but one of his ships was caught trading arms with Muslims by the Captain of Cabo de Gué, presumably in the 1530s. Tristão Borges escaped to Castile, but in 1552 he was back in Guarda farming rents for the Church.[46] A large number of sailors and ship masters ended up owning ships or parts of ships, and these included Francisco Baião, André Fernandes, Gil Vaz, Estevão Nogueira, João Salvado, Vicente Anes, and Gomes Pereira, all of them presumably Old Christians.[47]

These cases help us to understand social mobility based on the significant risks and profits of smuggling, which opened possibilities for investment, money lending, and partnerships. The case of Tristão Borges shows that political and religious constraints could be damaging, but he had sufficient capacity to re-create himself and gather intelligence to choose the right moment to return. I have included Old and New Christians involved in trade because contraband with North Africa clearly indicates association between merchants of both origins. It was partly because of this entanglement of interests that the king intervened to stop the inquisitorial enquiry. If my interpretation is correct, the links between these two communities may have contributed to the protection of New Christians. At this early stage of the Inquisition in Portugal, the financial power of New Christian merchants, with strong links with the royal family, was still respected. Limited market for consumption in Portugal (even in Europe for some products) played a role, that is, the Crown needed New Christians to place imported Asian products in North Africa, especially in a delicate political situation of withdrawal.

The investment involved in this trade was quite significant, for example, the 1,000 quintais of sealing wax bought from the king in 1549 by the partnership led by Bento Rodrigues and Duarte Álvares must have cost 45,000 cruzados, because sealing wax then had a value of 45 cruzados a quintal.[48] The staggering quantities traded are difficult to explain, but besides sealing letters, this wax was used for dyeing. In most trips to North Africa, between 500 and 2,000 cruzados of Indian and European textiles was at stake; risk and profits were significant, and we know that Vicente Lourenço started his trade with a capital of only 50 cruzados.[49] The most profitable trade concerned butts and axes for sugar mills (the profit on these could reach a staggering 1,500 percent) and arms, in general, spears and swords from the Basque Country or Andalusia (1,000 percent).[50] Ransoming captives was also a significant business since many Christians were detained in war, seized for piracy, or imprisoned for failing to fulfil contracts. Investment in naval construction, generally small and midsize caravels, was comparatively cheap: the two cases we found had cost 165 and 225 cruzados.[51] However, the freight rates could be expensive—from 50 to 200 cruzados—because of the risk involved. French piracy increased those risks because many caravels were taken with their cargo, but Portuguese and Castilian fleets also seized ships and cargos involved in illegal trade, not to mention the usual possibility of shipwreck.

The penalties imposed by the Inquisition on illegal trade with Morocco were significant, although the wealthiest merchants were spared. Sentencing to the galleys and banishment to Brazil targeted sailors and ship owners, probably none of them New Christians. Francisco Baião received the heaviest penalty on May 12, 1555, having confessed to the illegal transport of Moriscos and masters of sugar mills, along with technological transfer that included map smuggling: ten years in the galleys, commuted by the general inquisitor on September 3, 1560.[52] Remarkably, he survived five years of the galleys. João Salvado and Francisco Vaz were condemned to two years of exile, plus 50 and 87.5 cruzados to be donated for pious works.[53] Merchants were subjected mostly to pecuniary penalties; for example, Pedro Martins, who was involved in arms trade, received ten years of banishment to Brazil and 100 cruzados to be donated for pious works;[54] Cristóvão Pais received the highest penalty, one thousand cruzados;[55] Vicente Lourenço was fined 500 cruzados;[56] João de Campos, 100 cruzados to be donated to the royal chamber;[57] Belchior da Costa, 50 cruzados;[58] Francisco Nunes, 20 cruzados;[59] and Diogo Rodrigues, 10 cruzados.[60]

In summary, New Christian merchants had contracts with the king and the queen, the royal treasurer, and other noblemen, all as personal investors involved in trade, but the case of the king is ambiguous since he benefitted from his political position and concession on monopolies. New Christians shared ships and freights among themselves while they also developed partnerships with Old Christian merchants, which might have reduced their exposure to the Inquisition. They had relatives and factors in Andalusia, different parts of Morocco, and Flanders. They also had contacts in Madeira involved in this significant network. Portuguese merchants did not hesitate to trade in sugar from Souss, even though it competed with sugar from Madeira. They insured their ships in Lisbon, an operation officially run in those days by Francisco Delgado, even when they were trading directly with Muslim ports, such as Safi and Agadir.[61] They kept their accounts in order so that they could show them to the inquisitors when requested, as was required of Bento Rodrigues. This wealthy merchant presented extracts from his accounts detailing trade with North Africa, including the dates of voyages, the names of ships and their masters, and the cargos for both outbound and return journeys.[62] There are also numerous references to the common practice of bills of exchange between Morocco, Castile, Portugal, and Flanders to move money between the various networks that existed and guarantee liquidity.

We know that the trading networks of these times were fragile: if one, two, or three ships sank or were seized with valuable cargos, bankruptcies could ensue and allow other merchants to emerge through the ranks. It was a relatively unstable world, although the Rodrigues and Caldeira families are traceable at the top level of operations for at least three generations. There were also Old Christian Portuguese captains of forts involved in illegal trade, such as the captain of Mazagan, Álvaro de Carvalho, while other captains, such as Francisco Botelho in Tangier, were willing to vouch for New Christian merchants, which reveals the sizeable links of solidarity and common interest the two groups had built.[63] The position of the Portuguese Jewish community in Morocco is well known, and the trial records of the Inquisition give new information on their involvement on trade, particularly the dealings of Rut, who had a factor in Fez, one Francisco Gomes, and the brother of this factor acting on his behalf in Cadiz, Andalusia.[64] The cases of Muslim rulers and notable men who escaped to Portugal and Spain following involvement in civil wars and political disgrace in Morocco testify to the firmly established contacts between the supposedly opposed worlds of Christianity and Islam. In

June 1553, the nephew of the former ruler of Velez, D. Pedro, and Cristóvão Teixeira, another Morisco, paid Francisco Baião 10,000 reais each to be illegally transported from Lisbon to Safi. The normal fee would have been 6,000 reais per person.[65]

The main features of these networks of New Christians help us to better understand their operators' scope and methods. Those involved entered into temporary partnerships around specific contracts and voyages of trade. The core of their business circle was the family, close relatives, and associates, but they also reached out to Old Christians; that is, they were involved in trade with the king and queen, and with some of the main noblemen, such as the Duke of Aveiro, the Count of Castanheira, and Rui Lourenço de Távora. They received protection from powerful political and social interests, both in Portugal and Morocco, which in time would be extended to Spain. They benefitted from the monopolies of the king and from the royal family's involvement in trade with Asia. The most important merchants became knights of the king's house and knights of military orders. They developed local connections in Morocco but also in Andalusia and in Flanders. They flourished within the royal framework of contracts and financial needs while exploring the fringes of the system and the channels available for smuggling between enemy powers. The informal side of the Portuguese expansion, well studied by Cátia Antunes, transcended borders and engaged with cross-cultural transnational exchange.[66] These networks of New and Old Christian merchants confirm this vision, although the involvement of the Portuguese royal family, the access to royal contracts, and the protection from different powers complicate the picture.

2. Simón Ruiz's Financial Web

The second case of partnerships that generated limited networks is even more loose than the first. In this case, I focus on multiple partnerships and personal financial relationships with Simón Ruiz, who was a banker in the Castilian town of Medina del Campo.[67] Ruiz was active from the 1560s to the 1590s and had a wide range of contacts, mainly in Spain, Portugal, Italy, and Flanders. Approximately 50,000 items of this banker's correspondence can still be seen, of which around 11,000 are letters from Portuguese merchants, mainly New Christians, who were living in various areas of Europe. This correspondence was studied in the 1950s and 1960s, with thousands of letters being published, primarily from the 1570s and 1580s.[68] In recent years, interest in this exceptional cache of documents has revived and motivated new research on financial, economic, and business history.[69] Using this and other documentation, I shall try to reconstruct the operations of several generations of important New Christian bankers and merchants from the 1560s through the early 1600s, as well as their connections in time and space. This section shall deal mainly with financiers, whereas the preceding section looked at interregional and intercontinental merchants. The financial context in which the bankers operated, including its widespread international ramifications, will be more visible, whereas the trade that in many cases was at the root of these banking activities will be less easily detected. This section will establish a bridge to chapter 7, which deals with property.

The records of the major figures involved in trading contraband with Morocco, Bento Rodrigues and Manuel Caldeira, allow us to analyse some ideal examples of connections between the first and second types of networks. These merchants' biographies show the links between the second and the third generations of Portuguese New Christian financiers and international merchants. However, it has been difficult to find more information, except for a brief reference in the notarial archives of Lisbon, about a dowry agreed to in 1563 by Bento Rodrigues and his wife, Leonor Caldeira, for their daughter, D. Filipa Caldeira, who was betrothed to Pedro de Lahos de Tapia.[70] I have been unable to trace any other records referring to this new member of the family, probably a Castilian merchant or notable.[71] The *Livro do lançamento da cidade de Lisboa de 1565*, a register of special taxation collected in Lisbon, records that the merchant Bento Rodrigues and his son, Fernão Rodrigues Caldeira, who was living in the father's houses at Santa Catarina, rua da Cruz, were both exempt from these taxes because they could prove they had arms and horses.[72]

The historian Magalhães Godinho, who did not know about Bento Rodrigues, rightly underlined the links between the Rodrigues and Caldeiras families. He pointed out that a list of contractors for the fleet that sailed to India in 1582 included Gonçalo Rodrigues Caldeira and Luís Caldeira, and he linked these names with that of a contractor for the fleet that sailed to India at the beginning of the seventeenth century, Jorge Rodrigues Solis. This last merchant undertook to send five ships to India and two to Malacca.[73] This hypothesis, which requires more research if it is to be proven, would relate the Rodrigues and the Caldeira families to the Solis family, who played an important role in the early decades of the seventeenth century. Duarte Gomes Solis boasted that he had helped a grandson of Manuel Caldeira, whose inheritance was blocked by the *provisor dos defuntos* (the official responsible for overseeing inheritances from the dead, in this case presumably in India), to invest the money in pearls that were insured in Flanders, Seville, and Lisbon, which guaranteed a 200 percent profit.[74] This could have been a simple financial operation between unrelated people, but several cases highlighted by Duarte Gomes Solis in his financial proposals to Philip III and Philip IV involved relatives.

Manuel Caldeira was identified by the Spanish historian Ramón Carande as one of the bankers to Philip II who subscribed to the second of the three *asientos* (contracts) put out to tender by Philip II in Brussels on January 20,

1556, for the sum of 55,000 ducados to be paid in money and one jewel in Antwerp.[75] At the time, Manuel Caldeira was associated with Philip's favourite courtier, the Portuguese Rui Gomes da Silva, who became Duke of Pastrana and Prince of Eboli.[76] This means that the Bento Rodrigues family made the jump from being bankers to John III to being bankers to Philip II. Furthermore, in 1556, Manuel Caldeira, who at the time was based in Antwerp, obtained a contract to import slaves into Spanish America—a contract that was extended into the late 1560s—and in this he was associated with Bento Rodrigues and Diogo de Crasto, with Melchior de Vega as their representative in Seville.[77]

Also in 1556, Manuel Caldeira supervised ship building in Flanders for the *carreira da Índia*;[78] in the 1570s, he farmed the customs payments levied in Portuguese ports; and in 1582, he obtained a contract to equip and provision five large ships every year for the carreira da Índia, receiving from the king 80,000 cruzados; that is, 16,000 for each ship.[79] He also enjoyed the privilege of choosing the captain of one ship and the general captain of the fleet for one of the journeys (outbound or return) every year. This last privilege was transformed into a gift for the wedding of Caldeira's daughter, Beatriz, with Luís Mendes de Vasconcelos (1542–1623), a nobleman who would serve as governor of Angola from 1617 to 1621 and as grand master of the Order of St. John (Malta) in 1622 and 1623.[80] This match is a very powerful example of a matrimonial alliance between Old and New Christian families.

Manuel Caldeira had been a fidalgo of the king's house, a knight of the Order of Christ, allegedly treasurer of the kingdom of Portugal, factor to King John III, and attorney for the Infanta Dona Maria, in France and Flanders. The grandson Rodrigo Caldeira, also knight of the Order of Christ, boasted that Manuel Caldeira had been honoured by the kings of his time, in particular by King Sebastian, who had awarded him the privilege of wearing the habit of Christ. In the letter conferring this honour, the king would have declared that Caldeira had the necessary qualities, according to the laws of the kingdom and certified by the *Mesa da Consciencia e Ordens*, which meant that his blood was clean.[81] All this new information from the archives enriches our perception of Manuel Caldeira as a major financier from the 1550s to the 1580s. However, we must approach this information carefully, because the grandson was pleading in favour of his father after the latter had been detained by the Inquisition, as will be shown in part III. Although I have found evidence that permission to wear the habit of Christ was granted and the financial roles in relation to John III and the Infanta D. Maria are documented, I have been unable thus far to find archival evidence of Manuel Caldeira's role as royal treasurer.[82]

Diogo de Crasto, later Crasto do Rio, who traded in North Africa, West Africa, and Asia, was already mentioned as an associate to both Bento Rodrigues and Manuel Caldeira. Curiously, very few traces of his activities exist in primary sources, and what we know is mostly from royal documents

Genealogy of the family Caldeira

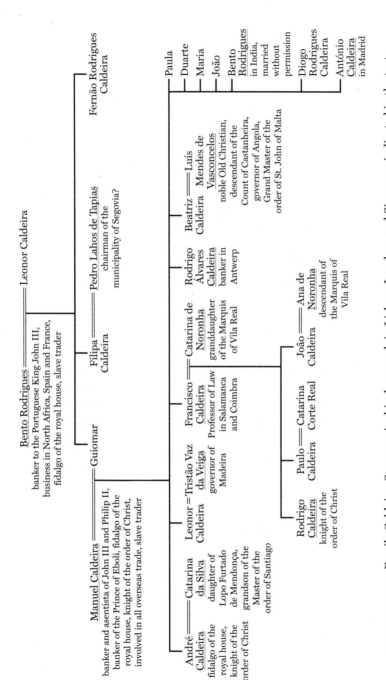

Genealogy 1. Family Caldeira. Sources: Archival research in Lisbon, London, and Simancas indicated in the text.

conferring favours on him. He was designated a fidalgo of the king's house in a letter dated October 2, 1532, and this letter was followed by two others conferring on him further privileges and rewards in 1533 and 1552.[83] In 1556, Diogo de Crasto was involved in the slave trade from Cabo Verde with Manuel Caldeira, both being guarantors for Bento Rodrigues.[84] By the late 1550s, Diogo de Crasto was a knight of the Order of Christ.[85] May 6, 1561, was the turning point for his fortunes—the date when the Queen Regent, Catherine, decided to appoint Diogo de Crasto (and his descendants) a "fidalgo and nobleman as if all his ancestors had been," naming him as a "fidalgo of a known manor (*solar*)" and declaring him, his brothers, and their descendants to be free of any blemishes relating to their birth. This blatant act of cleansing a family's blood was justified because Diogo de Crasto had provided armies, ships, soldiers, and munitions to assist the Portuguese forts in North Africa and India and had lent money to the Crown, sometimes more than 100,000 cruzados.[86]

We shall return to this financier in chapter 7, because his trajectory is both more complex and more revealing than might be supposed. The fact is that Diogo de Crasto do Rio and Manuel Caldeira, although in an apparently peripheral way, became part of a large set of financiers related to the banker Simón Ruiz in Medina del Campo. The pair wrote few letters, but it is probable that Manuel Caldeira had other connections apart from this Castilian banker, even though he offered the contract for pepper to Simón Ruiz in 1578, which Ruiz wisely declined since he did not know the intricacies of that business.[87] More dubious is the position of Diogo de Crasto do Rio and his son, Martim. They expanded their international connections early—namely, to Antwerp, where they were associated with an extraordinary financier, Rodrigo Álvares Caldeira. The latter was identified by Henrique Nunes, the son of the famous Nuno Henriques banned by John III in 1544 as an agent of Diogo de Crasto do Rio, probably in his youth.[88] This Rodrigo Álvares Caldeira, identified by the historian Hans Pohl as a son of Manuel Caldeira, wrote regularly to Simón Ruiz, subscribed to a significant number of asientos in the 1570s and 1580s, and played a major role as Portuguese consul and treasurer in Antwerp.[89]

Among the first Portuguese associates of Simón Ruiz in Portugal in the 1560s were the Gomes de Elvas family, a branch of the New Christian Castilian family Coronel (António and his son, Luis, followed later by Gomes de Elvas's other son, Manuel, his brother, Carlos Nunes, and his nephew Luis Gomes Angel, who was to become an important financier in Castile). Also involved were the Morales de Elvas family, who had interests in Merida.[90] The Gomes de Elvas, António Fernandes de Elvas (another important New Christian with houses facing the Convent of Carmo in Lisbon), and Tomás Ximenes families invested in asientos through Simón Ruiz. In the last decades of the sixteenth century, the Ximenes family obtained a significant share of the trade in indigo from India and from Central America into Castile, where it was used in textile production in Segovia. Heitor Mendes de Brito, considered the richest man in Lisbon from the 1580s to the 1610s, also sent money through Simón Ruiz to finance the business dealings in Castile of his brother, Nuno Dias, and his nephew, Francisco Dias, both from Trancoso.[91] In 1581, Mendes de Brito obtained the contract for the rents on sugar from Madeira, with Manuel Duarte, and in 1592 he participated in the contract for pepper with the Ximenes, Solis, and Elvas families.[92] The Rodrigues de Évora complete this collection of rich families, with branches in Antwerp, Lisbon, and Madrid, although there were other important families associated with this core group.

Philip II's bankruptcy between 1575 and 1578 presented Simón Ruiz with an opportunity to enter the profitable business of asientos for lending money to the king, generally paid out in Antwerp, Genoa, Frankfurt, Paris, or Geneva, to be reimbursed with high interests in Spain using silver transported from the Americas.[93] These operations involved an enormous amount of money, necessitating the organisation of consortia of financiers. To do this, Ruiz drew on his close relationship with Portuguese bankers in Lisbon, mainly the New Christians Luís Gomes de Elvas and António Fernandes de Elvas, who contributed 10,000 and 5,000 escudos, respectively, and facilitated the collection of a further 44,000 escudos (16,940,000 maravedis), guaranteed in Antwerp by, among other bankers, Jerónimo Lindo, Herman Ximenes, and Rui Nunes, all New Christians. During this period, Luís Álvares Caldeira also guaranteed payments in Antwerp, whereas Tomás Ximenes and Manuel Gomes were the bankers for this network in Lisbon.[94] For another asiento, in 1583, Simón Ruiz involved Lisbon merchants Jerónimo Duarte, André Ximenes, Heitor Mendes, Francisco Rodrigues de Elvas, Hernando de Morales, Luís and Manuel Gomes de Elvas, Rui Lopes, and Lopo Rodrigues de Évora.[95] The asiento of 1591 was successfully bid for by a consortium that included the Ximenes, Rodrigues de Évora, Caldeira, and Jorge families, all of them New Christians with professional and family relationships with each other.[96]

The last third of the sixteenth century saw a widening of the hitherto narrow milieu of the New Christian financiers, owing to the emergence of families from the Alentejo, mainly from Elvas and Évora, connected to Castilian Extremadura, who would play a major role in the following century. Families from Porto, such as the Paz family, were also active in this period, and Trancoso and its region produced a significant number of financial families, of whom Heitor Mendes de Brito was an important example. The increasingly diverse origins of rich New Christians went hand in hand with the concentration of capital and the recruitment of new merchants. Converging interests were expressed through consortia, particularly for the various types of asiento, such as those for distributing pepper, lending money to the king, farming royal rents, and taxation. These families followed the newly created hubs of trade and capital in Europe. They created branches in Antwerp, already the choice of the first generation of bankers, and in Madrid, the new capital of the Iberian Union of Crowns, while maintaining their business roots in Lisbon and enlarging their sphere of activity to include Italy. In this period, the flow of New Christian migration contributed to the extension of networks and the creation of new possibilities.[97] The second half of the sixteenth century saw a relative shift from trade to finance, the one clearly related to the other. We need to stress that these merchants were acting in a wider context than one strictly based on ethnicity or kinship: New Christians around Simón Ruiz were a minority engaged with cross-cultural investment in different parts of the world.

CHAPTER SIX

Migration

NEW CHRISTIAN MIGRATION, pushed by merchants but involving artisans and poorer people, is difficult to assess quantitatively. The two main questions—how many moved from a given location, and what were their ultimate destinations—cannot be answered with precise figures when dealing with a prestatistical society. For both origins and destinations, we must rely on an interpretation of scarce evidence and individual testimonies, although there is more information about local communities at the destinations. Moreover, we need to understand that this was a permanent displacement of migrants for whom religious persecution and poverty were the most pressing reasons for seeking a life in exile that, with a few exceptions, was difficult. We also have to consider strategies of relocation within families and partnerships due to apprenticeship abroad, establishment of agents, and the appointment of reliable associates in crucial hubs of international trade.[1] In any case, there is sufficient, although fragmented, information to suggest a global picture of the main destinations.

1. Eastern Mediterranean and Asia

Tomé Pegado de Paz, whose trial before the Inquisition in the late 1570s was briefly analysed in the Introduction, left a trail of denunciations of New Christians and Jews related to the Ottoman Empire. Some denunciations probably resulted from intelligence gathered in the 1550s by his father, Duarte de Paz. This must have been the case with the Jew Moses Hamon, then chief physician of Sultan Suleiman the Magnificent, who was accused of having tried to persuade the Sultan to conquer the *Estado da Índia* under the influence of New Christians from South Asia.[2] Another conspirator supposedly advocating seizure of the *Estado da India* was Jácome d'Olivares, a New Christian from Cochin, who had been taken into custody in the local enquiry of 1557 and sent for trial to Lisbon, where he was sentenced by the Inquisition, before managing to escape to Constantinople.[3]

Connections between the eastern Mediterranean and Italy were also addressed in this set of denunciations. First, Mateus Beiçudo, a New Christian who lived in Aleppo, was an alleged spy for the Portuguese king. Tomé, prompted by the Duke of Naxos, had failed to convince the Ottoman authorities to detain Beiçudo.[4] The latter then moved to Perugia and was admitted to the Roman court. Tomé lamented that such a dangerous man could circulate freely, implying that Beiçudo might be a double agent. He also denounced António da Fonseca, a very wealthy New Christian resident in Rome whose career will be discussed later, claiming he was in correspondence with the Duke of Naxos and had alerted the Duke and the Sultan to Christian military activities in the Mediterranean. He maintained that Fonseca would have alerted them to the well-equipped army of Juan de Austria before the battle of Lepanto but that his letter arrived too late.[5] António da Fonseca had two brothers, Jacob Aboa and Messa Aboa, who went to Constantinople and there publicly professed their Jewish faith. Jacob had two sons in Constantinople, one of whom, Moses, had been in Rome with his uncle and had returned with a gift of 800 cruzados.[6]

João Ribeiro, a New Christian living in Venice, was denounced by Tomé as a regular correspondent of the Duke of Naxos. The brother of a wealthy New Christian merchant living in Lisbon, António Dias Viegas, was accused of living in Constantinople as a Jew called Arrobas. Viegas had once sent 20,000 cruzados in money and cochineal to this brother and to a sister who was married to Isaac Ergas.[7] Tomé also claimed to have met in Constantinople the publicly professed Jew Henrique Nunes, who was a relative of the wife of the Duke of Naxos and had two sisters married there. He had also known Simão Correia, a publicly professed Jew and physician to the Sultan, who had two brothers, one of them called Henrique Correia. Finally, he denounced the son of the New Christian Bentalhado, from Porto, who had escaped to become a Jew in Constantinople.[8]

In 1557, the first enquiry in Goa against New Christians led to the detention of twenty people, drawn equally from Goa and Cochin. The trials were initiated in Goa by the ecclesiastical tribunal, and the proceedings and accused were moved to Lisbon, where further interrogation and sentencing by the tribunal of the Inquisition took place from 1560 to 1561. I shall highlight two cases drawn from the wealth of information on these trials, much of it already well studied.[9] Most of those accused had gone to India taking the maritime route around Africa, but some had decided on the European route, travelling through Castile and France to Antwerp, then to Italy, then from Venice to the Ottoman Empire, and finally to the Persian Gulf and South Asia.

In 1545, a New Christian, Diogo Gomes, born and resident in Santa Marinha, Seia, Portugal, having sent his wife and children ahead to Lisbon with his parents-in-law, went to Antwerp by land. He then moved to Italy, and thence to Salonika, where he converted to Judaism under the name of Jacob Beirut and married a second time, claiming that his first wife had died. From Salonika, he moved to Constantinople and thence to Cairo, where he failed in his first attempt to reach India. Back in Constantinople, he set off for Aleppo, where he left his second wife. He reached Basra through the valley of the Euphrates, then travelled to Ormuz, Chaul, and Bassein, where he was recognised as Portuguese by the captain, Francisco Barreto, and forced to reassume a Christian identity after his former status was established. Gomes claimed to have been captured by the Ottomans and forced to convert to Islam, thus explaining his circumcision. He then entered the employ of Francisco Barreto, who became governor of India, serving particularly as a justice official for the Portuguese fleets, and travelling all over the Indian Ocean and even to China. In Cochin he renewed his contacts with the local community of Jews, but he did not reconvert. He was finally exposed as a runaway New Christian by a fellow countryman from Santa Marinha who had travelled to India.[10]

This story, which is not so unusual, raises many questions. Why was Diogo Gomes relentlessly trying to reach the Portuguese *Estado da Índia*? Why did he not stay in Salonika, where he married; and why did he leave his second wife in Aleppo after being forced to sign a *guetzeman*, which is a conditional divorce in case of non-return after a certain period of time? In all these places, he received support from Jewish communities, but he chose to risk being recognised by the Portuguese authorities and face an inquisitorial enquiry, which was what eventually happened. Did he prefer to be among New Christians in a risky but more promising environment, where he knew he would have more opportunities?

The second story is less interesting from the viewpoint of the itinerary followed, but richer in social and economic issues. It concerns a wealthy New Christian, Diogo Soares, born in Lisbon to Castilian parents, whose grandfather, Gómez Suárez, had been made a *hidalgo de solar* by the Catholic king in 1495 (another case of blood cleansing). Around 1525, at the age of 16, Diogo Soares went to South Asia on the *carreira da Índia*. Having established himself in Goa, he married Leonor Fernandes, and the couple went on to have thirteen children and live an opulent life in Goa, owning good houses on the main street and a farm next to the sea. Diogo Soares managed the royal contract for drugs in Ormuz, and then the contract for royal rents in Salcete and Bardez. He made significant loans to captains and noblemen; he participated in warfare with three of his sons, bearing his own arms and using his own horses; and he was member of the main confraternities of the city of Goa, being well known among the local elite. Then eight trials were initiated in Goa that involved him and some of his relatives.[11]

Despite all the loans, alms, and military service he had contributed, Diogo Soares was unable to avoid inquisitorial persecution, which made it impossible to pursue his usual activities between 1557 and 1565. He eventually confessed to Judaism in Lisbon, on February 26, 1561, involving a Jew he had met in Hormuz in 1538 and the mother he had summoned to Goa in 1542.[12] The accusations against him, initially obtained from slaves, concerned the observance of Jewish ceremonies, such as the Sabbath, Yom Kippur (the day of atonement), Purim (the festival celebrating the rescue of the Jews by Queen Esther from the annihilation planned by Haman), and Pesaḥ (the Passover or feast of unleavened bread that commemorates the exodus from Egypt). He was also prosecuted for the methods used to kill the animals his household consumed, such as extracting the heart, as well as for his refusal of bacon and lard. Even cooking with olive oil was considered suspicious. Accusations that he had a secret room for religious ceremonies and a Torah in vellum were denied.[13] Francisco Barreto and several captains opposed the proceedings against the New Christians, probably because they had interests in common with the latter. We also know that the Dominicans and Franciscans were reluctant, although they eventually joined the operation, forced to do so by the Jesuits, who used it to obtain the creation of a local tribunal of the Inquisition in 1560. (It will be shown how the position of the Jesuits in relation to the Inquisition changed in time.) In any case, much suffering was caused to Diogo Soares and his family. He managed to take six or seven of his children with him to Lisbon, but one daughter died on the voyage, while the eldest son, Lopo Soares, who had been in the king's service in Japan and China, was killed in Lisbon after the trial. Diogo Soares was forced to persuade the other detained members of his family to confess to avoid excommunication and execution, and he himself was paraded in the auto da fé of March 3, 1561. It was not until four years later, on January 16, 1565, after repeated displays of penitence, that he was authorised to return to India with the remaining members of his family. He claimed to have spent 2,500 cruzados since he had left India, and back in Goa he needed to call in personal debts of 7,000 pardaus (approximately 5,250 cruzados).[14]

The enquiry of 1557 was just a prelude to the persecution of New Christians in the Portuguese territories and enclaves around the Indian Ocean and East Asia. The establishment of the tribunal of the Inquisition in Goa in 1560 foreshadowed two decades of repression that were renewed in the 1630s.[15] This tribunal had jurisdiction over all the *Estado da Índia*, which included Portuguese possessions (primarily trading enclaves) from East Africa to East Asia. Although most of the New Christians prosecuted lived in Goa, denunciations and reports show that a significant number of New Christians in Cochin, Ormuz, Malacca, Macau, and Japan were affected.[16] This indicates that regular royal decrees prohibiting New Christians from travelling to the East Indies in 1532, 1545, 1567 (cancelled the year after), 1580, and 1587 were not thoroughly implemented.[17]

In 1579, a letter written by a Jesuit estimated the population of New Christians in Macau as half of the total population of 600. In those years,

António Dias Cáceres, linked to the Dias Milão family, travelled from Acapulco to Manila and then to Macau, an itinerary also followed by Manuel Rodrigues Navarro, born in Beja, who escaped the Mexican Inquisition to eventually establish himself in Nagasaki, a destination chosen by other New Christians, such as the Peres family (also called Fernandes or Rodrigues) from Viseu. Japan had been a destination for New Christians since the 1540s, when Francisco and/or Diogo Zeimoto first visited. Persecution was less effective in places outside direct Portuguese jurisdiction. For this reason, Japan was favoured, as was the informal Portuguese empire in the Bay of Bengal, not to mention the constant flow of people to Asian-ruled destinations. New Christians were changing place regularly, partly because of the constant threat of persecution. However, they did have the support of some captains and Jesuits. Even though the number of New Christians among the Jesuits needs to be the subject of further study, we know that Pedro Gomes was Vice-Provincial of Japão (1590–1600), Duarte Sande made an impact in Macau, and Luís de Almeida and Aires Sanches were also active in the Far East.[18]

The connection between the two Iberian empires in the Pacific was well represented in the last decades of the sixteenth century by the New Christian Diogo Fernandes Vitória, who was related to the brothers Diogo and Duarte Fernandes in Brazil and was a business associate of Simão Rodrigues also in Brazil, António Dias in Porto, Francisco and Fernando Tinoco in Lisbon, and Fernandes d'Aires in Goa. Born in Porto around 1530, Diogo Fernandes Vitória traded slaves and developed sugar plantations in Brazil, first in Pernambuco for a cousin, Bento Dias Santiago, and then in São Vicente with another cousin, Manuel de Medeiros. In 1570 he moved to Mexico, and ten years later to Manila, where he became a member of the municipal council. He traded in American silver to buy Chinese silk, among other commodities, and included Macau and Malacca in his networks. His investment of capital in various trades was evaluated at 450,000 cruzados.[19]

2. Europe

In Europe, Antwerp played a crucial role in the escape route from Iberia to Italy and the Ottoman Empire. Until the end of the sixteenth century, this city must have registered the highest concentration of New Christians in Western Europe outside Iberia. I shall concentrate on two very successful families to understand their strategies for rising through the social hierarchy. Several members of the Rodrigues d'Évora family had lived in Antwerp since the mid-sixteenth century. Manuel Rodrigues (1506–1581) settled there in 1553. In 1576, the company he owned passed to his sons, Nicolau and Simão, while his other sons, Rui Lopes and Lopo Rodrigues, were active in Lisbon. Nicolau married Maria Gomes, sister of the powerful Álvaro Mendes, a member of the Order of Santiago and a banker diplomat, who served the Portuguese

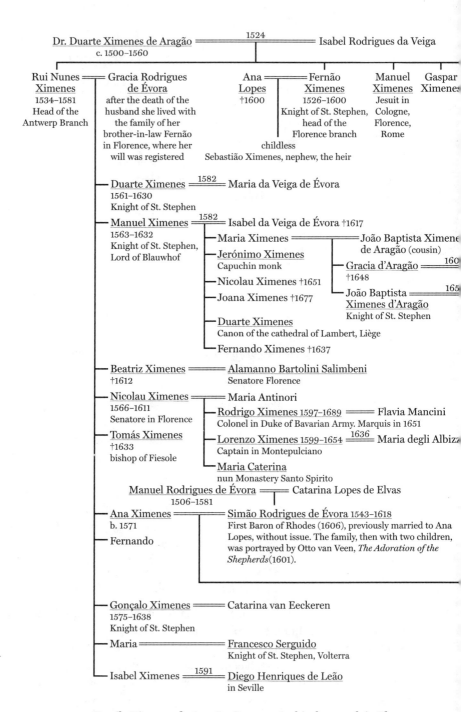

GENEALOGY 2. Family Ximenes de Aragão. Sources: Archival research in Florence and Lisbon indicated in the text; Christine Göttler, "Emmanuel Ximenez: A Merchant's Inventory in 1617 Antwerp": www.ximenez.unibe.ch; Hans Pohl, *Die Portugiesen in Antwerpen (1567–1648): zur Geschichte einer Minderheit* (Wiesbaden: Franz Steiner, 1977); Carlo Segrebondi, *Familie patrizie fiorentine*, vol. 1 (Florence: Carlo Cia., 1940); M. Gustave van Hoorebeke, *Le nobiliaire de Gand* (Gand: A.-I. Vander Schelden, 1849), 165–174 (for the Rodrigues de Évora family).

Genealogy of Ximenes de Aragão

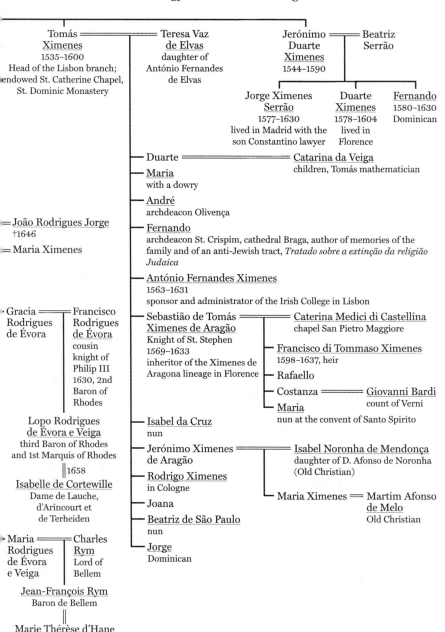

Tomás Ximenes 1535–1600 Head of the Lisbon branch; endowed St. Catherine Chapel, St. Dominic Monastery == **Teresa Vaz de Elvas** daughter of António Fernandes de Elvas

Jerónimo Duarte Ximenes 1544–1590 == **Beatriz Serrão**

Jorge Ximenes Serrão 1577–1630 lived in Madrid with the son Constantino lawyer

Duarte Ximenes 1578–1604 lived in Florence

Fernando 1580–1630 Dominican

Duarte == **Catarina da Veiga** children, Tomás mathematician

Maria with a dowry

André archdeacon Olivença

Fernando archdeacon St. Crispim, cathedral Braga, author of memories of the family and of an anti-Jewish tract, *Tratado sobre a extinção da religião Judaica*

António Fernandes Ximenes 1563–1631 sponsor and administrator of the Irish College in Lisbon

Sebastião de Tomás Ximenes de Aragão Knight of St. Stephen 1569–1633 inheritor of the Ximenes de Aragona lineage in Florence == **Caterina Medici di Castellina** chapel San Pietro Maggiore

Francisco di Tommaso Ximenes 1598–1637, heir

Rafaello

Costanza == **Giovanni Bardi** count of Verni

Maria nun at the convent of Santo Spirito

Isabel da Cruz nun

Jerónimo Ximenes de Aragão == **Isabel Noronha de Mendonça** daughter of D. Afonso de Noronha (Old Christian)

Rodrigo Ximenes in Cologne

Joana

Maria Ximenes == **Martim Afonso de Melo** Old Christian

Beatriz de São Paulo nun

Jorge Dominican

João Rodrigues Jorge †1646 == **Maria Ximenes**

Gracia Rodrigues de Évora == **Francisco Rodrigues de Évora** cousin knight of Philip III 1630, 2nd Baron of Rhodes

Lopo Rodrigues de Évora e Veiga third Baron of Rhodes and 1st Marquis of Rhodes ‖1658 **Isabelle de Cortewille** Dame de Lauche, d'Arincourt et de Terheiden

Maria Rodrigues de Évora e Veiga == **Charles Rym** Lord of Bellem

Jean-François Rym Baron de Bellem ‖ **Marie Thérèse d'Hane**

crown in France and England, supported D. António in the war of succession of 1580 against Philip II, and migrated to the Ottoman Empire in 1585, where he assumed a Jewish identify.[20] Simão (1543–1618) married Ana Ximenes and became the baron of Rhodes, one of the most striking cases of New Christian ennoblement.[21]

The powerful Ximenes family had links with the Rodrigues d'Évora family that stretched back many years. Duarte Ximenes de Aragão (ca. 1500–1560) had married the sister of Manuel Rodrigues, Isabel Rodrigues da Veiga, and they sent their sons, Fernão Nunes (1525–1600) and Rui Nunes (1529–1581), both also called Ximenes, to Antwerp in the mid-sixteenth century, while two other sons, Tomás and Duarte, maintained their business operations in Lisbon. Rui Nunes Ximenes married Graça Rodrigues d'Évora, daughter of Manuel Rodrigues d'Évora, with whom he had thirteen children, several of them active in business. A daughter of Rui Nunes, Ana Ximenes, married Simão Rodrigues d'Évora, creating a third generation of marital relationships between the two families, this time with a relationship that cut across two generations, which was not uncommon.[22]

The integration of these families into the local elite and aristocracy followed a well-trodden path. In 1586, Fernão Ximenes, who had moved to Florence, asked for and obtained from the Pope, Sixtus V, a document declaring that he had been born of an Old Christian lineage, an act of blood cleansing similar to those performed by the Castilian and Portuguese kings. In the early 1590s, Fernão Ximenes and his nephew Sebastião Ximenes were made knights of Saint Stephen, a significant military order created in 1561 in Florence by Cosimo I de' Medici, which underlined their attachment to that city. It was Sebastião who would be the founding father of the powerful Ximenes dynasty in Florence, as will be shown in chapter 7. Fernão was authorised to refer to his house on the Meir in Antwerp as a commandery (or estate) of Saint Stephen. Because he did not have children, he was succeeded in Antwerp by his nephews, Duarte and Manuel, who married two daughters of Rodrigo da Veiga d'Évora, Maria da Veiga and Isabel da Veiga, following the pattern of making their marital choice amongst their close kin. However, the next generation of both Ximenes and Rodrigues d'Évora abandoned the practice of endogamy to extend their alliances to include members of the local aristocracy, thus integrating themselves into the elite.[23]

If this line of enquiry were extended to other families of New Christians in Antwerp, such as the Fernandes, the Jorge, the Leão, the Duarte, the Soeiro, the Caldeira, the Correia, the Francês, the Godinho (or Godines), the Paz, the Henriques, the Teixeira, the Andrade, the Rodrigues de Lisboa, and the Rodrigues Serra families, it would show similar patterns of close alliance, with some of these also marrying into the local elite in the third generation. The areas in which New Christian families established themselves for purposes of business included Madrid, Seville, Italy, and Brazil. These families retained membership of the Portuguese nation, appearing here and there on lists of Portuguese consuls.[24] However, none of them managed to replicate the access to local aristocracy acquired by the top families.

Now, consider New Christian migration to join Jewish communities abroad; although generally successful, in some cases, New Christian migrants returned to their former communities. Some people—in general, younger people with poor relationships with their parents or those who had been orphaned—went back to Portugal and confessed to the Inquisition to obtain reconciliation and reintegration (although remaining under permanent suspicion) into the Catholic community. Confession necessarily meant denouncing others: those who had transported them or helped them, the relatives with whom they had escaped, the routes they had taken, and the names of the other apostates at the final destination. The Inquisition had early intelligence on all these issues, either from Old Christian travellers or from the apostates themselves when they fell into its network of tribunals. In this period, many reconciliations and trials occurred at the tribunal of Lisbon. In this chapter we will consider just two cases: those of Francisco Ferreira and Duarte Caldeira. They give good information on unstable migration that could be reversed.

On September 5, 1567, Francisco Ferreira went to the tribunal of Lisbon to be reconciled with the Catholic Church. He declared himself to be thirty years old, single, and to have been born in Castelo Branco or Castelo de Vide (Alentejo, Portugal) to Pedro d'Aires and Ana Lopes. Eighteen years previously, his mother had taken him along with his brother and his married sister, Ines Aires, from Lisbon to Antwerp, where they stayed one year before going on to Ancona, where they all assumed the identity of Jews and henceforth respected the Sabbath and the main Jewish ceremonies. Ferreira was circumcised and received the name Samuel. After five or six years, the three went on to Salonika. There, Ferreira himself decided to go to India, but because he could not find a way of making the journey, he went back to Italy, where he served as a soldier in Tuscany. After several years, he boarded a ship owned by Lucas Giraldo in Livorno to Alicante and, after reaching Lisbon by land, he obtained a place on the *carreira da Índia* as a soldier. On his arrival in the East, he lived in Goa, fought as a soldier in Malabar, and was involved in trade with China as a merchant. In China, he declared, he returned to Christianity as a result of being exposed to Jesuit preaching. On October 20, 1567, he abjured his errors and received reconciliation.[25] This is a difficult case to evaluate, because the capital Ferreira accumulated from his trade may have encouraged him to settle in Lisbon, where he may have had undeclared relatives. It is also possible that his reconversion was sincere.

The case of Duarte Caldeira is even less straightforward. When he was detained in Lisbon on August 26, 1576, he claimed to be twenty-five years old and to have been born in Lisbon but taken as a child to Ferrara, where henceforth he had lived as a Jew and learned Hebrew. His father, António

Caldeira, had been an attorney for the municipality of Lisbon, and his mother, Ana Gomes, was a daughter of Fernão Gomes *das naus* ("of the ships," meaning that he was the well-known shipowner, Fernão Gomes, with interests in the *carreira da Índia*). Taking the route through Flanders, the family had gone on to Ferrara, where they had assumed a Jewish identity. Duarte Caldeira had been known there as Salomon Zarco, his father as Guedelha Zarco, and his mother as Reina Barrocas. There were two aunts in Ferrara: Esther, who was married, and Luna, who was single. In Portugal, there remained an uncle, Manuel Caldeira (probably the banker), and there were cousins in Porto, as well as an aunt, Leonor Caldeira; in Lisbon there was another aunt, Branca Caldeira, whose home he had lived in when he first returned to Lisbon, but from which he had been expelled with the sum of 300 cruzados to help him on his way.

Caldeira had been in Lisbon since at least 1570, with his return possibly provoked by the death of his father. In Lisbon, he had gone about his business with the Star of David, the symbol of Judaism, on his clothing, and although he claimed to have gone to the Inquisition for reconciliation in 1570, later inquisitors did not find any record of this. In 1576, he was denounced by Luís Mendes of Ferrara, Luís Franco (whose wife was a relative of his), and Henrique Nunes and detained by the Inquisition. Duarte Caldeira admitted to having been in France with David Cohen, who had escaped from the Inquisition of Valladolid; he also denounced Jacques of Bordeaux, a former Portuguese New Christian; and finally, he confessed that he had kept his Jewish faith after his reconciliation five years previously. He was condemned to formal abjuration of his Judaism, perpetual detention, and a penitential habit, being paraded at the auto da fé of March 16, 1578. Thereafter, he lived two years within the precinct of the Congregation of the Doctrine of Faith, and three years in its neighbourhood, before his penalty was commuted on April 4, 1583.[26]

These case studies provide good examples of the welcoming and educational roles played by Jewish communities in Italy, creating a network that simultaneously fed and was fed by New Christians who wanted to return to the religion of their ancestors. We can also draw on general documents collected by the Inquisition as they sought to establish lists of New Christians turned Jews. One such document was appended to the papers for the trial of the merchant-banker Heitor Mendes, who underwent two periods of interrogation, first in 1568–1570 and again in 1601–1602 (on both occasions he was acquitted for absence of proof, owing to a very good defence and probable bribery). The paper, based on information given by Fr. André de Lisboa, a Capuchin, and Fr. Gabriel de Santa Clara, a Franciscan, arrived at the General Council of the Inquisition on July 31, 1601. It mentioned several relatives of Heitor Mendes, and therefore it was transcribed into the record of the trial. It gives more than fifty names, but I shall concentrate on those for whom family and other relationships are indicated.

In Venice there lived the following named individuals: Paulo Lopes, originally from Coimbra, relative of the Soeiro; António Fernandes Seco, originally from Porto, previously resident in Lisbon, relative of Gabriel Ribeiro and friend of Manuel Medeiros; Jerónimo Freire, surgeon, born in Tancos, who had a wife and children in Lisbon and a brother in Venice, and who corresponded with António Faleiro, who in turn was associated with Simão Fernandes Trancoso, turned Jew in Pisa; Diogo Dias Mendes, banker at the Jewry, known as Mosem Abendana, and brother of Heitor Mendes; Baltasar Lopes, brother of Rui Lopes, born in Lisbon, relative of the Ximenes family and nephew of a professor of medicine at Coimbra University, who turned Jew and then Muslim; Rui Lopes, his wife, Leonor Rodrigues, and another brother, Jerónimo Rodrigues, who corresponded with Girolamo Stella, Italian merchant in São Paulo, Lisbon; Pero de Pina Freire, born in Lisbon, son of Ambrósio de Taíde, and his brother Francisco Álvares de Pina, who was called Jacob Cohen, and who had an uncle, Mosem Cohen, in Lisbon; and Diogo Gonçalves de Lima, relative of Duarte Furtado a Cata-que-Farás, who lived in Lisbon.

In Pisa—although the difference between local communities in Italy was generally blurred because of the high level of migration into the area—the document named Simão Fernandes Trancoso, previously a factor in Lisbon of João Batista Rovelasco, called Abraham Israel, who was married to a niece brought from Lisbon, and who had in Florence a nephew called Joseph Israel, also from Lisbon. The document indicates that the Fernandes family had other relations: António Dias Franco; Manuel Dias da Beira, who escaped with Gonçalo Mendes Cabedo, proclaiming that he would go to Rome for a dispensation; Manuel Aboabi, who corresponded with Manuel Drago in Lisbon; Jorge Francisco, brother of Heitor Mendes; and Duarte Dias, son of Gaspar Dias and nephew of António Dias Franco, and his brother Damião Dias, a physician. In Lisbon was Rui Teixeira, whose son in Florence, António Teixeira, lodged escaped New Christians. Francisco Duarte, a banker now living in Lisbon, had lodged with António Teixeira when travelling from Rome. Finally, the Inquisition's document listed a sister of Gaspar Ximenes who had gone from Lisbon to Florence, where she was married to Valério de Abrunhosa, a man of letters from Serpa. As a witness to the veracity of its contents, the document indicated a converted Jew, Miser Abraham, who was lodged at the residence of the archbishop of Évora awaiting confirmation as a Christian.[27]

This document belongs to a genre of inquisitorial enquiry that started much earlier, indicating that intelligence was continually gathered by disciplinary institutions. The presence of New Christians in different places was noted to identify the links between them, check who became openly Jewish, who played a double role, and what connections they had with people still in Portugal. This information would stimulate further enquiry and suggest who might be prosecuted. Information was mainly collected by peripatetic monks but also by merchant travellers, disaffected members of Jewish communities who wanted to return or convert to Christianity, and New Christians who denounced their brethren because of disagreements or diverging religious allegiances. This highly subjective and arbitrary genre, which was bound to feed suspicion and further enquiry, could have political motivations. The purpose of this survey of Italian communities was most probably to direct the attention of the Roman Inquisition towards New Christians who had returned to the Jewish faith. Such documents had been produced as far back as the 1550s, when the diplomatic pressure they represented stimulated Pope Paul IV to order the repression of the community in Ancona.

A similar set of documents at the Roman Congregation of the Holy Office, compiled from 1594 to 1602, coincides in some cases with the one described above, but provide more information, particularly on good and bad Christians. There was no distinction between Portuguese and Castilian New Christians and Sephardic Jews: they were all mixed up, confirming the unsuitability of an anachronistic national approach to research such as this. The Roman report on Pisa added the following names: the captain Gian Francesco Pavia (or Paiva), the Henriques family, Melchor Pérez and his family, Antonio Lorco, David Lombrosi, Manuel D'Alva, João Lopes, José Navarro, Miguel Fernandes (son-in-law of Rodrigo Teixeira), and Fernando Mendes (known in Pisa as Daniel Ferro, who had a brother in Venice). According to this Roman report, Diogo Luís, who was the father of the physician Rodrigo Fonseca and the brother-in-law of António Fonseca in Rome, and his family, were considered good Christians.[28]

In the Roman reports, Nuno da Costa, another "good Christian," provided information on the Venetian community. In Venice, António Fernandes Seco had dealings with Lisbon and was associated with the important Italian merchant, Giovanni Francesco Aldobrandini. A nephew of António Fonseca, known in Venice as Aboabi, was hesitating to collect his legacy from the deceased uncle. Francisco Lopes had become Jewish; and his father, Diogo Lopes Rivito, once a master of writing in Lisbon, and his mother, had died in Constantinople as Jews. Another son of this couple, João Lopes, lived in Florence as a Jew. António Teixeira, son of Rui Teixeira, having returned from Brazil, lived in Florence as a Christian but never went to church. In Venice, three brothers—Rui Lopes, married to Leonor Rodrigues, Diogo Rodrigues, married to Isabel, and Jerónimo Rodrigues—lived as Christians but never went to the church and had dealings with the Jews of the ghetto. Miguel Vaz do Porto lived there with a big family brought from Antwerp. Pedro de Pina, son of Ambrósio de Taíde, who had stayed in Lisbon, had brought his wife and children to Venice. Rodrigo Mariana, a Castilian, had taken his family to Pisa and then to Venice, where he had dealings with the Jews of the ghetto. His brother, Diego Mercenas, was in Pisa, in the service of the Muslim king of Morocco, and his nephew, Alonso Pérez de Montalban, travelled between Pisa and Morocco. Lorenzo López de Padilla, who had returned from the Indies with 120,000 scudi, was also in Pisa, living as a Christian, but he was a Jew. Others came from Peru (for example, Álvaro Mendes, who had then moved from Venice to Constantinople). The brother of Heitor Mendes, Bendana, lived in Venice as Jew; another brother, Jorge Francisco, lived in Pisa as a Christian with a nephew, Francisco Dias; and a third brother, Gaspar Dias, was in Venice with his family, in particular his son, Duarte Dias. The brothers João Rodrigues Pardo and Domingos Rodrigues Pardo had two other brothers in Madrid. In Florence, Sebastião and Nicolo Ximenes were considered good Christians, as was the Dominican, André Teixeira, in Rome.[29]

This report on New Christians listed many more names than can be summarised here. The document estimated there were 120 households of Portuguese Jews in Pisa. Other reports compiled in the same codex provided more information on Daniel Rodrigues de Bragança, a resident of Venice who was married to a niece of Manuel Drago from Lisbon. Filipe Dinis had been circumcised in Venice after being the subject of an enquiry by the Inquisition, but his children lived as Christians after being Jewish in Ragusa (Dubrovnik). Diogo Rodrigues also lived in Venice and was married to a daughter of Jorge Rodrigues Brandão, who had escaped from Portugal to Hamburg after being denounced to the Inquisition. The Pimentel family had a member, Álvaro, who had gone to Constantinople to become Jew and had been circumcised by Micer Dominico, who had later converted to Christianity. Jorge Fernandes Machorro (also written Mochorro), born in Covilhã, Portugal, had taken the name Joseph Machorro in Venice; he had a brother, Diogo Gomes do Bemfazer, who migrated from Seville to Ferrara and then to Venice, and who had left behind two sons. In Modena, the banker Franco married the daughter of Simão Soeiro, resident of Antwerp, who was called Mor Soeira, and then married Dona Alumbre. Henrique Gomes, called Isaac Aboab in Pisa, was the brother of Bento Dias Santiago and Miguel Dias Santiago and had been born in Porto. His son-in-law, Mateus Nunes, went back to Lisbon, where he had dealings with Manuel Drago and a certain Caminha. The three traded in sugar from Brazil through the factor for sugar mills, Fernão Buco. Bento Henriques, known as Cabilho, married a daughter of Dr. Calhandra and took all the family to Constantinople. The family of Manuel Fernandes Serralvo was in Ferrara.[30]

The person bearing witness against these people suggested making enquiries in Antwerp about Simão Soeiro, Filipe Jorge, and Luís Álvares Caldeira. He also questioned the Christian beliefs of business partners in Seville, such as Rui Fernandes Pereira, a relative of Jorge Fernandes Machorro, Carlos Rodrigues, a relative of the same Machorro, Gaspar Dias Murça, brother-in-law of António Vaz, a physician who escaped from Portugal after being reconciled by the Inquisition, and Jorge Vaz, son of Miguel Vaz do Porto, who was about to travel to the West Indies. The main business partners in Lisbon of all these accused were allegedly Manuel Drago and Heitor Mendes.[31]

This list of names may seem tedious, but it can provide useful information to further identify networks. This small sample provides insight into continuous long-distance and regional migrations; dealings between Italy and the West and East Indies; families regularly split between Christianity and Judaism; conversions with possible returns, hesitations, and second thoughts; religious conviction and ambiguity; clarity of choice and financial interest; economic opportunities; and local religious possibilities. It confirms the role of Italy as a special place for transition between Christianity and Judaism, in both directions, and between Christian Europe and the Ottoman Empire. We have focused on the merchant elite, who experienced downturns in their fortunes owing to economic crises or inquisitorial persecution that could strip them of all their assets, but many ordinary refugees struggled to survive and had to be helped by local Jewish relatives or New Christian charity. Regular returns to Portugal and Castile, even under the threat of the Inquisition, can only be explained by the dire straits some found themselves in, which meant they were willing to grasp, as a last resort, at the possibility of claiming money left by a previous generation or at help from relatives who had remained behind.

These compilations rely heavily on local information. The motives for denunciations are clear in the letter from the "good Christian" and denouncer, Nuno da Costa, to Fra Zaccaria (or Zacarias), in which he asks for the mediation of the monk with Monsignor Santa Severina, or even with Cardinal Farnese, to obtain their intervention with the Duke of Ferrara for payment of a debt which has been blocked by the heirs of Isaac da Fano. In another letter, Nuno da Costa asks for mediation to obtain from Cardinal Santa Severina an intervention in Ragusa (Dubrovnik), where his adopted son Bartolomeu da Costa, a man who has become a Christian, has been detained with the goods he is dealing in and falsely accused by Jews. On December 4, 1594, Nuno da Costa writes directly to Cardinal Santa Severina.[32] This sequence of letters, which were curiously kept in the same file, shows how economic interests were linked to denunciations, and how good Christians could be moved by motives other than religious zeal. But there is more. Going back to the list appended to papers for the trial of Heitor Mendes, this same Nuno da Costa is named as someone whose father and brothers converted to Judaism in Venice. He wished to keep his Christian faith and had obtained from the pope an order granting him guardianship of a brother of minor age. He had also fought for D. António during the War of the Portuguese Succession in 1580, escaping to Madrid after his side's defeat.[33]

The special case of the Fonseca family in Rome, and their links to the Paz family, will allow us to progress further in this search to uncover the strategies used and the constraints experienced by merchants. The presence of Portuguese New Christians in Rome can be traced back to the 1530s, following the first generation of Castilian *conversos*. Many stayed there as merchants and merchant-bankers, some obtaining positions, particularly as jurists and physicians. In the 1540s, the Furtado family (led by the physician Pedro Furtado) and the Fonseca family, escaped from the Inquisition in Lamego and went to Rome. There they obtained documents of protection from the Pope, who ordered the Inquisition to release several of their relatives. Jácome da Fonseca, married to Justa de Paz, lived in Rome as an important merchant trading spices from 1543 to 1555 and acted as the New Christians' representative to the pope. Nevertheless, he ended up assuming a Jewish identity in the Ottoman Empire, under the name Jacob Aboabi.[34]

Documents show that Jácome's brother, António da Fonseca (1515–1588), was present in Rome from 1556 on. Jácome had two other brothers, Jerónimo Fernandes and Rui Fernandes, the latter being the author of the *Descrição do terreno ao redor de Lamego*.[35] Rui Fernandes died in 1559, and António persuaded the Portuguese ambassador in Rome, Lourenço Pires de Távora, to write to Cardinal Henrique asking permission for the widow to travel to Rome. Besides his relationship with the ambassador, António da Fonseca had close relationships with Diogo de Andrade and the Carmelite Eliseo, son of Bishop Martinho of Funchal, who were chamberlains to the pope from the 1560s to the 1580s. His best friend in Rome was a New Christian, Monsignor António Pinto, from Mogadouro, who had become a doctor in canon law in Bologna after studying in Coimbra. Pinto's father had been condemned by the Inquisition, and his uncle, Diogo Vaz Pinto, known as the Hieronymite Diogo de Murça, had been rector of the University of Coimbra. António Pinto himself had the status of knight of Saint Peter and was secretary to the Portuguese Embassy, having conducted business related to the Inquisition, accumulated ecclesiastical benefices, supported Philip II's claim to the throne in 1579, and was a member of the Council of Portugal in Madrid from 1588 until his death in 1592. During his time on the council, he voted against the exclusion of New Christians from the university. António da Fonseca had associates and correspondents in Lisbon who included the bankers Giraldi (father and son) and Heitor Mendes.[36]

António da Fonseca's networking is even more interesting than the preceding outline of his relationships has already suggested, and it clearly reached beyond the New Christian sphere; so, this research needs to be taken further. First, he became a member of the Confraternity of Saint Anthony of the Portuguese, in whose registers he appears from 1560 to 1585 as governor of the confraternity and governor of the hospital, rotating the position with António Pinto, the banker Francisco da Costa, Aquiles Estaço, a man of letters and secretary to the Pope, João da Veiga, Rodrigo Vaz Cernache, Dr. Jorge Fernandes, his associate Manuel do Quental, the chamberlains Diogo de Andrade and Eliseo of Portugal, Gaspar Homem, Dr. António de Gouveia, and António Pinto's nephew, Francisco Vaz Pinto, who later succeeded his uncle in Rome, among others.[37] Here we see Old and New Christians merrily mixed, because the distinction was not recognised in Italy. The famous jurist (Old Christian) Martin de Apzilcueta Navarro, who was a professor at the University of Coimbra and who defended Archbishop Bartolomé Carranza in his inquisitorial trial when the latter was called by the pope to Rome, donated a house at Campo dei Fiori to the confraternity and was buried at the church of St. Anthony of the Portuguese, where a magnificent sculptured bust of him was placed on the wall.

This shows how António da Fonseca used the confraternity to enlarge his connections. But he went beyond this simple move: he foresaw the accession of Philip II to the Portuguese throne, and in 1579 he wrote to Philip expressing his support. It was an action he had cannily reflected on and coordinated with António Pinto. That same year the Confraternity of the Most Holy Resurrection, located at the Church of San Giacomo degli Spagnoli in Piazza Navona, was created with the purpose of gathering all the Hispanic nationals in Rome. It was a curious initiative, which reveals the careful planning that went into Philip II's bid for the throne of Portugal both inside and outside Iberia. António da Fonseca immediately established links with the new confraternity, and when his wife, Antónia Luís, died in 1582, he decided to buy the rights to the Chapel of St. Peter and St. Damian at San Giacomo's Church and transform it into the Chapel of the Resurrection, for the burial of his family, with a significant donation to the church.

In 1585, António da Fonseca hired the painter Baldassare Croce to provide new decoration around the theme of the resurrection of Christ: God the father surrounded by the prophets (Daniel, David, Isaiah, and Elijah) who predicted resurrection; apparitions of Christ after the resurrection; St. Anthony of Padua worshiping the child Jesus; and the descent of Christ to limbo, an important old topic in New Christian painting. On the outside of the Chapel was the coat of arms of António da Fonseca and statues in stucco of John the Baptist and San Giacomo degli Spagnoli. The two columns of the portal of the Chapel had inscribed references in Latin to "António da Fonseca Lusitanian from Lamego made it" and "In honour of the resurrection of Our Lord Jesus Christ, year 1584."[38] This choice of an iconographic programme certainly reflects the focus of the confraternity, but it is interesting that the celebration of the resurrection should have been a matter of such importance to a wealthy New Christian in Rome. There was no subject that could have better defined the family's religious allegiance and squarely asserted its position among the divided allegiances of the New Christian community. Yet there were zones of ambiguity within António da Fonseca's family, as the next chapter will show.

New Christian and Jewish migration to the western coast of France, particularly Bayonne, Saint-Jean de Luz, Bordeaux, and Rouen, became important in the first half of the seventeenth century and was based on the textile

FIGURE 6.1. Inscriptions in the portal of the Chapel of the Resurrection, old church of San Giacomo degli Spagnoli, Piazza Navona, endowed by António da Fonseca. Photos courtesy of the author.

trade from the North and the sugar and spice trade from Brazil and South Asia. However, some degree of movement was already in place long before that because of a pragmatic reluctance by the French authorities to enquire about people's faith, even though Judaism was forbidden during this time.[39] The first royal letter explicitly protecting the Portuguese New Christians, identified as merchants, was issued on December 22, 1550. They were authorized to reside, trade, move inside and outside the kingdom, acquire property, and enjoy all the privileges and freedoms of the French subjects and inhabitants of the cities where they chose to live.[40] The second royal letter, issued on November 11, 1574, confirmed the same rights to the Spaniard and Portuguese residents in Bordeaux.[41] It shows that New Christians were strong enough to lobby for these royal letters by the mid-sixteenth century. The freedom of movement and status obtained by New Christians concerning residence, property, trade, and privileges, in line with French subjects, is remarkable.

By the turn of the seventeenth century, Amsterdam and Hamburg had also become significant destinations because of the religious tolerance exhibited, particularly in Amsterdam. Jacob Tirado, already living in Amsterdam in 1598, played an important role in the creation of the first Jewish congregation, the Bet Jacob, in 1603, but other former New Christians were also involved. Some of these New Christians, such as Garcia Pimentel, had migrated from Venice, and others—Duarte Nunes Belmonte, members of the Lopes Homem/Lopes Pereira family, Manuel Carvalho, and Henrique Garcês, maternal grandfather of Baruch Spinoza—came from Portugal because of the harsh inquisitorial persecution of the 1590s.[42] The conversion of New Christians to normative Judaism started to be defined in this early stage: Manuel Carvalho declared he had not professed Judaism until 1616. Henrique Garcês, who lived outside the ritual life of the community, although he had been taxed for the purchase of land for the cemetery, was only circumcised after his death in 1619 so that he could be buried at the Jewish cemetery. Miriam Bodian pointed out the main factors for the formation of the normative community: the Calvinist Dutch's preference for the clear Judaism of the New Christians over any ambiguous Catholicism or even atheism (as Hugo Grotius feared in 1615), the psychological need for religious legitimacy, and the advantages of a shared identity based on a religious project finally recognised by the burgomasters of Amsterdam in 1616.[43]

In Hamburg, a parallel influx of New Christians occurred, which was relatively protected by the Senate, although fear of competition by local merchants and the antisemitic sentiments of the Lutheran clergy caused some difficulties.[44] The famous physician Rodrigo de Castro was one of the first to settle there in 1591. Among the denunciations that have been preserved from inquisitorial trials, João da Costa accused Manuel Álvares da Costa and Jorge Pires Brandão, the latter with three children, plus the two Cardoso brothers of being the main Jews of New Christian origin in Hamburg in the mid-1590s. The accuser added that João Faria, born in Viana, son of Gonçalo Faria and nephew of Leonardo Fróis, resident in Lisbon with business in Hamburg, could give more information.[45] A document from the session of the Jewish community of Hamburg on April 13, 1617, and further denunciations at the Inquisition of Lisbon by Heitor Mendes Bravo, indicated Rui Fernandes Cardoso (alias Elihau Aboaf), João Ribeiro (alias Jacob Guedelha), Álvaro Dinis (alias Semuel Jahya), Rui Peres Brandão (alias Ishac Hoeff), Gonçalo Lopes Coutinho (alias Jacob Coronel), David Neto, Fernão Dias Mendes de Brito (alias Abraham Abendana), son of the banker Heitor Mendes de Brito, among the first generation of migrants.[46] In 1608 and 1609, twenty Portuguese merchants paid the *werkzoll* (duties for navigation markers for the Elbe), which indicates that the Jewish community of New Christian origin in Hamburg had reached around a hundred people.[47]

3. Africa and the Americas

New Christians controlled the royal contracts for trade with Guinea from the end of the fifteenth century onwards. There was a very early forced migration (more accurately, a deportation) of abducted Jewish children to the area, followed by a constant flow of New Christians to West Africa, first to the Cape Verde islands and the area of Senegambia (roughly, from present-day Senegal to Sierra Leone), and later to the Gulf of Guinea, based on Elmina and extended to the islands of São Tomé and Principe. There were two points of attraction in West Africa: the relative absence of Portuguese institutions, except in the Cape Verde islands, mainly in Santiago; and the openness of African populations, who simply accepted the lineages of foreign merchants. New Christians could openly profess their Jewish faith among the African populations, while displaying a superficial Catholic religious allegiance in their necessary contacts with the Portuguese authorities of the Cape Verde islands. The New Christians' background helped to promote the introduction of Portuguese influence into the region, as they revealed an extraordinary capacity for adaptation, including the absorption of local rituals and practices. They mixed with local populations, got involved in the politics of chieftaincies, and created new families with links to local lineages. The creation of a creole culture and language, already visible in the 1520s and 1530s, was very much a result of this flexibility, shaped by the New Christians' situation, although there were distinct experiences in Upper Guinea and the Cape Verde islands of Fogo and Santiago, partly affected by proximity to or distance from Portuguese institutions.[48]

By the mid-sixteenth century, stimulated by the establishment of the Inquisition in Portugal, the presence of New Christians in Guinea had increased; one witness calculated there were 200, a significant number if we consider the very high mortality rate for Europeans in the region.[49] In São Tomé, a royal representative lamented that New Christians made up one-fifth of the local Portuguese population, while there were complaints against the *ouvidor* (magistrate), Aleixo Lopes, who came from this same ethnic background.[50] Other witnesses mention the spread of New Christians to Kongo, while their presence in Cape Verde, early linked to the Canary Islands, is well attested not only in the inquisitorial files but also in complaints to the king in which local officials were accused of having "stained blood." Complaints were even made against the *corregedor* (head magistrate) of Ribeira Grande, Pero Moniz, the second source of authority over the islands after the captain.[51] Some of the New Christian merchants operating both in Upper Guinea and the Cape Verde islands—such as Manuel Garcia; Vicente Nunes; Francisco Lopes; Bartolomeu Garcia; and Manuel, Mécia, and Branca Dias—were denounced to the Inquisition because of commercial rivalry.[52] Diogo Henrique de Sousa, the contractor of Cape Verde trade in the 1570s, was the richest *lançado* (migrant among Africans) living in Guinea; he left twenty vessels to his son Mateus Fernandes, who became the leading trader in Sierra Leone, monopolising salt from Cape Verde.[53]

New Christians played a major role in the Portuguese presence in West Africa in this period, already structured by slave trade with the Americas. Their expansion in Flanders, including in Amsterdam, by the turn of the seventeenth century, meant direct connections between West Africa and that region. Estevão Rodrigues Penso (born in Elvas), Filipe de Sousa and his brother Diogo de Sousa (born in Lisbon), Luís Fernandes Duarte (born in Faro), Gaspar Nunes, Pero Rodrigues Veiga, Gaspar Fernandes Dias, Diogo Martins Bomdia, Jorge Carneiro, and Jerónimo Nunes were some of the merchants involved in this route, most of them Amsterdam Jews, using ships hired from Diogo Lobo Leitão, Simão Rodrigues Pinhel, Jerónimo Freire (or Jacob Peregrino), and even from the royal factor in Cachéu, Baltasar Lopes de Setúbal.[54] By that time, Sebastião Fernandes Cação was considered one of the main traders on the rivers Geba and Grande.[55] Some of these names will have a special meaning for our story, because they belonged to families on both sides of the religious divide and will come up again later in this book.

The importance of West Africa for the structuring of the Atlantic World has been highlighted by several authors, along with the role played by New Christians. The families Carvajal and Leão established a direct link between West Africa and the Spanish Americas. Duarte de Leão, whose brothers Álvaro and Jorge de Leão had been detained by the Inquisition in 1544 and released because of the general pardon of 1547, obtained the post of royal treasurer and comptroller in Cape Verde in those years. He decided to take his eleven-year-old nephew, Luis de Carvajal, born in Mogadouro, with him. It was a typical case of escape from possible inquisitorial persecution, such as had been undertaken by many New Christians in West Africa. Another of Luis de Carvajal's relatives in that region was his uncle, Francisco Jorge, factor of Duarte de Leão in Bugendo (Casamança); but Luis de Carvajal had more relatives who tended to move with him, and it was they who were accused of disrespecting the Virgin Mary on Christmas Eve 1562.[56] In 1580, Luis de Carvajal was appointed governor of Nueva León in northern Mexico and given the responsibility of pacifying the Chichimecas and expanding the region's population. He had gained a reputation for dealing well with natives, perhaps owing to his previous experience in West Africa. He took with him a significant number of relatives who, in 1589, were all accused of Judaism. Luis de Carvajal was reconciled in the auto da fé of February 24, 1590, but several family members, including a nephew with the same name, who were more vocal about and rooted in their Jewish faith and who claimed they were still waiting for the coming of the Messiah, were executed then or in a later auto da fé.[57]

The number of New Christians in Spanish America was already significant in the 1590s, because many had arrived early from Castile and others arrived later from Portugal. The lists of sentenced persons presented at the autos da fé in the 1590s and the early 1600s include a significant number of New Christians accused of Judaism, among whom was António Dias Cáceres, a friend of Luis de Carvajal, who had travelled to Macau and was reconciled at the auto da fé of March 25, 1601, in Mexico City.[58] The New Christian presence in Lima was not so visible at this time, but a significant number had arrived through Panama, and many had travelled through the Rio de la Plata, because Buenos Aires was considered a port of call less tightly controlled by the authorities and open to contraband. The autos da fé of 1600 and 1605 recorded proceedings against dozens of New Christians accused of Judaism, with some of these people being excommunicated. The general pardon took time to be implemented there, but several New Christians serving sentences, such as Gaspar de Silveira, were finally released.[59]

The migration of New Christians to Brazil started in the 1550s with the first stage in the development of sugar plantations. This movement of people became the counterpart of migration to West Africa, because sugar production depended on slave labour brought from Africa. New Christians became integrated into the colony as artisans, merchants, and sugar plantation owners. The Inquisitor Heitor Furtado de Mendonça visited Bahia (1591–1593) and Pernambuco, and Itamaracá and Paraíba (1593–1595) and identified sixty-nine New Christians from various backgrounds. However, many other documents exist, for example, registers of those plying particular trades and enquiries about access to military orders, that complete the picture.[60]

In Pernambuco, the wealthiest New Christians in this period were probably the bankers João Nunes Correia, Manuel Cardoso Milão, and Duarte Lopes da Costa. João Nunes Correia represented his brother Henrique Nunes Correia of Lisbon and later became an important contractor in Seville. Manuel Cardoso Milão was the eldest son of the powerful Henrique Dias Milão of Lisbon, who had three brothers with him (all went to Amsterdam following the detention of their father, who was later executed). Duarte Lopes da Costa went to Amsterdam and became Jacob Tirado, the founder of the first Jewish congregation, as previously mentioned.[61] New Christian merchants in Brazil included Francisco Lopes Homem and his nephew Manuel Lopes Homem (who temporarily migrated to Amsterdam); João de Paz; Luís Dias; Manuel de Azevedo from Porto; Afonso Serrão; Jorge Tomé Pinto from Porto; Pedro de Morais Sampaio from Lisbon; Manuel Rodrigues Vila Real; Henrique Gomes and Isabel Nunes; Manuel and João Nunes de Matos; and Miguel Dias Santiago. In the late 1560s, Bento Dias Santiago created a sugar mill at Camarajibe, but there were other New Christian sugar plantation owners, such as Fernão Soares, Filipe Dinis do Porto, André Gomes Pina, and Duarte Dias Henriques.[62] Similar cases of New Christians in business in Bahia and in the

FIGURE 6.2. Zacharias Wagner, *Slave Market in Recife*, 1637–1641, watercolour, part of a Thierbuch, 212 x 335 mm, inv. nr. Ca 226/106. © Kupferstich-Kabinett, Staatliche Kunstsammlungen Dresden. Photo: Herbert Boswank.

captaincies of the south, mainly St. Vicente, have been identified.[63] The concentration of wealthy New Christians was already significant in this period, but it would increase during the seventeenth century.

In the second half of the sixteenth century, New Christian migration favoured Italy, not only because Rome was a big hub for financial transactions but also because there was a relative tolerance and protection in several cities for Jewish communities. New Christians did not face prejudice, integration into Christian society was much easier than in Iberia, and at the same time they could maintain a certain level of relationships with their relatives in the Jewish ghettos. The transformation of Livorno into an important maritime hub in the Mediterranean by the Medici family in the 1590s, based on an invited Jewish community, played a major role. Moreover, New Christians could emigrate without making up their mind which community they would integrate into. In Italy they could decide to return to the normative community of their ancestors or even migrate to the Ottoman Empire and live entirely outside the Christian world.

The acceptance of New Christians in different cities of western France increased during this period, and they obtained favourable treatment from the French king, which reveals a capacity to lobby at the highest level for their interests. There were two advantages: access to French textile production in a position where they could mediate trade between southern and northern

Europe, and the rooted practice of French authorities to avoid enquiries on religious beliefs. The main trading maritime cities of Amsterdam and Hamburg—the former controlled by Calvinists after breaking away from Habsburg rule and the latter by the Lutherans—also saw the advantage of accepting active Jewish communities, thus attracting New Christians.

Emigration to Spanish and Portuguese America became important in this period. New Christians could keep their ties in Iberia and live a quiet life without much religious enquiry (at this stage). Emigration to western Africa, South Asia and East Asia still meant living in (and outside) Iberian colonial enclaves, but there was a significant freedom until the Inquisition of Goa was created in 1560. The creation of Luso-African lineages and Luso-Asian families followed. New Christians were both victims and perpetrators of abuse, because they became heavily involved with the slave trade and plantations based on slave labour.

CHAPTER SEVEN

Property

HOW DID THE New Christian trading elite invest the money they accumulated as capital? Would a route to ennoblement be opened by an investment in real estate and in royal interests (or bonds, as they would be called today)? Would perseverance in trade and finance be rewarded with wealth for the family and a guarantee of future security? How did this elite react to loss and even penury following bankruptcy or inquisitorial persecution? An investigation into property ownership will allow us to look at investment, forms of inheritance, rules of succession, matrimonial alliances, and social mobility, upward and downward. We shall revisit some of the families who have already been mentioned as we follow the main threads of our analysis. I shall engage simultaneously with economic and social history, because the two are intertwined, and to do this I shall privilege wills and trials. Wills were important because inheritance—that is, the division of accumulated assets—was (and is) a vital part of life, and names and dates given in records of inheritance were generally accurate, simply because these documents were legally binding. Inventories of property and notarial records are part of the same legally binding setting. Trials are important for two opposing reasons: for what they reveal, which invites decoding; and for what they hide, which stimulates the imagination. Finally, unlike traditional studies of genealogy, I shall highlight the importance of women in this story.

1. Crasto do Rio

Diogo de Crasto do Rio, whose blood was cleansed by royal decree and whose family was elevated to a status where it could claim spotless *fidalgo* ancestry, was mentioned in chapter 5. The status of the family was further improved by a recognition of its coat of arms, signed by the regent, Queen Catarina, on July 15, 1561, and the creation of a *morgado*, based on an entailed estate in Sacavém (near Lisbon along the Tagus River), which was recognised by King

Sebastian on July 6, 1568.[1] In 1575, the year he died, Diogo de Crasto do Rio had a family chapel instituted at the convent of the Franciscans in Lisbon.[2] Two of his sons were regular clergymen, one a Franciscan and the other a Trinitarian, and three other sons, Martim, Luís, and Duarte, were businessmen. The register of special taxation in Lisbon in 1565 recorded a significant number of houses owned by Diogo de Crasto do Rio and rented to various merchants, which means that he had decided to invest in real estate.[3] The dowry of one daughter, Maria, at 50,000 cruzados, facilitated a crucial matrimonial alliance, a pattern shared by other upwardly mobile families.[4] This reveals the extraordinary wealth of the family, because it was one of the highest, if not the highest, dowries of that time. Diogo was succeeded by his eldest son, Martim de Crasto do Rio, but the division of the family fortune was still being disputed in the 1590s. In time, the family became integrated into the higher ranks of the nobility through wealth and matrimonial strategy, eventually bearing the title of Viscount of Barbacena, having established family ties with the Count of Linhares and the Marquis of Castelo Rodrigo.[5]

There is a reference to the will of Diogo de Crasto do Rio in the notarial archives, but not the will itself. However, research eventually revealed the postmortem inventory of Luís de Castro do Rio, second son of Diogo de Crasto do Rio, signed by a judge of the Orphans' Court and the widow, Filipa Saldanha, on August 31, 1588. There were two children, Antónia, 10 years old, and Diogo, 9 years old. The inheritance of 4,872,350 réis (around 12,180 cruzados, less than what Martim would have inherited, due to the free third part of the parents' assets generally favouring primogeniture) was divided so that half went to the widow and half was divided in equal parts between the children. All the wills and postmortem inventories I consulted in Portugal for this research were drawn up according to this rule of equal division. However, the will of Luís de Crasto do Rio included additional interesting features. The deceased had been marginalised socially for having married Filipa against the wishes of his family, and in his will, he manifested signs of regret over this. His elder brother, Martim, and his sister, Brites, were indicated as executors of his will, and he requested that Martim should become the guardian of his children, although nothing of the sort materialised.

The widow, Filipa Saldanha, placed herself under the protection of the judge of the Orphans' Court in Lisbon (although she and her children were living near Pombal) and vigorously pursued a more favourable settlement. She was still presenting petitions related not only to her husband's estate but also to that of her father-in-law, Diogo de Crasto do Rio, in 1592. Luís also expressed a wish in his will that all his family—his wife and his children—should henceforth spend their lives in convents. This too does not seem to have happened, because the daughter married some years later. Finally, this postmortem inventory, with its degree of gender equality and indication that there were strong-minded women involved, reveals a staggering level of debt. The household was in decline, but it was still part of the elite. Much of the inventory was taken up with an enormous list of sizeable debts owed to the family—both private and public debts, since royal rents were involved, in both Portugal and Castile. Debts were also owed by bankers, such as Nicolau Giraldes (or Giraldi), Giacomo dei Bardi, and Diogo Rodrigues de Lisboa (in this case 132,000 réis due to the Crastos, complicated by the division of property following Diogo Rodrigues's death). The deceased's family themselves owed money to a significant number of people, including servants. Some of the servants were owed arrears of wages stretching back over fourteen or fifteen years, and these included the manager of the family's properties (100,000 réis), whereas arrears of between one and eight years were owed to other servants.[6] These debts explain the lengthy procedure involved in the execution of wealthy families' wills, which could last decades.

The Crasto do Rio family looks like a model of upward social mobility, with Diogo deciding to secure his wealth with safe investments in property. Yet the case of the second son, Luís, alerts us to the risks of downward mobility that this model of real estate investment could bring with it. He was disadvantaged by the rules of primogeniture and a marriage against the family's will. The next generation of financiers tried to prevent this kind of inequality developing within the family. The creation of a chapel to fulfil to both physical and spiritual needs, with a legacy to the Franciscans to seal the contract with them, would guarantee a burial place for the descendants and a memorial for the founder of the family, which was a crucial step in asserting the social and religious goals of full integration into the noble order at the highest level of court society.

The enormous dowry given to Diogo de Crasto do Rio's daughter, Maria, reveals the importance of matrimonial alliances for New Christians; it shows how the usual Portuguese practice of sharing inheritances equally between male and female heirs could be modified in favour of women to obtain strategic alliances with noble Old Christian families. This phenomenon also indicates the need of noble Old Christian families for injections of money and brings us to our last reflection on this case, which concerns debt. The Iberian kings were generally immersed in debt, and the richest New Christian families accumulated the debt owed them, some of it accruing through their activities as lenders and pawn brokers. However, they also had their own debts, particularly wages owed to their employees. Even those who owned an immense amount of property were not protected from droughts and bad harvests. Significant investment in royal interests (on taxation or monopolies) was not completely safe: royal bankruptcy could be around the corner, while short-term loans to the king in the form of *asientos* could be difficult to recover, owing to the risk of suspended payments from allocated sources of income. Finally, tribunals were slow, and determining rich inheritances could take decades. A significant part of a family's wealth could be virtually unrecoverable.

2. Nunes/Henriques

The upward social mobility represented by Crasto do Rio's primogeniture line is not as straightforward as it looks, including the matter of religious allegiance. The enquiry into the family of the famous financier Nuno Henriques was ordered by the Inquisition in 1572, almost thirty years after he had been banished by John III in 1544, and revealed deep-rooted suspicion about how his escape was arranged. His escape provoked strong reaction at court, but the long-term consequences are still surprising. The enquiry concerned the next generation. Diogo de Crasto do Rio, a fidalgo of the king's house, declared that Nuno Henriques's children, Jerónimo and Henrique Nunes, who were then twelve or thirteen years old, had migrated to Flanders. He knew that Jerónimo had died, but nothing else, and he suggested that probably Manuel Caldeira, "the son-in-law of Bento Rodrigues, knows more," a subtle way of shaking off any involvement in the matter. Manuel Caldeira, identified as a knight of the Order of Christ, was more talkative but firmly protective of the Henriques family. He declared that they had been good Catholics and that he knew that Jerónimo had died and his fortune had been inherited by Henrique. The latter was a gambler, who had lost most of his inheritance playing with the Duke and Duchess of Florence, which was something Caldeira claimed to have heard on one of his trips to Madrid. This information was confirmed by the testimony of Giacomo Bardi, another important contractor and financier in Lisbon. It was Bardi who revealed that Nuno Henriques and his family had fled Lisbon in 1545 or 1546 (it was 1544) after being condemned to pay 30,000 cruzados.[7]

These testimonies give context and historical depth to the itinerary of the Nunes family. Manuel Caldeira appeared to be dangerously close to this family, given that he had kept some connection with them. The story unfolded further in 1576 when Henrique Nunes was finally caught by the Inquisition on one of his regular trips to Lisbon. He spent six years in jail, was presented at the auto da fé of April 1, 1582, and was forced to spend another three years under house arrest, following which he was finally allowed to go to Castile in 1585.[8] It was only after three of his six years in jail that he decided to denounce other New Christians who had embraced Judaism and finally confessed that he had been baptised, which he had denied at the beginning of the investigation.

What matters now is that Henrique Nunes declared that those who had protected him on his risky trips to Lisbon were Gomes Pires, Leonor Dias, and Fernando Rodrigues Caldeira. Probably, these people had already escaped or died, but the reference to Fernão Rodrigues Caldeira, son of Bento Rodrigues and brother-in-law of Manuel Caldeira, was compromising. The main revelation would be left to a later stage of the trial: at that point, Henrique Nunes told the inquisitors that his father, mother, and one of his sisters had, in 1544, taken refuge in the house of Diogo de Crasto do Rio, who was not yet married and who lived with his brother, Luís. This implied that Crasto do Rio had helped the Nunes family to secretly embark for Flanders. In an impulse to protect the family's protectors, he declared that Diogo and Luís did not know that the Henriques family were Jewish.[9] When he was asked whether he had gone to mass when in Lisbon, he confessed that he would only go to the Franciscan church, where he liked to see the tomb of Diogo de Crasto do Rio.[10] Thus, Henrique Nunes paid tribute—or to put it better, reverence—to his father's friend who had saved the family.

The Inquisition did not prosecute the Crasto do Rio or the Rodrigues Caldeira families as protectors of apostates. Diogo was dead, and the whereabouts of Fernando were unknown, but at that time the main financiers were not (yet) threatened by the tribunal of faith. This story reveals courage displayed in the protection of friends, people's willingness to risk their own life and wealth, and a solidarity between New Christians that challenged personal interest. It also reveals the precariousness of life. The illustrious story of the Crasto do Rio family, who later became the viscounts of Barbacena, might have ended in 1544 without any blood cleansing or ennoblement, and without any wealth to be inherited. But the story of the Nunes family leads to the divergent case of those who reverted to the Jewish faith.

Henrique Nunes was born in 1531, probably in Lisbon, at the home and headquarters of the family in Rua Nova da Madalena (they also had property on the outskirts of Lisbon). His father kept a diary and Henrique later read this, so he knew all the events of his lifetime and their dates, such as the tremendous earthquake in the year he was born. In 1536, after the establishment of the Inquisition, Henrique went to Antwerp with his paternal grandmother, Leonor Henriques, and his aunt, Violante Henriques, and her children. There they lived in the house of Gabriel de Negro, who acted as a rabbi (he circumcised Henrique Nunes) and who later fled from Flanders when accused of Judaism. The rest of Henrique's family arrived in 1544 (his parents, six sisters, and two brothers). They were accused of Judaism in 1547, detained (Henrique escaped, claiming to be Flemish), and only released against payment of 45,000 cruzados, guaranteed by João Rebelo and João Micas. The family then moved to Venice, where they lived as Jews until the Venetian authorities expelled the Portuguese New Christians in 1550. At this point they went to Ferrara but returned to Venice some years later when the ban was lifted. The father (known as Seneor Benveniste) died in Venice, and most of the remaining family went to the Ottoman Empire.[11] Henrique Nunes had a first trial by the Inquisition in Venice in 1570, escaped from prison, and several years later resurfaced in Lisbon. He never explained to the inquisitors why he had returned to Lisbon several times, but his visits could only have meant that he needed to collect money there due to his gambling losses. Who might have owed money to his family? Or whom might he have been able to blackmail?

The inheritance of the Henriques, recorded in 1549, is very interesting. Half of the fortune was inherited by the mother, Violante; the other half was (slightly) unequally shared by the children, with the eldest brother, Jerónimo, receiving 10,000 ducati, while the other brothers and sisters—nine siblings were alive—received 6,000 ducados each among other bequests (presumably jewels and precious stones; unfortunately, we do not know about the portable property).[12] Henrique Nunes named the siblings Jerónimo and Rodrigo (Mair Benveniste); Reina (Marquesa Henriques), a widow living in Constantinople who had been married in Portugal to one of his uncles; Simacha (Beatriz), married in Constantinople to Abraham Benveniste (Agostinho Henriques, half brother of Diogo Dias de Andrade, who lived in Lisbon); and Palomba and Rachel, both living in Salonica. Two other sisters of Henrique Nunes had stayed in Ferrara: Leonor, already deceased, who had been married to the lawyer Manuel Reinel; and Gracia Benveniste, who had been married to Leão Abravanel and was still alive.[13]

The value of the fortune is important. Even after the family had been forced to pay huge sums and had undertaken successive migrations, there remained 58,000 for the widow, plus 58,000 for the children, a total of 116,000 ducati, without considering jewels and other possessions. This was a family that had been banned from Lisbon (with a loss of at least 30,000 cruzados), and then from Antwerp (another loss of 45,000 cruzados). I have not seen the inventory of property that would have been written before the father's death and which would have confirmed the bequests in this will, but according to witnesses, the will was implemented with the part concerning dowries and advances taking effect in the father's lifetime. If this was the case, it demonstrates, in the face of dramatic change and harsh conditions, a financial success that can only be compared to the extreme wealth of the Nasi family, with whom the Henriques had a close relationship. The Henriques family maintained some contact with the Rodrigues Caldeira and the Crasto do Rio families, probably fed by ethnic if not religious solidarity.

In this period, thousands of New Christians decided to follow their Jewish faith outside the country of their birth and paid a high price. Many had been reconciled by the Inquisition but saw relatives excommunicated and executed; others died on their way into exile; and a significant number faced dispossession and poverty following their stigmatisation. Despite the signs of solidarity shown by various Jewish communities, reception once the New Christians arrived was not always enthusiastic. The Jewish prayer books had been confiscated in Iberia, the Jews' spiritual leadership had been lost, and their attempts to keep the old faith had led to hybrid forms of worship. Embracing normative Judaism and integrating into traditional communities who had not suffered the same persecution was not an easy path. The case of Henrique's family was obviously a special one: you needed to have enormous capital, a strong will, and an efficient network of support to resist banishment, denigration, and the pan-European reach of persecution. Other cases are found of immigration into the Jewish communities established in Italy; France was also particularly attractive, although the Jewish religion was formally forbidden there; but the New Christians were divided, and it is difficult to establish their true religious allegiance. We shall return to this issue in part III, to see the consequences of access to northern Europe.

3. Caldeira

Most wealthy New Christians in Portugal and Castile chose the path of integration. Manuel Caldeira's family is an interesting case, with the next generation clearly focused on royal service. Manuel's eldest son, André Caldeira, was, like his father, a fidalgo of the king's house and a knight of the Order of Christ, and also a *comendador* (benefice entitlement) of St. Fagundo. He was captured in North Africa while taking part in the ill-conceived expedition of King Sebastian that was heavily defeated in Ksar el-Kbir, he was ransomed, and in 1587 he was married to Catarina de Silva, daughter of Lopo Furtado de Mendonça, a comendador of Loulé and grandson of the Master of Santiago. Another son, Francisco, became a famous professor of law (*catedrático de prima*), first at the University of Salamanca, then at the University of Coimbra for three long terms of service. He was appointed *ouvidor dos agravos* (royal judge/attorney) of the *Casa da Suplicação* in Lisbon, and he was a fidalgo of the king's house. Francisco's son, Rodrigo, became a knight of the Order of Christ in recognition of the service of his father. A third son of Manuel Caldeira, Rodrigo served in various wars and died fighting the English in the army of the Count of Feria. This Rodrigo had been married to Catarina de Noronha, granddaughter of the marquis of Vila Real.

We saw earlier (chapter 5.2) how the privilege of choosing ship captains of the *carreira da Índia* was transformed into a gift for the wedding of Manuel Caldeira's daughter Beatriz, a maid of honour to the infanta D. Maria, to Luís Mendes de Vasconcelos, a future governor of Angola and Grand Master of the Order of Malta, grandson of Álvaro Mendes de Vasconcelos, Ambassador of the king of Portugal to the court of Castile, and of the Count of Castanheira, secretary of finances to King John III. This is a very powerful example of a matrimonial alliance between Old and New Christian families, and it draws attention to the role played by the courts of the female members of the royal family in providing advancement for maids of honour or ladies in waiting. Another daughter, Leonor Caldeira, married Jerónimo da Veiga Cabral, son of Tristão Vaz da Veiga, Lord of the towns of Machico and Santa Cruz, and governor general of the island of Madeira. The grandsons of Manuel Caldeira, who were the sons of Francisco, pursued the same pattern: Paulo married Catarina Corte Real and João married Ana de Noronha, granddaughter of the marquis of Vila Real, two women who belonged to the main noble houses of Portugal.[14]

The last, and valid, will of Manuel Caldeira was written on June 5, 1593, a few days before his death. His wife, Guiomar, had died without leaving a will, and the distribution of her inheritance was integrated into her husband's will, although what was at stake was the *terça* (third) that the parents could dispose of, since the major part of Manuel Caldeira's wealth (the *legítima*) would be divided equally by all children, male and female. There were thirteen living children: André, Francisco, Beatriz, Paulo, Duarte, Rodrigo, Leonor, Maria, João, Bento Rodrigues (in India, married without consent), Diogo Rodrigues Caldeira, and António, who was living in Madrid. The other name is unknown. The total fortune of Manuel and Guiomar, to which, curiously, the two contributed equally, can be evaluated at 146,628,247 réis, or 366,570 cruzados, an extraordinary amount. The eldest son, André, received half of Guiomar's third when he married, and 75 percent of Manuel's third (the rest went in pious legacies), plus his share of the legítima from both parents, all of which consisted of entailed property due to the principal heir, according to the rules of morgado or primogeniture. The total amount of money André received was 40,356,405 réis, or 100,861 cruzados. The other twelve siblings must have received 19,083 cruzados each, although there were some peculiarities: Manuel Caldeira decided that those who expected to join religious orders should leave part of their inheritance for the dowry of Beatriz, the dowry being transformed into entailed property, an interesting arrangement for a morgado whose recipient was a woman, and one made as a guarantee for her heirs. The other two daughters, Leonor and Maria, would also receive dowries on their marriage.[15] These dispositions are in line with other forms of inheritance arranged by wealthy New Christians when they were eager to integrate into the nobility, creating privileged dowries that might be needed for marriage into that social order.

The organization of property interests undertaken by Manuel Caldeira during his life is typical of this social elite. He invested heavily in Lisbon urban property: the main houses where he lived and had his headquarters, at the bottom of the Calçada do Congro, and on which he had spent more than 6 million réis; another house nearby; and a set of houses at the Travessa do Padrão Maior and the same near Santa Catarina and on the main street, Rua Nova. The value of these properties was between 700,000 and more than 2 million réis, and most of them he rented out. He had major rural properties around Lisbon, for example, at Paradela, in which he had invested more than 4 million réis, and at Casal dos Reais in Loures (an investment of 387,000 réis), in addition to properties at Casal da Barroca and Casal da Granja. There were significant financial investments placed at interest (royal *juros* and *censos*, or bonds, but also tax rents), particularly in Madrid. A significant quantity of pepper was also part of the legacy he left, as well as ready money (approximately 5.6 million réis were left to André). To my knowledge, the inventory of all his assets has not been yet found, which is a pity because there are references to two retables depicting Christ's descent from the cross and several items of dress.[16] Finally, in his will, Manuel Caldeira invoked the Trinity, Jesus Christ, and the Virgin Mary—although not in a standard manner—and gave orders that he should be buried at the Convent of Our Lady of Esperança (a convent of the Poor Clares, who were attached to the Franciscans), next to his wife in the family vault he had taken there. He left provision for the creation of a chapel for him, his wife, and all the family. This is in line with his other bequests, but in this case he should have made the arrangements for the chapel himself, for it is not known whether his wishes were fulfilled.

4. Fonseca

António da Fonseca presents us with an extremely interesting case of New Christian migration to Italy, and particularly to Rome. The wealth of documents relating to him give some answers to our questions about the movement of New Christians. Careful analysis of his will, written on June 23, 1586, with an important codicil added on February 17, 1588, produces some surprises. António strongly recommended to his heir that the old contract he had entered into with Cardinal Farnese (1520–1589) should be respected. My reading of this will reveals that the New Christian António da Fonseca had managed the Cardinal's ecclesiastical rents in Portugal, rents offered by King John III as an inducement for the establishment of the Inquisition. The monastery of Santo Tirso paid 1,600 scudi annually; the bishop of Viseu paid 2,750 cruzados, with half due by St. John's day and half by Christmas; the bishop of Porto paid 500 cruzados; and the bishop of Lamego paid 750 cruzados, with half due by Easter and half by St. Michael's day. The heir had to pay all the ecclesiastical pensions due in Portugal each year, which amounted to 2,900 gold scudi. The Canons of Braga, Cristóvão Leão, the archdeacon, Pedro Borges Coutinho and Francisco da Costa, the Canon of Porto, Miguel Lopes, and the Canon of Lamego, António Lopes, were explicitly indicated as intermediaries who collected and sent the money.[17]

This extraordinary operation reveals how far António da Fonseca extended his power in Rome, which obviously had consequences in Portugal for his position as financier to Cardinal Farnese and collector of his rents. The network of canons linked to this operation, and personally identified, is also staggering, because it implicitly means that they were entitled to receive a financial reward for work well done. This will was placed under the protection of Cardinal Farnese and Cardinal Medici, with these high-level ecclesiastics being nominated to see that its contents were respected. Monsignor António Pinto, who refused to accept any legacy, was the executor of the will, and he promised to supervise the heir and guarantee a smooth transition of the inheritance.

António da Fonseca's nephew, Jerónimo da Fonseca, and his wife, Violante, Antónia Luís's niece, living in Rome, each received 2,000 gold scudi, having had their marriage arranged by António da Fonseca, who at the time had given them 3,000 scudi. A nephew, Manuel da Fonseca, who was living in Madrid, received 300 gold scudi and had his debts forgiven. Francisco de Fonseca, another nephew living in Rome, brother of Jerónimo and Manuel, received 200 scudi. Dr. Eduardo Lopes received 300 gold scudi. Jerónimo de Paz of Lisbon got 300 cruzados. Branca Nunes and Justina de Quental (niece of António da Fonseca, wife of Teotónio Nunes) received 800 scudi for dowries for their daughters, on top of 200 scudi already given by Antónia Luís. In his will, António da Fonseca declares great love for his companion, Heitor Mendes, a banker in Lisbon, leaving 500 cruzados for the first of Mendes's daughters to marry. He also mentions with great affection Heitor Mendes's mother-in-law, the wife of the *licenciado* (graduated) Nuno Dias.

Francisco da Costa, a relative who had lived with António da Fonseca for many years, received 200 cruzados for a dowry for his daughter. António de Quental, apparently his accountant, who lived in his house, received 500 gold scudi. Filipa de Paz, wife of Fernando Ramires of Lisbon, received 200 scudi; and a relative in Lisbon, Rodrigo Pereira, got 1,500 cruzados for the dowries of his three daughters. A relative, Fernando Peres, living in Chaves, Portugal, received 300 cruzados for the dowry of a daughter. For the eldest daughter of Simão Lopes, his nephew who lived in Venice, António da Fonseca left 50 gold scudi. João Henriques, son of his great friend Bento Henriques, received 300 cruzados for the dowry of his daughter. Francisca Henriques, niece of Antónia Luís, received 300 cruzados for dowries for her daughters. He forgave a debt of 130 scudi lent to Diogo Brandão, who was poor, and gave him 50 scudi. He also left money to all his servants (two women and three men); and he settled his debts, particularly those owed to António Nunes Caldeira in Spain.[18]

Institutional legacies were also part of the will. António da Fonseca left 400 scudi to the Spaniards' hospital, with the interest on 360 scudi to be paid in perpetuity for the dowries of six poor maidens in Portugal or Castile, the money to be invested in the Monte di Pietà nonredeemable fund, which was managed by the administrator of the Spaniards' hospital; and he left 200 gold scudi to the hospital of St. Anthony of the Portuguese in Rome. He authorized an investment of 3,000 cruzados for the perpetual assistance of the poor of Lamego, Portugal, whose rent would be managed by the dean and treasurer of the cathedral of the town, plus the *provedor* (manager) of the Misericórdia. Finally, he instructed that he should be buried in his Chapel of the Resurrection at San Giacomo degli Spagnoli, in the same tomb as his wife, over the portal, and he left donations for the perpetual celebration of masses for his soul in various churches.[19] In terms of its generosity to relatives, friends, and its charitable bequests, António da Fonseca's will was difficult to match; but the scale of the bequests and the exceptional sense of social responsibility and warmth towards fellow human beings revealed here were not uncommon among wealthy New Christians.

The inventory of António da Fonseca's property includes exotic items, the result of his trade with the East Indies, such as Indian leather chairs and a litter, wooden boxes, services of porcelain, and bezoars.[20] There were two sets of neighbouring houses, one in the neighbourhood of Parione and the other in the neighbourhood of Campo Marzio. The latter, which was near the Church of Santa Lucia della Tinta, had a loggia bearing the name "Fonseca" and was simultaneously a residence and a bank. In his residence there, António da Fonseca had two paintings of the Virgin Mary; another of the apparition of Jesus to Emmaus; another with Jesus praying in the garden; ten portraits of popes; a portrait of the Portuguese King John III; another, in a gold frame, of King Sebastian; another of Philip II; another of Emperor Maximilian II; another two of queens (not identified); a small painting of St. Francis; nine paintings of biblical scenes; one small world map; and another map, in a golden frame, showing just Portugal, which was most probably the one designed by Fernando Álvares Seco (another New Christian), printed in Venice in 1561 under the patronage of Aquiles Estaço, and dedicated to Cardinal Sforza.[21] The map of Portugal was deliberately intended to underline his political allegiance to the kings of Portugal and the Habsburg, as well as his religious conformity. Although he had been denounced by Tomé Pegado de Paz as a Jew who showed great favour to relatives in Constantinople, António da Fonseca seems to have played by the rules as a Catholic right up to his death.

António da Fonseca did not have children from his marriage, but he had a natural son who had been educated in his house and legitimised by Pope Gregory XIII. The son's name was Manuel Fernandes da Fonseca, and he was indicated in the will as the sole heir, receiving the lion's share of the inheritance, which included 10,000 gold scudi, plus more money to be made available to him should he marry. In the original will it was 13,000, plus 5,000 invested in a nonredeemable fund at the Monte di Pietà mutual bank, which would have yielded perpetual interest. He also inherited the position of patron of the family chapel at San Giacomo degli Spagnoli.[22] The problem was that, at the time of António da Fonseca's death, Manuel was a clergyman with ecclesiastic benefices. He was certainly the D. Manuel da Fonseca, named as archdeacon of the cathedral of Viseu, who witnessed the doctorate in canon law of Diego Solis da Fonseca, another New Christian, at the university La Sapienza in Rome, on April 4, 1587.[23] He later became a layman, married a Fonseca from Venice, had a significant number of children, thus guaranteeing the perpetuation of the family. In 1615 he created an imposing palace at the Piazza Minerva, behind the Pantheon and close to the Dominican Church of Santa Maria Sopra Minerva, which is now the Hotel Minerva.

Manuel Fernandes da Fonseca inherited the social positions his father had acquired; that is, he was an active member of the Confraternity of St. Anthony of the Portuguese, playing various roles in this organization between 1586 and 1620, mainly as *camerlengo* (representative) and treasurer.[24] He also played

FIGURE 7.1. Palazzo Fonseca, nowadays Hotel Minerva, built by Manuel da Fonseca in 1615, Rome, next to the Pantheon and Santa Maria Sopra Minerva. Photo courtesy of the author.

a significant role in the Confraternity of the Resurrection at San Giacomo degli Spagnoli, and in 1590, he was prior of the Confraternity (a function rotated between him, Francisco Vaz Pinto, and Jerónimo de Fonseca in those years).[25] In 1592 he was appointed procurator of the associated confraternities of Nostra Virtutum, linked to the Dominican Monastery in Lisbon, and of Sanctissimi Sacramenti, linked to the Dominican Monastery in Porto.[26] This is another interesting development, because these associated confraternities needed procurators in Rome for their requests to the Pope, which meant an extension of the patronage he had at his disposal. In the 1590s, the Confraternity of the Resurrection listed fifteen associated confraternities from Portugal and overseas, and the procurators of these were mostly New Christians (João Álvares Pereira; Valério Manrique, who had been elected camerlengo in previous years; Teotónio Nunes, also camerlengo; Dr. António Gomes; and António da Fonseca's nephew, Duarte Paulo). Don Rodrigo de Paz, Don Luís de Paz, Pedro and Timóteo Ximenes, and Luís da Fonseca were also active in the confraternity in these years.[27]

In a fitting conclusion to this extraordinary case study, we shall look at the will of Jerónimo Fonseca, nephew of António, and in fact the son of his cousin, António de Fonseca de Miranda.[28] Jerónimo had been indicated by António as second in line for the position of principal heir, in case his son Manuel died without heirs.[29] Jerónimo died in 1596, leaving a significant inheritance, although not as opulent as his uncle's. The will, signed on August 29, 1596, was designated as being under the protection of Cardinal Baronio ed Mantica, whose attendants witnessed it. Jerónimo was to be buried at the Chapel of the Resurrection founded by his uncle, and he left donations for masses and prayers to be said for his soul. He left his wife, Violante, the amount of her dowry due to her and a quarter share of his wealth, according to the statutes of Rome, plus the interest on 6,000 scudi while she lived, the principal to pass to his heirs. He left to his sister, Maria do Espírito Santo, who had entered the Convent of the Poor Clares in Porto, an annual rent of 40 scudi from an investment at the Monte di Pietà, with an indication that if the convent appropriated the money, the legacy would be cancelled. In both cases, the principal would return to the heirs after the death of the beneficiary of the interest.

Jerónimo Fonseca also left to the daughters of his sister, Justina da Fonseca, wife of Diogo Fernandes Pina, 500 scudi for dowries or endowments for their entry into religious orders. He did the same for the daughters of his sister, Filipa da Fonseca, wife of Henrique de Carvalho. The son of Filipa da Fonseca, António da Fonseca, received 1,000 scudi. For Manuel da Fonseca, his lawyer brother, who had managed money for him in Portugal, he stipulated that any debts he accrued should be forgiven, and he was to receive 1,000 scudi. To his other brother, Francisco da Fonseca, Jerónimo left 500 scudi; to his brother-in-law, Rodrigo da Fonseca, 100 scudi; and to his sisters-in-law, Dionísia and Graça Dinis, 50 scudi each. To his brother-in-law, Dr. Eduardo Lopes, he left a room of new leather wallpaper coloured green. To another brother-in-law, António Gomes, he left his coach with horses and accessories and money for straw.

Bartolomé Ollala de Rosas, Jerónimo Fonseca's business associate in Seville, received two large paintings of St. Susan and Saint Cecily. Of his properties, he bequeathed the house at Campo dei Fiori, rented for 200 scudi a year, to the Confraternity of the Resurrection to provide dowries for four maidens who wanted to marry into Portuguese families. The children of his brother, António da Fonseca, were declared his sole heirs: he left them 10,000 scudi guaranteed by investments at the Monte di Pietà, to be managed by António da Fonseca until the children were 25 years old, at which point António was to move to Rome and live with the other brother, Manuel Fonseca, to instruct him and guide him in business.[30]

This story echoes, although on a different scale, the will of Jerónimo's uncle, António Fonseca. It shows the same generosity to relatives, the same charitable bequests, expressed as dowries for poor maidens, and the same affection for Portugal. This legacy, surprisingly, was one of the few picked up by the Spaniards' confraternity, which always struggled with lack of donations. But there is a coda to this story that I found buried in the documentation on New Christians compiled by the Roman Congregation of the Inquisition. On May 25, 1595, António da Fonseca, the third of his family to bear that name, who was the son of Filipa da Fonseca and Henrique de Carvalho, and who lived with his uncle Jerónimo, denounced Rodrigo Teixeira, with whom he had had a conversation in Rome on Christianity and Judaism, in which

Rodrigo, then sixty-five or seventy years old, became enraged when António da Fonseca defended Christianity.[31]

There is a follow-up to this story in the same compilation. A priest, Fr. Francisco de Goes, denounced a group of twenty New Christians who had travelled with him from Spain to Italy by ship, having heard conversations among them in which they excluded the young António da Fonseca as a possible suitor for their daughters because he had denounced a New Christian as a Jew and declared that the vast majority of New Christians were Jews.[32] An anonymous witness declared that Jerónimo da Fonseca had left his fortune of 70,000 ducati to his brother, António da Fonseca, "il vecchio," a dependent of Duke Giuliano Cesarino, while his nephew of the same name, who had lived with him and was expecting to be his universal heir, was left almost with nothing because he had accused a relative of being a Jew.

Michele di Lavagna, auditor of the ecclesiastic tribunal in Florence, and a friend of the young António da Fonseca, confirmed this story and added that António considered his uncle Jerónimo to be Jewish, pointing out that no Christian clerics entered the house when he was dying, and that in his final moments he invoked only God, not Jesus Christ.[33] It is difficult to assess whether these details about the death of Jerónimo da Fonseca are true, owing to the resentment the young man was likely to have been feeling; but the radical downgrade of António's share in the will is plausible, not as a result of his uncle's Judaism but in response to the breaching of family solidarity, which should have been maintained despite the religious divide. It is my opinion that it is the issue of family values that is at stake here, values that are also expressed in the correspondence maintained by the old António da Fonseca with his relatives turned Jews in the Ottoman Empire and in Venice.

5. Ximenes

The next case is much more complex, based on the scarcely used archive of the Ximenes family that has been preserved in Florence.[34] In this archive I found some of the main wills of the different branches of the Ximenes family in Lisbon, Antwerp, and Florence, doubtless archived together since the family's massive inheritances were entangled for several generations, with many entailed properties at stake. The origins of the family are uncertain. Their ancestor has been indicated as Inigo Ximenes of Aragon, one of whose progeny, Fernando Ximenes, was captured at the battle of Toro and brought to Portugal. Reliable information about the next generation suggests that Duarte Ximenes de Aragão (ca. 1500–1560) married Isabel Rodrigues da Veiga, another New Christian. Their children included one very successful Jesuit, Manuel, who travelled to Cologne, Florence, Rome, and Macerata. Manuel gave the family respectability by supporting its upward movement, providing spiritual assistance, and becoming a major figure referred to in all the family's wills. Five other males—Fernando

FIGURE 7.2. Pieter van der Borcht, Tournament with the Ximenes houses in the background (Meir, Antwerp). Engraving in Johannes Bochius, *Descriptio publicae gratulationis, spectaculorum et ludorum, in adventu Sereniss. Principis Ernesti Archiducis Austriae* (Antverpiae: Ex Officina Plantiniana, 1595), pp. 140–141, 331 × 428 mm. Reproduced by kind permission of the Syndics of Cambridge University Library.

(1526–1600), Rui Nunes (1534–1581), Tomás (1535–1600), Jerónimo Duarte (1544–1590), and André (1547–1619)—excelled in business, apart from a certain Gaspar, who did not leave much trace in the archives. There is no information about any of the female members of the family.

In these two first generations, the Ximenes family established matrimonial alliances with the Veiga/Rodrigues de Évora, the Fernandes de Elvas, the Rodrigues de Elvas, the Serrão/Paz and the Lopes, all well-known New Christian families involved in trade and finance at the highest level. Gracia Rodrigues de Évora, daughter of Manuel Rodrigues de Évora (1506–1581), and then Catarina Lopes, married Rui Nunes Ximenes. Gracia's elder brother, Simão Rodrigues de Évora (1543–1618), who became the Baron of Rhodes in Flanders, married one of Rui Nunes and Gracia's daughters, Ana Ximenes. Tomás married Teresa Vaz de Elvas, daughter of the famous António Fernandes de Elvas. Tomás created his own houses in what was called the "Terreiro dos Ximenes" in Lisbon. Fernando married Ana Lopes, lived in

FIGURE 7.3. Anonymous, *The Holy Family*, end of the sixteenth century, oil on wood, 109×77.5 cm, inv. nr. 1743 Pint. © Museu Nacional de Arte Antiga, Lisbon, Photo José Pessoa (DGPC/ADF). Representation of the patrons and coat of arms of the family Rodrigues de Évora; possible patron Simão Rodrigues de Évora.

Antwerp, and founded the branch of the family in Florence; but he kept his interests, investments, and family attachments in Lisbon and Antwerp. Rui Nunes Ximenes and his family also moved to Antwerp, where he and Fernando instituted another chapel at the Cathedral of Antwerp. Tomás became the head of the branch of the family in Lisbon, supported by his two brothers, André, who married Maria, yet to be identified, and Jerónimo Duarte, who married Beatriz Serrão, daughter of Jorge Serrão and Isabel de Paz.

An extraordinary tally of births contributed to the power of this family, except for Fernando, who was childless but played a pivotal role in the success of the family. André had at least seven children, Rui Nunes had thirteen,

Tomás had twelve, and Jerónimo Duarte had three. Thirty-five children in a single generation, but there were certainly more who must have died. All these children are mentioned in wills, which means that they survived childhood. They kept strong ties between them, helping each other, opening new branches of their business in different cities, and providing replacement family members when there were breaks in the succession to entailed property. When Gracia Rodrigues Ximenes was left a widow by the death of Rui Nunes in Antwerp, she went to live with her brother-in-law, Fernando, in Florence, where she wrote her will. Jorge Ximenes Serrão, son of Jerónimo Duarte Ximenes, opened a branch of the family business in Madrid, probably in the 1590s, and it was in Madrid, in 1600, that his wife gave birth to their son, Constantino, who was to become a lawyer. Jerónimo Duarte Ximenes died in 1590, and he left his property entailed on his eldest son, Jorge. Jerónimo determined that his remains should be transferred to the Augustinian monastery of San Felipe el Real in Madrid, which was then under construction. Probably, he had endowed a family chapel there.[35]

The first two generations of the Ximenes family reinforced ties with some of the best-known New Christian families, obtained acceptance into military orders (André was a knight of the Order of Christ; Fernando a knight of the Military Order of Santo Stefano in Florence) and reached the status of fidalgo of the king's house (as Tomás did). The third generation followed a mixed path, establishing matrimonial alliances with the Old Christian nobility, while many became religious, taking on the Christian values of those around them. The children of Tomás Ximenes are a case in point: Fernando was archdeacon of Saint Crispin, in Braga; André was an archdeacon in Olivença; Isabel and Beatriz took the veil at the Convent of Esperança, Lisbon; Jorge became a Dominican; António Fernandes (1563–1631), despite his father's wishes, did not marry, and apparently became a Jesuit, a patron and administrator of the Irish College in Lisbon; Duarte married Catarina Veiga, and Maria married her uncle, André; but Jerónimo first married an Old Christian noblewoman, Isabel Noronha de Mendonça, daughter of D. Afonso de Noronha, and after her death he married Madalena de Faro; the case of Rui Ximenes, who spent some time in Cologne, needs further research; Joana married the nobleman Henrique Pereira, in Lisbon. Finally, Sebastião (Sebastiano) Ximenes (1568–1633) went with his uncle Fernando to Florence, where he became a knight of Santo Stefano and married Caterina Medici, daughter of Rafaello (1543–1629), who was a *commendatore* and admiral of the Order of Santo Stefano, an ambassador of the Medici, a senator of Florence, and a member of the secret council.[36] Thus, Sebastião achieved a significant alliance with a noble family, clients of the Medici clan, and he too endowed a chapel for the family in Florence at the Church of San Piero Maggiore.

If we consider the children of Rui Nunes and Gracia Rodrigues Ximenes, we find similar stories. Tomás (1571–1633) became bishop of Fiesole; Catarina took the veil; Ana sought a dispensation that would allow her to marry her uncle Simão Rodrigues de Évora; Joana died without marrying; we have no information on Fernando; Duarte (1561–1630) married Maria da Veiga and Manuel (1564–1632) married Maria's sister, Isabel da Veiga, the two wives being daughters of Rodrigo da Veiga de Évora; and in 1591, Isabel Ximenes married Diogo Henriques de Leão in Seville. All these marriages were with New Christians, but Beatriz Ximenes married Alamanno Bartolini Salimbeni, a senator of Florence; Niccolò Ximenes (1566–1611), who himself became a senator in Florence, married Maria Antinori, the daughter of local aristocracy; and Gonçalo (1575–1638) married Catharina van Eeckeren, the daughter of local aristocracy in Antwerp.

Fernando Ximenes, the founder of the Ximenes clans in Antwerp and Florence, was probably the family's most gifted member. He was already involved in trade with Italy in the 1580s, and on August 23, 1586, he obtained from Pope Sixtus V a brief recognising the nobility of the Ximenes family and authorising Fernando to use the Pope's own name, Peretti, which he did.[37] On one of his trips to Florence, the Grand Duke of Tuscany, Ferdinando I de' Medici, convinced him to stay, offered him the use of a palace, and welcomed him into the military Order of Santo Stefano, which guaranteed him easy access to local nobility. The early 1590s were the years when the Grand Duke issued the Livornine or Leghorn laws, intended to attract merchants to Livorno, and which included freedom of religion. In the case of Fernando Ximenes, Ferdinando I had lured a significant international merchant and banker to join local nobility. As we have seen before, the divide between New and Old Christians never crossed the Pyrenees; it did not become rooted in Italy, despite enormous efforts by Iberian ambassadors and inquisitors. The invitation by Ferdinando I must have triggered the quest for a papal brief of nobility. For this, Fernando had to prove his noble background, which in Lisbon at that time might not have been easy.

Fernando became a knight of the Order of Santo Stefano and immediately, in 1591, founded a *commenda*, an estate consisting of his house and the surrounding land, in Antwerp, using this as entailed property for him and his successors, and endowing it with an annual income of 1,125 Brabant florins. This foundation, created under the name Fernando Ximenes Peretti, was authorised by the Council of Brabant and approved by the Grand Duke on April 8, 1593, which was the date of Fernando's investiture as a knight and commendatore of the Order of Santo Stefano. In this same year, using the same papal brief, Fernando established a contract with the bishop and the chapter of the Cathedral of Antwerp to endow a chapel for the family there, paying a fee of 1,200 florins. In addition, he made another payment to the alms foundation of the city to maintain the tomb, epitaph, and arms; to arrange to have masses sung; and to manage the provision of dowries for two poor orphans.[38] He planned to create a foundation in Lisbon, with entailed property assigned to his brothers and nephews, but he gave up, partly because his nephew, the son of Tomás, Rui Nunes Ximenes, who had been an agent in Cologne, did not agree to manage the foundation. He revoked several decisions concerning the branch of the family in Lisbon in the last codicil of April 4, 1600.

Fernando left the lion's share of his estate to his nephew Sebastião, who had followed him to Florence and who received several properties, villas, and forests. The other nephew, Niccolò, who would become a senator of Florence, also received several properties. These bequests of interest would have been subject to the same rules as governed entailed property. Fernando also left investments, from which the interest would provide dowries for poor young women (either to marry or to take the veil), assistance to orphans, and support for convents. The properties Fernando had in Antwerp went to his nephews there, the children of Rui Nunes and Gracia, who had been under the formal guardianship of Fernando since their father died. Fernando's wife, Ana Lopes, declared her support for the decisions in Fernando's will and died in the same year as her husband. They decided to be temporarily buried in the monastery of San Clemente in Florence, with their remains then to be transferred to the chapel at the Cathedral of Antwerp, an instruction that was executed in March 3, 1610.[39]

Extended family solidarity by a childless patriarch was coupled with massive charity, which supported numerous convents, nuns, poor women, and orphans. The will of Gracia Rodrigues Ximenes, who lived in Florence after her husband Rui Nunes Ximenes passed away in Antwerp, confirms this balance between extensive charity and a relatively equal distribution of wealth among the children, male and female. Although the wealth Gracia herself inherited must have been a share of previously divided wealth, it is probable that she had been given half of an inheritance, as well as her dowry. Pious legacies to the cathedral of Santa Maria dei Fiori in Florence and the Jesuit college in Antwerp (through her brother-in-law, the Jesuit Manuel Ximenes) were followed by a distribution of the remaining estate to the thirteen children still alive, seven males and six females, who each received roughly 1,500 pounds (Flemish livres), with calculations based on twelve portions, which means that the dowry of the nun, Catarina, was not included here. The eldest son, Duarte, knight of Santo Stefano, received a surplus of 4,000 "fat pounds" from Flanders, part of the inheritance of Rui Nunes, under the rules of the *maioratus* (primogeniture) created for him. In 1601, a codicil mentioned dowries for the married daughters, without indicating the sums involved, added another dowry, for the daughter Ana, specified a maioratus of 4,000 pounds in customs revenues in Lisbon, and another sum of 5,333.3 pounds for Duarte, which was approved by the Portuguese King.[40]

The dowry agreed upon in Lisbon by Tomás Ximenes for his daughter Joana is one of the most amazing pieces of this labyrinth of wealth distribution. On November 13, 1598, Tomás established an entailed property through the dowry he created for Joana, who was about to marry the nobleman Henrique Pereira, a fidalgo of the king's house and member of the house of the Count of Feira. Tomás promised 45,000 cruzados, a staggering sum, much higher than the shares of his inheritance envisaged for his other children, as we shall see. Five thousand cruzados was to provide a house, this sum to be payable in coins of gold and silver, tapestries and furniture; 40,000 was to be invested in real estate and other interest-yielding investments—namely, at Lisbon's *Depositário Geral*, to create a morgado established for the person of Joana and her descendants (the places where investments were to be made and the houses and farms involved in this operation were indicated). This property, which constituted an inalienable entail, would always be inherited by the eldest son, or, in the absence of a son, by the eldest daughter. Joana and her husband could enjoy the rents of this entailed property (600,000 réis annually), for the first six years of their marriage. Tomás defined clear rules in case Joana or her husband died without children: the successor would be the next male heir of Tomás's line, and his heirs would have to invest half of their third part of the general inheritance in the morgado. Property acquired during the marriage would be divided equally between Joana and Henrique; and if Henrique died first, Joana would retain her dowry and half of the property thus acquired. Henrique renounced the right to pursue private litigation related to this contract, which was placed under the jurisdiction of the civil judges (*corregedores*) of the city and royal court.[41]

But there is more of interest in this document: one of the witnesses to the contract was Tomé Pinheiro da Veiga, then a student of law in Coimbra and a knight of the Order of Christ, who would become a famous jurist in the next fifty years, and whose participation in the restoration of the independence of Portugal is well-known. As a Veiga, he was certainly a relative of the Ximenes. Another witness was Tomás's nephew, Duarte Ximenes, which reminds us of the constant travel between Antwerp, Florence, and Lisbon undertaken by these merchants. In any case, this is an extraordinary dowry, coupled with the designation of property to be entailed upon a daughter in which the noble husband had very little to say, except for enjoying the rents for a certain time. The division of the acquired property into halves, a common rule, could not have better protected the interests of the bride. Moreover, her successors were constrained by the laws of primogeniture to use the surname Ximenes, otherwise they would lose their right to the inheritance.[42] The amount of money involved was inferior only to the dowry of Maria, daughter of Diogo de Crasto do Rio, but Tomás could not have arranged the contract more carefully in favour of his daughter. He had succeeded in finding a nobleman to help distance the family from their New Christian origins, but he must also have had one of the best lawyers in Lisbon to devise this precious legal document. The message this will conveys, loudly and clearly, is that women could be extremely important, cherished, and cared for.

Tomás Ximenes's will, signed on June 6, 1600, confirms the extraordinary value of the dowry. His daughter Maria, who married her uncle André, received a 9,000 cruzados dowry, and 4,000 was still due to her as the rest of her legitimate inheritance. Duarte, who had died, had received 10,000 cruzados; his widow received another 3,500, and there was more to come from their inheritance. Their houses, valued at 3,000 cruzados each, were entailed on their eldest grandson, Tomás, who had already received 2,000 cruzados from an inheritance from his grandmother, Teresa Vaz. Antonio Fernandes would receive a significant amount of entailed property—the grand houses where Tomás lived, bought from D. Antão de Almada, were estimated at 8,000 cruzados; and the farm of Fonte Boa was estimated at 11,000 cruzados—on condition that he invested 300,000 réis in customs interests (explicitly not in the houses of India or Mina, clearly considered unreliable at the time). António Fernandes would be obliged to pay 40,000 réis a year to a certain person who would give him a document from Tomás (secrets of life were involved here). This morgado was conditional: António Fernandes would have to marry according to the advice of his uncle André and the brother André Archdeacon of Olivença, executors of the will. In the case of his refusal, the morgado would be passed to the other son, Jerónimo, as it happened.[43]

Archdeacon Fernando received a sum of 14,000 cruzados, and there was still more for him from his legitimate share of the inheritance. Sebastiano, Prior of Romagna, husband of Caterina de' Medici, had already received 11,000 cruzados as his legitimate share of the inheritance (with still more to come); on top of all that, he received 6,000 cruzados. Tomás declared that he had helped found the *priorado* (property linked to the military order) besides having made gifts of jewels to Caterina. Isabel da Cruz had received 3,000 cruzados as a dowry, 2,000 for the ceremony where she took her vows and her trousseau, plus 30,000 réis of interest; when Tomás died, she would have 20,000 réis a year for the rest of her life. Rui, who had been in Cologne and was now in Antwerp, already had 5,600 cruzados inherited from his mother, and he received another 2,000 to cover debts and travel expenses. What remained from his legitimate inheritance was to be entailed, together with half his property. Beatriz, the nun, received 8,385 cruzados, of which 3,000 was for her dowry and 3,600 for the convent. Ninety thousand réis of interest from customs was also allocated to the convent, of which she would consume 40,000 in her lifetime (10,000 after Tomás died), plus 600 cruzados for the ceremony and her trousseau, and 80,000 réis for the other nuns of the convent as a friendly gesture. It was noted in the will that Beatriz had freely contributed 5,000 cruzados to the dowry of her sister, Joana, whose financial arrangements have been detailed here, and a significant sum still remained to be paid.

Jorge, who took his vows as a Dominican, received 4,000 cruzados to provide 100,000 réis of interest when it was invested in customs in Lisbon, as agreed with the friars. There were 200,000 réis more for the ceremony where he took his vows, his bed, and his habit. Jerónimo, the last son, received 4,000 cruzados, which were to produce 100,000 réis of interests (this would have meant an interest rate of 6.5 percent) when invested with the Count of Tentúgal in Cadaval, and more money for business, totalling 2,107,000 réis (5,267.5 cruzados). He would receive the farm of Odivor, which belonged to D. Diogo de Sousa, estimated to be worth 5,500 cruzados, on condition that he added the 100,000 réis from Cadaval to create an entailed property. He was to pay to Isabel da Cruz 20,000 réis every year and 10,000 réis to Beatriz de São Paulo after Tomás's death (there were penalties for not complying, as happened with António Fernandes). Tomás mentions the estate of his father-in-law, António Fernandes d'Elvas, who had left 70,000 cruzados to his sons Jorge and Diogo Fernandes. When the estate (in which Tomás's deceased wife had some financial involvement) was divided, there were 10,000 or 12,000 cruzados less than stated, because debts had to be recovered.

Tomás decided he wished to be buried at the Misericórdia (200 cruzados for annual masses, plus a gift of wheat and wine), followed by masses the same day in several churches and 500 masses at the end of the month, to be divided between the Dominicans, the Franciscans, the Augustinians (Graça), the Trinitarians, the Marianos, and the Misericórdia. The final place of burial would be the Chapel of Saint Catherine at the Dominicans' Church in Lisbon, where the remains of his wife and son Duarte were to be transferred. He left annual interest of 600,000 réis in perpetuity for dowries for orphans, clothing for widows, and assistance for other people he designated to the executors of the will. He also left 30,000 réis to his employee, Jorge Dias. He invoked Jesus, the Virgin Mary, and the saints at the beginning of the will and advised his heirs at the end that the most important thing in life was to reach heaven.[44]

These details have been given at such length so that readers can understand the thinking of the richest New Christian merchants and financiers who decided to integrate into Christian society, establishing strong links with the Church and noble Old Christians. The capital declared and distributed by this will amounts to more than 162,000 cruzados, but there was certainly more, as Tomás constantly hints. The dowry to Joana represents 28 percent of the total, which is clearly disproportionate in the context of twelve children (eleven alive, and the one deceased with heirs). However, although the will shows relative inequality, it shows reasonable distribution. Besides, this distribution was covered by the thirds (terças) of the parents, which they could freely dispose of. The distribution of the legitimate inheritance came after this and was generally equally shared, unless there were contrary legal dispositions, for example, renunciation by heirs who had decided to take religious vows. All the male heirs in this will received entailed properties, with the major items going to the eldest and lesser ones to the other two. Jerónimo would receive most of the entailed property because of the renunciation of his brother, António Fernandes.

Sebastiano, despite being the last-born male, had his position in Italy recognised and assisted from the beginning, being heavily favoured by his uncle
Fernando as his heir. Sebastiano received and bought many properties, including the fief of Saturnia (with the title of marquis), where he developed a magnificent palace, and the palace Del Monte at the entrance to Naples, not to
mention the palace in which he lived in Borgo Pinti, Florence.[45]

In 1615, Sebastiano asked for his son Tomás to be admitted into the Order
of Santo Stefano. It required an enquiry into his noble background in Lisbon, which was arranged by the viceroy and the archbishop of Lisbon. It was
declared that Tomás had been enrolled in the books of the fidalgos of the kingdom. Several witnesses indicated the family's noble background: the grandfather, Tomás, had been related to the house of the Count of Feira through
the marriage of his daughter Joana, while his son Jerónimo had married into
the house of D. Afonso de Noronha, a major nobleman of the kingdom; one
niece had married D. Luís Coutinho, son of the Count of Redondo; a granddaughter had married D. João de Almada; and another granddaughter had
married Nuno Álvares Pereira, all from important noble families. António Fernandes de Elvas, Tomás's father-in-law, had been a fidalgo of the house of the
infanta D. Maria, and King Sebastian had asked him to host foreign ambassadors. Luís Gomes de Elvas Coronel, Tomás's nephew, who had been elevated
by Philip III in 1606 to a title and the office of postmaster general, had married
into the noble house of Abranches.[46]

The strategy paid off in the case of Florence, since in Italy, unlike in Iberia,
there was no prejudice about blood purity. The alliance with the Medici clan
was a strategy duplicated in Lisbon, but when used by the Lisbon branch of
the family, it did not dislodge rooted prejudices, despite successful alliances
with major noble houses, as will be shown in part III. However, this case study
has allowed us to better understand the wide range of possibilities for entailed
property, in which the interest on investments was included alongside traditional real estate. It has also shown that women could be the vehicle for the
creation of primogeniture inheritances and could even themselves inherit in
the absence of male descendants.

Women played a major role in strategies of upward social mobility, not
only through matrimonial alliances, but also through the social world of
convents and the courts of infantas and queens. If we believe the witnesses
reporting on the New Christians attached to the court of the infanta D. Maria,
in which D. Afonso de Noronha was majordomo, we can better understand
where links were established and matrimonial alliances prepared.[47] The presence of a certain number of Ximenes in convents that were very well supplied
with generous contributions may have created possibilities for matrimonial
alliances. These convents were places for the aristocracy, and in some cases
for the royal family, and the impact of this New Christian sponsorship and the
regular arrival of female New Christians would have created bridges for direct
financial assistance or to explore the matrimonial market.

Finally, the importance of the quantity of clergymen among the Ximenes clan cannot be underestimated. One witness giving evidence to the enquiry into the noble background of the Ximenes family, when they asserted access to the Order of Santo Stefano in 1615, highlighted the patronage of the Irish College by the family. Certainly, their presence among the Jesuits (since the second generation), the Dominicans, and the Franciscans, and also other religious orders, provided them with some support, as well as visible evidence in the form of the chapel at the Dominican Church in Lisbon.

The disadvantage of this investment in entailed property, which in the Ximenes case went far beyond traditional investment in primogeniture, and involved all male and even female descendants, is that trade was progressively abandoned in favour of investing capital in fixed-interest assets and real estate. I have compared the account book of Niccolò Ximenes from 1592 to 1596 with the book recording the income and expenses of the heirs of Prior Tommaso Ximenes from 1648 to 1666. The first, and then one of many, Ximenes family members involved in trade, Niccolò recorded an enormous number of transactions: gifts (a chain of gold to the Jew Brignosa, who had converted to Catholicism); silks from Venice; textiles from Segovia; wheat from Flanders to Spain; sugars from Lisbon to northern Europe; cochineal from Spanish America; business relationships with Antwerp, Pisa, Livorno, Hamburg, and Cadiz; precious stones from India to Cologne and Venice; a farm inherited in Brazil; partnerships with Simón Ruiz in asientos in Antwerp; a share in the contract for pepper; and a multiplicity of agents and partners, such as Fernando Ximenes in Hamburg and also in Antwerp, Antonio Ximenes in Madrid, Francesco and Niccolò Capponi in Placencia, Jorge de Matos in Pisa, Juan Bautista de la Moneda in Burgos, Filippo Lucchini in Bologna, Francisco de Bobadilla in Medina del Campo (with the Ruiz), and Diego Enríquez León in Seville (this last already in debt).[48]

It is an extraordinary account book, overflowing with permanent transactions involving different continents, but also noting the displacement of people who might have been expected to settle in one place. It contrasts with the book of income and expenses from 1648 to 1662, which is full of rents from urban property, rural property, and salt mines, interest from deposits at the Monti di Pietà, records of taxes, debts, and wages of employees.[49] The impression here is typical of the affairs of an urban/rural bourgeois/aristocrat of central or northern Italy, and the shift from trading and financial speculation to investment in real estate seems clear. It is possible that some branches of the Ximenes clan might have still been deeply involved in trade at that time, but it seems, at this stage of research, that in Italy and Flanders they had invested in land.

{⸱⸱⸱⸱⸱⸱⸱}

The cases of these wealthy New Christian families indicate the beginning of the shift from trade to investment in real estate and royal interests. However, land and bonds would not guarantee long-term security because of seventeenth century war and climate change, not to mention royal suspension of payments. The Ximenes family was an extreme case of extensive diffusion of entailed property among nonecclesiastic male members. The participation of women in projects of social mobility and ennoblement through dowries to buy matrimonial alliances with aristocratic Old Christians was clear in some of these families. Control of dowries arguably gave women more power within the families. This sample is focused on integrated families pursuing ennoblement, except for the Nunes/Henriques family, who decided to re-create their ties with Jewish communities. We know that many merchants and financiers maintained an important degree of activity, both in Lisbon and Madrid, then and in the following century. It is too early to define the shift from trade as a betrayal of the bourgeoisie, as Braudel put it. In part III and part IV, we will explore how wealthy New Christians developed different social and economic strategies in response to growing extortion and persecution.

CHAPTER EIGHT

Values

THE IBERIAN UNION of Crowns, established in 1580, favoured renewed contact between New Christians across borders. Lisbon lost its position as a monarchical centre of decision with a royal court. The centrality of Madrid attracted a growing number of New Christian merchants and bankers who were farming taxation, leasing royal monopolies, and lending money; they needed to negotiate their contracts with the king. New Christian ethnicity, therefore, reinforced their economic and financial position. They also enlarged their sphere of social activity, but whilst this led to growing political influence, it also caused uneasiness among the traditional Castilian elites. The conflict of values that had been brewing during the sixteenth century—merit against blood, innovation against conformism—changed in its degree of intensity in the last decades of the sixteenth century and in the early seventeenth century. It is this process that will be addressed through an analysis of the economic and legal thought that placed merchant culture at the centre of their reflection. The extension and quality of this reflection in Castile needs to be better integrated, because it highlights the background of the New Christian elite's activities. The innovations introduced (and contributed) by New Christians in different areas of knowledge, mainly in political and legal thought, spiritual movements, literature, and natural history, will be analysed. It is not by coincidence that the turn of the seventeenth century registered the opening of the debate on blood purity and the inquisitorial backlash that would lead to the general pardon issued in 1604 and implemented in 1605. The last sections of this chapter will interpret this sequence.

1. Merchant Culture

New Christians contributed to the extraordinary development of intercontinental trade in the sixteenth century, but they also benefitted from late medieval commercial law within the *ius commune* (common law), which reflected the economic growth of the main Italian cities and their counterparts in western and northern Europe.[1] Rich merchant communities needed a stable institutional framework for their business. Commercial law was influenced by Roman and Byzantine compilations of laws, mainly the Theodosian code (438 A.D.), present throughout the Middle Ages; the *Corpus Iuris Civilis*, issued between 529 and 534 A.D. under the Byzantine Emperor Justinian, reintroduced in the twelfth century; but also the *Basilica*, completed about 892 A.D. under Leo VI, known as the Wise, and who was also responsible for the *Book of Eparch* on the regulation of trade and commercial organisations in Constantinople.

Commercial law developed with the practice of bills of exchange, *commenda* (goods entrusted to a merchant under certain conditions), *accomandita* (limited liability of the business partner), insurance (shared risks), written guarantees, creation of commercial institutions (such as associations of merchants with legal and judicial privileges), and commercial and maritime laws compiled in the fifteenth century, such as the *consolato del mare*, which was translated into different languages.[2] However, it is important to avoid the anachronistic vision of a common European *lex mercatoria*, diverse arrangements developed within local areas with state interference.[3]

The importance of contracts had been emphasised since the thirteenth and fourteenth centuries, as well as the level field that should exist between buyers and sellers, and the equity (justice) that should inspire the interpretation of law.[4] Thomas Aquinas (1225?-1274) and Peter John Olivi (1248?-1298), among other authors, contributed to the foundation of this tradition.[5] The debate on usury, which loomed from the thirteenth century onwards, contributed to keeping interest rates low, as John Maynard Keynes sharply observed.[6] Many authors acknowledged that nobody would lend without interest, since money was diverted from other uses and repayment was not guaranteed.[7]

Bills of exchange were extensively used to circumvent the prohibition of usury; that is, they facilitated the transfer of money but took account of the way currency rates differed from city to city. Credit has always been a crucial issue, but the late medieval and early modern period registered new needs and methods to obtain it.[8] State-building benefitted from the development of trade through customs fees and taxation raised on transactions, while groups of international merchants created a new culture based on systematic information on markets and the conditions that affected exchange rates, currencies, and commodities, including reflection on the setting of prices and the definition of value.[9] Commercial institutions with judicial capacity, such as guilds of merchants, trading exchange (bourses), and state legislation to regulate contracts and trade, emerged during the commercial revolution of the Middle Ages.[10]

In the Iberian case, guilds of merchants (*consulados*) were created in several Mediterranean ports and interior cities, like Burgos, for the wool trade, while royal institutions were established to regulate contracts on specific types of trade and solve conflicts, particularly those related to the *Casa da Índia* in Lisbon and the *Casa de Contratación de las Indias* in Seville.[11] The legal notion of a contract was developed to comprehend new investment in state bonds, while state contracts were designed to cover the farming of taxation or the obtaining of loans payable in different parts of Europe, as was necessary in Spain during the war in Flanders or the Thirty Years War. Titles of interest on loans could be sold on the market, while bills of exchange were traded and redeemed at the main financial fairs of Europe.

New Christian merchants were involved from the beginning in all these financial operations, as was shown in chapters 2 and 7. They contracted with the Iberian kings to farm taxes; enjoyed monopolies on trade in various parts of the Atlantic and Asia in return for hefty annual fees; guaranteed the payment of royal knights, judges, and guards, supported by specific sources of royal income; invested in state bonds in return for interest payable on customs or taxes; and lent significant sums of money against silver carried from the Americas by the *carrera de Indias*. They contracted for the sale of spices, sealing wax, and sugar with the king and members of the royal house in Portugal; they obtained exclusive rights to trade in specific products with certain regions of the Iberian kingdoms; they leased mines and salt pans under royal monopoly; they contracted to provision forts in North Africa and armies and fleets in various parts of the Iberian world; and they made extraordinary profits trading in precious stones, furniture, and textiles from India, porcelain and silk from China, and indigo and cochineal from the Americas.

New Christians guaranteed steady investment in both the carrera de Indias and the carreira da Índia: slave trade in the Atlantic, and sugar plantations in, and sugar trade with, Brazil. The source of their financial power was in intercontinental trade and contracts with the Iberian kings, but they also invested in land, state bonds, and loans. *Censos al quitar*, defined as irregular contracts of financial investment by Bartolomé de Albornoz, played an important part in the New Christian merchants' portfolios by the late sixteenth century.[12] In this period, New Christians were involved in the creation of entailed property, *morgado* in Portugal, *mayorazgo* in Spain, and *fidecommesso* in Italy (not exclusively related to primogeniture), which included urban and rural property, and also guaranteed interest on loans to the state and investments in customs and tax income. This investment strategy exposed wealthy families to extortion by the Iberian kings, as we will see in part III, in contrast to other New Christian families who took refuge in tolerant Italian cities, Amsterdam, Hamburg, and the Ottoman Empire in order to follow their Jewish faith.

Sixteenth century economic and legal thought in Castile was developed mostly by Old Christians, who reflected on local conditions of the market, mechanisms of fair trade, contracts, usury, bills of exchange, credit, and investment, shedding light on the specific framework and constraints that the New

Christians had to face, as other merchants, in their daily activity. The theologian Saravia de la Calle drew many examples from Medina del Campo, a major Castilian fair that had started as a centre for the international wool trade and become a major centre for the clearance of bills of exchange.[13] Saravia de la Calle asserted the importance of commutative justice, understood as equality in contracts between the different parties, equity between what one pays and the other receives, fairness in commodities delivered undamaged and corresponding to their description, with the promised weight, quantity, and quality respected.[14] He also reflected on payments in cash, and payments advanced or guaranteed, which had different costs and were (the latter two) exposed to usury.[15] He drew attention to "dry exchange," which meant covering up usury through the use of simulated bills of exchange applied to advanced or guaranteed purchases.[16] However, he accepted that lending with interest should not necessarily be defined as usury in the case of significant damage or loss, or the compensation of the lender for possible loss of profit.[17] He also recognised that the concept of a fair price was related to the conditions of selling and buying, the availability of merchandise and money, the quantity of buyers and sellers, the benefits of using the goods, the amount of work involved, the costs and hazards of production, and the costs of transport.[18]

Luis de Alcalá, a Franciscan, and specialist in moral theology, made his points with reference to the market city of Toledo. The city received large quantities of silk produced in Valencia and Granada, and goods brought to market in Toledo avoided the risks associated with maritime trade (shipwreck, piracy, merchandise deterioration). The most interesting section of his treatise offers a discussion of lending or selling with deferred payment, a practice he sees as producing illicit profit, meaning usury, because interest will always be involved. He acknowledges opposite opinions, which highlight the economic burden and human suffering that will result should these practices be forbidden. And he himself ended up accepting moderate interest for lending money, considering that the amount of profit depended on the circumstances of the loan and the use it was put to, for example, whether the profit was compensation for possible loss of money being held against the delivery of goods.[19] He accepted the arguments against this being classified as usury mainly in relation to maritime insurance, owing to the high risks involved.[20] What is interesting about his treatise is that Luis de Alcalá gave precise amounts for what constituted reasonable profit, which is something that has rarely been quantified. He indicated that in normal years moderate profit should be around 7 or 8 percent (annually), while in difficult years it could increase to 9 or 10 percent.[21] This is really very interesting, because it confirms the impression that the debate around usury was carried on with the intention of keeping interest rates as low as possible, since nobody would consider undertaking economic activity without access to money paid with interest. Martin de Azpilcueta Navarro, one of the most famous professors of law in the sixteenth century, who also acted as a lawyer and a consultant to kings and popes in Castile, Portugal, and Rome, published a treatise on exchange that contributed to the development of the theory of money and the impact of importing precious metals from Spanish America.[22] He absorbed the medieval debate on usury, including the distinctions between real and dry exchange and pure and impure exchange, although he acknowledged that the extraordinary increase in exchange, the productivity of money, and the possibility of lending at interest was beneficial to the republic.[23] He accepted that money could be seen as another form of merchandise, a theory that had been dismissed by the Aristotelian tradition.[24] He assimilated Baldus's justification for bills of exchange as being necessary for long-distance trade and as not representing usury.[25]

Martin de Azpilcueta considered that risk needed to be compensated and financial work should be remunerated. He gave the example of the Monti di Pietà, created in Italy, which collected interest to pay the salaries of those administering the money, but he also considered that those exchanging money should receive due remuneration for their work as holders of deposits, guarantors, and accountants.[26] He criticised the idea of dead money, which did not benefit anyone when it was not invested, but he nuanced his opinion by making the scarcity or abundance of money a consideration.[27] Kings, landlords, and merchants were criticised for borrowing money from bankers paid with bills of exchange drawn on other cities in Europe without coverage.[28] Usury in international contracts was the target of much criticism, but the overall impression is that the debate on usury was intended not to shut the door to lending with interest but to keep interest rates low.[29] In any case, this is another treatise reflecting the importance of well-regulated trade for the republic.

Tomás de Mercado, a theologian and Dominican, had links with the market established in Seville, having dedicated his *Suma de tratos y contratos* to the Consulado de Mercaderes de Sevilla (a merchant guild created in 1543 in Seville). He insisted on equality and equity in contracts (quoting Thomas Aquinas) and placed contracts under natural law. He advocated making equivalent dissimilar things, such as a horse and a Black slave, both valued at 100 ducados.[30] He added that the value of the work involved should be considered in the evaluation of contracts.[31] He praised bills of exchange that facilitated long-distance business as necessary, owing to the different currencies and values of money, and he highlighted the interdependence of merchants, whose situation was fixed by credit and debt, but who also suffered losses in dealings between places, according to the abundance or scarcity of money.[32] Naturally, he considered usury to be linked to speculation in exchange and monopoly in commodities, including in money and precious metals, which would lead to an increase in prices and interest.[33] He addressed the necessity of institutional frameworks, lamenting the absence of merchant guilds in Burgos, Medina del Campo, and Lisbon.[34]

Tomás de Mercado justified moderate interest related to the cost of transport, the risks of maritime trade, and the time during which the money owing to the seller of the goods was tied up.[35] He reflected on salaries, on investment in particular fields, and on taxes as contributing to the setting of prices.[36] Tomás de Mercado denounced deliberately inaccurate scales, weights, and measures; fraud in the presentation of property; dissimulation of defects in goods; and agreements between merchants to keep certain prices low and others high in situations of monopoly.[37] He also raised the issue of the legitimacy of the slave trade, given the cruel conditions of abduction and captivity.[38] Finally, he promoted the notion of honour in relation to trade and accumulated wealth, noting the familiar ties established between knights and merchants, as well as the creation of mayorazgos (entailed or inalienable property) by big merchants.[39]

Bartolomé de Albornoz, a doctor in law who lived for a short period in Mexico, wrote one of the clearest and most comprehensive treatises on contracts, which reflected the enormous development of commercial law and the law of obligations, including matrimonial contracts, warrants, mortgages, donations, loans, investment in state bonds and interest on rents, bills of exchange, inheritance and succession, dowries, and legitimate and illegitimate children.[40] He produced one of the best reflections on censos al quitar, investment at interest in royal rents, well defined as subordinate to (or inspired by) the emphyteutic contract, which established an equivalence between rents on land and interest on royal rents, mainly obtained from transactions and customs.[41] Albornoz rightly dated this investment in royal rents as beginning after the 1500s. He also pointed out that these censos al quitar could be entailed and transformed into a mayorazgo, one of the financial novelties of the sixteenth century.[42] But he considered censos al quitar as ruinous, because the king or the issuer of the censo could buy it out.

Moreover, in Albornoz's view, the whole of society was becoming dependent on interest and debt, undermining productive work, a lament that would be repeated by other authors.[43] He criticised Tomás de Mercado for his lenient position on usury in exchange, but he further developed Mercado's criticism of slavery and the slave trade. In his opinion, to buy kidnapped slaves showed a lack of conscience, and to enslave people or breed slaves was a work of the devil. He refuted head-on his contemporaries' argument that it was better for enslaved people to become slaves because they would become Christians, arguing that it was not the law of Christ that freedom of the soul should be paid for by servitude of the body. Natural law, he insisted, made men free.[44]

This unusual outlook was linked to consistent praise for merchants. Albornoz considered that trade sustained the world, being honourable, and making the merchant the equivalent of a gentleman. He gave the examples of Venice, Florence, and Genoa as maritime republics based on trade, where merchants were highly valued, being part of the local aristocracy, whereas in Spain manual work and commerce were not considered noble. Albornoz lamented the prejudice against merchants in Spain, but he pointed out with irony that virtue and honour, paradoxically, were the vassals of money.[45]

Martín González de Cellorigo, a lawyer at the *Real Audiencia y Chancilleria de Valladolid* (royal high court of Valladolid) and a lawyer of the Inquisition, wrote a first important *Memorial* in 1600, in which he reproduced the same arguments and some of the examples provided by Bartolomé Albornoz to condemn the mistreatment of merchants, because he viewed them along with peasants and artisans as the productive part of the republic's population.[46] But Martín González went further, strongly criticising the idea of living off rents, investing at interest, and the widespread creation of entailed property, which together meant the abandonment of productive activities, the withdrawal of land from taxation and from the market, and a decrease in production and wealth.[47] González de Cellorigo also pointed out that the clergy should contribute to the country's economy, thus challenging their exemption from taxation.[48] A critique of the excessive number of people at court completed his arguments against a parasitical way of life.[49] His was a strong opinion in favour of a change in economic policies, one that would place a premium on productive activities, while financial investments and the creation of inalienable property were considered parasitical and unproductive.

This favourable attitude to commerce and productive activities represented a shift in values, contrasted with the disdain for manual labour expressed by the traditional aristocratic occupations of war and ecclesiastic spiritual service. New Christians did not invent merchant culture, analysed here through legal and economic thought, but they contributed to and benefitted from it. Their pragmatic position is interesting, because they invested in a wide range of activities concerning trade and industry (more on this later) and also in the bonds and entailed property so much criticised by the sixteenth-century treatises. The conflict of values would play a role in the blood purity debate and the perceived threat of New Christian upward social mobility.

2. Innovation

Innovation is considered here as the alteration of something established, the introduction of new ways of doing and thinking. It involves a certain degree of imagination, emotion, creativity, and inventiveness. It supposes a curiosity to develop new enquiries and pursue different paths that can lead to challenging standard knowledge and perceived norms. Innovation requires, in general, a certain level of organisation or at least information exchange between a group of people interested in the same subject.[50] This is still an underresearched area in the early modern period, probably because it is not easy to reconstitute information exchange or identify informal and formal groups and organisations, although the history of science, medicine, and technology registered an extraordinary development.[51] We will deal here with new information, new practices, new methods, and/or new issues in different fields, from penal law to religious quest, from literature to natural history, in which New Christians made significant contributions.

The New Christians themselves pushed the debate on social values further, and thus had an impact on political, economic, and legal thought. Successive generations of New Christian procurators in Rome argued in favour of the free movement of people, because prohibitions on migration and selling property damaged trade. They also pointed out that trade contributed to the creation of wealth and increased royal finances. The issue of tyranny, discretely raised in Rome, was occasionally taken on board by the popes, particularly Clement VII, who asked his *nuncio* (ambassador) in Lisbon to confront King John III over the prohibition on New Christians leaving the country, representing it as an enslavement of part of the population.[52] Aspects of the penal process were constantly questioned by the New Christians, for example, conviction on the evidence of a single witness, secrecy in criminal procedures where the circumstances of an accusation and the names of the accusers were withheld, detention of relatives to extort denunciations, and the lengthy imprisonment of accused persons to obtain confession. New Christians also asserted their right to hold public office and to achieve honours based on merit and service to the king.

The most consistent protest of New Christians in Rome was produced by Gastão de Abrunhosa, a well-established notary in Lisbon, who went to Rome in 1602 and challenged the procedure of the Inquisition, following the detention of his mother and the dishonouring of his family, who until then had been considered Old Christians entitled to enter religious and military orders. This is a very interesting case of a fight between factions in the small town of Serpa, in which the Melo family mobilised an official of the Inquisition in Évora to obtain testimony against their rivals from detained New Christians. Gastão de Abrunhosa focused on conviction on the evidence of a single witness and the scandal of accepting false accusations by prisoners who knew they would be released if these produced convictions. He compared this scandal to that of convictions for lèse-majesté, in which the accused would be burned, together with those accused of being his accomplices, arguing that the acceptance of false accusations in both procedures and the rewarding of denunciations by the Inquisition was a path to dishonour for the whole of society. Nobody, he insisted, could claim a purely Old Christian background, since all were descended from Muslims, Jews, Aryan Visigoths, and other non-Catholic peoples.[53]

Abrunhosa was probably inspired by the well-known jurist Duarte Nunes de Leão, another New Christian, who compiled laws and wrote legal treatises and (significantly) chronicles of Portugal under the Iberian Union of Crowns. Abrunhosa also had access to relatives in Italy with legal expertise, such as Valério de Abrunhosa, who had been a judge of the ecclesiastic tribunal in Florence. The new atmosphere favourable to debate about blood purity enquiries in Spain clearly influenced his discourse, which shows traces of Salucio's demographic argument. He finally went to Spain to present his case to the king in person, and apparently he then withdrew to Barcelona. His family managed to obtain their release from detention, because they benefitted from the general pardon of 1604–1605, and his brother's expulsion from the military order of Avis was unexpectedly reversed owing to the intervention of the Council of Portugal. However, the name Abrunhosa disappeared from the records, probably replaced by another family name, a regular practice at the time.

The long-term impact of New Christians on Iberian society and beyond needs to be reassessed beyond political and economic thought, penal procedure, and social values. New Christian contribution to literature, art, the sciences, religion, and philosophy has been acknowledged, although more can be done in a comprehensive way. In religion, we have seen how New Christians played a role in the *alumbrados* movement and among the Erasmians. This participation created a background of practices and references that helped to resist boundaries imposed by the Inquisition, extending the New Christian presence to the creation of the Society of Jesus, the movement for preaching and education inspired by Juan de Ávila in Andalusia, and the new forms of mysticism explored by Teresa de Ávila and Fr. Luís de León (all three were New Christians). I shall highlight these innovative religious trends within Catholicism, though it is obvious that many New Christians stayed in the mainstream of the Church. However, even a conventional New Christian like the Dominican Melchor Cano (1509–1560), who took issue with Catholic spiritualists and reformists such as the Jesuits, and with the Old Christian archbishop of Toledo, Bartolomé Carranza (another Dominican famously prosecuted by the Inquisition), was a more complex figure than depicted.[54] Not only did he advise Philip II to take a stance against papal intervention, but he also wrote several theological treatises, mainly *De locis theologicis*, which provided new reflections on authority, the oral tradition, and the pursuit of reason in science and history.[55]

The case of the Society of Jesus is well known, from the original initiative of the Old Christian Iñigo de Loyola, together with New Christians who were influenced by Erasmus (Simão Rodrigues, Nicolás Bobadilla, Jeronimo Nadal, Diego Laynez, who became second Superior General of the Society and played a significant role in the Council of Trent), to those joining the Company immediately after its foundation, such as Juan Alfonso Polanco and Pedro de Ribadeneira, most of them Castilians.[56] In this case, there was a spiritual search and also an organisational innovation towards a centralised set of communities oriented towards preaching and conversion in Catholic areas, alongside missions to religiously disputed European areas and overseas. These aims were embodied in a new educational plan (*ratio studiorum*) that scandalised the

Dominicans, who were keen to perpetuate the scholastic principles of Thomas Aquinas. However, the Jesuits managed to overcome some fierce opposition with their avowal of submission to the pope and the doctrine of the Church. The most important hurdles they had to overcome were the blood purity statutes in Spain, and the opposition to the Society of the Archbishop of Toledo and Cardinal Juan Martínez Silíceo (1477–1557). In 1547, a blood purity statute imposed by the archbishop in his cathedral, supported by the Emperor Charles V, contradicted the Jesuit effort to make conversions, and the Jesuits resisted the adoption of a similar statute until 1593.[57] Such statutes, which were preceded and followed by fierce internal debate, later received qualification, while several Jesuits, such as Pedro de Ribadeneira, made statements against the merit of blood purity.[58]

The position of the Jesuits in Portugal was, from the beginning, much more aligned with the Inquisition and royal power. In Castile they were identified as a new spiritual movement that had to come to terms with accusations concerning the influence of Erasmus on them and their closeness to other movements, particularly the *alumbrados*, whereas in Portugal they favoured informal constraints on the acceptance of New Christians and positioned themselves as a pillar of orthodoxy, respectful of Rome and seeking to promote Christianity overseas using new educational methods. Their militant side and their willingness to work with the Inquisition convinced the royal court. In 1541, the Old Christian Francis Xavier went to the East as papal nuncio, accompanied and followed by other Jesuits, while in 1549 Manuel da Nóbrega (another Old Christian) headed the Jesuit mission to Brazil. In a few decades, the Jesuits became the religious mainstay of the Portuguese Empire. They became confessors to King Sebastião and Cardinal Henrique and consultants and censors to the Inquisition. They pushed for the creation of a tribunal of the Inquisition in Goa. And with Cardinal Henrique's leadership of the institution, they achieved a presence on its general council. However, just as their involvement was about to intensify with new nominations for posts as inquisitors, in the 1580s, the policy of the institution was reversed, and their involvement was frozen at the level of consultancy and censorship.[59]

My hypothesis concerning the freezing of the Jesuits' involvement with the Portuguese Inquisition is that it was probably directed from Madrid, where the Jesuits never reached the same level of political trust, while they inspired opposition from other religious orders. It is this opposition to the Jesuits within the political establishment, and their sudden distancing from power, that may explain the later alignment of the Portuguese Jesuits with the independence movement in Portugal. However, in recent years, research by Lúcio de Sousa and Miguel Lourenço, among other scholars, has shown that New Christians had a much stronger presence among the Portuguese Jesuits than supposed.

In other religious orders, the impact of New Christians involved in new spiritual movements was less visible, although their ideas held a strong attraction for the Franciscans, and this was reflected in Portuguese confraternities abroad, mainly in Rome and Madrid, placed under the patronage of St. Anthony of Lisbon (or Padua). Franciscan monasteries and convents accepted chapels from prominent New Christian bankers, and although the Dominicans also benefitted from such New Christian largesse, this was arguably on a minor scale. If we look at all the religious orders, few were untouched in one way or the other by New Christians. We have seen how important these religious positions were for New Christians, not only for reinforcing their relationship with the Church but also for improving their reputation and building trust.

The role of women in the spiritual movement is well known and testifies to the profound change in gender power relations after forced conversion. The mysticism of the Carmelite Teresa de Ávila (1515–1582) can be considered an extraordinary expression of this spiritual search. Granddaughter of Juan Sánchez de Toledo, a New Christian cloth merchant reconciled by the Inquisition, and daughter of Alonso Sánchez de Cepeda, a wealthy New Christian wool merchant who pleaded for (and obtained) *hidalgo* status using forged documents and bribed testimonies, Teresa showed an extraordinary resilience in the face of the various enquiries into her faith that suspicion of *alumbradismo* (literally enlightenment) stimulated.[60] She showed determination to reform her order, bringing it under clear rules, including that of poverty, and showing intellectual consistency in justifying her mystic path, which followed the steps of ascesis (or self-discipline), contemplation (or enlightenment), and union with Christ (or spiritual matrimony).[61]

The main mystical text that Teresa de Ávila wrote, the *Interior Castle*, was very much influenced by two ideas: one of a memory palace and the other of seven heavens, the latter composed of seven mansions within a castle, visualised as a diamond or a crystal, in which the central or innermost mansion was inhabited by God.[62] The castle was the soul, which discovered itself through prayer, discipline, and self-abandonment to God. It represented a process of learning and self-consciousness, passing over successive hurdles from mansion one to mansion seven, until it received the divine grace. This process was coupled with an acute perception of the phenomena of ecstasy and mystical union with God, with their impact on the body clearly described. Teresa de Ávila, who managed to obtain the support of the main theologians and religious orders of her time, never questioned the validity of the methods of the Church, always expressed her submission to its doctrine and rituals, and validated the path she followed by obedience to successive confessors. She wrote extensively on her experiences and produced philosophical reflections on her method that had a long-lasting influence. Hers is a clear case of the power of writing to transmit mystical experiences and still assert conformity to the Church's teachings. In 1616 she was beatified, in 1622 canonised, and between those dates there was a debate as to whether she should become the national saint of Spain. In 1970, she was declared a doctor of the Catholic Church.

In many cases, New Christian clergymen and nuns were under suspicion, attributable both to widespread ethnic prejudices and to their religious and intellectual quests. Fr. Luis de León (ca. 1527–1591), responsible for the publication of the main texts by Teresa de Ávila in 1588, is a case in point: an Augustinian and professor of theology at the university of Salamanca, he was twice sent for trial by the Inquisition accused of translating the Bible, criticising its Latin version by Jerome, and considering the Hebrew version superior. He was also accused of Pelagianism because of his sympathy for the individual's search for transcendency. He managed to be acquitted with minor penalties, resumed his academic teaching, and was appointed a provincial of his order. He also played a major role on the literary scene because of his extraordinary poetry, in which I highlight here the quest for self-awareness and a life of withdrawal from the world, comment on religious and mythological themes, and reflection on past and contemporary Spain. His father was the royal court jurist, Lope Ponce de León, while an uncle was a professor at the university of Salamanca.[63]

Juan de Ávila (ca.1499–1569) is another case of a priest who chose very early a path of asceticism and spirituality. His father, Alonso de Ávila, a New Christian, owned a silver mine in Sierra Morena. Juan studied law in Salamanca and then arts and theology in Alcalá de Henares, where he was a student of Domingo de Soto and met several members of the new generation of theologians and future bishops of Spain. His parents died when he was pursuing his studies, and in 1526 he sold their property, distributed the money to the poor, and began an ascetic life outside holy orders. When he attempted to join Catholic missions in the Americas, the archbishop of Seville and general inquisitor, Alonso Manrique, persuaded him to concentrate his efforts in Andalusia, where he stayed for the rest of his life.

Juan de Ávila survived a first trial by the Inquisition in 1531–1533, when he was accused of Erasmian ideas but acquitted. His preaching had a significant impact on Andalusia, where he created a vast network of colleges, the most important of which was located in Baeza. He supported the establishment of the Society of Jesus and had many conversations on joining the Society, having sent them several disciples. His project of having his various educational centres and disciples welcomed into membership by the Society was not fully accepted, probably owing to the number of New Christians among his followers.[64] He left a significant body of work on asceticism, of which the most important volume was probably the *Epistolario spiritual para todos los estados*, published in Madrid in 1578.[65] The famous Dominican Luis de Granada wrote a biography of Juan de Ávila in 1588, and this was followed by another one by Luis de Muñoz in 1635. The process of beatification was requested by the congregation of St. Peter in Madrid in 1623, but Juan de Ávila was only beatified in 1894, declared the patron saint of the Spanish clergy in 1946, and canonised in 1970.

There were also New Christians who risked their lives and publicly returned to their old faith, and even Old Christians who joined the Jewish tradition. Fr. Diogo de Assunção, a Capuchin monk, was excommunicated by the Inquisition, executed in 1603 for Judaism, and allegedly became a martyr in New Christian circles.[66] The trial, which lasted from October 25, 1599, to August 3, 1603, the date of the auto da fé, began with an unlikely story. Fr. Diogo de Assunção had escaped from the convent of St. Anthony of Castanheira (in Merceana, a parish of Alenquer, not far from Lisbon) and was heading for the Tagus river. He wanted to obtain lay clothing so he could escape to Flanders or England via Setúbal, and he stopped in Cachoeira at the house of a New Christian merchant, Gaspar Bocarro, who (maliciously) advised him to ask help from D. Diogo de Sousa, a fidalgo with a villa in Cadafais.

To this stranger, Fr. Diogo de Assunção revealed his lack of belief in Jesus as God incarnate, and he went further, declaring that Mary had given birth not only to Jesus but also to St. James and St. John, all fathered by Joseph. The apostles were relatives of Jesus, and there were no such things as saints. Martin Luther had abandoned Christianity in protest against the sacraments. New sects were created out of the vanity of men. Even if the doctrines of Jesus were good, how could they be communicated in the lands of Black people and in many other places where there was no bread or wine? This mockery was extended to holy relics, particularly relics of the true cross, which if all put together would create several forests. Testimonies on the stigmata of St. Francis or the burial site of St. James were derided as invented and incompatible with each other. D. Diogo de Sousa called the friars of the local monastery, who came to his house and detained the runaway brother, then advised de Sousa to denounce him to the Inquisition, to which they would deliver him.[67] The story sounded unlikely, and the inquisitors asked whether the friar looked to be in his right mind (a question that arose several times).

Fr. Diogo de Assunção carried with him extensive writings about his beliefs, and these were confiscated by the Capuchins and delivered to the Inquisition. The runaway had shown them to D. Diogo de Sousa and had read out parts to support his declarations. At the Inquisition of Lisbon, he straightway confessed, but the confession was not considered acceptable. He later declared that he was increasingly being shown the light by God. He was Jewish and did not believe in the Trinity, nor did he believe in the divinity of Jesus as the Messiah who was to come. The inquisitors made enquiries in Aveiro and Lorvão about the family, until they discovered that his maternal great-grandfather had been a New Christian.[68] But Fr. Diogo de Assunção declared that he was not aware of a New Christian background, and that his family was as blind as any other on religious matters. It was God who had enlightened him. Two Jesuits, Manuel Correia and Gaspar Ferraz, were brought by the inquisitors to bring him back to the Church. They failed, but they declared that he was not mad, having a consistent and clear discourse, without deviations.[69]

The sentence of Fr. Diogo de Assunção, published at the auto da fé, might have had an impact among New Christians, since some of them were eager to receive guidance in the absence of religious books and rabbis. Even if the sentence did not repeat the accused's declarations about the Virgin Mary, it detailed Fr. Diogo de Assunção's denial of the doctrine of the Catholic Church (rejection of the Trinity, of the divinity of Christ, of the resurrection, of the Gospels, of the sacraments, and of the saints), his allegations about the baseness of Christians as gentiles, his refusal to recognise any power of forgiveness in the Church or the Inquisition as human institutions, and his conviction that God would restore the Jews to their former status and send the Messiah.[70] It is not known what occurred during the auto da fé, but it is possible that Fr. Diogo de Assunção reiterated his Jewish allegiance before being burned.

There was much more at stake, from a religious viewpoint, than a return to Judaism or conformity to Catholicism, as we can see from these various cases. A revelation of Judaism to Old Christians might have occurred, given an unusual set of circumstances. And it is impossible to identify factions here, because crypto-Judaism could coexist with anti-Judaism among New Christians, while a deviant religious sensibility could be shared between Old and New Christians. It is the search for alternative spiritual paths and purified religious experiences, the refusal of conventional practices, the conception of faith as enlightenment, and the investment of belief in religion as love and charity, that can be related to a certain extent to the New Christian condition. The importance of salvation of the soul can be identified in this search, even among those who returned to Judaism. The relationship of these spiritual issues to our argument is also clear from a social viewpoint: almost all these New Christians had a merchant or liberal professional background.

Secular literature received an extraordinary boost from New Christian writers. In 1552, the Castilian Alonso Núñez de Reinoso, friend of the Portuguese Feliciano da Silva, Bernardim Ribeiro, and Sá de Miranda, published in Venice a novel *Historia de los amores de Clareo y Florisea, y de los trabajos de Ysea* dedicated to Juan Micas (João Micas), alias Joseph Nasi. Maritime adventures, deaths, a return from the dead, praise for love that makes men wise, and a passage through hell contribute to a succession of events that lead the female character, Ysea, to return to Spain alone. The travails of the pilgrim are recurrent, the pain of memory is favoured over forgetfulness, and there is a theme of persistent exile until at last refuge is found on an idyllic island, after entrance to a convent has been refused for having neither a 1,000 ducados for the dowry nor "known" (or better, "clean") lineage.[71] Constance Hubbard Rose has underlined the dual allegiance of the New Christians, who could not break away from their links to their original land. She has highlighted the pastoral framework shared by Ribeiro and Montemayor.[72] But there is an irony in Núñez de Reinoso's text that has escaped analysis, as far as I know: the references to precious and valued lineages present at the coveted convent are followed by the precise names of Elvira de Guzmán, Francisca Pimentel, Juana de Mompalau, Teresa de Ayala, Maria Manrique, Mariana Imperial, Ambrosia de Chaves, Isabel de Silva, Antonia Aguilar, and Ana de Carvajal, all of which suggest a mockery of New Christian names.[73]

In 1554, in Ferrara, the Jewish printer Abraham Usque published a novel, *História de Menina e Moça*, by Bernardim Ribeiro, who was most probably a New Christian.[74] The novel's first part is a long lament by two women about separation and exile, which has been interpreted by Helder Macedo as expressing the trauma of disruption and displacement imposed on the Jewish community by their forced conversion to Christianity.[75] The novel also offers oblique references to the Kabbalah and to the new role of women in the New Christian ethnicity as keepers of tradition.[76] The narrative is set in a bucolic environment, and this builds on the idea of disdain for court intrigue and idealises the life of a simple shepherd in a natural environment. Love drives this narrative, which deals with individual feelings and inner conflicts but also touches on collective emotions. Together, individual melancholy and a collective sense of loss develop the feeling of *saudade*—nostalgia for what was and will never be again. *Saudade* as a noun was not invented by the New Christians, the word having been used before, for example, by King Duarte (r. 1433–1438) in his treatise *Leal conselheiro*, which revealed an important capacity for introspection.[77] However, it is arguable that New Christians, particularly Bernardim Ribeiro, contributed to its spread and its wide acceptance.

The seeds for the picaresque novel were sown in 1554 with the publication, in Alcalá de Henares, Burgos, and Antwerp, of *La vida de Lazarillo de Tormes y de sus fortunas y adversidades*,[78] the author of which was never identified. The protagonist is a poor boy who grows up serving various characters represented as different social types. Lazarillo learns all the arts of deception and petty extortion, while he himself is exploited along the way. Its hyper-realistic approach to the underside of a society plagued by poverty and malign practices, and opposed to an ideal of virtue, defines this genre, which was inspired by Fernando Rojas and Francisco Delicado. Unscrupulous clergymen, residing in monastic establishments but involved in forbidden ways of life, were among the main characters of the novel, which probably justified its prohibition by the Inquisition.

The New Christian writer Mateo Alemán renewed this genre in 1599 to 1604 with *Guzmán de Alfarache*. Here, the autobiographical genre is again the source of the novel's format, since the main character speaks in the first person and establishes a straightforward complicity with the reader, who is addressed in the second person. The rhetorical complexity of the text reaches new heights, integrating the different traditions of confessional writing, social satire, and short stories; and the novel is enriched by aphorisms, refrains, and proverbs. The tension between a lie and the truth is at the core of the text, while the moralising purpose is reinforced by a character driven more by vice than by hunger.[79]

In natural history, the contribution of New Christians was probably more significant. Pedro Nunes (1502–1578) was a mathematician who studied in Salamanca and Lisbon and taught at the latter university before and after its transfer to Coimbra in 1537. He was the instructor of the princes Luís, Henrique, and, later, Sebastian. The governor of India, João de Castro, who left important scientific work carried out on the Persian Gulf and the Red Sea, was also his disciple. Considered a mathematical genius in his time, Pedro Nunes understood spherical trigonometry, commenting on Ptolemy in the light of Euclidian geometry. He created a new measuring device known by his Latin name, the *nonius*, to improve the astrolabe's accuracy, and this was later developed into the Vernier scale. Nunes also suggested the loxodrome, an arc or rhumb line crossing all the meridians of longitude at the same angle and defining a spiral with a constant bearing relative to the magnetic north. And it was Nunes who solved the problem of how to fix on the day with the shortest duration of twilight for any given location.[80] Mercator's projection of the globe resulted from Pedro Nunes's suggestions, and Nunes also influenced Christopher Clavius, probably his disciple at Coimbra, who made important modifications to the proposal for a modern Gregorian calendar. While Nunes was never bothered by the Inquisition in his lifetime, and his children Pedro Areas and Apolónio Nunes served King Sebastian, his grandchildren, Matias Pereira and Pedro Nunes Pereira, were accused of Judaism and detained by the Inquisition from 1623 to 1632.[81]

Some of the mathematical ideas Pedro Nunes developed concerned nautical problems that arose when Portuguese navigators began circling the globe. In 1529, he became a royal cosmographer, and in 1547, chief royal cosmographer. He worked with pilots, helping to improve their skills of orientation at sea, and with cartographers, who constantly updated the information collected by Portuguese navigators. The Portuguese school of cartography had been developing since the fifteenth century. Among other figures whose ethnic background still needs research, the New Christian Pedro Reinel (ca. 1462–ca. 1542) was the creator of one of the oldest signed nautical charts, in 1485, and of the earliest nautical chart of the Atlantic, which had a scale of latitudes and a wind rose, in about 1504. His son, Jorge Reinel (ca. 1502–ca. 1572), who drew maps of the Atlantic, was involved with his father and another New Christian cartographer, Lopo Homem (active from the 1510s to the 1550s), in the elaboration of the Miller Atlas of 1519, with a dozen charts of the world. Diogo Homem (1521–1576), son of Lopo, was another member of this school of cartography, although he was forced into exile after committing a criminal offence, and lived in England and then in Venice, where he drew a significant number of nautical charts and atlases, many of them of the Mediterranean.[82]

João Rodrigues de Castelo Branco, known as Amatus Lusitanus (1511–1568), studied medicine at the university of Salamanca and went to Antwerp (1534), having already travelled in Flanders and France. He then lived in Italy, particularly in Venice, and in the 1540s he was teaching anatomy at the university in Ferrara, where he regularly dissected cadavers in public discussions with colleagues and students. He gained the reputation of being one of the best medical doctors of his time, having treated aristocrats, relatives of the pope, and Pope Julius III (r. 1550–1555) himself. In 1547, Amatus moved to Ancona, but the new pope, Paul IV (1555–1559), who as Cardinal Carafa had been a member of the congregation of the Roman Inquisition, launched what became a notorious persecution of New Christians accused of Judaism, in which Amatus was targeted. Amatus escaped to Pesaro, leaving behind his possessions and some of his manuscripts. From there he moved to Ragusa (Dubrovnik) and then on to Salonika in the Ottoman Empire, where he assumed the Jewish faith. He died there twelve years later, the victim of an outbreak of plague he was trying to fight. The books written by Amatus Lusitanus were bestsellers in sixteenth century Europe, with the most important, *Curationum Medicinalium Centuriæ Septem*, going through eleven editions in different European cities between 1551 and 1628. In each of the seven volumes were recorded one hundred clinical cases, with the sex and age of the patient, the forms of treatment tried, and the development of the disease. These were major works that even provided information on the social milieu and food habits of the patients. Amatus Lusitanus also discovered the circulation of the blood and the function of the venous valves, while he contributed to discussions on the treatment of many diseases. Finally, he was a polyglot who knew Latin, Greek, Hebrew, Portuguese, Castilian, Italian, French, and German.[83]

Gonzalo Fernández de Oviedo (1478–1557), who was the target of contemporary insinuations of Jewish ancestry, claimed noble origins but never gave his father's name, although he published books on heraldry and genealogy. Certainly he had royal secretaries among his ancestors, and he himself started his life as a page and then secretary to princes in Castile and Italy before obtaining an appointment in the Spanish Indies, for which he had the support of highly placed New Christians.[84] He was a prolific writer, but what matters to us here is the *Sumario de la Natural Historia de las Indias*, published in 1526, and the first volume of *Historia General y Natural de las Indias*, published in 1535, which contain the first extensive descriptions of the natural phenomena of the New World. The *Sumario* was completely dedicated to the natural world, while the *Historia General* included ten books, volumes VI to XV, that focused on the same subject, significantly extending the knowledge available at the time. The descriptions of animals, including sea life, domestic plants, trees, roots, and fruits, complete with discussions of the medicinal uses of certain plants and minerals, included some 200 new items with illustrations.[85] This represented a significant new body of knowledge from other parts of the world to be integrated into the European knowledge of nature inherited from the classical world.

This revolution in European knowledge was further augmented with information from Asia provided by the medical doctor Garcia d'Orta (ca. 1501–1568). Born in Castelo de Vide to converted Jews who had taken refuge from Castile (Valencia de Alcantara), Garcia d'Orta studied medicine and the liberal arts in Alcalá de Henares and Salamanca. When he returned to Lisbon in 1526, he became a royal physician to King John III and a lecturer at the University of Lisbon, but in 1534, he decided to sail as chief physician with the fleet of Martim Afonso de Sousa, which was bound for India. Eventually, Garcia d'Orta settled in Goa, where he wrote a crucial treatise, *Colóquio dos simples e drogas e coisas medicinais da Índia*, which was published in 1563 and was based on a dialogue between himself and a European physician, Doctor Ruano, who had recently arrived with his mind filled with classical knowledge. In the *Colóquio*, Garcia d'Orta extensively described not only Indian flora, but also Indian fauna and minerals, particularly precious stones. He expressed his admiration for the medicinal knowledge of the Arabs, considered better than that of the Greeks, and showed himself to be open to consideration of Hindu traditions, from which he collected much of his information.[86] His treatise formed the basis of a book by another New Christian, Cristóvão da Costa (ca. 1525–1594), who lived in India as head physician of the royal hospital in Cochin, until he returned to Europe in 1572 to live and exercise his profession in Burgos, where he published, in 1578, an enlarged *Tratado de las drogas y medicinas de las Indias orientales* under the name Cristóbal Acosta.[87] The impact of both books in Europe was guaranteed by Carolus Clusius's translation into Latin.[88]

In 1543, Garcia d'Orta married a wealthy cousin, Brianda de Solis, with whom he had two daughters. His mother and two sisters had problems with the Inquisition in Lisbon—there are records of the trial of his sister Catarina in 1547—and so in 1549 Garcia d'Orta convinced them to join him in India, an unusual journey for women.[89] We have already come across several members of both Solis and Orta families who became important merchants. Garcia d'Orta traded in precious stones as well as fulfilling his important position as chief physician in Goa. He possessed an impressive house in Goa and received the lease on a significant manor in what was to become Bombay from the viceroy, D. Pedro de Mascarenhas. The year after his death, the Inquisition detained his sister Catarina, who confessed to having Jewish beliefs, and she implicated her brother. Catarina was excommunicated and burnt at the stake, while the corpse of Garcia d'Orta was eventually exhumed and burnt as well.[90] This is one of the signs that the Inquisition was turning to the regular persecution of notables, who up to the 1560s had been relatively protected.

Many New Christian physicians contributed to the advancement of medicine; for example, Rodrigo de Castro (ca.1546–1627), born in Lisbon, whose father and uncles (Manuel Vaz was the most distinguished) treated the king of Portugal and members of the royal family for several decades. Castro studied in Salamanca, worked in Évora and Lisbon, travelled to Antwerp and then to Hamburg, where he settled in the 1590s, and probably in the late 1600s assumed his Jewish allegiance under the name David Namias. His two sons were also physicians, André (alias David Namias) and Bento (Baruch Namias). Rodrigo treated the Count of Hessen, the king of Denmark, and the bishop of Bremen, an aristocratic practice extended by his son Baruch to Queen Christina of Sweden. The most important book published by Rodrigo de Castro was *De universa mulierum medicina* (1603), in which he studied the anatomy, the functions, and the diseases of women, contributing to the development of gynaecology and obstetrics.[91] In the book *Medicus-Politicus* (1614), he engaged with the ethics of medicine, integrating classical, medieval, and Renaissance authors, including Jews and Arabs.[92]

Filipe Montalto (1567–1616) was born in Castelo Branco, Portugal, studied medicine in Salamanca, exercised his profession back to his country, but in 1600 decided to move to Italy and assume his Jewish allegiance. In 1606, in Florence, he published a book on optics, *Optica intra philosophiae et medicinae aeram.*[93] In the meantime, his reputation spread and in 1612 he was invited by the French regent Marie de Medicis to join the royal court. Two years later he published his treaty on psychiatry.[94] In it, he follows the mainstream references to Greek medicine, but he builds on his extensive clinical experience to address mental diseases, refuting any supernatural origin and stressing the relationship between organic and psychic functions. The most interesting sections concern headaches, in which the extreme variety of causes and expressions are diagnosed, and melancholia, very extensive, in which the variety of afflictions and therapies are analysed.

Innovation was certainly not exclusive to New Christians. The cases discussed here of their searches and creativity in religion, penal procedure, literature, natural history, and medicine are significant, but they need to be placed in their historical context. New Christians dialogued with other believers (and some nonbelievers), jurists, men of letters, naturalists and physicians, even if the paths they chose reflected in one way or the other their liminal condition. The ambition to push further with their intellectual and religious searches has a hint of collective desire, either when they decided to stay within Catholicism or publicly returned to the faith of their ancestors.

3. Blood Purity

The blood purity debate reflected the multifaceted impact of New Christians but also the decline of the Hispanic monarchy and the growing discussion on policies to counter it. This period coincides with the most important sequence of suspensions of payments (or bankruptcies) by the Spanish Crown in 1596, 1607, and 1627, only surpassed by the period from 1647 to 1663, with its peak of partial and complete suspension of payments from 1660 to 1663.[95]

We know now that the best period of economic output and living conditions in Spain, compared to the rest of Europe, was before the Black Death (1347–1351), followed by sharp recovery in the 1390s, and prolonged until the end of the sixteenth century, despite the political turmoil during the fifteenth century. This period from the 1270s to the 1590s was characterised by relatively high wages and food consumption, resulting from a high land-to-labour-ratio frontier economy based on livestock (mainly sheep), trade in wool, and growing urban areas. The second period (or economic regime), from the 1600s to the 1810s, was defined by urban retraction combined with a low wage, densely populated countryside, and agricultural economy.[96] The blood purity debate coincided with the transition between the first and the second periods, when the change started to be sharply felt by the royal finances and the notion of decline infiltrated the political discourse, never to be abandoned.

Blood purity statutes had been promulgated and used in Castile and Aragon since the second half of the fifteenth century, despite initial royal and papal opposition on the grounds that they were blatantly against the notion of a universal Church and negated any notion of an integrated monarchy. By the mid-sixteenth century, a significant number of statutes had been formally endorsed by the king and the pope, but the general picture remained uneven, with some religious orders, chapters of cathedrals, confraternities, and guilds declining to participate in the new system of ethnic division within Christianity. However, the second half of the sixteenth century saw an increased use of these statutes, particularly in the kingdom of Portugal, which had previously been untouched by the phenomenon: in 1558 a papal brief blocked access by New Christians to the Franciscan Order; in 1565 the Order of St. Jerome obtained recognition for the same procedure, followed by the Dominicans; in 1572 the New Christians were excluded from the Order of Christ, followed by the other two military orders; in 1574 a royal decree prohibited the access of New Christians to the municipal offices of Vila Flor; in 1593 the Society of Jesus finally accepted the blood purity rule, although restrictions had been in place since its establishment in Portugal. From 1580 onwards, following the Iberian Union of Crowns, not only did the use of blood purity statutes become more widespread in Portugal (involving the university of Coimbra, colleges, cathedral chapters, tribunals, confraternities, and municipal and royal offices), but their implementation became more severe.[97] The question is: Did these statutes achieve their purpose of discriminating against, and segregating, New Christians?

Enrique Soria Mesa has shown how, in Castile, New Christians systematically worked their way onto municipal councils, a movement intensified by a massive sale of offices in the last third of the sixteenth century; how they reached some level of integration into the Church, even with the spread of blood purity statutes blocking access to religious orders and cathedral chapters; how they were not entirely excluded from the *colegios mayores* (major colleges); and how they had a very significant presence in the royal administration. They also managed to establish matrimonial alliances with titled nobility.[98] However, we do not know what proportions of applications for office were unsuccessful. The case of a request from Fernando de Añasco to wear the habit of the Order of Santiago, rejected by the Council of Orders in 1595 despite clear royal support for the petitioner, was certainly not isolated.[99] It might have had something to do with the number of generations scrutinised for the enquiry. A request for blood cleansing was an alternative. Initiatives like that of Don Pedro Osorio de Velasco, *gentilhombre* (gentleman) of Philip III, to have his family's blood cleansed by papal brief and royal letter in 1604 (previously blocked by the Council of Orders for stained blood) were not frequent in Castile.[100] But we know that New Christians developed different strategies according to local conditions. Because of the early establishment of blood purity statutes in Castile, New Christians there preferred to subject themselves to these enquiries to avoid the permanent stigma of being declared a royal exception, while in Portugal, before the widespread use of blood purity statutes, they obtained the selective support of the king to become Old Christians.[101]

In any case, in the second half of the sixteenth century a growing number of conflicts around blood purity were recorded, caused by the increasing use of these statutes. This triggered reactions from the New Christians and their supporters, including theologians from other countries, such as the Franciscan Henri Mauroy in 1553.[102] From the 1550s to the 1570s, several other theologians expressed their concern about the division of the universal Church, particularly the Dominicans Domingos Baltanás and Bartolomé de Medina, and the Franciscan Antonio de Córdoba.[103]

The Franciscan Gaspar de Uceda wrote a very articulate treatise against the statutes in 1586. His main arguments underlined the universalism of the Church, defended by St. Paul against Jewish exclusivism; the refusal of a sectarian stance and its divisive impact by St. Augustin, St. Anselm, and Pope Nicholas; the insistence on openness to all humankind by St. Peter; God's praise of virtue over lineage or personal status; and the consistent universal approach of the Roman Church owing to the grace bestowed by baptism. All these arguments were reflected in the granting of access to dignities and public office, papal bulls against division as a provocation by the devil, and the condemnation of blood purity statutes as contrary to reason and natural law. Gaspar de Uceda then addressed the usual accusations against New Christians: that they were rebels and ambitious. He suggested that the reverse was true and the accusations were falsehoods against innocents. In his opinion, the statutes were scandalous because they offered an invitation to sin by stimulating hate, exclusiveness, schism, and blasphemy. Moreover, they were an affront to the nobility, many of whom had married New Christians. Elvira Pérez Ferreiro has rightly pointed out that most of these arguments had been elaborated in the fifteenth century by the main treatises of famous New Christians, such as Alfonso de Cartagena, bishop of Burgos, Lope de Barrientos, bishop of Cuenca, and Cardinal Juan de Torquemada.[104]

There were also members of the elites who perceived themselves as Old Christians and reacted against close relatives being excluded from honours and military orders because of distant Jewish ancestors. This was the case with Cardinal Francisco de Mendoza y Bobadilla, bishop of Burgos, who apparently, before his death in 1566, wrote the *Tizón de la nobleza de España*, in which he denounced stained blood in almost all the titled nobility, thus taking revenge for the obstacles that had been raised against the two sons of his brother, the Marquis of Cañete, entering military orders.[105] The implicit message was obvious: if everyone was "stained" by having Jewish blood, there was no point in supposedly rigorous enquiries.

Bobadilla's argument was made explicit by his follower, Pedro Gerónimo de Aponte (ca. 1530–ca. 1580), who wrote several genealogies, including a supplement to Bobadilla's. At the end of his *Discurso sobre la limpiesa de los linages de España*, Aponte concluded that none of the noble houses of Castile, Aragon, or Portugal, all related, could claim blood purity. He produced the demographic reasoning that would later be developed by Salucio: going back ten generations would produce 1,200 ancestors, so who could presume to have clean blood?[106] The *Tizón* itself was followed by many other books of the same genre, the *Libros Verdes*, which were generally produced by Old Christians called *linajudos* (proud of their lineage), who assumed a dubious function as gatekeepers of genealogical enquiries on blood purity (open to bribery).[107]

Enrique Soria is right to point out the high proportion of the population who would have had Jewish blood, challenging the previous vision of segregated and endogamous New Christians. He is also right to highlight the significant number of families who were denied access to various organisations but who obtained that same access within one or two generations. The question is: how many passed the barrier? Even with all the recent research it has been difficult to find evidence for massive circumvention of rules, although many Christians joined municipal councils, were involved in the royal administration, or had aristocratic connections; while access to religious orders, cathedral chapters, and colleges became relatively more difficult. However, Old

Christian status did not mean permanent and stable recognition—it could be challenged after two or three generations.

The issue should be seen in the context of the conflict between the established and the outsiders: What were the mechanisms of social protection that facilitated the manipulation of blood purity rules? It becomes clear that even if the system accommodated a certain level of corruption and illicit crossing of boundaries, despite inquisitorial enquiries into false declarations of blood purity, these boundaries must increasingly have become a part of the system. This is consistent with a strictly normative discourse and a formal refusal to admit those with stained blood, so as to keep boundaries in place and maintain a certain level of control on ethnic and social mobility.

What eventually changed was that New Christian ideas and aspirations, benefitting both from the assertion of a merchant culture and the weakness of the royal finances, started to be publicly discussed, at about the turn of the seventeenth century. We have already pointed out that the two royal bankruptcies (or suspensions of payments) closest to each other were in 1596 and 1607. It was precisely between these dates that a window of opportunity opened for new ideas and the political influence of a wealthy merchant group that had been undermined for more than a century, for racist and religious reasons, despite their crucial role in intercontinental trade and royal finances. This short period also coincided with the last years of the long reign of Philip II and the beginning of the reign of the young Philip III, which suggests weaknesses in the position of the monarchy.

In this period the claims of merit against social legitimacy based on blood were argued over in a more methodical and consistent way. But most important of all, the impact of the blood purity statutes, and the methods used and the unlimited scope of enquiries into blood, were brought under serious scrutiny for the first time. It is well known that Philip II created a *junta* to assess the way the statutes were being implemented, probably following a refusal by the Council or Orders to grant access to military orders to two distinguished military officers, both supported by the king, in the mid-1590s. We have no record of the deliberations of that junta, but there are other texts that reflect a new social atmosphere. Interestingly, most are linked to merchant culture, which temporarily became the common ground for strategic action by New and Old Christians interested in social, political, and cultural change driven by an inclusive vision of society.

The public debate on the blood purity statutes received an extraordinary degree of encouragement from the *Discurso acerca de la justicia y buen gobierno de España en los estatutos de limpieça de sangre*, published in 1599 by the Dominican Fr. Agustín Salucio, the son of an Italian money changer.[108] Salucio considered that the statutes were harmful to good government because they militated against justice and mercy. He denounced them as contrary to the principles of the universal Church instituted by Paul of Tarsus;

they prevented the conversion of people who were thus unable to find their place either in Christendom or in the republic.[109] The power of these statutes should be curbed, since they were against distributive justice, against the division of land and public office in fair proportion and according to merit, and against good reason and equity.[110] The perpetuation of the infamy of caste, according to Salucio, damaged the people's will to serve their king, embedding inequality and harsh treatment in society.[111] He also derided pretentions to blood purity in the face of demographics: one single man could have a million descendants in thirty generations.[112] When he wrote about the common benefits that curbing the statutes would bring, Salucio was clearly inspired by the notion of reason of state.[113] He knew that the defenders of the blood purity statutes were difficult to defeat, so he ended up suggesting the limitation of enquiries to three generations.

A lesser known text by Agustín Salucio, *De origen de villanos que llaman christianos viejos*, engaged further with the origins and genealogy of the Old Christians, looking at how these would have emerged after the conquest of Iberia by the Muslims.[114] Salucio noted that the vanquished withdrew to the North of Spain, while many Christians who did not withdraw infamously submitted to the Muslims. These Christians were called *mozarabes* and their communities shrank in size over time, because some of their members converted to Islam to avoid paying tribute. Salucio related the notion of superiority of lineages to that of prizes for conquest, meaning access to property and the advantage of having a *solar* (manor), the origin of nobility and *hidalguia* status.[115] When the Christians were once again victorious, the mozarabes became subordinated to these new conquerors and became known as *villanos* (plebeans or rustics). In time, superior and inferior Christians mixed with each other, while the latest (Christian) conquerors tried to assimilate Jews and Muslims. Salucio opposed the policy of gentle conversion, suggested by Alphonse the Wise at his time, to the later policy that sought the exclusion of New Christians from military orders, colleges, and churches. Christians resulted from this long-term reorganisation of allegiances due to successive conquests; they were descended from Muslims, Jews or mozarabes, just as Muslims had descended from converted Christians.[116] The text is abruptly interrupted at this point. What matters here is not historical accuracy but the argument of successive changes, assimilations, and reassimilations resulting from conquest; it challenges assertions of long-term blood purity.

The arsenal of arguments against the blood purity statutes was thus well developed by the end of the sixteenth century. These arguments were shared by a significant number of laymen and members of other religious orders, particularly the Jesuits. Pedro de Ribadeneira, Antonio Possevino, Diego de Guzmán, García Girón de Alarcón, and Juan de Mariana were among the Jesuits who sought to intervene, but they were unable to prevent the introduction of blood purity status in their order in 1593.[117] The defenders of blood purity statutes were more powerful in the royal court, aristocracy, colleges, military orders, some cathedral chapters, religious orders, and municipalities. The junta created by Philip II to reform the implementation of the statutes did not reach a conclusion, and the attempt to extend this initiative to the early years of the reign of Philip III by the Duke of Lerma was defeated.[118] The discussion around the expulsion of Moriscos, implemented between 1609 and 1614, temporarily removed the blood purity debate from the forefront of politics, but it came back in the 1620s and 1630s.

4. General Pardon

The conflict of values—blood against merit, enquiries into blood purity against integration provided by baptism, entitlement of those of supposedly pure ethnic descent over the newly converted, discrimination based on ethnic prejudices against a universal Church—had reached a new intensity by the end of the sixteenth century. Four factors contributed to this exacerbation of the conflict of values: first, renewal of the New Christian elite connections, presence, and public participation within the Iberian Union of Crowns; second, the public debate that followed, in which values of merit, capacity, and ability were promoted to force the boundaries of access to public jobs and honours; third, the beginning of the secular economic downturn; and fourth, the financial crisis of the Iberian Crowns, mainly caused by growing commitments in various fields, including the breakdown of the territories under Habsburg rule with the revolt in the Netherlands, and the increasing costs of war. At the turn of the seventeenth century, the first significant cracks began to show in the Habsburg control of a good part of Europe. At the same time, the Union of Crowns achieved by Philip II in 1580 meant the absorption of the Portuguese Empire, which stretched from East Asia to the Americas. This overstretching created new possibilities for dynamic social groups, mainly the New Christians, but at the same time imposed new commitments and new protection costs on the monarchy, owing to the extension of the war in the Netherlands to the Atlantic and the Indian Ocean.[119]

While New Christian migration to tolerant cities in Christian Europe and the Ottoman Empire had been driven by inquisitorial persecution in both Castile/Aragon and Portugal at various periods between the 1480s and the 1570s, the Union of Crowns meant new possibilities for investment and trade. New Christians were in a particularly good position, because they had accumulated capital through trade in spices, precious stones, textiles, and porcelain from Asia; slaves from Africa to Iberia and the Americas; sugar from Brazil; and gold, silver, hides, and cochineal from the New World. They could face the financial crisis in Spain in 1575 and the Portuguese defeat in North Africa in 1578. Despite prohibitions on moving abroad or to other parts of the Iberian world, that is exactly what many wealthy and not so wealthy New Christians did. Seville and Madrid became the major destinations, but Havana, Vera Cruz, Mexico, and Lima were also favoured. These movements brought renewed connections between Portuguese and Castilian New Christian families, increased their presence in trade in the West Indies, and facilitated their participation in contracts to farm rents, provide fleets, and lend money to the Crown in Castile.[120]

New Christians became more vocal as these changes proceeded. They were supported by the development of economic thought, which argued in favour of trade and industry to produce wealth and keep the royal finances afloat, and which reflected the creation of a strong merchant culture. The value of their aptitude for production and trade, coupled with their capacity for negotiating and supporting the financial needs of the king, led to a new assertiveness among them concerning merit and the right to be considered for honours as a reward for royal service. The ability and capacity of New Christians were understood by some of the Old Christians involved in public administration, but traditional elites felt threatened by this competitive new elite, whose forced religious integration had made them eligible for all public and ecclesiastical jobs.

The diffusion of blood purity statutes in Portugal responded to the debate in Madrid around enquiries into blood purity. Gestures in favour of the limitation of enquiries were contradicted by renewed inquisitorial prosecution, primarily in Portugal but also in Castile.[121] In the meantime, the turn to the seventeenth century proved to be one of the most fragile periods for royal finances. Suspensions of interest payments by the Crown, also called bankruptcies, occurred in 1596 and again in 1607. They were followed by the renegotiation of the debt, because the Spanish state could not survive without borrowing money.[122] However, it meant that the Spanish government was unable to service the debt in the final years of the reign of Philip II and the initial period of the reign of Philip III. War with the Netherlands explains part of the burden, because the Crown needed to borrow the money it paid out in Flanders, using the silver cargoes from Spanish America as a guarantee. War with the Dutch extended to the Atlantic and Indian Oceans, resulting in heavy trade losses and reduced royal income.

For New Christians, this turmoil meant loss, but it also opened a window of opportunity because of the informal breakdown of rules. The growing presence of New Christians financiers in this period would lead, in the late 1620s, to an incomplete shift from Genoese bankers to *converso* bankers. During this time, New Christians built up their financial strength, supported by increased access to West Indies trade and royal contracts in all fields. Contrary to the opinion that the arrival of Portuguese New Christians compromised the relative integration obtained by their relatives in Castile, the former apparently renewed their family links across borders and reinvigorated the ethnic presence at the political centre.[123] Under pressure from New Christians, the old system of privileges was shaken up, although not defeated. An analysis of this new level in the values struggle will complete this section, with a focus on increased persecution by the Inquisition, which was met with protest, appeal, and denunciation of their persecutors' methods by the victims.

The Union of Crowns created a new dynamic of inquisitorial repression. The numbers in Castile are not overwhelming in this period, but we know that several traders and financiers were already targeted. The case of Portugal is easier to elucidate, owing to better archives and estimates by the Inquisition itself: 8,363 trials, excluding the tribunal of Goa, from 1536 to 1605, and between 60 percent and 80 percent of New Christians accused of Judaism.[124] The number of trials increased by more than one-third in the 1580s, compared with the previous decade, and more than doubled in the 1590s.[125] This extraordinary increase in trials came with a parallel strengthening of the control of blood purity. The Union of Crowns brought new statutes to Portugal— the major expansion in the use of blood purity statutes occurred precisely between 1580 and 1640—and, most importantly, a new zeal in implementing the exclusion of New Christians.[126] This Portuguese side of the blood purity debate has been neglected, but it played a crucial role both in Portugal and in Castile.

The escalation of persecution of, and restrictions on, New Christians came as a response to their growing presence in religious orders, military orders, and public jobs, primarily in Portugal but also in Castile. However, the widely accepted idea that the arrival of Portuguese New Christians would have had a tremendous impact on Castile after the 1580s, an impact that would have negatively affected the long-term integration of Castilian New Christians, has been rightly made more nuanced by Pilar Huerga Criado. This historian has demonstrated that many local communities in Castile at the time, mainly in Andalusia, Murcia, Extremadura, and La Mancha, showed signs of resilience, having kept their cohesion despite suffering inquisitorial persecution. Huerga Criado found a significant number of New Christians condemned to autos da fé in those regions during the second half of the sixteenth century, mainly from the 1560s onwards, who had not migrated from Portugal but belonged to old, well rooted local communities of New Christians who were accused of Judaism.[127]

My own research, based on individual cases, has shown that old links between the Castilian and Portuguese branches of families had not been broken. The well-known case of the Gomes de Elvas Coronel family and many others at various levels reveal the propensity of New Christians to travel between Portugal and Castile, where they obtained support for requests to the Crown or, eventually, passage to Rome. The migration of Portuguese New Christians after 1580 renewed those links and contributed to supporting New Christian communities in their struggle for social and political mobility. However, an undeniable national problem was posed by the arrival of many successful, wealthy Portuguese New Christians in Castile and the Spanish Empire, because they had allegedly violated the rule of separation of empires and in many cases had not obtained permission to travel. Although many bought their way into local communities and managed to obtain recognition and permission to stay (including through matrimonial alliances), when conflict or crisis arose they were an easy target because of the readiness of anyone they crossed to hurl accusations of Judaism. In part III, how this defensive strategy towards local competitors became more intense in the first third of the seventeenth century will be shown, but signs of conflict already existed in the last decades of the sixteenth century.

The escalation of inquisitorial persecution in those years led many New Christians to appeal to Rome. In 1596, two artisans, both named Manuel Fernandes, who had been reconciled by the tribunal of Évora, decided to denounce in Rome their conditions of detention and the way they had been forced to produce confessions to save their lives. In 1598, three other New Christians, two brothers, Afonso Duarte and Duarte Pinto, and their cousin, Jerónimo Duarte—in this case, members of a wealthy merchant family—travelled to Rome, where they placed themselves under the authority of the pope and the Roman Inquisition to respond to the accusations levelled against them by the Inquisition of Évora. Again, the unfairness of the Portuguese inquisitorial procedure was denounced. In this case, the pope asked the Inquisition of Évora to send him the accusations, which the Inquisition put off doing for as long as they could.[128]

More serious was the case of Ana de Milão, wife of Rodrigo de Andrade, detained by the tribunal of Lisbon in 1602 under the accusation of Judaism. The husband, then a New Christian procurator in Valladolid where he was negotiating a general pardon for the New Christians, went straight to Rome, where he appealed to the pope and the Roman Inquisition, because he believed his wife had been detained in retaliation for his initiative. The pope issued a brief ordering the trial to be moved to Rome, which was done after renewed papal orders.[129] However, successive delays meant that Ana de Milão was only released in January 1605 because of a general pardon issued by the pope and implemented by King Philip III, following a donation of 1,800,000 cruzados from the New Christians.

The first denunciation of Ana de Milão, made by an Old Christian servant, Francisca da Costa, occurred on January 16, 1601, triggered by the servant's new confessor, a Jesuit. The previous confessor, the priest Domingos Fernandes from the Church of St. André, who came to confess all the family at the Church of St. Mamede, never mentioned to the servant the need to denounce what she saw in the house.[130] Francisca da Costa denounced the family's refusal to eat pork meat or fat, their practice of clearing the fat from the meat when they prepared beef and chicken, the removal of blood from meat with water and salt, and the frying of onions and broad beans with olive oil. She also mentioned strange prayers intoned at the window whilst those praying looked at the sky. The inquisitors took note and asked for other witnesses. It took a year for the inquisitors to request the testimony of other servants of Ana de Milão, the first being questioned on January 21, 1602, when Rodrigo de Andrade was already in Valladolid, and a month before his wife's detention.

The same type of accusations were produced, focusing on culinary practices—apparently Old Christians favoured pork fat for frying, and so Moriscos and New Christians could be accused or religious deviance for frying with olive oil. Margarida Antunes added that when they stayed on the Palma farm in Alvalade, near Lisbon, Ana de Milão cried for the New Christians executed in the auto da fé saying that it was sad whether they had indeed committed crimes or whether they were innocent.[131] Luzia Ferreira, a Japanese aged thirty, who had been living in Portugal for nineteen years, having been freed in Malaca by João Ferreira because, as a Japanese, she could not be a slave, had also served the family. She defined herself as an Old Christian, in a second session where she confirmed the previous denunciations and added that rabbit, hare, and seafood were also excluded from her employers' cuisine. Ana de Milão's rosary did not have a cross, and the scripts she used to pray were psalms in the vernacular (the scripts were taken by another servant and shown to the Jesuits).[132]

It was on the testimonies of these three servants that Ana de Milão was detained, a tactic the Inquisition deployed in numerous trials. The decision to take testimony from the other two servants was clearly made to justify the trial. Rodrigo de Andrade was right in his assumption: it was retribution, a standard practice of the Inquisition. Resentment resulting from punishments or unfulfilled promises made to her was a possible motive for the first witness, but extortion should not be excluded, and this was an accusation levelled by the sons of Ana de Milão—Francisco de Andrade and André Rodrigues—who tried to convince the servants to deny their previous declarations (as they further declared to the Holy Office).[133] The inquisitors had all the means they needed to accumulate information on the household's activities. They knew that Ana de Milão's daughter, Beatriz de Andrade, had married the merchant António da Veiga, who was living at the Ximenes' Terreiro (the Ximenes family compound). They knew all the names of relatives from witness testimonies and from the first session of the tribunal, which dealt with the genealogy of the accused.

It is obvious that the family knew who had denounced them, which also raises the issue of leaks from the tribunal by jailers, secretaries, deputies, or even inquisitors. Wealthy New Christians had their channels of information, but they were under constant threat, mainly from their servants. It is also worth noting the cooperation in those years between the Jesuits and the Inquisition, even at the risk of violating the confidentiality of the confessional.

Ana de Milão firmly denied the accusations and produced *contradictas* against the (supposed) witnesses, accusing them of basing their evidence on enmity owing to punishments and promised marriage dowries that failed to material-ize (as in the case of Luzia Ferreira).[134] She was liberated on January 25, 1605, after three years in jail without a sentence, only because of the publication of the general pardon. Along with all the other prisoners, she was released after taking an oath to respect the confidentiality of what she had experienced and seen at the Inquisition.[135]

The turn of the seventeenth century thus saw a significant increase in appeals to Rome, primarily by New Christians but also by Old Christians who felt provoked by the Inquisition. This was the case with the priest Miguel Lac-erda, who had supported the general pardon when consulted by the authori-ties, and also in his sermons, and who was subjected to the usual retribution by being prosecuted. He denounced the secrecy of inquisitorial procedure as invented to grant indemnity to rebels, brazen enemies of people defamed, and malefactors eager to spread calumnies and stain innocents who had no rem-edy, while he insinuated that the Inquisition was more powerful than the all-powerful hand of God.[136] At the same time, there was a sequence of initiatives by New Christians who, between the 1580s and the 1600s, petitioned the royal court trying to enhance their own social position and have the Inquisition restrained. This sequence of actions seems to have started earlier than the records of the Inquisition suggest, because there are signs that a pardon might have been discussed in 1587.[137]

In 1591, a first recorded representation to Philip II requested access to honours, offices, and benefices, as well as authorisation to seek a general pardon from the pope.[138] The banker Heitor Mendes de Brito seems to have been responsible for this petition, with the contractor Manuel Gomes de Elvas. This contractor was at court dealing with the affairs of D. António Prior of Crato, the defeated pretender to the throne of Portugal, while supervising a new contract for the provisioning of forts in North Africa, in which were also involved Jerónimo Duarte Ximenes and later Tomás Ximenes.[139] Mixing contract negotiation with requests for honours and a general pardon for New Christians seems plausible, and such negotiations occurred at various times.

In 1594, another New Christian delegation went to Madrid with the same purpose. They suggested cancelling the 225,000 cruzados owed by the Crown on a contract, made by King Sebastian, which guaranteed the free move-ment of New Christians. King Henrique had promised to reimburse the New Christians should he break this contract, which he did, but he had only paid 25,000 of the total. In addition to this, 150,000 cruzados had been owed by the Crown to the New Christians since the time of King John III. On top of this the New Christians offered to pay 400,000 cruzados.[140] This strategy was particularly clever: it reminded the king of large debts owed because of breaking contracts signed with New Christians, promised to forgive those debts, and offered more money.

The death of Philip II and the accession to the throne of Philip III, in 1598, created another window of opportunity resulting from royal financial problems and the growing blood purity debate. New Christians wanted to offer 675,000 cruzados, 300,000 immediately and the rest in October 1599, plus a loan of 500,000 ducados, without interest, to be applied to provisioning the *carreira da Índia* and reimbursed in the form of pepper, half in 1600 and the other half in 1601.[141] The Portuguese Inquisition was already aware of these proposals and sensed a change in attitude at the top. They made representations opposing the proposals, and they mobilised the bishops— particularly the archbishop of Évora, the bishop of Leiria and the bishop of Algarve, the latter two of whom would become general inquisitors. In 1599, the bishops wrote letters to the king opposing the pardon, while the governors of Portugal promised a payment of 800,000 cruzados, which was immediately opposed because it required approval from the *cortes*.[142]

In 1600, New Christian merchants Jorge Rodrigues Solis and Rodrigo de Andrade went to Valladolid to negotiate the contract for farming Portuguese customs rents, and at the same time they renewed the request for a general pardon, with the support of João Nunes Correia, then a major contractor in Seville.[143] This time, Philip III decided to take the matter seriously and organised a junta of notables from various councils to consider the offer. Even more threatening to the Inquisition, the king decided to launch an enquiry into the management of property confiscated by the Inquisition. The enquiry revealed a chaotic situation with an absence of control by the general council, arbitrary procedure, and embezzlement. Radical changes were discussed but never implemented.[144]

The turning point came in April 1601, when Philip III authorised travel and the sale of property by Portuguese New Christians against a payment of 170,000 cruzados, increased later by another 30,000 cruzados concerning settlement in the Spanish dependencies.[145] This explains why the debate around these decisions, which was prolonged until the 1620s, always mentioned the 200,000 cruzados of the contract with the New Christians. In October 1601, the king suspended autos da fé in Portugal and ordered his ambassador in Rome, the Duke of Sessa, and Martim Afonso Mexia, representative of the Crown of Portugal, to ask the pope for a general pardon for the Jewish sins of New Christians. The brief should mention the payment of 800,000 cruzados, besides the 225,000 owned by the Crown to the New Christians.[146] This sequence of actions prompted a series of strong communications from the Inquisition and the bishops to Rome and Valladolid, which again revealed a structural articulation between the interests of the two institutions.[147] The three Portuguese bishops—of Évora, Lisbon, and Braga—went to Valladolid, accompanied by Martim Gonçalves da Câmara and the Jesuit Francisco Pereira, who opposed granting any pardon to the New Christians.

The next two years saw an impasse owing to the enormous pressure on Valladolid, while in Rome the cardinals and the pope opposed any reference to the service payment in a papal brief. In 1603, a junta created by Philip III voted to approve several articles for Inquisition reform, but these were never implemented. In the meantime, an absence of general inquisitor in Portugal, following the forced resignation of António de Matos de Noronha in 1599, was not remedied by the appointment of Jorge de Ataíde in 1600, because the latter never took up his post, nor by the brief appointment in 1602 of Alexandre de Bragança, archbishop of Évora, because one year later he was removed from the post.[148]

In 1604, the Portuguese New Christians renewed their offers to the king through Afonso Gomes, assisted by the contractor João Nunes Correia, while the king renewed pressure on his ambassador in Rome to obtain the brief he wanted. In June that year, the king again stopped holding autos da fé. On August 23, 1604, the papal brief *Postulat a nobis*, with a general pardon, was finally issued, although it was not published in Portugal until January 16, 1605, when it led to the liberation of 410 prisoners from the tribunals of the Inquisition. D. Pedro de Castilho was appointed both general inquisitor (in August 1604) and viceroy (in December 1604) and charged with supervising the implementation of the papal brief of general pardon, in which role he was unable to prevent a series of riots that were followed by judicial action and punishment.[149] For the general pardon, King Philip III was promised 1,700,000 cruzados by the New Christians, while the old debt of 225,000 was cancelled. The Duke of Lerma received 50,000 cruzados, and other dignitaries of the royal court another 50,000 cruzados.[150]

The New Christian strategy of seeking a general pardon was not supported by all the community. Gastão de Abrunhosa, while in Rome, kept his distance from the request for a general pardon, stating that he did not want mercy but justice.[151] Internal division among the New Christians only became public nine months after the publication of the general pardon, on October 31, 1605, when a group of sixty-eight New Christians signed a petition to the Council of Portugal in Madrid, and to the viceroy, asking to be excluded from the lists being compiled for the levy. They denigrated the procurator of the New Christians, Afonso Gomes, who was considered a person of little quality or wealth, as well as the others involved in his initiative, whom they claimed had vested interests resulting from the detention of relatives by the Inquisition. The petitioners claimed to be the substantial businessmen (*homens de negócio de substância*) in the kingdom with notable ancestors, who had offered their services to the king in times of difficulty. They considered themselves to be united with the "Old Christians" of the kingdom, with whom they were in one "mystical body." They denied the existence of a "republic" or "government" of those of Jewish descent and rejected any separation into a category of "New Christians" for the purpose of paying for the general pardon.[152] Their arguments were substantially similar to those used in the debate about blood purity in Madrid.

The petitioners declared that they had previously informed the Inquisition of their disagreement concerning this initiative, and they had nothing to be pardoned for. They were against innovation and freedom of conscience. They objected to being penalized financially for an initiative they did not support. They considered it was an offence against them to have their names listed and stained forever in public records, because many of them were fidalgos, senior judges, knights of military orders, and other servants of the king related to the most illustrious lineages of the kingdom, whose ancestors never had any stain upon their name. They claimed that money was being extorted from them by people at a low level, who did not have the means to furnish the sums they had promised to pay.[153]

It seems that this petition was rejected, because the royal court considered participation in the general pardon compulsory for New Christians, with the partial exemption of New Christians married to Old Christians. Lists of New Christians were compiled and supervised centrally, with the payments being allocated by area: from the community of Lisbon 718,377 cruzados; from the remaining communities in Portugal 736,053 cruzados; from the communities of Castile 200,000 cruzados; from the communities in Spanish America and Brazil 87,055; and from the communities of India and the Far East 75,000. The collection of the contributions, seen as another tax imposed on a section of the population (and the New Christians had already been targeted several times), was spread over several years; by 1610, 1,549,225 cruzados had been collected, but there are indications of an outstanding debt in Madeira in 1618 and in the Estado da Índia in 1629. James Boyajian rightly notes how this exceptional tax was added to several other financial demands made on New Christians in the same period, particularly for the provisioning of the *carreira da Índia*, which was under constant threat from the Dutch.[154]

The petition of these New Christians against the general pardon points to serious internal divisions in the community, which surfaced in this tense situation but also at other moments of crisis.[155] Well-known names are involved: the petitioners named as their procurators in Valladolid, Rui Lopes de Évora and Luís Gomes de Elvas, both residents of Lisbon, and António Gomes de Elvas, a resident of Valladolid. The prominent Gomes de Elvas family is well represented here. The following year, the same Luís Gomes de Elvas obtained royal authorisation to purchase the important position of postmaster general of Portugal, which the family would hold for two centuries, despite harsh denunciations of their Jewish origin. There were other members of the extended family among the petitioners, such as João Gomes de Elvas, but not Manuel Gomes de Elvas, who was identified with the group seeking a general pardon. This may indicate that divisions also occurred within families.

Related families, such as the powerful Ximenes (António Fernandes, Gaspar, António), the Rodrigues de Évora (Gonçalo, António), the Veiga (Manuel, António, Joana, Rodrigo, Catarina), the Angel (Rui Dias, Jerónimo de Oliveira, Antónia, Jerónimo Fernandes), the Fernandes de Elvas (António, Jorge, João), and the Soares Sampaio (Gaspar and Manuel) families signed the petition, as did other important merchants, such as Francisco Duarte, João Godines, Diogo Nunes Caldas, Manuel Mendes Cardoso, Diogo Lopes Cardoso, and Cosme Damião; but the rich banker Heitor Mendes, identified as the initiator of the move for a general pardon, did not sign.[156]

There were also ambiguities in the groupings. If António da Veiga was the same António da Veiga who was the son-in-law of Ana de Milão (there were always people with the same name), it seems odd that he should have signed a petition which denounced the instigators of the general pardon as having vested interests, given that he had a relative detained by the Inquisition. In any case, the petitioners did their best to portray themselves as integrated, although the divide between them and the instigators of the general pardon cannot be clearly defined as being between the established and the outsiders. There were blurred areas on both sides, and integration was (nearly) always under threat.

My interpretation is that the petition expressed the concerns of a wealthy group, who saw their strategy of social promotion and integration as being put at risk by the retribution that would inevitably follow from the Inquisition. They were either trying to save themselves from this, or they simply considered that the general pardon was useless, an argument expressed several times.[157] In any case, it does seem that the accusation of extortion, insinuated here and voiced later by other New Christians, such as Duarte Gomes Solis, was accurate; Philip III and his ministers saw the opportunity to impose another levy. This does not look like a concerted action by the wealthiest members of the community. Who were the instigators of the move for a general pardon? The memorandum on the New Christians who negotiated the pardon was published without date.[158] It needs to be properly analysed, but it must have been written between 1632 and 1634 because it mentions that the heir of João Nunes Correia, a contractor in Seville, was being tried by the Inquisition. I have identified this heir as the banker, Juan Núñez Sarabia, imprisoned in those years by the Inquisition of Toledo.[159] Therefore, the memorandum was written thirty years after the events it describes, which is significant. The purpose of this document was to identify, and smear, the people involved, both New Christians and their Old Christians supporters. It is possible that these were the actual names of those involved, but we do not know up to what point or whether some of them withdrew along the way.

The author of the memorandum tries to demonstrate that all these New Christians were struck down in some way and came to a sticky end as a result of their involvement, and he implies this was the result of divine retribution.

He also mentions the archbishop of Évora, Teotónio de Bragança, who died in Valladolid opposing the general pardon, but that he certainly enjoyed a peaceful death. All this reveals the atmosphere of deep hatred towards New Christians fostered by the Inquisition both in Madrid and Lisbon, which reached its climax in the 1630s. It is possible that João Nunes Correia died demented after years of prison and exile, suffering on top of this punishment a fine of 300,000 cruzados, punctually paid. It is also possible that Manuel Gomes d'Elvas died mad, with his property confiscated as a punishment for usury. Allegedly, Afonso Gomes died in prison and his heir and nephew, Pedro Gomes Rodrigues, nominated collector of the general pardon by Philip III in 1605, was detained for debt and later prosecuted by the Inquisition.[160] If these gloomy details were correct, divine retribution seems to have been largely inquisitorial retribution, accompanied by the usual risks to royal bankers and contractors of themselves being prosecuted for debt.

The general pardon, to sum up, revealed the divisions among New Christians resulting from permanent persecution by the Inquisition, involving confiscation of property, and permanent demands from the royal court, eager to alleviate growing financial deficits. Some wealthy traders refused to be involved in the negotiations and the payment of the general pardon, because involvement could mean they would be listed and their strategy of integration as Old Christians exposed. It is a crucial moment, since it corresponds, in a distorted way, to efforts to reform the Portuguese Inquisition by New Christians, linked to the debate around blood purity that was looming in those years in Madrid. The contribution of New Christians to innovation in different areas, fuelled by the reinforcement of legal and economic opinions in favour of merchant culture, was part of a general debate on economic, social, and political strategies to respond to the perceived crisis of the monarchy. New Christians were considered a threat to traditional society, not only because they were competitors at all levels, but also because they contributed to the assertion of values based on merit against blood, service, and reward against racial discrimination.

An analysis of merchant culture shows the growing support for trade and merit related to economic output in which New Christians found support. It is true that the values of work and merit did not displace the values of blood and noble descent, but the repugnance for manual work became arguably less pronounced. Innovative behaviour by New Christians is attested in the spiritual searches of St. Teresa de Ávila, Luis de León, and Juan de Ávila; in works of literature in which the pastoral and picaresque novel were used to convey New Christian feelings about the past and the present; and in natural history, in which New Christians (and New Jews) were involved in the development of mathematics, new knowledge of the world of botany, the search to understand the circulation of the blood, and the foundation of obstetrics and psychiatry. Legal arguments against singling out minorities due to ethnic prejudices were part of this intellectual atmosphere. New Christians were certainly not the only agents of change, but they did play a role in this period. The blood purity debate results from the economic and financial crisis of Spain, but also from the new assertive position of New Christians in all areas of the economy and knowledge. The growing persecution they suffered as a result of the threat they represented to a social order based on blood purity led to a debate about whether to issue a general pardon, an action finally taken by the pope in 1604.

Conclusions to Part II

THIS SECOND PART of the book has analysed the expansion of the New Christian merchant elite in the second half of the sixteenth century. These traders' accumulation of capital was visible on different fronts, particularly in the Atlantic, where it was structured by the slave trade and the emerging trade in silver, hides, and dyes. The economic relations between the Atlantic and the Indian Oceans, and later the Pacific Ocean, were forged by the Portuguese and then by the Castilians, around spices and precious stones, but also around Indian textiles and Chinese porcelain. We have concentrated on specific networks around the trade with North Africa and the financial hub of Simón Ruiz in Medina del Campo to understand the economic and financial possibilities explored by New Christians within a transnational and interethnic setting.

The deployment of New Christians across the globe in pursuit of business was rapid. They reinforced their position in West Africa and the Americas and reached the Far East; in doing so, they created links to new and old Jewish communities, particularly in the Ottoman Empire but also in South Asia and those cities in western and northern Europe that were more welcoming to New Christians and Jews. The diversified portfolios of rich New Christians have been reconstituted, based on case studies of specific families with interests in trade, real estate, royal contracts, bonds, and tax farming in different European cities. Sometimes these rich New Christians even managed to gain positions among the titled nobility.

The contribution of New Christians to merchant culture and the assertion of values based on expertise, competence, professional skills, merit, service, and reward, has also been analysed. A summary of innovations in religion and literature has shown developments that started very early and reflected the possibilities created by the liminal position in which this ethnic group had been placed. The impact of New Christians on the sciences was particularly significant in mathematics, cartography, medicine, and natural history. They were at the forefront of those seeking to identify and collect new information concerning diseases, mineralogy, flora, and fauna in other continents.

Different times of inquisitorial prosecution of the New Christian elite in Castile and Portugal have been reconstituted to understand the turning point of the 1590s and early 1600s, seen here as a window of opportunity but also as an escalation of repression under economic crisis. The blood purity debate showed not only the new possibilities that opened for the New Christian elite at a central level with the Iberian Union of Crowns but also the retribution these people suffered from disciplinary institutions.

The analysis of the long and painful negotiations for the general pardon of 1604, which involved vast amounts of money paid to the king and the pope, and their main advisors, shows the frustrations of the conflict between persecuted and gatekeepers, between outsiders who were more and more present and integrated at different levels and the established who wished to keep barriers and exclude competition from a racialized ethnic group. These negotiations also showed the divisions among New Christians, because a good part of the wealthy layer considered payment for the general pardon another levy, following which their names would be listed for further discrimination and extortion in the future.

We have set out here the main features of a conflicted society partly driven by the struggle around honour, merit, and reward in which New Christians played an important role. Part III will show how this conflict produced contradictory outcomes in the following fifty years.

PART III

Resistance
(1600s–1640s)

THE TURN OF THE seventeenth century saw economic and financial crisis in Iberia, the Dutch asserting themselves in revolt against the Habsburgs, the creation of the English and Dutch East India Companies, which entered strong commercial competition overseas, and colonial exploration of North America by the English. In the first third of the seventeenth century, the capacity of the New Christian elite to expand their affairs in the Iberian world improved, thanks to the Union of Crowns. They were also attracted by the (virtual) absence of discrimination in France and Italy and by the possibility of reconnecting with the faith of their ancestors in the Ottoman Empire and in the new Jewish communities created in Livorno, Amsterdam, and Hamburg. The enlargement of intercontinental trade, even under growing competition, benefitted the New Christian elite, but the pressure on the Iberian empires by Dutch and English rivalry would create a dynamic of divergence between Portugal and Spain. This divergence would lead to the restoration of Portuguese independence in 1640. How did this new political reality impact the New Christian merchant elite?

The royal financial crisis during this period stimulated fresh ways of looking at how the economy was working, because the amount of money collected in taxes and contracts for regular loans depended on production and trade. Many Old Christians were aware of the difficult situation of the Crown and the kingdoms involved. New Christians suffered from internal divisions concerning religious allegiance and political strategy. The values debate, which was part of the blood purity debate, inspired the publication of a series of documents (*arbitrios*) proposing new economic policies. Both New Christians—who, arguably, wanted to show their engagement with the problems of the state, as well as signal their availability as lenders—and Old Christians contributed to this development. The publication of *arbitrios* declined after the 1630s, just when the efforts to reform the process of blood purity enquiries were dropped, and this confirms the link between the two. The first half of the century was a relatively open period, in which public opinion found ways to express itself, but it was punctuated by fierce persecution of New Christians by the Inquisition.

Reassertion of Old Christian institutional power was at stake after the general pardon of 1604. Even if New Christians were divided in their attitudes to the pardon, the Inquisition felt the papal and royal decision as a major blow to their prestige and status that required a response. Retribution was a persistent rationale for the activities of the Inquisition, and the history of the New Christians could be analysed as a cyclical pattern of distress caused by massive growing persecution, leading to a call for intervention that would result in temporary relief (paid for at a high price) through pardons and permissions to circulate freely, followed sooner or later by another period of retribution through increased persecution.

But the Inquisition was not alone in its involvement: its activities were favoured by the king, even when he appeared interested in compromise, while other ecclesiastical and civil institutions also intervened. Many bishops, both in Portugal and Spain, had started their careers at the Inquisition and collaborated with, or supported, the Holy Office in various ways.[1] Private interests were always at play, with Old Christians attacking New Christians for access to economic resources.

The chapter on conflict addresses the first years of this period, which centred not only on the blood purity debate but also on the constant battle surrounding New Christian privileges. These are referred to as *privileges*, since the ancien régime was not a society of rights. The chapter will be extended to the mid-1620s to observe the crucial period of 1618 to 1623, in which anger at the conflict became increasingly significant, and following which a new political atmosphere started to coalesce, expressed by the pardon to Portuguese New Christians, disguised as an edict of grace, imposed by the king on the Inquisition in 1627.

The Portuguese revolt of 1640 had an undeniable impact on New Christians, but it is not taken as a *terminus ad quem* to this part, because it is much more interesting to follow attitudes and behaviour before, during, and after major political events. In the chapter on politics, these features will be analysed to understand continuities, disruptions, and subtle changes. Royal bankruptcies could be devastating, but the restoration of independence in Portugal was a major political change. The effect of the revolt on the status of New Christians will be assessed both in Castile and Portugal, because each of the kings became more exposed. Royal finances, already overstretched, received a new blow in Castile, while in Portugal new resources were needed for the war of independence. Prosecution of New Christian bankers by the Portuguese and the Castilian Inquisitions certainly would not help the war effort.

The end of the 1640s seems a good point at which to conclude this part. In 1649, the Portuguese king's decision to exempt New Christians from confiscation of property, in return for investment in the Company of Brazil, had a major impact on the Inquisition. It was the equivalent of the general pardon of 1604, except that it moved the debate from the strictly religious to the economic issues of freedom of trade in the Atlantic. The company focused on protecting trade and recovering Brazil from the Dutch, which could hardly be opposed; while the link between New Christian financial support for the war of independence and politics related to the Inquisition was clearly stated, removing the initiative, temporarily, from the tribunal of faith.

New Christian elite managed to reach high positions as financiers to the Iberian king, and these positions were strengthened in the late 1620s and 1630s. This period could, therefore, be defined as one of consolidation by New Christian bankers. However, at the same time, inquisitorial persecution reached new levels, which created insecurity among merchants and worked as a push factor for emigration. Political disruption in Portugal affected different interests among New Christians, depending on whether their business was connected to the Atlantic or to the Indian Ocean, while in the 1640s it created a new social dynamic that deepened the divergence of interests among New Christians. Some of the financiers and major merchants made their choices and moved from one country to another, but many stayed where they were to protect the main assets and investments they depended on.

These trends were also affected by international politics, including the long war of Dutch Independence, the Thirty Years War, and revolts in Catalonia, Portugal, and Naples. The idea of resistance is a better way to approach the New Christians in this period. The background to their struggle needs to be better defined, which is the purpose of the chapter on business, where the evolution and constraints related to the main sources of New Christian revenue and contribution will be shown. The search for new markets and participation in Spanish America is one of the most important issues, but the well-studied development of Brazil and the resilience of New Christians in Asia need to be part of the picture. We shall be guided here by those names and families of merchants that have proved useful in previous parts of this study; again we shall see continuities and renewal.

The following chapter, on identities, is important because some of the main New Christian scientists, authors, and artists were directly linked to important merchant families, while others came from a more modest merchant or artisanal background. This chapter helps us to reflect on the religious and philosophical issues raised by the New Christian status. The issue of the Immaculate Conception of the Virgin Mary needs to be considered, not only for its long-term consequences but also for New Christian involvement. Moreover, the impact of New Christians on literature did not diminish in this period as a result of the new importance of theatre. Our investigation will be flexible enough to include authors who started writing in the 1630s or the 1640s and reached their prime in the 1650s, even though this takes us beyond the period fixed on for part III. The presence of New Christians in art still needs further research, and some of the findings are open to debate. The analysis will be limited to one case that has a clear link to the debate on values pushed by the New Christians who flourished in this period.

CHAPTER NINE

Conflict

WHAT WAS THE reaction of the Inquisition to the general pardon of 1604? How did the conflict of values evolve in this period? Were blood purity enquiries moderated following the indications of the debate launched by Philip II in the last years of his reign? How did the royal government define its policies concerning New Christians as it came under pressure from different sides? What strategies did New Christians put in place to enhance their position and access the upper layers of society? These questions will be dealt with in this chapter, but their political impact after the late 1620s will be left for another chapter, which will deal with political changes in the last crucial decades of the first half of the seventeenth century.

1. Reaction

The general inquisitor and viceroy of Portugal, Pedro de Castilho, decided to avoid any immediate exacerbation of the conflict over the New Christians, preferring to prepare the ground for a new assertion of the tribunal's powers. He even responded positively to pressure from the king, in November 1605, to rescind the penalties imposed on New Christians before the general pardon. He ordered visits to district tribunals and investigations into confiscated property, which confirmed the claims of bad management by the tribunal in Madrid. With the material accumulated from his investigations, Castilho prepared a new set of internal rules, which were finally printed in 1613, replacing the previous rules issued in 1552 and 1570. Procedures were not changed, but there was a more comprehensive and tight set of norms that were to be followed to avoid criticism of arbitrary practices. In the meantime, the general inquisitor extended the diplomatic contacts of the Portuguese Inquisition both in Rome and in Madrid, using this network to insist that pardons would only make New Christians bolder, because they would never change their ways. He learned how to deal with the new political situation in Madrid, which he knew firsthand, having been involved in consultations there in 1603 and 1604. In 1608, with the agreement of King Philip III, he appointed the royal favourite, the Duke of Lerma, to promote the interests of the Portuguese Inquisition.[1]

This soft policy bore fruit. In 1606, the king limited what had been the free circulation of New Christians to mobility only with special authorisation, and this in turn led to a full prohibition in 1610, thus violating the contract established with the New Christians in 1601, a legal issue still being discussed in the 1620s. In 1607, a royal decree promised an annual contribution to the Inquisition of nearly 7 million réis from the monopoly on gaming cards, although this proved difficult to implement. In the same year, the king imposed a decree of perpetual silence on a New Christian proposal to rent confiscation of property for 200,000 cruzados for ten years, which publicly exposed one of the main goals of inquisitorial persecution, extortion, transforming it into another levy, regular and predictable.[2] In 1608, the tribunal's power of detention on the evidence of a single witness, revoked under pressure in 1603, was reinstated.[3]

The list of prohibitions on New Christians from entering royal service and from social integration is staggering: in 1607, from tax collection; in the decade from 1610, from being judges and attorneys, medical doctors, and apothecaries; from joining confraternities and holding municipal jobs, although not in a systematic way; in 1613, from receipt of *tenças* (regular royal rents granted as a reward for service); and in 1614, from marriage with noble Old Christians.[4] Needless to say, some of this legislation was not systematically implemented, but it defined new legal barriers for New Christians and represented a clear reversal of policy by the king. It expressed an eloquent repudiation of the general pardon, which again placed New Christians in a defensive position.

Inquisitorial diplomacy in Rome was also successful. In 1612, Pope Paul V announced that New Christians would no longer be admitted to religious orders, nor could they provide care of souls (curacy); in the same year, the pope confirmed the exclusive jurisdiction of the Portuguese Inquisition on questions of bigamy. In 1613, the pope confirmed the jurisdiction of the Portuguese Inquisition over cases of confessional solicitation, which gave the inquisitors further control of clergymen. In the same year, access to the main collegial churches in Ourém and Guimarães was forbidden to New Christians.[5] The period of Pedro de Castilho as general inquisitor (1604–1615) was thus defined by apparent acquiescence in persecution and reassertion of the jurisdiction of the Holy Office, while the campaign to exclude New Christians from royal rewards, ecclesiastical jobs, and social integration reached new heights.

However, inquisitorial activity was not limited to diplomacy and bribery. The number of trials in the three tribunals of Lisbon, Évora, and Coimbra clearly declined after the general pardon: they went down from 2059 in the 1590s to 1275 in the 1600s (a drop of 38 percent) and to 865 in the 1610s (a further drop of 32 percent).[6] In fact, all the files and denunciations accumulated by the inquisitors for future trials lost their potency with the general pardon. The inquisitors had to start all over again with the work of collecting denunciations, because these had to relate to the period after the date of publication of the papal bull.

In the meantime, the inquisitors launched enquiries into professions "infested" by New Christians, compiling not only lists of New Christian clergymen, particularly those condemned or reconciled at autos da fé, but also lists of doctors of medicine and apothecaries accused of poisoning Old Christians.[7] They also launched new enquiries into New Christian migration, using information collected over several decades. The results of one of those enquiries, probably from the mid-1610s (the end of January 1614 is the only available date within many hundreds references), showed how systematic the inquisitorial spying at the local level had become—the names, family relationships, and destinations were compiled for people who disappeared from small towns in different parts of the country. The register mainly recorded recent departures, but there were also references to people who had escaped twelve, seventeen, and even thirty years previously.[8]

The towns in the interior presented the highest numbers of departures; for example, Serpa, Fundão, Monsanto, Celorico, Penamacor, Covilhã, and Guarda. The vast majority departed because they or close relatives had been reconciled by, or denounced to, the Inquisition, but others lost their livelihoods when they were discovered to be New Christians. Brás Camelo, an ecclesiastical attorney in the diocese of Miranda do Douro who went to Rome with his brother, was one such case. Most went to Spain, mainly Seville, Toledo, Badajoz, Murcia, and Llerena, which suggests family connections on both sides of the frontier—a suggestion confirmed by a close reading of inquisitorial trials, in which we find constant movement from Castile to Portugal, but also in the other direction. A significant number of migrants went to Italy, mainly to Rome but also to Livorno, Pisa, Ferrara, and Venice, because of the relative absence of prejudices against New Christians and the existence of established Jewish communities. A smaller number of migrants went to France, where communities of New Christians had been established in Saint-Jean de Luz, Peyrehorade, Bayonne, Bordeaux, Nantes, La Rochelle, and Rouen. There were people of all ages, in some cases entire extended families of fourteen or fifteen members, and nearly all the men were artisans and merchants, while the significant number of women is striking. Accusations of Judaism were noted next to some names in the register of departures. This document reveals an extraordinary level of permanent surveillance of the population throughout the urban network.[9]

New Christians of increasing economic status were persecuted over these years, sending a clear message that the wealthy would not be protected. The most flagrant case is the detention of Henrique Dias Milão and his family, on October 28, 1606. Milão was married to Guiomar Gomes, a sister of Ana de

Milão, whose trial provoked an upheaval in Rome, as was mentioned in the previous chapter.[10] Retribution was clearly behind this set of trials. Milão, then seventy-eight years old, born in Santa Comba Dão and resident of Lisbon, had been a contractor for *terças* (third part of municipal taxes) in Portugal and had traded with Brazil. One of his children, Manuel Cardoso de Milão, was the contractor for pau-brasil and lived in Pernambuco. Altogether, Henrique Dias Milão had five surviving sons (Manuel Cardoso; Gomes Rodrigues; Fernão Lopes; António Dias, also in Pernambuco; and Paulo) and four daughters (Beatriz Henriques, married to Álvaro Dinis in Hamburg; Leonor Henriques, married to the physician Henrique Rodrigues; Ana de Milão, who had the same name as her aforementioned aunt and whose husband, Manuel Nunes, was in Brazil; and Isabel Henriques), all between fifteen and thirty-six years old. Except for Leonor Henriques, all the daughters who lived in Lisbon lodged in the houses owned by Henrique Dias Milão at Pampulha, Alcantara, which faced the convent of Nossa Senhora da Quietação, founded in 1582 by Philip II for Flemish nuns.[11] They were all detained with their father.

The procedure was standard. The Inquisition asked the Franciscan confessors who assisted at the convent, particularly Fr. Gaspar d'Ayala, to place the houses under surveillance and collect any information that might be useful for the trial. On September 23, 1606, the weak link, Francisco Barbosa, a servant from a poor New Christian family whose parents had died, and who had been rescued from Madrid by Henrique Dias Milão, presented himself "spontaneously" to the Inquisition after being ordered to do so by his Jesuit confessor (one of several cases of close Jesuit assistance to the Inquisition in this period). He denounced the usual infractions of keeping Jewish fast days, observing Jewish food restrictions, and celebrating Saturday as a holy day, claiming that these involved all the family, including those relatives who had lived or were living at the Milão home, such as António Dias Milão, brother of Henrique, who had returned from the West Indies, and António Dias Cáceres, a widower who was also a brother of Henrique.[12]

On October 18, ten days before the decision to detain the whole family, Fr. Gaspar de Ayala was called to produce the results of his spying. These included keeping windows open late on Saturday, wearing freshly washed clothes on that day, and cleaning the house on Friday.[13] The detention of the whole family on the same day produced, under threat, the necessary reciprocal accusations. The interrogation had clearly been carefully prepared by the Inquisition. All family members were forced to confess, in the case of parents, after the draft of a sentence of excommunication had been read to them. Henrique Dias Milão refused to denounce his family, and he was accused of avoiding full confession, excommunicated, and delivered to the secular arm to be burned.[14] All the others were condemned to property confiscation, formal abjuration of apostasy, and perpetual incarceration, after being forced to learn the Catholic doctrine in the Escolas Gerais (the site of the old university in

Lisbon), which functioned then as a secondary detention site. After leaving the Escolas Gerais, they were placed in a supervised residence and compelled to wear the *sambenito*, the infamous garment used at the auto da fé to stigmatise condemned heretics, and one that would immediately be recognised by all who saw them.[15]

This important family was destroyed on very little evidence: they had to go through the humiliation of denouncing each other and all their friends, and were finally brought together at the auto da fé of April 5, 1609, objects of public shame, to witness the excommunication (equivalent to a death sentence) of their father and husband. The case of Fernão Lopes Milão reveals that the degradation caused by the system had no limits. This member of the family went back to the inquisitors after the publication of his sentence at the auto da fé to denounce the friends who had first alerted him to the family's denunciation at the Inquisition and had promised to help them. He probably committed this infamous act to prevent being arrested a second time, should these people decide to denounce him, which would mean straight excommunication.[16] When a first denunciation was openly known in the city, fear would stay with the victims and their friends all their lives. The famous secrecy of the Inquisition was never unbreakable. There were channels of information between New Christians and the tribunal's staff, and probably the wealthiest people had one or two inquisitors on their payroll, although jailers and clerks were easier to bribe (some cases will be mentioned later).

The outcome of the Milão family's trials, which imposed three years in jail, an average length of detention, plus another year in a designated residence after the auto da fé, is revealing: in addition to confiscation of the family's property, the inquisitors asked for a bail payment to dispense them from perpetual incarceration and the wearing of the sambenito. Fernão Lopes Milão managed to get away with pledges of gold and silver to cover 100,000 réis of bail instead of 500 cruzados (200,000 réis), because the inquisitors refused to accept pledges offered against the credit of relatives in Santa Comba Dão.[17] Guiomar Gomes, the surviving matriarch, had to pay 1,000 cruzados to free herself and several of her children, double the sum initially requested, because her daughter, Isabel Rodrigues, their servant, Vitoria Dias, and her sons Paulo and Fernão Lopes had already escaped without permission or payment, presumably to Flanders (dispensation obtained on June 2, 1610).[18]

On February 5, 1611, information was received by the Inquisition from the *alcaide* (responsible) of the Escolas Gerais that Guiomar Gomes and all the others left behind—Leonor Henriques, Ana de Milão, and Gomes Rodrigues Milão—had escaped to Flanders.[19] In fact, the family ended up in Hamburg, where they had links with the family Dinis, joining the Jewish community under the names Abensur and Israel, and recovering part of their economic status.[20] A final note on Gomes Rodrigues Milão: we know from requests for dispensation from punishment made by Guiomar Gomes that he suffered from epilepsy, which led to frequent accidents.[21] He stayed three years in jail and was condemned, on top of all his other penalties, to five years in the galleys, of which he served several months before he managed to collect 300 cruzados to buy his release.[22] Two years was the average life expectancy in the galleys;[23] five years was a certain death sentence. This penalty was another cruelty inflicted by these self-righteous guardians of Catholicism, but it was not gratuitous; it was obviously imposed to extort more money, as was common practice with releases from and reductions in penalties.

2. Radicalisation

Fernando Martins Mascarenhas's service as general inquisitor in Portugal (1616–1628) represented a dramatic increase in persecution. In the decade of the 1610s, 865 trials were recorded, but in the 1620s, 2,827 were instructed— more than three times as many. This was one of the highest levels of prosecutions in a decade of all time. Mascarenhas deliberately, as we shall see, used the instruction of trials and the presentation of victims at autos da fé as proof of New Christian perfidiousness. He repeatedly sent letters to the king and to the pope claiming that New Christians were all Jews at heart who only pretended to be Christians, that they should not be honoured by the king, and that they should be excluded from benefices by the pope. At the same time, there are indications that he kept links with New Christians.[24]

There were two consequences of this radicalisation of public discourse: first, it triggered discussion on the expulsion of all New Christians from Portugal, in the same way as the Moriscos had been expelled from Spain between 1609 and 1614; second, it contributed to a reassertion of the blood purity statutes, whose criteria for enquiry, mainly the number of generations investigated, had been discussed since the turn of the century. In the period from 1618 to 1623, a huge amount of conflict was centred on the New Christians of the Iberian world, owing to the exacerbation of the blood purity debate in the final years of Philip III and the initial period of Philip IV. Political weakness, coupled with the replacement of political personnel at the top, always represented open periods in which changes might be possible. In this case, both looser criteria for blood purity and rewards offered to New Christians for their growing activity at court might have been perceived to be on the table again, having been withdrawn from 1607 onwards. This would have stimulated new action by interest groups from both sides of the debate.

The visit of Philip III to Portugal in 1619, postponed since his acclamation, contributed to pressure on the New Christians, a development largely ignored by the available bibliography.[25] In 1618, Philip's advisers were eager to find local resources to pay for his trip. They ended up raising a levy on the municipality of Lisbon (610,000 cruzados), another levy on customs duties (30,000 cruzados), a loan from the *Casa da Índia* (65,000 cruzados), and a levy on the confiscation of property from New Christians by the Inquisition (40,000 cruzados).[26] There were traces of resistance by the general council of the Inquisition because the trials were not concluded, but the general inquisitor swiftly guaranteed "with legitimate and secure conscience, that the king could count on that money, and on even more if needed."[27] Subsequent events indicate that the general inquisitor took advantage of this levy to increase persecution and expedite the practice of property confiscation, with that property being sequestrated in advance, without waiting for the conclusion of trials. He thus seems to have found, two years after his nomination, a way of keeping the king happy while he himself was free to develop his persecution of the New Christians. Fernando Martins Mascarenhas declared at the end of his life that during his rule (1616–1628) the Inquisition had given 400,000 cruzados to the king.[28]

This same year of 1618 saw the collective detention in Porto of New Christians engaged in international trade. These merchants had congregated in Porto to escape the more intense surveillance of contraband activities in Lisbon. On September 17, Paulo Lopes da Cunha (a banker), Álvaro Gomes Bravo (one of the top merchants in Brazilian sugar), Pedro Aires de Vitória and his brother, Álvaro Eanes, Baltasar Fernandes Mendes, Francisco de Almeida, Simão Lopes Pinheiro, João Baptista, António da Fonseca, Cristóvão Lopes, and Manuel de Andrade were detained.[29] Other detainees were not merchants, such as the patriarch Lopo Dias da Cunha (a medical doctor aged eighty-three years who was excommunicated and executed); his wife, Inês Henriques; and his children, Luís da Cunha (also a medical doctor), António Dias da Cunha (a canon of the cathedral of Coimbra), Angela Henriques (wife of Cristóvão Lopes), and Gracia Espírito Santo and Filipa de São Francisco (nuns at the convent of Monchique in Porto). The merchants' wives were also detained two or three days later, while other merchants were caught a month later.[30] The memory (and long arm) of the Inquisition is confirmed here: Manuel de Andrade was the son of Rodrigo de Andrade and Ana de Milão, the couple mentioned earlier, who had clearly taken refuge in Porto for safety and economic reasons. The collective detention of New Christian merchants in Porto made an impact in Madrid, as can be detected in the correspondence of the Council of Portugal.

Still in 1618, the Council of Portugal, whose members engaged in the New Christian debate on both sides, suggested to viceroy Diego de Silva y Mendoza, Marquis of Alenquer, that condemned New Christians should be exiled. Although in 1627, the king gave the power of expulsion of those reconciled *in forma* and *de vehementi* to the Portuguese Inquisition, the tribunal never exercised it.[31] The only purpose of fierce rhetoric on the subject was to defame and marginalise New Christians; the Portuguese inquisitors never had any intention of losing their main clients and the reason for their existence. The discussion of this issue was kept alive in various meetings of members of the

Church and the Inquisition up until the *Junta de Tomar*, in 1629, without any other purpose than to keep up pressure on the king and keep New Christians on the defensive.

The two-faced behaviour of the Council of Portugal is revealed in their response to a request from a New Christian group for free circulation, guaranteed by contract in 1601 and suppressed in 1610, to be reinstated. In this case, the Council supported the request for legal reasons (the validity of the contract) and for economic reasons (the importance of New Christians in trading with sugar plantations in Brazil, increasing the country's wealth, and supplying the financial needs of the king). They went even further, praising the activity of New Christians in all areas, including the creating confraternities and providing churches and convents. Because New Christians were excluded from offices and honours, the Council stated, only trade was left to them as a way of life; otherwise they would exist in conditions of tyranny and servitude, contrary to the tenets of pious kingship and support for faithful vassals. They concluded that the contract for the free circulation of New Christians should be respected.[32]

But consultations by the Council were one thing and royal decisions another. In those years, the political situation was extremely fluid. A decree issued on April 20, 1619, forbade New Christians departing for France with their capital and families, and ordered control of ports.[33] Also in 1619, New Christians lodged another petition against the unfair procedures of the Inquisition, and this move was regularly repeated in the following years, while the *cortes* (Portuguese parliament), gathered in Lisbon for the visit of King Philip III (II of Portugal), presented an opposite petition to exclude New Christians from royal jobs in justice and finance.[34]

3. Defence

In 1619, an astonishing report was published, in which Portuguese New Christians' claims were presented by a member of the Old Christian nobility, Martín González de Cellorigo, who had been a lawyer for the Real Cancillería of Valladolid in Spain and for the Inquisition, before being appointed a judge for the confiscation of property.[35] Cellorigo was approached by an unidentified group of New Christians and agreed to present their grievances to the king via the royal confessor and general inquisitor, Luis de Aliaga. He justified his role as the voice of the New Christians by insisting that the notion of a republic relied on the fair government of many families by a supreme authority that guaranteed order, justice, and happiness.[36] The claims and grievances of the New Christian nation were based on the idea that hostility and mistreatment from Old Christians, owing to the honours and enrichment obtained by New Christians, had prevented the latter's assimilation in Portugal, contrary to what had happened in Spain. This was a very disputable idea still reproduced by Spanish historiography, but useful for Cellorigo's argument, which can be translated as Old Christians resenting New Christian competition for resources. Cellorigo also emphasized that the promises made by King Manuel that there would be equality between Old and New Christians, no enquiry into matters of faith for a period of twenty years, no property confiscation, and free circulation had been broken by the inquisitorial procedure.[37] He even gave a very plausible figure for Jews forced to convert in Portugal in 1497—80,000—which historians have not noted.[38]

Cellorigo highlighted the principal grievances of the New Christians, particularly those related to special inquisitorial procedure that led to the condemnation of innocents: names of witnesses and circumstances of accusations kept secret; false accusations accepted; false confessions and random accusations encouraged by long-term detention; condemnation of those who refused to confess what they had not done, a vicious system that had led Old Christians wrongly accused to confess to being Jewish; unwillingness to recognise injustice and absolve people falsely accused, who always thereafter had to endure some suspicion of heresy, which meant their public dishonour; and unwillingness to unmask false accusers and condemn them.[39] In addition, Cellorigo voiced grievances concerning the immediate sequestration of accused people's property, which was frequently sold before the conclusion of their trial and left many families in poverty. He also criticized the exclusion of New Christians from ecclesiastical and civil occupations, because this impeded them from earning a living and participating in the society to which they belonged. And, finally, he railed against prohibiting New Christians from leaving the country.[40]

Cellorigo proposed a general pardon to promote civil harmony and ensure the integration of these important members of the republic and the return of many of them from foreign countries. He argued that without the previous general pardon, the migration of New Christians would have been fatal to Portugal's interests; that guarantees concerning the security of New Christians' property and capital should be given; and that the aim of such measures should be the enrichment of Spain and the impoverishment of its enemies.[41] His opinion was that prosecutions should proceed with all speed, that the names of witnesses and the circumstances of the accusations should be revealed, that false witnesses should be prosecuted, and that a system of appeal to the general council of the Inquisition in Madrid (or that the Portuguese council should be moved to Madrid) should be created.[42] He also questioned the cruel destruction of families by the expulsion from their homes of relatives of those detained, so that the homes could be sequestered and sold. Accused persons, with their families, should live in their homes until their trial was concluded, and their property should only be sold in the case of a conviction. Provision should be made for spouses and children whereby they could avoid poverty and their inheritance would be guaranteed. Cellorigo rightly concluded that the arbitrary system being pursued was responsible for migration and for the transfer of capital to the Netherlands, France, and Italy.[43]

The idea that people should be stigmatized by being labelled New Christians was condemned by Cellorigo. He considered exclusion from religious orders and ecclesiastical benefices to be against the sacred canon and the practice of the Catholic Church. Exclusion from royal and civil jobs was also condemned as being against the idea of reward for merit and service. The main goal of the nation should be social harmony. The passage of one hundred years following conversion seemed sufficient, for Cellorigo, to prevent suspicion against New Christian descendants, and he thus aligned himself with those who requested a three-generation limit for enquiries into blood purity. He also raised the issue of universal law (he meant natural law) based on the equitable treatment of individuals, who could not be blamed as a result of collective assumptions.[44]

Cellorigo supported free circulation, basing this on long-held ideas about the economic advantages of trade and the fundamental importance for the kingdom of New Christian merchants and their role in intercontinental commerce. He also signalled the binding nature of the contract concluded between King Philip III and the New Christians, considering that its revocation was illegal. However, he added an interesting argument, that the free circulation of all true Christians would help to separate them from Jews. Cellorigo concluded his report by highlighting the wealth produced and brought to Portugal and Spain by the New Christians, detailing all the benefits in Iberia and overseas, and recommending a policy of harmony to overcome divisions.[45]

This short period of time can be defined as a rare favourable moment for New Christians in certain circles of the political elite. Political pressure against New Christians by the king was reiterated in 1620, when the viceroy of Portugal, the Count of Salinas and Marquis of Alenquer, Diego de Silva y Mendoza, was asked to give an opinion on a new financial project that proposed forcing New Christians to accept a reduction in the *juros* (interest on investments in the king's rents) taking this from 14 or 16 *el millar* (a thousand units) to 20 *el millar*, which meant they would receive interest of 1 cruzado on every 20 cruzados invested (5 percent) instead of 1 on 14 (7.14 percent) or 1 on 16 cruzados (6.25 percent).[46] The marquis was fiercely against the proposal because it would break the laws of contract, which were sovereign and should be equally binding on all subjects of the king, lords and vassals alike. In his opinion there was no reason to single out New Christians; the law would not allow it.

According to Diego de Silva, the proposal would also call into question the prohibition on New Christians selling real estate (*bens de raiz*, to which *censos* were equated), since they would need to reorganise their portfolios of assets. If the buying of juros had been fair, their retention must be accepted. The only way the king could revise the payment of his interest would be to squarely buy back the investments made. The marquis then went into detail, arguing that the main New Christians who had bought the rights to this interest would not accept the proposal, naming the family of the *Correio Mor* (postmaster general), the Gomes da Mata, descendants of the Coronel family; Heitor Mendes de Brito; Manuel da Veiga, the son-in-law of Francisco de Sá de Meneses (the name is a reminder that New Christians had married into the traditional nobility, a group that could be extended to include relatives of the Castro, Almada, Coutinho, and Ataíde), the Briandos; and Antonio Fernandes Ximenes, Rodrigo Ximenes, and others with this surname. He underlined that Manuel Gomes d'Elvas, the person with the most juros, had bought them at a rate of interest of 7.14 percent, and would never accept a change to 5 percent.

Diego de Silva pointed out that many juros were entailed, to avoid these assets being squandered by the purchasers' successors. In this case, the owners might be open to the reduction if it overruled the law of *morgado* (or *mayorazgo*). He also considered the case of New Christian women married to Old Christians, whose children would be damaged by this decision. The marquis reiterated that "His Majesty cannot in good conscience interfere in the matter of contracts with the people of the Nation only because of the latter's blood and cannot force them to accept demands not imposed on other vassals."[47] He then engaged in a disquisition on natural law and God's punishment for breaking it, citing the example of the Egyptians and their harassment of the Jewish people, and that of the Romans who committed atrocities against Christians. He concluded with further reasoning on the rule of law and the impossibility of allowing exceptions to contracts beyond any stipulated therein. The rule of law was here used against arbitrary discrimination and made explicit in a serious way.

The theologians and jurists consulted by the Marquis Diego de Silva were in sympathy with this strong opinion. Fr. Pedro Calvo, a royal preacher, also opposed the proposal, saying that it would be a scandal and against the law.[48] The Dominican Fr. José de Santa Maria considered selling juros to be the same thing as selling real estate, which was forbidden when New Christians were involved. The law must be protected by the king. A contract must be respected, and the only way out for the king would be to buy back the juros. He quoted Azpilcueta Navarro on licit contracts of censos, situating these in common, natural, divine, and human law. The reference to natural law underlined what was considered good, fair, and lawful. And Navarro expounded on the obligations established by a contract that could not be evaded by one of the parties to it. In this case, the transaction was fair, and the contract was licit, which meant the seller had to respect its terms entirely.[49]

Pedro da Costa, Professor of Law at the University of Coimbra, expressed the same opinion: the king was subject to the terms of the contracts he made and had to respect his obligations, including to New Christians. He signalled that New Christians could take legal action against the king in his secular courts to make him respect the contract, both as a person who had signed a contract and as a king and public person who must safeguard the law, including both contracts between his vassals and contracts between his vassals and him. The king was obliged to respect contracts with New Christians with the same *igualdade* (equality, but also equity) as those made with any other vassals. Pedro da Costa quoted Alexandre III, Augustine of Hippo, and Thomas Aquinas on the fair treatment of Jews.

Pedro da Costa was of the opinion that the equality of nations in the matter of contracts was paramount: there was no room for special dispensations in favour of the prince or those holding positions of honour in the republic. He refused the argument that any suspicion that citizens wanted to flee the country justified a breach of contract. And he went further, claiming that New Christians invested in juros and in real estate of great importance, which they improved with significant works; they contracted with the royal treasury; they invested their capital in many trades, and lent money to the army and the *carreira da Índia*; and they held prestigious jobs in the republic, had a good reputation, and were linked by marriage to the main noble houses of the kingdom. He concluded by insisting on the equality of all parties to a contract, quoting Luis de Molina (after having quoted Gomes, Lynus, Baldus, Bartolus, Paulo de Castro, Abbas, Joannes Andreas, and Innocentius).[50]

A final and lengthy opinion was given by Diego de Llereda, who also upheld the principle of equality between the parties when a contract was signed between Old and New Christians. Llereda pointed out that many juros bought by New Christians were now the property of Old Christians who belonged to the nobility or enjoyed other significant privileges, and he highlighted the ecclesiastical immunity of many New Christians owners of juros. He went even further than his colleagues in contesting the logic of suspicion against New Christians, insisting that they were people who remained in the country and invested large amounts of money in trade, which enriched the country and thus increased the customs income and the royal treasury. These were the people who were least interested in emigrating. He remarked: "There is nothing more satisfying to human understanding than distinctive judgement based on difference of reason and difference of foundation," a subtle pre-Voltairean assertion that prejudice represented lack of judgment.[51] He also looked at a significant number of biblical and historical examples of unfounded collective accusations. He dismissed what he saw as unfair discrimination against New Christians, pointing out that travellers usually carried plenty of hidden money with them, and no theologian would suggest sequestering anyone's money or property purely on the basis of suspicion. Finally, Diego de Llereda countered rumours and suspicions with clear facts, suggesting that if the king bought back New Christians' juros, he might impose on them the acquisition of real estate with the money received.[52]

This is probably the best set of opinions by Old Christians (supposedly—the background of the law professors is not clear), themselves part of the circle of power, opposing discrimination against New Christians as contrary to the rule of law. They reveal a surprisingly open legal and political discourse against discrimination, challenging royal policies designed to abuse *conversos* as fair game. However, the reduction of interest was eventually implemented. The voluminous collection of documents related to the chapel contracted as a burial place for the family on September 7, 1609, by the postmaster general, António Gomes da Mata at the Augustinian convent of Nossa Senhora da Graça in Lisbon (in the transept, on the side of the Gospel) indicates that in 1621 the interest bought at the customs of Lisbon, which was used for prayers in, and the fabric of, the chapel was reduced from 16 *el millar* (6.25 percent) to 20 *el millar* (5 percent), representing a lowering of the annual rent from 140,000 to 112,000 réis.[53] This decision is confirmed by a contemporary document concerning the chapel of the archangel Raphael in the same convent contracted by Diogo Lopes Ulhoa in 1610, which states that the king decided to reduce all interests he owed in Portugal in that proportion.[54] If this is correct, it means that the interest cut was implemented but it coincided with a similar cut in Spain decided on October 8, 1621, affecting both New and Old Christians.[55]

4. Exacerbation

The zigzag of royal policies concerning New Christians lasted from the later years of Philip III's reign to the early years of Philip IV's. These policies bowed to growing pressure to exclude New Christians from ecclesiastical and civil positions. In 1621, after many years of negotiations in Rome, the pope agreed that the blood purity rules should govern access to the chapter of the cathedral of Coimbra. In 1622, the archbishop of Évora imposed blood purity rules on the chapter of his cathedral, an initiative extended in 1625 to the cathedral of Porto, in 1638 to the cathedral of Elvas, and in 1641 to the cathedral of Lamego.[56] The ever widening use of blood purity statutes in Portugal never reached the same level as in Spain, but the period of the Iberian Union of Crowns created a curiously convergent dynamic in which Portugal, because of its belated take-up of blood purity enquiries, encouraged a backlash in Spain against attempts to limit the scope of such enquiries. At the same time, in this crucial period of 1618–1623, divisions among New Christians themselves became increasingly marked: while some, such as Duarte Fernandes and Manuel Rodrigues de Elvas, in 1621, were asking for a general pardon, others, such as António Gomes de Elvas, Melchior Gomes de Elvas, and Ruy Diaz Angel, opposed this request and clearly expressed their disagreement.[57] The divisions of strategy among New Christians would cut across the main families.

In these years, the Portuguese Inquisition prepared another coup, this time against New Christians at the University of Coimbra, in which the latter had held significant positions since the sixteenth century, particularly in medicine and law. The trial of the professor of canon law and canon of the cathedral of Coimbra, António Homem, detained on November 24, 1619, is well known, but is still in need of comprehensive study.[58] Homem was one of the best jurists in the country, regularly consulted by bishops and kings. He had contributed to the process of the canonisation of Saint Isabel (1271–1336), queen of Portugal, completed in 1625. However, he had accumulated enemies, particularly the inquisitor of Coimbra, Francisco de Meneses, a direct competitor, who had applied for the same position as canon of the cathedral and who later became rector of the university. It was another canon, Álvaro Soares Pereira, who first denounced Homem in 1616.

The Inquisition visibly put all its effort into producing evidence: the trial drew on around 1,600 folios and all methods of enquiry, including torture, were used against Homem and other members of the university. Accusations of sodomy were also pursued, with enquiries launched in various places, particularly in the convent of St. Eloy, Porto. The Jewish ceremonies described by witnesses seem unreal, and if those making denunciations had wanted to underline the absurdity of their accusations, they could not have done better, with tales of Homem presiding over celebrations of the main feasts, such as the Yom Kippur, in white clothing and a gold mitre, with the image of Moses on the altar as a Jewish patron saint. There were also ludicrous accusations of a fake confraternity devoted to the memory of Diogo de Assunção, a New Christian Franciscan friar executed in 1601 who proclaimed his Jewish faith until the end. His image would be placed on the altar for the ceremonies reported, another accusation of idolatry among New Christians.[59]

The story in summary is that António Homem, a New Christian only on his father's side, was condemned for both Jewish apostasy and sodomy and was burnt at the auto da fé of May 5, 1624, having denied all wrongdoing, even under torture. His became a famous case, used by the Inquisition from the moment he was detained to reinforce its propaganda that all New Christians were Jews, and that they had infiltrated academia and the chapters of cathedrals. It was also referred to by New Christians, in their regular petitions, as a clear case of the condemnation of an innocent. This case was related to thirty other trials of members of the university and of the cathedral's chapter. Manuel Lopes da Silva, for example, another New Christian canon of the cathedral of Coimbra, was burnt at the same auto da fé, having denied all accusations until the end.[60] Fernão Dias da Silva, also a canon of the cathedral, had been burnt at the auto da fé of June 18, 1623 in Coimbra.[61] The canon António Dias da Cunha, son of Dr. Lopo Dias da Cunha, had been arrested but was released on March 20, 1620. He went to Rome and wrote long letters to the pope and the general inquisitor exposing the conditions of detention and revoking all his confessions and denunciations.[62] However, in the short term, the Inquisition had the winning hand: in 1621, a royal decree forbade New Christians to apply for chairs at the University of Coimbra.[63]

The attack of the Inquisition against New Christian scholars, members of the chapters of cathedrals (then considered a top ecclesiastical position with access to significant rents), and other clergymen enjoying benefices did not stop there. In the same year, the Inquisition extended the persecution to dozens of New Christian nuns in five convents in Coimbra and the surrounding area.[64] Some of the nuns accused had their sentences read at the auto da fé of May 4, 1625. The full list of all those condemned at that auto da fé was printed—perhaps the first time this had happened—with the names of the convents in which each condemned nun had professed. At the end of the list, the total was clearly underlined—"one hundred eighty-nine people, including twelve nuns"—in case this had gone unnoticed. It reveals that the object was to defame New Christian nuns. This practice obviously contributed to what was becoming a spiralling scandal, and the following lists from autos da fé did not reveal the names of the convents of condemned nuns. The reason is obvious: those nuns who had been reconciled were still struggling ten years later to recover their convent places, which were denied them by their sisters, who tenaciously opposed reintegration in face of both papal briefs and inquisitorial orders.[65] They obviously wanted to "cleanse" their convents of the stain of deliberate public stigmatisation.

It has not yet been clearly established when the long-term collaboration between Jesuits and the Inquisition was disrupted. Révah places it at around 1623, but António Homem's trial might have played a role. He had been educated by the Jesuits and was certainly accompanied at his execution by Jesuits, who specialised in that function, and might thus have come to realise that many of the condemned were sincere Catholics. The way property confiscation was managed in these situations might also have played its part by arousing resentment. Homem's library was apparently not sold but given to the College of St. Paul, where it was used by Sebastião César de Meneses, then deputy inquisitor of the tribunal of Coimbra, while the big houses owned by Homem between the cathedral and the College of St. Cross were occupied by the treasurer of inquisitorial confiscations, Pedro Homem de Resende, who had allegedly obtained authorisation from the general inquisitor. It was widely considered that those houses should have been knocked down as major sites of Jewish rituals, whereas it was the smaller houses owned by another condemned man, Miguel Gomes, which were destroyed and ritually sprinkled with salt.[66]

Resende and other members of the tribunal, such as the inquisitor Sebastião de Matos de Noronha (in 1625 nominated bishop of Elvas, and in 1635 archbishop of Braga, making him primate of all Portugal, despite rumours that he had New Christian ancestry), appropriated services of silver and gold from António Homem and other condemned people and had their own family arms engraved on these. All this corruption was unveiled in 1628 by the inspection of Francisco Leitão, judge of the *Relação do Porto*, who interrogated builders, booksellers, and jewellers involved in the evaluation of the property and the engraving of the services. There is no clear indication, however, of what happened to Homem's Quinta da Capoeira property and its contents.[67] There is an important coda to this story: the inquisitor Gaspar Borges de Azevedo repented before he died. In 1627, he produced a document confessing his misdeeds and signed it in front of witnesses. This document listed irregularities in trials, particularly in the case of António Homem, and accused the inquisitor Simão Barreto of forging proofs and forcing confessions. This denunciation triggered inspection visits to the Portuguese tribunals in 1630, but predictably the general inquisitor threw out its content.[68]

5. Appeasement

The ascendance of the Count-Duke of Olivares, who became head of government with the accession of Philip IV in 1621, saw a considerable lessening of royal pressure on New Christians. There was first an effort to clean up corruption at the highest level, by confiscating the properties of the Cardinal-Duke of Lerma, replacing the president of the council of Castile, and the stripping power from the council's members, which brought the execution of the Cardinal-Duke of Lerma's favourite, Rodrigo Calderón, the arrest of Pedro Téllez-Girón, Duke of Osuna and former viceroy of Naples, and the exile of the Duke of Uceda and Luis de Aliaga. A *junta de reformación* was created in 1621, which discussed economic and administrative reform. The economic model of the northern countries was on the table, as was the valuable input of New Christian merchants. Reflection on the money supply and the state's damaging dependence on Genoese bankers, which had been discussed since the turn of the century, was reintroduced. The *arbitristas* played a new role, particularly the elderly Baltasar Alamos de Barrientos, while the inner circle of the Count-Duke of Olivares, the Jesuit confessor Hernando de Salazar, and the lawyer José González became very active. The challenge was to increase trade and industry, which would improve royal finances, crucial for the political project of resisting Spanish decline in Europe.[69]

In this vision, the management of New Christians was at stake, but financial and (limited) social integration was implemented with inquisitorial pressure. This apparently contradictory line of policy is immediately visible in the first years of government: in 1623, there was a royal order for New Christians procurators to withdraw from the court, with an indication that further petitions would not be admitted.[70] The same year, after renewed discussion of the blood purity statutes, genealogical enquiry was limited by royal decree to four generations, although it does not seem to have changed the rooted practices of various institutions.[71]

The battle for influence can be followed through petitions and *arbitrios*, correspondence and pamphlets. In 1621, Cristóvão de Sousa Coutinho presented a protest against António Gomes da Mata holding the job of post-master general claiming that the position had been in his wife's family for several generations; his father-in-law, Manuel de Gouveia, had been the last postmaster general of the family, leaving the job as a dowry to his elder daughter. The petitioner, who had exercised the job following the death of his father-in-law, from 1598 to 1608 (the dates are incorrect; it must have been from 1595 to 1606), had seen the job's confirmation refused in 1603, and three years later the position was sold to Luís Gomes de Elvas Coronel. Coutinho stayed at court for several years without his claim being satisfied, although he insisted that, with five daughters, three sons serving in the army of the East Indies, and a family background of governors of India, his claim was supe-rior to that of António Gomes da Mata, who was a Hebrew [sic], and whose elevation to the job contradicted royal and divine law [sic], in a period when most people of that nation were detained by the Inquisition or had run away from the kingdom. He offered to pay back 70,000 cruzados to the Gomes da Mata family (the cost of the job), while he promised an annual rent of 1,000 cruzados towards the maintenance of the carreira da Índia.[72] His request was not accepted, but the terms offered show how racial prejudices were explicitly mobilised when there was competition for positions and assets.

In this period of acute struggle all possible arguments were used against New Christians, some of whom joined in for obvious reasons: they wanted to be seen as Old Christians. Anti-Jewish literature was published in Portu-guese and Castilian and circulated widely. In 1621, João Batista d'Este, a Jew who had converted to Catholicism, published *Diálogo entre Discípulo e Mes-tre Catechizante*.[73] The following year saw the publication of one of the most racist texts of all, *Breve discurso contra a heretica perfidia do judaismo*, by Vicente da Costa Matos, which summarised all the previous prejudices and appeals for discrimination and segregation, and favoured expulsion.[74] Fernão Ximenes de Aragão, a member of a famous New Christian family established in Florence, contributed to this anti-Jewish trend with *Doutrina catholica para a instrução e confirmação dos fiéis e extinção das seitas supersticiosas e em particular do judaismo*, published in 1625, which might have been writ-ten to support the request for authentication of their blood purity presented in Madrid by the family's Lisbon branch (a request that failed.)[75] In 1631, the Carmelite Luís da Apresentação also published a text in this genre, *Demon-stración evangélica y destierro de ignorancias judaicas*, although this was less prejudiced than the other texts.[76]

Pablo de Santa María (1352–1435, converted in 1391, bishop of Burgos) and Alfonso García de Santa María (or Alfonso de Cartagena, 1386–1456, who suc-ceeded to his father as bishop of Burgos) wrote significant texts against Jewish theological tradition and in favour of Christian doctrine. They were part of the anti-Jewish model of debate, but they advocated the integration of the newly converted and the importance of baptism. The sixteenth and seventeenth century flow of anti-Jewish texts by Old and New Christians became less tolerant, stressing hereditary heresy and apostasy. These texts did not deny their authors' origins, but writers such as Ximenes de Aragão placed clear emphasis on the divide between sincere and false conversion and suggested appropriate rewards and punishments. Aragão's text, dedicated to General Inquisitor Fernando Martins Mascarenhas, advocated the expulsion of New Christians condemned by the Inquisition.[77] This was in line with the rhetoric of the Portuguese bishops and even of the general inquisitor, as voiced years later at the *Junta de Tomar* in 1629, although these advocates left the criteria for expulsion to the Inquisition to decide.[78] The general expulsion of New Christians, debated more intensely since the expulsion of the Moriscos in 1609–1614, had been rejected by the Inquisition, because they would lose the main reason for their existence and their financial resource.[79] There were also practical reasons: the inquisitors estimated that 200,000 families were New Christians, including families that had marriage alliances with Old Christians of all social groups, including noble families.[80]

It is against this background that we have to understand the petition presented in 1622 to King Philip IV by Duarte Gomes Solis, in which he suggested that responsibility for the carreira da Índia should be passed, under contract, to powerful businessmen; that control of the *consulado* (guild of merchants) should be returned to the merchants, who would use the associated taxes to improve the coastal fleet; that the rates of exchange at different fairs should be moderated by a counsellor; that silver coins should be mixed with other metals, as in Flanders, to prevent massive exports of silver; that the contract concluded with the New Christians at the beginning of the seventeenth century (1601), but since revoked, which allowed free circulation, including overseas trade, should be honoured, because New Christians had paid 200,000 cruzados for those privileges; and finally, that Jews should be allowed to establish communities in India, as they had in Rome and other parts of Italy, to promote trade. This last suggestion had never been formally presented before and the official responsible for reviewing the petition, Pedro Álvares Pereira, considered it an affront to suggest that baptised Christians should be allowed to return to Christian lands as Jews, although he favoured the free circulation of New Christians and permitting them to trade in both Indies.[81]

Duarte Gomes Solis has been rightly considered by historians to be a major voice speaking on behalf of New Christian and bourgeois entrepreneurship.[82] However, it is interesting to note the nuances in the opinions of Gomes Solis's contemporaries, as expressed by Pedro Álvares Pereira, an old member of the Council of Portugal. Pereira conceded that Gomes Solis had experience of the East and should be heard but maintained that the arbitrista did not represent New Christians and he was too prolific and confused in his writing. The counsellor synthesized Gomes Solis's reasoning in six points and made him sign a record of these. Moreover, he pointed out that Gomes Solis lacked control in the governance of his own affairs: his property and the inheritance of his daughter had been placed under the administration of his father-in-law, Heitor Mendes de Brito.[83]

That same year Gomes Solis arranged to print the full petition, with its complaint about the bad treatment of merchants, who were the most efficient resource of the state when needed, and who were men of truth and credit whose support rested on reason, weight, and measure.[84] He pointed out that merchants who were not Portuguese could negotiate freely in all Portugal's conquered territories, as, for example, the Jews and *Bania* (merchants) did in India, while Christians vassals of the king were still oppressed after three or four generations and condemned to successive impositions, such as payment for the general pardon of 1604, which provoked the flight of many New Christians to the Netherlands. Gomes Solis classified the general pardon as another levy, exposing its true nature. He mentioned merchants who, having become *fidalgos*, had relinquished their work as contractors and left projects unfinished, advising "de mercader caballero no fíes tu diñero, de caballero mercader guardate del" (don't trust your money to a merchant-knight, beware of the knight-merchant).[85] He criticised the withdrawal of the contract for the provisioning of the *carrera de Indias* from João Nunes Correia, the best contractor in his opinion, for the exclusive gain of people related to the *Casa de Contratación*.[86]

Duarte Gomes Solis also criticised New Christians, advancing a contradictory argument lamented by Pedro Álvares Pereira: on one hand he maintained that they were reliable, rarely reneging on their business deals; on the other hand, he criticised many for returning to Judaism, advising the king not to give them honours (to avoid envy), to keep a distinction between aristocratic Old Christians and New Christians, and to erase Old Christians who had intermarried with New Christians from the books of the *fidalguia*.[87] He went even further, saying—probably with some insight—that many New Christians were neither Christian nor Jewish, but he added later that New Christian merchants had spread Christianity in Japan.[88] Leaving these sections aside, the arbítrio is full of expert knowledge of trade in Asia, advice on naval construction, and discussion of interest rates on loans in Spain, access to credit, and the problems of excessive taxation.

In 1623, Jerónimo de Ceballos published *Arte real para el buen gobierno de los reyes y principes*, in which he proposed the creation of *erarios*, following the Italian model of *Monti di Pietà*, mutual banks based on low interest rates, but the project failed because of the opposition of local urban elites. He also reflected on Portugal's complicated system of taxation, suggesting the reduction and concentration of taxes to make them more efficient. Finally, he engaged in discussion of royal service and the need to develop distributive justice based on reward for merit, opposing the blood purity statutes as divisive and unproductive.[89]

These years produced an increase in conflicting visions, but there was a change of political atmosphere at work. In 1626, when the judge (then *ouvidor*) Francisco Caldeira was detained by the Portuguese Inquisition, his son Rodrigo Caldeira, knight of the order of Christ, made an immediate petition to the royal court (probably the Council of Portugal). He claimed that the detention had caused a furore (*estampido*) all over Spain, since the honour of many children, siblings, and relatives of a family linked to the most noble families of the kingdom had been called into question. He went on, "We children and those who met him know perfectly well that the accusation is false; it has caused to be detained and accused of being a Jew and an apostate a man who is a true Christian and a firm Catholic."[90] This is a very interesting case, because no traces have been found of any related trial at the Inquisition. It is not impossible that the trial record has been lost, since lists of the autos da fé in Lisbon were only kept systematically after 1632, but the best hypothesis is that the scandal was too big and the special pleading of the family with the authorities was so efficient that a discreet release was obtained. If this is the case, it was a rare example of the Inquisition bowing to government pressure, which would not happen after Portuguese independence.

{⚬⚬⚬⚬}

To conclude this chapter, it is important to note how the New Christian elite maintained a significant presence at the royal court, protecting their precarious position during the backlash promoted by the Portuguese Inquisition. The first two decades of the new century clearly represented the development of discrimination in Portugal, with the king and the pope reinforcing the position of the Inquisition in every possible way as compensation for the general pardon. The main benefits obtained by New Christians were revoked, particularly freedom of circulation, although their migration, either to other parts of the Iberian world or to countries outside it, never stopped. The Portuguese Inquisition accumulated new files and launched new enquiries, reaching an extraordinary level of surveillance of the movements of New Christians through the network of small towns. The period from 1618 to 1623 represented an exacerbation of the conflict, with successive projects for extorting money from the New Christians opposed by consultations and *arbitrios* in their favour, though the latter were not always very efficient.

Legislation against New Christians was produced even after Philip IV's accession to the throne, while the expulsion of New Christians was always on the table, particularly after the Moriscos' expulsion from Spain in 1609–1614. Practical entanglements resulting from extensive intermarriage hindered the operation, as well as the deep-rooted interests of the Inquisition, which did not want to lose its main market of "clients" (or victims). However, financial considerations, which always played a role in any struggle involving New Christians, and a change in the political atmosphere with the new government of Olivares, who favoured social appeasement and limited integration under constant threat, temporarily improved the position of the New Christian elite. We shall see in the next chapter how there was a turning point, followed by fierce new political struggle.

CHAPTER TEN

Politics

THE PUBLICATION of a new general pardon disguised as an edict of grace and imposed by Olivares on the Inquisition of Portugal in 1627 represented a turning point, not because it would interrupt inquisitorial activity but because it was part of a package negotiated with New Christian financiers in Madrid to encourage their rich associates in Portugal to migrate and upgrade their activity as bankers to the king. The same year saw the first bankruptcy (or suspension of payments) of Philip IV's reign. It opened the way to renegotiate the debt, at a loss to the Genoese bankers, who until then had been the predominant financiers, and produced a new informal agreement with the Portuguese bankers, who stepped in and filled the void to a certain degree.[1] The Portuguese had been acting as royal bankers for a long time, but now they had the opportunity to change their position in the power structure. Since the turn of the century, a long-standing resentment had endured against the Genoese bankers, who sent their profits back to their own country.

The idea of favouring a caste of natural bankers who would invest their money in the Iberian world had been developing over the years and was clearly in line with the interests of New Christians. However, this turning point was not followed by peaceful integration. The Inquisition, both in Portugal and Spain, did its best to derail this agreement, while the rooted interests of traditional elites were increasingly voiced against the newcomers, who threatened privileges of blood. It was a renewed struggle between the established and the outsiders, as Norbert Elias would put it for another context, in which New Christians turned Old Christians through fabricated genealogies and sham blood purity enquiries had their place on the inner side of the divide.[2]

The edict of grace of 1627 was used to obtain the collaboration of New Christian bankers in Madrid. Olivares opened the door for Portuguese financiers to contribute to royal loans now that the suspension of royal payments was having an impact on traditional Genoese predominance in this sphere.

Slow replacement—the Genoese did not disappear—was envisaged with this policy, which responded to numerous *arbitrios* that, since the turn of the century, had called for the involvement of native Iberian bankers in these financial operations. An informal invitation to Portuguese New Christian financiers followed, while the free circulation of New Christians was finally reinstated in 1629 against the investment of 250,000 cruzados in interests.[3] These three years represented a significant lifting of the extraordinary pressure imposed on New Christians since the general pardon of 1604–1605, but the outcome was mixed.

The edict of grace was a temporary solution swiftly pieced together to provide relief from the extraordinary levels of inquisitorial pressure on New Christians, but it did not create a new dynamic. The obvious advantage was that it avoided long and complicated negotiations with Rome. The disadvantage was that, as an edict of grace, it did not generate a real pardon; it accepted, under exceptional conditions, the confession and absolution of repentant New Christians. This meant that all the previous files of denunciations and confessions were not wiped out, as had happened with the general pardon of 1604–1605. It explains why the rhythm of inquisitorial instruction of trials only faltered briefly in 1627 and 1628 and was followed by a renewal of the previous level of persecution; there was no break. In the 1620s there were 2827 trials versus 2743 trials in the 1630s, defining a high plateau, which would be followed by a decline in the 1640s, probably a result of political turmoil (1426 trials).[4] There was also a political response from the Inquisition and its supporters: in 1627, there were riots against New Christians in Lisbon, Setúbal, Torres Novas, Santarém, Portalegre, Évora, and Coimbra, which placed Olivares in a defensive position. There was another riot in Coimbra in 1630 under the slogan "Death to the Jews"; and in 1631, the law professor Francisco Velasco de Gouveia, who would play an important role in the restoration of independence in Portugal, was reconciled by the Inquisition, which led to the retirement of most of his colleagues.[5]

Inquisitorial persecution continued undisturbed, but two events in the early 1630s created a new dynamic in the unfolding story of the New Christians: the violation of the church of Santa Engrácia in Lisbon, from which precious liturgical gold and silverware were stolen, along with consecrated hosts; and the claim made by a child in Madrid that his Portuguese New Christian parents whipped a small statue of Jesus Christ on the cross they had at home. The Lisbon case was judged by the civil tribunal, but the Inquisition helped to collect information. A New Christian merchant, Simão Pires Solis, was accused of the violation and robbery, without any evidence, just because he had been seen outside the church on the night of the event. He was condemned to have both his hands cut off, before being burned at the stake, with his ashes disposed of in the river Tagus.[6] The merchant's brother, Henrique Solis, a Franciscan, protested his brother's innocence and himself fled to

Amsterdam, where he assumed a Jewish identity. He was burnt in effigy by the Inquisition of Lisbon on March 11, 1640.[7]

The real culprit, an Old Christian, only confessed to this crime later, but naturally Pires Solis's name was not publicly cleared.[8] Simão and Henrique were both children of Duarte Pires Solis, an *asentista*, who was living in the Netherlands, according to the people who denounced Henrique. Most of his denouncers were from Paraíba, Brazil, having been detained and brought to Amsterdam by the Dutch during the (temporary) conquest of the territory from the Portuguese. They managed to go back to Lisbon, but there were more denouncers from different origins. Diogo Lima, a Jew converted to Christianity, declared that he had been present when Henrique Solis was circumcised in Hamburg, at the house of Diogo Nunes da Veiga, a man condemned in Lisbon one year previously. Henrique Solis had married a Jewish woman, had fathered children, and was living in Amsterdam.[9]

In Madrid, the case of the Cristo de la Paciencia, the small statue supposedly beaten by Portuguese New Christians, which allegedly involved bleeding and laments from the talkative artefact, gave rise to an inquisitorial trial. Some confessions were extorted, but the persons accused continued to reject the accusations. The statue was not found, having supposedly been burnt. The accused parents were excommunicated and burnt at the stake in the auto da fé of Madrid on July 4, 1632, a scene witnessed by the king and Olivares.[10] The general inquisitor in Spain at that time was Antonio Zapata, who had an anti-New Christian stance and supported the Portuguese Inquisition. These two cases exacerbated public opinion against New Christians and had an impact on King Philip IV.[11]

The first result of this was that New Christians were immediately persecuted in various parts of Portugal, mainly in Lisbon, where a significant number of murders was recorded, and in Coimbra, which was shaken by a riot of Old Christian students.[12] The second was an exodus of New Christians, with Francisco Manuel de Melo and Manuel Severim de Faria writing of the departure of several thousand New Christians from Lisbon for Madrid and Seville, and for France, Italy, and the Netherlands.[13] Reporting these departures might have been a deliberate attempt to destabilize the position of the growing number of New Christians in Madrid.[14] In any case, dramatising these events produced a change in public opinion and placed New Christians in a defensive position in relation to political power in Iberia.

1. Trials

The well-known trial of the Portuguese banker Juan Núñez Sarabia (or Saravia) was launched in July 1632, twenty-three days after the auto da fé of the Cristo de la Paciencia.[15] Apparently, it was to this banker that Olivares had given guarantees to attract more Portuguese New Christian financiers to Madrid. The case is also interesting because it calls into question the way inquisitorial trials have been dealt with by most historians. It has been accepted that Sarabia was secretly a Jew—"un fanatico de la religion hebraica," wrote Caro Baroja—when not even the inquisitors themselves managed to prove it after five and a half years of detention, torture, and intense prosecution.[16] There are enormous flaws in the available analyses of the trial: the chronology of the trial has not been pieced together; the date of imprisonment, the dates of the accusations, and the dates of the interrogations and enquiries have not been considered; the quality of proof has not been discussed; and the defence of the accused has not been reviewed. For example, Domínguez Ortiz laments that the origins of Sarabia's wealth were unknown, when they are clear from a careful reading of the trial proceedings; and Sarabia's designation of his future place of burial has been ignored, whereas it is obviously an issue if one wants to discuss religious allegiance.[17]

July 27, 1632, was the date of imprisonment.[18] Antonio Zapata, the general inquisitor, was then eighty-one years old.[19] Ten days earlier, on July 17, the king had issued instructions to nominate Antonio de Sotomayor to this position, who was considered by all authors to be an ally of the Count-Duke of Olivares. Antonio Zapata duly resigned on September 6.[20] The detention of Juan Núñez Sarabia was thus decided by a lame general inquisitor, though one considered by Gutiérrez Nieto to be a fierce defender of blood purity.[21] It does not look as though the king or his ministers were consulted. If Zapata wanted to leave with a salvo against the policies of the king, he could not have chosen a better target. It is surprising, however, that the trial went on after Zapata's departure, and that the Inquisition threw everything it could against Sarabia, despite that this was supposed to be a period of leniency by the Spanish Inquisition.

My hypothesis is that the Supreme Council of the Inquisition was very much behind this move, making a withdrawal difficult. Moreover, it is possible that Antonio de Sotomayor was not such a good friend of New Christians as has been supposed. We need to reject simplistic suppositions about court factions pursuing coherent strategies. Courtiers changed their tack in response to sudden turns of events. It is also possible that Olivares decided to let the Inquisition prosecute Sarabia to keep the Portuguese bankers under pressure.[22] The trial was triggered by very weak evidence: an accusation by one Juana de Silva that was based on hearsay, because the accuser had never seen the accused.[23] She was a blackmailer and this was not the first case: in 1621, Juan Núñez Sarabia presented a memorial at the Inquisition indicating the name of blackmailers who were threatening to denounce him to the tribunal as Jewish.[24] This case is unconvincing from the beginning. Following Juana de Silva's denunciation, the accuser was murdered, with the Inquisition deciding that this had been arranged by Sarabia. The Inquisition tried to prove the involvement of Sarabia but failed in its endeavour (another black spot in the analyses of the trial).

It was only after Sarabia's detention and the sequestration of his property that the Inquisition tried to collect more denunciations: they wrote to the tribunal of Coimbra asking for denunciations involving the accused and his relatives, but nothing major surfaced.[25] They sought information from the tribunals of Spanish America, also without much success.[26] Then they decided to detain and try close relatives of the accused, a classic strategy used by the Inquisition to extort denunciations. The accused's brother, Enrique Núñez Sarabia, who was petitioning the king, and his nephew, Bartolomé Febo, a major merchant and financier with links to Rouen, son of Antonio Rodrigues Lamego, another important banker, were detained.[27] But what the Inquisition did in December 1632 under its new general inquisitor, Antonio de Sotomayor, was without precedent.

The general inquisitor nominated the secretary of the tribunal of Seville, Juan Bautista de Villadiego, to make enquiries among the New Christian communities in France, where they did not have jurisdiction and could have come into conflict with the French authorities.[28] Other motives might have contributed to this decision, but the direct link to Sarabia's trial shows the eagerness to find proof, even if it meant taking risky initiatives. Some witnesses who came forward during these enquiries ended up in Madrid, fleeing from the French authorities and accusing themselves of being Jewish, as well as ratifying their testimonies before the general inquisitor, whose direct intervention in this activity can be classified as unique.[29] The whole plot failed to find definitive proof. Sarabia asserted his innocence until the end, refusing to give in even under torture. He had already been in very weak health, and the doctors advised against torture, but the General Council overruled that advice on September 3, 1637. Sarabia suffered torture for one hour and a half without confessing.[30]

The final verdict was abjuration of vehemently suspected heresy, coupled with a fine of 20,000 ducados. The penalty was extorted from the widow before the publication of the sentence on December 13, 1637, not in private as promised, but at the church of St. Peter Martyr. The penalty is exceptional for "vehement suspicion," and, with the rest of the trial, is perhaps the most extreme case I have read, with the Inquisition eager to use all possible tricks against an accused. It showed the inquisitors' limits, but it guaranteed the downfall of Sarabia. After nearly five and a half years in jail, he avoided property confiscation but was discredited and ruined, a usual outcome of inquisitorial action.[31]

There are two other unsatisfactory aspects of the available analyses of this case. The first concerns the *contradictas*, or the defence by the accused. The only way to invalidate the accusations was to prove that they were produced by enemies. This was a well-known tactic, and anyone accused who did not want to confess would launch counteraccusations and indicate lists of witnesses. The defence mounted should be part of any trial analysis because it reveals the network of the accused, their relationships with Old Christians, and the reality of rivalry within the New Christian community. The integration of the accused in the parochial framework, the donations to important Christian charities, particularly the hospital of Saint Anthony of the Portuguese, and generous dowries given so that poor young women could marry or to guarantee the acceptance of girls into convents are all features visible in the case of Juan Núñez Sarabia. In his defence, Sarabia indicated members and secretaries of the royal councils of War and Finance, such as Manuel Lopes Pereira, several clergymen, such as the Jesuits Isidro de Arce and Francisco Crespo, several financiers, particularly García de Yllán, and even Count Olivares, as witnesses.[32]

Included in information about Sarabia's network are crucial details about his uncle, Juan Núñez Correa, with whom Sarabia had worked at the beginning of his professional life. Correa was an important contractor to the king in Seville, for whom he ran soap factories, provisioned the *carrera de Indias*, and was involved in contracts for trading slaves from Angola to Spanish America. We know that in the 1580s he lived in Olinda, Brazil, as the owner of a sugar plantation and mill, and there he had been accused by the visiting inquisitor. Sent to Lisbon in 1593, he was absolved and released for lack of proof, after being bailed (for 4,000 cruzados) by Rodrigo de Andrade and Jerónimo Henriques (whom we will come across later). In 1597, he was authorised to move to Madrid to negotiate contracts for pau-brazil, the Angolan slave trade, and later the pepper trade, dying there in 1625.[33] According to Sarabia, Correa had transformed the chapel of Christ at the convent of Carmen Calzado in Madrid into a burial place for himself and his family, having concluded a contract with the church administrators.[34] That Sarabia expected to be buried there means that he most probably inherited the fortune of his uncle and took on responsibility for matters concerning the chapel.

The endowment of a chapel as a burial place for the family was a common practice of New Christian financiers, exemplified by Diogo Crasto do Rio in Lisbon in the 1560s and replicated by many others, such as Antonio de Fonseca in Rome in the 1580s. It was generally combined with the creation of entailed property. Although it is difficult to be certain about the religious allegiance of New Christians, the endowment of a chapel and the creation of entailed property would be at odds with plans to escape and become Jewish elsewhere, even if these investments cannot be taken as a guarantee of Catholicism.

This was an exceptional trial, not only in its length, but also in the enormous effort the Inquisition made—vainly—to convict the New Christian banker to the king. Huge sums of money were invested in it. The study of literally thousands of trials has rarely revealed such a level of hate and an irrational pursuit of conviction so far beyond the usual extent of enquiry. Sarabia was personally targeted for a confession; all means were deployed for the purpose, but they failed because the inquisitors were dealing with an unusually strong character, from whom torture could not extract a confession despite his already very poor health (the doctors opposed it because of the subject's gout and hernia).[35] When Sarabia finally heard his sentence, he was fifty-three or fifty-four years old. Several drafts of the conclusion agreed on by the inquisitors over the previous three years of the trial had had to be withdrawn for further enquiry. The final paper of the trial, produced the day after the sentence, gives a sinister insight into the nature of the Inquisition: Sarabia was asked whether he had any complaints to present against the treatment he had received in jail and those responsible. Despite his lengthy imprisonment, he declared that he had been well—even punctiliously—treated.[36] It is obvious that the inquisitors did not want him to go, and so set up a trap, but one that he avoided; complaints would have meant an extended stay in jail for further enquiries. After this extraordinary treatment, Juan Núñez Sarabia's name is never again seen in archival documentation, but his brother Enrique would reemerge in Bordeaux ten years later as a business associate of the Portuguese merchant and banker Duarte da Silva.[37]

The position of the king and the Count-Duke of Olivares in this trial is not obvious. Any intervention by them, had it occurred, would have left no traces; it would have been informal, directed at the general inquisitor. But the inquisitorial procedure does not seem to have been modified in any way. On the contrary, an ally of Olivares, Antonio de Sotomayor, who only resigned after his patron was himself forced to resign, in 1643, took the initiative of extending the enquiry to France and supported further action to collect information in other countries. How should this direct challenge to, and demolition of, a banker of the king, who should have been protected, be interpreted? The detention and the initial enquiries of the Portuguese Inquisition were triggered by the outgoing general inquisitor, Antonio Zapata, who found a way to take revenge on the royal court and hit it where it would hurt most, in the area of its finances, while contributing to reversing the direction of the blood purity debate. The scandal had consequences for the declining prestige of the New Christians.

The action of the new general inquisitor appears inexplicable, but it is tempting to push the preceding hypothesis further: since the trial had already started, the Count-Duke of Olivares probably decided not to intervene but rather to extract some benefit from the negative turn of events.[38] The way Juan Núñez Sarabia was left unprotected to be destroyed by the Inquisition could be useful as a warning to other bankers with *asientos* to keep the interest low and be more willing to help the king in a deepening crisis of the Iberian monarchy.[39] If that was the calculation, it had mixed consequences: New Christian bankers in Madrid did not abandon the city, but merchants did migrate, while trade significantly declined in the Iberian Empires, owing to the Dutch War of Independence, Dutch economic and military competition in the south Atlantic and Asia, and the Thirty Years War.

Bartolomé Febo, a young financier (no more than twenty-five years old when he was detained, on April 14, 1633), had established a literary and musical salon in his house and was made of the same stuff as his uncle.[40] He did not know the Christian liturgy well, but he stayed calm and confident, denying all accusations and facing two sessions of torture. In these he accused his accusers, but also, implicitly, the inquisitors: "They want to make me Jew, I will die as a Christian."[41] He denied until the end any involvement in Jewish practices or beliefs, holding out until he fainted at the end of the second session of torture, which went all the way.[42] Although he always defended his father as a good Christian, he produced a perfect argument in the final stages of the trial: "If my father had broken his obligations as a Christian Catholic, it would not be my fault, since I did not do the wrong; it is well known that this is maliciousness on the part of the witness."[43] The inquisitors did not have enough proof: they decided on abjuration of mildly suspected heresy, a fine of 4,000 ducados, and exile from the area of Madrid and twenty leagues around, an astonishingly heavy penalty for mild suspicion. The Supreme Council reduced the penalty to 1,500 ducados, revoked the exile, and ordered abjuration in front of the inquisitors, the accused being spared the auto da fé.[44] It is difficult to ascertain whether there was any political intervention here from Olivares; but with so little proof, and the strong character of the accused, even the final verdict was well beyond normal practice.

We shall return to this trial in the next chapter, but there are several interesting pieces of information to consider here. One witness, Pedro Fernandes Correa from Rouen, declared that the family of António Rodrigues Lamego were *judios judaizantes* (Judaizing Jews), thus making a clear separation between ethnic origin (*judios*: they were and would always be Jews) and religious allegiance (*judaizantes*: they followed Jewish rites, although they could be practicing Christians).[45] This formula appears elsewhere, and attests to a semantic separation that confirms the power of labelling. Bartolomé Febo refused to marry the daughter of António Cáceres, an arrangement suggested by his father. This indicates, once more, close links among powerful New Christian houses. The son declared that he avoided the Portuguese in Madrid, who were loud, singing and begging on the streets, and who harboured envies and jealousy. It is implied that rich New Christians were a target for poor New Christians. Blackmail must have been rampant, despite the regular and significant practice of charity. Fierce competition among rich New Christians for asientos was also mentioned, and we have seen this before. Bartolomé Febo declared that he wanted to socialize with knights, men of letters, and musicians, underlining the elite leanings of rich New Christians.[46] Social division among New Christians was an important issue. The sections of contradictas in trials, such as the one on Bartolomé Febo, need to be analysed, for they give much information on debt, rivalry, hate triggered by frustration, and envy resulting from refused requests for loans, scams, and broken promises.[47]

Richer families kept up their relationships with poorer branches of the family and tried to help them, and sometimes poor New Christians were singled out to become the heirs of rich relatives, owing to the latter's lack of progeny. At other times, they showed unusual skill and secured a favourable position in richer relatives' business. There certainly was social mobility among the New Christians, but also bitter division.

There is another crucial element in these trials: both Sarabia and Febo declared that they were Old Christians.[48] In Portugal this would have been unthinkable in this period, when half or one-quarter New Christian had become the normal classification for many accused persons in prison, which attests to a very mixed society; this explains why the project of expelling the New Christians had to be abandoned. Fernão Soeiro, a merchant in Loulé who was detained on August 21, 1629, when he was fifty-three years old, denied all accusations of heresy, even under torture, although he declared with no prevarication that he was "of the nation."[49] At the auto da fé of Évora on October 21, 1633, Soeiro was given a verdict of vehement suspicion of heresy, which he had to abjure, and he was released one month after that. Later we shall hear about one of his sons, Manuel da Gama de Pádua.

Pedro de Baeça, who had reached an important position as a financier, was a knight of the Order of Christ and was enrolled in the lists of *fidalgos* of the royal house. He was also the nephew of the homonymous asentista active in Madrid in the 1590s and 1600s, and he was detained on November 18, 1631, when he was forty years old. He denied all accusations of Judaism, even under torture, and was condemned to abjure a heresy of which he was pronounced only mildly suspected. But he heard his sentence given out at the auto da fé in Lisbon on January 9, 1633. He also declared that he was a New Christian, but these proceedings were in Portugal, where it would have been easy to find records that referred to his relatives and to conduct local genealogical enquiries.[50]

Sarabia's and Febo's claims to Old Christian identity are thus striking. They can be analysed as a clever strategy: the two accused decided not to give any clue to the inquisitors; the judges would have to do their homework and prove their accusations of Judaism. The accused knew perfectly well that the status of New Christian was crucial to the accusation, or, to put it another way, they were in prison precisely because they were New Christians. But their claims were more than a simple strategy of defence. Denial of New Christian status was an important step to challenging the whole strategy of the inquisitors: it exposed the subjective nature of these classifications, and the attitude of the two accused coincided with the opinion of many Old Christians; that is, that blood purity enquiries should not go beyond three or four generations. Also, if they did not perceive themselves as New Christians, accusations based on weak evidence would have less impact. This strategy was also evident in other trials in Spain in the second half of the seventeenth century.

The inquisitors had the upper hand in this game. With hindsight, we know that there was no chance of reversing a procedure of racist enquiry that had been used for more than one hundred years and that functioned as the basis for any accusation of Judaism. This procedure went on, both in Portugal and Spain, until the mid-eighteenth century. However, in the early 1630s, a spirit of openness in the blood purity debate explains Sarabia's and Febo's daring strategy. Failure simply reflected the risks taken by these two generations of New Christian financiers. However, the escape route was present from the beginning; that is, to get through the procedure of blood purity enquiry by various institutions and, against all odds, mainly through bribery, obtain recognition as an Old Christian.

2. *Debate*

In the meantime, other documents discussed trade and banking by New Christians. A clever memorial by García de Yllán, a New Christian already mentioned, written on behalf of all businessmen (as it declared), was probably printed in the late 1620s or the early 1630s, and reflects this period of powerful positions under threat. Yllán insisted on the idea that trade was the soul of the monarchy, and mistreatment of merchants was the main reason for its decline. He exposed the discrimination suffered by merchants, who were excluded from honours and barred from the noble life. Moreover, he denounced persecution by ministers of justice, who would fall on merchants the moment they believed there was money and property to be extracted. Yllán considered merchants to be unfairly dependent on ministers of justice, detained by them without accusation or instruction from a judge. This daring reasoning strongly implies the writer is referring to the extortions practiced by the Inquisition and the king. The merchant (and Yllán meant the New Christian) was abused by a variety of officials of the state.[51]

But Yllán went further, lamenting the likely outcome of all this pressure: the merchant would apply his capital to the *juros*, *censos*, houses, and offices of the republic so that he and his children could consider themselves as noblemen, free from the extortions he had suffered as a merchant. Yllán denounced all the tricks of bad merchants, who bribed officers to cover up fraud, used the pretext of dowries to avoid paying debts, and claimed a noble background to avert judicial prosecution. His was a plea in favour of good businessmen, whose behaviour could be aligned with that of many emperors, kings, philosophers, and jurists who traded and contracted without staining their nobility. He also suggested a university (or guild) of merchants at court, and the foundation of new *consulados*, particularly in Madrid, in which the main financiers and contractors could develop trade under the rule of law.[52]

Three issues in this memorial seem crucial: the importance of the rule of law and the institutions organised by merchants to impose good practice, along with justice and fairness; the acceptance of differentiation among merchants, because bad merchants damaged the economy, creating debt and a bad reputation for businessmen as a whole (there is a clear elitist vision of financiers as gentlemen); and the denunciation of unfair harassment of honest merchants by officers of justice, which led to investment in land, interest, and offices—in brief, to the ennoblement of financiers who abandoned their trade at a cost to the republic.

This is exactly what Yllán did later in Antwerp, following the example of other rich New Christians there; but there were also examples of such behaviour in Rome and Florence, where New Christian merchants were generally not persecuted for their ethnic descent, while others in Lisbon and Madrid forged attestations to their blood purity and merged into the local aristocracy.[53] This strategy contrasted with that of other wealthy New Christians who managed to escape to cities where they could assume their Jewish faith, either in Christian countries or in the Ottoman Empire. Religion mattered because belief contributed to migration choices; but the push of the Inquisition and the pull factor of local conditions also played a crucial role. The betrayal of the bourgeoisie, as Braudel put it, had a twist in Iberia, where it was the consequence of systematic racism against New Christians of Jewish origin, combined with deep prejudices against merchants.[54]

This line of argument—that is, praising merchants for their contribution to economic and financial wealth—was accompanied by a reflection on the origin of the nobility and the role of the king, in which the value of blood and lineage was discussed. Another pamphlet, *Memorial sobre la nobleza*, written circa 1632, questioned the idea of an intrinsically or innate superior quality of noble blood. Noble status was bestowed by (or dependent on) the king as a reward for outstanding services. The idea of immutably noble blood was derided, because nobility had always been a dignity acquired through service, with the king playing a crucial role in promoting loyal vassals and defining a hierarchy of nobility. A well-governed republic should be based on such a hierarchy, and inequality within the nobility was considered important to stimulate service through reward (and enable punishment through demotion).[55]

According to this pamphlet, the freedom of the king to bestow noble distinction as a reward had been hindered by the idea of an intrinsic quality of nobility, which separated the acquisition of *hidalguias* (based on the sale of privileges) from access to military orders, while the blood purity statutes created an obstacle to promotion and reward for service and loyalty. The pamphlet asserted that the king had the power to cleanse blood and set aside all defects in it through acts of ennoblement. Well-known cases relating to the lineage of *moros*—the Granadas, the Venegas, the Cegris—were accepted in Spain, which raised the issue of why others should not also be accepted. The natural decline of the old aristocracy, which needed to be renewed, was another argument. The vision here expressed was that all kinds of service, including facilitating increases in trade and navigation, so important for the maintenance of the monarchy, should be rewarded, and grades of aristocracy should be opened up and reinvigorated.[56]

It is against the background of this intense conflict of values that we can understand the meaning of the *Execración contra los judíos*, written by Francisco de Quevedo and dated July 20, 1633, in which extreme hatred against New Christians, labelled Jews, was expressed with reference to the favourite of the king himself, the Count-Duke of Olivares, who was rumoured to have Jewish blood. The text was intended to heighten the emotion provoked by the appearance in Madrid of pamphlets written in Portuguese proclaiming "Long Live the Law of Moses and Death to the Christian Law." In Quevedo's pamphlet it is the language that matters, not the content, because we are confronted with a reiteration of the case against New Christians, labelled a vile and low rabble, a drop of whose blood could motivate riots against Jesus Christ and could pollute any clean blood with which it was mixed. Quevedo praised the establishment of the Inquisition by the Catholic kings and the decree of expulsion, contrasting such deeds with the acceptance of Jews by the Portuguese, which was punished when the New World was discovered by Columbus. Jews could only be dealt with by persecution and death, claimed Quevedo, who revelled in phrases such as "to burn and condemn Jews is just punishment . . . to burn and transform their money into powder and make them drink it is medicine."[57]

Extreme anti-Judaism was pushed further by Quevedo in *La isla de Monopantos* (written ca. 1636), in which a barely veiled Count-Duke of Olivares and his advisers participate in an international conspiracy fomented by Jewish rabbis and New Christians who declare themselves atheists and worshipers of the god money and who are all engaged in ruining Christian countries through perfidious financial tricks. This short story has been considered the first consistent attempt to embed the idea of an international conspiracy of Jewish people seeking world domination—a vision that would lead to the infamous *Protocols of the Elders of Zion* in the early twentieth century.[58] By the time he wrote this short story, Francisco de Quevedo was a fierce opponent of Olivares, although he had been close to him at the beginning of Philip IV's reign. The attack against New Christians was an easy way of channelling hate towards the favourite and his policies.

The pamphlet, *Comercio impedido por los enemigos de esta monarquía*, printed in Madrid in January 1640 without the name of the author, José Pellicer de Ossau y Tovar, drew on decades of accusations against New Christians, in particular one that insisted they had used the freedom to circulate granted them in 1628 (actually 1629) to occupy the important maritime ports of Spain and then to migrate to Bayonne, Bordeaux, Nantes, and Rouen; to Dunkirk, Antwerp, Rotterdam, and Amsterdam; to Lübeck, and Hamburg; and finally to Havana, Cartagena, Portobello, Lima, Buenos Aires, and the ports of New Spain. Instead of bringing wealth to Spain, they acted as the factors of an enemy, working for escaped relatives in northern Europe. They would invest their capital in the Netherlands or in the synagogues of Italy, but not in Spain, treating that country just as the Genoese had when they brought about the decline of Burgos and Medina del Campo, and Castile in general, with their usury.[59]

According to this pamphlet, the Portuguese financiers had fled the Inquisition and used royal finances for their own purposes, exhausting local wealth by insisting that interest on loans was paid in Flanders. This was part of a transfer of wealth from Lisbon to Amsterdam and the Dutch conquests in Brazil, Africa, and Asia, which had been instigated by Jewish communities escaped from Portugal. In this text, New Christians were haphazardly labelled as Jews, or as Portuguese who hated their homeland and their religion, conspiring against their natural lord as his enemies. France was viewed as an unproductive country that lived off Spain, while the Castilians paid all the taxes and undertook the most difficult work, losing out because of the unequal trading terms for precious metals versus manufactured textiles and glasses. Jews condemned by the Holy Office, as had recently happened in Peru, turned out to be involved in asientos worth millions, and the money ended up in northern Europe, while debts were accumulated in Spain. The petition also reproduced the idea that Portuguese Jews (never mentioned as New Christians) did not belong in the country and engineered the removal of wealth from Spain to countries where they were not confronted by the Inquisition and could publicly assume the religion of their ancestors. The final proposal of the petition was that these people should once again be forbidden to circulate freely, should be prohibited from living in ports, and should be excluded from royal rents, asientos, and trade with northern Europe.[60]

This pamphlet, like the texts from Quevedo, offered a catalogue of reactionary political ideas. Political decline was never the responsibility of the authorities, never the result of reverses in war or economic policies mistakes. Political decline was caused by the perverse misdeeds of Jewish traitors, who hated the religion in which they were born (after the forced conversion of their ancestors, never mentioned), and their natural lord. Unfaithful believers were always considered as unreliable subjects of the king. Economic decline resulted from the parasitism of other countries, aggravated by usury and the financial burden imposed by Jewish people in the wake of the Genoese, who were the first to invest elsewhere. The flow of precious metals to northern Europe was attributed to financial malice and contraband trade. Unequal economic development was lamented as the work of unworthy people who colluded with the enemy. It was not the result of an absence of policies to promote industrial development.

In this line of reasoning, inquisitorial persecution was never seen as the cause of the transfer of wealth to other countries. According to a pamphlet that revelled in its own extreme rhetoric, more prohibitions and the enslavement of New Christians was the solution. Disaffection and division eventually prevailed against the period of relative openness of debate between the late 1590s and early 1640s. *Arbitrios* declined, as the discussion to limit blood purity enquiries lost its traction. The ideology of blood purity triumphed not only because of the rooted interests of those who had had their Old Christian status certified but also because of the ambiguity of royal policies produced to keep New Christians under constant threat for financial gain.

3. Revolt and Naturalisation

On December 1, 1640, a revolt in Portugal terminated the Iberian Union of Crowns that was created in 1580. Once the Portuguese kingdom recovered its political independence, nearly three decades of war proved insufficient to resubjugate it, and the peace treaty of 1668 recognised an irremediable divergence. The main historical interpretations underline either the tenacious collective feeling of the Portuguese against Castile or the factional fighting within the political elites that led to the breakdown of the Union of Crowns.[61] Most likely, it was a combination of both factors. Factional fighting was crucial to triggering revolt, because the discontent of the Portuguese nobility had grown in the previous years. The nobles resented having to fight wars they did not feel were their wars in various parts of the Spanish Empire, particularly conflicts in the Netherlands and the Thirty Years War, and this situation was aggravated by the revolt of Catalonia, which broke out in May 1640, imposing more military recruitment on Portugal. The political and social elites in Portugal became detached from Madrid, feeling distant from the king and the centre of decision-making.

The imposition of new taxes in the 1630s, owing to the growing need of the monarchy to fund military commitments, contributed to the resentment of the population and those who had to collect the taxes and keep order. Revolts broke out in various parts of Portugal in 1636, and these took time to quell because the noblemen and local military forces resisted intervention.[62] Merchants involved in the Atlantic world were becoming disaffected because of the Dutch control of part of Brazil. Although the main Portuguese *asentistas* in Madrid were linked to the *carreira da Índia*, the situation in Asia was also eroding fast, with growing economic competition and the military presence of the Dutch and the English. In sum, the benefits brought by the Union of Crowns in 1580 had evaporated. The tipping point had probably been reached in the 1620s, while an accumulation of problems in the 1630s, and particularly in 1640, contributed to the preference for separation among a good part of the nobility, clergymen, and merchants.[63] However, to commit the country to a long war took much more than disaffection among the social elites; there was a visible collective anti-Castilian feeling that explains the tenacity and sacrifice of lives on the part of the Portuguese. Moreover, people were willing to pay heavier taxes to support the war, in contrast with previous revolts.[64]

The impact of Portuguese independence on New Christians was significant on both sides of the Iberian frontier and in the overseas territories. The economic issues will be discussed in the next chapter. Here, we shall limit our analysis to the status of Portuguese merchants in Castile and the Spanish Empire and the processes of naturalization they underwent. The activity of the Inquisition both in Spain and Portugal will also be addressed in this chapter because it can be seen simultaneously as an expression of the conflict between the countries and as a crucial push factor in migration, the outflow of capital and the destruction of resources.

Portuguese New Christians could obtain citizenship in a specific town in Castile following long-term residence and a locally contracted marriage, the two main criteria for integration that overrode rules against migration.[65] However, the new citizens needed, in principle, to receive naturalization from the king if they wanted to get authorisation to enter into contracts and trade with Spanish America. They were considered foreigners, even during the period of the Union of Crowns, and this was a matter of contention. The guild of merchants (consulado) in Seville used the power it derived from its control of trade with Spanish America, shared with *Casa de Contratación*, to maintain a constant pressure on the king against the naturalisation of foreigners.[66] However, the king needed capital, and foreign merchants had access to external sources of this, provided they could trade with America, while silver was always a crucial resource for the reimbursement of their loans to the king. It is between these two opposite poles of pressure, from established and outsiders, that we need to assess the variations in royal and local policies of naturalization.[67]

The naturalization of Portuguese, Flemish, French, and Italian residents started quite early. Documentation on naturalizations is preserved from the 1570s onwards, but there is evidence for many cases earlier. Naturalizations had then been controlled by the Casa de Contratación, which made enquiries into applicants' length of residence, marriages contracted since arrival, and capacity to mobilise their own capital. A licence from the king was necessary if merchants were to trade with their own capital. There were also naturalizations without express authorization to legitimise contracts of trade with Spanish America. Gold, silver, and pearls sent to unlicensed foreigners in Seville would be confiscated. The argument of the university (or guild) of merchants concentrated on foreigners as enemies of the Crown who would send capital and information abroad. New Christians were accused very early, from the turn of the sixteenth to the seventeenth century onwards of favouring Dutch, English, and French competitors of the Iberian Crown.[68]

The king produced a string of laws to control the naturalization of foreigners, revoking previous licences and forcing merchants to apply for new ones.

This practice had three causes: the administration's incapacity to keep a central record, owing to the local nature of the enquiries instructed by the Casa de Contratación; the desire to keep a constant pressure on foreign merchants, which could be quite difficult to do in periods of war or civil unrest; and the administration's need of the money obtained from licence renewals. In any case, we find laws concerning the naturalization of foreigners promulgated on July 14, 1561, July 27, 1592, October 1, 1608, December 25, 1616, and April 22, 1645, and these confirm the relatively mild period of Olivares.[69] The law of 1608 and, particularly that of 1616, defined the main criteria for naturalization: residence in the kingdoms for more than twenty years, identifiable property, and marriage with a woman native to the country.[70] Extensive research into the cases found in the files of the Casa de Contratación confirms the implementation of those criteria and the laws imposing the renewal of licences.

Among the cases of New Christians who became citizens of Castile in this period is that of Diego Enríquez, who was naturalized in 1608 when he was thirty-two years old. Born in Guarda (Portugal) and now living in Seville, the naturalized Enríquez travelled to Cartagena de Indias under royal licence, and there, on July 10, 1609, he obtained authorisation to trade and enter into contracts with Spanish American merchants.[71] Simão Lopes de Noronha, born in Castelo Branco, Portugal, and neighbour of Seville, who was married to Beatriz Enríquez, a native of the city, received authorisation to enter into contracts in 1609.[72] Jerónimo Fernandes renewed his licence to trade in 1609 and again in 1616, following the promulgation of laws making new licences compulsory.[73] Enrique de Andrade, Agustín Pérez, and Diego de Paiva received licences in 1618 and again in 1624.[74] Juan Rodrigues de Mesa, who was born in Estremoz (Portugal) and resident in Cartagena de Indias, but had spent long periods in Granada and in Madrid, obtained a royal licence to trade on August 8, 1625, more than a year after obtaining authorisation to travel to Cartagena in order to collect money owed him.[75] In the same year, a licence was issued to Jorge Antunes de León, another New Christian born in Castelo Branco (Portugal) and resident in Seville.[76] And Simón de Fonseca Pina, living in Seville, obtained a licence to trade in 1631.[77]

The impact of Olivares's policies is visible not only in the dropping of the administration's insistence on the renewal of licences, a requirement that could have upset foreign merchants, but also in the new practice of granting naturalizations and licences for trade as part of the negotiation of asientos. The Portuguese made extensive use of the new leverage they had acquired in the late 1620s to obtain these coveted licences to trade. Duarte Fernandes de Acosta (or da Costa) and Filipe Martins de Acosta were naturalized on March 15, 1629, following the arrangement of an asiento according to which the king was lent 655,000 escudos by Duarte Fernandes (the father of the aforementioned), Manuel de Paz, and Simão Soares. Gonzalo Núñez Sepúlveda was naturalized on April 4, 1630, after an asiento had been arranged by Manuel de Paz. Simão Rodrigues Bueno, resident of Seville, was naturalized on April 20, 1630, benefitting from an asiento negotiated by Duarte Fernandes. Diego de Paiva was naturalised the same day, thanks to an asiento of 633,421 escudos negotiated by Simão Soares. And Simão (or Simón) de Fonseca Pina, naturalised on May 22, 1631, benefitted from an asiento of 55,000 escudos negotiated by García de Yllán.[78]

Duarte Rodrigues de León (or Leão) was naturalized on September 20, 1632, following an asiento arranged by the brothers Diego and Alfonso Cardoso for the provisioning of the ocean fleet. This gave them the right to nominate five people for naturalization, with Diego and Alfonso themselves being the other recipients of citizenship. Jorge Paz da Silveira and Alfonso and Gaspar Rodrigues Pasariño (or Passarinho) were naturalized on February 6, 1632, at the conclusion of an asiento costing 100,000 escudos. Marcos de Góis de Morais was naturalised on November 8, 1632, as a result of an asiento costing 50,000 escudos, to be paid in Flanders, an investment shared with Jorge Paz da Silveira. Francisco Fernandes de Solis was naturalized on December 20, 1632, probably as part of the same asiento negotiations, and on July 8, 1634, Domingos de Herrera was naturalised based on an asiento by the same Paz da Silveira.[79] Francisco Lobo de Acuña benefitted from an asiento negotiated by Duarte Fernandes costing 300,000 escudos, to be paid in Flanders and Germany, a transaction that also brought Fernandes authorization to trade and enter into contracts in the Spanish Indies, a licence issued on August 17, 1635.[80]

Antonio de Ribeiro Carvalho was naturalised on December 15, 1634, following agreement on an asiento of 66,000 escudos to be paid in Flanders, Milan, Germany, and Genova concluded by Manuel de Paz.[81] Jorge Mendes de Chaves, who participated in an asiento with Marcos Fernandes Monsanto, Filipe Martins D'Orta, and Beatriz de Sampaio, widow of Simão Soares (all major New Christian bankers, and note the continuation of her dead husband's business by Beatriz de Sampaio), was naturalized and received a licence to trade on September 26, 1635.[82] João Rebelo, Manuel de Aguiar e Acuña, and Bento de Mesquita, who had participated in an asiento costing 55,000 escudos, received naturalization and a licence to trade in the same year.[83] Manuel Coronel was naturalized on October 19, 1635, after an asiento costing 300,000 escudos, to be paid in Flanders, was arranged by Manuel de Paz on February 14, 1634. This agreement indicated that two naturalisations for the Indies would be made available without further cost. And Simão Soares Peres was naturalized on August 27, 1639, following an asiento concluded by Duarte Fernandes that provided for two naturalizations.[84]

The Portuguese independence of 1640 did not stop this flow of naturalizations linked to asientos, although the few records of naturalizations taking place after 1645 are evidence of a very swift decline. Manuel Mendes de Miranda was naturalized on December 7, 1643, following an asiento he entered into, along with Francisco Garcia Prieto, Francisco Fernandes de

Solis, Lanfran David, Diego Cardoso, Pedro Lopes de Puerto, Juan de Soto, and Alfonso and Gaspar Rodrigues Pasariño, costing 55,000 escudos, which was celebrated on December 19, 1642. The size of the group participating in this contract, an average one as far as the sum of money was concerned, is a clear indication of the financial difficulties of the time. Antonio Ferreira, a captain, and Antonio Mendes Chillón were also naturalized on December 7 and December 19, 1643, respectively, as a result of this same asiento, which provided for three naturalisations. Henrique de Andrade, living in Seville, was naturalized on April 20, 1643, following an asiento into which he entered with Juan Ventura Tirado, Pedro de Vila Real, López de Robledo, Francisco de Soto, and Gaspar de Contreras that cost 51,794 escudos.[85] Nearly all these naturalisations concerned direct or indirect (subcontractor) participants in the asientos who took advantage of the financial needs of the Crown to get a share of trade with the Indies. It was a curious cycle of lending money to the king on the one hand and being reimbursed in American silver on the other, while the bankers also needed access to American trade to raise money for lending.

New Christians could convert their accumulated local influence or military service rewards into naturalizations. Bartolomeu Nunes, living in the city of Santiago in Guatemala, received his naturalization on July 20, 1629, having been proposed for it by the Count of Gomera, governor of the province, who had a royal *cédula* (document) for the purpose.[86] Melchior Mendes de Acosta, resident of Seville, claimed he had rendered service to the king in peace and in war and received his naturalization on March 8, 1631. Antonio Nunes Gramaxo, resident in Cartagena de Indias, was naturalized on June 8, 1631, having put his arms, horses, and servants at the disposal of the Crown, as his uncle Jorge Gramaxo had done before him; he also declared an enormous quantity of property.

Surprisingly, the possibility also existed of obtaining naturalizations as part of negotiations for royal pardons. Captain Gaspar Ribeiro, resident in Cuba, was naturalized on January 7, 1633, as part of an agreement for a royal cédula of pardon for Antonio Nunes Gramaxo, then resident in San Cristóbal de Havana, Cuba, who had traded and entered into contracts with merchants in the Spanish Indies without a royal licence. Supplying a special shipment of slaves, which were in high demand, could also be rewarded with naturalization, as occurred in the case of Manuel da Fonseca Henriques, who received his naturalization on September 27, 1634. Matias Rodrigues de Oliveira, resident in Seville for fifteen years, claimed naturalization as recompense for his father's service to the king in Portugal, in peace and in war, and received it on November 16, 1635.[87]

The records show several dozen naturalizations received by Portuguese New Christians as part of the terms of asientos, and many of these were granted to important bankers, their relatives, and their associates. A significant number of merchants who married in Seville and invested their capital there were able to obtain letters of naturalization and licences to trade without pressure on the king. All they had to do was to pay for enquiries to show they fitted the criteria for naturalization. However, only a few elite had the means to obtain these privileges of trade.

On several occasions, the administration ordered the Casa de Contratación to establish lists of naturalized foreigners. A document dated March 30, 1643, a crucial moment because Seville had allegedly been deserted by a good number of Portuguese in the previous two years, gives us a list of foreigners who were naturalised between 1602 and 1642. Of about 160 merchants, almost all were located in Seville. Sixty-nine are Portuguese (43 percent), and many of the aforementioned names are included here. Among the others are Flemish, Italian, and French names, as well as some English and German ones. The list of naturalizations between 1628 and 1631 indicates twenty-nine people, of whom ten were Portuguese, seven Flemish, seven Italian, four French, and one Corsican. The presence of the Portuguese increased in the 1630s, but in any case, we have confirmation here of the reduction in the numbers of the elite previously mentioned. The Portuguese New Christian community in Seville had been one of the most important. The very limited numbers of naturalizations after 1645 (arguably a maximum of ten Portuguese between then and the end of the century) reflected a divergence between the Iberian kingdoms and the impact of long-term inquisitorial activity against New Christians.[88]

4. Repression

Inquisitorial activity played an important role in opposing the struggle for recognition and ending the integration promoted by New Christians. Access to Spanish America was important, not only to the important market for the area's products—for example, silver, which flowed across the world and paid for loans to the Iberian king, sugar, hides, cochineal, indigo, chocolate, and tobacco, which became important from the 1620s onwards—but also to the market it opened for consumer products such as European metalwork and textiles and Asian spices, porcelain, and textiles. Despite Philip II's 1587 prohibition of New Christian migration to Spanish America, many travelled there without a licence. They were allowed to migrate without a licence in 1601, and again forbidden from migrating without a licence in 1616, until free circulation was reinstated in 1629. In the meantime, enquiries into Judaism were instigated by the king, particularly in 1596. In 1602, Philip III ordered the expulsion of Portuguese who had migrated without a licence before the authorisation issued the year before and accused them of collaborating with the enemy (presumably the Dutch).[89]

The impact of these contradictory policies was delayed as a result of the extent to which New Christian networks had become embedded in local societies. New Christian participation in these societies was crucial from a financial viewpoint and, in general, they obtained (and paid for) protection from local authorities and even from viceroys. From 1570 to 1635, in Lima, Peru, there were eighty-one New Christians tried for Judaism: sixty-two Portuguese, thirteen Castilians, and some Creoles and other mixed-race people, one born in Bordeaux and another in Greece.[90] The list of the accused, which includes Diego Pérez de Acosta, brother of the famous bishop of Tucumán (Córdoba), Francisco de Vitoria, exposes the fiction that New Christians were exclusively Portuguese and reveals a mixture that had developed locally and defied simplistic ethnic definition. The majority were merchants, and several of them died refusing to deny their Jewish faith. However, in the following years the persecution of New Christians in Lima reached new heights.

On January 23, 1639, seventy-one people accused of Judaism were presented at the auto da fé. Their trials had been prepared in the previous five years and involved consultations with the General Council (Suprema) in Madrid because of the numbers involved (around 200 New Christians had been accused, but some had been sentenced before the main auto da fé) and because of the status of the accused, who included the richest man in town, Manuel Bautista Pérez. This man resisted torture and was executed for refusing to confess to Judaism. His main associate and brother-in-law, Sebastião Duarte, was also executed, having revoked a first confession he made and returned to a state of denial and refusing to confess even under torture.

By contrast, the impenitent physician Francisco Maldonado de Silva, who wrote remarkable philosophical and theological texts, challenged the inquisitors head-on concerning their own faith and died as a Jewish martyr defending his faith, an event celebrated by Menasseh ben Israel in *The Hope of Israel*, published in 1652.[91] A total of twelve people were handed to the secular authorities for immediate execution (one in effigy form); the others were reconciled, and eight were absolved. Of the sixty-three executed or reconciled, forty-five were Portuguese, sixteen were Castilians, one originated from Brazil, and one from Tucumán.

Lima could be reached via the Rio de la Plata, a very important smuggling route, but also through the isthmus of Panama, the difficult Andean passage, and the maritime route. The district of the Inquisition of Lima comprehended a very diversified territory on the west side of South America. In 1641, the number of New Christians resident in that district of the Inquisition was estimated by a commissioner as 540, without counting Lima and Buenos Aires, where they might have doubled this number.[92] The collective prosecution of this rooted community represented a major scandal, not only in Spanish America, but also in Iberia, because of the connections of the main persons accused in Lisbon, Seville, Madrid, and West Africa.[93]

Mass detentions of New Christians by the Inquisition in Mexico started later, in 1642, after Portugal had achieved independence. The outcome of these detentions was also remarkable: in successive autos da fé lasting from 1646 to 1649, 172 New Christians were accused of Judaism (some of them were accused of relapsing), among them the richest man in Mexico City, Simón Vaez Sevilla. These numbers of accused were not nearly as high as those dealt with by the Portuguese tribunals, where an average of 100 annual trials during the busiest decades was normal, but for Spanish America they were extraordinary. The tribunal of Mexico had only twenty cells at its disposal, and the enormous numbers of prisoners forced it to enlarge the building. After the big auto da fé on April 11, 1649, ninety-nine prisoners remained in the cells of the tribunal because their trials had not been concluded. Property confiscation reached three million pesos in those years, a staggering sum, way above the best years in Iberia.[94] This vast operation does not seem to have ever been repeated, and a substantial number of those condemned to exile obtained a reduction in their penalty, while others never arrived at their destination, and many suspects fled Mexico City before being caught.

In the cases of both Lima and Mexico, and in that of Cartagena de Indias, the economic and social power of the New Christians prosecuted was dealt a severe blow from which the community never recovered.[95] If the first case triggered an alarm among New Christians all around the Atlantic world, revealed by dozens of lawsuits around debts left by the condemned and claimed by other merchants, arguably contributing to the success of the revolt in Portugal and the consolidation of its independence, the second partly resulted from panic at the idea of a possible revolt of Portuguese communities in the main ports and cities of Spanish America.[96] In any case, the Inquisition served as an instrument for stirring up local factional fighting and disrupting alliances and protective relationships carefully built up over the years by wealthy New Christians. This ethnic group was also subject to internal divisions between rich and poor, as Solange Albero clearly highlights, not to mention the permanent envy felt by some members for other members' social and economic success.[97]

These trials had an undeniable political impact in Spain, where they contributed to the widespread opinion, instigated by conservative Old Christians (and some New Christian insiders), that all New Christians were Jews. Such an atmosphere in the late 1630s and 1640s was critical because of revolts in Naples, Catalonia, and Portugal, which triggered, in the latter cases, long-term wars involving France on the side of Catalonia and the unstoppable success of the Portuguese independence movement. Portuguese bankers in Madrid stayed there, partly because they had to recover previous loans and investments, but also because they had obtained entry into military orders as a reward for their service, had created chapels in the city, and had buried relatives there. The evidence suggests that the situation of the Portuguese community in Seville was not identical; apparently many returned to Lisbon or moved to other cities, partly because of an emergence of inquisitorial persecution.

Caro Baroja considered that the Inquisition in Spain continued to exert significant pressure on wealthy New Christians in the 1640s, citing three significant trials: that of Diego de Sarabia, a "veinticuatro" knight of Granada, who had 150,000 ducados in gold and silver plus 100,000 ducados in coins sequestered; that of Manuel Enríquez, who subcontracted the asiento for the administration of the dry ports to Henrique Álvares Brandão (in Castilian: Blandon) and the royal monopoly of playing cards in Madrid to Manuel Nunes Navarro, having entered into a contract for the administration of the treasury in Oviedo for three years from 1640; and that of Alfonso Rodriguez Borges, another asentista.[98] More research is needed, but it does not seem that repression peaked immediately after the resignation of the Count-Duke of Olivares. Financial, political, and military crises exposed even more need for financial resources, whilst the anti-New Christian stance of the general inquisitor Diego de Arce y Reynoso (1643–1665) would contribute to increasing the number of trials on Judaism in those decades.[99]

The situation in the Portuguese Empire was not significantly easier for New Christians in this period. An inquisitorial visit to Bahia in 1618–1620 had targeted New Christians there and thus weakened the city of Salvador to the point where the Dutch laid siege to it and occupied it in 1624. It was reconquered the following year by the Iberian monarchy, but the Dutch occupied most of the northern captaincies of Brazil from 1630 to 1654, when they were finally expelled.[100] Between 1632 and 1636, and again between 1644 and 1649, there were bursts of inquisitorial activity against New Christians in the empire, this time in Asia, undertaken by the tribunal of Goa.[101] Again, this persecution weakened the capacity of the Portuguese to resist military conflict and economic rivalry with the Dutch in Asia. However, the 1640s did not register the same high level of persecution as the 1630s in Portugal, probably owing to the war of independence.

Meanwhile, in Portugal, the general inquisitor, Francisco de Castro, became involved in the conspiracy of 1641 against the new Portuguese king, John IV, along with the archbishop of Braga, the marquis of Vila Real and the counts of Caminha and Armamar. Unlike his co-conspirators, Castro was released two years later, after confessing and submitting (an echo of the practices imposed on the victims of his tribunal), and was received joyously back into their midst by fellow members of the tribunal and their supporters.[102] The king's generosity did not pay off, however. During the last ten years of Francisco de Castro's life he was involved in several conflicts with the monarch as a result of his continual manoeuvres against New Christians, whose financial support proved to be vital for the war of independence against Castile.[103]

Pedro de Baeça, an important New Christian merchant and asentista, was also involved in the 1641 conspiracy against the Portuguese king and ended up being executed. However, this is the only major case of political action in favour of Philip IV among the New Christians in Portugal. Diogo Rodrigues de Lisboa and his son Jorge Gomes de Alemo, two other important New Christian merchants and financiers from Lisbon, were also detained when the conspiracy was discovered, but they managed to convince the authorities of their innocence. Pedro de Baeça was a major merchant trading with Asia, via the carreira da Índia, who also had asientos from the Spanish king, and his decision to side with Philip IV was clearly motivated by the focus of his economic interests.

Work is still needed to assess properly the number of New Christians involved in Castilian asientos who decided to depart to Portugal and abandon their investments, but likely they were very few. Obviously, several New Christians were caught in Lisbon during the war and found themselves unable to return to Castile, just as some who were in Castile were cut off by the outbreak of war and a prohibition on travelling. However, there were cases of merchants in Seville who, allegedly, decided to return to Portugal; the Casa de Contratación complained in 1641 that it was not possible to conclude contracts for the slave trade because all the merchants had gone to Lisbon ("todos se habían marchado a Lisboa").[104] So, Portuguese New Christian loyalties were divided between Philip IV and John IV, and it seems that location and investment were often crucial—often, but not always.

Duarte da Silva, the most important banker, financier, and merchant of Lisbon in the 1640s, was detained by the Inquisition on December 9, 1647, having presented himself after the *familiares* (civil members with powers of representation) of the Holy Office had conducted a three-day search.[105] He had recently guaranteed an enormous amount of money for the construction of several ships in the Netherlands for the Portuguese. The famous Jesuit Father, António Vieira, then in that country on a mission for the Portuguese king, and a friend of the banker, declared that when the news of the detention reached there it was a blow to Portuguese independence in that the exchange rate increased by 5 percent, the commission was immediately suspended, and all credit for Portuguese business evaporated. In a letter to the Marquis of Nisa, Vieira lamented, in a rage, the imprudent step and the incapacity of the government to prevent or redress it.[106]

Francisco Sousa Coutinho, Portuguese ambassador in the Netherlands, spoke with irony of the political purpose of the operation and exposed how little power the king had: "Duarte da Silva . . . was never a Jew, except when he provided 300,000 cruzados for the construction of frigates in the Netherlands; the news [of the detention] arrived first, then the credit, which it nullified. . . . [Duarte da Silva] was in prison five years; when he knew he was about to be detained, he alerted the king, who advised him to accept detention because he would release him . . . the inquisitors had more power than the king; he only got out of jail to the gallows [auto da fé], where he was watched by the king."[107]

This episode was thus interpreted by contemporary diplomats as a political coup against Portuguese independence by the Spanish faction, although we know that it coincided with a wave of persecution of New Christians in Castile. Duarte da Silva was detained with his second son, Francisco Dias da Silva (sixteen years old), his eldest daughter, Catarina (seventeen years old, who avoided detention for one month), and his brothers-in-law, Jorge Dias Brandão and Rodrigo Aires Brandão, who were his associates in trade.[108] All of them were tortured, Duarte da Silva, his son, and Jorge Dias Brandão twice. All of them resisted the temptation to produce false declarations and false denunciations to win their freedom, thus thwarting the main purpose of the inquisitorial machine. The inquisitors had virtually nothing against them other than hearsay denunciations, but they were presented at the auto da fé on December 1, 1652, to hear a verdict of vehement suspicion of a heresy which they had to abjure, even though there had been no confession. They all stoically endured five years in jail.

The inquisitorial coup against the Portuguese war of independence generated a countercoup to safeguard crucial financial support from the New Christians. In 1649, King John IV exempted them from property confiscation by the Inquisition because of the creation of the Company of Brazil, which would play a decisive role in securing trade with Brazil, recently much damaged by Dutch corsairs, and would support the reconquest of the territories occupied by the Dutch.[109] Duarte da Silva managed to recover his financial and political standing; the trial showed that he had informers inside the Inquisition, such as the notary Gaspar Clemente, and friends there, such as Fr. João de Vasconcelos and Sebastião César de Meneses. At the outset of the inquisitorial threat, he even took refuge in the house of none other than the king's secretary, Pedro Fernandes Monteiro.[110]

Duarte da Silva had been born in Alter do Chão, in the province of Alentejo, Portugal. He had married Branca da Silva, the daughter of his cousin Joana Brandão, and in 1647 their surviving children numbered seven, ranging in age from eighteen years to seven months: four sons (Diogo Pinto, Francisco Dias, Simão Henriques, and João) and three daughters (Catarina, Serafina, and Joana). Duarte da Silva had lived in Castile, Brazil, and in Viana do Castelo, Portugal. He was able to point to extensive acts of charity and donations to confraternities and churches. It was proven that every year he ordered a significant quantity of ham from Lamego and Porto, plus *marrans* (piglets) and *chouriços* (sausages) from Alentejo for domestic consumption.[111] The inquisitors even had their own physicians check whether he had been circumcised, showing that they believed in their own speculations. Father Vieira, the Count of Óbidos, the Count of Odemira, Luís Gomes de Barros, an attorney of Lisbon, Gonçalo Pinto Soares from the house of the Marquis of Nisa, the postmaster general Luís Gomes da Mata (also a New Christian), Diogo Bernardes Pimenta, a royal high judge, Pedro Fernandes Monteiro, and Jorge Pereira, a close associate of members of the Inquisition, were among the witnesses for the defence.

Among Duarte da Silva's enemies were several merchants: Francisco Dias Mendes de Brito and his brother Diogo Mendes de Brito, whom da Silva had discredited; Gaspar Fernandes and João Rodrigues Mesa from Estremoz, whose representations to the king he had refused to support; and Domingos de Medeiros, from Viana, and Pedro de Mesquita, Jerónimo Serrão Pimentel, and Francisco Soares Serrão from Lisbon, with whom he had come into conflict over various matters, including money owed him. Intrigue at court, competition, debt, envy, and blackmail among New Christians were rampant. There were rumours that Manuel da Gama de Pádua, who was involved in the Companhia do Brazil, had used his influence to liberate his brother Jorge Lopes da Gama from the Inquisition and was informing Branca da Silva of everything that happened to her husband Duarte in prison.[112]

The verdict of vehement suspicion of heresy was coupled with five years' exile to Brazil, but there is no sign of any property confiscation, which Duarte da Silva avoided because he refused to confess. His guarantor was Manuel da Gama de Pádua, an emerging New Christian power broker who was to exert considerable influence in the following decades. A bail of 1,000 cruzados was paid for Duarte da Silva to remain at home until he recovered from ill health that had resulted from his stay in prison (two sets of torture must have left marks). This was agreed to in a document signed on December 10, 1652, and the signature is still that of General Inquisitor Francisco de Castro. In April, the inquisitors summoned Manuel da Gama de Pádua, as Silva's guarantor, to implement the exile to Brazil, but this never took place. Apparently with the support of the king, and emphasising his services to the Crown, Duarte da Silva applied to the General Council, which exempted him from exile on July 31, 1653.[113] Francisco de Castro had died at the beginning of 1653. The General Council probably did not want a first serious clash with the king when there was no replacement in sight, owing to the virtual absence of diplomatic relations with the pope, who did not recognise the kingdom of Portugal until the peace treaty between Portugal and Spain in 1668.

Duarte da Silva regained his health and quickly recovered his economic and political position. John IV died in 1656, and the queen regent, Luisa de Guzmán, showed more firmness in facing the Inquisition and the institutions controlling blood purity. On February 14, 1659, Duarte da Silva's son Francisco was given a *comenda* and allowed to wear the habit of the Order of Christ; on June 23 of the same year, a similar privilege was bestowed on the other son João, both explicitly opposed by the *Mesa da Consciência e Ordens*, because they were New Christians, and the first had been presented at the auto da fé along with his father and other relatives. This opposition was firmly disregarded by the queen regent, whose decision was supported by a papal brief. In addition, in April 1662, Duarte da Silva became responsible for arranging the credit for, and delivery of, the dowry of Catarina of Bragança on her marriage to the English king, Charles II. At the same time, he obtained the privilege of nominating a recipient of the habit of the Order of Christ, with a *tença* of 20,000 réis attached. He nominated Álvaro da Silveira; and then obtained another nomination, this time to the Order of Santiago, with a *tença* of 20,000 réis, which he gave to his son-in-law, Francisco Nicolau da Silva.[114] This son-in-law had married Joana, who at the time of the detention of her father by the Inquisition had been three years old. We shall see in part IV how important Francisco Nicolau da Silva later became in Rome.

Duarte da Silva proved to be a constant thorn in the flesh of the Inquisition. He contributed to the fight against the Holy Office all his life, first in London and then in Antwerp. It seems that he never went back to Portugal, although he continued to have his correspondents and supporters there. If we believe his declaration of his age to the Inquisition, he must have been born in 1596. By the time he died in Antwerp in 1677, he was eighty-one and had led a life that exemplified both the success New Christians could achieve in the seventeenth century and the insurmountable problems they faced in seeking full integration.[115]

{⟨≈≈≈⊙⟨W⟩⊙≈≈≈⟩}

The benefits of the Iberian Union of Crowns for the New Christian elite lasted until the 1610s, but the 1620s, with the end of the truce with the Low Countries, created a new dynamic of divergent interests in the Iberian world. Rivalry between merchants played a role in the downfall of the New Christians in Spanish America, which accelerated the divergence between Castilians and Portuguese in Iberia. The restoration of the independence of Portugal in 1640, in turn, aggravated the backlash against New Christians in Spanish America and created a division between financiers loyal to the Castilian king and to the Portuguese king. This division weakened the New Christian merchant elite.

This chapter has shown how general inquisitors in Portugal and Spain made their mark on Iberian society and has shown their involvement in factional fighting, but it should not be assumed that the conflicts they entered into with regard to the New Christians evolved according to simple institutional political allegiances. The members of the Inquisition were divided in their political opinions, as various pieces of information and indications of internal support for different parties have shown. Nevertheless, there was a logic to the way they operated, reproduced their practices, and imposed their uncompromising policy that would eventually prevail, even during periods when there was no general inquisitor. This argument is well justified by the exemption of New Christians in Portugal, in 1649, from confiscation of their property, which is the terminus ad quem of this part of the book.

CHAPTER ELEVEN

Business

THE NEW CHRISTIAN diaspora became a worldwide phenomenon as a result of push and pull factors. Amongst the former was New Christian experience of political pressure, financial extortion, and inquisitorial persecution; amongst the latter was the existence of countries with friendly policies, established communities with shared interests, and business opportunities. Migrants came from Portugal and Castile and mixed with established communities of Jews, New Christians, and Old Christians in Europe and Asia (where they also mixed with natives of the countries where they settled). They developed their communities in Africa and the Americas, there mixing with natives and Old Christians. We shall now make a journey to the different parts of the world where New Christians chose to deploy their activities.

1. Asia

By the end of sixteenth century, the annual amount invested by New Christians in maritime trade with Asia via the Cape of Good Hope was estimated at 1.5 million of 2 million cruzados, that is, 75 percent of the total, while investment in trade with Mexico via Manila was estimated as close to 500,000 cruzados of 1.5 million cruzados, that is, 30 percent of the total. These trading ventures brought a profit of 150 percent, with the *carreira da Índia* worth at least 5 million cruzados in Lisbon (if we do not consider shipwrecks). New Christians controlled, on average, 44 percent of the total Portuguese capital circulating in Asia, 4.3 million cruzados, which brought substantial profits. They had access to local credit from south Asian bankers, pioneering long-term practices that would be imitated by Dutch and English.[1] Christian confraternities, mainly *misericórdias* sponsored by the king, played a crucial role in lending money to governors and captains for their military needs, guaranteeing legacies, and transferring back to Europe large inheritances left by merchants deceased in Asia.[2] The extraordinary wealth accumulated by misericórdias was partly invested in New Christian ventures, while merchants frequently used bills of exchange to transfer money, including inheritances and pious legacies to the Catholic Church.

Dutch and English competition in Asia after the turn of the seventeenth century dramatically raised protection costs and the sums paid to the *Estado da Índia*, while a decline in the quality of shipping and naval management, reflected in a high percentage of shipwrecks, represented a significant loss on returns. However, the Portuguese managed to pursue their trade successfully during the first two decades of the seventeenth century. The turning point for Dutch naval supremacy in Asia occurred in the 1620s, but the Vereenigde Oostindische Compagnie (VOC) was still heavily in debt; profits only became regular in the followed decade.[3] In the 1630s, the Portuguese still controlled between 2 and 3 million cruzados of trading capital annually, significantly more than the Dutch, while New Christian investment of 1 million cruzados in return cargo represented one-third of the total Portuguese trading capital for all Asia, owing to the significant extent of the network involved.[4] It was the combined persecution of New Christians by the tribunals of the Inquisition in Lima, Mexico, and Goa in the 1630s and 1640s, just as Dutch competition started to bite, that contributed to reducing Portuguese capacity for investment and trade in Asia.

The story of Pedro de Baeça, or Baeza (1555–1611?), offers a good starting point for investigating New Christians in Asia. A member of the extensive Silveira family, Pedro de Baeça was the son of Fernão de Baeça and Leonor de Paz, both of whom belonged to successful New Christian merchant families. He married Catarina de Crasto (ca. 1570–1600) first, then married Ana Maria Bobadilla de Alarcón from Madrid.[5] He was taken to Asia when still quite young and gained experience of trade in India, Malacca, Southeast Asia, Macau, and Nagasaki. He returned to Portugal, invested in the carreira da Índia, and went to Madrid, part of the first generation of the Portuguese New Christian migrants to go there after the Union of Crowns.

However, like his compatriots, he did not lose his attachment to Portugal. In 1587, he entered into a contract to provision the Lisbon galleys, and in 1602 he agreed to rent the Portuguese ports' customs duties for ten years.[6] In 1611, he obtained the post of royal factor in Ternate, but apparently he died during the journey there.[7] This is a typical career for a contractor who had cut his teeth on Asian trade. What is interesting is the series of memorials he wrote in Madrid in the last years of the first decade of the seventeenth century. He was one of the first to calculate the negative impact that the Dutch would have on Portuguese trade in Asia, mainly on pepper, although by that time this commodity's value accounted for only 6 to 7 percent of the total value of return cargo, which was now dominated by Indian cloth, precious stones, and other spices.[8]

In 1608, Pedro de Baeça asked for clarification of changes that had been made in previous years to government policies concerning the Asian trade.

According to him, in 1564, the regent Cardinal Henry had confiscated all merchandise arriving in Lisbon, accusing the merchants of dealing in contraband. There was a riot, and the merchants had refused to make ready any ships for India. The regent had had to return the confiscated merchandise and tax it. He had then liberalised trade on all spices and taxed them at one-fifth, plus 18 ducados (of pieces of 10 reales) for each *quintal* of pepper, 30 ducados for the same weight of cloves and cinnamon, 35 ducados for indigo and nutmeg, and 40 ducados for mace.[9] It is impossible to trust *arbitrios* or *memoriales* on dates or values, or even official documents giving retrospective data. It may be that the event dated 1564 relates to the reform of Asian trade in 1570, studied by Magalhães Godinho.[10]

Pedro de Baeça evaluated Portuguese losses in the Asian trade as follows: 30,000 to 40,000 quintais of spices now traded by Sumatra to Suez, and 25,000 quintais of spices brought by the Dutch to northern Europe; the Dutch had sent fourteen ships of 800 tons, with 45 to 50 cannons each, and carrying 4,500 soldiers and sailors, to conquer Ternate, since the Moluccas were worth 22,000 to 24,000 quintais of cloves every year. As a consequence, the Portuguese trade had been reduced to a fraction of its previous value, with Portuguese merchants handling only a third of the spices they had traded previously. The income of the *Casa da Índia* from pepper alone went down from 1.5 million to 400,000 cruzados.

The memorial indicated the values of spices and other commodities: nutmeg and mace from Banda were bought for 1 to 2 ducados and were worth 8 ducados in Malacca; in Spain, a quintal of nutmeg was worth 120 to 130 ducados, and a quintal of mace 240 to 250 ducados, but in northern Europe they were worth much more, and the Dutch were now bringing to Europe 2,500 quintais a year against the 500 to 600 being brought by the Portuguese; sandalwood was worth 2 to 3 ducados a quintal in Timor, but in China it was worth 30 to 35 ducados, with the Portuguese taking from Timor and Solor 25,000 to 30,000 quintais every year. He also suggested trading spices via the Philippines through the Pacific, for security reasons.[11]

The homonymous nephew of Pedro de Baeça, Pedro de Baeça da Silveira (1591–1641), has regularly been confused with his uncle in the available bibliography up until the present day.[12] We have come across him before. He was the son of Diogo Lopes de Lisboa and Filipa de Paz, sister of Pedro de Baeça. When he was detained by the Inquisition of Lisbon in 1631, he pointed out that he held the contract for the import of pepper from India, still a significant trade. He also indicated that he had spent seven years, at the beginning of his professional life, in the fleets of Castile, Guinea, and the West Indies.[13] From 1627 to 1630, he spent several months of each year in Madrid, where he was involved in negotiating contracts by Portuguese New Christians. In 1627, he had entered into a contract to rent the taxation of the dry ports of Castile, which he had given up after receiving an offer of 15,000 silver ducados. He also pointed out that he had lent a great deal of money to the king, sometimes sums of more than 150,000 cruzados, while he had also imported equipment for the royal fleets. For all of this business he had been honoured with the habit of the Order of Christ.[14] Later, in the final years of his life, Pedro de Baeça da Silveira was to sign a significant number of notarial documents concerning freights (he was using English ships), money lending, and contracts for property, and these, when added to the activities he indicated to the Inquisition, present the full range of activities of a major merchant and royal contractor.[15]

Pedro de Baeça da Silveira, having been received into minor orders, was very familiar with the doctrine of the Catholic Church and never confessed any heresy. He pointed out that he had endowed a chapel under the patronage of Nossa Senhora da Guia, at the convent of São Francisco in Lisbon, to which he had donated 52,000 réis of annual interest. Moreover, he emphasized that his four sisters were nuns at the convent of Vilalonga, and two of his daughters had been admitted to the convent of Santa Ana eight days before his detention.[16] That detention did not have a long-term adverse effect, and Pedro de Baeça da Silveira continued to enjoy the king's favour following his presentation at an auto da fé in January 1633. In 1637, he obtained permission for his two sons to wear the habit of the Order of Avis, against a loan of 200,000 cruzados to the king, while, with Jorge Gomes de Alemo as his merchant associate, he managed to get a contract on brazilwood production and trade under royal monopoly. In that year Philip IV owed him more than 500,000 cruzados, not counting interest, due on loans to support trade with the East Indies and Brazil.[17]

It is estimated that the total debt of Philip IV to this group of merchants, which included Diogo Rodrigues de Lisboa, Simão de Sousa (brother-in-law of Pedro de Baeça da Silveira, and master of the Lisbon mint), Álvaro da Silveira, and Francisco Botelho Chacão, would have exceeded 2 million cruzados, a staggering sum. If we were to add the money owed to Pedro de Baeça's brother, Jorge de Paz, who became Baron da Silveira and was one of the main *asentistas* in Madrid, the amount of debt would be even higher.[18] This is an interesting case of trade in different parts of the world being based on a framework of family links extending from the financial centre in Madrid, and it explains Pedro Baeça da Silveira's final and fatal political allegiance to Philip IV.

In 1615–1616, the capital invested by New Christians in the Goa-Lisbon stretch of the carreira da Índia reached 1.3 million cruzados. The investment was made by Duarte Fernandes, Manuel de Paz, and his half brother Fernando Tinoco (all three future royal financiers in Madrid, with Fernando Tinoco becoming treasurer of the Council of Portugal in Madrid in the late 1630s), and by Fernandes's uncle, Simão Rodrigues do Brasil, his cousins Francisco Tinoco de Carvalho and Manuel Fernandes Tinoco, Francisco Mendes de Castro (acting on behalf of thirty-three investors), Francisco da Silveira and Fernão Jorge da Silveira, Pero Gonçalves Brandão, Valentim Garcia, António

Vaz Mendes, Henrique Rodrigues da Silva, António Fernandes de Sampaio, Gaspar Lopes Pereira, Manuel Cardoso, and Rui Soares de Vilaboa.[19]

There were other significant New Christian investors in the carreira da Índia who had a diverse portfolio, such as Duarte Pires Solis and Manuel Rodrigues do Porto. Investors in Brazil or in the Spanish *carrera de Indias*— such as the prominent contractor Juan Núñez Correa; the future major asentistas Marcos Fernandes Monsanto, Simão Soares and Duarte Brandão Soares; and also Diogo Teixeira de Sampaio, Duarte Dias Henriques, António de Azevedo, Luís Fernandes Gramaxo, Gaspar Bocarro, Simão Vaz de Sevilha, and Fernão Gil and Manuel Rodrigues Lamego (these two cousins of Pedro de Baeça da Silveira)—were also investing in the East Indies trade from Lisbon.[20]

These financiers had relatives, associates, and correspondents in Asia. The early persecution of the New Christian community in Goa from the 1560s to the early 1580s did not lead to extinction, while the new wave of persecution in the 1630s and 1640s contributed to the decline of the Estado da Índia. António Bocarro, who became royal chronicler and archivist in 1631 and wrote the extraordinary *Livro das plantas das fortaleza* in 1635, was a New Christian whose life testifies to shifting allegiances between Christianity and Judaism, and finally back to Christianity.[21] The presence of Ximenes, Solis, Vilasboas, Vilhegas, Cáceres (Dias Milão), and Lopes d'Elvas' relatives is well known, while there was a significant number of New Christian merchants in Kochi and in other territories.[22] East Asia had a concentration of *conversos* who had escaped both from the Inquisition of Goa and the Inquisitions of Spanish America. The community in Macau was strong enough to block several attempts by the authorities to launch religious enquiries in the 1580s and 1600s, while the community in Nagasaki, arguably supported by New Christian Jesuits (Pedro Gómez, Luís de Almeida, Aires Sanches), managed to overcome an attempt to detain five people accused of Judaism by the bishop Luís Cerqueira at the end of the sixteenth century. In the first decades of the seventeenth century, the merchants Francisco Rodrigues Pinto, Manuel Rodrigues Navarro, Afonso Vaez, Francisco Vaez, Diego Jorge, Vilela Vaz, Paulo Gonçalves, and Pero Rodrigues Nabo carried on a well-documented trade between Nagasaki, Macau, Indochina, Goa, Manila, and Acapulco.[23]

2. Seville and the Slave Trade

The migration of New Christians from Portugal to the main financial and commercial centres of Spain, Madrid and Seville, started before the 1580s, and the Iberian Union of Crowns stimulated the flow, despite contradictory policies, which included frequent prohibitions until 1629. Seville gave access to the rich trade with Spanish America, while Madrid controlled the market for loan contracts to the Crown, paid for by American silver, and also for contracts for tax farming and various monopolies (e.g., spices and tobacco), which brought significant profits by the mid-seventeenth century. Seville was regularly forced to give significant donations to the king, as happened in 1621, 1629, and 1645, while the loans imposed on the *consulado* (guild of merchants) reached 18 million ducados during the seventeenth century.[24] The practice of sequestration of property carried by the *carrera de Indias*, launched by Charles V, was repeated in 1629, an operation valued at 1 million ducados, and again in 1649, which brought an even higher amount.[25] New Christians suffered a good part of these exactions.

In the 1630s, Portuguese investment in the transatlantic trade handled from Seville represented at least 20 percent of the total, not counting the slave trade, and almost all was in the hands of New Christians.[26] The links between major merchants in Seville and the asentistas in Madrid are well known. A case in point is Duarte de Acosta, who acted in the 1630s as an agent in Seville for Alfonso Cardoso, Fernando Ladrón de Guevara, and Duarte Fernandes, in the matter of the contract to provision the ocean fleet in the 1650s. He was eventually offered a place at the Contaduría Mayor de Hacienda and became one of the few asentistas who continuously received consignations of silver at the *Casa de Contratación* in Seville.[27] Marcos Fernandes Monsanto, another important asentista, a cousin of Simão Soares, one of the richest men in Madrid, with whom he negotiated loans to the king, was responsible for conducting his business between Lisbon and Madrid, while his son, Luís Correia Monsanto, rented the customs duties in Seville. Luís Correia involved Felipe Martínez D'Orta in the administration of this contract, and when the contract was extended up to the 1650s, Ruy Diaz Angel, Francisco Lopes Brandão, and Manuel Rodrigues de Andrade were also involved.[28]

The contracts for the slave trade to Spanish America, under royal control, were regularly renegotiated after the 1590s. Carrying contraband was rampant in this trade, and had been since the very beginning, a result of (arguably) low margins of profit and customs inefficiency. Negotiations were concluded with a single contractor, who would have overall responsibility for the trade, being authorised to issue licences to other merchants for up to a certain number of slaves against payment of an annual lump sum to the Crown. For the contractor, the business could be very profitable because it offered multiple possibilities for carrying contraband under the pretext of supplying slaves, the contraband being mainly nondeclared slaves and Indian textiles traded for American silver, cochineal, indigo, and sugar.[29] On the Portuguese side, as we have seen, there had been autonomous contracts for trading slaves from Cape Verde and Angola since the sixteenth century. The Iberian Union of Crowns did not manage to integrate the two sides of the trade, production and distribution, on a regular basis, but in some cases, the *Consejo de Hacienda* (council of finances) or the *Contaduria Mayor* (royal office of accounting) did bring them into line by putting them under the same contractor. The first three contractors in our list (see below) controlled both the slave trade contract from Angola and the contract to provide Spanish America, but this did not prevent the system from breaking down.

The contractors for the slave trade to Spanish America were, from 1595 to 1600, Pedro Gomes Reinel, who combined this contract with one for trading slaves from Angola (he was to lead Cosme Ruiz, inheritor of the famous Simón Ruiz bank, into bankruptcy in 1606); from 1601 to 1604, João Rodrigues Coutinho, who also combined the contract with one for slaves from Angola; from 1605 to 1609, Gonçalo Vaz Coutinho, brother of the previous contractor, although the contract for trading slaves from Angola was held by Duarte Dias Henriques from 1607 to 1614, a hiatus due to direct administration by the Crown; from 1615 to 1622, António Fernandes de Elvas, who combined this with contracts for trading slaves from Cape Verde and from Angola; from 1623 to 1631, Manuel Rodrigues Lamego, brother of António Rodrigues Lamego, who conducted his business first in Madrid and then in Rouen while both brothers were associated with Juan Núñez Sarabia; and from 1632 to 1638, Melchior Gomes Angel, in association with Cristóvão Mendes de Sousa.[30]

These contractors were New Christians except for João Rodrigues Coutinho and Gonçalo Vaz Coutinho, the former knight of the Order of Christ, member of the Council of Portugal, governor of Mina, and in 1602 nominated governor of Angola (where he died the following year). The annual payment during the period of Pedro Gomes Reinel was 100,000 ducados, increased to 170,000 under João Rodrigues Coutinho, but cut to 140,000 ducados under Gonçalo Vaz Coutinho. António Fernandes de Elvas agreed to pay 115,000 ducados annually (his competitor was Juan Núñez Correa, who offered more but whose conditions were not acceptable); and Manuel Rodrigues de Lamego obtained the contract for 120,000 ducados annually (bidding against Luís de Fonseca and his uncle André de Fonseca, Simão Pires Solis, Rui Dias Angel, and his father-in-law Francisco Duarte).[31]

The last contract, in 1632, brought the king only 95,000 ducados a year, but from 1638 to 1639, the bids for the new contract, which were disrupted by the independence of Portugal, were higher again, with André Rodrigues de Estremoz (brother of the counsellor Fernando Arias de Mesa, who went to Naples) offering 130,000 a year but without a limit on the number of slaves. While the contract with João Rodrigues Coutinho stipulated at least one slave for each ton of the ship, thirty-eight years later André Rodrigues promised to transport thirty pieces (one piece corresponding to one prime male slave) per ton, this language indicating the scale of the dehumanisation of this trade.[32]

There was certainly an enormous potential for profit: from 1595 to 1610 there were 498 ships and 75,389 slaves registered, a dramatic increase from the previous period, most of whom were transported to Cartagena de Indias and the Caribbean islands, but many became a form of contraband, disappearing down the route through Rio de la Plata to Potosi, despite successive attempts at control by the authorities.[33] In 1614, a meeting of the Consejo de Hacienda complained that three years without a contract had represented a loss of 360,000 ducados for the Crown of Castile and 300,000 for the Crown of Portugal.[34] The opening of the slave market in Angola had a significant impact on the transatlantic slave trade, which grew during the seventeenth century, before it became the huge trade in human beings of the eighteenth and first half of the nineteenth century.

The involvement of New Christians in this infamous trade went beyond the crucial role of asentistas. There was a vast network of subcontractors, associates, and correspondents at different levels, including regional fairs and local ports. The case of Gonzalo Núñez de Sepúlveda (1585–1655) is perhaps the most successful. Born in Lisbon from a family involved in the Asian trade, he went to Luanda and worked as representative of the slave trade contractor António Fernandes de Elvas (and the latter's widow), then represented the contractor Henrique Gomes da Costa. In the late 1620s, Gonzalo Núñez moved to Seville, where he joined the financial operations of the bankers linked to Manuel de Paz, who guaranteed his naturalisation, as we have seen before. He married Mencia de Andrade, sister of the banker Enrique de Andrade, and was given access to the military Order of Santiago by the king in 1639. In the 1650s he decided to institute a chapel at the cathedral of Seville for him and his family, the chapel of Concepción, from which the remains of Christian conquerors of the city from the Muslims in 1248 had to be removed.[35] The chapel included an impressive baroque altar with sculptures by Alonso Martínez of the Immaculate Conception, St. Joseph and St. Paul, and on the sides sculptures of St. Gonzalo and St. Anthony of Padua, (a regular reference among New Christians of Portuguese origin). The coat of arms of the Sepúlveda are part of the iconographic programme. North of the cathedral, next to the Hospital of Virgen Macarena, there is still a street named Gonzalo Núñez de Sepúlveda.

It is estimated that the slave trade to Spanish America generated 100 million pesos for Portuguese merchants between 1595 and 1640, which sum represented half to three-quarters of the slave trade to Brazil in the same period.[36] A total of 250 million pesos for all the transatlantic slave trade in that period may be a reasonable estimate, equivalent to 181 million ducados. However, the cost of political protection and bribery at both origin and destination, shipping, wages, food, medicine, and commissions to a succession of agents, would have made the business quite perilous, even if we do not consider the mortality rate of the slaves. Contraband, which could include carrying three times the registered number of slaves, as well as goods such as textiles, would have made the investment profitable.

The operation was extremely complicated from the beginning. The contractor needed to bid higher than his competitors, which narrowed the profit margin. Moreover, he needed to pay upfront an extraordinarily large deposit

FIGURE 11.1. Alonso Martínez, sculpture of the Immaculate Conception for the chapel of San Pablo, Cathedral of Seville, ca. 1655, endowed by Gonzalo Núñez de Sepúlveda. Courtesy Cabildo de la Catedral de Sevilla. Photo courtesy of José Manuel Díaz Blanco.

of money to guarantee the annual rent due to the Crown, defined with precise dates, and he needed to obtain guarantees from other merchants in case of default. António Nunes Caldeira, nephew of Manuel Caldeira, who had a solid financial background, was outbid by Pedro Gomes Reinel, who had to combine this with other contracts, each helping to finance the others. Reinel eventually went to jail, accused of fraud for not paying the agreed deposit of 100,000 ducados. He renounced the contract, returning the rights to the Crown, in 1599 (the contract was valid until 1604), but he had to manage it for the following year, until a new contractor was found. João Rodrigues Coutinho was due to pay an upfront deposit of 250,000 ducados, and he had to commit to delivering at least 38,500 slaves in nine years, plus one thousand for the king.[37] These obligations led to his property being (temporarily) sequestrated after his death. Gonçalo Vaz Coutinho was suspended in the first months of his contract, but managed to recover his rights and sold an enormous number of licences in the final years of his contract.[38] António Fernandes de Elvas went bankrupt with a set of contracts in arrears, and it was left to his widow, Helena Rodrigues Solis, the daughter of Jorge Rodrigues Solis, to try and save part of the investment.[39]

The required guarantee against possible default was generally given by other merchants, but João Rodrigues Coutinho decided to involve dozens of individuals in specific small towns, particularly in Herencia, Ciudad Real, and Tembleque in the region of Toledo. This became a good example of the "empire of paper," as Fernando Bouza defined royal administration in Spain, because the recorded guarantee occupies three volumes with around five thousand folios each. This operation, based on the estimated value of rural and urban property that guaranteed the slave trade contract reflects the financial ambitions of countryside small property owners, men and women.[40] However, the risks of this investment were denounced by the Trinitarian Fr. Bernardo Monroy, who attacked it from the pulpit in Tembleque and insisted that investors would be stripped from their assets, to the disgust of Jerónimo de Hernández, the agent for João Rodrigues Coutinho.[41] The return on this gigantic operation is nowhere to be seen, but management costs must have been high, particularly when added to payments to numerous factors, most of them New Christians, who controlled the transport and delivery of slaves in the main ports of the Atlantic.

The economics of acquiring slaves in Africa, transporting them, keeping them alive, and selling them in Spanish America have been very well analysed in relation to the expeditions of 1613–1614 and 1616–1619, from Cachéu (Guinea) to Cartagena de Indias (and then Lima), by the merchant Manuel Bautista Pérez, who became the wealthiest merchant in Lima in the 1620s and 1630s.[42] On the first trip, he was an agent for several investors; on the second, a minor partner in an investment put together by his uncle, Diogo Rodrigues de Lisboa, who provided two ships he owned. The margins of profit were not particularly significant—between 25 percent on the trade from Guinea and 10 percent on that from Angola (distances mattered)—because of the significant mortality rate, taxation, the cost of keeping the slaves alive (food, medicine, and doctors), buildings rented along the way, freights, and the amortization of ships.

The time taken to realise the profit was long: the second voyage by Manuel Bautista Pérez lasted two and a half years, and this merchant decided, unusually, to undertake the last part of the trip from Cartagena to Lima himself. He was right to do so, because this section produced the highest profit—the value of a slave varied from 270 to 310 pesos in Cartagena to 600 in Lima. In any case, the investment required several years of risky waiting, during which there might be shipwrecks or piracy. This explains the rampant contraband in Indian textiles and undeclared slaves, the real numbers of which were more than double the numbers declared and taxed. Moreover, each trip required over 150 types of commodity for trading in Guinea (seventy from Europe) and around 100 people were involved in buying and selling slaves. Manuel Bautista's main support in Cachéu was his brother, João Bautista, who died there in 1617.[43]

Manuel Bautista Pérez, born in 1589 in Ançã, in the district of Coimbra, Portugal, benefitted from the support and network of his uncle, Diogo Rodrigues de Lisboa (1568–1648), in fact a second uncle who was Manuel Bautista's maternal grandmother's nephew. The uncle occupied a major position in Lisbon until the 1640s, and was involved in the slave trade, regularly took on the contract for pepper, and traded with Brazil. He was associated with other major merchants, such as Pedro Baeça da Silveira, Manuel Rodrigues de Elvas, Juan Núñez Correa, Fernando Tinoco, Duarte Fernandes, Duarte Dias Henriques, and Simão Soares, with whom he combined resources to provide the loans they were forced to make to the Crown and the carreira da Índia, despite having protested about repeated extortion.[44] Diogo Rodrigues's trial at the Inquisition, from January 11, 1632, to January 9, 1633, was one of the fastest on record, and the weak accusations brought against him were not substantiated. He denied everything and insisted, with many ecclesiastical witnesses, mainly Jesuits, on his Christian practice and charity. Typically, he was reconciled rather than absolved, following a verdict of mild suspicion of heresy. His trial followed hot on the heels of the previous one, that of Pedro de Baeça da Silveira, sentenced the same day and also reconciled following a verdict of mild suspicion after he refused to confess. A concerted action against two of the major merchants of the period had failed.[45]

3. Spanish America

In 1627, in Cartagena de Indias, Manuel Bautista Pérez married Guiomar Henriques, daughter of his cousin João Vaz Henriques. António Nunes Gramaxo, a leading New Christian merchant, then in Cartagena, was their godfather. Manuel Bautista Pérez had lived in Seville with his father, Francisco Pérez from Granada, and his mother, Isabel Gomes of Lisbon, who had died when he was a child. He had established himself in Lima in 1619, and there he had built an extraordinary palace, known as the Casa de Pilatos, near the Plaza Mayor. The house's long frontage faced the Convent of St. Francis, nowadays the headquarters of the Constitutional Tribunal of Peru, but Manuel Bautista Pérez owned other premises, including offices, stores, and shops, that were built around this palace. A very good library, with books on religion, history, geography, law, philosophy, mathematics, and accountancy, was part of the main palace.

Manuel Bautista Pérez's household has been defined as a cluster of four families: his own; that of his wife; that of Sebastián Duarte, a close associate who had married Manuel Bautista Pérez's sister-in-law, Isabel Henriques; and that of another brother-in-law, Luis de Vega; fifty-eight people in all.[46] A captain of the militia, member of the main confraternities, known for his charity and relations with viceroys and ecclesiasts, Bautista Pérez was part of a network of bankers and merchants based in Seville. The network included Afonso and Gaspar Rodrigues Passarinho, Antonio Nunes Gramaxo, Enrique de Andrade, and Duarte Fernandes in Seville; Juan Rodrigues Mesa, Luis Fernández Suárez, and Blas de Paz Pinto in Cartagena de Indias; Juan de Silva in Portobelo; and Sebastián de Vaez Sevilla in Mexico, to name only the most important members; but it extended to Luanda, Cachéu, Acapulco, Manila, Potosi, Tucumán, Buenos Aires, Rouen, Antwerp, and Madrid.[47]

Many of these New Christian merchants travelled around the Atlantic ports, visiting both Iberian empires, first as agents and then as full partners or independent merchants with associates, as happened with Manuel Bautista Pérez or Antonio Núñez Gramaxo, until they made a significant fortune and settled in the place they considered most advantageous, drawing on the networks they had gradually built up. The main trade that created the Atlantic geographical and historical complex was the slave trade, combined with silver, but there were many other profitable trades from the Americas.[48]

Cochineal, made from drying and pressing a parasitic insect found on cacti in Mexico, became extremely important as the perfect red dye.[49] Indigo from Central America competed with south Asian imports to Europe and was used to make a strong blue dye; in 1577, already more than 400 farms produced indigo in Central America and Yucatán.[50] Hides produced in the Caribbean and in South America had an impact in Europe. Pearls collected in the Caribbean and on the northeast coast of South America competed with pearls from the Persian Gulf, the gulf of Mannar in Sri Lanka, and Brunei. Tobacco transformed European, African, and Asian habits from the 1620s onwards.[51] This last crucial product still needs further research, but we know that Francisco de Ávila, Jorge de Acosta, and Fernando Lopes de Acosta were very early accused of smuggling it to northern Europe through the Canary

Islands, and through Portuguese and Galician ports.[52] Tobacco was made the subject of a state monopoly in Spain in 1631, and the taxes on it were generally farmed to New Christians, both in Portugal and Spain, until the early eighteenth century.[53] The contractors of the royal monopoly of tobacco in Castile from the 1630s to the 1690s were nearly all New Christians, such as Antonio de Soria, Luis Mendez Enríquez, Juan de Rosales, Diego Gómez de Salazar, Jorge Bautista Carrafa, Simón Ruiz de Pessoa, Francisco Lopes Pereira, Manuel de Aguilar, Luís Marques Cardoso, and Manuel de Cáceres.[54] The impact of tobacco on royal finances in the Iberian world is well known; for example, in India, it significantly helped the Portuguese finances during the seventeenth century, when it was reexported via Lisbon from Brazil.[55]

However, New Christians were not limited to trading enterprises. A major merchant, Simón Vaez de Sevilla, resident in Mexico City, organised a "putting-out" system (domestic subcontracting) with imported fabrics given to local seamstresses who would sew them into clothes for the markets in the mining towns of Northern Mexico.[56] The other most successful merchant, Manuel Bautista Pérez, had a large farm near Lima, with many dozen slaves, which sent its produce to the local market.[57] Another significant New Christian merchant in Cartagena de Indias, Blas de Paz Pinto, possessed a cattle ranch near the city to supply its need for meat.[58] Although these New Christians specialised in trade, for reasons that included the necessity of being ready to depart in case of persecution, they also invested in the productive sectors previously mentioned. The supposed separation between production and trade needs to be nuanced.

The riches accumulated by the primary merchants in the 1630s in Spanish America have been estimated at between 400,000 and 900,000 pesos per merchant; but only part of this investment would have been in the form of real estate or state rents, because most of the money was invested in trade that would have taken years to yield a profit.[59] These merchants were at the head of a very complex hierarchy ranging from large and midsize merchants with regional businesses to local shopkeepers and poor peddlers, the last two of whom were indebted to a chain of suppliers. The primary merchants were also dependent on suppliers, and on top of this they received significant investments from other people for whom they had to produce interest, while they loaned money as bankers to the royal finances and to local people. It is estimated that the tribunal of Cartagena realised around 200,000 pesos in 1635–1639 through the confiscation of New Christian property, and the tribunal of Mexico realised 528,255 pesos in 1642–1649 from the same procedure; but we know that in some cases, such as that of Manuel Bautista Pérez in Lima, Peru, the Inquisition was still trying to collect debts ten years after confiscating the property.[60]

The reaction to inquisitorial activity by victims' families—which might range from partial recovery from disaster to decline into total indigence is difficult to assess; it would require specific research into the material situation of the widows and children, who might have changed their names and migrated, a common reaction. The two sisters Guiomar Henriques and Isabel Henriques, widows of Manuel Bautista Pérez and Sebastián Duarte, both excommunicated by the Inquisition and executed, with five and four children, respectively, suffered severely from the confiscation of their property. We know that they pleaded to retrieve their dowries, which should have been protected by law, finally denouncing the poverty in which they had been left after a fortune worth more than 200,000 pesos had disappeared, and asking for a pension.[61] We do not know the result of these requests, but in 1656, the will of Joan de Nolete, by then probably the wealthiest merchant in Lima, recorded that he owed 15,240 pesos to Guiomar and 8,533 pesos to Isabel.[62] Apparently, they had continued to take action to improve their lot and had decided to invest part of the money eventually recovered.

Everyone in this society was in debt to someone else, although at different levels. Wealthy New Christians also knew how to hide property and how to leave account books that declared they had borrowed money from colleagues who were not under suspicion by the Inquisition; these colleagues would then claim the money from the latter after confiscation of the accused's property. The persecution of New Christians in 1635–1649 in Spanish America disrupted significant networks of trade, triggering the collapse of the slave trade to that area for several decades and diverting it to Brazil and the emergent Dutch and English colonies. The claims of numerous merchants in Seville, Lisbon, and Madrid concerning investments and commodities entrusted to prisoners of the Inquisition, rather than owned by them, took many years to verify and satisfy.

The tribunal of Lima became infamous for systematically avoiding compliance with financial orders from the king and even from the General Council. Inquisitors and their close associates were involved in the disappearance of assets. The wealthy merchant Enrique de Paz, for instance, was detained in 1635 and reconciled in Lima in 1639. His property had been seized and sold as soon as he was detained, and the familiar of the Holy Office, Francisco de Sosa, had become the depositary for his assets. In 1638, Manuel de Monte Alegre, who was responsible for the defence of the prisoner, launched a prosecution of Francisco de Sosa to ascertain the whereabouts of the assets. A significant number of creditors presented their claims, among whom was the prisoner's business partner Francisco Gutiérrez de Coca, by coincidence himself a familiar of the Holy Office, who claimed 25,000 pesos of profits from his investment in the company.[63]

The combined activities of the creditors of Diego López de Fonseca and Antonio de Acuña, both detained in Lima in 1635 and reconciled in 1639, was even more significant, because in 1633 the prisoners had brought with them to Portobelo 200,000 pesos worth of merchandise, while they had instructions to collect 30,000 pesos in outstanding claims. They would earn 6 percent commission on the sales and 2 percent on the money collected for creditors. It was a typical contract, although the amount of the investment involved was unusual. The most important merchants in Seville, the Passarinho brothers, Enrique de Andrade, Francisco Fernández de Solis, Francisco Antunes, Simón Rodriguez Bueno, and Manuel Mendez de Acuña, father of the prisoner, and also Jorge de Paz da Silveira in Madrid and Manuel López de Noronha in Cartagena de Indias, were involved. We are talking here about hundreds of names in a trial involving many very rich people, with numerous documents, including printed declarations of cargos with the names of shipmasters, memoranda, and copies of contracts.[64]

Despite some involvement of Old Christian merchants, viceroys, and local authorities in New Christian business, it was local conflicts, divisions between rich and poor within the community, the crude financial demands made by the tribunals and, eventually, the political disruption of the Iberian Union of Crowns that may explain the huge amount of inquisitorial activity against New Christians from 1635 to 1649 in Lima, Cartagena, and Mexico.[65] In 1642 in Mexico City, the last place to launch massive detentions, the protection of the viceroy, the Duke of Escalona, collapsed before the determination of the bishop of Puebla, Juan de Palafox y Mendoza, a visitor from the Inquisition who manipulated the uprising in Portugal to persecute the New Christian community by building on a panic reaction to rumours of uprising in various ports of the Spanish Empire that had a significant community of Portuguese merchants, sailors, and soldiers.[66]

4. Brazil

Although New Christians in Brazil were also targeted by the Inquisition on various occasions, particularly during the visit of 1618–1620, the region was under the jurisdiction of the distant tribunal of Lisbon.[67] In spite of numerous denunciations, particularly during the enquiry of 1646 (studied by Anita Novinsky), there was not a corresponding number of detentions: in the whole seventeenth century, fifty-nine New Christians were prosecuted, in contrast to 484 in the eighteenth century.[68] There was nothing similar to the massive and disruptive detentions in Spanish America in the 1630s and 1640s. Thiago Krause notes that no member of the political elite of Bahia, classified as unusually open, was prosecuted by the Inquisition. He highlights that during the visit of 1591–1593, half of the New Christians in Bahia were married to Old Christians, as were two-thirds of the New Christians in Pernambuco. The area of Rio de Janeiro was not touched by the Inquisition until the repressive wave of the early eighteenth century.[69] This high level of intermarriage was certainly a result of the significant demographic disproportion between the male and female populations of European origin, as Evaldo Cabral de Mello has already noted. Ambrósio Fernandes Brandão, a New Christian collector of the tenth for the contractor Bento Dias Santiago, merchant, and sugar planter, who wrote one of the best descriptions of Brazil, was accused twice at the Inquisition but apparently suffered no trial.[70]

It is tempting to talk about realpolitik in the case of Brazil as a growing colony, but at the same time, in Asia, the Inquisition of Goa launched two waves of detentions against New Christians in the 1560s–1570s and the 1630s–1640s that had economic and military consequences. There was also a big wave of New Christian prosecutions in Brazil, mainly in Rio, in the early decades of the eighteenth century. Two generations of refugees from Portugal, a sudden and high concentration of New Christians, less intermarriage, and tougher standards imposed by the Inquisition are possibly the combined factors that explain the latter development. In the first half of the seventeenth century, a significant number of New Christians in Brazil—merchants, farmers, and sugar mill owners—acted as factors, correspondents, and associates of important contractors in Portugal and Spain. There was a freedom of speech unthinkable in Portugal, attested to by the different enquiries. We will balance here an analysis of the contractors involved with Brazil and the economic agents active in the colony.

The enslaved people traded to Brazil, some of them smuggled into Spanish America down the Rio de la Plata, had become increasingly important, because the Portuguese controlled both the production in Africa and the distribution across the Atlantic. Luiz Felipe de Alencastro rightly stated that Brazil was formed in Africa, that is, the sugar plantations, and after the 1620s, the tobacco plantations depended on this infamous trade.[71] Nor was there any clear division between merchants and the owners of farms in the Americas. Duarte Dias Henriques (1570–1631), for example, invested simultaneously in sugar plantations in Pernambuco and the contract for slaves in Angola; and he traded down the Rio de la Plata, exported sugar and tobacco to Amsterdam, had interests in the carreira da Índia, bought *padrões de juro* (the interest on the Crown's rents), participated in *asientos* in Madrid, and rented the customs duties from the dry ports and the tithe from the sea ports.[72]

The Portuguese economy of the Atlantic had a reputation for free trade because there was only royal control of the main contracts for the slave trade, which would in any case be subcontracted and licensed to many private merchants, while dealing in contraband was embedded in the system. On the Spanish side, the carrera de Indias was under tighter control, but there was room for private arrangements. At first, only the sugar trade paid customs duties, but in the early 1630s, part of the tobacco trade became controlled by the Crown, which established contracts for the acquisition, transport, and distribution of tobacco in Spain and Portugal. The contract for the import and export of brazilwood, which had always been under the Crown's monopoly, was reckoned to be worth 61,000 cruzados a year around 1627. In the

1630s, the contract was held by Álvaro de Azevedo (who had been sentenced by the Inquisition in 1627), and he traded with Rio de Janeiro and Paraíba, in partnership with Luís Vaz de Resende.[73] The peace with the Netherlands from 1609 to 1621 favoured the expansion of trade with northern Europe, and this was facilitated by the New Christian and Jewish communities in Antwerp, Amsterdam, and Hamburg. The growing presence of these communities in Italy in that period, mainly in Livorno, Pisa, and Venice, also promoted trade with Brazil.

The disruption provoked in the south Atlantic by the war with the Dutch from 1621 onwards led to the capture of 547 Portuguese ships between 1623 and 1638, followed by the capture of 249 in just one year in 1647 to 1648, which suggests that over a thousand were taken in the period 1621 to 1649, most of them involved in the sugar trade.[74] This situation naturally increased the costs of maritime freights and the insurance of these, while the closure of the ports of Brazil in 1634 to 1636 represented a painful disruption to trade. The war also implied constant requests to merchants and New Christians for special donations, particularly for the reconquest of Bahia in 1624 (200,000 cruzados) and for the (failed) reconquest of Pernambuco in 1631 (500,000 cruzados).[75]

A decline in the royal finances had a domino effect, with tougher controls on contraband in Lisbon, which led to the transfer of merchants' capital to the northern ports of Aveiro, Porto, Viana, and Vila do Conde, and also to Setúbal (one of the two hubs, with Aveiro, for salt export), where the unloading of Brazilian sugar and trade with northern Europe developed in those decades, while maritime trade in Lisbon stagnated.[76] Risks at sea and Dutch conquests led to the imposition of royal contracts for the supply of the main ports of Brazil in that period, such as the contract signed by Pedro de Baeça da Silveira and Jorge Gomes Alemo in 1638. This contract involved the sequestration of ships and provoked protests from private merchants in Porto and was instigated by Manuel Fernandes de Morais, an associate of Duarte da Silva in Lisbon, thus indicating the rivalry that existed between competitors for contracts.[77]

Despite the arrival of peace between Portugal and the Netherlands after the acclamation of John IV, the war in the colonies went on unabated as the Dutch sensed an opportunity to make territorial gains. Conflict occurred in Asia with significant losses for the Portuguese, but the Dutch were beaten in the south Atlantic because of the superior numbers of Portuguese settled in the area who decided to take matters into their own hands. In 1648, an expedition led by the governor of Rio de Janeiro, Salvador Correia de Sá, managed to reconquer Luanda and São Tomé from the Dutch, cutting off their supply of slaves.[78] In 1649, the creation of the Company of Brazil was supported by the exemption of New Christians from the confiscation of their property by the Inquisition. New Christian participation was imposed as a matter of course because of divergent interests between private merchants. The Company played a crucial role in protecting trade by using armed convoys, and thus it made a successful contribution to the war in Brazil against the Dutch West Indies Company, which was finally ousted in 1654.

The Company of Brazil reflected an association between New Christian and Old Christian merchants that contradicted simplistic assumptions about exclusive New Christian networks or inquisitorial persecution supported by public opinion. Among the sixteen merchants on the board of the company (nine deputies and seven counsellors) were the New Christians Baltasar Rodrigues de Matos, Francisco Botelho Chacão, Gaspar Dias de Mesquita, Afonso Serrão de Oliveira, Álvaro Fernandes d'Elvas, Manuel da Gama de Pádua (who would play a major role during the period that followed), Duarte da Silveira, and Diogo da Silveira. Among the Old Christians were Gaspar Pacheco and Gaspar Malheiro (both of whom had denounced the economic impact of the persecution of New Christians), with Francisco Fernandes Furna, Matias Lopes, João Guterres, and Sebastião Nunes. There is no information on the social status of the remaining two board members, Jerónimo Gomes Pessoa and Luís Dias Franco, although their names suggest New Christian kinship.[79] Further research is required, for example, into whether some Old Christians names were in fact New Christians who had satisfied the blood purity enquiry, but in any case, an entanglement of interest is revealed here.

The significant presence of foreign merchants in this period, attested by the records of inquisitorial visits to ships and also by these merchants' participation in the fleet and in the trading investments of the Company of Brazil, must be related to the persecution of New Christians. Despite the extraordinary resistance of these merchants, who benefitted from the communities created abroad by the Jewish diaspora, trade between Portugal and northern Europe became increasingly controlled by the English (who specialised in salt cod and textiles), and the Dutch, the French, the Flemish, and the Germans (who specialised in cereals, arms, and munitions).[80] Foreign merchants always had a presence in Portuguese commerce, particularly from the late Middle Ages to the sixteenth century, and enjoyed royal privileges granted to attract their capital and encourage them to develop trade.[81] The Iberian Union of Crowns made the system less open, with harder restrictions on foreign access to the Iberian colonial world, but the need for transport allowed the circumvention of these restrictions, until the 1630s and 1640s registered a shift towards more openness that would deepen in the following decades.

Anita Novinsky identified New Christian families involved in the government of Bahia—namely, Mateus Lopes Franco, Diogo Lopes Ulhoa, António Gomes Pessoa, Diogo da Costa Carvalho, Bento da Silva Bravo, Diogo de Leão, Duarte Álvares Ribeiro, Lopo Rodrigues Ulhoa, and the relatives of Duarte da Silva who temporarily worked in Bahia, Jorge Dias Brandão and Rodrigues

Aires Brandão.[82] They were all merchants, but also plantation and sugar mill owners.

The family Ulhoa is an interesting case. André Lopes Ulhoa (or Ilhoa), illegitimate son of Manuel Lopes Ulhoa (or Ilhoa), born in Lisbon around 1572 and living in Bahia since 1602, was interrogated by the Inquisition in June 1620. He declared a large plantation, half of the island of Cajaíba, rented at one-fifth of the production for around 80,000 réis annually, which was received as a dowry for his marriage to the Old Christian Ana Silveira in 1612. The dowry included an enclosure for cattle near the river Paraguaçu. He was manager of a sugar plantation and mill belonging to his uncle, Diogo Lopes Ulhoa (the same name as that of the future secretary of the government) and benefitted from the estate's production owing to inheritance arrangements. André also owned houses in Salvador in Bahia, a property on the street of the Company of Jesus rented to Fernão Nunes at 60,000 réis annually, and another property on the street of Our Lady of Ajuda rented to António Rodrigues Chaves at 40,000 réis annually. André declared a rich collection of furniture and jewels. He had debts, as usual, to several merchants, including Diogo Rodrigues de Lisboa, one of the main bankers of the kingdom. He had relatives married to the Orta family in Antwerp, and in 1617, his uncle had sent him to the royal court in Madrid, although André did not give details of his business there.[83]

The uncle Diogo Lopes de Ulhoa must have been a very rich and powerful man. In 1610 he invested in the chapel of the archangel Raphael at the Augustinian convent of Nossa Senhora da Graça in Lisbon as the burial place for his wife, who had died the previous year, for himself and his descendants (he mentioned his brother, António Lopes Ulhoa, married to Florença Gomes). He paid 400,000 réis upfront with the signature of the contract and guaranteed 60,000 réis of annual interest, invested in the royal taxes for Lisbon, for daily masses and annual offices.[84]

André Lopes Ulhoa's case at the Inquisition was one of several dozen brought against New Christians from Brazil in the seventeenth century. André benefitted from the fact that he had taken advantage of the time of grace during the inquisitorial visit in 1618 to confess his Jewish mourning for a deceased aunt in 1609. His emotion is understandable. Diogo Lopes Ulhoa and Branca Gomes did not have children and he had been educated by them. He considered Branca Gomes as his mother. He received a judgment of abjuration of mildly suspected heresy, spared both from the auto da fé and the penitential habit.[85]

If this case attests to the economic capacity of the New Christians, the next generation, represented by Diogo Lopes Ulhoa, whose relationship to André and the homonymous Diogo still need to be verified (probably he was son of António Lopes Ulhoa) combined political, social, and economic power. Diogo

Lopes Ulhoa was secretary to the governors Diogo Luís de Oliveira, Count of Miranda (1627–1635) and Fernando de Mascarenhas, Count of Torre (1639), represented the merchants at the meetings of the municipal council, supported the defence of the city, donated money to the government, possessed three sugar mills, and engaged in diplomatic activity on behalf of Portuguese independence in northern Europe in the 1650s.[86]

The progression of the family was not linear. There was a first setback with the son, António Lopes Ulhoa, who saw his application for the habit of Santiago refused on May, 5, 1641, because of New Christian background on both sides, plus the fatal kinship to the uncle Simão Rodrigues Solis, executed by burning for the desecration of the Church of Santa Engrácia in 1630.[87] This situation was reversed with money and diplomatic activity. On July 5, 1655, Diogo obtained 50,000 réis of *tença* from the Order of Santiago.[88] On May 4, 1663, he obtained acceptance into the Order of Christ against the opinion of the council, with a papal dispensation from "blood defect" supported by the king.[89] He had been responsible for the royal treasure in Brazil (*provedor-mor*), when he obtained the transmission of the job to his son António on November 8, 1661.[90] His son António obtained 50,000 réis of annual tença for himself on October, 18, 1673, 200,000 réis of tença for his five daughters, and he guaranteed the transmission of the job of provider of services to the royal treasurer to his son José on October 14, 1675.[91] António's other son, Diogo, obtained the status of both knight and fidalgo of the royal house with *moradia* on July 10, 1709.[92] Thus three generations of aristocratic status were obtained through having the right sponsors, lending and donating money to the king, and engaging with and contributing to diplomatic activities of the Portuguese restoration.

The relationships between Jews and New Christians have been well studied for Dutch Brazil, a place of exceptional religious tolerance.[93] Several Jews were detained in a military campaign there by the Portuguese, but others dared to go to Bahia, where they were arrested. This was the case with Isaac de Castro, who had apparently been baptized in Tartas, in the South of France, by New Christian parents who had escaped from Bragança and who later went to Amsterdam, from where Isaac went on to Recife. The defiance of Isaac de Castro, who strongly affirmed his Jewish faith during the inquisitorial process and was executed after the auto da fé on December 15, 1647, in Lisbon, became famous in Europe.[94] This case calls attention to the international connections of Jews and New Christian in Brazil. Several New Christian merchants had been in northern Europe before settling in Brazil, particularly Manuel Homem de Carvalho in Amsterdam and Hamburg, Gabriel Mendes in Hamburg, and Miguel Francês (a well-known family) in the South of France, Antwerp, Amsterdam, and Hamburg.[95] Circulation in Europe might have contributed to commercial expertise and the reinforcement of merchant networks.

5. Madrid

The financial power of the Portuguese New Christians in Madrid has been relatively well evaluated. Their investment in the asientos for loans to the Crown from 1626 to 1650 is estimated at 81 million ducados.[96] In 1647, when the second bankruptcy of Philip IV occurred, there was a total of 13 million ducados of debt. Among the main creditors were the baroness Beatriz da Silvera (or Silveira), Duarte Fernandes, Violante Correia, João de Silva Lisboa, Salvador Vaez, and Duarte Brandão Soares, all New Christians.[97] The first generation of New Christian financiers of the 1620s, led by Juan Núñez Sarabia (until his trial by the Inquisition), Duarte Fernandes, Manuel de Paz, Simão Soares, Duarte Dias Henriques, Simão and Lourenço Pereira, Marcos Fernandes de Monsanto and García d'Yllan (or Ilhão), was quickly replaced by a second generation, as will be shown. Some of them managed to survive change and inquisitorial persecution; others, such as García d'Yllan, moved to Antwerp.

Two New Christian women, Beatriz da Silvera and Violante Correia, were among the main creditors of the Spanish Crown in 1647. A serious study should be conducted on the role of New Christian women in business, because many looked after the investments of their families when they became widows, whilst others had been equal partners before being widowed or had even been investors in their own right.[98] Widows whose deceased husbands had managed to obtain noble titles carried on using these and, in the more frequent case of membership of military orders, they pleaded for their sons to inherit the privileges if the issue had not already been settled. They benefitted from the fact that inheritance law in Portugal was relatively egalitarian between male and female heirs, while dowries protected women's assets when they married. This explains how wealthy women came to invest and be involved in business on their own account.[99]

New Christian women had an acknowledged role in carrying on the traditions of their community, but their competence extended to participation in trade, as a result of inheritance law, the regular absence of husbands involved in trade, and inquisitorial persecution. Dowries were regularly used to protect assets from confiscation and to reinforce business alliances, for example, in the 1630s, Gaspar Rodrigues Passarinho married three daughters to important merchants, all New Christians, and paid more than 20,000 cruzados each, a very important sum.[100]

The list of seventy-four participants (under seventeen contractors) in asientos from 1626 to 1650 shows that eight were women: Francisca Gomes Pacheco, sister-in-law of Manuel de Paz; Isabel Denis Pacheco, widow of Manuel de Paz; Violante Correia, widow of Fernando Tinoco; Mariana Tinoco, cousin of Manuel de Paz; Beatriz da Silveira, widow of Jorge Paz da Silveira; Beatriz de Sampaio, widow of Simão Soares; Leonor Brandão, mother-in-law of Duarte Brandão Soares; and Lucrécia Nunes, aunt of Juan Núñez Sarabia (the only one of them in Lisbon; the others were in Madrid).[101]

Several of these women were their husbands' partners in business before they became widows, and when widowhood came, they went on investing, endowing chapels, and managing the family wealth that was the inheritance of their children. Some New Christian women had strong heads. In 1626, Diogo Rodrigues de Lisboa lamented in a letter to Manuel Bautista that his daughter, then living in Seville, refused a suitable match. He was resigned to sending her dowry (4,000 pesos, quite mean for that level of merchant, probably in revenge) to her, but added that he might need to travel to Seville to help her find a husband, a task that was "no different from buying merchandise."[102]

Asientos were the most important business in Madrid, but in many cases, they needed to be attached to other contracts to guarantee liquidity. An accumulation of contracts, however, could lead to trouble, as in the case of the contract for renting the *almojarifazgos* (customs) for Seville when it was held by Marcos Fernandes Monsanto.[103] When, as sometimes happened, asentistas became secretaries of the Consejo de Hacienda, or even members of the Contaduría, this would reinforce their position when it came to reimbursements, which were generally in arrears. Their position at the royal court would also favour access to the private credit market, and there were several cases like that of António Rodrigues Lamego, who, before he moved to Rouen, lent money to the titled aristocracy. Lending between asentistas and other contractors was a normal practice.

Asentistas were also in an ideal position to bid for contracts to rent dry and sea port duties, taxation on sea trade (such as the *averia*, a tax on the Indies trade for armed protection), customs duties on salt, cacao, tobacco, playing cards, and mercury (for silver mining) monopolies, duties on wool exports, and taxes on various types of commodities traded into the big cities. The contract for tobacco, for instance, would lead to subcontracts that would go right down to the shopkeeper and involve an extraordinary number of people, but it was always threatened by the trade in contraband and local production that continued to spread in Iberia. These contracts required a significant network of merchants to guarantee collateral in case of default.

The main New Christian asentistas kept their political allegiance where their investment was, in Madrid. This was the case with Manuel de Paz, even though, around 1639, he had passed his business to his half brother, Fernando Tinoco (treasurer of the Council of Portugal), and his son-in-law, Filipe Denis Pacheco (who had made a fortune in the East Indies). Duarte Fernandes, the son of Álvaro Fernandes, treasurer to the infanta Maria, is another case of trading longevity; he was active until the end of the 1640s. He had been based in Seville, trading in slaves, indigo, and precious stones from the East Indies, but he had a powerful network of relatives (his brother, Fernando Lopes, in Lisbon; his sons Álvaro Lopes da Costa in Lisbon,

Fernando da Costa in Seville, and Duarte Fernandes da Costa in Madrid) and associates (particularly Simão de Sousa in Lisbon and Filipe Martins D'Orta in Seville). Jorge de Paz da Silveira died in 1647 and was succeeded by his nephew, Diogo da Silveira. The size and extent of the Paz and Silveira families guaranteed that a significant number of relatives would involve themselves in their asientos; the Passarinho brothers were also involved before they moved to Antwerp to escape the Inquisition.[104]

Marcos Fernandes Monsanto is also an interesting case. This merchant owned plantations and sugar mills in Espírito Santo, Brazil, before moving in the 1620s to Seville, where he entered a partnership to invest in the asientos, first with Simão Soares and later with Salvador Vaz Martins. Among his associates were Rui Dias Angel in Madrid, Simão Rodrigues Bueno in Seville, Diogo and Francisco de Paiva in Seville, and Manuel Rodrigues de Andrade and Francisco Lopes Brandão in Seville. In 1641, his property in Brazil was confiscated.[105] Duarte Brandão Soares is another case of an asientista who stayed in Madrid and was associated in business there with his brother-in-law, António Nunes Gramaxo. Duarte Dias de Olivares and João da Silva de Lisboa complete the list of major New Christian financiers who stayed in Madrid.[106]

Financial documents before and after the revolt in Portugal give an extraordinary picture of the inertia of royal procedures and the constraints on business. The reaction to the Portuguese revolt was only visible on December 19, when King Philip IV sent (fruitless) letters to the viceroy of Brazil ordering him to divert ships from Brazil to ports in Andalusia, Galiza, and Bizcaya free of charges, and to ports in Spanish America, where they would pay half normal customs duties.[107] Other orders to governors of islands and forts in the Atlantic followed. The king also tried to reach the viceroy in India, but it was a bad time of the year for maritime communication. Petitions for entry into military orders never ceased to arrive, in fact, the number increased, probably because supplicants sensed the weakness of the king.[108] Manuel Cortizos, who was involved in the contract for pepper and delayed in Badajoz, asked to be allowed to go to Madrid (apparently routes were blocked).[109]

The most immediate consequence of the Portuguese revolt was the disbursement of significant maintenance payments to noblemen, soldiers, and merchants who were in Spain and cut off from their sources of revenue in Portugal (the Count of Feira, the Countess of Benavente, and the Count of Tarouca, for example, but also Jorge Lopes Brandão and Luís Brandão, who claimed to have left 200,000 ducados of property in Brazil).[110] In Spanish America, the wealth of Portuguese who stayed in Portugal was sequestered.[111] Portuguese monks living on the frontier between Castile and Portugal were ordered to move to the interior of Spain, a curious political intervention that conflicted with the statutes governing these religious orders.[112] Having first been viewed as a series of "alteraciones" or "incidents," the Portuguese revolt became a "rebelión" in May 1641. On August 17, 1641, ships sailing from India were ordered to divert to Cadiz or Coruña, but to no avail.[113] The hospital of Santo Antonio in Madrid, which had been created alongside the confraternity of the same name by the city's Portuguese merchants, was cut off from its rents in Portugal.[114] On June 17, 1641, Portuguese soldiers in Madrid were ordered to join the tercios in Catalonia.[115] In the meantime, decisions were made as if nothing had happened. For example, on July 3, 1641, the contract for soap factories in Covilhã was passed from Gil Góis de Silveira, who had died, to Fernando Tinoco.[116]

6. Lisbon

In the first decades of the seventeenth century, the situation with contracts in Portugal, as discussed between the royal councils in Lisbon and Madrid, gives us an idea of the chaotic realities of business involving the Crown, with permanent arrears and petitions for payment of old debts related to contracts, bids for new contracts, disputes over access to offices, and negotiations for the main offices, such as that of viceroy of India or governor of Brazil, which might involve the bestowing of a noble title. I decided to replicate in the following paragraphs the chaos in the royal administration as revealed by the archives. It looks unreadable, but at the end the reader may have a better idea of daily royal business administration.

On November 11, 1612, the king decreed that all who held minor offices in the justice system should show that they were fulfilling their duties within one month; otherwise their positions would be considered vacant.[117] The following year, judge Francisco Machado Brandão required confirmation of his appointment to the office of accountant for the royal finances in Porto, with the right to appoint and oversee the customs officials in that city.[118] Miguel Ferreira offered 34 million réis to rent the taxation of wine in the district of Lisbon for three years, while Fernão Bocarro, Salvador Pires Magriço, and Tomás da Silva offered more than 4.6 million réis to rent the taxation of olive oil in the same district.[119] The taxation of meat in the district of Lisbon was rented to Tomé Antunes and Miguel Carvalho for three years for 21.4 million réis.[120] Brás Gomes de Elvas entered into a contract to rent the customs duties from the dry ports in Portugal for six years, paying 32 million réis a year.[121] There was discussion over a payment of 48 million réis for the contract to trade in slaves from Angola, São Tomé, and Cape Verde. The heirs of João Rodrigues Coutinho had abandoned the contract for Angola, which meant the Crown had lost an income of 24 million réis a year. The counsellors agreed to drop the obligation to trade slaves via Seville, owing to the high mortality rate of 50–60 percent; the direct transatlantic trip would mean a loss of 14–20 percent of the cargo.[122]

In 1613, a report of Manuel Gomes Galego, contractor for the provisioning of the Tangier and Mazagan forts in North Africa, listed ships and wheat sent. This contractor was paid by different rents, including the *bula da cruzada* (indulgencies sold for the needs of the crusades and then of the Church); he claimed 20 million réis in arrears.[123] In 1605, Jorge Rodrigues Solis, who had been treasurer and contractor for the customs of Lisbon and other maritime ports of Portugal in 1602 and 1603, requested that the king reduce by 12 million réis the money owed on the contract; the matter was still not solved in 1613.[124] Diogo de Meneses claimed payment by the king of a debt of 3,000 cruzados, which he had inherited (with entailed obligation) from his father-in-law, Lopo Rodrigues de Évora, who had lent the money to equip the carreira da Índia in 1606. Meneses suggested that he could add 1,000 cruzados to the sum owed (giving a total of 4,000 cruzados or 1.6 million réis) and that he should receive a *padrão de juro* (royal bond) for 100,000 réis a year (indicating an interest rate of 16/millar, meaning 1/16 or 6.25 percent) derived from customs duties or from the taxation of wine in Lisbon. This proposal does not seem to have been accepted, the opinion of the council being that the 3,000 cruzados should be paid, with one-third in money and the rest in pepper.[125]

On a claim by the heirs of Gonçalo Rodrigues Angel for 150,000 réis that the merchant had lent for equipping the carreira da Índia in 1600, the council's opinion was that the sum should be repaid in pepper.[126] The council was still evaluating the damages caused by war (English and Moroccan corsairs) to the receipts of the contractor Diogo Lopes Pinto and the heirs of contractors Afonso da Costa and Diogo Gomes on *almadravas* (tuna fishing) from the Algarve, sardines from Lagos, and the toll from Faro in 1595 and 1600.[127] The Jew Abraham Vilhalão claimed 418,000 réis on merchandise sequestrated for a ransom in North Africa, but this claim does not seem to have been met.[128] The executioners of the will of the Infanta Maria (1521–1577) claimed the disbursement of 12,475,000 maravedis of interest (a staggering sum) deposited in Madrid and refused to accept bills of exchange because they would lose a lot of money.[129] And there is conciliation of a debt by André Ximenes, who had entered into a contract for the royal monopoly on brazilwood in 1607 for 23.2 million réis a year.[130]

In 1620 the situation was similar. The contract agreed upon with Manuel Moreno de Chaves to provision the coastal fleet in Portugal and the ships of the carreira da Índia was discussed at various levels (sometimes the king would dissolve a previously agreed contract because he favoured another merchant). The bids by André Lopes Pinto and Duarte Fernandes for the contract for pepper were still being evaluated. The councils inclined towards André Lopes Pinto, who offered new money upfront, but finally Manuel Moreno and Francisco Duarte promised to deliver 175,000 cruzados in March and obtained the contract.[131] Francisco Rodrigues Vitória had been executed for debts on his contract for the island of Madeira (generally involving sugar and customs duties), and now there was discussion of new bids for the contract by Álvaro Fernandes de Elvas and André Soares.[132] We also learn that to unload three large ships (naus) of the carreira da Índia took 86 days in 1619, which was considered better than in the previous year.[133]

The councils also reviewed inspections of construction work on ships for India being undertaken in Lisbon by Vicente Caldeira de Brito and Simão Soares.[134] António Fernandes de Elvas and Brás Gomes de Elvas were already in trouble over the payment of money owed on their contracts, and there was a request for the execution of the two merchants by Vicente Caldeira de Brito, Luís de Figueiredo, and Miguel Godinho.[135] António Fernandes de Elvas ended up in prison and lost his share of the contracts for the slave trade in Angola and Cape Verde. This triggered a complicated process of reconstitution of the contracts, with an offer of 50,000 cruzados by the detained merchant being accepted under reserve, which involved other debtors of António Fernandes and guarantors in Seville.[136] In the same year of 1620, there is a sequence of letters from the king to the general inquisitor ordering the sale of property confiscated from New Christians to finance the carreira da Índia.[137]

It is tempting to skip drawing detailed conclusions from this apparent chaos, because the contracts make obvious the cycle of high royal demands, corresponding bids, necessary defaults, detentions, renegotiation, and part-renewal by the merchants involved. The management of debt involves permanent delay, partial payment, and the use of different sources and processes by all the parties involved. Appropriation of offices, bought or obtained as reward, was seemingly linked, in some cases, to the privilege of appointing holders of other minor jobs. The problem of an infinite number of office holders who would subcontract their jobs to people who would do the real work was also pointed out. Finally, the time taken to unload the ships of the carreira da Índia was noted, because it had financial consequences.

The political change in Lisbon in December 1640 was arguably made possible by a group of New Christian and Old Christian merchants involved in Atlantic commerce who played a major role in the huge business of financing the war of independence. From May 25 to June 3, 1641, a consultation was held by the *Junta dos Três Estados* (a council created with representatives of the three orders to manage royal finances), and the record shows loans provided by Francisco Botelho Chacão, Baltasar Rodrigues de Matos, Diogo Rodrigues de Lisboa, and Duarte da Silva.[138] As we have seen before, New Christians were on both sides of the political divide between the new Portuguese king, John IV, and Philip IV.

On August 1 and 2, 1641, another consultation held by the Junta dos Três Estados requested an inventory of the property possessed by Pedro de Baeça da Silveira, Diogo Rodrigues Lisboa, and Jorge Gomes Alemo (the latter were father and son) in Bahia, Rio de Janeiro, and Madeira so that it might be confiscated.[139] These New Christian financiers had been involved in the pro-Castilian conspiracy of 1641, which would lead to the execution of Pedro de Baeça on August 26 of the same year. The evaluation of the confiscated properties of Pedro de Baeça, including a large quantity of sheep in the region of Santarém and a significant loan of 22,500 cruzados to D. João de Mascarenhas, *comendador* (title linked to rents in a military order) in Mértola, proved to be difficult to execute.[140] The release of Diogo Rodrigues de Lisboa and Jorge Gomes Alemo, who denied everything, even under torture, might have been related to a timely loan made by the former. On October 10, 1649, Jorge Gomes Alemo was involved with Jerónimo Gomes Pessoa in a loan to the king towards the cost of the reconquest of Pernambuco from the Dutch.[141]

The execution of Pedro de Baeça da Silveira and the confiscation of Marcos Fernandes de Monsanto's property cleared the way for the rise of other merchants in Lisbon after the restoration of independence, and these were men who had emerged during the 1630s. Perhaps the most visible case is Duarte da Silva, who made his fortune trading in sugar, slaves, diamonds, coral, and textiles. After Portuguese independence, Duarte da Silva became one of the top bankers to King John IV, investing heavily in provisions and ammunition for the troops and the frontiers in the war of independence, the naval fleet, and the Brazilian captaincies. He had close business associates, such as Diogo de Aragão Pereira, António da Silva Pimentel, Paulo Antunes Freire, and Diogo Moniz Teles in Bahia, Brazil; Bento Bravo in Pernambuco; Manuel Fernandes de Morais in Porto; Francisco Botelho Chacão and Fernão Rodrigues Penso in Lisbon; Francisco Mendes in Viana de Foz de Lima; his brothers-in-law, Jorge Dias and Rodrigo Aires Brandão from Viana da Foz de Lima, who moved to Bahia and then to Lisbon; Manuel Fernandes Camacho and then Manuel de Cea in Madeira; Francisco Nunes Sanches, Rui Lopes da Silva, and Gaspar de Paiva in Rome; Pedro Franco de Albuquerque and Henrique Gil da Veiga in Livorno; António e Simão Mendes de Almeida, Antonio de Franchi, Manuel Fernandes Brandão, and Manuel Machado in Venice; Enrique Núñez Sarabia in Bordeaux; Manuel Rodrigues Nunes and Agostinho Coronel Chacão in Rouen; Gaspar Rodrigues Passarinho in Antwerp; Bento Osório in Amsterdam; Dirck Stork in London; the widow and heirs of Duarte Esteves de Pina in Hamburg; and Manuel Dias de Paz and Afonso Manhós in Goa.[142]

Duarte da Silva's business was mainly sugar from Brazil, silk from Italy, textiles from Castile and India, diamonds from India to northern Europe, cod from the North Atlantic, and coral from the Mediterranean to India. The king owed 30,000 cruzados to him and Francisco Botelho Chacón, to be paid in Bahia, plus 25,000 cruzados from the asiento on Brazil, three debts over 1.2 million réis for the provision of gunpowder, and 25,000 cruzados for other munitions and armours. Part of the asiento for provisioning the frontiers was to be delivered from Hamburg. He guaranteed credit of 100,000 cruzados for construction of six galleons in Holland. Then there were debts in India, Brazil, and Europe (many thousands of cruzados), with retained merchandise and cargoes to be delivered. Many merchants owed him money from consigned commodities, but Duarte da Silva also lent money to the postmaster general,

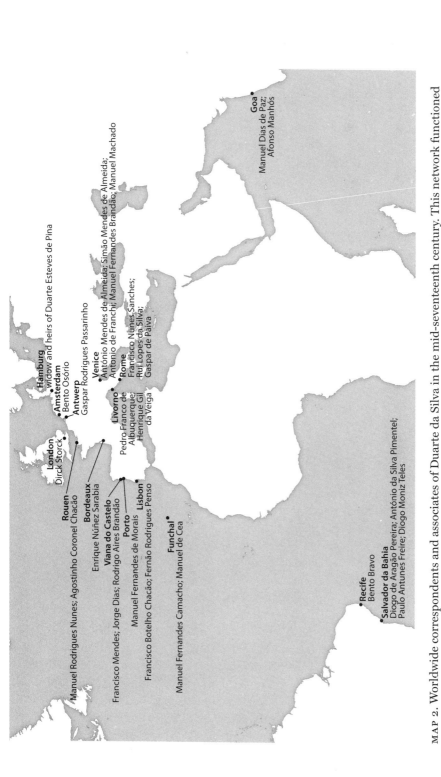

MAP 2. Worldwide correspondents and associates of Duarte da Silva in the mid-seventeenth century. This network functioned while Duarte da Silva was in Lisbon. Sources: Trials of the Inquisition indicated in the text.

Luís Gomes da Mata; Juliana de Noronha; João de Mascarenhas; the Count of Óbidos; the Count of Prado, Luís de Góis de Matos; the Convent of St. Dominic in Benfica, Lisbon; the provider and prior of the hospital of Nossa Senhora da Luz in Lisbon; Jorge Fernandes de Elvas; and the heir of Afonso Barros de Caminha.[143]

Fernão Rodrigues Penso financed the Portuguese embassies abroad after independence and was replaced in that function in 1644 by Baltasar Rodrigues Matos, another New Christian, who had a father, Nuno Álvares de Matos, living in Rouen and a brother, Manuel Rodrigues de Matos, living in Rome and involved in negotiations with the papal court. In 1648, Fernão Rodrigues indicated Gaspar Pacheco, an Old Christian, as the best person to finance the embassies, and his suggestion was accepted.[144] In 1642–1647, significant contracts were issued for supplying provisions (arms, munitions, food, clothes) to troops and fortifications in Alentejo, to support the war against the Dutch in Pernambuco and for provisioning embassies. In 1643, a specific contract for 1.5 million cruzados was offered by the Crown and was subscribed to by the Old Christians Gaspar Pacheco, Gaspar and Manuel Malheiro, and the New Christians Baltasar Rodrigues de Matos, Pero Lopes Serrão, and Jeronimo Moreno.[145] The practices surrounding investment in Brazil changed, as we have seen, with the creation of the Company of Brazil in 1649, which provided New Christians with temporary relief from expropriations, but the way they were forced to support the company was, again, abusive.

The divisions between Old Christians and New Christians, visible in local riots in 1627 and 1630, do not seem to have fractured the relationship between noblemen and merchants. The case of the Old Christian António Teles da Silva, who was active from 1634 to 1650 as captain general of the Índia fleet and governor of Brazil, attests to the similarity of the two groups' interests. His fortune was evaluated at 80,000 cruzados, not small by any standards, even if substantially inferior to that of the main merchants. His primary financier was Sebastião Nunes. He maintained commercial relationships with New Christians João da Fonseca Chacão and Fernão Rodrigues Penso, to whom he consigned merchandise, but he himself also engaged in lending money. On July 7, 1648, António Teles da Silva lent 1.6 million réis to Fernão Rodrigues Penso, who paid back the total with an interest of 77,000 réis (this represented nine months at an average rate of interest) on April 1, 1649. He also had business with the merchants João Malheiro Reimão, from Viana, and Francisco da Serra, Rodrigo Aires Brandão, Manuel da Gama (de Pádua), and Manuel Rodrigues da Costa in Lisbon. When he died, he still had investments in South Asia through João Rodrigues de Lisboa and in the Levant through Gaspar Rodrigues in Seville, while bills of exchange had been left in the hands of Manuel Rodrigues da Costa and Gregório Mendes in Lisbon.[146] However, António Teles da Silva supervised the enquiry into New Christians in 1646 while governor of Brazil, putting all his effort into obtaining denunciations.[147]

7. Europe

Europe beyond the Pyrenees will be addressed in this section, being of interest because it continued to offer refuge to New Christians, who migrated to the Mediterranean and northern Europe as a response to intensive periods of persecution. Antwerp, which had functioned as a precarious platform for migration to Italy and the Ottoman Empire in the sixteenth century, lost its attraction for this purpose in the first half of the seventeenth century, but kept a significant New Christian community, probably because it became less repressive as a result of the Habsburg war in the nearby Netherlands. Economic developments must be considered; although Antwerp had lost its position as a centre of a world-economy to Amsterdam by the end of the sixteenth century, it kept a share of the diamond trade. Its geographical closeness to Amsterdam, Cologne, and Paris was important. Prolonged war between Spain and the Netherlands also contributed to the resilience of Antwerp, whose financiers played a major role in implementing loans contracted by the Spanish king in Madrid for the payment of troops in the North.

The Florentine branch of the Ximenes family seems to have invested in land, noble titles, and alliances in this period, projecting an aristocratic behaviour far removed from that of merchants. In 1630, when Francesco di Tommaso Ximenes married Maria Gerini, sister of the Marquis of Gerini, her dowry was 13,000 scudi, a significant but not outstanding sum, whilst he himself would inherit the titles and fief of his father, Sebastiano.[148] The wills of both male and female members of the extended family, who lived in Florence, showed a significant number of nuns and monks, enormous amounts left in pious legacies, and the successive endowment of chapels and marble sepulchres, but also entailed property and legacies of privileges.[149] Niccolò Ximenes, a senator in Florence, created an entailed property for his elder son and left a significant number of legacies to convents, to the family chapel (12,000 scudi), and to family members who had entered religious establishments. He declared in his will that the family business in Florence should cease, and the money should be invested in rents and in the Monte di Pietà in Rome.[150]

The Ximenes family branches in Lisbon and Antwerp kept their investments in business, even though they developed similar strategies of aristocratic alliances and purchases of titles. In Antwerp, Duarte Ximenes (1561–1630) married Maria da Veiga; his brother Emmanuel (1563–1632) married Isabel da Veiga (Maria and Isabel were sisters, daughters of Rodrigo da Veiga de Évora); and the third brother, Gonçalo (1575–1638), married a local aristocrat, Catharina van Eeckeren. They were all knights of the order of St. Stephen and all, at different times, held the position of Portuguese consul. They continued their trading activities with Brazil (sugar), West Africa (the slave trade), and South Asia (precious stones), and they had agents in Amsterdam and the main Dutch cities and used Dutch ships to carry freight for them. Nor was the aristocratic

FIGURE 11.2. Antonius Sanderus, Castle Logenhaghen, in Steendorp, known as "Blauwhof" in the first half of the seventeenth century, owned by a branch of the Ximenes family, engraving from *Flandria Illustrata* [1641–1644], tome III (Hagae Comitum: Apud Christianum van Lom, 1732). Reproduced by kind permission of the Syndics of Cambridge University Library.

project put on hold: Emmanuel became lord of Blauwhof, while his uncle, Simão Rodrigues de Évora (1543–1618), who had married the sister of the three knights, Ana Ximenes, became Baron of Rhodes.[151] Within two generations the number of descendants of these families—the Ximenes de Aragão, the Rodrigues de Évora, the Veiga de Évora, the Fernandes de Elvas, and the Henriques de Leão (Diogo had married another of the three knights' sisters, Isabel)—would reach several dozen directly related members, including members of the local artistocracy.[152]

Many other New Christian families were in Antwerp, although the total numbers throughout the seventeenth century would be modest—fewer than one hundred in any randomly chosen year. In the 1600s, the brothers André and António Faleiro emerged as consuls and merchants, as did Francisco Godines and Nicolau da Veiga; in the 1610s, Francisco de Sousa, Jorge de Andrade, João de Paz (brother of André de Azevedo, also in Antwerp, and Álvaro de Azevedo, in Porto), and Francisco Rodrigues Serra followed the same path; in the 1620s, it was Francisco Lopes Franco, Miguel Dias Santiago, Diogo Teixeira de Sampaio, and Vasco da Veiga; and in the 1630s, Bento Rodrigues de Lisboa, García de Yllán, and Garcia Gomes de Vitória.[153] Gaspar Rodrigues Passarinho arrived in Antwerp in the mid-1640s, but he kept

FIGURE 11.3. Otto van Veen, *The Adoration of the Shepherds* (1601), triptych with the patrons Simão Rodrigues de Évora and Ana Ximenes, oil on wood, 230.5 × 204.5 cm (central panel), 238.5 × 94.5 (right panel), 237.7 × 95 cm (left panel). © Collection and photo Maagdenhuis Museum / Stad Antwerpen (B), inv. nr. 95. Simão Rodrigues de Évora commissioned the painting for the women's chapel of St. Anne's Almshouse he founded for twelve women.

a low profile. The wealthiest families made matrimonial alliances with the local aristocracy, while many other families established links with them. All the New Christians had relatives or associates in Porto and Lisbon, and in some cases these ties extended to Brazil or Goa.[154]

The material culture of New Christian financiers in different parts of Europe, or even the world, should not have been particularly different. Local habits and possibilities must have had an impact, although we know through inventories of property that silver cutlery, glass from Venice, bedspreads and clothing from India, porcelain from China, and furniture made of tropical wood could be seen in New Christian houses in Rome, Seville, Madrid, Antwerp, Lisbon, Salvador of Bahia, or Lima. Differences, however, could be detected in appearances. The contrast between two portraits of New Christian financiers who stayed within Christianity is striking: Filipe Godines, tax collector for the Spanish king in Antwerp, portrayed by Anthony van Dyck circa 1630, and António Gomes da Mata, from the well-known Seneor/Coronel/Elvas New Christian family, whose portrait is still to be better researched, anonymous, but probably contemporary. António inherited from his father Luís (1558–1607), who received a coat of arms in 1600, bought the position of postmaster general in 1606, and became a fidalgo in 1607.[155] Godines looks flamboyant in silk and lace, as does his wife, Sebilla van den Berghe, from a

FIGURE 11.4. Anonymous, portrait of António Gomes da
Mata Coronel, ca. 1630–1640, oil on canvas, 70 × 57cm.
© Museu Nacional de Arte Antiga, Lisbon, inv. nr. 1743 Pint.
Photo Luís Pavão (DGPC/ADF).

local merchant family, painted at the same time; but Gomes da Mata looks
austere. There is no trace of a portrait of Gomes da Mata's wife. Fashions,
apparently, did not mirror each other between Lisbon and Antwerp. It is also
possible that Gomes da Mata was underplaying his wealth.

The Jewish community in Amsterdam was established in the 1590s, after
the end of the embargo declared by Philip II on Dutch ships (1585–1590).
Manuel Rodrigues da Veiga (or Vega), born in Antwerp, son of Luís Fernandes,
importer of sugar and spices, was one of the first New Christians to settle
there.[156] Garcia Pimentel arrived from Venice in 1596. His brother Manuel
Pimentel, who had enjoyed a short period of success in Paris, where he had
earned an enormous amount of money gambling, had an impact on the Jewish community, among whom he was known as Isaac Abeniacar between his
arrival in 1613 and his death two years later.[157] The Lopes Homem family took
refuge in Amsterdam after the trials of some members by the Inquisition in
Lisbon, but some of them went back to Iberia, with António Lopes Pereira
becoming an important figure at the court of Philip IV.[158]

Religious ambiguity is underlined by the case of Fernão Álvares Melo, who
went to Amsterdam, where he seemed to be indifferent to religion. However, in

FIGURE 11.5. Anthonis van Dick, portrait of Filipe Godines, ca. 1630, oil on canvas, 211.5×137.5 cm, inv. nr. 995. © Bayerische Staatsgemäldesammlungen, Alte Pinakothek, München.

1609, having returned to Lisbon, he was detained, committed for trial and reconciled by the Inquisition, which prompted him to escape back to Amsterdam, and then Hamburg, where he remained thereafter and where he converted to Judaism under the name David Abenatar Melo.[159] Bento Osório, reputed to be the second richest man of the Amsterdam Jewish community, was importing salt from Aveiro in the 1610s, when the contractor in Portugal was André Lopes Pinto, but he was also involved with sugar and other trades. From 1615 to 1617, he sent 200 ships to Portugal. When the West Indies Company was created, he became a shareholder.[160]

Lopo da Fonseca Ramires, known as David Curiel, became a pillar of the Jewish community in this period, while his brother, Duarte Nunes da Costa, known as Jacob Curiel, went from Tuscany to Amsterdam and finally to Hamburg. They both served the Portuguese king after the restoration of independence.[161] The Jewish community numbered around 800 people in the 1610s, remaining at the same level in the following decades, before growing again in the 1640s and

FIGURE 11.6. Anthonis van Dyck, portrait of Sebilla van den Berghe, ca. 1630, oil on canvas, 210.5 × 136.7 cm inv. nr. 201. © Bayerische Staatsgemäldesammlungen, Alte Pinakothek, München.

1650s to about 2,000 individuals.[162] Difficult issues of identity were rightly underlined by Yosef Kaplan, who labelled this community "New Jews."[163]

The experiences of the Jewish community in Brazil under the Dutch West Indies Company, which conquered most of the northern captaincies in the 1630s and 1640s, before withdrawal and final defeat in 1654, must be taken into consideration. Jews in Brazil played a significant role between Portuguese Catholics and Dutch Calvinists, introducing Jewish practices that reinforced New Christian deviance, particularly in Paraíba.[164] The impact of this small community in the New World cannot be overestimated. They provided the expertise for the transfer of sugar mills from Brazil to those Caribbean islands that the Dutch gained control of, they stimulated Jewish migration from the Netherlands to the New World (New Amsterdam, later New York, the Caribbean islands, and Surinam), and they participated in that exceptional experience of religious tolerance involving various Christian confessions and Judaism in the New World.[165]

The Jewish community in Hamburg was established in the last decades of the sixteenth century, following the long-term relationship between Lisbon and the city. Rui Fernandes Cardoso imported sugar from his brother, Gonçalo Cardoso, in Lisbon and their nephew, Diogo da Fonseca, in Brazil, until the latter two were detained by the Inquisition in 1618. In the following decade, Gonçalo Lopes Coutinho, brother-in-law of the famous merchant Álvaro de Azevedo from Porto, was a major importer of sugar, owned ships, and established a sugar refinery in the newly founded city of Glückstadt, in Schleswig-Holstein, then Denmark.[166] In that period, Rodrigo Pires Brandão, Álvaro Dinis, and Manuel Bocarro Francês (Jacob Rosales) are supposed to have held Jewish religious services in their houses, along with Rui Fernandes Cardoso. By the end of the 1610s, Abraham Senior Teixeira had arrived from Antwerp. And in the early 1620s, Diogo Carlos, Duarte Esteves Pina, Manuel Rodrigues Isidro, Pedro de Palácios, and David Abenatia Melo arrived from Amsterdam, confirming the close ties between these northern cities, which would be joined by London with its own Jewish community by the mid-seventeenth century.[167]

The Jewish communities in Italy had strong ties with New Christian communities both in Iberia and in Italy but also with Jewish communities in the Ottoman Empire, North Africa, and northern Europe. New Christian communities continued to thrive in Italy because of the virtual absence of concern about blood purity. The tendency for major merchants to become titled noblemen became more marked in the seventeenth century. We will include here the case of the kingdom of Naples, then under the control of the Spanish kings, where the Jewish community had been enlarged as a result of the expulsion of Jews from Sicily in 1492, only to suffer expulsion in its turn in 1541.

From the 1580s to the 1650s, the organization of the New Christian community became increasingly controlled by two main families, the Vaz from Portugal and the Vargas from Aragon.[168] The history of the Vaz family is well known: the financier Miguel Vaz, who went to Naples in the late 1580s with his two brothers, became a major merchant in wheat, textiles, and wine, contracted customs rents, administrated noble fiefs, invested in public debt, and bought a significant number of rural and urban properties, mainly in Puglia, and obtained the title of Count of Mola in 1613. The support of those holding political power was crucial for his ascent, particularly that of the Count of Lemos and the Count of Castro, successive viceroys; he was involved in reform of royal finances in the kingdom and influenced the work of the famous economist, Antonio Serra.[169]

However, the Count of Osuna reversed this situation, leading to an accusation of conspiracy in 1616 and the first denunciations of Judaism. At this point Miguel Vaz, having taken refuge at the convent of the Celestine monks, built the imposing church of Saint Michael at the centre of Naples, on which he spent 19,000 ducados; in his will in 1623, he declared 240,000 ducados and annual rents of 23,000. The next generation studied law, became senior magistrates, and obtained the titles of Duke of Casamassima and Duke of San Donato. Several women married into the traditional Neapolitan aristocracy, including marriages with the Duke of Belcastro and the Duke of Spezzano.[170]

While the Vaz family kept their close kinship, despite marrying into titled nobility, the Vargas family seems to have become more dispersed, fostering links to the Gaetani, Barone, Rossi, Barbuti, and other aristocratic families. They followed a similar itinerary of social mobility, from merchants and bankers to high positions as magistrates, although they rarely engaged in matrimonial alliances with the aforementioned families. In the 1640s, Alonso Vargas became judge of the *Magna Corte di Vicaria* and then counsellor at the *Sacro Regio Consiglio*. The Marquis de la Guardia became the linchpin of the family, and part of the family became rooted in Salerno. Political changes brought about by Portuguese independence in 1640, the Neapolitan revolt of 1647, and the plague of 1656 created new strains within these New Christians families. There were denunciations from branches whose fortunes were waning, and correspondence with the Jewish community of Livorno was intercepted.

However, the abundant information that exists on the affairs of Miguel Vaz, though at a much earlier point, does not sustain a vision of exclusive trade among New Christians. His associates were foreign merchants, Genoese, Flemish, and French. The intercepted correspondence might have been with relatives owing to traditional links. In any case, the primary noble New Christians were condemned by the Inquisition in 1661 and the majority of their property was confiscated. This provoked a conflict with local aristocratic institutions, which had supported the victims through extended attachments. The inquisitor was expelled, and New Christians merged into the titled nobility.[171]

The New Christian community in Rome managed, in certain cases, to overcome the third generation "curse," proving to be more resilient. They found their way to titles directly through the papal administration and cardinals, while they asserted their positions within the Portuguese and Castilian communities through investment in the latter's confraternities. The Banco di Santo Spirito, created by Pope Paul V in 1605 to provide capital for hospitals and churches in Rome, immediately attracted deposits from several New Christians, such as Antonio Pinto, Francisco Navarro, Luís Fonseca, Manuel Fonseca (the son and heir of the important merchant António Fonseca), Jerónimo da Costa Brandão, João Brandão, Gabriel Fonseca Rodrigues, and Manuel da Costa Brandão, a well-known banker in Rome.[172] The sums involved in this period were still relatively limited.

New Christians mixed with Old Christians through the confraternities, although they always sought to control the main functions, particularly that of treasurer. In the Spanish archconfraternity of the Santissima Resurrección, the registers were created in 1603. In that year, one of the counsellors was Manuel da Fonseca, son of the famous António da Fonseca, and the *camerlengo* (administrator of property and revenues) was Luís da Fonseca. In those early years of the seventeenth century, several women were involved, although without special functions, such as Ana de Fonseca, Maria Jorge, Maria Galvão, Madalena Ximenes, Mariana da Costa Brandão, Catarina Gomes, Gracia Henriques, Gracia Mendes, Isabel Henriques, Isabel Cardoso, Isabel Gomes, Leonor Gomes, Beatriz de Paz, Branca de Paz, Violante Nunes, Violante Galvão, and Violante Gomes.

Antonio da Fonseca is identified as the patron of the chapel of the Santissima Resurrección in 1639. Fernando Galvão, from Lisbon, was registered in 1604; Francisco de Paz Tinoco, from Badajoz, in 1606; Gaspar de Andrade, from Lisbon, in 1610; Diogo da Silveira in 1612; Gabriel da Fonseca, from Lamego, in 1613; Diogo Nunes Henriques, from Lisbon, in 1617; Gabriel da Veiga, from Viseu, in 1618; Francisco Vaz Brandão in 1623; and João Brandão, from Lisbon, in 1623. Alexandre Brandão, declared a native of Rome, was registered in 1624; Fernando Nunes, from Viseu, in 1624; Fernando da Costa Brandão, from Lisbon, in 1624; Francisco de Almeida, from Coimbra, in 1625; Custodio Vaz from Elvas in 1625; Duarte Rebelo from Guarda in 1628; Francisco Nunes Sanches, from Guarda, in 1629; Blas Nunes Caldeira, from Lisbon, in 1638; and Gaspar da Silveira, from Coimbra, in 1647.[173] The new members indicated, in general, the diocese of origin, not the town or village.

In the same archconfraternity of the Santissima Resurrección, the general congregation registered in 1614 included Rodrigo Galvão, Rodrigo Álvares, Francisco de Andrade, Simão da Costa, Diogo de Silveira, Gabriel da Fonseca, Jerónimo Duarte, António de Paz, all of them New Christians among Old Christian names (of 109 members, twenty were Portuguese). In the following years, other New Christians arrived, particularly Henrique de Paz, Manuel do Quintal, Manuel Henriques, Manuel Nunes, Henrique de Orta, Sebastião Touro Godinho, Luís Álvares Pereira, and Rui Botelho Feo. In 1619, the camerlengo was Bartolomeu Francês, and in 1622 it was Francisco Vaz Brandão. In 1623, the banker Manuel da Costa Brandão registered as a member of the general congregation, and in 1625 he assumed his first function, accepting responsibility for the confraternity's Portuguese altar. In 1628, the most important New Christian of all in seventeenth century Rome, Francisco Nunes Sanches, who became a marquis, appeared in the record for the first time as one of the Portuguese almsgivers, with João Baptista Francês as the camerlengo. In the following year, João Gonçalves Bravo was secretary of the archconfraternity. In 1630, the almsgivers from Portugal were Fernão da Costa Brandão and Rui da Costa from Castelo Branco.[174]

The records of membership at the confraternity of St. Anthony, in the old church and hospital of the Portuguese in Rome, reveal a duplication of some of these names. In the 1610s and 1620s, those participating in the activities of the congregation included Manuel da Fonseca, Fernando Galvão, João Brandão, Francisco de Andrade, Manuel Nunes, Manuel Brito de Almeida, Manuel do

Quintal, Manuel Dias Rangel, Rui Botelho Feo, Henrique de Paz, Luís Álvares Pereira, Sebastião Touro Godinho, António Dias da Fonseca, Duarte Gomes Coronel, and Cristóvão de Paz. It is obvious that some of these New Christians were only temporarily in Rome. A certain Duarte da Silva appeared in 1631, but we do not know whether he was the future banker to John IV. Fernão da Costa Brandão is another case. Francisco Nunes Sanches, the future marquis, arrived in 1636, later than his first appearance as a member of the archconfraternity of the Santissima Ressurreccion (1628), but he soon assumed informal and formal functions as treasurer, banker, and lender to the confraternity. Afonso Peres Vergueiro, Francisco Nunes Sanches, Braz Nunes Caldeira, and Alexandre de Abreu Barreto (this last was probably an Old Christian, like many of the members) became governors of the confraternity in 1639.[175] The revolt in Portugal in 1640 is nowhere mentioned in the records of this and the Spanish confraternity, but references to the ambassadors of the two countries vanish at this time. There were consequences of the political change in the long term, although the unfolding of the Portuguese presence within the Spanish confraternity took several decades.

{⤞⊙⊷}

In this period, New Christian business experience was extended to different parts of the world. The commercial connection between Mexico and Manila became important, establishing a bridge with the Far East and adding to the previous connection between Macau and Japan. A relative cooperation between Spaniards and Portuguese, to which New Christians contributed, was interrupted by the expulsion of the Portuguese from Japan in 1639, after a string of edicts against the activity of the Jesuits, and the independence of Portugal in 1640. In the meantime, the carreira da Índia from Lisbon to Goa managed to resist the competition by the Dutch and English until the 1630s. New Christian merchants controlled more than 30 percent of trade between the Americas and Manila and close to 45 percent of trade between Lisbon and Goa, while they also had a hand in interregional Asian maritime trade. Some of the main New Christian families (e.g., the Ximenes, Solis, Dias Milão, and Lopes d'Elvas) were present in all the Asian regions involved in maritime trade and had agents there. Prosecution of New Christians by the Inquisition of Goa in the 1630s, exactly when the Dutch competition was gaining momentum, had an impact.

In the meantime, trade from Seville to the Americas via the carrera de Indias also had a significant investment by New Christians, who placed agents in the main Spanish American ports. New Christian families—the Reinel, Henriques, Fernandes d'Elvas, Lamego, Angel—were then heavily involved in slave trade from Africa to the Americas. However, the major financial and commercial positions of Manuel Bautista Pérez in Lima and Simón

Vaez de Sevilla in Mexico were suppressed by the wave of inquisitorial trials, which targeted the wealthiest New Christian merchants in the 1630s and 1640s. In Brazil, by contrast, New Christians were not particularly targeted, probably because there was no local tribunal and the experience of the conquest of Bahia by the Dutch in 1624, after an inquisitorial visit, dissuaded further enquiries. The investment of New Christian in plantations was already significant. The experience of Dutch Brazil was important from a religious tolerance point of view, because there was a Jewish community alongside Calvinists and Catholics, although it was short lived.

New Christian bankers and financiers in Madrid kept their positions during this period despite inquisitorial prosecution extended into the 1650s. The political disruption produced by the independence of Portugal introduced a divergence of interests that did not exist before, with the new centre of power in Lisbon attracting merchants involved in trade with Brazil, who contributed to the financial needs of the war. The resilience of New Christian bankers in Madrid (e.g., Paz, Tinoco, Fernandes, Monsanto) is an interesting feature. However, the New Christians of Seville seem to have been more vulnerable, probably because of the crackdown of the Inquisition in Lima and Mexico. In Lisbon, it was precisely in the 1630s that the careers of the main New Christians, such as Duarte da Silva or Manuel da Gama de Pádua, started.

In Europe, the wealthiest New Christians in Italy continued to pursue their integration into the nobility, a move extended to Antwerp, while the New Christian communities in west and southwest France became rooted. The established Jewish communities in Amsterdam and Hamburg registered a significant growth in this period, creating a basis for business for New Christians in northern Europe. The role of David Curiel and Jacob Curiel is well known, but there was a much larger group of merchants trading in Brazilian sugar and Portuguese salt. The mid-seventeenth century can perhaps be defined as a peak of New Christians activity in business, associated in several cases with activity by Sephardic Jews in northern Europe.

CHAPTER TWELVE

Identities

THIS CHAPTER WILL investigate religious identities, understood as fluid and changeable, and will present an analysis of examples of literary and artistic expression by New Christians that may provide the basis for reflection on the plurality of perceptions, values, and visions of their place in society and also of the structure of society. Political allegiances will be included that are based on examples dealt with in this book or raised by other authors, and these may offer some clues as to how the New Christian trading elite positioned themselves. The literary and artistic expressions selected are not, in general, the direct creations of this merchant elite, although most authors and artists had links to merchants as relatives or sponsors. We shall also discuss the decoration of chapels and palaces commissioned by New Christian merchants that reveal iconographic programmes. Inventories of property provide some insight into material culture, including choices of images and thematic books.

The chapter is structured around collective and individual identities to underline how permanent change was brought about not only by external constraints and possibilities but also by the internal dynamics of intellectual and spiritual searches. The word *identity* is generally linked to sameness, unique and continuous properties, and unchanging individual or social characteristics.[1] It can be related to the sense of belonging, social status, and relationships of duty and obligation, understood under temporary allegiances, which make it possible to use textual or visual signs to reconstruct meanings. Sociologists, social psychologists, and philosophers have done their best to include change in the notion of identity; it is this path that we will develop by addressing a framework of moveable and changeable conditions.[2]

1. Religion

Religious identity has been the big issue for debate concerning New Christians. The present study seeks to place this issue in a wider context, showing that New Christians cannot be seen purely in black and white, either as Christians or as Jews, as was the predominant approach up to the 1960s. Most New Christians stayed in Iberia or migrated to the Iberian colonial world, a segment mixed with Old Christians, and many were persecuted. However, a significant number migrated to other parts of Europe, where they either became New Jews, as in Rome, Ancona, Venice, Ferrara, Pisa, Livorno, Amsterdam, Hamburg, and the Ottoman Empire, or they (apparently) kept their Christian faith, as in Antwerp, Rome, Venice, Pisa, or Florence.[3]

The return of many New Christians to the traditional religious practices of their ancestors reveals the superficiality of a faith imposed through violent conversion, even after three or more generations. Migration under difficult conditions, in many cases losing wealth and facing poverty, suggests a strong desire to live according to the faith of their ancestors. The fact that several New Christians excommunicated by the Inquisition refused to die as Catholics and declared their Jewish faith to the very end showed deep reflection and a courageous choice under enormous pressure from the clergymen assigned to "comfort" them and bring them into the Christian fold on the way to execution and in the face of insult and rage from the mob.

The major impact of permanent persecution cannot be denied, both in reinforcing the feeling of ethnic discrimination or New Christian status and in pushing many to migration. An analysis of many hundreds of inquisitorial trials fails to show systematic examples of clearly irrefutable accusations. In many cases, denunciations were based on hearsay, rather than anyone having witnessed the practices denounced. In other cases, the main accusations were collected in jail, from detained relatives who fell into a state of despair and decided to satisfy the judges and get out of prison. These denunciations and the confessions that followed them were quite repetitive: they responded to stereotypes of Jews secretly fasting and declaring allegiance to the "law of Moses." Many read as though the detained needed to have a very strong character to avoid producing a false accusation or confession in a setting where everything had been prepared to obtain this. There were, however, those whose characters were sufficiently strong for them to refuse to confess what they had not done or to decide to protect their family and loved ones. Some of these detainees died at the end of their courageous stance; others got out of jail to live the rest of their lives completely broken, physically and materially; but some recovered their full capacity as family members and social beings.

Whatever the outcome, the Inquisition certainly provided a crucial push factor. Many of those reconciled feared another accusation, which would lead to them being executed as relapsed sinners, while the children and other relatives of those condemned might decide to change country and live in a freer atmosphere, where prejudices against Jewish ethnic descent either did not exist or had a relatively minor impact, as in Italy. This is not to say that New Christians did not have their convictions as Jews: many proved they had. However, we should appreciate that many who felt that they were Christians nonetheless continued the cultural practices inherited from their ancestors, such as fasting on some days, or preparing funerals with traditional rituals such as washing the body of the deceased, dressing it in burial clothes, and wrapping it in a fresh sheet. Such cultural practices were interpreted by the Inquisition as signs of religious allegiance or as a clear indication of beliefs. We need to maintain critical detachment from sources that seek to legitimise the logic of prosecution and inquisitorial penalties.

Accusations of Judaism were generally based on suspicions that Jewish food rules were being observed, particularly the well-known Jewish taboos on eating pork, goat, rabbit, fish without scales, and seafood. Even cooking with olive oil could be an indicator of Jewishness (or adherence to Islam), which proves that the northern Iberian habit of cooking with lard still functioned as an ethnic divider in the sixteenth and seventeenth centuries, before a Mediterranean diet conquered all Iberia. Duarte da Silva proudly boasted that every year he bought two large baskets of ham to be consumed in his home in Lisbon—a sure proof of his Christian allegiance.[4] More serious was the accusation of respecting Saturday as the Sabbath, meaning not working on that day and preparing the house the day before. The house of Henrique Dias Milão, for example, was placed under surveillance from the convent nearby, at the direct instigation of the inquisitors, who prompted the confessors frequenting the convent to request that this be done.[5] This was a society of institutionally organised surveillance that left its imprint on the collective consciousness right up to the dictatorships of the twentieth century, when the labels of *malsíns* (from the same word in Hebrew, meaning informer or denouncer) and *bufos* (originally, traps for birds) reappeared.[6]

In spite of the many confessions extorted, a careful study of the trials of the Inquisition (that is, of whole trials not just the sentences pronounced by the inquisitors) leaves the reader feeling that the New Christian frenzy in the Iberian world was not entirely dissimilar from the witch frenzy that devastated a good part of Europe (at the opposite end, curiously, in central and northern Europe), also from the fifteenth to the seventeenth century.[7] Recognizing parallels between the two persecutions (victimisations) should not be seen as promoting far-fetched analogies. Many historians nowadays think that the inquisitors were right about the Jewishness of New Christians, either because the latter really were apostates or because they were not convinced Christians. But many don't hesitate to dismiss the accusations of witchcraft as baseless. However, the tens of thousands of witches who were executed over two centuries in central and northern Europe, in Protestant as well as in

Catholic areas, were interrogated by ecclesiastic and civil judges. Was it only these interrogators who acted on unfounded prejudice? Or, to put it another way, why should we accept that the inquisitors, unlike their witch-hunter counterparts, pursued their purpose without bias?[8]

We could consider the Iberian inquisitors as "New Christian hunters," because the labelling of someone as a New Christian was the first circumstance that could lead to accusations of Judaism, a trial, and the confiscation of property. The Iberian Inquisitions were driven by prejudices of ethnic descent against converted people from Jewish and Muslim origins. Racism was clearly at play, transferring to converted people previous prejudices against the other (racialised) religions of the book.[9] But there is more: the inquisitors decided what the label "Judaism" involved and imposed an idea of religion that was already implicit in Christian reasoning. David Graizbord rightly highlights the fact that the premodern Hebrew language did not have a word for religion (nor for prayer) and people did not designate their situation as "Judaism," a Greek word. The correct collective name was "Israel." The biblical and rabbinical culture handed down to Israel was a comprehensive way of life, with behavioural duties based on a legal covenant with a deity. The idea of an interior faith focused on the salvation of the individual soul did not have any meaning outside the normative public community of Jews. Graizbord also points out that under Christianity religion was considered to be a set of beliefs in certain theological propositions, linked to prescribed rituals of God worship and associated ethical requirements. The idea of crypto-Judaism, meaning a belief in the law of Moses as offering salvation of the soul, as the Inquisition would have put it—and made those denouncing and those confessing repeat it—was therefore a Christian fantasy.[10]

I have followed David Graizbord's thinking closely here, because he exposes the fallacies of the Inquisition concerning Judaism better than anybody else. However, the New Christians' situation was arguably unstable, poised between the Jewish and the Christian worlds, assuming features of cultural resistance and nonconformism that simultaneously flirted with and departed from hybridism.[11] The search for Jewish practices (in many cases distorted) was part of that situation, while adopting a Christian framework could lead to the reversing of established Christian rituals, imitating narratives heard in the autos da fé, and producing absurd accusations, such as that Moses was worshiped as a saint, or the ludicrous idea that a simulated confraternity to celebrate the Jewish martyr of an auto da fé in Lisbon had been created in Coimbra. This imposed framework certainly had an impact on New Christian consciousness, particularly with the absorption of the notion of salvation. We must keep in mind that the rabbinic world had collapsed with forced conversion: there was no study of the scriptures, no renewal of culture, no guidance. For the transmission of traditions, New Christian communities depended on women, whose status rose significantly in the Iberian Christian context, owing to the absence of rabbis but also to the relatively egalitarian Iberian inheritance system, which even allowed, in defined circumstances, cognatic succession to entailed property with the possible return of property to the original branch of the family. Inquisitorial persecution reinforced the importance of this inheritance system, with wealthy New Christians seeing the possibility of protecting money through dowries and entailed property.

Fragmentary and distorted versions of traditional practices among New Christians have baffled the best historians in this area, such as Nathan Wachtel. Wachtel acknowledges the clear Jewish commitment of several New Christians, such as Francisco Maldonado da Silva, who was well acquainted with the Scriptures and rejected the Christian interpretation of these at the cost of his life. In other cases, such as that of Manuel Bautista Pérez, there was very little content in the accusations, which Bautista Pérez rejected from beginning to end. Wachtel suggests that if there was a deviance in the accused's attitude to Catholicism, which is not obvious in many cases, the memory of her/his Jewish ancestors' faith might have been a major factor.[12] I would slightly modify this interpretation to consider a memory of ethnic belonging that linked to Bautista Pérez's knowledge of, and loyalty to, his ancestors and, crucially, to his relatives, making sense of their struggling position in a Christian world. There was certainly a desire to preserve ethnic ties in the strange world into which they had been forced to integrate through baptism, only to be discriminated against immediately afterwards. The sense of belonging had its risks of persecution and condemnation; on the other hand, it offered solidarity and assistance against adversity.

The complexity of New Christian intra-ethnic relations, however, does not allow a romanticised vision of solidarity. Conflict and internal division were a constant in New Christian communities that were plagued by jealousy, envy, and revenge channelled through denunciation. David Graizbord starts his book, *Souls in Dispute*, with the tale of a New Jew, a former New Christian, who decided to reconvert and, as proof of his sincerity, denounced more than a hundred other New Jews who were former New Christians.[13] In similar cases in this book, many of the trials started as revenge for a refusal of assistance, a rebuffed offer of matrimonial alliance, or broken commercial ties. Once there were Jewish communities that could be reached, in Italy, Amsterdam, or Hamburg, New Christians could become normative Jews, but porous frontiers meant passage was possible in either direction. The Inquisition defined the terms of reconversion, which implied massive denunciations to feed their appetite for prosecutions.

2. States

Early modern states contributed to the definition of religious frontiers alongside political ones. The Calvinist Netherlands could cope with Jewish communities better than with Catholic communities.[14] New Christians were welcomed as Jews, not as Catholics. There were cases of New Christians who kept their Christian faith, mainly at the beginning, but they were in an uncomfortable position. The opposite occurred in France, then a Catholic state which excluded Jews, where New Christians established communities in Saint-Jean de Luz, Bayonne, Bordeaux, Rouen, La Rochelle, and Nantes. With a few exceptions, those joining these communities were not investigated as to their religious beliefs, but they needed to present a Catholic façade even when they perceived themselves as Jewish. These conditions changed in the early eighteenth century.[15] In Iberia, by contrast, there was zero tolerance for concealed Judaism and a high degree of surveillance that easily transformed New Christians into Judaizers.

It is not surprising that the same man could be a Jew in Amsterdam and a Catholic in Lisbon or Seville. If he wanted to trade between these places on his own account, without an agent, he needed to change his religious allegiance from town to town. There were many such cases of merchants plying their trade between Italy and Iberia.[16] In these situations, the erosion of religious conviction was also not surprising. The idea that each person could be saved in his/her own religion, which has been studied by Stuart Schwartz, became quite important in the sixteenth century, as a result of the good behaviour observed among Muslims in the Ottoman Empire and in North Africa, and also among Jewish communities.[17] Finally, the emergence of religious indifference, in some cases, of outright atheism, cannot surprise us in circumstances where atrocities were regularly perpetrated in the name of religion. We have already met several cases, such as that of Fernão Álvares Melo before his trial by the Inquisition, in which their treatment by Christians decided the accused in favour of allegiance to Judaism. Finally, a libertine atmosphere in the seventeenth century would lead to more serious philosophical reflection, labelled by Jonathan Israel as radical Enlightenment.[18] New Jews of New Christian origin, such as Baruch Spinoza, played a crucial role, underlining the liminal position of these communities open to experiment.

Religious tolerance in Dutch Brazil, during the short period in which the northern captaincies were occupied by the Dutch West India Company (1630–1653), was a peculiar situation, with Portuguese Catholics settled in the area, together with their slaves, whom they had converted, while the Calvinist Dutch were a tiny minority of conquerors, who had brought with them loyal Jews from Amsterdam. The coexistence of the two Christian confessions with a Jewish community was unique in the Western world in this period, which Jonathan Israel and Stuart Schwartz rightly underline.[19]

There had been a (difficult) coexistence of the three religions of the book in medieval Iberia, but the division of Christianity following the Reformation had created a new situation that took time to be accepted, a situation aggravated by the expulsion of Calvinists (the Huguenots) from France in 1685. Religious tolerance in the New World was thus a surprisingly successful phenomenon, but a short-lived one; although it had parallel pockets in central Europe, it only became widespread in the nineteenth century. With the expulsion of the Dutch from Brazil, Jews had to return to the Netherlands, although some relocated to Dutch America. Those who wanted to stay in Brazil, Jews and Calvinists, had to convert to Catholicism.[20]

Political allegiance became extremely important after the restoration of the independence of Portugal in 1640. To stay in Spain or Spanish America, or return to Portugal or the Portuguese territories overseas (and vice versa) was the agonising choice facing many New Christian migrants, some of whom had newly acquired naturalisation or locally recognised citizenship. Political disruption forced choices, as ever, and as far as we can see, these choices were guided by where the profession, the money, or the family was, although we have indications that most Portuguese New Christians based in Seville might have deserted the city. Family may have had some weight in these choices, but a serious study still needs to be undertaken on this issue.

It is also true that Portuguese New Christians were persecuted in Spanish America both before and after the revolt in Portugal, first for economic reasons (the competition they represented), then for political reasons. In Spain itself, the breach of trust on Portuguese New Christians might have led a significant number to return to Portugal, but the main bankers and merchants stayed where their main investments were, as did many soldiers caught in their duties away from Portugal. In the meantime, the intensity of inquisitorial persecution in the 1640s was extended to the 1650s. Support for the Portuguese in their war of independence from Jewish bankers in Amsterdam and Hamburg who had fled the Inquisition is another enigma of this story. Possibly they were betting on a more lenient Inquisition in a country where diplomatic relations with Rome had been relatively disrupted by the revolt— formal relations were only reestablished after the Peace Treaty with Spain in 1668. But there was an undeniable sentimental attachment to Portugal, probably because of the long-term business and emotional ties with relatives and associates who had stayed there.

It is even more difficult to evaluate feelings of belonging in other cases, such as that of emigrants to Antwerp, Amsterdam, Hamburg, Italy, and the Ottoman Empire. The resilience of Antwerp in the face of its sharp decline vis-à-vis Amsterdam is surprising. Although the numbers of Portuguese emigrants were low, the city still attracted major bankers, such as García de Yllán and Gaspar Rodrigues Passarinho in the 1640s, and Duarte da Silva in the 1660s. These merchants obviously did not want to stay in Iberia, where they faced threats or even a major trial from the Inquisition, but they did not want to move to Amsterdam, which they could easily have done. This suggests that they did not want, or did not feel it convenient, to become Jews. But it is difficult to tell exactly how they felt. They may have simply been trying out the possibilities offered by various cities.

The idea of a portfolio in business should be extended to a portfolio in politics, with multiple claims to citizenship and stakes in various states and cities.[21] In Amsterdam and Hamburg, most New Jews were apparently happy and grateful for the protection given by local authorities, but a section of the community lived in poverty, and some decided to return to Iberia against all the odds.[22] In Italy, New Christians lived side by side with Catholic and Jewish communities in Venice and Pisa, to name only the main centres. Some of them changed their religious identity when they travelled outside their cities, mainly when they travelled to Iberia, as we saw with the case of Henrique Nunes Righetto. Removal to the Ottoman Empire meant, in principle, there could be no return, because of the immigrants' integration into normative Jewish communities. However, there were cases of return and even of travel to the *Estado da Índia*.

The vexing question is the constant labelling of New Christians as Portuguese. There are clear nationalist reasons for this. In particular, it is supposed that in Spain New Christians had been violently persecuted and uprooted in the first forty years of the Inquisition, but had become relatively integrated by the time the Portuguese New Christians arrived in the 1580s, bringing with them practices that had been all but forgotten, but which now stimulated new persecution.[23] Several authors have tried to correct this simplistic narrative, showing how many supposedly Portuguese New Christians had been born in Castile, how family ties had always been maintained across the frontier, and how New Christian migration in both directions had fed the permanent renewal of many local communities in Iberia.[24]

In Spanish America, the diverse origins of New Christian arrivals (from Portugal and Spain, with internal variety, but also from France, Italy, the Low Countries, and elsewhere) has been confirmed.[25] New Christians in Portugal represented a significantly higher percentage of the total population than in Spain, but this does not mean that they were the exclusive focus for suspicion concerning Jewish practices. Many trials of New Christians in Portugal showed that the accused had Spanish origins or family links, and records of trials of New Christians in Spain in the first half of the eighteenth century present many cases of people whose families had lived in Spain for several generations.

The ease with which New Christians crossed a fairly porous frontier, paying scant attention to laws against migration that could not be adequately implemented (contrary to the better control exercised in ports such as Lisbon), makes difficult any assertion concerning their political allegiance. On top of this, the notion of nation was relatively loose before the eighteenth century, subsumed in allegiance to a crown, although there was clearly a diffuse notion of collective belonging as Portuguese or Castilians.[26] Curiously, the notion of nation had been regularly applied to Jews and their descendants since the sixteenth century, which may have made it easier for them to accept a collective identity as New Christians. It underlined Jewish descent and separation from Christendom. A clear complication derived from this labelling is that Portuguese merchants were identified in North Europe as Jewish, even when they were not New Christians.

Let us see how this notion was integrated by dictionaries. The *Vocabulario Portuguez e Latino* by Raphael Bluteau defines *nação* as a collective name for people who live in a large region or kingdom under the same lordship. It differentiates nation from people, since a nation may comprehend several peoples. For example, in the case of Portugal, the Beirões, Minhotos, Alentejanos, and others, compose the nation of Portugal, while the nation of Spain is composed of Castilians, Aragonese, Andalusians, and so on.[27]

The *Diccionario da lingua portugueza*, compiled by Antonio de Morais Silva, gives a much more succinct and efficient definition, once the distinction between New and Old Christians in Portugal has been abolished: "Nation: people from one country or region with its own language, laws and government, e.g. the French, Spanish, and Portuguese nations. People of the nation: descendants of Jews, New Christians. Race, caste, species."[28] Nation is here equated with race and caste. The definition accurately includes the historical application of the notion to the New Christians, while introducing the modern notion of nation as based on language, law, and government, and thus showing a change in concept and attitude, in the Portuguese case, between the 1720s and the 1780s. The entry for "Marrano," which says, "adj. insult addressed to a Moor or Jew who abstains from pig meat" suggests a significant detachment.[29] "Cleanness of blood is attributed to someone who descends from nobles and does not have a Jewish, Moorish or Mulatto caste."[30] The ambiguity and detachment persist, although the uses of these racist expressions are duly recorded.[31]

The first Spanish dictionary *Tesoro de la lengua española* by Sebastián de Covarrubias, published in 1611, did not elaborate on the noun nation, or *nación*, "from the Latin word *natio*, which is kingdom or extended province, such as the Spanish nation."[32] New Christians are not mentioned under this noun; and the noun *converso* is not included. Only under race (*raza*) is it indicated that "concerning lineages it is taken as a bad thing to have some of the race of Moor or Jew," after defining caste in terms of its use in relation to horses and fabric.[33] Covarrubias defines marrano in a partisan way, "It is the person recently converted to Christianity, and we have a bad concept of this person, because they have simulated conversion." Then the author tries to reflect on the origin of the word and considers that "the Moors call a year-old pig a marrano and it may be that for this reason, and for not eating pig, that the new convert is called a marrano."[34] This is dramatically different from the detached way Morais Silva deals with the entry marrano more than one and a half centuries later. By then, the notion of New Christians of Jewish origin being collectively called a nation is no longer current.

3. Literature, Politics, Art

Perceptions and reflections by and on New Christians concerning their religious status and social position can be found in literature, political thought, and art. It is important to extend our approach to culture, understood here as a set of meanings, since we need to understand the context of conversos' ways of doing and thinking, engaging with critical dispositions that give us some clue about resistance in daily life. The reflection on the divide New/Old Christian by authors whose origin is unknown can also highlight different approaches that do not conform to the disputable supposition of uniform anti-converso attitudes among Old Christians.

The ethnic origin of Miguel de Cervantes is still much debated. There is no unequivocal document that proves his Jewish descent, although several writers have pointed to a mercantile and medical background. However, a study of his books reveals plenty of hints of mockery at both blood purity and Old Christian rusticity and illiteracy.[35] The explanation of the main character's name in *Don Quixote*'s first chapter points to the example of Amadis of Gaul, who had added to his name his kingdom and native country, and concludes: "[He decided] to call himself Don Quijote de la Mancha, which, in his opinion, energetically declared his lineage and native country, honouring them by taking them as a surname."[36] La Mancha is a region of Spain, but it also means stain, which could hint at New Christian "tainted" blood. There is here a double irony, because the region (or stain) and lineage are considered honoured by being included in Don Quixote's name. The reference to lineage makes this interpretation plausible, and it may be reinforced by a reading of Francisco López de Ubeda's *La pícara Justina*, published in the same year, 1605. Here, the main character, Justina, laments her stain, also used as a metaphor, while several references to her ancestry play on the same line of crude irony, such as a reference to her grandfather, "que se mató en la cruz" (who committed suicide on the cross, meaning he was a Jew), and to other "grandfathers" who were from beyond Mount Tabor (with the same meaning).[37]

The rusticity and common sense of Sancho Panza may be seen as mocking Old Christians and their prejudices about blood purity. In one dialogue, Quixote's squire comments, "Thank God that I am Old Christian, and to be a count, that is enough," to which Quixote replies, "More than enough, and even if this is not the case it does not matter; because if I were the king, I would confer nobility on you, without you buying it or serving me."[38] Arbitrary ennoblement is thus derided in what was a risky exercise, given that it exposed both the prejudice and contradictory practices of promotion, here based on an affection, but juxtaposed to the common practice of selling titles or using them to reward service regardless of stained blood. In the second part of the novel, when Sancho Panza is made governor of the island of Barataria and asks who is to be his secretary, someone says, "I am, because I know how to read and write, and I am a Biscayan," to which Sancho Panza replies, "With that explanation you could well be secretary to the emperor himself."[39] Here Cervantes mocks the pride of people from the northern mountains (or the Basque Country) in not being stained by Jewish blood—this area was frequently claimed as their homeland by New Christians pretending to have blood purity, but it is true that Biscayans had the reputation of being good secretaries.

Miguel de Cervantes pushes his capacity for discreetly deriding prejudices even further when, at the end of the second part of the novel, the character Ana Félix, a beautiful young woman expelled from Spain with the other Moriscos (a recent event, 1609–1614), remains a Catholic in Algeria but returns to Spain to recover the family's treasure. Captured with her galley near Barcelona, she is saved by the viceroy and meets her father, who has returned from Germany, where he has found a peaceful place to live with his family.[40] The message about migration to places in Europe with freedom of conscience (a notion already coined and discussed) could not be clearer.

Fernão Mendes Pinto (ca. 1509–1583) is an even more difficult case in asserting family identity. He lived from 1537 to 1558 in Asia, where he acted as a soldier, merchant, missionary, and diplomatic agent. He joined the Jesuits for a short period of time in the 1550s. He was captured several times, sold, and ransomed. He wrote a remarkable book, *Peregrinação*, that was published in 1614, more than thirty years after his death. This book can be defined as a hybrid between memoirs, autobiography, travel account, and picaresque novel. It is an anti-epic text, based on an extraordinary repository of stories in which constant plunder of the Portuguese is candidly exposed and criticised. Fernão Mendes Pinto stages many different scenes and conversations between explorers and local rulers, who challenge the Portuguese motives and uncover their greed and ruthless methods. It is this radical criticism and the visible influence of the picaresque novel that allow his inclusion here as an example of detachment and experimental writing possibly linked to a New Christian environment.[41]

Francisco Rodrigues Lobo's *Corte na aldeia*, published in 1619, is a massive book on court etiquette, dealing with various types of correspondence, formal manners, forms of address, dress codes, moral values, conversational conventions, announcements and narrative accounts, aphorisms, and behaviour in military and educational settings.[42] It offers a vast programme, very well written—basically it is a dialogue between several friends of different social origins—and providing more than just an update of Baldassare Castiglione's work. It also has an attractive setting: a court held in a Portuguese village, implicitly attributable to the absence of the royal court from Lisbon during the Iberian Union of Crowns. There is no doubt about Rodrigues Lobo's (1580–1622) Jewish descent, since the records show that his brother, Miguel Lobo, was tried by the Inquisition in 1626–1634, accused of Judaism.[43] The book praises the Hebrew language, declared sacred because of the honesty of its words.[44] We have to place this brief but quite pointed reference in the context of a long discussion about the history of classical languages since the Renaissance, including the intervention by the Hebraist Johann Reuchlin opposing the destruction of Jewish books in early sixteenth-century Germany.[45]

The second interesting aim of the book is to convey the importance of communication with foreigners in providing an understanding of the civility of other courts, the laws of other kingdoms, the beauty and kindness of foreign ladies, the styles of other kings, and the habits and instincts of other peoples. We could classify this approach as cosmopolitan because the author clearly states that variety is important for enriching understanding and memory.[46] The book's classification of four main social types at court is also unusual: kings, princes, and lords; ambassadors; gentlemen; merchants. The justification for the inclusion of the fourth type is, again, cosmopolitanism: in pursuit of trade, merchants have been in the main *praças* (cities or markets) of the world, absorbing information on habits, conditions, and laws.[47] Merchants were defined by their liabilities, financial power, size of business, networks, trustworthiness, creditworthiness, integrity, and common sense. Rodrigues Lobo, who was a clergyman in minor orders receiving an ecclesiastical benefice, highlighted trade across the world in metals, precious stones, textiles, ivory, perfumes, alabaster, furs, paper and glass, coral, hides and leather, woods, cereals, and wines—all listed with the main places they came from.[48] This is in line with the praise of merchants we found in sixteenth-century Iberia, but here it is pushed a little further as part of the ideal court society.

A third and crucial point is made by the way in which the book touches on the Inquisition. The message here is: "I do not want to deal with conscience, because it is a dangerous matter, but there are many who do great damage in this area." At first sight, this looks too innocuous (or too implicit) to be related to the Inquisition; but the logic of the sequence makes it clear. The paragraph states at the beginning that "God gave men of great esteem three things, body, wealth and conscience, which men of letters have been harming; with their purges, syrups and bleedings, physicians cause more damage than the invention of gunpowder; the constant demands, quarrels and collusions of lawyers prevent truth from being asserted and exhaust wealth."[49] It is obvious that the author means that conscience has been abused and wrecked by those who were supposed to help keep it true: the inquisitors.

Anger at the persecution of the New Christians in the 1630s, both in Portugal and Spain, produced much more explicit critiques of the Inquisition in literature than Lobo's. The case of Antonio Enríquez Gómez is well known.[50] Born in Cuenca around 1600 and dying a prisoner of the Inquisition in Seville in 1663, this descendent of Castilian New Christians—a merchant, a poet, and a playwright—moved from Cuenca to Madrid, then in 1635 to Bordeaux, and then to Rouen to escape the Inquisition. He returned to Spain (Granada and Seville) around 1650 to recover debts, and lived there under the name of Fernando Zárate until he was caught by the Inquisition in 1661. He wrote many plays in Madrid; then anti-inquisitorial and philo-Jewish pamphlets, plays, and memoirs in Bordeaux and Rouen; and finally Christian comedies in Seville.

The *Academias morales de las musas* is an extraordinary poem on exile, printed in 1642 in Bordeaux and reprinted six times in Spain between 1647 and 1734. In it, Gómez declares that he has been dispossessed of his freedom, refuge, and soul by exile, and that he lives without rest, care, or guidance, a display of strong New Christian feelings of loss and nostalgia for the world left behind that clearly touched his compatriots.[51] An important reflection on the illusions of the world is offered in the fourth part of the poem, in which the author complains that

> the century of freedom of conscience is proclaimed, no doubt, but each day's experience tests this truth; I see tyranny growing in power, the wise man abhorred, the ignorant loved, and I espouse this cause as my own. Who would not suffer pain and anger when the poor are abhorred by the rich, and the virtuous despised? I see the just alone and dejected, the good person beset by troubles and oppressed by criminals. When will this venomous existence have an end? . . . I abhor life and close my lips when I see an arrogant person lacking in justice who has dominion over a wise man.[52]

It is certain that Gómez had the inquisitors in his mind when he wrote these verses.

Antonio Enríquez Gómez was not completely free to publish what he thought because he probably hoped that at a future date the book would be printed in Spain, but at several points he castigates the malsín, or informer, who ruins the lives of other people with venomous and false accusations, moved by envy and ambition. Moreover, he uses the biblical case of Saul to denounce those who pretend to be zealous defenders of the faith to kill innocents, comparing them to cruel wolves pursuing innocent lambs and advising kings to watch lamentable tragedies in public theatres. The allusion to the auto da fé is thus thinly veiled, but he reinforces his critique when he exposes the hypocrisy of those zealous defenders of the faith (the inquisitors), who lament the ruin they create, regret the damage they do, and pretend that their tyranny is just compassion for humankind.[53]

The revolt of the Maccabees against the tyranny of the Seleucid emperor, Antiochus Epiphanes (175–164 B.C.E.), who forbade the Jews to practice their rituals and forced them to worship idols, was not part of the Jewish scriptural canon, but texts referring to it had been collected by the early Christians, and in the sixteenth century it had become the part of a debate between Protestants and Catholics on apocryphal and canonical scriptures.[54] The revolt was transformed into a literary topic by New Christians, who used it as a metaphor to denounce their own persecution by the Inquisition, supported by the Iberian kings. Theirs had also been an experience of politically imposed religious change, with all the pain implied in responding to violent profanation of temples, ceremonies, and daily practices. The theme was addressed by the New Christian Miguel de Silveira in a poem with the explicit title *El Macabeo*, in 1638.[55] Antonio Enríquez Gómez, in another pamphlet, *Politica Angelica, Segunda Parte*, published in Rouen in 1647, used the subject to compare Antiochus Epiphanes, with the Iberian Inquisitions and to criticise the latter as even worse than the former because they showed less mercy, concealed the names of witnesses, and in their insatiable cupidity justified the confiscation of property even from repentant sinners.[56]

The Inquisition was directly addressed by Gómez in various texts he produced while living in Rouen in the 1640s, particularly in the *Romance al divín mártir Judá Creyente*, a tribute to Lope de Vera y Alarcón, who had converted to Judaism and been excommunicated by the tribunal of Valladolid in 1644. But it was in the prose satire *Inquisición de Lucifer y visita de todos los diablos*, probably written the following year, that the writer managed to make his critique more systematic and more satirical. In *Politica angelica*, he played with the idea of the transmigration of a soul into bodies representing various social (and psychological) types, but here it is the devil who decides to join forces with prisoners of the Holy Office to hold an Inquisition of the Inquisition. In doing this he challenges the logic of the tribunal, revolted by the unfair competition initiated by the inquisitors, who are seeking to occupy the field of spiritual judgment reserved for God and that of eternal punishment reserved for Lucifer.

The devil questions his usurpers' right to detain those they accuse for many years, to subject them to torture and other villainies, to dishonour whole lineages by forcing members who have committed no sin to appear in their parishes in *sambenitos* (penitential garments worn by those condemned by the Inquisition), denouncing these procedures as tyranny against the souls of those thus treated.[57] The practice of concealing the names of witnesses, which forces those detained to guess who might have denounced them when trying to invalidate accusations, is criticised.[58] It is the confiscation of property, not salvation of the soul, that is at stake here.[59] The Inquisition is considered not holy but sinful, while it is suggested that the inquisitors must have studied to be executioners, not theologians, jurists, or philosophers, because they concentrate on detaining, condemning, torturing, killing, and robbing.[60] The obsession with genealogy is questioned, because the dead are interrogated to judge the living, and lies replace truth in an attempt to steal honour, life, and wealth.[61] The Inquisition, seen as a company of thieves in the guise of people who would save souls, denying mercy and being arrogant enough to usurp the place of God as spiritual judge, is the recurrent theme of this pamphlet.

The real beliefs of Antonio Enríquez Gómez are elusive, despite the enormous quantity of plays, pamphlets, and poems he wrote. As pointed out earlier, in the last period of his life, when he was living in Spain, he even wrote Christian comedies under the name of Fernando Zárate. He confessed in jail to the sins he was accused of and died as a Catholic, having the honour of being paraded in effigy as reconciled with the Church. It is absurd to try to define what his beliefs were: he clearly led several different lives and decided to live each to the full, adapting to local circumstances and the possibilities and frameworks for activity they offered. The critique of the Inquisition clearly came from his heart, as did the philosophical reasoning about the failed promises of freedom of conscience in his century. He was talking too early, and in the wrong place; Rouen was part of France and the practice of Judaism was not allowed, although matters of faith were not rigorously enquired into. The fact is that Gómez never decided to migrate to Amsterdam, which he could easily have done. And in his pamphlets he demonstrated that he was very familiar with other Christian confessions. It seems very likely that he was a New Christian freethinker (or *libertin*, a noun that evolved from meaning "emancipated" in the late fifteenth century to meaning "independent from all subjection" in the seventeenth century) who flirted with various strands of belief, and at times with nonbelief, according to the community he was living in and the possibilities offered by local society.[62]

More dramatic is the case of Gómez's friend, the New Christian Manuel Fernandes Vila Real (1608–1652), who lived in Rouen and Paris and had access to Cardinal Richelieu, whom he kept informed of the events of the Portuguese Revolution in December 1640. Vila Real styled himself a captain because of his early military service in Tangier. He was a merchant and a journalist, who launched the *Mercure de Portugal* in Paris in 1643 and contributed to other gazettes of the time. In 1664, in recognition of his services, King John IV appointed him a knight of the royal household and a consul in France. He was highly praised by the Portuguese ambassadors in northern Europe, played a major role in the promotion of the Portuguese Restoration in Europe, and made every effort to obtain material support abroad for the war of independence.

Vila Real was a political writer who questioned the legitimacy of the Inquisition and supported freedom of conscience, although in a veiled way, and without challenging the absolutist order. He returned to Lisbon in 1649 to receive a new appointment from the king as a commissioner of the *Junta dos Tres Estados*, with special responsibilities in relation to the war of independence. However, that same year he was detained by the Inquisition, just as he was about to leave the country under royal orders, and after a long trial, which forced him to make belated and fruitless confessions (and denunciations), he was excommunicated by the Inquisition and executed (burnt) by the secular arm.[63]

Vila Real's political output was not particularly innovative. He favoured a strong monarchy, although one sustained by low taxes, and favoured limited just wars fought with the support of a people released from the burden of poverty. In his view, the sinews of the republic were trade, which must increase wealth and stimulate industry and agriculture. He was against monopolies as hindering freedom of trade. Merchants of proven quality should be involved in royal institutions and contribute to their activities. Merit and service rather than noble descent should be rewarded. Censorship, however, was supported as being necessary to protect the reputation of the republic (his model was France; his book *Epítome genealógico* focused on Cardinal Richelieu). Vila Real considered that equality for all before the law must be the cornerstone of any monarchy; the sovereign must obey the rules and protect vassals and foreigners allowed into the country from the tyranny of bad ministers or local lords. Justice, in the sense of fairness and equity, sustained the republic. Revolt against tyranny was justified, as in the recent cases of Catalonia and Portugal.[64]

Vila Real's reasoning became more subtle when he talked about religion and policies concerning people forced to convert. The expulsion of the Moriscos by Philip III of Spain in 1609–1614 merited a long discussion on exile and the ruin of the state. The decision was considered cruel, because many Moriscos were Catholics, innocent of the accusation that they had reverted to their former faith. Even nuns and monks had been forced to abandon their congregations, all being subjected to the most atrocious tyranny and extortion during their painful voyage. Many people had been forced to leave—cities were depopulated, fields were emptied of farmers, and several regions suffered significant population decline. The pretext that Catholicism required such acts was rejected because King Henry IV had intervened in favour of those dispossessed. The decline of Spain and the reinforcement of the Muslim states of North Africa were the outcomes of this politically inept act.[65]

But there was more. Manuel Fernandes Vila Real wrote in favour of freedom of conscience several times, opining that the sovereign was obliged to protect the secrets of the soul rather than render them public. He stated: "It is not in the power of the Prince to scrutinise the secrets of the soul. It is sufficient that the vassal obeys his laws, observes his precepts, without introducing his dominion into the most mystical of thoughts and into the intimacy of the heart. If there is no scandal, no bad example, what is the point of reckless judgment and speeches more motivated by hate than by reason? [The Prince] cannot replace God; his power is only human."[66] This line of reasoning would be developed in the eighteenth century.

I have not included Sephardic thinkers in this book except for New Christians recently returned to Jewish communities, as was the case with Uriel da Costa. The case of Benedictus (Baruch) Spinoza (1632–1677) is difficult to avoid because of his New Christian origins and his recognised status as one of the most original thinkers of the Enlightenment. It is disputable whether his family ethnic and religious origins contributed to his radical philosophical stance, although the difficulty of becoming reintegrated into a normative community and the presence of other New Christians with an alternative way of thinking might have played a role. Isaac de La Peyrère, who launched a pre-Adamite hypothesis as part of his criticism of the Bible, and Juan de Prado, a deist from Andalusia, were in Amsterdam in 1655. However, Jonathan Israel has convincingly argued that Spinoza's system of thought was well developed way before his excommunication by the Jewish community in 1656, pointing out that if there was some stimulating influence it came from the ex-Jesuit and scholar Franciscus van den Enden (1602–1674). But Spinoza developed his own system of thought very early, without visible dependence from van den Enden.[67]

The main issues developed by Spinoza concerned the strategy of reading the Scriptures in the same way as any other text, enlarging the search for the philological and historical context; the identification of God with nature, as having immanent infinite properties with their own motion; and the departure from Descartes's doctrine of two substances, the material body and the mind, considered as a single identity. Spinoza developed this system of thought in his successive writings. The identification of God with nature excluded the idea of a personalised God embodying divine Providence, who could intervene to reward or punish. The desecration of the Scriptures meant the rejection of a revelation, produced through messages sent by God, which structured the religions of the book. Spinoza's vision of nature would also contradict the idea of miracles or, even more important, the idea of immortality of the soul. His contemporaries understood well the consequences of this line of thought, making redundant the religions created for individual or collective salvation. Finally, Spinoza conceived freedom of conscience within a radical theory of toleration and re-evaluated the notion of constituent power and right of resistance within the republican tradition.[68] This extensive philosophical programme represented a complete departure from both Christian and Jewish backgrounds.

The impact of New Christians on art does not reach the same level as in literature or political thought; alternative and nonconformist forms are difficult to identify. They contributed to the mainstream themes and patterns, but in some cases they engaged with controversies. The work of particular painters within a converso environment would justify further scrutiny, relating paintings to precise historical events. There are stimulating interpretations of Velázquez's paintings, mainly linked to secrecy and dissidence in *Christ in the House of Martha and Mary* and *Kitchen Maid with the Supper at Emaus*, to torture and accusation in *Christ after the Flagellation Contemplated by the Christian Soul*, and to Bacchus as pacifier in *The Triumph of Bacchus* (or *Los borrachos*); but more research is necessary.[69] We will concentrate here on one important case.

The cult of the Immaculate Conception, publicly supported by the Franciscans and Jesuits (and other religious orders) against the Dominicans, who fiercely rejected it, exploded in Seville in the 1610s with extraordinary violence, triggering the preaching of fervent sermons, the distribution of pamphlets in which religious orders insulted each other, and accusations of Judaism lodged by the Dominicans at the Inquisition against supporters of the cult.[70] The archbishop of Seville, Pedro de Castro, who when he had been in Granada had accepted the authenticity of documents forged by Moriscos claiming early conversion, which included references to the cult of the Immaculate Conception, rallied against Dominican condemnation and organised a delegation to convince the king, Philip III, to support a request to Rome for the dogma to be recognized.

This initiative would have long-term consequences in the Iberian kingdoms where, by the mid-seventeenth century, religious belief was defined by attitudes to the cult of the Immaculate Conception of the Virgin Mary. In the 1610s, Rome was clearly too divided for an outright assertion of the dogma, and the pope intervened only to suppress its condemnation. Indeed, the dogma of the Immaculate Conception of the Virgin Mary was not formally declared until December 8, 1854, through the bull *Ineffabilis Deus*.[71] The reasons for the powerful and unstoppable reemergence of this cult in Seville, and its subsequent promotion on an Iberian—and eventually a Latin Christian—scale, have recently been the subject of study.

Felipe Pereda rightly highlights the role played by visual culture in the seventeenth century assertion of the cult of the Immaculate Conception, finding that new points from the Bible, particularly from the Book of Revelation by John the Evangelist, were being discussed. Some of these were integrated into a major canvas painted by Juan de Roelas and sent to Philip III in 1616, in which the artist depicted a multiethnic society engaged in celebration, with children of different skin colours and the overarching theme of the Virgin's protection of motherhood through the notion of pure milk.[72] The argument was that milk suckled at a pure breast could be equated with pure blood, thus contributing to the integration of minorities in a society shaken by the expulsion of the Moriscos in the previous years. Pereda refers to Cervantes's Ana Félix (second part of *Don Quixote*, in an episode already mentioned), a character whom the novelist claimed had imbibed the Catholic faith through her mother's milk, thus contradicting blood purity prejudices, since her mother was a morisca. Briefly, the cult of the Immaculate Conception can be interpreted as a counterclaim to blood purity controversies—a counterclaim that stressed the inclusion of all ethnicities, thus enhancing the project of a harmonious imperial society that could appeal to the king.

New Christians were deeply involved in this controversy in Seville, where they had a visible presence in all areas of activity. The Jesuit Juan de Pineda, who played a major role in the promotion of the cult in Seville, was accused of

FIGURE 12.1. Juan de Jauregui, design of the print, *The Woman of the Apocalypse*, in Luis de Alcázar, *Vestigatio arcani sensus in Apocalypsi* (Antuerpiae: Apud Ioannem Keerbergium, 1614). Reproduced by kind permission of the Syndics of Cambridge University Library.

Judaism. The Confraternity of the Pomegranate, which also played an important role in the diffusion of the cult and was supported by archbishop Pedro de Castro was the subject of enquiries by the Inquisition, which suspected them of connections with the alumbrados, a spiritual movement that, as we have seen before, had strong links to the New Christians. The cult of the Immaculate Conception of the Virgin Mary was built on the identification of the Virgin with the woman of the apocalypse, a figure who featured in the works of several painters, from Juan Pantoja de la Cruz (1553–1608) to, in a different context, Diego Velázquez (1599–1660). The visual positioning of the Virgin, on a convex moon, which defined the iconography of the Immaculate Conception

FIGURE 12.2. Juan de Jauregui, design of the print, *The Apocalypse*, in Luis de Alcázar, *Vestigatio arcani sensus in Apocalypsi* (Antuerpiae: Apud Ioannem Keerbergium, 1614). Reproduced by kind permission of the Syndics of Cambridge University Library.

in those years, responded to comments by the Jesuit Luis de Alcázar on the book of Revelations. These comments were illustrated by Juan de Jauregui, in work in which the parallel functions of the woman of the apocalypse and the Virgin Mary were clearly suggested.[73] Both Luis de Alcázar and Juan de Jauregui, an artist and poet who later became a member of the circle of the Count-Duke of Olivares, were New Christians.[74] It seems that New Christian circles used the cult to promote the vision of a purified and spiritualised Church that could be reformed and made more inclusive.

However, this contribution of New Christians at the very beginning of the new assertion of the cult of the Immaculate Conception of the Virgin Mary in Spain is relatively absent from recent research. José Javier Ruiz Ibáñez and Gaetano Sabatini organised an excellent volume on the issue, structured around the religious and political use of the cult to redefine the Hispanic monarchy in a period of decline and involve all local communities across the empire.[75] The assertion of purity through the example of the Virgin Mary is there related to rooted prejudices against New Christians and Moriscos. The Introduction to this volume touches the issue of inclusion, while the chapter by Jean-Frédéric Schaub provides a good reflection on the ambiguities of blood stain and blood purity. I believe that the first moment of New Christian intervention, so well studied by Felipe Pereda, needs to be taken onboard, because it shows the possibilities of subverting the ideology of blood purity and extending inclusion to discriminated-against minorities. This first moment did not lead to real change; but it is part of the history of resistance by New Christians that can alert us to seek similar movements in history.

The first half of the seventeenth century registered developments of New Christian religious allegiance that were influenced by the possibilities of reconstituting Jewish normative communities in northern Europe, mainly in Amsterdam and Hamburg, followed by London, in the 1650s. This functioned as the pull factor, very much instigated by significant New Christian migration. The push factor was obviously increased repression by the Inquisition, which started to target financiers and merchants, who were largely spared between the 1520s and the 1570s. Political allegiance, which was already important to explain the acceptance of Sephardic communities in northern Europe and in the Mediterranean, owing to mercantilist policies, registered a division in Iberia triggered by the independence of Portugal. New Christians revealed a strong capacity for adaptation through migration, naturalization, and citizenship, although they largely lost their connection to Spanish America, while keeping and enlarging their presence in Brazil.

New Christians contributed directly and indirectly to new reflection in literature and political thought and, marginally, in art. Mockery of pretensions to blood purity was expressed by major writers, while the political fairness of the expulsion of Moriscos was clearly questioned and the restrictions to freedom of conscience started to be discussed. New Christians who lived in France could publish more daring reflections on the illegitimate substitution of God's final judgment by the Inquisition, while political pamphlets promoted the idea that neither the monarchy nor the Church should enquire on private matters of conscience not made public.

In the meantime, the movement to promote the Immaculate Conception of the Virgin Mary, supported by some religious orders (Carmelites, Franciscans, Jesuits) and New Christians against the Dominicans, received an extraordinary development in the area of visual culture. The idea of the purity of Virgin Mary and the regenerative qualities of her milk for all believers implied the inclusion of all minorities, overcoming the rigid barrier of blood purity. Furthermore, it was possible, in paintings, to introduce veiled references to precise cases of discrimination against New Christians. At the heart of all these developments was the discussion on divisions provoked by blood purity enquiries. This intellectual movement was suppressed by the 1640s, owing to the backlash of conservative elites, but it left seeds of new ideas that would be influential in the future.

Conclusions to Part III

THE FIRST HALF of the seventeenth century registered increased persecution of New Christians, with resistance and enlargement of the scope of their actions by the trading elite. The commercial possibilities opened up by the Iberian Union of Crowns were fully explored by the New Christian elite; they developed their presence in Seville, in Madrid, and in Spanish America, obtaining naturalisation. They invested in the slave trade from Africa to the Americas, controlling most of the contracts both on the Portuguese and on the Castilian side. They also reinforced their presence in Italy, both in Christian and Jewish communities, as well as in the southwest and west France, where public allegiance to Judaism was not allowed but religious identity was not enquired into. The creation of Sephardic communities by Iberian New Christians (and Jews from Italy) in Amsterdam and Hamburg, at the turn of the century, established a new basis for shared trade in northern Europe. Commercial connections between Iberia and Iberian America or Iberia and the East Indies, through the Cape of Good Hope and across the Pacific, grew in this period, despite the competition from Dutch and English companies. The share of trade by New Christians was significant on these maritime routes: from 30 to 45 percent. The expulsion of the Portuguese from Japan in 1639 was the first blow to the New Christian networks, while competition from the Dutch East India Company started to be heavily felt after the 1630s and 1640s.

Inquisitorial response to the general pardon of 1604, negotiated by some New Christians, materialised in the 1610s when royal policies concerning New Christians were reversed and the pope reinforced support for the tribunal of faith. The Inquisition of Portugal launched new waves of persecution from the 1610s to the 1630s, followed by the Inquisition of Spanish America in the 1630s and 1640s. In the latter case, the main *converso* merchants were wiped out from Lima and Mexico. In the meantime, in Madrid, but also in other parts of Castile, the Inquisition prosecuted *conversos*, including financiers and bankers, mainly from the 1630s onwards. The tribunal of the Inquisition of Goa launched new persecution of New Christians in the 1630s and 1640s, which contributed to the weakening of the *Estado da Índia*. The blood purity debate, which loomed from the 1590s to the 1630s, concluded with the defeat of the reformers, whose real intention has been scrutinised here. The radical writings of Quevedo, who launched the first conspiracy theories attributed to Jews, expressed the rejection of any attempt to reform the ideological configuration of blood purity.

The last years of the reign of Philip III brought new misery to New Christians in Portugal, resulting from the exceptional demands for money from the merchants, the city of Lisbon, and the Inquisition itself. The tribunals of faith launched a fierce wave of persecution in 1618, with immediate confiscation and selling of property at the moment of detention, before trial, that defined a new practice with heavy social consequences. The accession of Philip IV to the throne in 1621 and the policies launched by his favourite, Olivares, gave some respite to the New Christians, who were viewed as an alternative to Genoese bankers, but the Inquisition, both in Portugal and Castile, did not suspend their persecution. The edict of grace of 1627 imposed on the Portuguese Inquisition from Madrid had only a temporary impact because it did not have the weight of a general pardon issued by the pope that would have invalidated all denunciations and confessions. Portuguese independence in 1640 created a complex political dynamic, because both Portuguese and Castilian kings needed financial support more than ever—in the Castilian case, for war on different fronts—but the Inquisition did not interrupt its prosecution of major financiers for long.

In general, New Christians kept their allegiances where their investments had been made, although the independence of Portugal created a significant division, visible in the relations between Macau and Manila in the Far East but also in the Portuguese community in Seville. The renewed persecution of Portuguese New Christians, which could alienate their support for the war of independence, led King John IV to create the Company of Brazil in 1649 with funds from New Christians that could not be confiscated, although lists for imposed investment were drawn up. A steady flow of New Christians to Jewish communities in Italy and northern Europe was visible in this period.

Finally, literary expression of the *converso* condition and reflection on the New/Old Christian divide developed in this period. In France, several texts by New Christians were published, mainly by Antonio Enríquez Gómez, in which the merits of the tribunal of faith were derided and the inquisitorial fantasy of playing God in the Last Judgment were exposed. Enríquez Gómez went as far as imagining a dialogue between an inquisitor and a devil, the latter outraged by the appropriation of his traditional competences by the tribunal. Literature also reflected the debate on blood purity, with clear derision of the pretentions of Old Christians. The idea of freedom of conscience started to spread in Iberia through literary texts. Political texts, again published in France by New Christians such as Manuel Fernandes Vila Real, boldly defined the support for freedom of conscience, stating that no one should enquire into ideas and beliefs not made public. Radical philosophy promoted by Spinoza, who had such an impact on the transition to modernity, cannot be directly related to his New Christian background; he departed from both Christian and Jewish frameworks. And finally, the impact of New Christians on art needs further research, but the movement in Seville in the early seventeenth century in favour of the dogma of the Immaculate Conception of the Virgin Mary included from the beginning a participation by New Christians, who argued for the comprehensive integration of all Christians by the Virgin.

PART IV

Decline
(1650s–1770s)

⟨━━◗⫶◖━━⟩

THE MID-SEVENTEENTH CENTURY marked a radical turning point in the history of the New Christians that has not been evaluated as such before. The number of prosecutions brought by the Inquisition in Portugal increased dramatically during the late 1650s and 1660s, up until the suspension of the Inquisition by the pope in 1674. These years represent the peak of roughly three centuries of inquisitorial activity almost exclusively directed against New Christians accused of Judaism. While the level of inquisitorial persecution in Spain in these years was significantly lower than it had been, it did not show any signs of further decline. New Christians in high positions in Madrid and Seville were a target, despite a change of general inquisitor and later the accession of a new king. My argument is that the initiative of the Portuguese New Christians in Rome, who asked for a general pardon in the early 1670s, was a response to decades of repression that had led to a calamitous eradication of trust and capital, hugely undermining the operational capacity of the primary merchants and bankers.

The suspension of the Inquisition from 1674 to 1681 did not provide New Christians with relief. The alliances established by the different intervenients, the opposition organised by the Inquisition, and its reestablishment and the consequent backlash against New Christians at all levels will be studied in this part of the book. The unfolding of the political fight both in Rome and in Lisbon will be considered. Contexts and rhythms of persecution of New Christian merchants will be analysed and related to changing conditions in the international markets. Finally, the major event of the War of Succession in Spain, which registered the last heavy financial involvement of New Christians in Iberia, will be scrutinised.

This part of the book, which opens with a chapter on the persecution of New Christians, will analyse the main trends of inquisitorial activity in Spain and Portugal and their consequences up to the 1660s. I shall study major collective detentions and the new procedures involved in these, drawing on extensive research in the archives. New Christians' wealth will be followed here, as well as their presence abroad and their links with Jewish communities. The growing presence of foreign merchants will be introduced to better understand the changing context of trade. The political intervention (or absence of intervention) of the Portuguese king will be investigated and compared with policies being implemented in Spain over the same period.

A chapter on the suspension of the Portuguese Inquisition will follow. This was a crucial moment in New Christian history, but it did not succeed as expected. The surprising alliance between New Christians and Jesuits did not coalesce into a powerful dynamic for change, and I will try to explain why. The involvement of the Portuguese regent, the future King Peter II, also needs to be better analysed over the whole period of his regency and reign. The political battle in Rome, which became the centre of the political struggle, showed the different interests at stake. An account of contrasting experiences in Portugal and Spain will conclude this chapter, offering a perspective on New Christian communities abroad, mainly in Italy. Overall, the chapter will offer a balance of focus between the collective and the individual activities of New Christian agents.

The chapter on the reversal of the New Christians' fortunes addresses the consequences of these developments. The reestablishment of the Portuguese Inquisition will be centre stage here, linked to the legal framework that was created for the occasion by the pope and the Portuguese king, a framework not hitherto deeply studied. New laws against New Christians had devastating effects that have yet to be properly assessed. The flow of migration did not stop, and I shall focus on specific cases. The importance of Brazil as a refuge for New Christians will be addressed. The breakdown of New Christian trading networks will be the focus here, although exceptions will be underlined. Defensive strategies of New Christians under decline both in Spain and Portugal will be centre stage. The participation of New Christian financiers in the War of Succession of Spain will complete this section.

The last chapter concentrates on the subsuming of New Christians into global society and the disappearance of major New Christian merchants. There were some surviving networks up to the 1740s, both in Spain and Portugal, and we will analyse a last wave of inquisitorial persecution in the 1720s and 1730s in Iberia, which provoked new migration and transfers of capital. The replacement of New Christians by Old Christians and foreign merchants accelerated the disappearance of a group hitherto firmly conscious of its own identity. Those who stayed in Iberia and their descendants integrated further into the local population. Pombal's abolition, in 1773, of the distinction between New Christians and Old Christians responded to political changes in the concept of the state, but it contrasts with the perpetuation of the concept of blood purity in Spain.[1]

CHAPTER THIRTEEN

Persecution

THE DATA FOR inquisitorial sentences carried out annually in Portugal, which are underestimated by the available sources, indicate 1,123 trials for the 1650s in the three tribunals of Lisbon, Coimbra, and Évora; 3,007 trials for the 1660s; 1,379 for the 1670s; 934 for the 1680s; and 529 for the 1690s, for a total of 6,972 trials in the second half of the seventeenth century. In this period, the tribunal of Lisbon tried 1,435 cases, Évora tried 2,879, and Coimbra tried 2,658, which demonstrates how thoroughly the territory was covered.[1] New Christians represented between 68 and 84 percent of the total number of accused in each tribunal, from the more cosmopolitan and diversified (Lisbon) to the more focused on Judaism (Coimbra and Évora).[2] It looks as though extreme circumstances led to more than 6,000 trials against New Christians in the second half of the seventeenth century.

The relative downturn in inquisitorial repression in the 1640s (1,426 trials compared to 2,743 in the previous decade) and 1650s (1,123 trials) was due to political disruption caused by the struggle for the independence of Portugal, and in 1649, there was a decree by King John IV exempting New Christians from property confiscation (and, even better, allowing for the return of some confiscated property) in order to encourage them to invest in the Portuguese General Company of Brazil.[3] The Inquisition's practice of confiscating property was reinstated in 1657, following the death of King John IV the previous year. The pope had already backed such a reinstatement in 1650, but his wishes could not be implemented against the clear opposition of the king.[4] This turn of events, which coincided with a decline in the fortunes of the Company of Brazil, from the abolition of its monopoly on trade in 1658 to its integration by the state in 1664, unleashed a major wave of trials by the Inquisition in the late 1650s and 1660s, the harshest of any seen in Portugal.[5] The average number of trials per year in the early 1670s continued to be very high, until the suspension of the Portuguese Inquisition by the pope in 1674. However, after the reestablishment of the Inquisition in 1681, there was a significant decline in trials because of the political policies established to force New Christians out of the kingdom and changes of inquisitorial procedure imposed by the pope.

The situation in Spain at that time was entirely different, even if the estimate of trial numbers, based on *relaciones de causas* (summaries of trials), assumes that records of half the trials have probably been lost. According to that estimate, there were 2,123 prosecutions for Judaism in the whole of the period from 1615 to 1700 in Spain, plus 250 trials in the Spanish Empire, which means many fewer trials than in Portugal in the second half of the seventeenth century.[6] The Spanish trials targeted low-, middle-, and high-ranking New Christians, including asentistas and bankers. Despite less-reliable figures, it is possible to say that the Spanish tribunals were relatively less aggressive than the Portuguese towards the New Christian financial elite in this period, and it is certain that the Portuguese tribunals developed a much wider and deeper focus on the persecution of New Christians in the countryside than their Spanish counterparts.

1. Castile

On June 29, 1654, an extraordinary number of victims were paraded at the auto da fé in Cuenca, among them a significant number of New Christian merchants. Jerónimo de Barrionuevo, who compiled *Avisos* (newsletters) in those days, reported a rumour that 200 New Christian families fled Madrid that night.[7] Fernando de Montesinos, a well-known asentista associated with Jorge Enríquez, who had the contract for salt produced in Galicia and Asturias and the contract to provision Ceuta, was presented at that auto da fé, along with his wife, who was a cousin of the major financier Manuel Cortizos. When Fernando Montesinos was finally released, with a heavy penalty of 10,000 ducados, and exiled, he left his business to his two sons, who developed it in the following decades. Fernando decided to live in Amsterdam, where he assumed the Jewish faith.[8]

The brothers Rodrigues Cardoso were another example of very wealthy financiers pushed to emigrate by the Inquisition. They had the contract for salt in Atienza and Espartinas as well as contracts for other royal rents and taxes. They had been blackmailed with threats of denunciation for Judaism to the Inquisition and had decided to report the case to the general inquisitor of Spain, but the latter did nothing. They then cleared their debts and escaped to Amsterdam, taking with them, according to rumours, 200,000 ducados in wool and another 250,000 in gold, claims impossible to check.[9]

Also detained at this time was Francisco Dias Mendes Brito, grandson of Heitor Mendes de Brito via his mother, Ana Mendes de Brito, who had married Jorge Rodrigues da Costa. Dias Mendes Brito was then forty-four years old. Having been the administrator for alcabalas (taxes on purchases) in

Cuenca, treasurer for the Council of the Indies, and the person responsible for issuing crusade bulls in Castile, he saw his financial career cut short by an exile from which he never recovered.[10]

In 1659, Diego Gómez de Salazar, a New Christian from Ciudad Rodrigo, a former accountant to the Royal Council of Finances and general administrator of tobacco in Spain, was detained by the Inquisition in Valladolid. He was associated with some of the main asentistas of the time, and several of his relatives were also involved with royal contracts. Reconciled by the Inquisition, he managed to assemble the family (other relatives had also been reconciled by the Inquisition) and all escaped to Bayonne, France.[11]

The case of Francisco Lopes Pereira, administrator for the *millones* (taxes on consumption, particularly on wine, vinegar, and meat) in Granada, who had previously had the contract for tobacco in Jaén and the contract for salt in Malaga, provides a good insight into inquisitorial methods and into the social promotion and family network of a midrange financier. The Inquisition started his trial (1658–1664) with the accusations of one single witness, Blanca Pereira, who had been detained in Madrid and herself accused of Judaism.[12] By the time the trial started, this witness had taken refuge in Bayonne and had written to the Inquisition with the help of a local priest to withdraw the false accusation she had levelled against Francisco Lopes Pereira.[13] The inquisitors recorded receipt of the letter, but they did not take it into consideration. They brought in other witnesses and kept repeating, right up to the point of sentencing, that the accused had already been tried at the Inquisition of Coimbra, an accusation which he vehemently denied. As a matter of fact, Francisco Lopes Pereira had had a first trial in Coimbra in 1651 to 1652, where he confessed and abjured at the auto da fé of April 14, 1652.[14] He risked excommunication and execution as relapsed.

Francisco Lopes Pereira persisted in declaring himself to be an Old Christian, arguing that his family had never paid the tributes imposed on New Christians (meaning they had not been so listed).[15] He was familiar with all the Christian prayers, commandments, sacraments, and mortal sins. He denied all accusations of Judaism, accused his enemies of illegal activities, gave lists of those who would testify to his integrity, and withstood two sessions of torture, the first lasting an hour and fifteen minutes.[16] He was finally condemned, without confessing, on the grounds of vehement suspicion of heresy, and sentenced to prison and to the wearing of penitential garments for two years. He was exiled from Granada and Madrid, and an area ten leagues around these, and from seaports and an area twenty leagues around these, for ten years. He was also required to pay a fine of 6,000 ducados.[17] His property had been sequestered when he was detained; and although it could not be confiscated as part of this sentence, the penalties that were imposed were extraordinary. The intention of imposing financial ruin and exclusion from trade without solid judicial proof is obvious.

This is a good case for an analysis of extended family networks. Francisco Lopes Pereira was born in Mogadouro, northeast Portugal, apparently in 1617 (he declared himself to be forty-one years old in the session on genealogy).[18] His father was a native of Chacim and his mother of Mogadouro. Both parents had migrated to Granada, where they still lived and conducted business at the time of the second trial.[19] Several relatives were from the same towns, plus Vila Flor and Muxagata, and were also merchants. Among the accused's many other relatives, his cousin, Manuel Duro, was working for the administrator of tobacco in Cordoba, while Gaspar Lopes Duro was employed at the tobacco factory in Granada. A brother, Diogo Lopes Pereira, lived with his wife in Francisco's house and participated in Francisco's business. A brother-in-law, Diogo Lopes Vale, born in Chacim, was the administrator for tobacco in Cordoba. Francisco had two sons and two daughters, the elder pair, fourteen and twelve years old, born in Mogadouro.[20] He had learned how to read and write in Mogadouro.

Lopes Pereira had been trading in textiles between Portugal and Castile since he was twelve years old, helping his uncles in Segovia, Medina del Campo, Salamanca, Madrid, and Toledo. In Portugal, he had sold merchandise in Braga, Coimbra, Guimarães, Aveiro, and Lisbon. He had traded on the frontier between Portugal and Spain, Bragança, Alfaião, Vale de Frades, Picote, Vilarinho, and Guarda, allegedly with the permission of the Duke of Braganza; but he was probably also involved with contraband. He had established himself in Castile around 1650, then in Peñaranda de Duero, Valladolid, Salamanca, Rio Seco, and finally Granada.[21] He had started as a peddler and was promoted to working with contractors for salt, tobacco, and taxation in Andalusia, very likely New Christians, such as the contractor for tobacco, Juan López Gómez, who was reconciled by the Inquisition. He was associated with some contractors in Madrid, such as Luís Nunes from Trancoso (Portugal). This suggests that the main contracts implied the use of subcontractors.[22]

Francisco Lopes Pereira seems to have withstood six years of detention by the Inquisition. He involved his elder son, Manuel de Aguilar, in his business, and this son maintained the family's commercial undertakings in the 1660s. In the 1670s, Francisco Lopes Pereira obtained new contracts to provision Ceuta and farm the tobacco rents. In 1682 he won a contract to exploit the salt pans of Granada. He resisted the Inquisition and enlarged his business. But there is more success within this family. Another Diego Lopes Pereira, relative of Francisco Lopes Pereira but one or two generations down the line, became an important tobacco merchant in Portugal and Spain, with associates in London and Amsterdam. Like many other New Christians, Diego supported the Habsburg claimant to the throne during the War of Succession, and following the latter's defeat, he went to Vienna and became a general administrator for tobacco there. His homonymous son received the title of Baron of Aguilar in 1726.[23]

Caro Baroja discovered a certain number of inquisitorial enquiries related to the families of the main New Christian financiers, such as Luísa Ferro, widow of Manuel Cortizos de Villasante, a famous courtier and asentista who had been a knight of the Order of Calatrava, Lord of Arrifana, secretary responsible for the accounts at the Consejo de Hacienda, secretary to the cortes of Castile and León, secretary responsible for the administration of the millones tax, and a general factor in the royal service. Manuel Cortizos had been at the centre of the royal financial system, owing his position to shrewd generosity, having offered and lent the royal family staggering sums of money in crucial moments of distress (reportedly 800,000 escudos on one occasion, 600,000 on another).

Manuel Cortizos died in 1650. In the following year, the Inquisition drew up a list of accusations against his widow and his son, Sebastián Cortizos, the latter also a knight of the Order of Calatrava. There was even an order for imprisonment against Luísa Ferro, though this was never executed. Caro Baroja suspected corruption, which may well have occurred, but royal protection seems unlikely when we consider how previous bankers had been left in jail.[24] The fact is that the son kept his position as one of the main financiers of the kingdom in the following decades. His successor, a nephew, Manuel José Cortizos, became one of the biggest asentistas and *contador mayor* (major accountant) of the three military orders. He acquired the title of Viscount of Valdefuentes in 1668 and that of Marquis of Villaflores in 1674.[25]

Carmen Sanz Ayán, who has produced some of the best studies on seventeenth century finances in Spain, considers that the New Christian financiers successfully withstood inquisitorial persecution and managed to keep a relatively steady position at the top of the system in the transition from Philip IV to Charles II and beyond, showing a decline only in the 1690s. They continued to be well placed in negotiating asientos, making payments in Castile and other parts of Europe, which implied guaranteed rents. The Portuguese New Christians controlled 66 percent of contracts for trading in *vellón* (silver mixed with copper) during the reign of Charles II, but among the asentistas classified as Spaniards by Carmen Sanz there were also New Christians, such as Ventura Donis, whose successor, Ambrosio Donis, became Marquis of Olivares in 1680.[26]

When Philip IV declared himself unable to pay on any of the asientos for vellón, in 1662, the Crown was estimated to owe 21,616,000 ducados to Portuguese bankers, which was an extraordinary sum. Portuguese New Christians dominated customs contracts at the time and provisioned the Castilian army of Extremadura, which was fighting against the independence of Portugal. They controlled contracts for the coastal fleet (Duarte da Costa in the 1650s) and obtained a significant portion of shares in the tobacco business, which was under royal monopoly. In the period from 1650 to 1665, Portuguese New Christians provided 39 percent of all the silver and 35 percent of the vellón that was handled by asentistas.[27]

In the second half of the seventeenth century, several of the major New Christian merchant houses survived inquisitorial persecution and kept their leading positions in trade and finance. This was the case with the brothers Manuel and Bartolomé Montesinos, who took over the family business from their father, Fernando, who was detained and reconciled by the Inquisition. They obtained contracts for provisioning military outposts, such as Ceuta (the only place in the Portuguese Empire which maintained its allegiance to Philip IV after the restoration of Portuguese independence), as well as the army in Galicia and Extremadura. They obtained contracts for salt in Andalusia, Galicia, and Asturias, and participated in asientos for silver supplied to Italy and Flanders. They were succeeded by Diego Felipe, Manuel's son, who kept the business going under difficult circumstances until the end of the 1690s.[28]

Simón de Fonseca Piña (Pina), who was born in Estremoz, Portugal, and married to Beatriz da Veiga, daughter of a financier condemned by the Inquisition, created another important house in this period. He obtained contracts for rents on wool, spices, and the taxation of maritime and dry ports, participated in asientos to finance the Crown, involved his brothers Antonio and Leonardo, and survived a long detention by the Inquisition (as did his brother Antonio).[29]

Francisco Baez (or Vaz) Eminente is another case of someone who had a long and successful life, first as a merchant and neighbour of Seville, then as a financier in Madrid, from the 1630s to the 1680s. He obtained contracts for taxes in Seville (almojarifados) and the Indies, and for provisioning the army and the royal fleet in Andalusia; and he obtained asientos for financial loans to the king, the rents on dry and maritime ports, and the provisioning of Larache. He also imported fabrics and hats from France and wool from England. When he was detained by the Inquisition in 1689 and his property sequestered, his business somehow managed to survive through his son, Juan Francisco Eminente.[30]

Diego Fernández Tinoco, son of a well-known Portuguese New Christian asentista, Fernando Tinoco, with his associate, Francisco Fernández de Solis, in Seville, provided a significant number of loans to the king in this period, obtained an honourable position at the *Contaduría Mayor*, and was excluded from the royal suspension of payments in 1662. As the royal debt to him accumulated, he succeeded in obtaining the title of Viscount of Fresno.[31]

Tomás de Aguilar Rondón, who was married to a daughter of the prominent financier Diego Gómez de Salazar, controlled the general treasury of the masters of the Spanish military orders and was responsible for provisioning the army. Despite being detained by the Inquisition, with his father-in-law, in 1659, which led to his exile from the royal court, his business interests were transferred to his brothers, Alonso and García de Aguilar, who kept the existing contracts and financial loans to the king until the early 1680s.[32]

These examples of prominent financiers—more could be added—reveal resilience and a capacity to safeguard the succession to their business interests in Castile, despite inquisitorial persecution. Three or more generations ensured the survival of these families, in which several branches of brothers, sisters, and nephews were on hand to keep afloat commercial and financial houses in moments of distress. The ennoblement of some of the top houses, even after the stain of inquisitorial trials, represented a continuity with previous practices that was maintained by the increasing financial needs of the Crown. New Christian financiers were in an ideal bargaining position because of accumulated royal debts. But many merchants in other ranks had to escape, or slipped into poverty, as a result of inquisitorial activities. What still needs to be better researched is the capacity to hide wealth, preserve assets under the names of associates and partners, and declare false debts by forging evidence in account books.

2. Portugal

On May 28, 1658, the inquisitors of Coimbra ordered the commissioner of the tribunal in Porto, the Dominican Manuel Caldeira, to open an enquiry on Policarpo de Oliveira, one of the main merchants in the city.[33] This decision had been prompted by André Vieira Veigão, an Old Christian merchant of the same city, a familiar (civil member with royal privileges and responsibility for detentions) of the Inquisition, who reported that Policarpo was widely rumoured to be planning to leave the kingdom to avoid detention by the Inquisition.[34]

Veigão was the first witness and provided the names of other witnesses for the enquiry, most of them Old Christians merchants (António de Brito, a contractor for royal rents, Manuel Duarte Pereira, and Inácio Leite). These men confirmed the rumours, stated that Policarpo had been asked to pay his debts and indicated that he had sent all his stocks of sugar to northern Europe and transferred a cargo of salt cod (bacalao) to an associate, Bento Ribeiro Torrado.[35] Veigão declared that Gaspar de Abreu de Freitas, a judge of the appeal tribunal *Relação* in Porto, told him that Policarpo was gathering witnesses to corroborate the enmity in which he was held by Henrique Fernandes Mendes, another major merchant in Porto, who had been detained on March 19 of the same year, in case Fernandes Mendes levelled an accusation of Judaism at him.[36] Veigão added that he had kept Mendes's three-year-old granddaughter with him out of pity (a typical justification for abduction), because the child's mother had also been detained. However, Filipa Nunes Tovar, a friend and the future mother-in-law of Policarpo de Oliveira, had asked him to give her the child, which he had done.[37] This was meant to imply that Henrique Fernandes Mendes could not have been an enemy of Policarpo. Veigão even boasted that Policarpo "changed colour" every time he came across him on the street.[38]

This enquiry collected denunciations of other merchants who were alleg-edly preparing their escape to other countries, mainly France, such as António Rodrigues Pinhel (who was accused of selling his houses to an employee, which was considered a fraudulent sale), Rafael Rodrigues, Miguel Rodrigues, Gonçalo Rodrigues Nardo, and Gabriel Rodrigues.[39] The reaction to Veigão's claims was speedy: the order to detain Policarpo de Oliveira came on June 2, sent to the same André Vieira Veigão. Policarpo was delivered on June 9 at the Inquisition of Coimbra by the inquisitorial familiar Bento da Costa.[40] He was detained on the declarations of one single witness, Henrique Fernandes Mendes, and on the supposed need for an enquiry based on Veigão's reported rumours. After detention there was, as usual, a deluge of denunciations from other prisoners who did not want to be accused of incomplete confession, which could lead to excommunication and execution (as we have seen before, activities in the Inquisition's jails were an open secret).

The operation against New Christian merchants in Porto had probably been in preparation since 1657, following the abolition of exemption from prop-erty confiscation. It gained new momentum with the detention of Henrique Fernandes Mendes, but May 1658 seems to have been a turning point, with new enquiries into escaped New Christians and preparations to escape. The enquiry against Policarpo de Oliveira was just the latest one of these.

A series of crucial detentions occurred simultaneously at midday on June 6, 1658, with the Inquisition helped by secular justice. This indicated coordination with, and involvement of, the civil authorities. The judge, Gaspar de Abreu de Freitas, was praised by André Vieira Veigão for his assistance.[41] On the very day of the detentions, the judge wrote a letter to the elder inquisi-tor of Coimbra reciprocating with praise for the zeal of Veigão, boasting that he had executed his orders, and claiming merrily that "within six days not a single New Christian will remain here."[42]

In this case, we have inside information on how the decisions were made. The level of surveillance over New Christians was staggering: every movement was monitored, intentions scrutinised, gossip spread. The intervention of Old Christian merchants and inquisitorial familiars, who decided to take advan-tage of the inquisitorial strategy to oust New Christian competitors from the market, is blatant. This story is in line with what we know from the Spanish side, where factional strife loomed at a local level using the Inquisition as a powerful tool.[43] In the case of Porto, it seems that a long-standing relationship of shared interests between Old and New Christian merchants was broken down on purpose. We know from the trial of Policarpo's younger brother, Nicolau de Oliveira, that the young man owed 230,000 réis (not a major sum) to a group of merchants that included André Vieira Veigão and António de Brito, but there was certainly much more at stake.[44]

The other important aspect of this case is the cosy relationship between Policarpo's Old Christian fellow merchant, who was an inquisitorial familiar, and the judge of the royal appeal tribunal in Porto. More research is needed on this issue, but I doubt that it reflects a pattern. Divergent interests existed among those involved, which sometimes gave rise to conflict between the civil and inquisitorial jurisdictions. However, this particular judge, Gaspar de Abreu de Freitas, used the matter to his advantage, advancing from the appeal tribunal of Porto to membership of the Royal Council of Finances, then becoming a royal envoy in London and Rome. We shall see him intervening several times on New Christian issues.

Now let us look carefully at the main New Christian merchants involved and assess the impact of the operation. Henrique Fernandes Mendes was the local administrator (treasurer) of the General Company of Brazil, created in 1649. This company played a significant role in the military recovery of northeast Brazil from the Dutch, completed in 1654, but its power then declined until its integration by the state in 1664.[45] New Christians had been listed and forced to contribute to the capital of the company against a promise of being exempted from property confiscation by the Inquisition. Detention of its local treasurer was another blow to the company now that exemption from confiscation for its investors had been abolished. Henrique's father, Baltasar Fernandes Mendes, had been detained by the Inquisition in 1618. Policarpo de Oliveira was one of the asentistas of King John IV and was financing Portugal's war of independence. His father, Luís de Oliveira, had been an asentista in Madrid, an associate of Juan Núñez Sarabia. They had relatives in Rouen, the famous Rodrigues Lamego family. Policarpo was the nephew of Manuel Fernandes de Morais, by this time deceased, who had been the agent of Duarte da Silva in Porto.[46] He was also related to Manuel Fernandes de Vila Real, who was excommunicated and executed in 1652.[47] In his *contradictas*, Policarpo tried to invalidate the testimony of Henrique Fernandes Mendes, claiming that he had refused a proposal of marriage to one of Henrique's daughters.[48] This is possible: such matters emerged as major reasons for hatred and division within the community in other cases.

Policarpo was thirty-two years old when he was detained. His parents were dead, but he had an enormous number of relatives, the Oliveira, the Morais, and the Vila Real families. He had six brothers and three sisters, all born in Madrid, two of them dead, four living in Rouen (Luís, José, Brites, and Leonor), two in Lisbon (António and Miguel), and one in Porto (Nicolau). He himself had spent time in Cartagena, Murcia, Rouen, Lisbon, and Porto.[49] In his inventory of property, Policarpo declared that he had not invested in real estate, he had only movable property, such as furniture: Moscow chairs (scarlet leather chairs), buffets of jacaranda, a big mirror, Indian counters of ebony and ivory, a counter of jacaranda, panels depicting stories from the Bible, trunks from India and Flanders, textiles from Brittany, buttons and linen held on behalf of Fernão Rodrigues Penso, light wools from Rouen held on behalf of António Rodrigues de Morais (a brother-in-law) and Duarte Rodrigues

Lamego, panels on which were depicted a world map, the Virgin Mary and the goddess Ceres, bedspreads, a bed of jacaranda with bronze ornamentation, feathers and dresses, and a new hat of beaver.[50]

Policarpo received part of the inheritance of his uncle, Manuel Fernandes de Morais, particularly a stock of brazilwood in which Salvador Correia de Sá (Governor of Rio de Janeiro and southern Brazil) had a stake. His assets included a significant amount of iron and canvas from Nantes; a cargo of salt cod, partly owned by Rodrigo Aires Brandão of Rouen and traded by Bento Ribeiro Torrado; nine boxes of sugar and four of tobacco sent from Viana to Lisbon, ordered by João Guterres; and letters of exchange to the Count of Miranda, José Garcia de Leão, João Vaz Silveira, and Fernão Rodrigues Penso, to be collected. He had debts to Alexandre Correia Brandão, António Mendes Leão, Bento Pereira Camelo, and Pascoal Cordeiro Lima, who had sent him wine from Vila Real, and further debts in Livorno (names of creditors not mentioned). He also had open accounts with Inácio Leite (a contractor for royal rents), Manuel Ramos, Gonçalo Vieira Veigão, Manuel Coelho Pereira, Manuel Pais Ribeiro, and António Fernandes Carvalhais of London. There were ongoing accounts of the Porto customs's contract with Fernão Rodrigues Penso. Policarpo owned one-third of a ship and had a stake in cargoes on many other ships, particularly English ships. Finally, he had received 6,000 out of 13,000 cruzados owed by Filipa Nunes de Tovar as part of the dowry for his marriage to her daughter, Violante.[51]

The relationship between Policarpo and his future mother-in-law, Filipa Nunes de Tovar, then forty-five years old, indicates the power of this woman, widow of a major merchant, Pantaleão Fernandes, who had bought herself one set of houses in Rua dos Mercadores (Policarpo went to live next door) and inherited another set of houses from her husband on the other side of the street. She passed the ownership of the latter houses to her daughter, although she retained managerial control.[52] She knew how to read and write, and she signed the records of successive sessions of interrogation. When the judge, Gaspar de Abreu de Freitas, detained Policarpo for having debts to the king, in April 1658, Filipa bailed him out with a consignment of light wool worth 900,000 réis, to be accounted part of the promised dowry for her daughter.[53] She had an impressive collection of silverware, and she was clearly in business herself, mainly in textiles, owing money to the English merchant, Thomas Pate. Half of her real estate belonged to her, half to her children, António Fernandes and Violante. Filipa had lived with her parents, António Nunes Xave (or Chaves) from Torre de Moncorvo and Isabel Fernandes Tovar from Porto, both now dead, in Medina del Campo and Madrid, until she had returned to Porto twenty-two or twenty-three years before these events.[54]

Two letters from Policarpo's brothers, António and Nicolau de Oliveira, were introduced as evidence at the trial. The first was taken during the sequestration of property following Policarpo's arrest. In it, António responded to a request from Policarpo to obtain a royal licence to go to France with his future wife to collect money from Jerónimo Rodrigues de Morais in Rouen. António advised against this move, because Policarpo owed money to the king on his customs' contracts and could be detained. The request would have to be registered by the royal treasurer, and this could only be done if the petitioner were without debts. António mentioned that he had asked the opinion of Vicente de Bastos on this subject. People absent without authorisation would forfeit their property to the king, as had happened to António da Fonseca. He suggested that the sugar sent by Gregório António Dias from Brazil should be addressed to António Rodrigues. Policarpo should also establish a faithful trustee and clear his accounts before any licence was requested.[55]

The letter from Nicolau was written on June 8, immediately after Policarpo's detention, which means that it had been intercepted. Nicolau regretted the loss of property and the detentions of Filipa Nunes Tovar, António Rodrigues Pinhel (brother-in-law of Filipa Nunes Tovar), Miguel Pereira de Leão, Francisco de Paz, Miguel Rodrigues, Rafael Rodrigues, Diogo Vale de Oliveira, Francisco de Oliveira, Domingos Lopes Pereira, Francisco da Costa Henriques, António Henriques da Costa, and António Mendes de Leão, "all men and women of the nation from this city."[56] He lamented the destruction of the city and declared that he had requested letters of favour from Dom Francisco Martins, who had been staying at the house of the Count of Faro. He applauded the good fortune of Mateus Mendes, António Mendes de Almeida, António Carvalho, Gonçalo Lopes, Francisco Nunes Xave (or Chaves), and Manuel de Leão, who had escaped (but we know that some of them, for example, Francisco Nunes Chaves, were detained later).[57]

While detained, Policarpo and Filipa engaged in a dangerous clandestine exchange of letters through an employee of the Inquisition, Antónia Gonçalves, which could have been fatal. The employee was eventually exposed and the letters were found and added to the trial as further incriminating evidence. Policarpo openly revealed his game to the inquisitors in these letters: he advised Filipa never to denounce her daughter, Violante, his fiancée, since her freedom was a guarantee of their future after the Inquisition; they could live on her dowry.[58] Policarpo and Filipa ended up with parallel trials for breaching of the Inquisition's secrecy. The endgame was nasty: to avoid excommunication and execution, they had to denounce each other and dozens of relatives and friends, including Violante, who was detained. Filipa denounced around 110 people (the most complete New Christian "Who's Who" in Northern Portugal, with links to Spain and France), Nicolau de Oliveira denounced seventy-seven people, and Policarpo denounced fifty. They all had their property confiscated, including Violante: her dowry had gone up in smoke.[59] They managed to survive, obtained reductions in their sentences, which initially included exile to Africa, and continued to live near Porto; but they disappeared from the records, probably sinking into poverty or managing to escape to Rouen to live on the charity of relatives. Filipa had a stroke in 1661, after which her left side was paralysed.[60]

The wave of repression was extraordinary. I have counted fifty-eight merchants and their wives and children detained in Porto in 1658, the vast majority in June—twenty-four men and thirty-four women.[61] We have seen how women were important in business, both in their own right and in standing in for their husbands. More people were linked to this wave, which ended up at the Inquisition of Lisbon. These included the important merchant Manuel Rodrigues Isidro, son of André Lopes Isidro, one of the main merchants of Porto in the 1630s. Rodrigues Isidro kept the Jewish fast days in jail and finally refused to eat at all, until he died. His bones were burned at the auto da Fé of Lisbon, on October 17, 1660, for the crime of apostasy.[62]

The first denunciation of Manuel Rodrigues Isidro was produced by a New Christian from Rouen, Simão Lopes Manuel, who went to the Inquisition of Coimbra to accuse a significant number of people, including Isidro's homonymous uncle in Hamburg, Jacob or Isaac Baruch, and the former's brother, Baltasar Álvares Nogueira, also living in Hamburg. Manuel Isidro had been an agent of Duarte da Silva in Angola and a factor of the Crown in Brazil. He was a bachelor, but he had a son by Jerónima Soares, Simão, who went to Brazil, and he had two daughters by Francisca do Espírito Santo in Porto. He was a founder of the Company of Brazil, in which he had invested 650,000 réis. He owned shares in three ships and had cargoes in transit on more than twenty ships. He dealt in Madeira wine, Brazilian tobacco and sugar, South Asian precious stones, slaves and ivory from Angola, iron from Biscay, cereals and salt cod, and in paintings and sculptures from Flanders. When he was detained, he was living in Lisbon and had business associates in Porto, Pernambuco, Bahia, Luanda, Goa, London, Rouen, Brussels, and Amsterdam; in nearly all these places he also had relatives. He was engaged in banking and insurance, and he also functioned as a pawnbroker.[63]

While Manuel Rodrigues Isidro acknowledged himself to be a Jew, the other cases were open to dispute. Francisco de Paz, an important merchant from Porto, engaged in imprudent behaviour in a cell crowded with other accused people, such as Policarpo de Oliveira, whose conversations and acts breaching the Inquisition's ban on communication between detainees were denounced by an Old Christian placed there. Francisco's inventory of property was significant. He had a silk shop valued at 1.4 million réis, perhaps the highest valuation I have seen for a single shop; he possessed the houses where he lived in the Rua dos Mercadores; but he declared debts owed to the English merchants Richard Peres and Thomas Tute; and he owed part of the dowry of his daughter, Brites Rodrigues, to his son-in-law, Mateus Mendes de Leão (who apparently escaped; I did not find any trace of his trial). In Amsterdam, he and his associates, Duarte and Manuel Faro, had fifteen boxes of sugar; and these merchants had promised him a cargo of Swedish iron for 150,000 réis.

The accusations were stereotypical. Francisco de Paz confessed and denounced many people, but it was not considered enough.[64] It is not clear why he was executed while Policarpo was not. Perhaps Policarpo denounced more important people or benefitted from the flood of Filipa's denunciations. Francisco de Paz complained of suffering from loss of memory caused by disease. And his show of repentance may have been less convincing. In any case, his death went to make up the minimum level of excommunications (followed by executions) considered adequate by the inquisitors to keep the New Christians in check.

The most telling inventory of property is perhaps the one declared by Henrique Fernandes Mendes. He possessed several houses in São João Novo and Rua dos Ferreiros, which he valued at 6,000 cruzados. He had the same kind of furniture as Policarpo, although he declared many more paintings— around forty panels valued at 100,000 réis. He owed 3,000 cruzados to Heitor Mendes in Gogim, Lamego, 5,000 to Manuel Maio, a physician in Porto, 4,500 to his sister Filipa Rodrigues (another case of women in business, she was the widow of Francisco Trevino), and 3,000–4,000 cruzados to the Company of Brazil. He also had more than 100 boxes of sugar in storage, linen, and letters of exchange that he had accepted and that were still to be paid (worth 150,000, 50,000, and 20,000 réis, respectively).[65]

More interesting from an organizational point of view is Henrique's declaration that he had never paid a salary to his assistant, Bento de Araújo, an Old Christian, who had worked for him on all his dealings for ten years; he had only paid maintenance and clothing. The assistant was owed 500,000 réis, that is, 50,000 a year. Henrique Fernandes justified the situation by saying that he was waiting for a favourable occasion to send this business assistant to Brazil with the money and various commissions, as other merchants did. He owed another assistant, António Amorim, 500,000–600,000 réis of sugar sent from Pernambuco in 1647. He listed all his debts: to masters of ships for freights; to associates in Lisbon, such as Manuel Martim Medina, a familiar of the Inquisition, and Domingos and Diogo Lopes de Silveira; and to Arnau Piper, agent of Henrique Belmann of Hamburg. Finally, Henrique Fernandes owed the abbey of Miragaia for a dispensation obtained in Rome to marry his daughter, Isabel, to her cousin Álvaro Gomes Sarzedo, son of António Gomes Sarzedo.[66]

This wave of inquisitorial repression provides a good case study of the second most important network of New Christian merchants in Portugal, with its connections, most of them through relatives, to Hamburg, Amsterdam, London, Rouen, Madrid, Lisbon, Livorno, Bahia, Recife, Luanda, and Goa. It shows how the Inquisition's operation was centrally planned with the help of local Old Christian merchants, familiars of the tribunal, who seized the opportunity to oust New Christians from the market. A sharp decline in their wealth, owing to loss of property and trust, meant the erosion of business standings of New Christians. We can also assess the diversity of New Christian investment in different types of trade and their vast network of connections encompassing northern Europe, the Mediterranean, the Atlantic and the Indian Ocean. The strategy of placing relatives in the main hubs of these networks was visible, although the special importance of Lisbon and Porto was undeniable, generally linked to the availability there of royal contracts for loans and for the farming of taxes.

The disruption of the New Christian presence in these main hubs would have consequences for the networks patiently built up over the years. The system of succession through dowries, to protect assets in a risky inquisitorial world, was clear, while women also played a major role not only as guardians of tradition but also as business assistants or entrepreneurs in their own right. The Inquisition was open to corruption, but the engagement of prisoners with its low-level employees implied a very high risk. The dismantlement of the New Christian network based on Porto needs to be better researched, but it seems that it had long-term consequences. In those years there was no equivalent wave of repression against merchants in Lisbon, but the high level of general detentions had some impact on New Christians in the capital.[67] We shall see in the next chapter how a new wave of detentions in the early 1670s intensified the New Christian sense of deep crisis.

3. Italy

Rome was the main hub for New Christians abroad, even more so in this period of the third quarter of the seventeenth century that was defined by new waves of persecution in Iberia followed by migration. If Amsterdam, Hamburg, London, and Livorno attracted New Christians willing to return publicly to Judaism in this period, Italy remained both the favourite place for a New Christian who definitely did not want to take that step and a possible destiny for those who hesitated to embrace the religion of their ancestors. Jewish communities in Venice, Pisa, and Livorno could keep attachments to New Christian relatives living in the same city or nearby. Antwerp was another place to which Iberian New Christians went, although its increasingly peripheral economic position led to a decline of this community.

Rome had several advantages that attracted New Christians. It was the seat of the papacy, which undertook or supervised numerous financial operations in Iberia; that is, it drew important revenues from issuing crusade bulls and responding to demands for marriage dispensations and from distributing ecclesiastic benefices and nominations to the position of bishop and cardinal. Cardinals in Rome with benefices in Portugal needed to collect the rents associated with those benefices. New Christians controlled the greatest part of these financial operations. The pope was also the source of the delegated powers of the Portuguese and Spanish Inquisitions. Any grievance with sufficient financial backing would end up in Rome. New Christians needed to keep brokers there who knew the cardinals and had access to the pope. Besides all

PALAZZO DELL'ILL™ SIG™ MARCHESE NVNEZ NELLA STRADA DE CONDOTTI
Architettura di Gio. Antonio de Rossi.
1. Facciata principale, 2. Fianco del Palazzo, 3. Strada de Condotti, 4. Palazzo della Religione di Malta.

FIGURE 13.1. Alessandro Specchi, Palazzo Núñez Sánchez, engraving [1690], in *Il Qvarto Libro Del Nvovo Teatro Delli Palazzi In Prospettiva Di Roma Moderna* (Rome: Domenico de Rossi, 1699), fl. 46. © British Library Board. All rights reserved / Bridgeman Images.

this, Rome was a big market as a flourishing city in the early modern period. It meant business.

Francisco Nunes Sanches (ca. 1600–1689) was certainly the most successful among the New Christian financiers. He was active in Rome from the late 1620s onwards, joining first the archconfraternity of the Spaniards and then the Portuguese confraternity of Santo António, where he assumed the most important functions. At the same time, he established links with several other prominent New Christian families, such as the Nunes Caldeira, the Peres Vergueiro, the Quintal, the Costa Brandão, the Azevedo, the Lopes da Silva, the Veiga, the Mendes Henriques, the Gomes Homem, and the Correia Bravo.[68] Nunes Sanches maintained this double affiliation all his life. In 1658 he obtained Roman citizenship, and in the following year he acquired the fief and title of Marquis of Cantelupo, which had been the property of the Orsini in the diocese of Tivoli.

Nunes Sanches possessed houses in the Campo dei Fiori, but his largest property, a palace, was built in the Via Bocca di Leone and occupied a whole block between the Via Condotti, the Via Borgognoni, and the Via Leoncino. His sisters, Beatriz, Ana, Catarina, and Grazia, arrived in Rome in 1642, followed by two nephews, Savio and Sebastiano. In 1645, his niece Dionora arrived. Dionora married the Marquis Afonso Peres Vergueiro, another New Christian who was an associate of Nunes Sanches. Nunes Sanches was married but childless, and the succession was guaranteed by his nephew Francisco, who married the noblewoman Girolama Gottifredi, daughter of Francesco and Costanza Del Drago. This couple had seventeen children, and their son, Vincenzo (1674–1740), became the main heir to the second Francisco. Most of these relatives married into the Roman aristocracy, helped by generous dowries from Francisco Nunes Sanches. In 1651, he endowed a chapel at the church of San Lorenzo in Lucina.[69]

Nunes Sanches specialised in money exchange and lending to prelates, but he was also involved in trade, as his association with Duarte da Silva in Lisbon attested. He controlled the money made from the issuance of crusade bulls in Portugal, channelling this to the construction of Saint Peter's Basilica. In 1645 to 1650 he was authorised to open a bank for lending money.[70] As Marquis of Cantelupo, he left traces in many different records, particularly at the Banco di Santo Spirito, which he used for some of his financial transactions.[71] He exercised the function of treasurer (among others) at the Iberian confraternities in Rome and invested money there for works and repairs.

Nunes Sanches's four-story palace on the Via Bocca di Leone, designed by the architect Giovanni Antonio de Rossi, had twenty-seven windows on the main facade and twenty-three on the lateral facade, and its size was nearly equalled by that of the building next to it on the same street, also owned by Nunes Sanches. The initial iconographic programme for the palace, conceived and executed by Francesco Grimaldi (1605–1680), focused on the Old Testament, particularly on Elias, Tobias, Jacob's dream, Moses, and Moses rescued from the water, but the three capital virtues were also prominent. The second programme, by Giacinto Calandruci (1646–1707), included images from the New Testament—the Sacred Family with John the Baptist, the baptism of Christ, Christ with St. Peter and St. Andrew, Christ and the Samaritan, and the Temptation of Christ. And as well as religious themes there were representations of the four continents.[72] It is difficult to decide whether these distinct sets of themes corresponded to shifting religious sensibilities.

Rui Lopes da Silva is another significant New Christian financier of this period. He was born in Lisbon towards the end of the sixteenth century, and around 1617 he went to Goa, where he and his half brother on his mother's side, Manuel Dias da Silva, were the agents of Fernão Lopes da Silva, Francisco Tinoco de Carvalho, and António Vaz Brandão. He moved to the Persian Gulf in 1633, then to Valencia in 1636, and in 1638 he moved to Madrid, where he participated in asientos with Manuel de Paz, Fernando Tinoco, and Francisco Tinoco de Carvalho. In 1643, after the fall of Olivares and news of the arrest of his cousin, Afonso Manhós, by the Inquisition, he went to Rome. In the 1630s he invested in the carreira da Índia, purchasing pepper, cowries, and cotton cloth from various markets in Asia, and he also invested in trade from Seville to Mexico and Cartagena de Indias.[73] In 1663, Lopes da Silva endowed the chapel

FIGURE 13.2. Gian Lorenzo Bernini, design of the Chapel Silva endowed by Rui Lopes da Silva at the church Sant'Isidoro of the Irish Capuchins in Rome, right side from the altar with the portrait of the sponsor and the representation of charity and truth, ca. 1663. Courtesy Aletes Onlus: www.aletes.it/cappella-da -sylva-nella-chiesa-di-santisidoro-a-capo-le-case/.

of Santo Isidoro, designed by Bernini, at the Church of the Irish Franciscans as a burial place for his family, which is indicative of his standing.[74] A parallel and contemporary case of a wealthy New Christian commissioning the decoration of an endowed chapel from Bernini is Gabriel da Fonseca (ca. 1586–1668), physician of Pope Innocent X, at the Basilica di San Lorenzo in Lucina, Rome. Bernini sculpted an excellent bust of Fonseca.[75]

Rui Lopes da Silva's activities in Rome seem relatively discrete, although he was listed as a knight (of the military order of Santiago, as we know from the Inquisition's trial of his half brother) in the register of the confraternity of Santo António in 1665.[76] He must have been extremely clever, because he escaped successive denunciations to the Inquisition, as the trial of his half brother, Manuel Dias da Silva, detained in Lisbon in 1646, attested. The

FIGURE 13.3. Gian Lorenzo Bernini, design of the Chapel Silva endowed by Rui Lopes da Silva at the church Sant'Isidoro of the Irish Capuchins in Rome, left side from the altar with the portrait of the sponsor's son Count Nicolau Lopes da Silva with the representation of peace and justice, ca. 1663. Courtesy Aletes Onlus: www.aletes.it/cappella-da-sylva-nella-chiesa-di-santisidoro-a-capo-le-case/.

denunciations collected from the trials of Baltasar da Veiga, Manuel Correia, Luís de Lemos Mascarenhas, and Afonso Manhós (this one in Goa) accused both brothers.[77]

The inventory of the property of Manuel Dias da Silva in Lisbon reveals investments in real estate, farms, and lending to the aristocracy, as well as debts of large sums, involving many thousands of cruzados. He was involved in the contract for cinnamon and was in trade with India in association with his half brother. He also exported wine and imported cochineal from the Americas. Strangely enough, he declared that he had recently invested large sums in two voyages to Japan, from where the Portuguese had been expelled. He declared an extraordinary debt to Rui Lopes da Silva, and although this was possible, it raises the possibility of fraud to protect capital. He had also invested in shares in the fortresses of Mascate and Sofala.[78]

FIGURE 13.4. Gian Lorenzo Bernini, bust of Gabriel Fonseca, chapel of Annunciation, Basilica di San Lorenzo in Lucina, Rome ca. 1668–1670. The chapel, designed by Bernini, was endowed by the same Gabriel Fonseca (ca. 1586–1668), physician of Innocent X, probably grandnephew of António da Fonseca. Photo courtesy of the author.

The trial's session on genealogy revealed the extent of the Silva and Man-hós families, with relatives in Castile, New Christian ancestors who were land-owners in Alentejo, a lawyer in Goa married to a noblewoman, and several relatives trading in different parts of India. Manuel Dias da Silva indicated that he had three sons and three daughters aged from seven months to ten years, while Rui Lopes da Silva, married to Brites da Silveira (a New Christian from Lisbon), had two sons, Duarte and Manuel, aged eight and six, and one daughter.[79] The name of Francisco Nicolau da Silva, son of Rui Lopes da Silva, who would have some importance in the New Christian negotiations in Rome in the 1670s, was not listed, suggesting that he was protected in some way. The outcome of this trial is unusual. Manuel Dias da Silva died a natural death in jail during enquiries into his contradictas (attempts by the defendant to invali-date accusations on the grounds they were motivated by enmity). His heirs were invited to pursue his defence, which they did. The sentence declared that the accused had been absolved because of lack of proof, and so his bones could be buried with Christian rites and his sequestered property should be returned.[80] There are no traces of how this verdict was brought about, but it was likely impossible without the long hand of Rui Lopes da Silva.

In the inventory of property at the trial of Duarte da Silva, Rui Lopes da Silva was indicated as one of his main business associates in Rome, involved in bills of exchange and payments for his assistance to Duarte's elder son, Diogo in Rome.[81] Rui Lopes da Silva is claimed, in the defence of Duarte da Silva, to be the uncle of this son, who had allegedly escaped from Lisbon in 1646 to avoid a marriage he did not want.[82] He had not been mentioned in the enquiry into Duarte's genealogy, which is normal, because Duarte was trying to reveal the smallest possible number of relatives' names.[83] There is a gap of almost five years between the session on genealogy (February 1648) and the enquiry into contradictas at which Rui Lopes da Silva was mentioned as Diogo's uncle (November 1652). However, Rui Lopes could not have been Duarte's direct brother-in-law, because Duarte's wife, Branca, was the daughter of a cousin, Joana Brandão, married to Francisco Dias from Viana.[84] Rui Lopes da Silva could have been Duarte's cousin; the designation uncle (*tio*) might have been extended. We still need to find the family links of Rui's wife, Beatriz da Silveira, not to be confounded with the homonymous wife of the asentista Jorge de Paz, in Madrid.[85] In any case, Duarte da Silva did not mention the children of his cousin Joana, except when he talked about his wife.

Duarte da Silva obtained several royal privileges in 1662, when he accompanied Catherine of Braganza to London to take up her role as wife to King Charles II, a match for which he guaranteed payment of the extraordinary dowry. Among these royal privileges was membership of the military order of Santiago, a position which Duarte da Silva passed to Francisco Nicolau da Silva, who was engaged to his youngest daughter, Joana da Silva, then fifteen years old.[86] In 1662, immediately after his arrival in London, where he was finally safe from the long arm of the Inquisition, Duarte da Silva sent his first petitions to the Portuguese king. In these, he protested against the inquisitorial persecution of New Christians, suggested royal authorisation for a synagogue to attract Jews back to the country, and made a proposal for significant New Christian financial support for trade with Asia in exchange for a general pardon.[87] Because of his position as a major financier and a member of an alliance of families—the Silva, Brandão, Solis, Leão, Dias, and Henriques—he played an important role in New Christian networks, and these spread from South Asia to Brazil, Lisbon, Madrid, Rome, London, and later Antwerp.

Florence did not attract a significant number of New Christians since it did not offer the same advantages of trade and market opportunities linked to the papacy as Rome. The exception was the Ximenes family, which had managed by the late sixteenth century to reach a position of titled nobility supported by the Medici family. Although they kept links with the other branches of the family in Antwerp and Lisbon, they withdrew from trade and invested their assets in land and a noble way of life, including military service. The case of Colonel Roderico (or Rodrigo) Ximenes, who fought in the Thirty Years War, is significant. On October 22, 1651, Ximenes received the title of Marquis from the ruler of the Palatinate, Wolfgang Wilhelm. Ximenes died without heirs, so the title was transmitted by Wolfgang's son, Philip Wilhelm, to Ferdinando Ximenes d'Aragona, cousin and feudal heir to the colonel, on October 16, 1689.[88] Ferdinando Ximenes, already Marquis of Saturnia and a knight of Santo Stefano, thus acquired a new title and the lands attached to it.

By contrast, the Lisbon branch of the Ximenes family had the usual problems of male inheritance. Jerónimo Ximenes de Aragão, a fidalgo of the King's house, had accumulated significant wealth and bequeathed an entailed property (morgado) to his grandson, Afonso Jorge de Melo Ximenes, guaranteed through his only daughter, Maria de Mendonça, who had married an Old Christian, Martim Afonso de Melo (whom Jerónimo Ximenes made the executor of his will). The daughter died and Jerónimo added a codicil naming his grandson, then married to Joana Coutinho, his outright heir. He also left legacies to a seminary he had founded for Irish Catholics, and of which he was patron (padroeiro), with instructions that he was to be buried there with his first and second wives, Isabel de Mendonça and Madalena de Faro. Other relatives mentioned in the will were his brothers, António Fernandes Ximenes and Fernão Ximenes, the latter an archdeacon; his nephew, Jerónimo de Aragão, a Dominican; and another nephew, also a cleric, Fr. Jacinto Ximenes de Aragão. The morgado left by Jerónimo's father would be inherited by his nephew, Rodrigo Ximenes de Aragão, the son of Jerónimo's elder brother Duarte, because no woman, or descendant via a woman, could inherit it. The morgado created by Jerónimo had 320,000 réis of annual interest in the almoxarifado (royal rents and taxes) of Évora; houses in São Cristóvão (Lisbon) rented out at 47,000 réis annually; large farms, particularly in Arraiolos and Coruche, worth 200,000 réis annually; 50,000 réis of interest in Cadaval; and three salt pans in Alcácer do Sal worth 340,000 réis annually.[89]

This case shows why large families kept track of their various branches. There were several entailed properties at stake, each generation created more entailed property, and the conditions of inheritance varied. Extended families functioned as a pool of possible heirs in case of death without male descendants, but this pool could trigger conflict. New entailed property could define the rules of inheritance differently from previous cases. This is what Jerónimo Ximenes did, allowing his daughter to succeed, on condition that the property passed to her son. In this case, we know how the conditions were worked out in advance, including an obligation for the heir to keep the name Ximenes. The concentration of property in a few hands would be the outcome of successive deaths of relatives who died without direct issue.

In the following chapters we shall see how some successful lineages of New Christians in Italy eventually lost their prominence because they lacked male heirs, became bankrupt, or suffered economic decline. Alliances with other noble families, particularly the Panciatichi, allowed the Ximenes to preserve their position in Florence for nearly three centuries. But it is important to ask whether allegiance to other New Christian branches of the family, and to New Christians in general, was still at work in this and other cases. Up to the mid-seventeenth century we still have entangled skeins of inheritance, and the various wealthy New Christian families functioned as a pool to guarantee successions, but we need to observe, in the following chapters, the evolution (or disintegration) of those ties.

Italy offered a privileged refuge both for those New Christians who wanted to keep their Christian faith—either out of conviction or for practical reasons—and for those who wanted to revert to the faith of their ancestors. By the mid-seventeenth century, Jewish communities had reached around 4,300 people in Rome, 2,650 in Venice, and 2,000 in Livorno.[90] By that time too, many more Jewish communities had developed in Verona, Padua, Ferrara, Mantua, Florence, Urbino, and smaller towns, although the numbers were smaller and they were affected by political and military upheavals. The coexistence of New Christian and Jewish communities in several towns, even with the limitations of the ghetto for the latter, revealed a permanent interaction that surpassed formal religious allegiances. The important role of women as keepers of the tradition and the return of New Christians to Judaism, particularly in Livorno and Pisa, has been studied.[91] Although several seventeenth-century crises (climatic, economic, and demographic) hit Italy, causing a stagnation in population size, it seems that the Jewish communities proved resilient in places not directly involved in war, where they could engage in trade, primarily in Venice and Livorno. This latter port strove to maintain its links to the eastern and southern Mediterranean, and to Lisbon, Amsterdam, and Goa.[92]

4. Northern Europe and Beyond

Antwerp had lost its central position in international trade, although financial services were more resilient because of Spanish dynastic interests in the region. New Christian community declined, but a significant number chose to stay or even to move there. There was no Jewish community in this Catholic city dependent on Spanish Habsburgs. However, it was sufficiently close to German and Dutch cities with Jewish communities to be a possible option for those who did not want to assume Jewish allegiance but at the same time wanted to distance themselves from the Iberian Inquisitions. Sometimes it was used as a first step to northern cities in the same way it had been a step towards Venice and the Levant in the sixteenth century.

The famous banker García de Yllán, who hosted Queen Christina of Sweden in his palace in Antwerp, was registered as consul of the Portuguese nation in 1638, 1645, and 1650.[93] He had married into the Brandão family, headed by Gracia Brandão de Mesquita. In 1652, three years before his death, he became lord of Bornival, and in 1674 his son Ferdinand received the title of Baron of Bornival.[94] This was a typical case of ennoblement of the sort to which Yllán himself had drawn attention in the early 1630s, while in Madrid, as an inevitable outcome of merchants' denigration and inquisitorial persecution in Iberia.

In 1650, Yllán shared the consulate in Antwerp with Francisco Lopes Franco y Feo, a member of the powerful Franco family (António Rodrigues Franco had been a consul in earlier years). In 1648, another well-known merchant and financier from Spain, Gaspar Rodrigues Passarinho, had been elected Portuguese consul. Meanwhile, the Duarte, Veiga, Pinto, Dias Vaz, and Teixeira Sampaio families were still active in the city in the mid-seventeenth century.[95]

Hamburg had been a destination for New Christians since the 1580s, many of them arriving directly from Lisbon, but also from Antwerp, Amsterdam, and Venice. There was a small flow in the following decades, facilitated by the traditional relations between the Hanseatic League and Portugal, and by a relatively neutral position on the part of Hamburg towards the Habsburgs that contrasted with the war for independence in the Netherlands. Sugar and dyes from Brazil and spices from India played an important role in the early days, as these were traded for cereals and textiles from northern Germany and iron from Sweden.[96]

Successive agreements with the Senate of the city in 1612, 1617, and finally in 1650 created a welcoming environment for the new Jewish community, despite opposition from Lutheran pastors and physicians, the latter incensed by the success of Jewish colleagues, particularly Rodrigo de Castro (ca. 1546–1627), one of the founders of gynaecology, and his son Bento de Castro, who treated Queen Christina of Sweden.[97] The famous free thinker Uriel da Costa (ca. 1584–1640), born in Porto, moved to Amsterdam in 1614 and then to Hamburg with his brother, Abraham Israel da Costa (Jácome da Costa Brandão). In Hamburg he wrote his first text contesting rabbinic tradition before returning to Amsterdam, where he developed his criticism, writing in favour of a natural religion based on reason rather than divine revelation, and refusing to accept the immortality of the soul. He was excommunicated twice by the community and eventually committed suicide in 1640.[98]

In the first decades of the seventeenth century, the main Jewish merchants in Hamburg were Abraham Aboab (António Faleiro), who married Ana, daughter of Filipe Dinis, a rich merchant of Venice; Elihau Aboaf (Rui Fernandes Cardoso); Ishac Hoeff (Rui Peres Brandão); Jacob Coronel (Gonçalo Lopes Coutinho), a sugar merchant and shipowner, who created sugar mills, soap, and silk industries in Glückstadt (then Denmark); David Abendana (Fernão Dias Mendes de Brito), whose relationship to the famous Heitor Mendes de Brito in Lisbon is still to be clarified; Ishac Baruch Isidro (Manuel Rodrigues Isidro), one of the founders of the Bank of Hamburg; Semuel Jahya (Álvaro Dinis), son of Filipe Dinis, director of the Danish mint in Glückstadt, who married Beatriz, the eldest daughter of Henrique Dias Milão; and Jehosua de Palacios (Pedro de Palácios), who married Isabel, another daughter of Henrique Dias Milão.[99] Three sons of Rodrigo de Andrade and

Ana Milão (Francisco, André, and Manuel) also migrated to Hamburg, where Francisco registered one of the highest turnovers of the Portuguese merchants in the 1630s and 1640s.[100] By the mid-seventeenth century, the Jewish community is estimated to have been between 800 and 1,200 members strong before it declined in the last decades of the seventeenth century.[101]

The period from 1650 to 1670 is considered to represent the peak of the Sephardic community's prominence in Hamburg, with Jacob Curiel (Duarte Nunes da Costa) and Isaac Seneor (Manuel Teixeira), another host of Queen Christina of Sweden, developing their wealth as merchants and bankers. Jacob Curiel also played an important role as financial backer and provider of crucial ships and munitions to King John IV during the war of independence against Castile, in association with his son, Jerónimo Nunes da Costa, alias Moses Curiel, in Amsterdam. They were also the representatives of the Portuguese Company of Brazil in Northern Europe.[102]

The Sephardic Jewish community in Amsterdam was arguably the wealthiest in Europe, created in the same decades as the one in Hamburg, and like Hamburg composed of refugees from Iberia, but growing particularly fast along with the new position of the city in the world economy. The 1630s and 1640s saw migration from Amsterdam to Hamburg and Brazil, but this trend declined in the following decade, with migration to London becoming significant. There was a constant flow from New Christian communities in Portugal, Spain, France, Italy, and Antwerp; in the third quarter of the seventeenth century, the community must have counted more than 3,000 people.[103] The opening of the new Portuguese synagogue in 1675 offered a symbol of the success of the community. In this period, Jerónimo Nunes da Costa, alias Moses Curiel (1620–1697), and Antonio Lopes Suasso, alias Isaac Israel Suasso (1614–1685), were the two leading Jewish financiers in Amsterdam, the first as an agent of the king of Portugal, the second as an agent of the king of Spain. This divergence of political allegiances during and after the Portuguese war of independence shows the structural trading link of the Sephardic community with the Iberian world, despite direct Dutch investment in the Caribbean after the 1650s.

The trade from Spain was based on wool, but also silver, cochineal, cacao, and indigo from the Americas, while the trade from Portugal was based on salt from Setúbal and Aveiro, sugar, tobacco and brazilwood from Brazil, and precious stones from India. From the Baltic, Jewish merchants exported wheat, barley, and rye to Iberia, as well as wood from Norway and Sweden and iron from Sweden. They were also involved in the cod trade from Newfoundland and England. Moses Curiel controlled the salt and brazilwood trades, while he fulfiled Portuguese orders for guns and ammunitions for the war of independence. He also played an important role in the negotiation of the Peace Treaty between the Netherlands and Portugal in 1661, keeping the role of Portuguese representative in the United Provinces until he died.[104]

Isaac Israel Suasso, the wealthiest Jewish banker of this period, had married Rachel de Pinto, daughter of Gil Lopes Pinto (alias Abraham Pinto), and the bride had brought a dowry of 130,000 gulden (over 69,300 cruzados, one of the highest dowries on record). Suasso became the Spanish king's banker in Amsterdam and was active in the wool trade with Spain and in trading precious stones and jewels. He was involved in negotiating the Spanish-Dutch alliance against the French from 1674 to 1675 and received the title of Baron of Avernas Le Gras, which referred to a domain he had acquired in Southern Brabant. He also became an important lender to Prince William. His successor, Francisco Lopes Suasso (alias Abraham Israel Suasso), who inherited the title, played a significant role in the campaign of William III in England, lending William staggering sums of money.[105]

The volume of Jewish trade based in Amsterdam increased more than fourfold from the 1620s to the 1650s but was followed by a steady decline. The Jewish community's share of the city's total trade was about 4–8 percent in 1634, which was a period of boom for both the East and the West India Companies.[106] This is significant, but it falls well short of the share of New Christian trade in Lisbon deriving from both Brazil and the carreira da Índia in those days. The decline is expressed by the relative concentration of successful trade in the hands of the two top merchants. Bankruptcies occurred; for example, that of Isaac Pessoa (originally Manuel Gomes Pessoa) in 1679, which has been studied by Daniel Swetchinski. Isaac's father was Jerónimo Gomes Pessoa (alias Abraham Israel Pessoa), who escaped with his family to Rouen at the end of 1650 and then moved on to Amsterdam in 1661, where he soon died. The single largest debt Isaac owed was to Fernão Rodrigues Penso, in Lisbon, for 47,355 gulden or 25,256, followed by other debts in Rouen, Hamburg, Frankfurt, Copenhagen, and Barbados.[107] The crucial case of Fernão Rodrigues Penso is discussed in the next chapter, but Penso was the son-in-law of Jerónimo Gomes Pessoa and was married to Brites Pessoa.[108]

The establishment of a Jewish community in London, negotiated by Menasseh ben Israel, became significant in the 1650s. At first this was dependent on Amsterdam, but it became increasingly autonomous as the English transport of Portuguese trade grew in the second half of the seventeenth century. The presence of the English in the Caribbean increased rivalry between London and Amsterdam and the navigation acts and the assertion of English naval power through war with the United Provinces contributed to the decline of the Jewish community in Amsterdam, which was visible from the 1680s onwards. In London, the community gained in numbers from the growing persecution of New Christians by the Inquisition in Portugal, but their share of trade was never very significant, despite particularly successful cases. In 1660, there were 41 Jews (male adults) in London. Fifteen years later there were 174 men and 84 women.[109]

FIGURE 13.5. Emanuel de Witte, The interior of the Portuguese synagogue in Amsterdam, 1680, oil on canvas, 110 × 99 cm, inv. SK-A-3738. Courtesy Rijksmuseum, Amsterdam.

Several members of the community came from Amsterdam, such as Manuel Martínez Dormido (alias David Abravanel Dormido), originally treasurer for royal taxation in Andalusia, who was detained and tortured by the Inquisition in Spain (1627–1632) and escaped to Bordeaux and years later to Amsterdam, where he took a leading role at the synagogue. Dormido had invested in Dutch Brazil (sugar mills), where he had sent two of his sons, Daniel and Salomon.[110] The first hakham (Torah scholar) in London, Jacob Sasportes, was brought from Amsterdam in 1663. However, other New Christians followed a different path. Agostinho Coronel Chacón, the agent for Duarte da Silva in Rouen and London, joined the Church of England and received a knighthood from Charles II in 1660. Fernando Mendes da Costa, another New Christian, who came from Lisbon with the Queen, seems also to have integrated into English society with his relatives, his son Álvaro da Costa becoming *moço da câmara* (chamber page) to the Queen.[111] Jewish people also migrated to the English colonies in the Caribbean, particularly Barbados, and the Dutch colonies in the area, mainly Curaçao, and they were trading (or more likely smuggling) to Spanish America and English America.[112]

The case of Diogo Rodrigues Marques, from the wealthy family Rodrigues Mogadouro, who escaped to London in the early 1670s with his wife, Marquesa Rodrigues, and their six children (three boys and three girls) is significant. The family had strong ties with Livorno, but instead this branch decided to join the Jewish community in London. Diogo Rodrigues Marques's will, dated November 11, 1675, reveals an extensive network of merchants who were associates and trading partners: João Machado in Goa; Gaspar Francisco in Rio de Janeiro; Rodrigues Marques's uncle and father-in-law, António Rodrigues Mogadouro and his brother, António Rodrigues Marques, in Lisbon; Bento Ribeiro Torrado in Porto; Gaspar de Robles and Diego Roldán in Bayonne; Rafael Henriques in Bordeaux; Jerónimo Nunes da Costa, the heirs of Simão Rodrigues Henriques, Joseph de Medina and Abraham de Sotto in Amsterdam, the latter dealing with an enormous quantity of Diogo's bills of exchange; the heirs of Lopes Dias da Silva in Genova; Francisco Carvalho Nunes, plus António and Simão Mendes de Almeida, in Venice; his uncle Jacob Henriques de Miranda, in Pisa; and Gabriel Medina and Roque Rodrigues in Livorno.[113]

The rapid integration of Diogo Rodrigues Marques into the local market can be seen in the extraordinary amount of his lending and investment in English companies and merchants trading not only in London but also in Lisbon, Cadiz, and Livorno: John Cook & Co, Charles Duncombe & Co, Benjamin Braseley, John Pargiter, William Bird, William Gulfe, John Pollexfen, Edward Barthwell, Jeremy Snow, and Joseph Horneby. Rodrigues Marques mentions Francisco de Liz and Alfonso Rodrigues in London, but there are names for which he gives no precise location, such as Solomon Medina, António Rodrigues Nunes, Luís de Morais, Isaac and Luís Álvares, Luís Gonçalves de Andrade, Manuel de Velázquez, Costa Furtado, Jacob Aboab, Manuel Dias Vaz, Gaspar Dias Brandão, Jacques Gonçalves, and Isaac Mainell. His close friends in London were Jacob Benathiell, Jacob Gómez, Jacob Fernandes Miranda, and Isaac Sequeira, who would assist his wife in the execution of his will. Clearly, the purpose of Rodrigues Marques's move to London, besides escaping the Inquisition, was to engage with an emerging world financial centre and develop the family's network in northern Europe without losing its established ties in India, Brazil, the Mediterranean, and Amsterdam, which continued to function as a main base for bills of exchange.[114]

Diogo Rodrigues Marques was active as a banker and an investor, placing investments on behalf of many other people; for example, "the widows of Guarda in Portugal, or those of Trancoso in Brazil," another case of the sort of female financial activity we have noted during the course of this book. By far the most lucrative trade he engaged in was diamonds from India, but he also traded in pearls, emeralds, silver and gold, textiles from India and from England, elephant tusks (he sent Gabriel de Medina in Livorno 123 tusks for Francisco Carvalho Nunes in Venice). We are talking about many thousands of cruzados of trade and an extensive expertise in diamonds, whose different qualities and prices were obsessively calibrated.[115]

Unfortunately, by the time António Rodrigues Marques, himself a widower without children, arrived in London in the early 1680s, his brother Diogo had died in 1675 and his sister-in-law had died in 1678. His eldest nephew, Isaac, had been disinherited by Diogo for disobedience, and the other two nephews were not mentioned by António in his own will, made on January 2, 1688. His mother, Sarah Henriques, who had rescued Diogo's inheritance after the death of Marquesa Rodrigues, was declared the outright heir to António's fortune, but he tried to guarantee the perpetuation of the family through the sons of Dr. Fernando Mendes, and through David de Medina, who was married to one of his nieces, and Samuel Ximenes, who was married to another niece, on condition they changed their name to Marques. For the execution of the will he counted on Peter Henriques Jr., Abraham Fernandes Nunes, Manuel Lopes Pereira, and André Álvares Nogueira.[116]

If we turn to another continent, the expulsion of the Dutch from northeast Brazil in 1654 terminated a rare experiment in coexistence among Catholics, Calvinists, and Jews, all openly allowed to perform their own rites.[117] There were New Christians from Brazil who decided to publicly declare themselves Jews, others who stayed Catholics, and even some who fell somewhere in between.[118] This gives us an insight into the relationship between religious allegiance and politics in an experimental place where freedom of conscience seemed possible but did not last long.

The main leaders of Jewish migration from Amsterdam to Dutch Brazil were Manuel Mendes de Castro, hakham Isaac Aboab da Fonseca, and Moses Rafael de Aguilar. The size of the Jewish community reached a peak in the mid-1640s, probably around 1,000, but falling to 650 in 1654.[119] The three main tax farmers of Dutch Brazil were Baltasar da Fonseca, Moses Navarro, and Duarte Saraiva (alias David Seneor Coronel). This last was probably the richest man in the community, the owner of four sugar plantations (with mills) and engaged in trade from Amsterdam to Rio de La Plata.[120] Some members of the community reverted to Catholicism after the Portuguese reconquest; the vast majority went back to Amsterdam; and then several groups travelled to the Dutch Caribbean colonies, where they established sugar plantations. In time, the Caribbean production contributed to displacing Brazil as the dominant world sugar producer. Inquisitorial persecution was again launched in the region, although New Christians there managed to hold out against this better than those in Spanish America, where dual status as New Christian and Portuguese proved to be fatal immediately before and after the Portuguese revolution of 1640.[121]

The case of Isaac de Castro, nephew of Moses Rafael de Aguilar, with whom he travelled in 1641 from Amsterdam to Dutch Brazil, offers an example of solid Jewish teaching in Pereyhorade, France, where he was born, and in Amsterdam, where the family had migrated. Isaac de Castro defected from Dutch Brazil to Bahia in December 1644, probably to escape a criminal enquiry, and was executed (burnt at the stake) by the Inquisition in Lisbon as a convicted Jew on December 15, 1547. His unalterable adherence to his religious convictions against constant attempts to make him die as a Catholic led to his being praised as a martyr by Jewish poets. Isaac de Castro left copious information on the Jewish community in Dutch Brazil, and at his trial he identified seventy-two persons by their birthplace: thirty from France (New Christian communities, mainly Bordeaux, Bayonne, and Peyrehorade), twenty-two from Portugal, nine from Brazil, eight from Castile, two from Spanish America, and one from Italy.[122] The high number of Jewish people he could identify from France was due to Isaac's own origins, but it is undeniable that New Christian communities established on the west coast of France played an important role in trade and ethnic allegiance between southern and northern Europe, in many cases providing a stepping stone for migration to Jewish communities in northern Europe and beyond.[123]

{⟨≈⟩×⟨≈⟩}

In the mid-seventeenth century, a resilient New Christian trading network continued to operate across the Iberian world, with well-developed links to Jewish communities in the Mediterranean and northern Europe. In Italy, France, and Habsburg Flanders, New Christian financiers thrived and some of them acquired titles of nobility. The independence of Portugal, relatively absorbed by New Christians in the short-term, had long-term consequences, imposing divergent interests and political allegiances. The fact that New Christians had been wiped out of Spanish America signalled the first serious cracks of their Atlantic presence, although they enlarged their presence in Brazil. In the 1650s and 1660s, steady persecution of New Christian financiers by the Inquisition, both in Spain and Portugal, created an erosion of their merchant networks, although many families resisted.

The Sephardic communities in Italy, mainly in Livorno, were still increasing in their numbers and activities with connections in different continents. The Sephardic communities in Hamburg and Amsterdam reached the peak of their influence around the 1650s. And the offshoot community in London managed to obtain recognition, compensating for the beginning of decline in Amsterdam. These communities had the capacity to send members to the Dutch and English colonies. The relative dependence of New Christian and Sephardic communities on Iberia has not been sufficiently acknowledged. We shall see in the following chapters the relentless erosion of the position of the New Christian merchants under the extraordinary volume of trials launched by the Inquisition in Portugal.

CHAPTER FOURTEEN

Suspension

THE SUSPENSION OF the trials prosecuted by the Portuguese Inquisition decreed by the pope in 1674–1681 must be analysed in the context of an unprecedented sequence of events: the increased inquisitorial persecution that began in 1658, immediately after the exemption from property confiscation was abolished; the response to that persecution of the New Christian leaders, who appealed to Rome; the involvement of the Jesuits, who supported the appeal; and the papal authorities' interest in recovering control over an important part of their jurisdiction. To all this we must add the weak political position of the Portuguese regent, Pedro.[1] Why did the New Christians target the Portuguese and not the Spanish Inquisition? Because the extraordinary increase in trials occurred in Portugal, where the merchant elite had been especially penalised with property sequestration and confiscation, which dramatically reduced their capacity to keep royal contracts and intercontinental trade. Their action must be seen as a desperate last card they needed to play for survival.

A volatile political conjuncture proved crucial. The Portuguese regent deposed his brother, Afonso VI, in a palace coup in 1667. The following year he managed to negotiate a peace treaty with Castile, which gave him international recognition, while the new institutional arrangement with Rome, after twenty-eight years of disruption, became open to renegotiation.[2] In the meantime, the relative autonomy of the general council of the Inquisition, from the death of the general inquisitor in 1653 to the new appointment of another general inquisitor in 1671, although the latter died two years later, contributed to an unrestrained activity on the part of the institution. Regent Pedro faced an empty treasury, so the offer of financial help from the New Christians in return for a general pardon, to be obtained in Rome with the support of the prince, was tempting. This offer, however, triggered a coalition of internal social and political forces in support of the Inquisition.

This conjuncture was similar to the one that affected New Christians during negotiations for a general pardon in the early seventeenth century, but with two major differences: then, the political fight had been between the Portuguese Inquisition and a strong, distant (seen as foreign) king presiding over a recent Union of Crowns that had a stable relationship with Rome; in the early 1670s, by contrast, there were two centres of power in the New Christian dispute, Lisbon and Rome. On this occasion, the ruler in Lisbon was weakened by his questionable legitimacy (Pedro became regent after ousting his incapable brother), while the relationship with Rome was much more uncertain. The New Christians would seem to have had some strong advantages, mainly in Rome, but the Inquisition was better placed to use the weakness of royal power to its advantage in Lisbon. This short period of time was exceptional because it stimulated a well-articulated set of grievances from New Christians, and these had political and legal consequences. They caused an unprecedented political action by the Jesuits against the Inquisition (one that required the involvement of the pope and the cardinals of the Roman Inquisition) and an extraordinary reaction by the Inquisition and the hierarchy of the Portuguese Church (one that mobilised the nobility and the third estate against the New Christians). It is a fascinating story that has been very well told by Ana Paula Lloyd, so I shall concentrate here on the New Christians and how and why their extraordinary political effort was eventually defeated.

Increased persecution of New Christians is an important starting point. If we consider only the short period from 1660 to 1674, we can count a total of 4,386 people sentenced in three tribunals, distributed thus: Lisbon 667, Évora 1,969, and Coimbra 1,750.[3] The vast majority were New Christians. We need to keep in mind that these numbers concern people whose sentences were carried out. The papal suspension came in 1674, but there was still an auto da fé in Coimbra, although not in Lisbon or Évora. There were also around 600 people detained before 1674 who stayed in jail during the suspension and were then presented at the autos da fé after 1681. The average number of people detained annually was well over 300, although Lisbon had a lower annual average than the other two tribunals. This discrepancy had one possible cause; that is, the cases tried in Lisbon were more complex. Another important indicator of the degree of terror raised against New Christian communities was the number of presentations, or better, spontaneous visits, by people to the tribunal to confess and denounce others. The inventory of trials of the Inquisition of Coimbra shows one and two presentations in the 1640s and 1650s, followed by 60 in the 1660s, 102 in the 1670s, and 210 in the 1680s.[4] I interpret these numbers as a sign of the interiorization of fear and the disintegration of solidarity.

This chapter will focus on specific trials and sets of trials directed against major merchants and bankers that might have contributed to triggering New Christian activity in Rome. As with previous instances when the pope was asked to intervene, there was a dramatic increase in the number of trials, combined with specific cases of prominent merchants targeted by the Inquisition. Then we shall discuss the main stages of those actions and the alliances established between New Christians and Jesuits up to the point where the Portuguese Inquisition was suspended. My main argument is that the different agendas of these unlikely allies contributed to the mishandling of this window of opportunity, but the existence of a much stronger coalition of political and social forces in favour of the Inquisition also needs to be acknowledged. The evolution of international trade will be tackled as a necessary background to understanding the development of this conflict. Finally, I shall analyse the conditions that led to the reestablishment of the Inquisition, which have not been entirely taken on board by existing studies.

1. Targets

In the 1660s and early 1670s, the richest merchants in Lisbon were arguably António Rodrigues Mogadouro, Fernão Rodrigues Penso, Manuel Rodrigues da Costa, Manuel da Gama de Pádua, Pedro Álvares Caldas (all New Christians), and Francisco Malheiro (an Old Christian), although foreign merchants, primarily English, had become more and more important, particularly since the business of transport (renting ships and handling freights) was put out to contract by the Company of Brazil. Most of these major New Christian merchants were prosecuted by the Inquisition at dates from 1667 onwards, with the exception of Manuel da Gama de Pádua and Pedro Álvares Caldas, who had been arrested before. These two became procurators of the New Christians and benefitted from the protection of the pope, but Manuel da Gama's family, as we shall see in chapter 15, would be targeted for retribution after the reestablishment of the tribunal. In my analysis of the trials of these major New Christian merchants I shall include Manuel da Costa Martins, who was not the equal of the others in wealth but played a significant role in incriminating them at the Inquisition.

Manuel Rodrigues da Costa, secretary of the *Junta dos Três Estados* (a body created to supervise finances, including special taxation for Portugal's War of Independence), was the first to be detained, on November 12, 1667, as the persecution reached its height. He was then fifty-six years old. The questioning to establish an inventory of his property was carried out over the period from November 26, 1667, to March 1671.[5] Manuel's strategy was clever: he denied any significant real estate ownership. All the real estate he bought had been recorded under the name of his son, Francisco Soeiro da Gama, a *fidalgo* of the royal house and an accountant to the royal treasurer, because it had been bought with money inherited from his first wife, Guiomar Soeiro, sister of António da Gama Nunes and Manuel da Gama de Pádua (who were thus his brothers-in-law).[6] He declared only 1,000 cruzados of rents drawn from the *estanco* (royal monopoly) on tobacco and the pottery workshops in Nossa

Senhora do Monte, Lisbon.[7] He had been involved with the *asiento* (royal contract) for all frontiers since the early 1650s, with the contract for Angola, and with the contract to provision Alentejo, a region crucial to the war of Portuguese independence. The value of this last contract was estimated at 1.3 million cruzados, with 700,000 cruzados being assigned from the *comarcas*, or the counties' taxation, and the king owing him and his partners 600,000 cruzados. The partners varied over time, and at different points they included Francisco Malheiro, Cristóvão Rodrigues Marques, Pedro Fernandes Lemos, Pedro Álvares Caldas, António da Gama Nunes, and Manuel da Gama de Pádua (after his brother António died).[8]

Moreover, Manuel Rodrigues Costa drew attention in the inventory of his property to his debts as a broker and holder of the contract to provision Alentejo. I have counted 352,500 cruzados invested by noblemen such as D. Francisco de Lima; D. Rodrigo de Meneses; Martim Afonso de Melo, Count of São Lourenço; the Count of Vila Flor; the Count of Vila Maior; and the Countess of Soure, and also by merchants such as António Rodrigues Mogadouro, Diogo Rodrigues Henriques, and Duarte Gomes da Mata; by the official responsible for the royal treasury, João Cabral de Barros; by the royal judge Domingos Antunes Portugal; by the lawyer Jorge Moreno; and by many others. This collection of debt was enlarged by the money Manuel Rodrigues Costa owed as the executor for several wills, which also totalled dozens of thousands of cruzados. The property brought by his second wife, D. Joana de Sousa, who had been born in Bahia, was valued at 11,000 cruzados.[9]

Manuel Rodrigues da Costa's message was that he had very few assets, only debts. His attitude at the Inquisition was as tough as his desire to safeguard his wealth. He stood firm for three and a half years, and he refused to confess anything, even under torture. He was released because of lack of proof, this time being given a sentence of light suspicion of heresy, for which he was paraded at the auto da fé of June 21, 1671.[10] It is likely important that Manuel Rodrigues da Costa's second wife, from Bahia, Branca de Sousa, was an Old Christian, as was the wife of his son, Filipa de Sousa, also from Bahia (were they mother and daughter?).[11]

While Manuel Rodrigues da Costa chose the risky but rewarding path of firm refusal of confession, Manuel da Costa Martins, detained on May 21, 1672, when he was forty-one years old, started to make a confession a month later and provided an extraordinary list of the New Christian community in Lisbon through his wide-ranging denunciations. He was a contractor for the customs and dry ports of Portugal, a business valued at 30,750 cruzados. His father, Francisco Martins Manuel, from Mértola, Alentejo, was a contractor for the Priory of Crato. It is fair to say that, unlike Manuel Rodrigues da Costa, Manuel da Costa Martins provided a significant number of accusations.[12]

Costa Martins did not possess a significant amount of real estate. He had houses in the Rua da Rosa in Bairro Alto that were rented to a sergeant major in the Order of Christ for 25,000 réis, and these were worth 600,000 réis; he had mills powered by animals in the Rua da Barocca (also in Bairro Alto) worth another 600,000 réis, and these were rented out against a payment of flour; and he owned marshland at Esgueira (Aveiro). He had furniture that included seven tapestries, allegedly from Arras, depicting the history of Marcus Aurelius, valued at 600,000 réis; seven or nine tapestries also from Arras representing the planets (the property of the heirs of his deceased brother, Lourenço Pestana Martins), also worth 600,000 réis; two cabinets of *pau-santo* (wood from Brazil) with twenty drawers each; one cabinet from India inlaid with ivory; six Moscow chairs and six drum stools of the same reddish-brown leather; twenty-three or twenty-four panels (paintings) in his living room, office, and another chamber, valued at 100,000 réis; a bed of *pitiá* (another wood from Brazil) inlaid with ebony, valued at 40,000 réis; and extensive cutlery and silverware, gold, and pearls. He also acted as a pawnbroker.[13]

Manuel da Costa Martins was married to Antónia Craveira, an Old Christian, and denounced nearly his whole family as practicing Jews. He also denounced the following: Francisco Carlos, treasurer of the *Junta do Comércio*; António Nunes da Veiga, knight of the Order of Christ and son of the former contractor Sebastião Nunes; Fernão Peres Coronel, Pedro Ribeiro, Jorge Ribeiro, and Manuel de Sequeira, all frequenters of the gambling house of António Dias Leão in Arcas street; another New Christian, Francisco Manuel Delgado, a contractor (whose father was Filipe Serrão, also a contractor, and whose sister was married to Manuel de Melo Coutinho, an Old Christian fidalgo); and the contractors Rodrigo Nunes, Diogo Rodrigues Henriques Mogadouro, António Rodrigues Mogadouro, Francisco Rodrigues, Pantaleão Rodrigues Mogadouro, Diogo Rodrigues Marques, son-in-law of António Rodrigues Mogadouro, and his brother António Rodrigues Marques.

The list of Costa Martins' denunciations did not stop there. It was extended to include Fernão Rodrigues Penso, a contractor, and his son-in-law, Pedro Gomes de Olivares; Francisco Nunes da Costa, a contractor and knight of the Order of Christ; João Lopes Pardo and Manuel Lopes Pardo, customs administrators; Dionísio Rodrigues and his brother, Luís da Costa, contractors; Sebastião Francisco de Pina, a contractor; Diogo de Chaves, knight of the Order of Christ, his brother Simão Rodrigues Chaves, his sister Luísa Maria Chaves and her husband Duarte Garcia de Bivar, a contractor and knight of the Order of Christ; José Pessoa, a merchant, his brother-in-law, Manuel Lopes de Leão, the medical doctor Miguel Lopes de Leão, and his brother Rodrigo Vaz de Leão; and also Gregório Gomes Henriques, Jerónimo Soares Leitão, Luís Álvares, and Bento da Silva Bravo and his nephew André Correia Bravo, a merchant and knight of the Order of Christ.

Other important figures were denounced, such as Domingos de Sequeira, a contractor for tobacco; João Serrão de Oliveira, a contractor for the tax on olive oil; Júlio Coelho, goldsmith; Gaspar Vaz de Sequeira, a merchant; Manuel de Mesa and his brother, Francisco de Mesa, merchants; Simão Gomes de Almeida, a merchant; Henrique de Vaz Pinto; Luís Lopes Franco; Rui Gomes Solis, the owner of a gambling house in the *Beco das Comédia* where he, Manuel da Costa Martins, met most of these people; Francisco Gomes Solis; Manuel Rodrigues Bueno; António Serrão de Castro, an apothecary; António Vaz de Lemos; João Moreno Lopes, a lawyer; Francisco Soeiro, a merchant, and his father-in-law, Gomes de Azevedo; Mateus de Sousa, a merchant; Jorge de Andrade, a contractor; Manuel da Silva Henriques, a contractor, and his father-in-law Manuel da Costa, a merchant; Pedro Álvares Caldas, a contractor; Manuel Gomes, a merchant; and Jorge Coelho Febos.[14]

The preceding list might seem over long, but it is useful in that it shows most of the royal contractors, main merchants, and New Christian knights of the Order of Christ to have been accused; and some of these played a significant role in this history, as will be shown in this and the following chapters. The fact is that Manuel da Costa Martins' trial, unlike most such trials, was expedited because of his extensive denunciations. He spent only one year and a half in jail, and on December 10, 1673, he was presented at the auto da fé, where he was reconciled in return for formal abjuration, which meant his property was confiscated and he was detained ad arbitrium. Although he was condemned to wear the penitential habit, this sentence was lifted on December 12, 1673.[15] The last document concerning Manuel da Costa Martins recorded an authorisation for him to attend the Holy Communion of his niece, Filipa Pestana (he did not have children of his own), on March 17, 1674.[16] However, the misfortunes of this serial denouncer were not yet at an end. On July 26, 1674, he was murdered, shot by a gun. His corpse was buried at the church of the Convent of St. Francis in Lisbon. The death was recorded on September 1, 1684, and a note of it was included in the file on António Rodrigues Mogadouro, who had died in an inquisitorial jail on July 8, 1679, while the decision on his trial was still pending.[17]

Manuel da Costa Martins must have made many enemies, and it is difficult to link his murder to a specific family. The inclusion of a record of the murder at the very end of Mogadouro's trial, five years after the latter's death in prison, revealed more about the inquisitors' embarrassment over an extremely unfair trial than about any real evidence available at that time. In any case, Manuel da Costa Martins' denunciations triggered the detention of several wealthy New Christians. On July 28, 1672, the inquisitors of Lisbon issued orders for the detention of António Rodrigues Mogadouro, his sons Diogo Rodrigues Henriques and Francisco Rodrigues Mogadouro, Fernão Rodrigues Penso, Francisco Carlos, Diogo de Chaves, and Simão Rodrigues Chaves. All the orders were implemented the following day.[18]

When António Rodrigues Mogadouro was detained, he was seventy-four years old, the patriarch of an extended New Christian family. He was noted in several documents by New Christian agents as being the wealthiest

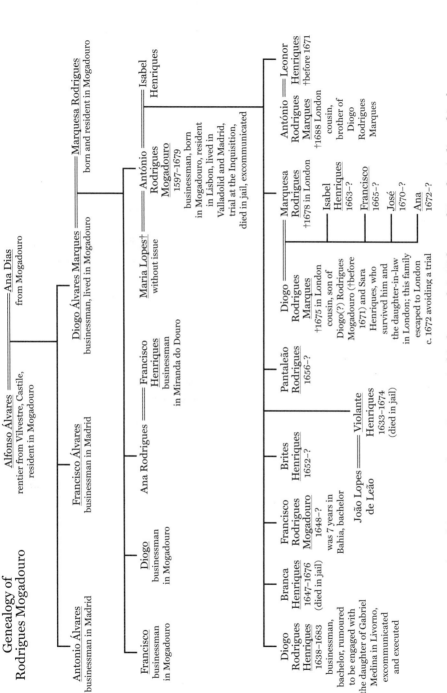

Genealogy of
Rodrigues Mogadouro

Afonso Álvares ══ Ana Dias
rentier from Vilvestre, Castile,   from Mogadouro
resident in Mogadouro

Diogo Álvares Marques ══ Marquesa Rodrigues
businessman, lived in Mogadouro   born and resident in Mogadouro

Antonio Álvares
businessman in Madrid

Francisco Álvares
businessman in Madrid

Diogo
businessman
in Mogadouro

Francisco
businessman
in Mogadouro

Ana Rodrigues ══ Francisco
Henriques
businessman
in Miranda do Douro

António Rodrigues
Mogadouro
1597–1679
businessman, born
in Mogadouro, resident
in Lisbon, lived in
Valladolid and Madrid,
trial at the Inquisition,
died in jail, excommunicated

Maria Lopes†
without issue

══ Isabel
Henriques

António ══ Leonor
Rodrigues   Henriques
Marques   †before 1671
†1688 London
cousin,
brother of
Diogo
Rodrigues
Marques

Diogo Rodrigues
Henriques
1638–1683
businessman,
bachelor, rumoured
to be engaged with
the daughter of Gabriel
Medina in Livorno,
excommunicated
and executed

Branca
Henriques
1647–1676
(died in jail)

Francisco
Rodrigues
Mogadouro
1648–?
was 7 years in
Bahia, bachelor

João Lopes ══ Violante
de Leão   Henriques
1633–1674
(died in jail)

Brites
Henriques
1652–?

Pantaleão
Rodrigues
1656–?

Diogo ══ Marquesa
Rodrigues   Rodrigues
Marques   †1678 in London
†1675 in London
cousin, son of
Diogo(?) Rodrigues
Mogadouro (†before
1671) and Sara
Henriques, who
survived him and
the daughter-in-law
in London; this family
escaped to London
c. 1672 avoiding a trial

Isabel
Henriques
1663–?

Francisco
1665–?

José
1670–?

Ana
1672–?

GENEALOGY 3. Family Rodrigues Mogadouro. Sources: Archival research in Lisbon and London indicated in the text.

merchant in Lisbon. The first denunciations against him were minor, such as that of João Rodrigues, who was black, from Angola, and a slave of António Rodrigues Marques, the nephew of António Rodrigues Mogadouro, who lived in the same house as his brother, Diogo Rodrigues Marques and was married to Marquesa Rodrigues, daughter of António Rodrigues Mogadouro. The denunciations, which were confirmed by other slaves called to testify, concerned food rules and keeping the weekly holiday. But what probably triggered the detentions was a rumour that Diogo Rodrigues Henriques, son of António Rodrigues Mogadouro, had arranged to put freight on an English ship on which he hoped to escape to Livorno. The captain of the ship would have given notice of its departure two days in advance. This rumour, initiated by Cesare Ghersi, an Italian merchant later called to the tribunal, was communicated by Pedro Ferreira, familiar of the Inquisition, on May 23, 1672.[19] This denunciation came two days after Manuel da Costa Martins' detention. There seems to have been a concerted action, suggesting that Costa Martins was considered a weak link in the New Christian community who could provide needed denunciations. The real target seems to have been the Mogadouro family.

Diogo Rodrigues Henriques supposedly arranged to marry the daughter of Gabriel de Medina, a Jew of Livorno who was a nephew of António Rodrigues Mogadouro. Manuel Preto Valdez, merchant, deputy of the Junta do Comércio and familiar of the Inquisition, had been to Rome with the Portuguese ambassador and would have taken letters from the Mogadouro family to Gabriel de Medina in Livorno and seen the houses being built in preparation for the marriage. But this was all hearsay. When Manuel Preto Valdez was called as a witness by the accused, he avoided these issues, although he did declare that António might be an apostate. Pedro Ferreira also had letters from Afonso Rodrigues Mendes, who had lived in Bordeaux and was now in Madrid, declaring himself scandalised by the Jewish behaviour of many New Christians in Bordeaux, among them members of the Mogadouro family. António de Castro Guimarães declared that Diogo Rodrigues Henriques had told him, Francisco Rodrigues Quinteiro, Manuel Gonçalves Campelo, and Domingos Maciel, all familiars of the Inquisition, that the Mogadouro family were building houses in Livorno to live there. He also claimed to have seen Diogo Rodrigues Henriques at the House of Insurance registering an enormous quantity of money and diamonds to be sent to Italy aboard the ship *Jerusalem*.[20]

This seems like a repeat of the main repressive inquisitorial wave in Porto in 1658, which was triggered by Old Christian familiars of the Inquisition. Initially, there was little reference here to Judaism, only to business connections with relatives in Bordeaux and Livorno. It was the classic trick of detaining younger members of a family—in this case the Mogadouro family—that brought more substantial accusations. Brites Henriques, the daughter of António Rodrigues Mogadouro, detained on January 9, 1674, an unmarried woman then twenty-two years old, decided after six months of detention to challenge the inquisitors. She declared herself to be Jewish and recited several prayers to Adonai (a Hebrew name for God) for help against the tyranny of the Inquisition.[21] Pantaleão Rodrigues Mogadouro, detained the same day, and aged nineteen, decided on a similar approach when interrogated on July 23, 1675—he refused to take the oath on the Gospels, insisting he did not believe in them, and he declared himself Jewish.[22] The defiant youngsters were later forced to recant and ended up declaring their allegiance to the Christian church. The same thing happened to a third brother, Francisco Rodrigues Mogadouro, twenty-four years old at the time of his detention, who was more cautious at the beginning, then confessed, and then revoked his confession twice.[23] They were all reconciled. The worst case was that of the eldest brother, Diogo Rodrigues Henriques, thirty-six years old when he was detained. This brother lost control, pretended to be mad, ended up being declared "negative," and was excommunicated and executed with property confiscation.[24]

The clue to the enmity between the Mogadouros and the Martins was given in a particular pair of denunciations: one by the mother-in-law and one by the wife of Lourenço Pestana Martins. These women hated the Mogadouros because they had tried to marry their daughters to Diogo and Francisco Rodrigues Mogadouro, to no effect.[25] Clearly the Mogadouros did not think they were a good match. There were also grievances about some boxes of sugar that the Mogadouros had managed to take out of customs. On April 20, 1673, Francisco Pais Ferreira wrote from Madrid to the Duke General Inquisitor with information on Pedro Lupina Freire, the dissident secretary of the Inquisition, who was on his way to Rome, Pedro Álvares Caldas, who was involved in negotiations for the general pardon in Rome, and the Mogadouro relatives in Bordeaux. He spread the rumour that António Rodrigues Mogadouro was the protector of New Christians who had escaped to northern Europe and of New Christians who had returned south and were now on their way to Brazil.[26]

More interesting was the declaration of Maria Pereira, who was called by the Inquisition on January 5, 1673. She reported a conversation with her former master, Pascoal Cordeiro de Lima, a blacksmith, whom she said had told her that if the Mogadouros managed to get out of jail they would have money to live on, since they had managed to remove from their house a large trunk with jewels, diamonds, pearls, and gold coins from Castile worth 100,000 cruzados. Pascoal had taken the trunk to the house of the Marchioness of Castelo Melhor and from there it went to Italy.[27]

The inventory of his property by António Rodrigues Mogadouro was in line with that reported in other cases; that is, he declared himself not to have any real estate. He had been a royal contractor in the past, and he indicated his recent involvement in the shipment of a large cargo of tobacco from Brazil. Sugar from Brazil was one of his main trades. He was also involved in trade with Goa via his associate, Simão Ribeiro, and with Livorno via Gabriel de

Medina. He indicated a significant amount of furniture, including cabinets and trunks from India, panels of paintings, tapestries from India and Italy, bags with gold coins valued at 733,600 réis, silver valued at 842,000 réis, silverware, a significant amount of clothing, bedspreads, and mattresses. He also operated as a pawnbroker, and he gave the names of several customers, particularly Doroteia de Gusmão, widow of João Mendes de Vasconcelos (3,000 cruzados lent at 6.25 percent interest, with jewels as collateral), and Henrique de Paz Pinto.[28]

António Rodrigues Mogadouro was a man of complete self-control. When the inquisitors asked whether they could keep any property not declared in the inventory and later found, he did not blink and declared that he was sure there were no other items. He insisted from the outset that he had nothing to confess, and he kept up his insistence without any deviations until his death in jail on July 8, 1679, certified by the physicians as being the result of dropsy. He had spent seven years in prison. The guards, the official in charge of the jail and the surgeon testified that he died repeating the name of Jesus many times. He had confessed to a Dominican several times, activities that were permitted because the Inquisition was in those days suspended by the pope; otherwise, confession in jail would not have been allowed.[29]

What is extraordinary is that legal proceedings against António Rodrigues Mogadouro were taken during the period when such trials were the subject of a papal suspension. On February 2, 1676, the inquisitors concluded the trial, deciding that the accused should be excommunicated as an apostate and his property confiscated, all this confirmed by the general council on March 17, 1676.[30] However, they decided not to publish the sentence in the first two autos da fé celebrated in Lisbon after the reestablishment of the Inquisition, which were held on May 10, 1682, and August 8, 1683, in which Mogadouro's four children were presented (three reconciled, one excommunicated and executed). They published only the very lengthy sentence against António Rodrigues Mogadouro, on November 26, 1684, at the auto da fé celebrated at the church of Saint Dominic. Then his bones were burnt with those of two of his daughters, Branca Henriques and Violante Henriques, who had also died in jail.[31]

The inquisitors were clearly uncomfortable about their dealings with this family. They kept the bones of António for five years and implicated him in the murder of Manuel da Costa Martins, even though he was in jail at the time. Branca Henriques denied any wrongdoing, contested the testimonies, and died in jail on August 28, 1676, after confession, and heard calling the name of Jesus. Violante Henriques, married to João Lopes de Leão, died in jail on February 18, 1674, more than one month after detention, without any session at the Inquisition. They were both excommunicated as apostates, and their corpses were unearthed to be burnt.[32] The excommunication and execution on the same day of the "negative" father and two "negative" daughters seems fitting—those who survived were those who confessed. If there is some evidence that Brites and Pantaleão had been practising Jews, there is no clear evidence for António Rodrigues Mogadouro. He had been the majordomo of the confraternity of the Holy Sacrament in the parish of Saint Nicolas, where he had invested a great deal of money in annual feasts and in charity and had been praised by the priest and the treasurer of the church, neither of whom had seen his behaviour as anything but that of a good Christian.[33] This would be normal for convinced Jews, dissimulation was considered inevitable, but to die calling repeatedly on Jesus seems excessive, even if one was persuaded that one's children would otherwise be adversely affected. He probably did not know what had happened to them, but this is not certain, owing to the accepted lack of secrecy in inquisitorial jails.

While António Rodrigues Mogadouro was discrete, composed, austere, Fernão Rodrigues Penso was a flamboyant womaniser who boasted about his adventures and talked too much at the Inquisition, although he behaved better in a second trial, as will be shown in the next chapter. They were both detained on the same day, July 28, 1672, which was not coincidental. The Inquisition had obviously decided to prosecute the richest New Christians. Penso, sixty years old at the time of his detention, spent eleven years in jail, was reconciled, detained again and, surprisingly, reconciled a second time without abjuration.[34] He was a businessman born in Badajoz of Castilian parents, the father allegedly an Old Christian from Merida and familiar of the Inquisition in Spanish America, the mother a New Christian from Badajoz, both from a peasant background. Penso's wife, Brites Pessoa, who died in 1649, was the daughter of a New Christian, Jerónimo Gomes Pessoa, who had joined the Jewish community in Amsterdam. Penso had two legitimate daughters, Ana Maria Penso, accepted into the Convent of Odivelas, and Mariana de Morales Penso, married to Pedro Gomes de Olivares. He also had eight illegitimate children by a married woman, Ana da Costa, whose husband was away in Castile. He gave each of these illegitimate children to wet nurses when they were newborns, and when they were five or six years old he received them into his house and educated them as his children. Two illegitimate daughters were also placed in the Convent of Odivelas.[35]

The inventory of Penso's property was substantial; unlike Mogadouro, Penso decided to go into detail. He had a farm in Palhavã, between the roads to Benfica and Nossa Senhora da Luz, and this was leasehold, valued at 20,000 cruzados. In 1667, he had absorbed into his original farm a neighbouring farm that had belonged to Jorge Dias Brandão, brother-in-law of Duarte da Silva, his best friend. He also had 200,000 réis of interest from the royal monopoly on tobacco. He owned shares in two caravels, one-quarter and one-third, respectively. The gold, silver coins, and diamonds he possessed were valued at 6,000 cruzados. The descriptions of his furniture and silverware are quite extensive and give details of finely wrought cabinets inlaid with ivory, wardrobes, a bed of *pítia* inlaid with ebony, paintings by a "good hand," tapestries from India, two litters, chairs, plus slaves, horses, and mules.[36]

Fernão Rodrigues Penso had had the contract for the *terças* (taxation) from municipalities since 1648; he had had the contract for Tangier until the city became part of the dowry of Catherine of Braganza; and he had the contract for Mazagan (North Africa). The king owed him 140,000 cruzados from the last contract for Mazagan, 3.3 million réis (8,250 cruzados) from the contract for Tangier, 3,000 cruzados on a loan, and 20,000 cruzados that Fernão had given as a deposit on the new contract for terças. Among the people owing him money on loans were the Marquis of Nisa (25,000 cruzados), the Count of Ribeira Grande (13,000–14,000 cruzados), the Marchioness of Castelo Melhor (4,000–5,000 cruzados), the Count of Castelo Melhor (4,000 cruzados), Domingos Pereira de Faria, treasurer for crusade bulls, Captain Baltasar da Cunha, Francisco de Barros de Almeida, treasurer for Lisbon's customs duties, the Count of Figueiró, the Countess of Sarzedas, Francisco de Noronha, the Count of Vidigueira, and D. Pedro Mascarenhas, governor of Rio de Janeiro.

There was a significant number of merchants with whom Penso had business debts to adjust, such as Bento Ribeiro Torrado from Porto (in 1658, an associate of Policarpo de Oliveira), Domingos de Sequeira (on the contract for Mazagan), and António Fernandes Pereira, his merchant partner in Terceira, Azores. Penso also had significant debts to an extensive list of merchants and lenders, such as Pedro Álvares Caldas (30,000 cruzados), João Vieira Matoso (14,000 cruzados), D. Antónia de Araújo, widow of Captain Manuel de Sousa Magalhães (12,500 cruzados at 6.25 percent interest, which was standard), Luis Correia de Paz, Bartolomeu de Gamboa, and João Duarte de Resende. He still owed money for the legitimate share of his wife's inheritance to Ana Pessoa, their daughter.

If all this information is useful to establish Penso's position as a banker and as someone responsible for placing financial investments on behalf of the high nobility and most prominent merchants, the confidences he furnished concerning his dealings on behalf of King John IV offer us new insights. He claimed to have placed 20,000 cruzados in Venice, without interest, to assist the infant Duarte, brother of the new King John IV, detained by the emperor after Portugal's declaration of independence. He also guaranteed money for the first ambassadors to Rome, France, and England. In England, he assisted Antão de Almada with 8,000 cruzados. His relatives in Seville sent boxes with music books and new compositions to the cathedral music master via England. During the regency of the queen, he provisioned the forts in North Africa.

Penso refused to make the mandatory contribution to the Company of Brazil (5,000 cruzados); and he asked to be left out of the exemption from property confiscation because appearance on the list was a "discredit to honourable and Catholic people." He claimed that the authorities had already tacitly accepted his position.[37] He had guaranteed the money—30,000 cruzados a year—to pay for the voyage and daily expenses of the deposed King Afonso VI in Terceira, Azores, and this he continued to do until the day he was detained by the Inquisition. Penso claimed that he had been promised the habit of the

Order of Christ and 200,000 réis of tença for the person who would marry his daughter, Ana. There was another *alvará* (royal order) for the *comenda* (benefice) of Ouriz, part of the Order of Avis, for his illegitimate son, Fernando, with a papal dispensation for his investiture. Finally, there were five *padrões de tença* (titles of royal pensions) of 200 cruzados each for his five illegitimate daughters.[38]

The confidences Penso related to his friend Duarte da Silva are also interesting, although impossible to check. Duarte presented himself to the Inquisition knowing that they did not have sufficient proof; he had used the time he had spent in hiding to alert possible witnesses. Moreover, Duarte da Silva had most of his wealth secured in banks in Holland and Venice, and the interest on this increased the capital by 3 percent a year. When Duarte went to England to guarantee the million cruzados for Catherine of Braganza's dowry, Penso had given him a cipher in case he needed to communicate urgently. Duarte had used this cipher in 1666 to ask Penso to make representations to the Count of Castelo Melhor when Duarte's wife, Branca, could not obtain a licence to leave the country. This Penso had done, and the authorisation had been issued.[39]

Fernão Rodrigues Penso denied the accusations against him and refused to confess during a trial that lasted almost ten years, from 1672 to 1682. The inquisitors continued to prosecute this trial during the period of suspension of the Inquisition decreed by the pope. Penso must have known when the Inquisition was reestablished by the pope, for he finally started to confess on March 10, 1682.[40] Strangely, he confessed that he had been a Christian for twenty-six years, then Jewish for nineteen, and then a Christian again for twenty-four years after being absolved by a Jesuit missionary.[41] Most probably he wanted to protect his family, whom he never denounced. On the other hand, he must have feared that his trial would be brought to a speedy conclusion with his excommunication.

In any case, partial confessions were the worst option at the Inquisition; for the accused could not even guess who the witnesses against him were. Finally, on April 14, 1682, Penso came up with three crucial names: Manuel da Costa Martins, Martinho Pestana, and Luís Álvares.[42] A trial that had lingered on for almost ten years was sorted out in one month. Luckily for Penso, the Inquisition was beginning to run short of witnesses: many had died, or were away, so it was not possible to ratify most of the denunciations for the sentence. The inquisitors were happy to wrap up the trial before other witnesses could disappear. On May 10, 1682, Penso was presented at an auto da fé held at Terreiro do Paço, where he formally abjured. He was reconciled with property confiscation and was sentenced to perpetual jail and wearing of the penitential habit. He was released with penances on May 22, 1682.[43]

This trial provides an ideal opportunity to study the strategies of both the Inquisition (the withholding of names and circumstances; times when pressure was exerted and others when proceedings seemed to have been abandoned; the final rush to a verdict) and of the accused (denial of the accusations;

identification of prosecution witnesses as enemies; name dropping and bragging about political influence; offering supposedly helpful information for the Inquisition). However, there was something crucial I have not mentioned: the anxiety of the accused who, while a wealthy man, was under permanent pressure from many people asking for loans, alms, and help in time of crisis, much of this attributable to the fall in business provoked by the Inquisition. The *contradictas* (legal objection against witnesses) are exactly about this pressure: how Penso had created enemies, because he had refused marriages, declined to support people in distress, and refused assistance to people who had known better days.

Two cases among the prosecution witnesses are revealing. Penso had promised the physician André Soares a boat to carry his family to a ship leaving the country after his reconciliation, and the boat did not arrive. The Soares family waited all night, and the next day the physician went to the Inquisition to accuse Penso.[44] The poet and pharmacist António Serrão de Castro was another witness. This man hardly knew Penso, but he had debts, and he could not replenish his pharmacy with medicine; so he asked Penso for a loan, which was refused.[45] Denunciations were (also? mainly?) about resentment and retribution. The life of these wealthy merchants and royal contractors was about risk management, not only of their investments (insurance against shipwrecks could reduce the risk; but there was no insurance against suspension or permanent postponement of payments by the king), but also, perhaps mainly, of how to deal with people who depended on or wanted to depend on them.

Relations between wealthy New Christians and the Inquisition should be analysed in terms of risk management. This is a difficult area of study because, naturally, this relationship left very few traces. Contacts were kept secret. However, we have seen in several cases that New Christians had informants inside the Inquisition, mainly secretaries and notaries willing to take risks; but some inquisitors were themselves informants; and some New Christians could and did access general inquisitors. Indeed, Fernão Rodrigues Penso, in his trial, let slip the information that he had once taken a letter he had received from a prisoner of the Inquisition to the inquisitor Luís Álvares da Rocha.[46] He did not go into detail, but it must have been uncomfortable for the inquisitors to have such dangerous relationships revealed in court. These links could accelerate or prevent inquisitorial action; many denunciations never triggered a trial, whilst others ended in rare absolution. The position of one inquisitor could make a difference.

2. Action

The idea of a new general pardon was floated in 1662 by Duarte da Silva immediately after his arrival in London. He must have understood that 1658 had been a turning point in Portuguese inquisitorial persecution. The only trace of this proposal is in Pope Alexander VII's brief *Ex omni fide*, issued on February 11, 1663. Duarte da Silva is there identified as a Portuguese Hebrew punished by the Inquisition and resident in London. The proposal contained the offer of an enormous amount of money for the navy and armed forces to defend the kingdom, in exchange for authorisation for a secure Jewish synagogue, a general pardon for those accused of Judaism, and publication of the names of witnesses in trials. Alexander VII sent the brief to the inquisitors, in which he declared his opposition to the proposal.[47] He must have been prompted by the general council of the Inquisition to issue this brief, given the lack of official relations between the Holy See and Portugal, in order to keep the pressure on the new king, Afonso VI. Duarte da Silva was right: the following years would bring decisive battles in Portugal's War of Independence.

The next ten years proved to be even more disastrous for New Christians in Portugal. The extraordinary increase in trials served the inquisitorial narrative that exempting New Christians from property confiscation in 1649 had made them bolder in their apostasy. In 1668, a meeting of the third estate of the Portuguese parliament (*cortes*) asked for the exclusion of New Christians from honours and distinctions, the expulsion from the kingdom of all those reconciled at autos da fé, and the prohibition of marriage between New and Old Christians.[48] In May 1671, the desecration of the parish church of Odivelas involving the theft of liturgical objects brought scandal, and this created a public commotion similar to that created by the events of 1630.

On July 22, 1671, Prince Pedro prepared a decree to expel all New Christians reconciled at autos da fé following confessions, with their children and grandchildren, and also those reconciled following a judgment of vehement suspicion of heresy and their children. Moreover, New Christians could not create entailed property or marry Old Christians.[49] This was clearly a racist law that singled out a large community by ethnic descent. A huge protest prevented publication of the decree, but it expressed a radical change of atmosphere. It was not until October 1671 that the peasant perpetrator of the robbery in Odivelas was detained. The man was given a civil trial and executed the following month, but the narrative of another New Christian outrage had become rooted.[50]

In May 1672, the general inquisitor, Pedro Lencastre, issued a strange sumptuary decree forbidding reconciled New Christians to use horses, litters, or coaches; to dress in silk or wear jewels or ornaments of precious metal; to hold public positions or receive positions of honour (in military orders); or to farm royal rents.[51] There were orders from the general council to the various tribunals instructing them to implement the decree; and there were protests from New Christians, for example, a petition from Pedro Álvares Caldas for the restitution of his use of horses and litters in which he cited the royal privileges he had received.[52] It is possible that the general inquisitor had been allowed by the king to decide what to do with reconciled New Christians, but the sumptuary decree represented extraordinary interference with the basic rule of royal monopoly on legislation, decrees being essentially the prerogative of the king.[53] In any case, the period during which the regent and King Pedro II governed was the richest in sumptuary laws, with two major general regulations in 1668 and 1677, which were reenacted in 1686, 1688, 1690, and 1698.[54] The detentions of July 28, 1672, ordered by the Inquisition were the last straw for the New Christian merchant elite: its members started preparations to appeal to Rome with the help of the Jesuits.

The Jesuit Baltasar da Costa, provincial of Malabar, who had been in London and was most likely contacted by New Christian and Jewish communities in northern Europe, particularly by Duarte da Silva, wrote to the Regent Pedro's confessor, the Jesuit Manuel Fernandes, with a new proposal: the New Christians would guarantee the initial transport of 5,000 soldiers to India and the payment of 20,000 cruzados for their annual maintenance; they would send 1,200 soldiers every year, as the need arose; they would create a trading Company of India with adequate capital; they would pay missionaries and pay for the delivery of papal letters dealing with the nomination of bishops in the East; and they would cover the expenses of the ambassador to Rome to the amount of 200,000 réis a year. All this would be in exchange for a general pardon, with the liberation of prisoners of the Inquisition and the reform of tribunal proceedings, including the ending of the practice of secret witnesses and condemnation on the word of a single witness.[55]

This proposal, first communicated by Baltasar da Costa to the prince in early September 1672, targeted the restoration of the Portuguese presence in the East.[56] It is obvious that the empire was the main source of both New Christian and royal wealth, and was used as leverage for negotiations, first in 1649 (focused on Brazil) then in 1672 (focused on India). The conditions of the offer varied slightly; the figures indicated resulted from an adjustment in March 1673.[57] There was a second (complementary but separate) offer that has not been mentioned: on June 12, 1673, Manuel da Gama de Pádua, joined by Pedro Álvares Caldas five days later, promised to redeem the interest paid by the customs of Lisbon, then 53,803,000 réis, in the next twenty years, an investment estimated at 100,000 cruzados.[58]

The first step was to obtain authorisation from the prince to present the proposal for a general pardon and the reform of Inquisition proceedings to the pope. The Inquisition immediately reacted to the rumour of the New Christian initiative, claiming that it would undermine royal prerogative and established tradition, and would contribute to the impunity of apostates. The Jesuits mobilised more than forty theologians, including bishops, to sign a document in which they declared that the New Christian appeal to Rome should not be impeded.[59] The Inquisition mobilised twenty-three theologians who declared the New Christian appeal unlawful.[60] In this fight, which reached its climax in August 1673, it appears that the Jesuits had the upper hand and the appeal was sent to Rome.

However, the Inquisition proved to have several crucial trump cards to reverse its initial disadvantage. The tribunal mobilised the mob against New Christians on the streets, instigating a number of insulting charivaris reported under the cry "Death to the Jews."[61] It stimulated pamphlets against New Christians and the main advisers of the regent, accusing the latter of collusion with the "perfidious race." On July 31, 1673, a pamphlet was posted over the door of the slaughterhouse of Lisbon in which the main courtiers were threatened: the Marquis of Fronteira, as financially dependent on António Correia Bravo, a "great Jewish scoundrel"; the Marquis of Marialva and D. Rodrigo de Meneses, "paid by New Christians" (Caldas, Lemos, Costa, Bravo, and De Pádua were named) with the money extorted from poor Old Christians and the royal patrimony. The populism of the pamphlet was completed with the lament that these courtiers called Old Christians "wicked villains."[62]

The tribunal stirred up the bishops, many of them former inquisitors, to write to the prince opposing the New Christian appeal. The bishop of Leiria and the bishop of Lamego became particularly vocal, while the archbishop of Lisbon had to backtrack on his original position.[63] The language used by the bishops was particularly violent, showing how the dignitaries of the Church in Portugal felt this was a decisive moment. They sided unanimously with the Inquisition in a crucial sequences of actions, well analysed by José Pedro Paiva in his excellent study.[64] In the meantime, the general council of the Inquisition (the general inquisitor, Pedro de Lencastre, had died on April 23, 1673) launched a series of counterappeals to the prince.[65] They put extraordinary pressure on Jesuit consultants to the Holy Office and theologians from other religious orders to change their vote on the New Christian appeal. The University of Évora had voted overwhelmingly in favour of the appeal, but the majority of voters at the University of Coimbra sided with the Inquisition.[66]

The gathering of the parliament (cortes) in early 1674 offered a major opportunity for the Inquisition to complete its mobilisation of Old Christian elites. It managed to obtain the support of the three estates to write to the pope opposing the New Christian appeal.[67] The procurators of the third estate, according to New Christians, were infiltrated by familiars of the Inquisition who asked the regent to oppose the appeal and condemned freedom of conscience.[68] This latter notion had never been floated by the New Christian procurators, who immediately denied that this was their purpose, but it reflected the inquisitorial fear of a change of values which was looming in northern Europe.

Who were the main actors in this violent dispute? The New Christian procurators who spoke for the community were António Rodrigues Marques, Manuel da Gama de Pádua, Pedro Álvares Caldas, Pedro Fernandes Lemos, Duarte Garcia de Bivar, and D. José de Crasto. Duarte Garcia de Bivar left very few traces in the archives: he received the habit of the Order of Christ on October 13, 1660, with a dispensation from the king and the pope.[69] Even less information remains about D. José de Crasto, son of Fernão Dias de Crasto, businessman in Madrid, and nephew, administrator, and heir to Francisco Carlos, a widower without children.[70]

António Rodrigues Marques, nephew and son-in-law of António Rodrigues Mogadouro, who kept Mogadouro's youngest children in his own household until they were detained early in 1674 by the Inquisition in retaliation, had been received into the Order of Christ with 12,000 réis of tença on September 26, 1662. The king overlooked his mercantile background (he traded with various parts of the Portuguese empire and northern Europe) after the enquiry had pronounced him "clean, without any trace of the infectious nation."[71] This is ironic, because he must have been the only procurator who ended up joining the Jewish community in London.[72]

Manuel da Gama de Pádua has appeared in this history several times. He studied liberal arts at the University of Coimbra, was received into the four minor ecclesiastic orders, was detained by the Inquisition in July 1636 when he was twenty-nine years old, was reconciled under vehement suspicion of heresy in 1640 without ever confessing (even under torture), and was released in March 1640 after almost four years in jail.[73] He started as a silk merchant and contractor for playing cards in Algarve. He became a major merchant and an asentista after Portuguese independence, played an important role in the Company of Brazil, and became treasurer for the custom duties of Lisbon.[74] When Duarte da Silva was prosecuted and reconciled by the Inquisition, Manuel da Gama guaranteed the money for his bail. He was a fidalgo of the royal house and received into the habit of the Order of Christ with the comenda of St. Francis of Ponte de Sor on September 27, 1658.[75]

Pedro Álvares Caldas was another royal contractor who developed his wealth after the independence of Portugal. He was detained by the Inquisition of Évora on February 9, 1655 when he was thirty-three years old, and he was reconciled (formal abjuration with property confiscation) at the auto da fé of April 18, 1660.[76] His wife, Catarina de Alarcão, and his daughter, Maria Álvares Caldas, were also prosecuted by the Inquisition.[77] When he was detained, he was a general administrator for terças (the royal share of municipal taxes) and a contractor for the provisioning of the Portuguese army in Alentejo (a strategic region during the war of independence against Spain). It seems that he recovered from the inquisitorial blow, and there is a record of 40,000 réis annual tença awarded to him by the king on July 8, 1667, and another record of 60,000 réis annual tença awarded on August 28, 1667, for his daughter Maria da Saudade.[78]

Pedro Fernandes Lemos was received into the Order of Christ on October 8, 1659, following a royal dispensation for his "defect" of blood. He had the contract to provision the Portuguese army in Alentejo when he presented

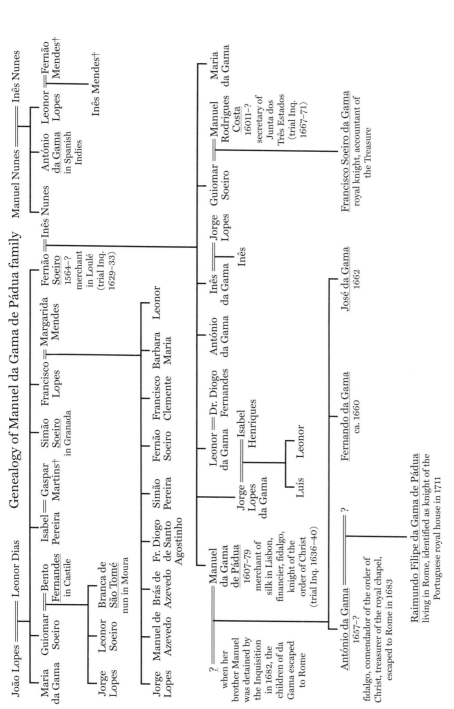

GENEALOGY 4. Family Da Gama de Pádua. Sources: Archival research in Lisbon and Rome indicated in the text.

himself to the Inquisition on December 12, 1662 (he was then sixty-six years old). He must have had information that the tribunal had gathered several denunciations from other prisoners and was about to arrest him, and so he presented himself at the tribunal, confessed, and was reconciled (formal abjuration), a rare "privilege," on November 19, 1663.[79] His son, who bore the same name and also belonged to the Order of Christ, presented himself at the Inquisition on October 17, 1663 (he was thirty-five years old) for the same reason as his father and was reconciled (formal abjuration) at the tribunal on November 20, 1663.[80] One of them was received into the comenda of Santo Ildefonso do Vale da Telha on March 3, 1666,[81] but it is difficult to tell which was the comendador—probably the father.

All the New Christian procurators had been prosecuted and reconciled by the Inquisition or had close relatives who were in prison at the time of the appeal. They risked being accused a second time, which would most probably mean excommunication and execution, but they had lived with this threat since they had been reconciled. The fact that they were procurators of the community, with an appeal outstanding with the pope, meant that they were temporarily protected, as was customary, by a special papal directive that placed them and their families under the protection of the pope until the appeal was decided. The Inquisition was hamstrung by this papal directive, and the detention of the young children of António Rodrigues Mogadouro at the house of António Rodrigues Marques, on January 9, 1674, was immediately denounced to Rome as a provocation against papal authority. It was argued that the persecution and destruction of the richest family in Portugal resulted from the basest motives of revenge.[82] These actions of the Inquisition, including the manipulation of the three estates, did not go down well in Rome; the inquisitors were seen as rebellious and an obstacle to further action from the pope.

The main liaison between these procurators and the prince was the Jesuit, Manuel Fernandes, his confessor. It seems that the procurators had established quite an intimate relationship with Fernandes. Manuel da Gama de Pádua and Pedro Álvares Caldas asked the prince to keep secret their proposal to redeem the compromised interest on the customs of Lisbon and to deal only with them. The purpose of the proposals to the Crown was to encourage the return of New Christians with their money to the kingdom and encourage the investment of their capital in trade. The procurators lamented that many New Christians did not want to sign the petition to Rome because they were afraid of being imprisoned. They confided that the brother of António Rodrigues Marques, Diogo Rodrigues Marques, had escaped to another country "free for his convenience" with 300,000 cruzados, but that he had had every intention of returning if the safety of New Christians could be established.[83] These letters are signed and dated June 17, 1673. We know that Diogo died in London in 1675 with a trading capital estimated at £36,000 (equivalent to 270,000 cruzados), of which he held £15,000 for the account of his brother,

António. He also left £1,000 in a trust fund to provide dowries for poor brides in the London Jewish community.[84]

The other Jesuits involved in these negotiations were António Vieira, who had been prosecuted by the Inquisition for his prophetic writings; Luís Álvares, provincial of the Society in Portugal and rector of the University of Évora; and Manuel Dias, Pedro Jusarte, and Baltasar da Costa.[85] António Vieira played a significant role in Rome, where he resided from 1669 to 1675, and supported the New Christian appeal at the highest level. In a letter that Vieira wrote to Manuel Fernandes, he reported that King John IV and Queen Luísa had declared that after the restitution of the kingdom of Portugal there was only one fortress to be conquered, the one in Rossio (the palace of the Inquisition), "Where," Vieira added, "so many traitors in those times and nowadays take refuge," concluding, "His Majesty now has the opportunity to demolish and subjugate the pride and rebellion of that fortress, not with his own hand but with the hand of the pope."[86] The motives and plans of the Portuguese Jesuits (or most of them) were here openly exposed, but we need to consider a wider context.

Three major issues explain the Jesuit intervention in New Christian action. First, they had fallen out with the Portuguese Inquisition owing to divergent political interests. There were Jesuit preachers censored by inquisitors for their support of King John IV, conflicts of precedence concerning access to the local market in Évora, and several Jesuits were prosecuted by the Inquisition, not just the famous royal preacher, Father António Vieira.[87] While the Inquisition relentlessly prosecuted New Christians in general and their merchant elite in particular, damaging the financial backbone of the war against Spain, the Jesuits were eager to have them on board as crucial financiers of an independent Portugal. They had recovered their position as the most influential religious order, with easy access to the sovereign—a position they had lost during the Iberian Union of Crowns—and they did not want to lose it again. In Spain, the Jesuits never reached the same level of influence. The nomination of the Jesuit Johann Eberhard Nithard as general inquisitor in Spain (1666–1669), resulting from his position as confessor to Queen Regent Mariana of Austria, was exceptional and did not last long. He was ousted by a military and palace coup and sent as ambassador to Rome, never to return.[88]

The second issue concerned the centrality of Rome in this New Christian initiative. The Jesuits managed to square the circle of total loyalty to both the prince and the pope. The autonomous and disruptive practices of the Inquisition were seen by the Portuguese Jesuits in this period as working against the interests of both the prince and the pope. The third issue concerned the long-term consolidation of common interests between the Jesuits and the New Christians. The latter financially supported Jesuit missions and created chapels in various Jesuit churches. The relationship between the New Christians and the Franciscans was also important, but not at the same level. Although there were also some dealings between New Christians and Augustinians, and even between New Christians and Dominicans, as we have seen before, these were not as close. Moreover, many decades of Jesuits ministering to those condemned by the Inquisition as they made their way to execution while still claiming a sincere Christian faith may have eroded this order's belief in inquisitorial methods. Father Manuel Dias compiled a list of "negative" (those who had not confessed) condemned and executed people who had died claiming their Catholic allegiance and a list of New Christians who had left the country and lived as Catholics elsewhere.[89]

The proposal for a general pardon and for reform of the way the Inquisition performed its duties guided negotiations between New Christians and Rome for the next nine years. It was in line with previous New Christian tactics, particularly, seeking a general pardon to relieve persecution and clearing denunciations from the inquisitorial archive. The crucial demand for reform of the way the Inquisition performed its duties was in line with continual criticisms from other sources concerning abusive inquisitorial penal procedure, particularly at the turn of the seventeenth century, and was the most important element of the proposal. My interpretation is that this dual strategy was influenced by the Jesuits, who wanted to permanently curb political interference from the Portuguese tribunal after it had been so damaging during the war of independence against Spain and to align its proceedings with those of the Roman Inquisition. Jesuit intervention went far beyond what might have been expected. I argue that this intervention supported the appeal at the beginning in a way that New Christians could never have dreamed of, but that it made any compromise much more difficult to reach because of the strong institutional position of the Inquisition and the support they received from the vast majority of members of the religious orders and the bishops. The Jesuits became isolated within the Portuguese Church.[90]

New Christian grievances were presented to the pope and the Roman congregation of the Inquisition in the summer of 1673 in a remarkable document that deserves deep analysis because its content had an immediate impact and long-lasting consequences, both legal and moral. New Christians understood that the Catholic Church was a legalistic institution, guided by canon law, which had created a tradition of minimum guarantees for the individual, including the recognition of rights to sovereignty and property for non-Christian peoples.[91] Keeping Christians separated from Jewish people and fear of Jewish contamination were embedded in canon law; segregation and discrimination were regulated. Practice frequently challenged this legal framework, as we have seen with the sixteenth century debates on papal intervention in Iberian expansion or the legitimacy of New Christian forced baptism in 1497 in Lisbon. The grievances of New Christians represented more than a century of reflection on, and appeal against, the abusive penal procedures of the Portuguese Inquisition. The systematic unfairness of the trials and the deeply rooted prejudices against New Christians, no evidence for which appeared in a canon law that recognised the sacrament of baptism as a transformative act, were at the core of the grievances. The strategy of stressing the violation and perversion of law resulted not only from the New Christian's tradition of appeal to Rome but arguably also from their recent support by the Jesuits, who knew only too well the important role legal debate would have to play if the power of the Portuguese Inquisition was to be quashed.

These grievances must have been formulated with a lawyer's touch, but in the copies I had access to they are presented in a crude way, with only a few quotes from authorities. They were probably reduced to their essentials for the purpose of comment or discussion.[92] The first grievance concerned property confiscation. Inquisitorial sequestration meant all property was taken immediately and the family was expelled from its home, becoming dependent on the charity of relatives and friends, since any request for a food allowance from the Inquisition implied long-term litigation. Creditors of the detained would be stripped of their rights, as would leaseholders and holders of *fidecommisso* or entailed property, because the Inquisition's exchequer immediately sold everything as unencumbered property. If the prisoner was liberated with restitution of property, it required many years of litigation to recover a fraction of what he or she had lost. This procedure, the grievances concluded, violated both the principle of confiscation only after sentence and the principle of not harming third parties. Length of prison time was the second grievance, based on a list of fifty-seven prisoners who had stayed in jail from four to fourteen years, simply because they had been accused without sufficient evidence and detention was used to extract confessions or to obtain more accusations.[93]

The scandalous unfairness of property confiscation that reduced families to poverty, coupled with malicious detention without legitimate evidence to extort confessions and denunciations from people singled out, were naturally placed at the top of the list of grievances. These grievances exposed the perversion of the basic principles of justice by the Portuguese Inquisition. The grievances were then extended to include the impossibility of freely choosing a lawyer, because prisoners could only choose among a limited number of lawyers accepted by the tribunal. These lawyers did not have access to the trial, only to the articles of the legal charge; the prosecution had free rein, while the defence could not even make allegations *in jure* (according to law); the lawyers accepted by the tribunal had to swear not to defend the accused if they found him or her guilty; in general, these lawyers terrorized the accused by insisting on the difficulty of the defence and encouraging him or her to liberate himself or herself through confession. Part of the grievance was the understanding that no lawyers were able to provide the accused with an independent defence; all were part of the tribunal.[94]

Inquisition corruption, which was patent in its property confiscation, was also exposed by its treatment of minors. Young family members were given into the care of a jailor, who would encourage them to confess so that they would earn part of the confiscated property.[95] Preparations for an auto da fé were used by the inquisitors to pressure detainees to confess, because the next one might not be celebrated for another one or two years. They also placed other prisoners (or even fake prisoners) in the same cells as the accused to denounce them and pressure them to confess.[96] Diminutive (meaning having insufficiently confessed) prisoners could end up being condemned for not having denounced their first- or second-degree relatives. They could be accused of acts of Judaism inside the jail, with no possibility of evidence from any third party. Those who presented themselves to confess could be accused of not having confessed fully, and could therefore be further denounced and still be tortured and excommunicated.[97]

Prejudices against New Christians based strictly on blood were the third set of grievances, this time disseminated through the various articles of prosecution. Defence against these articles was impossible because the testimony of other New Christians was not accepted. For their defence the accused needed to present six Old Christians (acceptable to the tribunal) for each article.[98] In this way, the Inquisition, while welcoming New Christians to denounce each other, excluded their testimonies from any defence. The bias towards condemnation without any guarantee of a defence was blatant. The evidence of Judaism resulted merely from genealogy. When there was proven innocence, the accused were never released but were subjected to the humiliation of being presented at the auto da fé to abjure their lightly or vehemently suspected heresy resulting from insufficient proof. If anyone accused of Judaism was discovered to be an Old Christian, he or she would immediately be liberated without any need for a defence. Accusations of Judaism were not accepted against Old Christians. If the denouncer was a New Christian, he or she would be prosecuted as a forger or a perjurer; the same applied to any Old Christian who confessed to Judaism.[99] Those accused of performing Jewish rituals who did not confess ("negative" detainees) could be condemned without any evidence of crime (any corpus delicti), such as liturgical objects, signs, or other clues, being found in the places where they were supposed to have held rituals.[100] By contrast, the theft of liturgical objects from Catholic churches was always supposed to have been committed by New Christians, while in many cases such thefts were proven to have been committed by Old Christians.[101]

All the grievances in the second section of the petition (another fifteen) were focused on the prejudice that existed against anyone who had any New Christian blood, and it was asserted that New Christians were more discriminated against than people who had converted from any other religion. This was behind the refusal of many Jewish families to convert. They knew they would continue to be a target for the Inquisition. The distinction—what we would nowadays call discrimination—comprehended every descendant of converted Jews. All these people, not just those condemned by the Inquisition, were subject to hatred and contempt, and excluded from dignities, respectable jobs, and ecclesiastical and secular offices. Their treatment could be compared with that of converts in France, Germany, and even Spain, where such people lived peacefully and without discrimination. It could also be compared with the treatment of people from a lower social stratum, with the way many peasants were assimilated into the population of Lisbon, which proved the effect of good treatment. The refusal of any division among Christians, advocated from the beginning by St. Paul and reiterated by Nicholas V, was pointed out.[102] The condemnation of those labelled "negative," detainees who did not confess, occupied a good part of the grievances, and there were abundant quotes from treatises by inquisitors such as Guidonis Fulcodii, Diego de Simancas, Francisco Peña, Prospero Farinacci, Antonio de Sousa, and Cesare Carena, and references to specific articles from canon law that advocated moderation and the protection of the innocent.[103]

Condemnation on the word of a single witness, considered the most important form of oppression of innocent people, was developed in this part of the petition. The quality of the witnesses accepted by the Inquisition, in contrast to the quality required by other tribunals, was exposed, particularly witnesses who were slaves who hated their masters, or were perjurers, or civil criminals.[104] Unlawful detentions, miserable conditions in the cells, and a complete refusal of spiritual assistance and administration of the sacraments (penance, extreme unction) to prisoners were also listed in the grievances.[105] The following articles developed the idea that the Inquisition did not seek to establish the innocence of the accused, but did everything to destroy innocence, forcing illegitimate confessions and persuading witnesses—single, inimical, disreputable, or even criminal witnesses—to falsely accuse. The formal, repetitive nature of the accusations (stereotypical we would say)—dressing in freshly washed shirts on Saturday, reciting the Lord's Prayer to God in the sky, respecting the two main annual Jewish fasts, refusing to eat pork, rabbit, or fish without scales, and taking care not to sweep the house in a reverse direction—exposed how confessions and denunciations were arrived at.[106]

The grievances also pointed out the contradiction between the inquisitors' claim that Judaism was an unstoppable plague and evidence from various parts of the world that showed the opposite, and they questioned whether this claim was anything other than a strategy of the Portuguese Inquisition. It was also pointed out that the inquisitors' acceptance of the word of perjurers and false accusers was a major problem they had never addressed. The grievances finally rejected the idea that New Christians would declare themselves Jews as soon as they reached another country, because they were all secretly Jews, arguing that this was a prejudice projected onto sincere Christians.[107] Unsurprisingly, New Christians did not raise the issue of torture, which was engrained in civil and canon law in Italy. It would take almost a century to see it systematically contested there, by Cesare Beccaria, and then abolished.[108]

This large set of grievances, the careful construction of which anticipated all analysis of inquisitorial trials by historians, made an impact in Rome, where the local Inquisition had (virtually) never engaged in a ritual such as the auto da fé: first because that Inquisition was at the core of the Church and did not need a specific ritual to assert its power; and second, because the disciplinary procedure that prevailed in Italy was based on a discrete manipulation of punishment and lenience, generally eschewing public humiliation and avoiding the systematic destruction of entire families.[109] The procedures of the Portuguese Inquisition were only possible with a targeted minority enslaved by their own king, as Clement VII commented to his nuncio in Portugal.[110]

The scale of the Portuguese Inquisition's corruption and its irregular procedures, even if not scandalous by Roman standards, went beyond perceptions of what constituted minimal acceptable justice in a country in which Roman law was embedded, along with commercial, civil, and canon law. Besides these grievances, New Christians presented lists of prisoners who had refused to confess and had been executed despite claiming to have been Christians all their lives. There were also lists of minors presented at autos da fé whose confessions should not have been accepted, and there was a list of 146 New Christians released from prison in recent years who could not recover their property, after the sentence cleared them of confiscation.[111] Briefly, the papacy's political interest in reviewing its relations with Portugal and the Portuguese Inquisition was matched by a real juridical debate about legal guarantees and the parameters of penal procedure concerning a minority vigorously persecuted and systematically accused of Judaism.

3. Intervention

It is now time to shift our attention to Rome, which was where most of the action occurred between 1674 and 1681. The way in which files concerning the New Christian appeal to Rome, dated July 1673, were preserved at the Archivio della Congregazzione per la Dottrina della Fede, indicates that an attempt was made to reconstitute the main lines of the historical relations between Rome and the Portuguese Inquisition. Papal briefs and bulls are mentioned; the record of exemptions is highlighted; previous New Christian appeals, mainly in the early seventeenth century, are studied; and a series of documents related to this latest appeal (for and against) produced in the 1670s and 1680s is recorded.[112] There are revealing copies of original instructions from Clement VII to the nuncio in Lisbon, particularly objecting to King John III's 1532 prohibition on New Christians travelling abroad. Clement VII asked for the revocation of this because it placed those subjects in the position of slaves, raising the suspicion that the Inquisition was not moved by religious zeal but by an intent to destroy these people. Clement VII added to his reasoning: "They would become worse than Jews, since they would perceive it as the captivity in Egypt . . . it is a minor evil that they would become Jews by their bad faith rather than by our iniquity; His Majesty cannot constrain the will that God made free, being better advised to use charity and piety with them, and give up violence that can never be good or fair."[113] This pointed advice, quite clear in its political analysis, is placed in the very first section of the first codex. Its sage meaning originally fell on deaf ears, but its retrieval after one and a half centuries suggests it came to be considered a principle on which analysis of the appeal would be based.

The first letters to Rome from New Christian procurators in Lisbon in the summer of 1673 confirm our hypothesis that the main goal was then a general pardon.[114] It is in António Vieira's letters from Rome to the royal confessor, Manuel Fernandes, in Lisbon, that we discover the Jesuits' insistence on the importance of grievances and their push for reform of the way the Inquisition was run, with precise instructions that testimonies should be collected from bishops and ministers of the Inquisition, if possible, and from religious men who accompanied the condemned to the stake and sensed their innocence.[115] Clearly, we have two different agendas that were put together: the general pardon eagerly requested by the New Christians to obtain immediate relief, and a reform of the inquisitorial process pushed by the Jesuits to curb the power of the Inquisition. These two agendas converged, not least because reform of the inquisitorial process had for a long time been on the New Christian agenda in Rome.

The nomination of New Christian procurators in Rome was not straightforward. A letter from July 24, 1673, written at the papal nuncio's house in Lisbon and signed by the six Lisbon procurators, nominated on behalf of "all Catholic descendants of the Hebrew Nation resident in Portugal" the following procurators in Rome: Marquis Francisco Nunes Sanches, D. Francisco Nicolau da Silva, Francisco Peres Vergueiro, and Baltasar Gomes Homem.[116] On October 20, 1673, the same procurators in Lisbon nominated the abbot Francisco de Azevedo New Christian procurator in Rome.[117] This change means that the previously listed candidates did not accept the nomination. António Vieira explained that they did not want to have a public assignment because they had relatives in high positions in Rome and Lisbon, although they were willing to support the appeal financially.[118]

The reason for changing the New Christian procurators in Rome is still a mystery. It is implausible that their names were put forward without them being asked for their consent. They must have changed their minds. This might have been because they feared the disclosure of their New Christian status would compromise their position with the Roman congregation, but it does not seem to have had any impact on their position in Rome. The distinction between New and Old Christians did not exist there; indeed, such a distinction was considered somewhat problematic in that it went against the universalist vision of the Catholic Church. It seems that the congregation did not disclose these names to any Portuguese residents, ambassadors, or agents of the Inquisition, but the secrets in Rome were difficult to hide. In 1675 the Portuguese Inquisition's agent, Jerónimo Soares, reported meetings at the house of Baltasar Gomes Homem on the "Jewish affairs" with the involvement of a secretary of the cardinal Colonna.[119] In any case, the change of mind by the New Christian procurators nominated to Rome must have been motivated to protect their interests in Lisbon, where they still had many business dealings, not to protect their interests in Rome, where they had a strong position.

Francisco Nunes Sanches (ca. 1600–1689) was the most important Portuguese financier in Rome, as was shown in the previous chapter. Born in the diocese of Guarda, he never mentioned his mother, while his father was only identified as Gonçalo. Initially classified as a merchant in the registers of confraternities, he first had an aristocratic "Don" added before his name and was finally identified as "Marquis," an extreme case of social mobility. He became a member of both the Spanish and the Portuguese confraternities in Rome, joining the first in the 1620s and the second in the 1630s, and assumed managerial and money-lending functions for both. He remained a member of both confraternities until he died, a revealing strategy for extending his social capital even after the independence of Portugal.[120] The sources of his wealth were already indicated in chapter 11, and I will add here that he lent money to prelates and noblemen, such as the Cardinal of the Santa Rota, the Duke of Infantado, the Count of Lerma, Count Filippo della Brodesiera, Cardinal of Aragon, Marquis Ottavio del Buffalo, Gran Condestabile Lorenzo Antonio Colonna, Duke Alessandro Caffarelli, Prince Savelli, Prince Livio Odescalchi, and Queen Christina of Sweden.[121] Francisco had several agents in Lisbon, particularly Jerónimo Nunes Peres.[122]

Nunes Sanches had two brothers, Gaspar de Paiva and Gonçalo Nunes Sanches, the latter a clergyman and a canon of St. Peter's Basilica, who accumulated benefices in Portugal.[123] Their sisters only arrived in Rome after 1640. Artemisia married Manuel de Palma; Catarina first married Gregorio Almeida and then the Count (future Marquis) Ottavio della Bordesiera, with a dowry of 15,000 scudi given by Nunes Sanches. Ana and Gracia became nuns. Their niece, Dianora (with a dowry of 14,000 scudi) married Afonso Peres Vergueiro, future marquis, who lived in accommodation belonging to Nunes Sanches on the Via Condotti. In the next generation, the most successful marriage of this ennobled family was by another Dianora, who married the Duke Alessandro Caffarelli with a dowry of 35,000 scudi, a marriage that had to be authorised by the pope.[124]

Francisco Nunes Sanches's will, dated July 9, 1689, modified a previous will from 1685 that had coincided with the creation of a fidecommisso for his nephew and heir, Francisco, son of his brother Gaspar. The modified will concentrated the greatest part of Sanches's wealth on the heir, in line with similar practices among these ennobled New Christian families. In the will, Nunes

Sanches mentioned a long series of relatives—the two sisters still alive in their convents; and several nieces and nephews, some of them already representing a third generation. He also left some money to the two confraternities, the Portuguese and the Spanish, with the former the more favoured. There was a long list of beneficiaries, both individuals (such as Francisco Nicolau da Silva) and institutions, and these included extensive payments to charities and payments for masses to be held for his soul in various churches, including the basilicas of St. Peter and St. John Lateran. He established rules for the succession to his fidecommisso, which, in the case of serial failures, provided for the succession of his grandnephew, Francisco Peres Vergueiro. Francisco Nunes Sanches declared that he worshiped the Holy Trinity in one God, the sacred humanity of Christ, the merits of his passion and mercy, and the protective intercession of the Virgin Mary, the angels and the saints. He chose to be buried in his chapel of San Lorenzo in Lucina.[125]

The other informal New Christian procurators in Rome did not have the same financial resources, but the one probably closest to Nunes Sanches was Francisco Nicolau da Silva, son of Rui Lopes da Silva, son-in-law of Duarte da Silva, knight of the order of Santiago (obtained for him by his father-in-law) and, later in life, count. He also had an account at the Banco di Santo Spirito, although this did not reach a high level of activity.[126] He was also a member of the archconfraternity of Ssma. Ressurrección, along with Baltasar Gomes Homem and Francisco de Azevedo.[127] Gomes Homem and Azevedo were very active members of the Portuguese confraternity, at least from the early 1670s on.[128] Baltasar Gomes Homem obtained papal bulls and briefs for the nomination of Portuguese bishops requested by the king, and many other documents concerning ecclesiastical benefices from the Datary. Gomes Homem's cousin, João Gomes de Moura, was his agent in Lisbon, and between them they guaranteed communication between the Portuguese ambassador in Rome, Bishop Luís de Sousa, and the royal court in Lisbon.[129] There is still research to be done into the affairs of Francisco Peres Vergueiro. He was probably the eldest son of Afonso Peres Vergueiro and Dianora, niece of Francisco Nunes Sanches. A gap in the recorded activities of the Portuguese confraternity in Rome between 1679 and 1695 makes it impossible to pinpoint when Francisco Peres Vergeiro acquired the title of marquis, but in 1696 he was designated as such in the records of the confraternity.[130]

In the 1640s and early 1650s, the close relationship of several of these informal New Christian procurators with the Datary had the support of Ferdinando Brandani (or Brandão), a financier and merchant in art, Conservatore of Campidoglio and Prefetto delle Composizioni at the Datary, whose portrait was painted by Diego Velázquez.[131] Ferdinando, brother-in-law of the banker Manuel da Costa Brandão and a close friend of Francisco Nunes Sanches, was involved in a scandal involving the forgery of papal documents that brought about his downfall, in spite of the protection of Cardinal Francesco Albizzi

FIGURE 14.1. Velázquez, Portrait of Ferdinando Brandani, ca. 1650, oil on
canvas, 50.5 × 47 cm, Museo Nacional del Prado, Madrid, inv. nr. P-7858.
© Photographic Archive Museo Nacional del Prado. Ferdinando Brandani was
a financier and merchant in art, Conservatore of Campidoglio and Prefetto delle
Composizioni at the Datary.

(1593–1684), whose mayordomo was Fernão da Costa Brandão, another
brother-in-law of Ferdinando.[132] Despite this setback, António Vaz Brandão,
son of Fernão, and António Gomes Homem, probably the son of Baltasar, were
involved as employees in the embassy of the Nuncio Ravizza in Lisbon in 1671,
which provoked a scandal in Lisbon.[133] In any case, there is evidence that the
relationship of New Christians financiers with the Datary, a crucial Roman
office for the issuing of ecclesiastical benefices and appointments, continued
for quite a while longer.[134]

These New Christian bankers and financiers had become firmly entrenched
in Rome in the upper echelons of extensive networks that included high offices
in crucial institutions of the Church and in the houses of the main cardinals.
They had inserted themselves into the Roman system of patronage, obtaining
cardinal protectors. For example, Francisco Nicolau da Silva asked that the
execution of his will be supervised by Cardinal Carlo Bighi, "mio signore et
unico padrone."[135] These cardinal protectors, any of whose death would create
a need for a replacement, were crucial for relative security in an ever-changing
world prone to constant intrigue and factional fighting for access to coveted
resources. Protection was obviously paid for, but relationships could become
quite well developed through shared interests in literature, art or sciences, and

even to sincere friendship, common values, and perceptions of justice, as New Christian grievances would reveal.

I agree with Ana Paula Lloyd's rejection of the traditional anti-Semitic view of material interest as the explanation for the New Christian appeal. The procurators were putting their positions and their wealth at risk, particularly in Lisbon.[136] Their exposed positions would be partially covered by papal protection during the appeal, but they knew they would pay a price in the long run—as they did. In the appeal to Rome there is clearly New Christian solidarity (ethnic, not religious), indignation at systematic injustice, and a genuine call for new rules (converging here with the Jesuit interest). Desperate reaction against the inquisitorial assault on wealthy New Christians that had radically eroded their reputation for trustworthiness, the basis for their economic and financial power, was obvious, but we cannot ignore the crucial issues of values and rights, which were very much in play at this period and were encouraged by the reformist tendencies of Pope Clement X and reinforced by Pope Innocent XI.[137]

This context helps us to understand the decisive action taken by Pope Clement X on October 3, 1674, in which he declared that he had decided to consider the appeal of the New Christians. He ordered the Portuguese inquisitors to interrupt their prosecutions of New Christians and any preparations for autos da fé. The inquisitors were suspended from their function and he, the pope, would take responsibility for the trials.[138] In Coimbra, the auto da fé planned for November 11 took place against the background of a threatened riot after agreement was reached with the papal nuncio. Most victims here were released without property confiscation, but this was not the case with the other tribunals, where detainees languished (some died) until 1681.[139] This unprecedented action, which reasserted the papal source of the jurisdiction of the Inquisition, had political consequences, specifically, the regent, Pedro, who was already having a change of heart because of pressure from the three orders of the cortes, turned against the New Christians.

The papal brief had been published by the nuncio without previous warning to the regent, who felt that his rights had been violated. He decided to change his representative in Rome, withdrawing Ambassador Gaspar de Abreu de Freitas, who had previously been the ambassador in London. We have met this character before as a zealous judge in Porto supporting the Inquisition during the repression of 1658. It seems that he played on both sides of this dispute, extorting money from New Christians.[140] The new ambassador, the bishop of Lamego, Luís de Sousa, was sent to Rome in May 1675, and consistently sided with the Inquisition, whose representative, Jerónimo Soares, was already there. They complained bitterly about the strong links between the New Christians and the cardinals.

The following years were an impasse. The cardinals proceeded to assess the appeal and appeared to agree with most of its grievances, but any hope of developments was blocked by the Portuguese Inquisition and Regent Pedro.[141] Clement X passed away on July 22, 1676, and Innocent XI was elected on September 9. Innocent simply reinforced previous policy concerning the Portuguese Inquisition, but he had to accept Regent Pedro's suggestion of Veríssimo de Lencastre, archbishop of Braga and one of the hardliners, as general inquisitor, and the archbishop was appointed on November 28, 1676.[142]

New Christians lodged a substantial denunciation of the scandalous life led by inquisitors and their deputies, accusing them not only of corruption, but also of concubinage. For example, they claimed that Manuel de Moura Manuel and Pedro de Ataíde had enriched themselves through the confiscations made by inquisitorial familiars in Coimbra; the general inquisitor had fathered several illegitimate children, and he had a new relationship with a nun from the convent of Esperança in Lisbon; Bento de Beja had fathered illegitimate children; Estevão de Brito Foios, Alexandre de Silva, and Manuel de Moura Manuel had abused and threatened women who resisted when their husbands were detained or about to be detained; Manuel de Moura Manuel had ordered the murder of a courier simply because the man wanted to be paid; and Manuel de Magalhães de Meneses, Pedro de Ataíde, and António de Vasconcelos had extorted money from candidates for the position of familiar of the Inquisition. These claims were presented with the names of the concubines and witnesses, particularly doctors and surgeons, and of abused husbands and fathers, some of whom had been forced to pay the dowries of concubines being placed in convents.[143] It is a bold picture of daily life under the Inquisition, with relationships of abuse between inquisitors and victims a regular feature. However, I consider it unlikely that this would have had a major impact on the cardinals.

From this period there also exists a long report on the devious practices of property confiscation by the Inquisition, a report that highlights the cases of Cristóvão Rodrigues Marques, a rich man of Elvas who was released without confiscation but did not have any property returned, not even his wife's dowry; Afonso Peres Paceto, a lawyer in Évora who had a large library; and Miguel Lopes Correia, another lawyer in Évora. There were individuals who appealed to Rome, particularly D. André, the son of Francisco Lopes Mendes from Évora, and Miguel Lopes de Leão, the son of Miguel Vaz de Leão from Lamego.[144] This issue of property confiscation and the underhand practices that went with it and were directly responsible for the poverty inflicted on numerous families is addressed in many other petitions from New Christians. The issue of restitution of property unfairly confiscated and sold clearly struck a chord among the cardinals. It is one of the items of the grievances that was unanimously supported. It was related to the basic rights of the accused, rooted in Roman law and renewed during the Middle Ages.

Innocent XI proved to be even more determined than Clement X to assert his rights as the source of inquisitorial jurisdiction. He asked for trials of New

Christians held since his election to be sent to Rome to be checked.[145] We know from the correspondence of the Portuguese representatives in Rome that he expressed his strong displeasure at the constant postponements introduced by the Portuguese Inquisition under various pretexts.[146] On December 24, 1678, Innocent XI issued a brief requiring the Portuguese general inquisitor to send him the records of five trials of negative offenders who had been excommunicated and executed within ten days. This order was countered by a strange move on the part of the regent, who ordered the archives of the Inquisition to be sealed, thereby invoking the power of secular justice.

The regent was clearly prompted by the inquisitors, who played the usual game of seeking protection from either the pope or the king, depending on the circumstances. This blatant disobedience did not go down well: Innocent XI issued another brief on February 18, 1679, suspending the general inquisitor and the inquisitors from their functions and attributing exclusive jurisdiction on heresy to the bishops. Although this was a major blow to the Portuguese Inquisition, the response had been prepared way in advance: the bishops, many of whom had started their careers in the inquisitorial bureaucracy, refused to accept the new jurisdiction given them by the pope. This refusal set the terms for negotiation for the next two years.[147]

In the meantime, there was a change of generation. António Vieira, who had played a crucial role in Rome—he had preached before the College of Cardinals, had been a regular at the literary salon of Queen Christina of Sweden, and had instigated and supported the New Christian appeal—returned to Portugal in 1675 to be confronted with a toxic political situation created by the Inquisition. In the following years, his absence did not seem to be felt in Rome, but it may have had an impact in the decisive period of 1679 to 1681. He was an old man, full of energy, with a papal bull exempting him from the jurisdiction of the Inquisition, but he found himself in an entirely hostile political field. He returned to Brazil in January 1681, probably anticipating defeat.[148]

Duarte da Silva was pulling strings against the Portuguese Inquisition in the 1660s, as we saw, and probably influenced (and financed) the appeal to Rome in the 1670s. He died on September 19, 1677, in Antwerp, at the age of eighty-two, having lived thirty years after his trial by the Inquisition of Lisbon. The reading of his will occurred the day after his death in the presence of his widow, Branca de Silva, his nephew, Jorge Dias Brandão (also detained in 1647), his second son, Francisco (detained in 1647, he had fought with the Spaniards in the Franco-Dutch war of 1672 to 1678 and been made Marquis of Monfort by the Emperor in 1682), Filipa de Castro e Silva, Luísa de Castro e Silva, Ana de Lima, and Duarte Brandão.[149] On November 8, 1677, the inventory of property revealed that Duarte's youngest son, João da Silva, had married Luísa de Castro e Silva, had died, and had left a son, Duarte João da Silva (who had been tutored by his uncle, Francisco); Jorge Dias Brandão had married Duarte's daughter, Catarina; and Duarte Brandão da Silva and Beltran de Morales had been the witnesses to the will. The inventory showed an enormous quantity of diamonds; dozens of paintings, including portraits of Duarte da Silva's children and grandchildren; painted *biombos* (Japanese screens); numerous tapestries (one set showing the history of Alexander); sculptures in marble of the four continents; furniture; and textiles from India.[150]

Manuel da Gama de Pádua was arguably the New Christian leader among the procurators in Lisbon owing to his long experience in trade, finance, politics, and in conflicts with the Inquisition dating back to the 1640s. He died on September 29, 1679,[151] at what was a crucial moment in the negotiations to obtain a solution to the political deadlock between Rome and Lisbon. The forces involved were too powerful for the absence of one man to derail the proceedings, but Manuel da Gama had made a difference at the very beginning of the process.

In Rome, the death of the Cardinal Protector of Portugal, Virginio Orsini, in 1676, did not have an impact: Orsini was peripheral to the negotiations. But the same cannot be said about Cardinal Francesco Barberini, who was responsible for the Congregation of the Roman Inquisition, Dean of the College of Cardinals, and head of the Fabbrica di San Pietro, and who passed away on December 10, 1679. He had played a crucial role in all the process of the suspension of the Portuguese Inquisition.[152]

The activities of the New Christians and the Portuguese representatives in Rome can be summarised with reference to a single question: How much could they influence the relevant cardinals and the pope? The correspondence of the ambassador, Luís de Sousa, offers abundant laments on the financial resources of the New Christians; their admission into, and even their presence, as masters and employees, in the cardinals' houses; and their ability to persuade others in favour of the appeal. Each movement is noted, confirming Norbert Elias's thesis of court society as a place of constant vigilance and observation of the rising or falling value of each agent, according to the prince's favour.[153]

In letters written between March and May 1678, Luís de Sousa sounds exasperated. He laments the power of Francisco de Azevedo, the New Christian procurator in Rome, who is spreading the idea that the regent has sent him, de Sousa, simply to appease the Inquisition; that he is partial to the tribunal because he has been bribed; that the inquisitors have been corrupted with money extorted from the New Christians (Azevedo has pointed to the sudden enrichment of João da Costa Pimenta in Évora, and the decision by Veríssimo de Lencastre to accept much less as General Inquisitor than the annual 50,000 cruzados he received as archbishop of Braga, suggesting he expects to obtain more from the New Christians); and finally that more than half the vassals of the Portuguese king, including the nobility, have New Christian blood, and any decision against the New Christian appeal would affect them all.[154]

According to an obviously stressed ambassador, Francisco de Azevedo has even offered to resign as New Christian procurator if he receives a clear order from the regent, implying that the prince secretly favours the New Christians. Luís de Sousa ends up asking the regent to denaturalise Francisco de Azevedo, although this never happened.[155] The ambassador was dismayed when he received information that Francisco de Azevedo had sent a precious gift of chocolate to Cardinal Cibo, secretary of state under Innocent XI, who had accepted it. Luís de Sousa feared that more important gifts would follow, despite Cibo's reputation for probity.[156]

The ambassador became even more nervous when he saw Azevedo in the same coach as Cardinal Colonna, who, with Cardinal Altieri, was frequently accused of being on the New Christian side. The New Christian procurator was, "on the left side of the back seat, where the Duke of Savoy or the Duke of Florence would be," and he concluded, "and this [Colonna] is one of the judges of our request."[157] In a long letter advocating the reinstatement of the decree expelling New Christians reconciled at the auto da fé, which would have meant the immediate exile of the procurators Pedro Álvares Caldas and Manuel da Gama de Pádua, the ambassador laments the presence of Abbot Brandão as chamberlain to Cardinal Albizzi, and of António Correia Bravo's son in the house of Cardinal Ottobono.[158] There are also many references to cardinals' servants being bribed to get them to act as spies, reporting on correspondence and discussions at meetings.

However, despite all the ambassador's efforts to collect information and have regular meetings with the cardinals and the pope, he only noticed two months later, on April 30, 1679, the issuing of the crucial papal brief of February 18, in which Innocent XI suspended the general inquisitor and all the inquisitors, transferring the jurisdiction of the Portuguese Inquisition to the bishops.[159] Luís de Sousa lamented the absence of frankness in Rome, since Cardinal Cibo had hidden the brief from him, repeatedly insisting that there was no news. Luís de Sousa had been wrong footed by the clever cardinals, who used the nuncio in Lisbon for speedy and crucial communication, knowing that if the information was conveyed first by the ambassador, the regent would take steps to avoid publication of the papal brief.

On this crucial issue of the suspension of the Inquisition, the diplomatic scene seems to have been in permanent flux both in Lisbon and Rome, that is, the ambassador expected to be rewarded by the king, and the nuncio expected to the rewarded by the pope. This is why the nuncio, under pressure from the New Christians, kept the Inquisition under surveillance and reported to Rome all its infringements of papal briefs. The allegiances in play were well defined, as were the interests at stake. To circumvent the Portuguese ambassador was part of the game. The brief was published without giving any notice to the regent, who felt aggrieved at what he saw as a disregard for his exclusive legal privileges, although until the eighteenth century these privileges were frequently in conflict with those of the pope.

Analysis of the role of these agents, the ambassador, Luís de Sousa, and the inquisitor, Jerónimo Soares, shows that they opposed the New Christian appeal the best they could and consistently reproduced the stereotype of a widespread Jewish apostasy that only the Inquisition could tame, a fragile assertion after almost one and a half centuries of intense prosecution.[160] They alleged that they represented the interests of the Portuguese Crown, which was denied by the New Christian procurators, and they invoked the threat of riots because of vast support for the Inquisition, a threat viewed by the cardinals as a sign of disobedience to the pope. Their role in obtaining intelligence, putting pressure on the Roman court, and contributing to defining policies back in Portugal, was decisive.

The ambassador had consistently advised the regent to resist any request for records of trials by the pope as an assault on the autonomy of the Portuguese Inquisition and the privileges it had received from the king. This was known in Rome via the Jesuits' (Manuel Fernandes) and the New Christians' access in Lisbon to the letters of the ambassador, and it contributed to the latter's relative isolation in Rome. However, the deadlock was an embarrassment for everybody. On top of this, the financial capacity of the New Christians in Rome was no match, in the long term, for the institutional advantages of Portugal.

Finally, the ambassador and the regent had to acquiesce to the pope's request for records of five original trials, which had been discussed since July 1679 and which a tenacious Innocent XI had refused to withdraw. It took another two years of continuous negotiation and selection of trials in Rome. The first trial was refused by the ambassador because it was "inadequate," meaning it would confirm the reasons for the New Christian's appeal. It took several months for the ambassador and the inquisitor, Jerónimo Soares, to select and order the translation of two trials they were willing to pass on, and these were finally submitted to Innocent XI on December 23, 1679.[161]

The final decision took more than eighteen months, having been delayed by the detention of one of the nuncio's servants in Lisbon, considered an attempt on ecclesiastic immunity, and also by the idea floated by Innocent XI that any reinstatement of the Inquisition would have to be accompanied by the replacement of the general inquisitor and all the inquisitors, a request later narrowed to focus on the inquisitors Manuel de Moura and Bento de Beja, who were considered disobedient and disrespectful of the pope.[162] In fact, no punishments for disobedience towards the pope were implemented, which confirmed the Portuguese Inquisition in its idea of victorious resistance, although this narrative needs to be nuanced, as we shall see in the next chapter.

The period of suspension of the Portuguese Inquisition is a rare case of an appeal that was lodged by a minority systematically persecuted through blatant racism, which was accepted by the pope for analysis by a council of cardinals linked to the Roman Inquisition. The justice of the procedure was at stake: whether accusations were based on blood prejudices; whether property should be confiscated immediately upon detention, long before sentencing; whether there should be different procedures for Old and New Christians; whether accusations should be accepted on the word of a single witness, or on the word of slaves or servants who had been manipulated; and whether practices of long detention and the detaining of relatives, including minors, to extort false confessions and accusations were acceptable. This is arguably one of the first cases in which the rights of a minority were brought clearly to the forefront of a legal debate. Most cardinals agreed with New Christian grievances. The latter's right to question the legality of the Portuguese Inquisition's procedures was thus supported in Rome, leading to the suspension of the Inquisition judicial procedures for seven years. This suspension became a crucial case of political experiment, with the different players trying to push the limits of their actions and floating various threats to make the others withdraw.

The Inquisition mobilised the three estates and swung the attitude of the prince when the matter became an issue of royal rights threatened by papal intervention, while the papal court used the New Christians and the Jesuits to reassert its power in Lisbon by seeking to control the Inquisition. The Portuguese Jesuits were wrong footed both by the successful reaction of the Inquisition and by the changing allegiances and political configurations in Rome. For example, Cardinal Colonna, who was a supporter of the New Christian appeal, was also a member of the congregation for the Propagation of the Faith (*Propaganda Fide*), and in this role he defended French missionaries against the Portuguese royal patronage of the Church in Asia.[163] In this struggle, the interests of the Portuguese Jesuits were at stake, and they needed the support of the regent and the ambassador in Rome against the *Propaganda Fide*.[164] The suspension of the Portuguese Inquisition was clearly political, and the endgame (full reestablishment of the tribunal of faith) revealed how the balance of political power had shifted; but the legal issues involved cannot be underestimated. They reflected and, up to a certain degree, preceded the debate about rights and justice that would loom large in the eighteenth century, entering the mainstream with the work of Cesare Beccaria nearly a century later.[165]

CHAPTER FIFTEEN

Breakdown

ON AUGUST 22, 1681, the papal brief *Romanus Pontifex* reestablished the Inquisition in Portugal. The endgame saw an almost complete triumph of the Portuguese Inquisition. There was no general pardon for the New Christians, and although the reestablishment of the tribunals had some significant strings attached, the tribunal returned to its old rhythm after two relatively timid decades. The general inquisitor and the other inquisitors kept their jobs. The political deadlock between Portugal and Rome had been concluded largely according to the conditions set by the Portuguese regent and the three estates. The pope had engaged with the New Christians' appeal, and he had tried to reform the inquisitorial procedure in Portugal, but there was a gap between the way Innocent XI conceived the reopening of the Inquisition and the way the tribunal received his brief and implemented it.

The following decades are crucial in this history of the New Christian elite. They need to be addressed in a systematic way, looking not only at Portugal but also at Spain and other countries, because the suspension of the Portuguese Inquisition had been a major episode on the international stage. New Christian networks were not restricted to one country, as I have demonstrated in this book, and the conditions of persecution in Portugal had an impact across countries and continents. I shall now tackle the reestablishment of the tribunals, the practices of the Portuguese Inquisition following their reestablishment, and the political consequences of the new framework. The international context will also be addressed, mainly in relation to the War of Succession in Spain, which impacted the New Christian elite second only to the reestablishment of the Inquisition in Portugal. The developments of maritime trade and world economies will be addressed in this chapter, because they too affected New Christian networks.

1. Reestablishment

The papal brief has been interpreted as a victory for the Portuguese Inquisition, supported by the king and the three estates.[1] I agree, but with two caveats: the intentions of the pope were distorted by the way the brief was celebrated and implemented in Portugal; and while the brief did reinstate the tribunals, it slowed down inquisitorial activity for two decades.[2] A proper analysis is necessary because of the clear gap between the perceptions of the authorities in Rome and the inquisitors in Portugal. This gap was identified by a carefully judged book published in London in 1730 on the history of the Inquisitions in Spain and Portugal, which presented the brief as "promulgated in favour of the New Christians" (these are the book's precise words).[3]

This book highlights thirty points from the brief and, in a reading that I would concur with, suggests they represent a refusal of racial discrimination, as we would put it nowadays, and an assertion of the rights of the accused, with the two issues shown as inextricably entangled. The first section of the brief can be summarised as follows: New Christian estates shall not be confiscated before sentence; an inventory of an accused person's property shall be made in the presence of a relative and given to him or her; an accused person's family shall be maintained by his or her estate and his or her creditors paid; accused persons shall not be detained without strong suspicion of breaking the law; accused persons shall not be kept in prison longer than necessary and shall be released as soon as possible, without having to wait for an auto da fé; a lawyer can be chosen by an accused person from outside those appointed by the Inquisition; a defence lawyer shall have access to all information concerning the trial, including the names of witnesses who will be called; the enquiry on the defense shall be dealt with according to canon law; New Christians shall be able to testify on behalf of the accused and against Old Christians; no proof of Judaism shall be deduced from a person's being of Jewish origin.[4]

The following points are also to be noted: no officers or wardens of the Inquisition shall be appointed guardians or tutors of any minors accused, and such people shall refrain from making suggestions as to guardianship; those accused without proof shall be discharged immediately; an accused who does not name someone who has denounced him in his confession cannot be judged as obstinate; refusal to denounce relatives cannot be taken as sufficient grounds for judging a detainee guilty; witnesses upon whose testimony accused persons are condemned shall be many in number and of good standing, and there shall be no question of their having testified falsely (thus condemnation by single witnesses or slaves is disallowed). The issue of proof is mentioned several times, particularly the exclusion of "things impossible" and "indirect proof"; the articles of accusation shall be presented in full to the accused and his lawyer; confessions obtained by force, disregarding the age, sex, or competence of the accused cannot be used; the prisoners shall be treated with charity and receive religious books.[5]

This set of rules can be considered relatively restrained, although they included almost every one of the New Christian grievances. They concerned procedure, which can always be interpreted with latitude. However, it was expected that they would be taken seriously; they showed the clash between different juridical cultures and the forward-looking nature of the New Christian grievances, which had guided the papal brief. The property rights of accused persons and their relatives was the first issue addressed by the pope, with clear condemnation of the abuses of immediate sequestration and selling of property at the point of detention. The newly established procedure was a response to almost a century of plunder by the Inquisition and its officers, the result of widespread corruption, as we have seen, which had thrown thousands of families into poverty and forced many to emigrate.

The integrity of the accused was another issue addressed here that reflected developments in legal culture; that is, the usual abuse of detaining relatives in order to obtain denunciations was exposed, although not resolved, while the protection of close relatives by the accused was implicitly considered acceptable. Respect for the property and the family of the accused were therefore the two main issues emphasized by the pope. The issue of proof was the third main concern, with condemnation on the testimony of a single witness being implicitly rejected, and condemnation on false accusations indicated for avoidance, while indirect proof (hearsay) and "things impossible" (the pope may have had in mind the accounts of invented Jewish rituals supposedly performed by António Homem and denounced by other New Christians, which were included in his files) were indicated for exclusion.

Banning the nomination of officers of the Inquisition as guardians or tutors to accused minors (below twenty-five years of age) should be seen as related to the exclusion of forced confessions (obtained under torture) obtained without regard for the age, sex, or competence of the accused. This is a crucial issue in relation to minors, women, and old or frail people, which again related to the integrity of the accused. Freedom to choose a lawyer and the tribunals' obligation to present all the accusations and the full scope of the trial to the accused's lawyer would create a different legal setting. The practice of keeping the detained in prison without proof, waiting for the collection of denunciations, was clearly dismissed, while rejection of the other abuse of forcing prisoners to wait for an auto da fé, sometimes for years, completed the papal assessment of the rights of the accused.

There was also a crucial acceptance of the New Christian complaints against ethnic prejudice, or as they would have put it, negative distinction, because of their Jewish ancestors. Pope Innocent XI, in this brief, declared that New Christians could be accepted as witnesses in favour of other New Christians or against Old Christians, while "no proof of Judaism shall be deduced from a person's being of Jewish origin." I repeat this phrase here, because it is an extremely important principle that exposed the racist foundations of the tribunal in Portugal.

The Portuguese Inquisition was an institution driven by racial divide, practicing systematic discrimination against, and persecution of, New Christians of Jewish origin from the 1530s to the mid-eighteenth century.[6] Although the Spanish Inquisition can be defined the same way, owing to its prodigious early prosecution of conversos (and then Moriscos), the Portuguese Inquisition's long-term overwhelming focus on New Christians, which increased over time, reinforced its racist impact on Portuguese society. It is true, however, that blood purity statutes were more widely used in Spain than in Portugal and had a long-lasting impact there. The context is important: fluid early modern Iberian states were shaped by interdependent relations and changing balances of power between social groups with their own agency. Where institutions were weak and fragmentary, the Church played a major role, monopolising the power to legitimate violence, define policies, and regulate social conflicts. The dominant role of the Inquisition, in alliance with the episcopate, amplified the Catholic Church's function of controlling ethnic exclusion from, or inclusion in, society through its blood purity enquiries. Papal admonition of the Portuguese Inquisition had to be acknowledged, even if the consequences were minor.

The papal brief basically accepted the legitimacy of the New Christians' grievances and sustained this position against (indeed, was probably reinforced by) all the efforts of the Portuguese ambassadors and agents to denigrate this ethnicity as intrinsically apostate. Political considerations did not allow the pope to extinguish the Portuguese Inquisition, but we cannot dismiss his public backing of a persecuted minority, even if the procedure and legal principles defined by the brief could be, and indeed were, eventually overturned by practice on the ground. From a legal point of view, New Christians won the day, although they felt bitter at the way the Portuguese Inquisition loudly celebrated the reestablishment of the tribunals without any penalties or dismissal of inquisitors. From a political and a social point of view, New Christians had lost their case. The reestablishment of the Portuguese Inquisition dealt a fatal blow after all the blows they had already suffered at the hands of the Iberian Inquisitions during the seventeenth century. But it required more than the reestablishment of the Inquisition to exclude the New Christian merchant elite from Portuguese society.

The failure of Innocent XI's attempt to satisfy both sides of the conflict between New Christians and the Portuguese Inquisition must be seen in its international context. He had struggled for several years with Louis XIV of France over the absolutist monarch's effort to exert his power over the Catholic Church in his kingdom, an effort embodied in the issuing of what were known as the Gallican Liberties. These four articles, approved on April 11, 1682, by an assembly of the French clergy, limited papal leadership to spiritual matters and stated that the pope's judgment was not irreversible, thus denying the infallibility of the pope, a feature that was only in fact defined as a dogma by the Catholic Church in 1870.[7] Long-term opposition between the theological and political visions of the Jansenists and the Jesuits was part of this conflict, with the Jesuits, who favoured the central position of the pope, obtaining the support of Louis XIV against the Jansenists, who were accused of siding with the Calvinists in matters of free will and divine grace. These conflicts would contribute to the revocation of the Edict of Nantes in 1685, through which Louis XIV tried to ease his tense relations with the pope. The situation in England was also closely monitored by Innocent XI, because Charles II did not have children and succession to the throne by his brother James, who had converted to Catholicism, was a strong possibility. James duly succeeded in 1685, although his alignment with Louis XIV became problematic to the pope.[8] Finally, negotiations for the provision of the bishoprics in the Portuguese empire were not easy either because of the debate around the royal patronage.[9]

These were crucial years. Innocent XI did not want to pursue a fight with the king of Portugal that he seemed to have no possibility of winning, given the Portuguese bishops' refusal to assume inquisitorial functions. On the other hand, Innocent XI was a sincere reformer, not only on matters of moral and administration—he was labelled "father of the poor," and he reduced nepotism and controlled sumptuary expenses—but also on matters of religious minorities, opposing the detention of Jewish people and curbing the campaign for their conversion.[10] His main adviser, the jurist Giovanni Battista de Luca, who was nominated cardinal in 1681, had denied a previous doctrine of the Church condemning Jews to a condition of servitude, a doctrine later reasserted by Benedict XIV.[11] The reform of justice was at the core of the papal brief *Romanus Pontifex*, which addressed the rights of the New Christians as a main concern. The impact of New Christian grievances on the reform of justice and the development of the rights of the accused still needs to be integrated into legal history.[12]

The way in which the papal brief was received in Portugal represented a perverted view of the document's intentions. There were feasts to celebrate the reestablishment of the Inquisition in Lisbon, Évora, and Coimbra with fireworks, lights at the windows, church bells ringing, popular demonstrations conducted by familiars of the Inquisition shouting "Long life to the Faith, Death to the Jews." In Coimbra, a straw statue identified as "Father António Vieira" was dragged through the streets to the doors of the Jesuit College, where the door was hammered on and insults shouted, before the figure was taken to the main street and burnt. The level of violence was such that the king had to send knights and soldiers onto the streets of Lisbon to avoid major incidents.[13] In Coimbra, the celebrations lasted four days.[14]

The brief had been sent with a recommendation to the papal nuncio in Lisbon that he should warn the king and the general inquisitor against any retribution against New Christian procurators who had presented the appeal to Rome. This was not respected. The reintroduction of the Inquisition was further celebrated by the organisation of autos da fé: in Coimbra, on January 18, with 67 sentenced presented; in Évora, on February 15, 1682, with 109 sentenced; and in Lisbon, on May 10, 1682, with 106 sentenced. In the auto da fé in Lisbon, three major New Christian contractors who had died in jail—Diogo de Chaves, Simão Rodrigues Chaves, and António Nunes da Veiga, son of Sebastião Nunes da Veiga, all knights of military orders—were absolved, which meant that they could finally be buried with Christian ritual.[15] But four New Christians were excommunicated and executed: Gaspar Lopes Pereira, the son of Francisco Lopes Pereira (whose trial in Spain was analysed in chapter 13), a merchant who affirmed his Jewish faith; António de Aguiar, a merchant and another case of pride in Judaism; Miguel Henriques da Fonseca, a lawyer who also persisted in his Jewish allegiance; and Pedro Serrão, half New Christian, son of António Serrão de Castro, presented at the same auto da fé, who refused to confess and died as a Christian.[16]

In the next two years, the Inquisition managed to hold various autos da fé to deal with prisoners whose prosecution had been blocked by the Inquisition's suspension. Diogo Rodrigues Henriques, son of António Rodrigues Mogadouro, who was excommunicated as negative, was presented on August 2, 1682.[17] His father, who had died in jail after spending his last hour saying the name of Jesus after confessing several times to a Dominican, was finally excommunicated postmortem and presented at an auto da fé in the church of São Domingos on November 26, 1684, more than five years after his death and three years after the papal brief. The inquisitors looked for likely heirs, including relatives in Mogadouro, asking them whether they wanted to represent the former contractor; however, they all declared they did not want part of the inheritance, probably knowing that it would mean a long and useless judicial process because the property had been confiscated.[18] This enquiry meant that the direct relatives had either been executed or escaped after reconciliation.

New Christians did not lose their voice after the reestablishment of the tribunals. They complained to Rome about the celebrations by the Inquisition; about the destruction of several New Christian houses following forced confessions, such as that of Fernão Rodrigues Penso, or that of António Rodrigues Mogadouro, who had never confessed, contrary to the rules defined by the brief; and about an excess of violence in jail that led to suicides, such as that of Rodrigo Nunes del Cano, and the case of Pedro Serrão, who died claiming to have been a Christian all his life.[19] They protested that the recovery of confiscated property had become no easier, and that all the prisoners who had been released were still waiting for their property to be returned. They also denounced the inquisitorial argument that condemned a refusal to confess by those who did not want to inculpate their children, when there were many clergymen, monks, and nuns who did not confess even under duress. And they noted that the Inquisition had started to nominate hundreds of new familiars, a tactic devised to reward and enlarge social support.[20] The Jesuits also wrote to the pope asking to be exempted from the jurisdiction of the Inquisition, because the position they had taken in favour of New Christians might be used as evidence of their having supported heretics.[21] The situation was extremely tense with an ongoing conflict between the Jesuits and the Inquisition that would take time to heal.

The celebrations and autos da fé represented a good political move to suggest support from Rome and score again against New Christians, but the general inquisitor was well aware that there could be a legal backlash. With the general council, he highlighted twenty-five important points in the brief that needed consideration: they concluded that thirteen were in line with what they were doing (this was not the case); and twelve looked likely to impose changes, particularly on property confiscation and acceptance of New Christian testimony.[22] But the implicit prohibition of condemnation upon one single witness, the free choice of lawyers, and the full access of the defence to the accusations were never implemented. Also, trials would now take more time to prepare and the activity of the Inquisition would be slowed down. The lists of sentenced persons presented at autos da fé that were compiled by António Joaquim Moreira show a peak in the 1660s, with 3,007 trials; then a contraction in 1670s, with only 1,379 trials, owing to the suspension of the Inquisition; followed by another contraction in the 1680s, with 934 trials, and a further contraction in the 1690s, with 529 trials.[23] The records for these two last decades show the lowest number of inquisitorial trials of the whole of the seventeenth century in Portugal. But we need to look at the royal policies of the era to get a full picture of the consequences of the reestablishment of the Inquisition.

On September 1, 1683, a law of "extermination of the Jews" (meaning exile) was published by Regent Pedro, two weeks before he was acclaimed king after the death of his incapacitated elder brother. The law reinstated the previous failed attempt to expel New Christians who had been reconciled by the Inquisition, but this time it was limited to those who had confessed and abjured in forma. João Lúcio de Azevedo dedicates three pages to this extraordinary law, highlighting the penalty of expulsion after two months' confinement in the college of the Doctrine of the Faith, with the option of remaining for spouses not themselves convicted, and a requirement that children under seven be left behind, with those aged two or three to be placed in a foundling wheel. The contrast with the charitable and profamily concerns of Innocent XI is striking. Azevedo concludes that the law did not have a major impact, suggesting that it may not have been implemented to any great extent.[24] But implemented it was, which made a big difference to the life and destiny of New Christians, because they could not return to the kingdom, under penalty of death and property confiscation, and similar penalties were applied to any who helped them.

The Marquis of Gouveia, majordomo (or master) of the regent's house and president of the Desembargo do Paço, was nominated to supervise the implementation of the law and received precise instructions relating to the transport and family arrangements of the condemned (wives could be sent to houses of seclusion, *recolhimentos*, next to convents). On October 8, 1683, the general inquisitor was required by King Pedro II to send a list of those New Christians who had abjured in forma.[25] Notes on the implementation of the sentences show the names of the convicted and specific letters for each of them, asking where they wanted to be transported. The list compiled in the year 1683 was followed by new lists elaborated in 1684, 1685, 1698, 1702, and 1703 for the implementation of the law.[26]

The slowdown imposed on the Inquisition by the papal brief was thus largely compensated for by the policy of expulsion implemented by the king. The law of extermination was suspended in 1704,[27] and this date coincides with an interruption of the sequence found in a codex created by the Marquis of Gouveia. Opposition to the Inquisition's expulsions finally won, defeating a policy previously explained by the New Christians to Rome in these terms: the inquisitors used the possibility of expulsion to extort false accusations, and confessions were extorted by the Inquisition and then denied by the victims at the confessional.[28] However, the political situation was ambiguous. The War of Succession in Spain had intensified and both the Portuguese king and the Habsburg candidate to the Spanish throne needed New Christian support. Let us look at a particular case to understand the full extent of the convergence of inquisitorial and royal racist persecution.

Fernão Rodrigues Penso (see chapter 14) had fallen into the inquisitorial trap of confessing to regain his liberty. There was no real proof that he had engaged in Jewish practices. Most probably, as one witness suggested in his trial, he was an atheist, or more likely, a freethinker. Without a confession, he could well have been excommunicated and executed. But the consequences of his confession were devastating. His economic standing had been seriously damaged on December 3, 1672, a few months after his detention by the Inquisition, when a warrant of attorney had been signed by João Vieira Matoso, probably an Old Christian, a fidalgo of the royal house, a knight of the Order of Christ, and the administrator of the property and house of Fernão Rodrigues Penso, including a contract for terças. Matoso named as his agents the previous administrators contracted in various judicial regions of Portugal (*comarcas*) by Rodrigues Penso, followed by all their names (twenty-one) and places.[29] João Vieira Matoso was the godfather of Fernão's son, which suggests that he stepped in with the agreement of Rodrigues Penso.[30]

Following his confession, Fernão was reconciled, with formal abjuration and property confiscation in 1682. Two days after he was presented at the auto da fé, a royal *alvará* ordered the erasing of Fernão's name from the register of fidalgos of the royal house, which meant that he lost privileges and judicial standing.[31] This was unprecedented. New Christians traduced in autos da fé could be awarded royal privileges soon after; they had never lost their royal privileges. This meant that Fernão's loss of citizenship and expulsion were preceded by exclusion from royal privileges. Recall that after 1681 there were apparently no more cases of New Christians granted exemption from blood purity rules so that they could access military orders.[32] To sum up, Fernão Rodrigues Penso's case highlights irrefutably the political turn against New Christians in Portugal.

The inquisitors were relentless in this case, as in many others. They went after Fernão's son, Fernando de Morales Penso, then twenty-five years old, who only confessed and denounced his father after being read a fake sentence of excommunication (meaning execution), a trick frequently used by the inquisitors when they did not have proof of Judaism and desperately needed a confession.[33] Fernão was again detained on August 3, 1683, for failing to mentioned his son in his confession (which was against papal guidance), and at this point he decided he had had enough of this vicious game. He insisted that the only new denunciation must certainly have come from his son, declared it was not true, openly complained about the practice of extorting denunciations from relatives, refused to confess or incriminate himself, accused the inquisitors of persecuting him based on only a single witness (he knew the papal brief), and then kept his mouth shut.[34] Now seventy-one years old, he was tortured but still refused to confess, was reconciled at a new auto da fé, and was sent into exile in Castro Marim for three years.[35] He had declared that he had an inheritance from his father, who had died in Lima, to collect in Seville, and if he survived all these ordeals that is where he probably ended up. In any case, he made no further appearance in Portuguese documentation.[36]

Now for a brief digression into inquisitorial methods. Fernão never saw his son after 1672. When he was presented at the auto da fé, on May 5, 1682, his son had been detained on April 25, 1682, ten days earlier. The son was paraded in the auto da fé on August 8, 1683; five days after Fernão was detained again by the Inquisition, but the son was then exiled to Brazil.[37] This revealing story demonstrates inquisitorial methods. The Roman cardinals were right to agree with New Christians that the Portuguese Inquisition needed to be reformed, but it was clearly incapable of reform; racist and inhumane behaviour were engrained in the institution.

In October 1683, Fernando Morales Penso wrote from Brazil to the Jesuit Manuel Ferreira, declaring that he had been a Catholic because he had been baptised, that his declarations to the Inquisition had been false, and that he had confessed to what he had not done for fear for his life. He also promised to present his case to the pope, and he finished by asking the Jesuit to present this declaration at the tribunal, which the Jesuit did. The declaration was appended to the trial record, probably waiting for other accusations; before the papal brief it was possible to take action following a confession of perjury.[38] The Inquisition also went after the two legitimate daughters of Fernão Rodrigues Penso, Ana Maria, a nun at the convent of Odivelas, who was detained on August 3, 1683, presented at the auto da fé on December 12, 1684, and released after being sentenced to abjuration of mildly suspected heresy; and Mariana de Morales Penso, detained August 4, 1683, and presented at the auto da fé on November 11, 1684, and released having been sentenced to abjuration of vehemently suspected heresy.[39]

2. Rome and Madrid

The consequences of the reestablishment of the Portuguese Inquisition were felt in various parts of Europe, particularly in Rome. The expulsion from Portugal of reconciled New Christians was followed by spontaneous emigration. The best-known case concerned the escape of Manuel da Gama de Pádua's sons to Rome in the early months of 1683. It should be remembered that Manuel da Gama was a procurator of the New Christians in Lisbon and a long-term financier of the Portuguese kings from the 1640s to the 1670s. The pope had protected Portuguese New Christian procurators against the retribution of the inquisitors, but several cases occurred in which these provisions were violated. This protection was reiterated by the pope and the nuncio alongside the brief of reestablishment, but to no avail.

The first of Manuel da Gama de Pádua's sons to arrive in Rome was José da Gama, the youngest (twenty-one years old), who complained that on January 5, 1683, the Inquisition had detained his uncle, Manuel Sequeira, the brother of his deceased mother. He wanted to place himself under the jurisdiction of the Roman Inquisition for any accusations of Judaism that might be levelled against him. Manuel Sequeira's detention was considered a sign of things to come, in line with the usual extortion of denunciations from relatives to reach the real targets. José declared that his brother António, the eldest of Manuel da Gama de Pádua's three sons, could not escape from Portugal because his privileges would be revoked and his property confiscated. However, after the middle brother, Fernando, arrived, he was finally followed by António (then twenty-six years old), a fidalgo of the royal house, knight and comendador of the Order of Christ, and treasurer of the royal chapel.[40]

The three brothers and another relative, Francisco Soeiro, presented themselves to the Roman Inquisition with the support of the abbot Francisco de Azevedo, a former procurator for New Christians in Rome, who obviously kept strong links with this family (he even functioned as interpreter in this presentation). António declared that he had left Lisbon on May 17, 1683, without permission from the prince (then, still regent); he left letters to the prince, the secretary of state, the archbishop of Lisbon, and the royal chaplain. His first session at the Roman Inquisition was on July 5, 1683. All his property in Portugal had been confiscated, including rents of 3,000 scudi a year, and he had lost the job of treasurer of the royal chapel, which had been in his family for thirty years and which had now been given to someone else.[41]

The king obviously had declined to give any guarantees to António da Gama, and the latter, all too aware of inquisitorial procedure, had preferred to abandon the comfort of his inherited positions rather than to risk detention, humiliation, and demotion. It seems that António da Gama de Pádua stayed in Rome and managed to reach some kind of accommodation with the Portuguese royal house, because his son, Raimundo (or Ranunzio) Filipe da Gama de Pádua, on March 16, 1711, was granted the title of *cavaleiro fidalgo* (fidalgo knight), the same status as his father and grandfather. This brought Raimundo 10,600 réis of moradia every month and one *alqueire* (bushel) of barley every day.[42] Raimundo had been involved in the business of ecclesiastical benefices at the Roman Datary with other well-known New Christians, such as Manuel de Andrade, Pascoal da Paz e Silva, Francisco Soeiro de Azevedo, and Gaspar Peres Vergueiro.[43]

The family Correia Bravo is another case of wealthy New Christians who decided to move to Rome after the reestablishment of the Inquisition. The process was smooth, they obtained the authorisation of the king, and the outcome was even more successful than it had been for the da Gama de Pádua family, because they quickly obtained the title of marquis. We have come across the names Bravo and Correia Bravo several times in this study. The head of this branch of the family was a royal contractor, André Gomes Bravo, who was married to Clara Mendes, the daughter of Domingos Coelho, a goldsmith. They lived in Rome in the first half of the seventeenth century and had two sons, António Correia Bravo, married to Filipa Santiago, another New Christian, and Bento da Silva Bravo, married to Brites de Gusmão, an Old Christian.[44]

António Correia Bravo, a fidalgo of the royal house, was a major merchant who left a vast fortune to his elder son, André, and money from the terça (taxation from municipalities) for the creation of entailed property for his grandson, António. He had another son, Francisco Correia Bravo, who became a secular clergyman (later an abbot), and three daughters, who all became nuns at the convent da Rosa in Lisbon.[45] António Correia Bravo received the habit of the Order of Christ, with a pension of 20,000 réis, on March 8, 1666.[46] On January 2, 1673, he was appointed a deputy of the Junta do Comércio (the council of trade).[47] António died in 1680, and his will had important consequences. His brother, Bento da Silva Bravo, also a merchant, was detained by the Inquisition in 1683, after its reestablishment. He accused his nephew and son-in-law, André, who was married to his daughter Clara da Silva, of Judaism.[48]

André was detained on August 8, 1683. Then thirty-three years old and a knight of the Order of Christ, he had three sons and two daughters: António, ten years old; Francisco, three; Carlos, two; Maria, seven; and Leonarda, six months.[49] Miguel Israel Vitória, the person who denounced him, declared that a significant number of members of the Bravo family lived publicly as Jews in Hamburg, that they maintained close relations with the Correia Bravo family, and that a young member of the Hamburg Bravo family had been hosted by André.[50]

In the inventory of his property, André indicated a vast fortune of 40,000 cruzados inherited from his father, plus another 30,000 from the disposable third part of his parents' assets, totalling 70,000 cruzados. His main investments were in the tobacco monopoly (2,500 cruzados), with the contractor Amaro de Barros, familiar of the Inquisition (8,000 cruzados), and in the Junta do Comércio (6,000 cruzados). There were other investments (less than 2,000 cruzados) with the fish merchant, Domingos Rodrigues, and the merchants Pedro de Figueiredo, Manuel Alves Falcão, and Jorge Maximiliano (a German). He also acted as a pawnbroker, making extensive loans to noblemen against collateral, particularly to Lourenço de Souto Maior, António de Azevedo Coutinho, Lourenço de Lencastre, the Count of Feira, the Count of Vila Flor, the Count of Atouguia, royal officers, priests, soldiers, merchants, and artisans. André must have been the major banker in Lisbon in those days, investing in public funds and private merchants' businesses with fixed interest of 6.25 percent, while engaged in substantial lending and pawnbroking activity against collateral. He declared an enormous number of jewels, mainly diamonds, silverware, cutlery, and tapestries. He also traded goods, for example, a bundle of coral sent to Goa worth 3,000 cruzados. Finally, he had two houses in the Rua da Galé and two others in the Alfama neighbourhood, and he was about to buy the houses of Dr. José Galvão Lacerda.[51]

The inquisitorial procedure was a mixture of old and new strategies. André Correia Bravo denied all accusations, his resolve probably stiffened by the law of extermination, which made any confession fatal. He was tortured but held out.[52] The new inquisitorial procedure stressed more clearly the need to obtain the truth, although torture, given the little proof the tribunal had, was clearly excessive.[53] The final sentence was lenient compared with those handed out previously: André was spared a public auto da fé and abjured *de levi* (mild suspicion) at the tribunal, an uncommon practice of the Portuguese Inquisition in the past and probably influenced by the Roman Inquisition, which deliberately refrained from public ceremonies.[54] The papal brief had an undeniable impact on inquisitorial procedure, primarily after 1683, and up to the early 1700s. This may explain the election as cardinal of the general inquisitor, Veríssimo de Lencastre, on September 7, 1686. This appointment was certainly proposed by King Pedro II and was granted by the same Pope Innocent XI.

The will of André Correia Bravo's father, António, signed on August 4, 1680, was used as a pretext for the family's escape to Rome. The three executors of the will were the bishop of Rio de Janeiro and secretary of state, the Dominican Manuel Pereira; António's brother, Bento da Silva Bravo; and his son, Francisco

Correia Bravo.[55] António had established dowries for his daughters' maintenance at their convent: for each one, 75,000 réis of tença, made up of 30,000 from an investment in the customs of Lisbon, 25,000 from the Lisbon fish house, and 25,000 from the monopoly on tobacco. He recommended increasing the dowry to 100,000 réis each, as one of the daughters had died. And he was to be buried within the cloisters of the monastery of Carmo, in Lisbon. Distribution of the bequests would only take place three years after his death. André and Francisco would be his heirs; and they would have to create an entailed property for his grandson, António, and his descendants.

The will's profuse pious legacies were accompanied by donations to the wives of Sebastião Jorge, Manuel Coutinho, and Sebastião Coutinho in Amsterdam, and to the family of José Nunes Franco and the daughters of Pedro de Baeça in Lisbon (the execution of these legacies, via Bento da Silva Bravo, is attested by notary's records from Amsterdam). The king and the Marquis of Fronteira owed money to the deceased (amounts not listed); and António mentioned account books for the identification of debtors in Hamburg, Venice, Livorno, and Goa. From the terça (the third part of the inheritance, which he was allowed to dispose of freely), 15,333,368 réis (or roughly 38,333 cruzados) was to be used to create entailed property for his homonymous grandson. This money was guaranteed by ten bags with *dobrões* of gold and silver, and by cargoes from Goa sent by António Diogo Martins de Moura traded in partnership with António Rodrigues Marques.[56]

There is a request by André Correia Bravo to move his house to Rome, because his brother Francisco had arranged a marriage there for the young António. He wanted to move his available money and create the previously mentioned entailed property there. On January 20, 1687, the king issued an alvará in which he accepted the request to move to safeguard the investment in an entailed property being arranged for the minor, António. However, André Correia Bravo needed to leave a guarantee, and this stipulation was accepted by Amaro de Barros on his behalf.[57] The papers related to the will included an apology from André for not being able to find the value of the terça, but apparently everything was sorted out and the family all went to Rome. Finally, on June 29, 1687, a certificate was issued in Rome, signed by João dos Santos Caria, apostolic notary at the archive of the Roman Curia, according to which the Count of St. Peter, Francisco Nicolau da Silva, had invested 18,000 scudi (about 54,000 cruzados if they were scudi d'oro) at the Secca (or mint), at 4–4.5 percent interest, an amount given by Francisco Correia Bravo, as executor of the will, for an entailed property for his nephew António.[58] But this is not the end of the story. The Correia Bravo family already had connections in Rome through the extraordinary trading network developed by António, who had also subsidised the Portuguese embassies from the 1640s onwards. However, in the 1670s he managed to place his son, Francisco, in the household (and under the protection) of none other than the powerful cardinal Pietro

FIGURE 15.1. Church of Sant'Antonio degli Portoghesi, engraving of the façade in *Studio d'architettura civile sopra varie chiese, capelle di Roma, e palazzo di Caprarola, et altre fabriche con le loro facciate, spaccati, piante e misure*, Part III (Rome: Domenico Rossi, 1721), p. 35. Courtesy Bibliotheca Hertziana, Max-Planck Institut für Kunstgeschichte.

Ottoboni, the future Pope Alexandre VIII (r. 1689–1691).[59] In 1675, Francisco Correia Bravo was elected governor of the Portuguese confraternity of St. Anthony, a function he took up on January 1, 1676.[60] The confraternity, as we have seen, was an ideal place to extend networks of solidarity. The involvement of Count Francisco Nicolau da Silva in their affairs is another indication of the family's immediate integration into Roman society.

André Correia Bravo soon obtained the title of marquis, but he died in 1694, whereupon the title passed to his elder son, António, who should have inherited from both sides of the family, because the only inheritor of Bento da Silva Bravo was his daughter, the Marchioness Clara da Silva. In 1700, Bento da Silva went so far as to buy the Mausoleum of Augustus, on top of which had been built the Pallazo Soderini, which was in a poor state of repair and which he set about restoring.[61] Bento's will, which was drawn up between 1700 and 1702 (he died in November that year), showed the first signs of divergence from tradition: he revoked a previous decision to make his grandson António his universal heir and gave this position to his daughter.[62] The executors were his nephew, Francisco Correia Bravo, and Francisco Soeiro de Azevedo. He wanted to be buried at the church of St. Anthony, next to his brother André.

With the exception of the Marquis of Fronteira, who owed him 6,000 cruzados, debts to Bento da Silva Bravo were owed him by his network of agents and associates including his half brother, Pascoal Pereira, in Pernambuco, then in Maranhão, where he died; 1,000 cruzados, to be recovered from the selling of houses in Lisbon to his friend Amaro de Barros, blocked by his grandson, António, who wanted to recover his inheritance; Miguel Osório de Almeida in Amsterdam (Jerónimo Nunes da Costa was mentioned as a witness, but he had already died, as well as a certain Gomes, brother-in-law of Álvaro da Costa in London); António Ribeiro Quaresma in Rio de Janeiro; Francisco de Aguiar in Bahia, who had died and left his wealth to the Carmelites; an inheritance, also in Rio, from Jacinto de Campos, his father-in-law, which included part of the dowry he should have received and money from farms he had sold (Jacinto's son-in-law, Duarte Ximenes, was to be charged); Francisco Esteves Barros and Miguel Carneiro da Costa in Pernambuco (also dead leaving debts); and in Lisbon António Casado de Gamboa, treasurer of the house of Aveiro, who had asked for 1,000 cruzados for the ransom of a cousin in Algiers, Manuel Casado, which had been taken care of but never repaid; Gabriel Arias in Livorno (a man of well-maintained accounts); João dos Santos Caria in Rome; and Agostinho Ribeiro and Manuel de Mota in Goa.[63]

It must have been after the death of his father that Marquis António Correia Bravo decided to take action to recover every last part of his inheritance. This action was mainly taken against his uncle Francisco; but, as we have seen, it was also aimed at his maternal grandfather, whose financial transactions in Lisbon had been blocked. An action against his uncle Francisco, now an abbot, for the sequestration of his property, particularly his houses in Lisbon, due to the abbot's failure as executor to implement the grandfather's will, was launched in Lisbon in 1704 through the procurator João Barbosa Barreto, who subcontracted the power of attorney to Manuel Fernandes Crasto and Francisco Trigueiro Góis.[64] This involved a request to rescind the declaration of execution of the will. António also declared that the certificate of investment in the Secca was not valid, for the executor of the will had kept the title to the investment, which had been made in Venice, not in Rome, where this type of investment did not exist.[65] However, the judicial action was not successful. Francisco Correia Bravo managed to defeat a similar action in Rome, and he sent the judgment in his favour to Lisbon, where the sequestration of property, ordered in 1706, was lifted in 1707.[66]

The Marquis António Correia Bravo, who in 1695, following the death of his father, had registered a full list of the properties he possessed in Portugal, in 1718 requested permission to sell those properties, bonds, and equities to concentrate his entailed property in Rome.[67] The Marquis lived a long life (1673–1760), and this request represented a clear intention to break with Portugal. His then agent in Lisbon, Alexander Hus (or Heusch), was named consul for the German nation in 1718.

It seems that the deaths of Marquis Francisco Nunes Sanches in 1689, Marquis André Correia Bravo in 1694, abbot Francisco de Azevedo in 1697, Count Francisco Nicolau da Silva in 1699, the knight Bento da Silva Bravo in 1702, and Marquis Gaspar Peres Vergueiro in 1708 marked a turning point for the links between New Christian communities in Rome and Lisbon. These were major bankers and financiers who had become noblemen. Their descendants would not have the same sense of attachment and New Christian solidarity as they completed their families' integration into the local aristocracy, as had already happened with the Marquis Ximenes in Florence. However, the lives of Raimundo Filipe da Gama, Manuel de Andrade, Pascoal da Paz e Silva, Francisco Soeiro de Azevedo, and other New Christians active in Rome in the early decades of the eighteenth century still need to be the subject of comprehensive research.

3. International Context

Jonathan Israel considers that the War of Succession in Spain (1702–1713) was the crucial turning point, after which the fortunes of the Sephardic Jewish communities of northern Europe declined. These communities supported the Habsburg candidate to the Spanish throne, Charles, who was defeated after a long international conflict and civil war in Spain. In doing this they aligned themselves with an international coalition that included the Netherlands, England, the Holy Roman Empire, and Portugal against France and (a divided) Spain. The change in alliances, from Spanish-Dutch in 1648–1698 to Spanish-French from the 1700s onwards, would have represented a decisive blow. The focus of Jonathan Israel's history is Jewish communities, not New Christian networks, but their destiny was connected. These communities and networks followed the interests of the countries where they lived and operated, and their axes of activity adapted to political and economic shifts. Bankruptcies among Jewish bankers and merchants at the end of the War of Succession partly explains the significant decline of such communities, but we need to understand why they invested so much, putting their survival at risk. Israel also highlights changes in international trade in this period, with the development of mercantilist policies by France, England, and the Netherlands, which certainly played a role.[68] This vision is useful, but it needs to be nuanced. The outcome of the War of Succession promoted French interests in the Atlantic, but the English also managed to reinforce their position. Jewish communities in southwest France and London thrived. Major New Christian families in both Spain and Portugal received a heavy blow, but they did not disappear, as we shall see.

The question that needs an answer is: Who replaced New Christians in the late seventeenth and eighteenth centuries as major royal contractors and financiers? The obvious successors would have been foreign merchants and Old Christians, whose background and new capacities need to be better understood. We know that Flemish ships traditionally traded salt from Setúbal and Aveiro in Portugal, playing a crucial role in preserving fish in northern Europe. English ships carried bacalao (salt cod) from Newfoundland to Bilbao in the Basque Country and Porto in Portugal, a trade initially shared by the French and Portuguese. Dutch, English, and French ships carried textiles to Spain and Portugal, and Jewish and New Christian networks participated in both the legal and the illegal strands of this trade. German ships traditionally carried cereals, iron, timber, and equipment for naval construction from the Baltic to the Iberian Peninsula. In the fifteenth and sixteenth centuries, the Portuguese king operated a policy of privileges (such as low taxation) for foreign merchants to attract capital and develop international trade.[69] In the seventeenth century, Italian and German merchants had a strong presence in Lisbon, followed by Dutch, English, and French merchants. From the 1570s onwards, Portuguese merchants lost control of trade between Portugal and northern Europe.[70]

Although Italian, Flemish, and German merchants participated in the first stages of overseas Portuguese expansion in the Atlantic and the Indian Oceans, the Portuguese king excluded foreign merchants from trade with his colonies. Portuguese merchants controlled most of the trade between Portugal and its colonies, but there were always partnerships with foreign merchants. The Castilian king excluded foreigners from the carrera de Indias very early, in 1504, but we know that Portuguese merchants moved to Spanish America in significant numbers. English and Dutch smuggling to Spanish America became extremely important in the seventeenth and eighteenth centuries.[71] In the meantime, English, French, and Dutch merchants established a strong presence in Seville and Cadiz.[72] The presence of foreign merchants was related to the inability of the Iberian countries to produce sufficient manufactured commodities for both the internal and overseas markets. Portugal also had a structural weakness in its cereal production, which meant it failed to feed its own population and needed to import.

The Dutch had built the most powerful commercial fleet in the Atlantic, although their activities were curtailed in the second half of the seventeenth century by a series of navigation acts passed by the English (and followed by Anglo-Dutch wars), in which transport by foreign maritime powers was forbidden.[73] The ironic, but unsurprising, result of northern European piracy was a dramatic increase in Portuguese and Spanish use of Dutch ships and freight carriers in the Atlantic, which was made possible in the Spanish case by the Peace of Münster, a treaty signed between Spain and the Netherlands in 1648. The reversal of alliances made by the Iberian countries with the Netherlands, in the Portuguese case reinforced by the expulsion of the Dutch from Brazil in 1654, increased Dutch naval capacity and triggered the passing of protective laws by England that allowed the development of the latter's own commercial fleet. The victory of the Portuguese over the Dutch in the Atlantic was followed by increased maritime cooperation, although this never existed in Asia, where the Dutch managed to conquer several important Portuguese cities and territories, such as Malacca, Kochi, and Sri Lanka.

Mercantilist policies in northern Europe increased in the second half of the seventeenth century, targeting commercial maritime transport and ownership. The decline of the Spanish navy was one component of this shift, while the Dutch and the English fought to gain the upper hand in this area. France also tried to strengthen its navy, but Louis XIV's advantage was in his territorial army, which started to represent a threat to the Netherlands.[74] This army would play a major role in the War of Succession in Spain. Meanwhile, improved English commercial maritime capacity had an impact on the Iberian Atlantic islands, particularly the Canary Islands, and to an even greater extent Madeira, which, from the mid-seventeenth century on drew a significant number of English merchants attracted by the wine trade and the position of the island as a staging post on the voyage from England to its newly acquired colonies in the Caribbean islands and North America.[75]

Partnership with Dutch, English, and German merchants became increasingly important in Porto and Lisbon during the seventeenth century, always linked to the colonial trade, mainly sugar from Brazil, but also spices, textiles, and precious stones from South Asia, where New Christian merchants started to use English ships for their trade with Europe. Access to American silver was crucial for foreign merchants in Spain, where it paid the deficit in the commercial balance. Meanwhile, a divergence developed between the international alliances of Spain and Portugal in the last decades of the seventeenth century. In Portugal, French ascendancy was visible at the royal court, partly because of Queen Marie Françoise of Savoy, whose influence eclipsed that of Queen Catherine of Braganza, the wife of the English king, Charles II. Initially, Portugal recognised Philip V, but it quickly changed sides. The Portuguese eventually decided on an alliance with the English, owing to the latter's growing naval power and the protection they could provide for Portugal's colonial empire. In Spain, the final decision to accept the Bourbon succession to the childless King Carlos II instead of the Habsburg candidate made sense, because it would accommodate the closer and more threatening territorial power.[76] This strategy would define a structural alliance that survived even the French Revolution.

These alliances were fuelled by the strategic considerations and political interests of the different countries involved, but at the same time, they impacted local communities of foreign merchants and were modified as a result of pressure from these groups. Such communities are generally excluded from political, diplomatic, and even economic history, but they played a role in developing markets and, at certain moments, in promoting the interests of their countries, while some themselves lost out or benefitted from shifts in international alliances. The history of these communities on the ground is still to be investigated in a systematic way, but it is crucial to collect every piece of information that may contribute to understanding the competition New Christian merchants encountered and the possibilities that existed for replacing them as major merchants and bankers. We have already seen several cases of partnership between New Christian and foreign merchants—Italian, Dutch, German, French, and English—as well as cases of competition for access to markets, particularly the attempt by Italian merchants to obtain a share of the Roman financial market, extremely important owing to its distribution of dispensations, and it briefs of nomination to, and transfer of, benefices, rents, and pensions.[77]

From 1641 to 1648, 907 foreign ships entered the port of Lisbon. Although the available information is fragmented, making aggregation by country of origin a hazardous operation, I note 236 Dutch ships, 229 English and Irish, 105 Hanseatic (mostly from Hamburg), 51 Danish, 34 Spanish, 30 Swedish, 17 French, 14 Genoese, and 14 from Livorno. We can already see there is almost parity between Dutch and English ships (which, with Irish ships, represented 25 percent of the total). If we jump more than seventy years, in the year 1720 alone, the port of Lisbon received 158 English ships, 58 French, 51 Dutch, 22 Spanish, and 9 from Hamburg.[78] These figures show a relative decline in Dutch and German ships, a consolidation of the French position, and the overwhelming importance of English trade and maritime transport, although none of this was achieved in a linear development. We must keep in mind the opening of Portugal to Dutch, French, and English trade during the War of Independence, while James II's defeat at the battle of Boyne in 1690, followed by repression and expropriation, triggered Irish and English Catholic migration. The War of Succession in Spain would have had contrasting impacts on English merchants in Castile and French merchants in Portugal.

Foreign merchant communities in Portugal never reached high numbers: English merchants in Lisbon were estimated to be around 33 both in 1673 and 1686, but seventy years later, when the earthquake of 1755 struck, they numbered 155.[79] There are no clear long-term figures for the Dutch or the Germans: 160 Dutch were counted in Lisbon between 1580 and 1620, and 28

Germans in 1605; but both numbers increased in the second half of the seventeenth century.[80] The number of French merchants active in Lisbon varied between 18 in 1686 and 56 in 1699, declined after the great persecution of 1705, but recovered after the War of Succession. There were around 35 French commercial houses in 1755.[81] With the exception of dangerous periods during the war, foreign merchants were in general well integrated.

Although the Iberian countries did not recognise freedom of conscience for Protestant merchants and sailors during the sixteenth century, which led to some notorious inquisitorial trials, peace treaties concluded in the early seventeenth century by Philip III with England and Hamburg, followed by a truce with the Netherlands in 1609, brought not a formal confessional recognition but a nonconfrontational practice, as long as members of these nations who had been born Protestant did not worship in public.[82]

The peace treaty between Portugal and the Netherlands in 1641 guaranteed, for the first time, "freedom of conscience, privately in their houses and ships" for all Dutch people in the territories of the kingdom of Portugal.[83] Moreover, many foreign Protestants converted to Catholicism, which proves that a tendency to local conformity was widespread and affected more than New Christians. Between 1641 and 1691, 151 Germans from Hamburg and nearby cities converted, while 58 Dutch and 4 Flemish took the same step.[84] Conversion was important for promotion, because being a Protestant would block any permanent honour or privilege, excluding ambitious men from the status of royal vassal or member of a military order.[85]

Northern European merchants, who generally migrated at a very young age as apprentices, married Portuguese women as well as women from their own group or other foreign merchant groups living locally. The project of social promotion was visible, and many of these foreign Catholic merchants succeeded. One of the main paths to raising one's status was to become a familiar of the Inquisition, which in principle required a blood purity enquiry, which was waived in the case of northern Europeans, who were considered of pure blood, as in the case of the Hamburg-born Diogo Timão, German consul in Porto; João Canjuel of Antwerp, consul for the Germans and Flemish in Évora; Pedro Pedrossen from Hamburg, who lived in Porto and obtained royal contracts; and the family Heusch, who became consuls for the German community for several generations into the eighteenth century.[86]

Another path for raising social status was to join a military order, which also involved a blood purity enquiry. Sebastião Lamberto, whose father João, born in Hamburg, had operated in Portugal and Brazil during the War of Independence, provided ships, marine equipment, and 50 looms for the production of sails in Portugal, recruited crews and artisans, and became overseer of the royal treasury in Brazil and a member of the Brazil Trade Board. He was rewarded with membership of the Order of Christ and the privileges of a cavaleiro fidalgo in 1694. Pedro da Maia (Maier or Meyer?) from Lübeck had financially supported the infant Duarte, who was detained by the emperor, and the Portuguese ambassadors to the Hanseatic league, had offered loans to the king, and had sent building materials for fortifications. He received a comenda of the Order of Christ, later transferred to his son Diogo da Maia, who also obtained a patent of cavaleiro fidalgo in 1664. Pedro Hasse and his son André outfitted the fleet to recover northern Brazil from the Dutch, made loans to the king, and secured 250 ships for Portugal between 1651 and 1690. André Hasse obtained membership of the Order of Christ in 1671, became a familiar of the Inquisition in 1675, was made a cavaleiro fidalgo in 1691, administered the taxation of Brazilian sugar, and was appointed to the Brazil Trade Board. His son, Pedro Hasse, inherited these positions and privileges.[87] There are no equivalent studies of Catholic Irish, English, or French merchants in seventeenth-century Portugal, although the ennoblement of 28 French merchant families in the eighteenth century followed a similar path.[88]

Traditional practices of social promotion by the king in exchange for financial support were therefore applied to foreign merchants at exactly the same time as the New Christians were losing status. This promotion was not new. In the sixteenth and seventeenth centuries, important Italian merchants became financiers to the king, both in Castile and Portugal, and obtained access to noble status. But these last decades of the seventeenth century seem to indicate an increase in the scale of these practices. We do not yet know the real extent of this shift, but some foreign merchants from northern Europe acted as financiers for the king, lending money, farming taxes, and participating in royal financial institutions. The situation in Spain reflected the strong presence of foreign merchants in various ports, mainly on the Mediterranean. In Madrid, Genoese (from the sixteenth century on) and New Christians from Castile and Portugal controlled the market for royal loans from the 1620s to the 1680s, slowly withdrawing from that investment in the 1690s, not really because of inquisitorial persecution but from monetary reform coupled with a chain of suspensions of payment.[89]

Cadiz played a major role because of its monopoly of the American trade after 1717, but before that date its position complemented that of Seville. Cadiz attracted a significant number of foreign merchants after it was licensed to ship European textiles to America in 1633, a licence extended to all trade with the Americas in 1679. A list of obligatory donations to the royal finances from 1662 reveals more than 105 foreign merchants, divided between Dutch (30), French (29), Genoese (23), English (13), and Flemish (10), besides Germans from Hamburg, Venetians, and Armenians.[90] The absence of Portuguese New Christians in Cadiz is significant and is confirmed by lists of donations for the following years. The few who stayed were most probably granted citizenship. But they still played a role in the War of Succession, as we will see.

French merchants had the upper hand in Spain in the last decades of the seventeenth century, even before the War of Succession. In 1686, the French controlled 39 percent of all the Spanish American trade through the demand for their textiles. The case of the Flemish merchant, Pedro Colarte, is quite exceptional because of the vast capital he accumulated during his life. Foreign merchants shared the monopoly with Castilians, and some of them were ennobled; for example, in 1700 the owner of the main French trading house obtained the title of Marquis of Villa Panés.[91] Barcelona and Valencia also attracted a significant number of foreign merchants, particularly Italian and French, as did Cartagena and Malaga. The northern ports of Spain played a constant part in maritime trade, particularly in shipping cod from Newfoundland to Bilbao, a trade controlled by English ships from the 1620s onwards, but did not attract an equivalent number of foreign merchants.[92] And it does not look as though any foreign merchants were involved in royal contracts and loans to the king at the level the New Christians had been until the 1680s.

The War of Succession in Spain precipitated changes. The acclamation of Philip V, grandson of Louis XIV, who was accepted as the real king in the first decade of his reign, protected the interests of France in Spain in a very direct way. In 1701, a slave trading contract with the Portuguese Company of Cape Verde and Cachéu was rescinded in favour of a new French company, which multiplied the French interests in Spanish America. The unilateral termination of the Portuguese company's contract by the Spanish king was followed by a promise of compensation of 300,000 cruzados on July 28, 1701, but this was never implemented. The promise was used to negotiate a peace treaty with Portugal, the idea being to prevent that country from becoming a member of the alliance in favour of the Habsburg candidate for the throne; but the attempt was unsuccessful. Governors in Spanish America felt free to put an embargo on the Portuguese company's ships, preventing them from landing in various ports (three embargoed from Cartagena, five from Havana) and to detain administrators accused of contraband, such as Gaspar de Andrade in Maracaibo, who subcontracted the import of slaves to the Dutch West Indies Company in 1700.[93]

The Portuguese company's asiento for the slave trade, agreed upon in Madrid on July 5, 1696, for six years and eight months, in exchange for a deposit of 200,000 silver pesos, had been supported by the Portuguese king on October 20, 1696, and registered in Madrid on January 22, 1697. Daniel de la Plaza, Gaspar de Andrade, João Barbosa da Costa, Jorge Fernandes Ferreira, Leandro Vieira, João Batista Machado, Pedro Franco de Paiva, Pedro Nunes Guedelha, knight of the Order of Christ, and Manuel Ferreira de Carvalho, resident of Madrid, were among the founders and administrators of the company. It was Manuel Ferreira de Carvalho, negotiator of the asiento, who launched legal action in Madrid (but failed) to obtain payment of the compensation promised by the king for losses incurred through embargos and nonpayment for previous deliveries of slaves. There is more research to be done on these names, but João Batista Machado was half New Christian, father of

Bento Bravo da Silva who had been prosecuted by the Inquisition in 1682 and sentenced with formal abjuration and property confiscation.[94]

In 1702, trade in Spain by subjects of the Holy Roman Emperor, the English, and the Dutch was forbidden, which triggered an alliance in favour of the Habsburg candidate, Charles. French merchants were favoured with exemptions from taxation, registration, and inspection of their ships, and they monopolised contracts for the provision of arms, munitions, and military equipment. The explicit purpose of French policies was to guarantee the dominance of French industry and French control of the markets in Spain and Spanish America.[95] The carrera de Indias suffered a clear disruption between 1700 and 1705, while French merchants took advantage of new opportunities. Many dozens of French ships traded in Spanish American ports, and it is estimated that, for example, between 1695 and 1726 they controlled more than 60 percent of the external trade of Peru.[96] French migration to Spain was already significant during the early modern period, but a reversal of alliances created a new dynamic. The impact on trade was significant, but it is difficult to evaluate the extent to which New Christians were replaced in various areas.

The group of royal financiers in the first years of Philip V's reign included the banker, Bartolomé Flon; the Basque treasurer to the Queen, Juan Francisco de Goyeneche; Juan Francisco Eminente (a New Christian), Hubert Hubrecht, Jean-Jacques Yon, and other French bankers based in Cadiz and Madrid; the Italians Rubini and Spinelli; and the Englishman, Francis Archer.[97] It seems that other Spanish financiers linked to royal institutions played a significant role, particularly as brokers during the sale of offices between 1704 and 1711. One of these was Tomás de Pomar y Mainar, a member of Philip V's Council of Aragon and later Marquis of Miana, whose father, from Aragon, had been a member of the Contaduría Mayor de Cuentas attached to the Council of Finances. Another was Ventura de Pinedo, an accountant at the Tribunal of Mayor de Cuentas.[98]

The Italians clung on; the French joined the circle of royal financiers; there was even an Englishman, and probably a German (this needs more research); and there is still one New Christian, so they were still active in royal finances and contracts, as we shall see. Old Christians became important, with the Basque network of relatives and associates of Juan de Goyeneche playing a major role in royal loans and contracts for provisioning the army and navy, obtaining concessions for the monopolies on salt and tobacco, and for the privilege of producing publications. Goyeneche was the editor of the *Gaceta de Madrid*, which indicates a new relationship between finances and communication.[99] The emergence of Basque financiers is not surprising. The Basque country had a long history of mining and exporting iron; Basques had managed the main port for the cod trade in Castile and Aragon; and in the War of Succession, the Basque country was the main point of entry for French troops, who then needed provisioning.

French territorial expansion threatened the very existence of the Netherlands during the Franco-Dutch war (1672–1678) and the Nine Years War (1688–1697), with the latter conflict already involving some of the main contenders in the War of Succession. Jewish bankers from Amsterdam, particularly Antonio Álvares Machado and Jacob Pereira, provided loans to the States General and obtained contracts for provisioning the army, while the Jewish financier Baron Francisco Lopes Suasso acted as Spanish Resident and another Jew, Baron Manuel Belmonte, arranged Spanish reimbursement for the Dutch expedition to defend Sicily from the French in 1675. During the War of Succession, these bankers renewed their contracts with the Dutch army and navy. Moreover, they were used by the Archduke Charles, along with other Jewish financiers, such as Baron Francisco (Isaac) Ximenes Belmonte, nephew of both Manuel Belmonte and Jerónimo Nunes da Costa, as representatives in Amsterdam and other Dutch towns.[100]

The New Christian Joseph Cortissos (probably related to the Cortizos), an associate of Machado, became chief contractor to the Archduke in the Iberian Peninsula. Joseph Cortissos had been born in Antwerp, the son of Abraham Senach Cortissos, who had joined the Jewish community in Amsterdam after trading in Spain and Morocco. However, Joseph did not follow his father to Amsterdam. Instead, he became a contractor for the army in Flanders during the campaigns of the 1690s, and then became a general contractor for the army of Archduke Charles during the War of Succession, an operation that included seeking supplies of horses and grain in Morocco.[101] The French called attention to the financial role played by the Jews in supporting the archduke, and this had an impact on the New Christian presence in Madrid, which had been weakened by the withdrawal of the Portuguese Marquis of Minas in 1706, a few months after conquering the city. The Castilian supporters of Philip V used the supposed threat posed by Jews and Protestants as propaganda against Archduke Charles.

French troops started to reverse the fortunes of Philip V after 1706. The vicissitudes of war were necessarily linked to financial support, and in the case of Archduke Charles, this support was uncertain. His expenses far exceeded the contributions promised by the various allies, which were always paid late and seldom paid fully, while Jewish and New Christian financiers invested too much money in a faltering enterprise that would never properly reimburse them. Military strategy was fiercely discussed at the time. The archduke was most concerned to hold Valencia and Catalonia, areas that would obviously support him against the French, but he never managed to control Castile. A divergence of interests among the allies emerged with a secret treaty that the British negotiated with the circle of Archduke Charles in 1708, but a change in the fortunes of war, and a new Tory government in Britain in 1710, led to direct secret negotiations with the French that would define the Treaty of Utrecht, which was concluded in 1713.[102]

In 1711, the accession of the archduke as Holy Roman Emperor Charles VI made his claim to the Spanish throne unviable. France and Spain made territorial concessions to the Holy Roman Empire in Italy and Flanders, to the British in the Atlantic and the Mediterranean (Gibraltar and Menorca), and to Portugal in the Rio de la Plata and the Amazon, while guarantees of their right to fortified frontiers were given to the Netherlands. The main winner was Great Britain, because it obtained the contract for the slave trade with Spanish America, and this market was opened to annual British shipping that totalled 500–650 tons.[103]

The outcome of the War of Succession represented a big blow to the Jewish bankers of Amsterdam and to those New Christian financiers who remained in Portugal and Spain after half a century of inquisitorial persecution. The defeat of Archduke Charles and the Peace Treaty of Utrecht left some bankers with heavy losses and they never entirely recovered their investment. According to Jonathan Israel, Joseph Cortissos, Solomon de Medina, and other contractors went bankrupt.[104] However, this statement needs to be qualified. In the case of Cortissos, he left relatives actively trading in London, such as Abraham Cortissos, and there is a trail of documents about his own continued activities.[105]

The case of Solomon de Medina is even clearer because of his involvement in a political and financial enquiry. The Tories, pushing for the peace treaty secretly negotiated with Louis XIV, used the testimony of several contractors to the army in the Netherlands to accuse the Duke of Marlborough of demanding bribes for signing agreements for the provisioning of troops, and of keeping for himself 2.5 percent of all the royal money allocated to the maintenance of the troops. The commission created to enquire into this accusation reported at the end of 1711 that the duke had illegally received £63,319 in the previous ten years for contracts to provision the troops, plus 2.5 percent of royal money provided to pay foreign troops, amounting to £177,696.[106]

The contractor who triggered the enquiry was Sir Solomon de Medina, royal knight, who denounced the scheme of bribes, citing payments for provisioning contracts made by him from 1707 to 1711 and by the previous contractor, Antonio Álvares Machado, from 1702 to 1706.[107] It is probable that Solomon de Medina made a significant financial loss on these contracts, which would explain the denunciation, but he left a clear trail of private and public cases of litigation, including over debts from the War of Succession, and these can be seen in the National Archives.[108] Solomon de Medina's will, written with his wife, Ester de Medina d'Azevedo, registered in Amsterdam on June 6, 1727, and translated into English in 1730, does not indicate an extraordinary fortune, but he did leave around £10,000, including his wife's dowry.[109]

{≈≈≈≈}

The reestablishment of the Inquisition in Portugal in 1681 dealt a major blow to the New Christians, followed by the disruption of the relative (and ambiguous) support they had received from the regent and King Pedro II. This king imposed the loss of privileges and expulsion of all the New Christians reconciled in forma (with confession) by the Inquisition. The War of Succession in Spain saw the majority of New Christians and Jewish bankers supporting the Habsburg candidate to the throne. Defeat of the Habsburg coalition, which involved Austria, England, the Netherlands, and Portugal, meant that loans were never recovered.

The assertion of national interests, in which control of trade and manufacturing privileges played a major role, became patent in the sequence of wars that ran through the seventeenth and early eighteenth centuries. Wars were fought to obtain new territories and new resources, but also to extract access to new markets, as happened with the French in Spain and Spanish America and the British in the Atlantic. The protection of a nation's merchants and manufacturers simply meant that these actors had managed to manipulate their states into defending their interests as state interests, a long story eventually theorised by John A. Hobson in 1902, but clearly understood by those involved in this period.[110]

Merchant transnational diasporas, such as the New Christians, became increasingly limited in their scope and possibilities. The uneven decline of Jewish communities in Venice, Amsterdam, and Hamburg in the late seventeenth and early eighteenth century was attributable both to international and local political developments, although the Jewish community in London thrived and the community in Livorno kept a high profile. These developments, in my view, cannot be separated from the disruption of the New Christian elite in Iberia and Spanish America as a result of internal policies. The War of Succession in Spain reveals how entangled these processes were. However, New Christian merchants did not disappear from one day to the next. They tried to survive on the peripheries and showed some resilience concerning state contracts in Spain.

CHAPTER SIXTEEN

Immersion

STUDIES OF NEW CHRISTIAN ethnicity in the eighteenth century are relatively scarce, with most scholarly attention focusing on the previous two centuries. The eighteenth century is rightly considered the period during which this ethnicity and its specifically plural identity disappeared, but the process of its immersion in a global society needs to be better researched. I decided to engage with the decline of New Christian merchants because I am against an exclusive focus on so-called glorious periods. Decline and disappearance are as significant and tell us a great deal about social reorganisation—in this case, how new political, economic, and social configurations made hybrid or plural identities very difficult or impossible to perpetuate. This period requires a much deeper exploration than I can provide here, but it will be useful to define the main issues, add some archival material, and raise a few hypotheses for further research.

I did not choose "Immersion" for the title of this chapter arbitrarily. New Christians ceased to be distinguishable as an ethnicity, but they did not vanish. This is why I prefer the word *immersion* rather than *dissolution*. In the first half of the eighteenth century, inquisitorial persecution was even more intense in Spain than in the previous century, as the studies by Julio Caro Baroja and Teófanes Egido demonstrate.[1] Migration to Jewish communities in northern Europe continued in a small steady flow from both Portugal and Spain until the end of the eighteenth century, which meant that a minority felt a strong ethnic and religious allegiance even after more than two centuries of forced conversion and indoctrination.[2] The strategy of immersion in the wider society failed in many cases, but the vast majority found ways to escape scrutiny, probably through intermarriage and name changes, in a repressive environment that did not change dramatically until the middle of the century. The demographic paradox, as highlighted earlier, was that while the Iberian societies were becoming increasingly mixed, the blood purity rules did not lose their strength. In Portugal from the 1680s to the 1700s they became even stricter, with New Christians reconciled with formal abjuration at an auto da fé being expelled and losing their status as royal knights and *fidalgos* or members of military orders.

International relations continued to develop, as did cultural exchange, but while in northern Europe the Inquisition had been drawn on to generate a new system of values, presented as a highly efficient and productive counter-example of religious intolerance, which should be avoided, this perception had had no immediate impact on southern countries. However, we need to search more assiduously for repudiations of the Inquisition in this period in Iberia, because some of these existed only in manuscript until the nineteenth century and even beyond.

The War of Succession in Spain defined a new division between Spain and Portugal, deepening the divergence caused by the Portuguese War of Independence. Communication between the New Christians of the two Iberian kingdoms became gradually less visible. In both countries, New Christians became less active in royal financial contracts, although their participation in the farming of rents and taxation did not disappear entirely. New Christians still had a hand in the tobacco monopoly, particularly in Spain but also in Portugal. In 1704, the king's decision to stop automatically exiling New Christians condemned by the Inquisition (labelled "extermination") could be interpreted as having been imposed by the new financial needs of the War of Succession, but it could also be seen as a response to pleas from the inquisitors, who were finding confessions (and denunciations) much more difficult to obtain.

The renewal of inquisitorial repression of New Christians in Portugal got swiftly under way in the first decade of the eighteenth century, whereas in Spain it had to wait until the 1710s, partly because the reform projects of Macanaz took precedence and partly because the Bourbon king lacked enthusiasm for an institution alien to the French tradition. In 1715, the reversal of Philip V's position concerning the Inquisition, imposed by the triumphant Spanish faction at court, can be interpreted as a final assimilation of the new king into the Spanish religious configuration. Opposition to the New/Old Christian divide subsided in Spain, whereas in Portugal by the mid-eighteenth century such opposition had become mainstream in government circles. The label New Christian was abolished in 1773 in Portugal, sealing a curious new divergence from Spain.

This is the setting for the final chapter of this book, a chapter that seeks to identify the main traces of New Christian ethnicity in the process of immersion into global society, probably facilitated by changes in inquisitorial strategy and the decline of alternative hybrid traditions. The chapter is organised in three sections: the persistence of New Christian presence, particularly in Spain; the withdrawal of New Christians to the peripheries of Portugal and Brazil, where they continued to be persecuted; and the ideological change concerning blood purity by the political elite in Joseph I's reign in Portugal. Within these sections, we shall try to address the difficult question of the relationship between New Christians and Sephardic Jewish communities in northern Europe—the latter also in decline—while the immersion of wealthy New Christian families in the aristocratic environments they chose, mainly in Rome but also in Flanders, anticipated similar strategies at different social levels in the Iberian world.

1. Persistence

Estimates of the numbers of trials in Spain and Portugal in the eighteenth century can give an idea of both the continuation of inquisitorial persecution and the resilience of New Christian communities. It is not easy to compile data for Spain, because no complete series of printed auto da fé records exist, while *relaciones de causas* (summaries of trials), although these were more abundant, repeated names when the trials lasted several years. The best estimates were made and compiled by Torres Arce for (roughly) the reign of Philip V and concern four tribunals. I have added data collected for Llerena by Martínez Millán for the period 1700–1730.[3]

	Logroño 1700–1746	Valladolid 1700–1745	Murcia 1700–1750	Granada 18th cent.	Toledo 1700–1745	Llerena 1700–1730
Judaism	77	627	109	398	126	178?
Islam	1	—	—	277	1	
Protestantism	3	—	—	—	—	
Alumbrados	28	9	1	—	3	
Propositions	43	32	23	47	32	
Bigamy	12	48	11	31	22	
Solicitation	30	43	32	37	23	
Acts against Inq.	21	27	—	—	12	
Superstition	81	21	70	92	40	
Varied	24	22	—	91	18	
Total	320	829	246	696/973?	277	193?

Adapted from M. Torres Arce, "Judaizantes y el Santo Oficio de Logroño en el reinado de Felipe V," in *Historia de la Inquisición en España y América*, ed. Joaquín Pérez Villanueva and Bartolomé Escandell Bonet, vol. 3, *Temas y problemas* (Madrid: Biblioteca de Autores Cristianos, 2000), 657–693, esp. 660–661 (tables); José Martínez Millán, "La persecución inquisitorial contra los criptojudaicos en el siglo XVIII. El tribunal de Llerena (1700–1730)," in *Historia de la Inquisición en España y América*, vol. 3, 557–656.

Proceedings against New Christians accused of Judaism represented 76 percent of all trials held in Valladolid, 57 percent in Granada, 45 percent in Toledo, 44 percent in Murcia and 24 percent in Logroño. The data for Llerena compiled by Martínez Millán is based on relaciones de causa, but the total is incomplete, and it is difficult to accept that 92 percent of trials were of New

Christians for Judaism, even if Llerena had the longest frontier with Portugal, the origin of most New Christians accused by that tribunal, although not by the other tribunals. The total number of those accused of Judaism in these five tribunals is 1,515, but this figure does not include New Christians accused at the tribunals of Seville and Cordoba, where we know that a significant number were prosecuted. At the tribunals of Aragon, Judaism was a minor crime in this period: Haliczer found fifty-one cases at the tribunal of Valencia between 1721 and 1727, the most repressive period, and there were only sixty-seven cases for the whole of the eighteenth century.[4] Martínez Millán added forty New Christian trials by the inquisitorial tribunal of the royal court between 1717 and 1722.[5] If we estimate between 2,000 and 3,000 trials for Judaism by Spanish tribunals in the first half of the eighteenth century we shall not be far off the mark. Much more data is now available, but Teófanes Egido's compilation of numbers of those who were excommunicated can still be useful. In the same period of Philip V's reign, 228 were executed in person or in effigy, of which 96 percent were New Christians. This would reinforce the estimate of more than 2,000 trials, because the number of executions must have been well under 10 percent of the total.[6]

The Inquisition in Spain scaled down its activities from the beginning of Philip V's reign to 1715. The main reason for this was the War of Succession, which reduced the activities of all tribunals between 1702 and 1713, but the French influence at the royal court in this period, reinforced by the growing influence of Melchor Rafael de Macanaz as royal secretary after 1705, general *Intendente* (administrator) of Aragon from 1711, and attorney general to the royal council from 1713, led to the development of a centralisation of power and an attempt to reinforce royal, secular jurisdiction against that of the Church and the Inquisition. These projects of reform, devised and promoted by Macanaz, generated fierce opposition, led by the general inquisitor, cardinal Francesco del Giudice. The death of Queen Luisa Gabriela de Saboia and the marriage of Philip V to Isabel de Farnesio in 1714 brought with them the expulsion of the French faction led by the Princess Orsini and the fall of Macanaz, who was exiled in February 1715.[7] The ascent of a conservative coalition was accompanied by the return of the Inquisition to its traditional activity of prosecution of heresy and apostasy, which was expressed in a new wave of detentions, mainly of New Christians accused of Judaism, and concentrated in the last years of the 1710s and in the 1720s.

This activity of the Spanish Inquisition was political, and New Christians were once more used to block projects of reform. The purpose was clearly to show the traditional power of the Inquisition and send a threatening message to all opponents, this time in response to those holding early Enlightenment views on the supreme jurisdiction of the secular state. Melchor Macanaz was committed for trial by the Inquisition and his property sequestered. Projects of judicial reform were largely shelved for another fifty years. The implicit equation of New Christians with innovative thinking was a well-used method of bringing a racial factor into opposing any promoters of reform who might undermine the privileges of the Church and the central ideological position of the Inquisition. Squashing any opposition by linking the struggle against it to the persecution of a racialised minority has been used at various moments of history, which should alert us to equivalent movements of repression in history that challenge common views on anachronism. It should also alert us to an unfounded but traditional and conservative view of the Inquisition as interested only in the religious issue of heresy. This long instance of renewed inquisitorial activity was openly triggered by political goals and pursued in the most aggressive way at the expense of the usual victims.

In Portugal, the Inquisition took more than twenty years to overcome the restrictions imposed by Pope Innocent XI in 1681. In the 1680s, there were 934 trials in the three tribunals of Coimbra, Lisbon, and Évora, largely necessary to clear the extraordinary number of prisoners that had accumulated before the suspension of the Inquisition in 1674. In the 1690s, the number of trials went down to 529, followed by a recovery in the 1700s to 1,136. The following decades showed a relatively constant high number of trials: 1,034 in the 1710s, 1,123 in the 1720s, and 959 in the 1730s. The decline started in the following decade: 775 trials in the 1740s, 634 in the 1750s, and 212 in the 1760s.[8] There is no reliable data for the last third of the eighteenth century, but the trials seem to have declined dramatically.

If we consider only the trials from 1700 to 1749 and compare these with the Spanish case, we have 5,027 trials. If 80 percent of these were New Christian trials, probably an underestimate for this period, that would mean around 4,000 trials concerning Judaism were held, almost double the Spanish total and in line with the previous concentration of the Portuguese Inquisition on this minority. The sudden Spanish concentration on Judaism is new, because the estimates for Spanish trials dealing with Judaism in this period vary between 24 and 92 percent (the latter figure is problematic) for the different tribunals considered earlier. To sum up, there was substantial renewed prosecution of New Christians accused of Judaism in the eighteenth century, in Spain concentrated in the late 1710s, 1720s, and 1730s, and in Portugal from the 1700s to the 1750s.

What, then, was the reason for the permanent decline in trials for Judaism after the 1740s in Spain and the 1760s in Portugal? The idea that New Christians had finally disappeared, absorbed into the global population, is tenable, given the steady rate of inter-ethnic mixing from generation to generation, although this mixing varied between core and peripheral locations. Inquisitorial classifications are an unreliable indicator of miscegenation: the 1660–1699 records for the tribunal of Évora reveal 1,786 part New Christians (one-half, one-quarter, or one-eighth New Christian ancestry) compared with 1,113 full New Christians; but the records for 1700–1769 show a reversal in these proportions from the beginning; that is, 293 part New Christians to 603 full New Christians, although the total of those whose details were taken was much smaller.[9]

Tailland's is the only systematic study available. Either the relative decline in the numbers prosecuted by the Évora tribunal led to a concentration on full New Christians, or reluctance in Rome to accept the likely Judaism of those with one-half, one-quarter, or one-eighth New Christian ancestry made the inquisitors blur the divisions. In any case, a complete merging of New Christians into global society is open to question, at least until the 1760s, probably because persecution contributed to the creation of identity. We should also remember that there had been previous occasions when persecution of New Christians seemed to fade away, only to be renewed with surprising strength, as happened in the late 1710s in Spain. When the Inquisition needed accusations of Judaism, they would find them.

Finally, to complete this complex puzzle, consider that migration from Iberia to Jewish communities in London and southwest France maintained a steady, even if small, flow during the whole of the eighteenth century. In my view, this problem can only be solved by transferring the focus from New Christian ethnicity to the Inquisition itself and its relationship with royal power. The political changes and ideological shifts that occurred in both Portugal and Spain in the third quarter of the eighteenth century need to be considered. The third part of this chapter will deal with this issue.

Caro Baroja identified a cluster of important New Christian families, resident in Madrid, who were prosecuted during the late 1710s and early 1720s. The status of these families reveals a certain continuity with the financial positions of those previously prosecuted, although it is not at the same high level as that of the defendants prosecuted from the 1620s to the 1680s. Francisco de Miranda, reconciled by the Inquisition in 1721 with property confiscation, had been involved in auctions for *asientos* to provision the Spanish army in Extremadura during the War of Succession and was considered the most important New Christian in Madrid under Philip V.[10] His close friend, Francisco de Torres, a rich merchant, was accused by the Inquisition of making an incomplete confession, because "as he would have his property confiscated, he hoped that, concealing, he could recover his wealth with the help of Francisco de Miranda."[11] Antonio Carrillo, a third head of this group of families, some of whose members were involved in the royal administration, was executed in 1721.[12]

Miguel de Robles was also in this group. He was born a Jew in Bayonne and married into the Pimentel family, one of whose most important members was Diego Felipe Montesinos. Montesinos was involved in the *millones* tax in Seville, was a contractor to provision Ceuta in North Africa, was an administrator for the royal monopoly on tobacco in Toledo, and was superintendent of the tobacco trade in Zaragoza.[13] The head of the Pimentel family,

Antonio, who was a contractor for the rent on cacao from the Indies, was prosecuted by the Inquisition but escaped. Antonio was linked not only to Francisco de Miranda but also to Diego López de Castro Paz Coronel Quirós, the head of another important family, who lived in Madrid, had dealings with Princess Orsini, and ended up being executed in 1723.[14]

Francisco was the public head of the Córdoba family. He was an administrator for the royal rents in Campo de Criptana and was accused of being looked up to as a rabbi by the other families (the Miranda, Torres, and Carrillo families) and having links to the Jewish communities of Livorno and Bayonne. His father, Alonso de Córdoba, also known as Diego López, who was a contractor for the millones in Granada, had been reconciled at the auto da fé in that city in 1691 and condemned to a penalty of 6,000 ducados and six years of exile.[15] Diego de Ávila is another case of a New Christian with assets at the centre of the Spanish financial world. He had been born in Malaga and ended up a general administrator for the royal rents in Castile, where he was detained by the Inquisition, died in jail, and was executed in effigy in 1721.[16]

Many other New Christians were in trouble with the Inquisition in Aragon and Castile in these years. Luis Villarroel is identified by Caro Baroja as a contractor for the royal monopoly on tobacco in Colmenar, having bid for similar contracts in Badajoz and Aragon, but it seems that he was a major investor in Aragon, where he was known as Luis Fernando de Villarroel, a general administrator of the royal monopoly in association with Antonio de Arroyo. He was detained by the Inquisition on charges of Judaism, which triggered a series of civil grievances brought by the heirs of Antonio de Arroyo and Bernardo de Solance about what had happened to their money. The accounts for the tobacco contract ended up at the Inquisition.[17] Raymundo Suárez de Mesquita was a contractor for tobacco and an administrator for munitions in Atienza; Manuel Mercado de Noroña was a contractor for the rent on soap in Llerena; José Delgado was an administrator for royal rents in Llerena; and Antonio Gómez was a contractor for tobacco, powder, and ammunition in Valladolid.[18] Baltasar de Castro, born in Madrid, was a major financier who lived in Zafra and was an administrator for royal rents; his brother José de Castro, who lived in Villanueva de la Serena, had a similar position; Fernando Zamora, resident in the same town, shared with Manuel Mercado the contract for the rent on soap in Extremadura.[19]

Most New Christian financiers prosecuted by the Inquisition had their investments in the southern areas of Spain. Francisco Baez Eminente was identified by Caro Baroja as being an asentista in the south; Juan Francisco Eminente, probably a relative, was involved as a contractor to provision the navy from 1698 to 1702, and as a contractor for the army and a collector of *almojarifazgos* (duties) in 1701; Francisco Eminente triggered a civil action related to payment of interest in 1724.[20] Francisco Diaz de Espinosa was an administrator for royal rents in Cadiz and Seville; Tomás Rodriguez del Castillo was an administrator for tobacco in Huelva; José de Silvera was a general administrator for the rent on tobacco in Jaén; Miguel de Oliveros Acosta y Meneses was an administrator for tobacco in Lucena; José de Sabariego was an administrator for tobacco in Murcia and Baeza; Pedro Alvarez Pereyra was an administrator for the rent on tobacco in Malaga; and Diego Pablo de Oliveros was an administrator for tobacco and soap in Antequera and Caceres.[21]

Sebastián Antonio de Paz was an administrator for tobacco in Almagro and was also involved with the production and distribution of lace in the region of Jaén. Alonso Pacheco de Tapia was an administrator for royal rents in Utrera; Sebastián Callado de Noroña was an administrator for tobacco in Antequera; and Antonio Diaz de Soria was an administrator for royal rents in Malaga.[22] Stephen Haliczer has pieced together the remaining networks revealed by the Valencia Inquisition's prosecution of New Christians, showing that tax farmers were in decline, and although they were holding onto the tobacco administration, the Inquisition's prosecutions dealt this business a final blow. The cases of Simón de Alarcón and Diego and Felipe de Paz were the most significant.[23]

The majority of New Christians committed for trial were poor people—artisans, peddlers, and people in lowly positions in the tobacco monopoly at the local level or involved in various trades as shopkeepers. Some of them collected rents for landlords and convents, as was the case with Francisco López de Laguna, a rent collector for the Bernadine convent in Aranda de Duero.[24] The decline in the position of New Christians during the eighteenth century can be plainly seen: very few were involved in royal asientos, although there were still asentistas of royal rents among them. The monopoly on tobacco was the main area where the remnants of the New Christian networks congregated.

As well as New Christians with local roots, the records contain traces of New Christians detained on their way to Livorno, as happened in 1699 when a large group aboard a Genoese ship was detained after the ship anchored in Cadiz. The group, apparently led by João Lopes Dias, born in Mirandela, and later resident in Chacim, Trás-os-Montes, Portugal, consisted of thirteen men, sixteen women, nineteen children, and one grandchild, a total of forty-nine people, and all were sent to Llerena. They had with them some merchandise, mainly Mexican silver coins, sugar, and tobacco, all destined for Gabriel de Medina in Livorno, a member of the Mogadouro family whom we have met before.[25]

If Llerena was the tribunal with the responsibility for controlling the passage and exchange of New Christians across the frontier with Portugal, through the plains of Extremadura and Alentejo, the tribunal of Logroño played a similar role in relation to the frontier with France which cut across the Basque Country. They were dealing with a long-standing contraband route fed by New Christian and Jewish communities in southwest France, but the main target was a regular flow of New Christians from Portugal and Spain into France and a flow in the opposite direction of Jews from various parts of Europe into Spain through that frontier and the ports of the Basque Country.[26]

2. Withdrawal

The Portuguese lists of autos da fé indicate the renewal of high levels of persecution from the 1700s to the 1730s, followed by a steady decline, until the 1760s reveal a very low level of persecution. The lists (not complete) show an overwhelming number of New Christians among those sentenced between 1700 and 1740, many of them of mixed ancestry (one-half, one-quarter, or one-eighth or less New Christian). There were 555 trials of defendants who had lived in Brazil in the first half of the eighteenth century, more than half the total number of trials of people from that region in three centuries, the vast majority New Christians.[27] This number is only 14 percent of the total of New Christians sentenced in this period, but a concentration of inquisitorial trials on the elite of colonial Brazil is clear. It is possible that many *conversos* had decided to withdraw to the peripheries of the kingdom and the empire, to Brazil and the South Atlantic, although a significant number of New Christian residents of Lisbon and Porto continued to be detained. On the other hand, all traces of New Christians virtually vanished from the records of the tribunal of Goa, although it is possible that local New Christians managed to stay unnoticed.

The discovery of gold in Brazil towards the end of the seventeenth century, followed by diamonds, and later by the production of spices and cotton in Maranhão, added to the traditional production of sugar and tobacco in the northeast, contributed to the transformation of the colony into the leading region of the empire. The attention to the role of New Christians in that colony therefore increased. Traditional migration may have registered a new push with the reestablishment of the Inquisition in 1681 in Portugal. In the Spanish empire, by contrast, New Christians had virtually vanished from the records from the last wave of inquisitorial persecution in the 1630s and 1640s until the 1710s.

The significant number of New Christians born in Portugal and detained by the Spanish tribunals is matched by those born in Castile and detained by the Portuguese tribunals. During these three centuries, frontiers clearly were crossed in both directions, according to economic, social, and political needs. It does not make sense to talk about Portuguese or Castilian New Christians as if they could be defined in this way.

There is another interesting issue. Excommunications leading to execution declined in the first two decades of the eighteenth century, only to increase again after the 1720s. In the early eighteenth century a significant number of detainees who had relapsed escaped the ultimate punishment, a phenomenon rarely seen before. It is likely that the impact of papal intervention from 1674 to 1681 was slightly more important than supposed.[28]

The geographic distribution of those detained is concentrated in the peripheries, primarily in Trás-os-Montes, Beiras and, to a less degree, Alentejo, contrasting with the distribution in the seventeenth century. This may show a lingering resilience in small communities in the interior, but it may also represent a withdrawal from the main urban areas nearer the sea to avoid detection by inquisitorial enquiries both in Portugal and Castile. The social status of New Christians sentenced by the Inquisition is clear from the lists of autos de fé: the majority were artisans and people without jobs, while there was a significant number of agricultural workers and other manual labourers. Among artisans, we need to highlight the important number of silk weavers from Bragança, to which we must add dyers and others employed in that industry, wool weavers from Covilhã and Alentejo, and manufacturers of stockings from Porto and Lisbon, who together numbered several hundred in this period.

A significant number of sugar mill and sugar plantation owners were among those prosecuted who had lived in Brazil. Liberal professionals, such as lawyers, physicians, and apothecaries, were still important, and some of these also had Brazilian backgrounds. There were peddlers, shopkeepers, retailers, and stallholders in local markets, but we still find a significant number of merchants and contractors for royal rents and monopolies such as tobacco. While Minho played an important role in migration to Brazil, the vast majority of New Christian detainees from that colony had their origin in Beiras and Trás-os-Montes, which can be explained by the various push factors at play.

The decline of New Christian contractors needs further research to produce a detailed chronology. The case of Diogo de Chaves de Carvalho, a major financier detained in October 1704 and sentenced at the auto da fé on February 1708, is significant, following as it does decades of determined prosecution of wealthy New Christians.[29] Thirty-seven years old at the time of his arrest, Chaves de Carvalho was living in Lisbon, having been born in Fundão. The inventory of his property occupies sixty-two pages of the record of his trial. He was renting a significant number of *comendas*, large properties owned by military orders and provided as benefices to knights as a reward for services to the king. He would pay a fixed amount of money to the comendadores in exchange for collecting the income from these properties. The contracts for twelve comendas, almost all in Beiras but one in Minho, involved an annual payment of more than 6 million réis, equivalent to circa 16,000 cruzados.[30]

Chaves de Carvalho had a brother, Simão Carvalho Chaves, who had a share in the investment and was responsible for collecting income, although Chaves de Carvalho also involved António Mendes Martins, a familiar of the Inquisition, his cousin Francisco Lopes Preto, and the contractor Manuel da Costa Silva in the running of the comendas. Chaves de Carvalho derived income from farming taxes in Lisbon and Setúbal, royal rents in Lamego, stamp duty in Pinhel and Guarda, the monopoly on playing cards, rents from the Junta do Infantado, rents from Eixo and Porto de Mós due to the House of Bragança, taxes on fishing in Setúbal, also owned by the House of Bragança, and rents from the entailed properties of the Count of Vimioso. He had contracts to provide cereals for the granaries of Tomar, and for collecting the tithe for Penamacor, Panoias, and Rumela due to the Bernadine nuns in Portalegre. He was also involved in the contract for provisioning the province of Beiras during the War of Succession. The values involved here are staggering, probably four times as much as the money involved in the comendas, but in several cases the business involved subcontracts and shares of much larger contracts.[31]

Chaves de Carvalho claimed property confiscated by the Inquisition, particularly his share in contracts held jointly with Manuel Fróis Nunes, worth millions of réis. He had traded in cereals, wine, olive oil, textiles, and sugar from Brazil. He had lent money to several people, including royal judges, Alvaro da Silveira de Albuquerque, the governor of Brazil, clergymen, royal clerks, masters of ships, and merchants. He had traded in bills of exchange, in one case involving a payment of 6,000 cruzados to Milner & Co. in Lisbon. He had accepted the position of guarantor for several contracts, which had increased his liability and involved several cases in court. His investment in property had, by comparison, been very limited, consisting of a large property in Fundão valued at 1,000 cruzados and an eighth of a caravel in Cascais, a share valued at 80,000 réis.[32]

The inventory of Chaves de Carvalho's property at home indicated, as would be expected, beds, sideboards, cabinets, chests, and caskets from India and Brazil, tapestries and bedspreads from India, tableware of gold and silver, desks, chairs, a chessboard inlaid with ivory, two stringed instruments (a *violão* and a *rabeca*), two wigs, two calivers, textiles, and clothing. It is difficult to assess the full scale of the investments he was involved in, but it should not be far from the mark to say that Chaves de Carvalho was directly and indirectly involved with contracts that could have been worth over 100,000 cruzados annually, although his liability was high. He declared that two of the comendas had been invaded by enemy troops, and he could not pay what was owed on them. The War of Succession had started to affect his finances. He also declared that he had paid 80,000 réis for the reconstruction of the fort of Sabugal.[33]

Chaves de Carvalho denied any wrongdoing and developed a strenuous defence and *contradictas*, until he was confronted with a sentence of excommunication as "negative." He then collapsed and confessed profusely. He was sentenced at the auto da fé on September 12, 1706, to formal abjuration, property confiscation, and exile for five years to Brazil. Because he was very sick, he petitioned to be treated at home, which was conceded. On February 1, 1708, when the inquisitors ordered his guarantor, Gonçalo Lourenço de Aguiar, a goldsmith, to take him back to the civil prison to implement his exile, Chaves de Carvalho claimed that he was still sick, producing an order from his doctors that he should be treated at the spa of Caldas da Rainha, while his mother, condemned to exile with him, was paralysed.[34] We know that he was alive in 1712, when his son, Francisco Carvalho Chaves, was detained by the Inquisition.[35]

The obsession with quantification that defines this period reached new heights with the case of Francisco Mendes de Crasto, another major financier, at the turn of the eighteenth century. A New Christian, heir to an entailed property (*morgado*), contractor and banker, a merchant engaging in business with senior members of the royal bureaucracy, the owner of extensive urban and rural properties, Mendes de Crasto and his family had chosen to invest in fixed assets, the opposite strategy to that of Chaves de Carvalho. The inventory of his property occupies 106 pages of the trial record. He declared a farm in Santa Apolónia, Lisbon, with old houses, olive trees, and an orchard. On the outskirts of Lisbon he had another farm assigned to his son, bought for 3,000 cruzados. In Lisbon, he had houses in the Fancaria de Baixo, a row of houses on the Rua do Alecrim where a royal judge, Crispim Mascarenhas, lived, other houses in the same street, including shops, a merchant's establishment in the Praça Nossa Senhora da Conceição, other houses in front of the Count of Vimioso's palace, and some large houses on the Rua das Flores.[36]

Outside Lisbon, Mendes de Crasto had a large farm near Alcácer do Sal, three small properties in Azinhaga, Santarém, a property called Moinho do Bispo in Montemor-o-Novo, and two farms near Beja. He had financial investments in rents in Carnide, Lisbon, on the monopoly of tobacco, and on the *almoxarifado* of Guarda. He was also a shipowner with shares in several caravels putting out from Sesimbra. He traded with Brazil, carrying sugar from Pernambuco, Bahia, and Rio de Janeiro, and cloves from Maranhão. Mendes de Crasto permitted investment in his trade by various people, in particular, 16,000 réis from the inheritance of a nun at the convent of Santa Mónica, Lisbon. He organised the production of pistols and calivers for Rio, imported fine textiles of velvet and damask from northern Italy, and exported wool from Portugal to the Netherlands.[37]

Mendes de Crasto lent money (in some cases, large sums), but he also had debts and a large number of cases in court. He declared a debt of 8,000 cruzados owed to his niece, Isabel Caetana de Tovar, the orphaned daughter of his sister, who was under his guardianship, and another debt of 12,000 cruzados to his brother, Miguel Teles da Costa, major captain in Paraty, both debts relating to the estate of his deceased father. He participated in contracts for the customs of Porto, the rent on salt in Aldeia Galega, and the granaries of Oeiras, Barcarena, and Benavente. He organised a trading company with João Saraiva de Carvalho, a royal judge, Luís Paulino da Silva, the secretary of the royal tribunal, André de Sousa da Cunha, a priest of Barcelos, and Nuno

Leitão Pereira de Almeida, a cousin, when the first of these collaborators became *ouvidor geral* (general judge) in São Paulo, Brazil.[38]

Portuguese society was immersed in dealings that involved royal bureaucracy, clergymen, and convents. An appointment to a senior judicial position in Brazil could be transformed into a good opportunity for trade. However, all these connections did not protect Mendes de Crasto from the Inquisition. When he was detained on September 30, 1707, he was more than fifty years old and sick. Born in Trancoso and resident in Lisbon, he was a man whose ancestors were not only rich but also well connected: his maternal grandfather, Diogo Mendes da Costa, had been the Marquis of Ferreira's treasury judge. Mendes de Crasto had been married three times, and had a surviving son from his first marriage and a daughter from the second.[39] He had been denounced by merchants and financiers, including his brother-in-law and former associate, Álvaro Nicolau Nogueira, José Nunes Chaves, who had been born in London, the contractors Rafael Luis de Medina and Gabriel Luis de Medina, born in Castile, and José da Costa, son of Manuel da Costa Brandão.[40]

Mendes de Crasto denied any wrongdoing and put up a strong defence and contradictas until he was threatened with a sentence of excommunication for being negative. He then made an extensive confession and was sentenced to formal abjuration, perpetual wearing of a penitential habit, service in the galleys for seven years, and property confiscation, this sentence being pronounced at the auto da fé on June 30, 1709.[41] At his age, condemnation to the galleys was a death sentence (even for strong men). The last documents from his physician, written in January 1710, declared that Mendes de Crasto had a tumour in his throat, had difficulty in urinating because of a kidney stone, had bouts of epilepsy, had a continuous fever, was deaf, and suffered from insomnia, loss of blood, and delirium. There was nothing left for him but the last sacraments.[42]

Mendes de Crasto's brother, Miguel Teles da Costa, was detained by the Inquisition on October 6, 1710, and presented at the auto da fé on July 26, 1711, a fast track to a similar sentence with property confiscation. Besides the inheritance from his father, Miguel Teles da Costa had relied on a farm in Rio das Mortes and houses in Paraty and Ouro Preto for his income. He was also involved in trade with Minas Gerais.[43] His brother-in-law, Álvaro Nicolau Nogueira, born in Madrid and resident in Lisbon, whose trial was prosecuted from 1704 to 1707, received a similar sentence, with five years in the galleys, although this sentence was commuted in 1709 and he received authorisation to live in Montemor-o-Novo.[44] These cases represented confiscation of an exceptional amount of property by the Inquisition.

It is useful to look at the variety of strategies of resistance to the Inquisition used in this period. Belchior Dias Mago is an interesting case. He was a local medium-sized merchant and administrator of rents resident in Fundão, son of a lawyer, when he was accused of Judaism by nine artisans and merchants who were on trial.[45] He was detained on September 6, 1706, when he was forty-four years of age, and had his property sequestered. He had houses in Alcaria and a vineyard and a forest in Fundão. He declared a debt to the royal treasury of 200,000 réis, and another to Pedro Alves Cabral, a priest from Alcaria, who had lent him 500,000 réis from the tithe he received at 6.25 percent interest.[46]

Belchior Dias claimed to be an Old Christian on both sides of his family, and to be married to an Old Christian, with whom he had four sons and one daughter. He acknowledged that there had been rumours about his mother's ancestors, but his uncles, Gaspar Rodrigues Nabo and António Dias Correia, were ordained as priests.[47] He even added a genealogical tree for the latter priest. He consistently denied all accusations, and even under torture he did not confess.[48] In the end, he was not presented at an auto da fé. The sentence, pronounced in a private session at the tribunal, declared that his "quality" (Old or New Christian) was not known. The accusations of Judaism were repeated, but taking into account his defence, his contradictas, and a lack of sufficient proof, it was decided he should only make an abjuration of mildly suspected heresy, and the sentence of sequestration of property was lifted.[49]

Belchior Dias was released on July 22, 1709, nearly three years after he was detained, and without even being given a clear absolution.[50] This was the norm for the tribunal—a norm which had been denounced in Rome by New Christians many times. But this was one case, among others, in which the accused challenged an inquisitorial classification and won. Belchior Dias's brother, a lawyer, Gaspar Rodrigues Nabo, was detained by the tribunal of Coimbra and endured the same ordeal from September 1705 to July 1709, almost four years, before also being released after denying all accusations, with an identical sentence pronounced in a private session.[51]

We have been focusing here on cases of New Christian merchants prosecuted by the Inquisition, but the continuous trend of New Christian immersion in society as Old Christians, with donations to the Church, seems to have been pursued unabated in the first half of the eighteenth century. One example, which needs more research, is the donation by Diogo de Brito do Rio, a fidalgo of the royal house, and his wife Aldonça da Mota, a descendant of the family Coronel, founders of the Jesuit College of Santiago in Elvas, Portugal, at the end of the seventeenth century. They commissioned a painting with their portraits at the time of their donation, and they had a marble tomb built for their remains at the college.[52]

The late 1700s saw a dramatic increase in cases from Brazil. The trials of the Vale family reveal what happened to a dense cluster of endogamous families who owned important sugar mills and plantations in the region of Rio and who had emigrated from Portugal in the period from the 1660s to the 1680s, the peak of inquisitorial persecution. Ana do Vale, the matriarch, was fifty-seven years old when she was detained in 1710. With her four sons, she

FIGURE 16.1. Anonymous, Portrait of Diogo de Brito do Rio, fidalgo of the royal house, and Aldonça da Mota, founders of the Jesuit College of Santiago in Elvas, Portugal, ca. 1700, oil on canvas, 159 × 120.5 cm. Private collection. Courtesy *Cabral Moncada Leilões / Vasco Cunha Monteiro*.

possessed a sugar mill and a property, Golambande, which was considered one of the best in the region of Rio. The property had been bought by her deceased husband, and they themselves had valued it at 70,000 cruzados, with the five and a half leagues they had added to it, 120 oxen, eight horses, and dozens of slaves. The harvest of 1710, gathered in before they were detained and sent to Lisbon, had been excellent, estimated at 10,000 cruzados.[53] Ana do Vale's brother, João Rodrigues do Vale, who was married to Leonor Guterres da Costa, ran the sugar mill and plantation their father had owned in Jacotinba,

FIGURE 16.2. Tomb of Diogo de Brito do Rio and Aldonça da Mota, founders of the College of Santiago, Society of Jesus, in Elvas, Portugal, 1702. Photo courtesy of Rui Jesuíno.

a quarter of which belonging to another sister, Catarina Gomes. The whole was worth 14,000 cruzados.[54]

The members of the family were condemned to formal abjuration, perpetual wearing of the penitential habit and detention, and property confiscation. The set of trials to which they were subjected also involved other family members, such as Ana do Vale's brother-in-law, António do Vale da Silveira or de Mesquita, born in Vila Real (probably where the Vale family originated); her daughters-in-law, Angela de Mesquita and Isabel Gomes; and her nephew and son-in-law, João Soares de Mesquita, owner of a plantation, brother of Alexandre Soares Pereira and married to Leonor Mendes de Paz, who owned a sugar mill and a plantation estimated at 60,000 cruzados and houses in the main street of Rio de Janeiro that he had bought for 7,000 cruzados (still to be paid). They all had similar sentences.[55]

The case of Manuel Lopes Henriques, a sugar mill owner in Bahia, shows how the past haunted those who had migrated to the periphery. The order to take him into custody was issued in 1705, but he was only delivered to the Inquisition in Lisbon on December 18, 1706, when he was forty years old. He had been the subject of two denunciations: one from his brother, João Henriques Ferreira, and another from Diogo de Chaves de Carvalho, whom we have already mentioned. Born in Covilhã, Manuel Lopes Henriques married the widow of a landowner from Bahia, Mariana Soares, who was also a New Christian. She already had three daughters, and the couple had two more daughters together. The inheritance of the stepdaughters, the eldest of whom was thirteen years old, had been legally set at 5,000 cruzados each, and their stepfather was paying 40,000 réis annually for the maintenance of each.[56]

The main sugar mill and plantation in Matoim had 125 slaves. Lopes Henriques did not declare the value, but we know from other cases that it could have been worth around 100,000 cruzados. He owned several sugar plantations in the region, one of which included a harbour, and each would have been worth about 20,000 cruzados. He also had houses in the city of Salvador, on the street leading to the Terreiro de Jesus, and these were valued at 5,250 cruzados, but he still owed 4,000 cruzados to the Misericórdia from this purchase, paying 6.25 percent interest every year. He had sent 40 boxes of white sugar and 110 rolls of tobacco to Lisbon, a cargo worth 3.1 million réis in Bahia, and he reported other cargoes of sugar valued at 4,000 cruzados. He also sent a significant amount of gold to Manuel Francisco Lima in Porto: 3 caps and 110 coins worth more than 900,000 réis. However, he declared that debts were owed to him from previous cargoes.[57]

Lopes Henriques listed his acquisition of two farms previously owned by António Moniz Barreto, deceased, although both these had been purchased in a state of indebtedness: one, next to the sea, by 1.9 million réis (4,750 cruzados), and the other, the Paço da Gamela, by 13,000 cruzados, of which 6,250 cruzados remained unpaid. He had jewels at home, silver tableware, wash basins and trays, chairs, a set of maps, two desks and two sideboards, and twenty boxes of tiles from Lisbon.[58]

Manuel Lopes Henriques denied any wrongdoing and stood by his denial. He was tortured but stood firm, refusing to confess. He ended up at the auto da fé on June 30, 1709, three years after he was detained, but through insufficient proof and the firmness of his defence and contradictas, he avoided property confiscation. However, the inquisitors imposed a sentence of abjuration of vehemently suspected heresy.[59] He must have been one of the wealthiest farmers and merchants of Bahia at the time.

The original cluster of Manuel Lopes Henriques's relatives and associates in Portugal, mostly from Covilhã but also from Guarda, Trancoso, Celorico, S. Vicente da Beira, Fundão, Moimenta da Beira, and Lisbon, about twenty people under trial between 1703 and 1706, did not fare so well. They were all detained and denounced each other and received sentences of formal abjuration and property confiscation. If we concentrate here on his close family, we find that his father had been a merchant, his paternal grandfather a tanner, and his maternal grandfather also a merchant. Of his five brothers, the eldest, Francisco Henriques Ferreira, became a dyer.[60]

António Lopes Henriques, João Henriques Ferreira, Diogo Henriques Ferreira, a physician, and Álvaro Henriques Ferreira shared the royal contract for the production of woollen cloth in Covilhã.[61] They all owned the houses where they lived in Covilhã, estimated as worth between 100,000 and 800,000 réis; Francisco possessed vineyards and farms producing cereals; Alvaro had vineyards and traded textiles for sugar with their brother in Brazil; and João possessed farms producing cereals, was involved in significant trade in textiles and cereals (wheat, rye), plus sugar from Brazil, had lent around 400,000 réis to local merchants and a nobleman at 6.25 percent interests, and owed 95,000 réis to Rodrigo de Sande de Vasconcelos for freight charges between Lisbon and Bahia.[62]

João was apparently the real manager of the factory, where he had at the moment of his detention 47 full bolts of cloth worth 30,000 réis each, a total of 1,420,000 réis, another 30 full bolts of cloth of lesser quality worth 25,000 réis each, a total of 750,000 réis, 40 arrobas (around 590 kgs) of alum, a mordant for dying, bought at 32,000 réis, and 5 arrobas of spun wool (around 74 kgs) worth 60,000 réis; and he valued the equipment in the factory in two separate sections: the printing section, with two presses of copper and ten scissors, was worth 400,000 réis; and the weaving section, with looms, combs, stripes, wheels, and cards, was also worth 400,000 réis.[63] It was João who received the harshest penalty from the Inquisition: five years in the galleys as well as property confiscation.[64]

This family is representative of local elites decimated by the Inquisition over three centuries of activity. They were not major merchants, although they were involved in trade with Brazil; rather, they were manufacturers in a country with a diffuse and relatively weak network of workshops and rural household production, and they invested locally in urban housing and agriculture. They were typical ancien régime non-noble local elites, in this case classified as New Christians. The silk industry in Bragança, with so many New Christian weavers and dyers (apparently all male) who were prosecuted by the Inquisition, would justify a serious study from this perspective.[65]

It is difficult to estimate how many New Christians returned to their occupations after being sentenced by the Inquisition. Probably the vast majority did; but the property confiscation from workshop owners meant a loss of investment, a reduction of fixed capital and a blow to mobile capital with disruption of networks, a fracturing of trust built up, and increased litigation to recover debts. Condemnation to the galleys meant, in most cases, a death sentence for important manufacturers. Trading networks could be reestablished by other people, but knowledge and expertise in an industry were more difficult to replace, even if at various periods foreign experts were involved.[66]

New Christian merchants and financiers were well represented in the lists of autos da fé from the 1710s to the 1740s. There were around twenty contractors for tobacco prosecuted by the Inquisition.[67] The total number of New Christian merchants, administrators of rents, and contractors prosecuted was much higher, although their status and financial capacity were tending to decline. By the end of the 1720s, we still have a significant case of wealthy families accused in Vila Real, Trás-os-Montes. Luís do Vale, merchant and administrator of rents, was detained by the Inquisition on December 17, 1726, and presented at the auto da fé on May 9, 1728, in Coimbra.[68] His account books were kept by the Inquisition, and they contain a record of income and expenditure for several investments jointly held with do Vale's associate and cousin, Diogo do Vale Cordeiro, including a share in the administration of rents in Mondim and the administration of rents in Passos and Sabrosa.[69]

The extended Vale family was probably the wealthiest in Vila Real, with relatives in Brazil and links to the Henriques, Vaz, Leão, Mesquita, and Nunes families, including Francisco Nunes Carvalho, morgado for Escarigo, who was absent from the kingdom.[70] The inventory of property owned by Diogo do Vale Cordeiro, who lived in Lisbon, included a farm at Telhada in Sever, Santa Marta de Penaguião, estimated to be worth 24,000 cruzados, and a house in Vila Real worth 3,500 cruzados. There were two rented comendas, that of São Martinho de Bornes, Vila Pouca de Aguiar, and that of S. João da Cova, plus a property owned by the chapter of the Cathedral of Braga, and these were held in association with other merchants in Goiões. Diogo also produced wine, the last crop promised to an Englishman in Porto, forty barrels at 33,600 réis (seven gold coins) each.[71] Diogo lamented the oppression of New Christians, whose children could not become clergymen, judges, or royal ministers. These associates, denounced by a significant number of relatives undergoing trial, were both sentenced to formal abjuration, which meant property confiscation.[72]

Surprising as it may seem, the methods of the Portuguese Inquisition did not change much until the 1750s. They patiently collected denunciations through a snowball procedure, targeting towns and families, whose members they detained, and squeezed them until they produced the necessary denunciations. António Manuel de Lima, born in Bragança and resident in Lisbon, a lawyer and merchant, was detained and sentenced in 1758, having been denounced by seventeen relatives and friends. He had some inherited property in Bragança and received some textiles from his brother to sell in Lisbon, which suggests he can be classified as a small merchant. He was sentenced to formal abjuration and had his property confiscated.[73]

Francisco Rodrigues da Costa, born in Chaves and resident in Leiria, an administrator of contracts, was detained on November 20, 1757, and presented at the auto da fé on August 27, 1758. He was denounced by thirty relatives and friends who were also on trial, including members of the Leão, Veiga, Martins, Sequeira, Chaves, and Pinto Ferreira families, and the aforementioned António Manuel de Lima. The accused administered properties in the area of Leiria, in some cases brokering acquisitions, but it was a small-scale operation. He was condemned to formal abjuration and property confiscation. The same sentence was given to his brother, Gaspar Rodrigues da Costa, the owner of some of those properties.[74] A third brother, João Rodrigues da Costa, cleverly escaped to Cork (Ireland) and then to London. He was excommunicated in absentia, and in August 1764, with the help of his confessor in London, he wrote letters to the Inquisition asking permission to be given absolution in the Portuguese chapel. This request was refused by the inquisitors, who ordered the accused to return to Lisbon. This does not seem to have happened.[75]

In the meantime, the profile of New Christians from Brazil detained by the Inquisition had changed, along with the economic situation they had helped to build, from owners of sugar mills and plantations to lawyers, physicians, gold mining contractors, merchants in diamonds, slave merchants, and tobacco manufacturers. The impact of political and military events can be seen in the inventories of property recorded; for example, the destruction of property produced by the invasion and plunder of Rio de Janeiro by the French corsairs commanded by Duguay-Trouin in 1711, during the War of Succession in Spain.[76]

José Pacheco de Azevedo, the owner of a sugar mill near Rio de Janeiro worth 50,000 cruzados and of houses in Rio's Rua da Croce worth 6,000 cruzados, was also a contractor for the royal taxes (*décima*) in Minas. In April 1714, producing an inventory of his property for the Inquisition, he declared that he had lost 40 percent of the 50,000 cruzados he expected to make on that contract because of French plundering.[77] This is a very interesting case. He was denounced by ten New Christians for Judaism, he declared he was an Old Christian on both sides, with a grandfather who was a knight, a nephew who was a comendador in the Order of Christ, and women in his family who were married to captains.[78] Even put to torture he did not confess. Despite a lack of sufficient proof, and although he had a strong defence and contradictas, José Pacheco was condemned to abjuration of vehemently suspected heresy and to a fine of 50,000 réis for the expenses of the tribunal, an unusually heavy penalty.[79] However, he escaped property confiscation and obtained authorisation to return to Rio on April 1, 1718, four years after his detention, when he was already sixty-six years old, though obviously a resilient man.[80]

Belchior Mendes Correia, also known as António Cardoso Porto, born in Celorico and resident in Bahia, having also spent a period of his life in Bayonne, France, was detained by the Inquisition in 1726, at the age of fifty-six. A slave merchant between Brazil and Western Africa, he also traded in textiles and ran a tobacco factory with two partners, one of them a servant of the Viceroy, Vasco Fernandes César. At his factory, he had stored 400 arrobas of tobacco (equivalent to about 6,000 kg). In his inventory, Belchior Mendes Correia also declared a musical instrument (viola) and collections of books covering both religion and comedy.[81] Faced with eighteen denunciations and an enquiry ordered by the Inquisition in Bahia, Belchior Mendes confessed. On June 17, 1731, after five years in jail, he formally abjured at the auto da fé and had his property confiscated.[82]

The decline in inquisitorial prosecutions of New Christians after the 1740s is also visible in Brazil, where fewer and fewer wealthy people were detained. We still find two or three cases in 1761, from Vila Boa de Goiás, in the interior of Brazil, but few denunciations and little property were involved. António Ferreira Dourado went bankrupt in Lisbon in 1750 with 25,000 cruzados of debt; escaped to Brazil to avoid jail; worked in the local judicial and fiscal systems; was detained in 1761; confessed; and was sentenced to formal abjuration and property confiscation. He had no real estate, but he was a poet who estimated the worth of his manuscript, an epic poem titled *America*, at 3,000 cruzados.[83] One witness accused him of considering the Inquisition superfluous and claimed the tribunal was responsible for draining millions from Portugal just to bolster the standing of the institution.[84] José Pinto Ferreira, a lawyer born in Tomar, had two farms and urban property in Goiás, slaves, and law books. His brother, Tomás Pinto Ferreira, born in Sardoal, had managed one of the properties but did not have real estate himself. The brothers were denounced by seven relatives in what was a typical local raid by the Inquisition. They confessed and were sentenced to formal abjuration and property confiscation.[85]

3. Ideological Turn

The classification "New Christian" or "converso" started to be challenged in the first half of the seventeenth century and became a matter of contention during the eighteenth century. We have seen how some defendants accused of Judaism claimed Old Christian origins, refused to make any confession, and managed to get away with light sentences. Genealogical enquiries were expensive and time consuming, and the Inquisition did not have the capacity to cover all cases. This failure to conduct widespread investigations did not mean that the notion of blood purity had lost traction; in fact, it had become rooted in society owing to compulsory enquiries into the backgrounds of those seeking membership of confraternities, military orders, the Inquisition, certain municipal councils, chapters of cathedrals, university colleges, and other institutions. Successfully navigating the blood purity barrier was part of the game, as we have seen before; the assertion of the rule itself became more important than the complete exclusion of New Christians. In the meantime, miscegenation between New and Old Christians from generation to generation had led to a significant degree of arbitrary assertion of blood purity by the mid-eighteenth century. We shall address what had become a conflict of perceptions through a problematic enquiry into blood purity triggered by an outraged family, the growing concern of people opposed to the perpetuation of such a division, and the radical change of perspective imposed by the governing elite in Portugal.

Manuel de Albuquerque e Aguilar, born in Castelo Rodrigo and resident in Vila Rica, Brazil, was a diamond merchant detained by the Inquisition in 1731, at which point he had precious stones worth 20,000 cruzados. He has been studied because of interest in his early trading activities, before his first royal contract in 1739, when he was a broker for shipments to Miguel Rodrigues Faro and Manuel Lopes Ribeiro in London, on one of which he declared a debt of 80,000 cruzados.[86] However, this trial is important for far more than the limited information on the diamond trade it gives us.

Manuel de Albuquerque was presented on July 6, 1732, at the auto da fé in Lisbon, where he was described as being part New Christian and was sentenced to formal abjuration and property confiscation for Judaism.[87] His name was included in a printed list of those prosecuted at the auto da fé that was circulated all over the country, a common practice that added humiliation and stigma to the families involved. He was identified as "38 [years old] Manoel de Albuquerque e Aguilar, part New Christian, businessman, bachelor, son of António de Sequeira Cabral, who lived of his wealth, born in the town of Castelo Rodrigo and resident in Minas de Ouro Preto, Brazil."[88] His relatives in Castelo Rodrigo and the surrounding region became extremely upset because, apparently, they had always perceived themselves as Old Christians. They rejected the label New Christian and petitioned the Inquisition to make an enquiry to clear their name. This was a rare move that needs to be properly analysed.

The petitioners were António de Sobral e Albuquerque, a priest with the title of abbot at Santa Marinha de Alheira (in the diocese of Braga), Luís Pinto Cardoso, a sergeant major in Armamar, married to the culprit's sister, Mariana Josefa, and Matias Caldeira de Vasconcelos, a familiar of the Inquisition, who was resident in Meda. They wanted to "redeem their credit, and the credit of numerous people, noble and clean families who would become dishonoured and denigrated by this unimaginable event."[89] They lamented that the culprit had forgotten his obligation as a Christian and his blood, birth, and upbringing at the house of his uncle, Manuel de Aguilar Macedo, a priest of Toens, and had lapsed and fallen into the perverse error of Judaism.

The petitioners claimed that Manuel de Albuquerque was not a New Christian, and there had never been such an allegation or rumor attached to his parenthood. They attributed his acceptance of the designation "New Christian" to presumption, hallucination, dread of prison, or a mistake on his part. And they pointed out another mistake: Manuel de Albuquerque had been identified as thirty-eight years old, when the register of baptism revealed that he was not yet thirty-one years of age.[90] They claimed that his confession of his origins was wrong and false and would result in great damage to his relatives and descendants. They pointed out similar cases at the Inquisition in Spain, in which false confessions by people supposedly from a New Christian background had been reversed after enquiry, restoring the credit of the defamed people. They petitioned for an enquiry to redress the situation. And they ended their petition by indicating the names, places of birth, and places of residence of the parents and grandparents of Manuel de Albuquerque e Aguilar.[91]

This was a very bold move, which could backfire—and it did. Neither the ideology of blood purity nor the correctness of the Inquisitorial procedure were questioned. These petitioners sought to give the impression of being clearly convinced of their status as Old Christians. They presented an account of the relatives and collaterals of the condemned man in the present and in past generations. These included Gaspar de Morais, a royal judge and knight of the Order of Christ; Cristóvão Pereira de Meneses, a major captain in Meda; Luís Caldeira Varjão, a familiar of the Inquisition; António de Morais, a royal judge in Évora; António Velho de Azevedo, a knight of the Order of Christ and general lieutenant of artillery in Almeida; Abbot António Pais Teixeira, a commissioner of the Inquisition; two brothers, António and Dionísio Cabral, who were Jesuits; another clergyman, André de Albuquerque, a familiar of the Inquisition; Caetano Alexandre, a major captain in Trancoso; Mauricio Saraiva, a canon of the cathedral of Coimbra; Domingos Saraiva, another major captain of Trancoso; João da Costa, a canon in Coimbra; Sebastião Saraiva, a familiar of the Inquisition; Father Manuel de Aguilar de Macedo, a commissioner of the Inquisition; João Álvares Sobral, a sergeant major and knight of the Order of Christ; Manuel Álvares Sobral, a knight of the Order of Christ; a Franciscan, João de São Carlos; three nuns at the convent of São Luís de Pinhel; Manuel de Afonseca, priest and abbot of Vilarinho de Agrochão; two monks of the Order of St. Jerome; Manuel de Afonseca e Albuquerque, a chaplain of São Luís de Pinhel; Abbott André Teles of Santa Maria de Pinhel, another clergyman; another Franciscan monk; a monk of the order of St. Bernard; Gaspar Veloso Metelo, a familiar of the Inquisition and knight of the Order of Christ; Pedro Cabral de Chaves, a knight of the Order of Christ; and Fr. Feliciano de Albuquerque, a member of the order of St. Bernard and professor of theology at the college of Coimbra.[92]

It is difficult to say whether the petitioners were naive or cunning. They exposed dozens of people with positions in the royal justice system, universities, cathedral chapters, military orders, religious orders, parishes, and the Inquisition itself, who, if they had been New Christians, would have managed to navigate the barrier of blood purity. Some were still active. In any case, on November 3, 1732, the inquisitors launched the requested enquiry, setting out ten questions to be asked relating to the family's blood purity and the veracity of the information contained in the petitioners' report. They nominated a commissioner to undertake the enquiry in Castelo Rodrigo, Vilar Torpim, Meda, and Pinhel; and they charged the petitioners.[93]

The commissioner interrogated fifty people in a first procedure at Castelo Rodrigo, and all of them guaranteed that Manuel de Albuquerque's father, António de Sequeira Cabral, a businessman, was an Old Christian. Some, however, raised the suspicion that his mother, Marina da Guerra de Albuquerque, might have had Jewish blood on her father's side.[94] This was sufficient for the commissioner to conclude, on February 4, 1733, that the mother had Jewish blood, raising the possibility that several members of the family included in the petitioners' report were stained.[95]

Apparently, the inquisitors took on board the commissioner's conclusions, but they did not act. It was obviously too embarrassing, because this enquiry exposed the lack of credibility of other enquiries; for example, some that had led to the investiture of familiars of the Inquisition. It is not impossible that some inquisitors realised the fragility of the whole concept of blood purity, a concept that became increasingly open to dispute from generation to generation. It was an application to become a familiar of the Inquisition, lodged in 1751 by a grandson of Mariana da Guerra, José Guedes Cardoso Pinto e Vasconcelos—the aristocratic fashion for long names had started to be imitated by local elites—that allowed this case to be completed and closed.[96]

The inquisitors ordered a new enquiry in Vilar Torpim with questions related to Filipe de Aguilar, the father of Mariana da Guerra. Twelve witnesses were interrogated, all of whom declared that he was an Old Christian. This is not surprising: Vilar Torpim was a very small town with only a few hundred inhabitants and a long tradition of being prosecuted by the Inquisition, which raises the issue of probable conflicts in Castelo Rodrigo that would have made unanimous answers to the inquisitorial enquiry unlikely. The inquisitors were not happy with this outcome in Vilar Torpim, and they ordered the interrogation of an old abbot who was supposed to have heard an already dead older woman declaring that the blood of the Aguilar family was stained.[97] The abbot confirmed the story, and the inquisitors finally obtained what they wanted: they decided that the branch of the family under investigation was New Christian and refused the application by José Guedes Cardoso, a decision supported by the general council in October 1752.[98]

How should this case be understood? The inquisitors were clearly uncomfortable with the initial, probably unintentional but blatant, challenge to blood purity enquiries. They tried to dissimulate and postpone, but José Guedes Cardoso's application to become a familiar forced a decision: either they would acknowledge the error of classifying Manuel de Albuquerque e Aguilar as a New Christian and accept the application; or they would assert the impurity of his blood and refuse it. They clearly chose the second option virtually without proof from Vilar Torpim. It was a political decision: they preferred to uphold the fiction of blood purity and rebuke a candidate who threatened the system. But they did not extend their enquiry to the familiars already in place. They probably knew it would open a Pandora's box.

One last word about Manuel de Albuquerque e Aguilar: in his first statement to the Inquisition he declared he was an Old Christian. Only later, when he started to confess and was denouncing many New Christians, did he indicate some Jewish background on his father's side. It is obvious that he had no clue. We know from the reports and enquiries that he had run away at a very young age to Lisbon and then Brazil. Therefore, he could not have been inducted into Judaism by his family. He declared as his Jewish mentor the physician Manuel Dias de Carvalho, who had escaped to France.[99]

This case unveils the ambiguities of blood purity and clarifies that its perpetuation was political. At a local level, the system had started to crack. Among the intellectual and religious Portuguese elite, discontent about caste divisions was being openly expressed. In 1707, immediately after the investiture of Nuno da Cunha as general inquisitor, the Jesuit Manuel Correia (1636–1708), then resident in Rome, wrote him a letter titled *Racional discurso sobre os desacertos de Portugal*, which contained the fiercest attack on the system.[100] He opened the letter by lamenting the ocean of infamy, ignominy, and discredit that had sunk the honour, fame, and glory of Portugal among other nations, because of the division between Old and New Christians and labelling the latter as Jews. He condemned the repeated autos da fé and the diffusion of lists of those condemned that circulated throughout the world, including to the head of the Church, which defamed all Portuguese as Jews. The enormous number of people involved in these exercises after so many years in a small country inflicted an injury on all inhabitants that was beyond repair. He also decried the theater [*sic*] of autos da fé, staged in main squares, to which foreigners were invited. The collection of penitential habits, *sambenitos*, in the main churches of Lisbon, Coimbra, and Évora, with the portraits of those condemned to wear them, were, in his opinion, an offence to the whole nation, involving as they did noblemen, people in holy orders, and members of the lower social strata.[101]

Manuel Correia reproduced some jokes from the time of Philip II in Lisbon, according to which Spaniards derided the similarities between those condemned by the Inquisition and familiars of the Inquisition: the former were public Jews, the latter were suspected Jews, meaning that nobody was exempt from fear. He remarked that the Spaniards were clever to declare that they had Jews among them, but they were Portuguese, thus contributing to Portugal's infamy, while many defendants at the Portuguese Inquisition had been born in Spain. The cure for this disease would be to eradicate distinctions of blood among the Portuguese. Baptism, in his opinion, always purged previous states of error. Converted Calvinists and Lutherans, Germans, English, Dutch, and Italians were considered Old Christians without any impediment to their ecclesiastical status. By the same token, indigenous peoples converted following conquest by Portugal were considered Old Christians. The infamy attributed to Jews was the result of a passion for vengeance whereby whole families and innocent generations were defamed. If the classification did not exist, there would be no memory of people's origins or descent.[102] This is the most comprehensive exposure of the racialisation of, and discrimination against, part of the population, touching all issues, from the promotion of foreigners to the defamation of Portuguese as Jews, attributed to the iniquitous practice of autos da fé.

Manuel Correia pointed to practice concerning the conversion of Jews in Rome, which was not followed by discrimination. All those converted could access honours and high status. He also mentioned the existence of a ghetto and a synagogue, which should be allowed in Portugal. And he added a daring jab: the head of the Church should not be moved by his own interests but by the well-being of souls. He also noted that foundling children were considered Old Christian in Portugal. The impoverishment of the Portuguese kingdom was attributed to this division, through emigration and the transfer of wealth, while other countries such as the Netherlands, England, France, and Italy benefitted. He highlighted Livorno, a former fishing village that had been transformed into a commercial centre by the Portuguese, but he pointed out that many New Christian emigrants there remained Catholic. He went further, suggesting the suppression of familiars of the Inquisition, since they were harming the monarchy and contributing to the perpetuation of the division of blood. The idea of blood purity, in his view, offended natural reason, justice, and the common good, creating an arbitrary logic of distinction among the subjects of the state and Church.[103]

The impediment to accessing religious orders occupied another section of the letter, in which Manuel Correia mentioned a holy man who had created a new institution (this is certainly Ignatius Loyola) and had been censored for not discriminating against New Christians. This man would have replied, "How can I exclude from the path to heaven those who are willing to abandon pomp, luxury, leisure, good food, and wealth?" The exclusion of those who embraced poverty, silence, fasting, and submission was classified as contrary to natural reason, truth, and justice.[104] The writer then addressed other issues, such as the money spent in Rome for the authorisation of marriage between close relatives, the excesses of religious people due to venality, the need to reform the system of nuns' dowries, and the excessive expenses of convents, all typical eighteenth century topics.[105] The final statement is the least convincing: that the writer had "no impure blood from any infect nation" (he had been born in Luanda, a Portuguese enclave for the slave trade in central West Africa), before asserting his objectivity and his dearest wish for his country to be cleansed of ignominy.[106] The main topics of the blood purity debate are here systematised and discussed by a professor of philosophy and theology at the university of Évora, a rector of the college of arts in Coimbra, a provincial of the Jesuits, and a participant in various congregations of the Society in Rome, where he was a Portuguese representative and general inspector.[107]

Even sharper was the text written in the 1730s and 1740s on the distinction between New and Old Christians by António Nunes Ribeiro Sanches, who was born in 1699 in Penamacor and died in Paris in 1783. Ribeiro Sanches studied medicine in Coimbra and Salamanca, practised as a physician in Guarda and Benavente, Portugal, had parents and close relatives sentenced by the Inquisition, and escaped to London in 1726. In London, he converted to Judaism but had doubts, then moved to Livorno, Bordeaux, Paris, and finally, Leiden, where he went back to university and had the best professors, such as the celebrated Hermanus Boerhaave. In 1731 he accepted an invitation addressed to the university of Leiden by the Russian empress, Anna, to send three physicians, and he lived in Russia for sixteen years, accumulating an extraordinary amount of experience as a physician to the army on various war fronts and also at the imperial court. He reverted to Catholicism in the mid-1730s, then finally asked to be released from his post and went back to Paris, where he was highly respected by the prominent scientists of the day, such as the comte de Buffon, with whom he had corresponded, sending the Frenchman the results of his observations and experiments in Russia. He wrote extensively on the treatment of various diseases and public hygiene and was consulted by several European governments on the reform of medical education. Portugal and Russia gave him annual pensions until his death.[108]

It is this background that makes an analysis of Ribeiro Sanches's pamphlet on the origins of the denominations "New Christian" and "Old Christian," probably written in 1735 and completed in 1748, compelling. It is an extraordinary case of a New Christian who became famous in his lifetime, reached a senior position in the republic of letters, engaged with the best physicians and scientists in Europe, and was so influential that he caught the attention of the Portuguese political elite. His manuscripts circulated in Portugal. His denunciation of the fatal division between New and Old Christians was based on three main ideas: the enquiries that had to be negotiated for access to civil and ecclesiastic jobs, confraternities, and colleges provoked an exponential increase in New Christians; the trials of the Inquisition were another major mechanism that diffused the stigma, because New Christians were prepared by their families, in case of detention, to confess and denounce as many people as they could to avoid execution, and to present themselves and denounce people recently detained whom they knew; and the autos da fé (nonexistent in Italy), the printed lists of the culprits, and the collections of sambenitos with the portraits and names of the condemned in the main churches had spread the idea through many countries that Portugal was a nation of Jews.[109]

This reasoning was not new. When Manuel Correia had expressed it, he had been reflecting a long line of grievances presented to the pope by the victims and by people distressed by the oppression imposed on this minority. Perhaps this was the right time to reassert this disquiet. In Ribeiro Sanches's view, the enquiries into blood purity and the trials of the Inquisition produced New Christians; they would have disappeared as a separate group without these mechanisms of distinction (or discrimination) and coercion. The stigmatisation of a minority born, baptized, and religiously educated in Portugal is contrasted with the acceptance into Portuguese society of foreigners, all considered Old Christian with very little enquiry into their background. Foundling children were considered Old Christians, another absurdity of classification. Mixed marriages, promoted by Afonso de Albuquerque in Goa, were praised by the author; the same policy used in Portugal would have unified all Christians. The exclusion of New Christians from privileges was considered the result of ignorance and blindness; if some New Christians opted for Judaism, this was caused by education, not by blood, "because all blood is red," a pertinent observation from a physician, debunking head-on prejudices concerning race.[110] Moreover, Ribeiro Sanches reflected on his own experience as a New Christian boy, constantly insulted and undermined as Jewish, subjected to gestures of derision as if he were emitting a filthy smell, or were a dog, or had a tail. He also lamented the restrictions placed on New Christian married couples, whose property could be easily confiscated and whose access to dignities obstructed.[111]

Ribeiro Sanches regretted the loss of so many subjects by the kingdom, the decline in trade, the desolation of the provinces of Trás-os-Montes and Beira, where so many manufacturers of silk, wool, and leather had disappeared, the ruin of many families that had depended on the condemned administrators of comendas and entailed properties. He pointed out the advantages given to many foreign merchants who got rich and took their profits back to their countries. He also underlined the decline of sugar production in Brazil, a consequence of property confiscation, which King John V tried to limit in 1728. He highlighted the Venetian policy of passing the property of those condemned by the Inquisition to their heirs.[112] This picture of economic and demographic damage to the kingdom was being painted at a time of jurisdictionalism, or assertion of the power of the state over the traditional privileges of the Church. The final remarks by Ribeiro Sanches in his pamphlet were strangely prescient—the pope had never managed to change the procedures of the Inquisition in Portugal; the king had always prevailed, facilitating the execution of the excommunicated without seeing the trials. He hinted that to have a country of united subjects, faithful and loyal vassals, change needed to come from the state.[113]

Ribeiro Sanches's friend and patient, Luís da Cunha (1662–1749), the ambassador and envoy of the Portuguese king in London, The Hague, Utrecht,

Madrid, and Paris from 1697 to his death, also condemned the label New Christian, the division between New Christians and Old Christians, and the inquisitorial procedure. If we compare the reasoning of Luís da Cunha on this issue with Ribeiro Sanches's text, the similarities are striking—they follow the same lines and reflect the same arguments, even at times using the same words. It is plausible to assume that Ribeiro Sanches gave Luís da Cunha his main lines of information and argument, because of his personal experience as a New Christian, although the reasoning developed by Luís da Cunha in favour of this oppressed minority had been current in diplomatic circles since the War of Independence in Portugal.

Luís da Cunha had his own experience of Judaism in the Sephardic community in the Netherlands; that is, he was invited to important weddings (for example, by the Suasso family), and he had a Jewish lover, Madam Salvador Pereira, who converted to Christianity. He had enormous prestige at the royal court in Portugal and had represented his country at all the main international diplomatic meetings where Portuguese interests were at stake, particularly that leading to the Treaty of Utrecht.[114] He dispatched many reports, recommendations, and pieces of information to the king and secretaries of state, offering opinions that no one else would dare to formulate. In a certain way, Luís da Cunha opened a small window for the royal court onto the evolution of ideas in Europe. He was not part of the political game in Lisbon, which gave him space to offer his opinions freely, apparently encouraged by the king. He became an authority. In his letter to Prince Joseph, the future king, written between 1747 and 1749 and later referred to as a political testament, he suggested Sebastião José de Carvalho e Melo, future Marquis of Pombal, for secretary of state.[115] His unambiguous attack on the New-Old Christian division must have carried far more weight than the pamphlet by Ribeiro Sanches.

Luís da Cunha stressed the idea of deserted towns with ruined factories, such as Covilhã, Fundão, Guarda, and Lamego in the province of Beira, and Bragança in Trás-os-Montes. This was the result of extensive inquisitorial detentions, which ruined those who were caught and made others flee abroad with their capital.[116] He labelled these actions as responsible for bleeding the country through property confiscation and instilling fear that affected numerous workers who could no longer find jobs. He quoted Fr. Domingos de São Tomás, who worked for the Inquisition and had stated that, "As there is a house that fabricates coins, there is a house at Rossio that makes Jews of New Christians, because he knew how they were prosecuted . . . ; instead of extinguishing them, they multiplied."[117]

In his opinion, the practice of secrecy concerning the name of accusers was responsible for the widespread denunciations of those detained, to avoid being considered deficient in their confessions and excommunicated, which meant executed. Luís da Cunha lamented the exclusion of Jews from the country while they were accepted all over Europe, including in Rome, a long-term topic of the community's grievances. He quoted the kingdom's legislation, according to which it was a secular duty to prosecute apostasy.[118]

Luís da Cunha derided the autos da fé, an entertainment called a triumph of faith that had been invented by the inquisitors to excite the curiosity of people; they were attended by Portuguese nationals as they attended bull fights and by foreigners as a fair where a variety of badges were exposed.[119] He asserted that all private tribunals for certain crimes would produce an enormous number of criminals, as had happened in France, where Louis XIV had instituted a special tribunal to enquire into sorcerers and poisoners and then had to close it down because of the extraordinary numbers of accusations. He regretted that King Pedro II lifted the order of extermination (or exile) of condemned New Christians who confessed because the Inquisition had decided it had produced a decline in denunciations and trials.[120] He observed that it was not the role of the Church, and still less that of the prince, to deal with internal beliefs, concluding that the republic did not have to go looking for secret Jews as long as they did not cause a scandal and kept to their houses. He regretted that the secrecy of accusations and condemnations on the word of a single witness had not been forbidden.[121]

More damaging to the tribunal, Luís da Cunha asserted that the king had the power to abolish the tribunal or to change its style (procedure).[122] He insisted that the Inquisition caused an increase in the number of New Christians with its procedure, as did confraternities and other institutions with their blood purity enquiries, which should be suppressed.[123] Property confiscation by the Inquisition should also be prohibited, imitating Venice's policy. Luís da Cunha regretted the destruction of property in Portugal and also in Brazil, "where the Inquisition mined the wealth of the Jews in Rio de Janeiro" by expropriating their sugar mills, until King John V intervened because of the great damage to trade.[124]

The issue of property had already been a major concern of the papacy from 1674 to 1681 and would become a major issue of jurisdictionalism in Europe, fully absorbed by the French Revolution. Protection of property rights against the arbitrary rule of the Church or the prince were at the core of the legal and political debate of the century. But Luís da Cunha went further in his criticism of the harm produced by blood purity enquiries and the Inquisition. He rejected the idea that Judaism contaminated blood and advocated eliminating the label "New Christian" and granting freedom of conscience for Jews to live according to their religion, as was practiced in many countries in Europe. Eliminating an injurious label, reinforced by penalties for those who dared to reproduce the old insults, would allow the full integration of the oppressed minority into the republic, with property rights guaranteed and access to all honours, which would result in unifying the republic and strengthening trade.[125]

The difference between this letter to the prince and the first one, probably written in 1736, responding to a demand for political instruction from Marco António de Azevedo Coutinho, is important. Although the first letter was probably written in 1736, it was not sent immediately, and we know only that it was sent before 1747. The coincidence between the dates of the two letters and the dates of the two stages of the preparation of Ribeiro Sanches's pamphlet is remarkable: 1736? and 1735, 1747/1749 and 1747. The first reflection on the Inquisition and New Christians, probably from 1736, had a wider historical scope. Moral and religious feelings were more explicit in the reproval of inquisitorial activity, because so many innocent people had been condemned in contravention of the legal and religious principle that it is better that one criminal should go free than that one innocent person should be condemned.[126] Luís da Cunha rejected the idea that one drop of Jewish blood would contaminate "pure" blood, and he repeated Ribeiro Sanches's idea that education, not blood, could create Jews. The Realpolitik of the French government, which accepted Jewish communities in Bayonne, Bordeaux, and Metz, was praised.[127]

Luís da Cunha disapproved of the inquisitors' prejudiced belief that all New Christians were Jewish. He pointed out that they were not circumcised, and they did not know the precepts of the written law. The arbitrariness of New Christian status was exposed and precise, with horrendous examples given. The production and multiplication of New Christians by the Inquisition and the blood purity enquiries were already at the core of his reasoning.[128] The suggestion to suppress the Inquisition, however, was rejected: the intention should be to reform the procedure, forbid property confiscation, and give freedom of conscience to Jews. The elimination of the label "New Christian" was not explicitly advocated, although the theme of regret at the loss to the kingdom of people and capital through inquisitorial prosecutions had already been developed.[129] The later letter to Prince Joseph also contained a reworking of da Cunha's earlier rejection of the autos da fé, then called "masquerades," and of the collection in major churches of penitential habits worn by the condemned, with the latter practice criticised as a perversion of memory.[130] Briefly, Luís da Cunha's final political advice to the prince on the Inquisition and the New Christians was much sharper and more decisive than his first to the secretary of state; that is, extinguishing an infamous label, suppressing blood purity enquiries, reforming inquisitorial procedure, and abandoning property confiscation.

Luís da Cunha also provides invaluable help to analyse the apparent absence of debate on New Christians in Spain in his time. The Duke of Ossuna, whom he met at the negotiations for the Peace of Utrecht, told him that Princess Orsini, who then informally ruled the Spanish monarchy, planned to abolish the Inquisition simply by not filling places that fell vacant. The project failed with the fall of the government. Luís da Cunha added that the project, if implemented, would have immensely damaged Portugal, since all New Christians would have moved to Castile, which they could have done without essentially changing their homeland. To avoid such an exodus, it would have been necessary for the Portuguese to replicate the Spanish project.[131] This remark underlined the idea that New Christian communities were in fact Iberian. After the French faction and the royal secretary, Macanaz, were defeated by the Spanish (and Italian) faction at court, led by the General Inquisitor Giudice, a new wave of persecutions of New Christians prevented any attempt to reform the Inquisition. However, that wave came to an end by the 1740s, which meant that prosecutions declined. The ups and downs of repression were never "natural" or spontaneous.

The second half of the eighteenth century saw a debate in Spain related to the Inquisition that curiously ignored New Christians. The blood purity statutes were not touched on, but they kept their formal validity until the mid-nineteenth century. A sequence of laws in 1835, 1837, 1845, and 1857 suppressed blood purity enquiry for public positions, but a general suppression, including enquiries prior to marriage, only came about on May 13, 1865.[132] The strategy of successive governments under Fernando VI, Carlos III, and Carlos IV was to reduce the autonomy of the Inquisition and curb the number of trials. As a result of this gradualist approach to taming the tribunal, the New Christians apparently ceased to be used as a proxy by the Inquisition to oppose moves towards reform. The persecution of conversos disappeared in the second half of the eighteenth century, but prejudices remained for a long time in several regions, mainly in Mallorca, where the *Xuetes* (local New Christians) were still stigmatised in the 1960s.[133]

The move to assert the legal rights of the state over the Church and Rome on secular issues, then called *jurisdictionalism*, drove the debate around the Inquisition and the Society of Jesus, with the two organizations conflated for the purposes of this conflict. While the Society of Jesus was suppressed in Spain in 1767, after it had already been expelled from Portugal (1759) and France (1764), the Inquisition was not touched. However, an imposed moderation of inquisitorial activity was extended to the censorship of books. The Spanish Inquisition in 1761 published a Roman edict of exclusion that banned the catechism produced by François-Philippe Mésenguy. This decision had an immediate backlash. It was used by the government to obtain the complete submission of the tribunal, and the general inquisitor, Quintano y Bonifaz, was exiled. Bonifaz petitioned for pardon, which was conceded in return for total obedience to the Crown and acceptance of royal scrutiny of any decisions imposed from Rome. A moderate Spanish Enlightenment that was represented by major royal ministers, such as Campomanes, Aranda, Floridablanca, Jovellanos, and Urquijo, never brought to fruition their projects to suppress the Inquisition, but together with the Jansenists, they succeeded in infiltrating the institution.[134]

The indirect and restrained way of appeasing the Inquisition and diluting the New Christian question in Spain resulting from the shift in the state's interests, which were no longer strictly aligned with those of Rome in a changing world, contrasted with the more direct policies adopted in Portugal on the same issues. However, Pombal also opted for soft control in the 1750s and 1760s while he was asserting his power and placing his men, including his brother Paulo de Carvalho e Mendonça, as members of the general council of the Inquisition. The number of trials declined significantly in those years.[135] In another significant development, printing and distributing lists from autos da fé, which took place from the 1620s onwards, was widely criticised as stigmatising families and bringing the country into disrepute and was finally broken off in 1759.[136]

The first law that favoured the New Christians was published on May 2, 1768. This required the collection and delivery to the royal treasurer of lists of all taxation being imposed on New Christians in the kingdom and its domains. These lists were considered hostile and abusive, because they unfairly increased the infamy and exclusion of New Christians, resulting in damage to the reputation and credit of many families. The new law forbade the reproduction and use of these lists for any purpose.[137] This was the first assault on the blood purity system.

The second assault on, and definitive demolition of, anti-New Christian procedures, came five years later, on May 25, 1773, when the distinction between New and Old Christian was eradicated. This distinction was now considered abusive and offensive, being contrary to the unitarian spirit of Christianity and the canons and practices of the Roman Church. The distinction was qualified as seditious, leading to the denigration, segregation, and oppression of the many vassals excluded from civil and ecclesiastic honours and jobs. All requirements based on blood purity were revoked. Anyone found using the distinction in oral or written language would be stripped of their nationality and exiled from the kingdom and its domains. Noblemen guilty of acting in this way would lose their positions; plebeians would be whipped and deported to Angola.[138]

The last law in this sequence was issued on December 15, 1774, and reiterated the revocation of what was now a seditious, barbarous, and impious distinction and clarified that those reconciled by the Inquisition were henceforth absolved on any crime, as were the children and grandchildren of the condemned, now considered free from all stain, while property confiscation was clearly excluded from spiritual (meaning the Church's) jurisdiction. This last clarification represented a major legal assertion of the rights of the state against the Church, striking at the core of two centuries of inquisitorial penal decisions that had been accepted without question by the state. The law also stipulated that those who disputed this ruling would lose their property; if they were judges, they would lose their jobs and the right to apply for other jobs.[139]

These laws matched the jurisdictionalist assertion of the state, being based on a desire to treat all vassals without distinction to create a certain homogeneity, a common sense of belonging, and of loyalty to the king. They were related to a growing freedom of movement and increased status enjoyed by natives of the Portuguese domains in the New World and Asia. We know that these laws were effectively implemented: there are many records of religious orders, military orders, and confraternities that show traces of articles on blood purity having been erased from their statutes. We also know that the university of Coimbra protested against these laws but was forced to obey.

The issue of timing is an interesting one. Why were these laws issued only eighteen and twenty-three years after the nomination of Pombal as secretary of state? Of particular importance are the earthquake of 1755 and the attempt to murder King Joseph in 1758, which allowed Pombal to assert his power, expel the Jesuits, and strike at the main noble houses. He also needed time to change the composition of various councils and tribunals to obtain institutional consensus. The laws were made after consultation with those institutions, including the general council of the Inquisition. It is no coincidence that this council was transformed into a royal council, with new rules for the Inquisition placed under the patronaged of the king and the Marquis of Pombal, and registered at the secretariat of state of the kingdom on September 9, 1774.[140] Briefly, the significance of blood purity as a concept was eradicated, and the Inquisition was placed firmly under the control of the government.

Conclusions to Part IV

THE BACKLASH of the reestablishment of the Portuguese Inquisition, complemented by royal legislation imposing forfeiture of privileges and exile on all reconciled with formal abjuration at autos da fé, dealt a final blow to the major New Christian merchants and contractors. We still find New Christians involved in the royal monopoly on tobacco, mainly in Spain, and administering royal rents and taxation in both Portugal and Spain; but their participation in financial asientos or major contracts declined dramatically in the first half of the eighteenth century. While production of sugar and trade with Brazil was still largely in the hands of New Christians at the turn of the eighteenth century, the wave of Inquisition prosecutions from the 1700s to the 1720s significantly reduced their share. In Spain, the major wave of prosecutions of New Christians in the 1710s and 1720s had a similar impact.

New Christians were generally replaced at the highest level by Old Christians and foreign merchants and financiers, promoted by the king and the Inquisition both in Spain and Portugal. It was a clear decision to suppress the economic power of a minority elite based on racial discrimination. Iberia became economically more dependent on foreign powers through this strategy of the Inquisitions, which prevailed over secular power up to the mid-eighteenth century. While jurisdictionalism by the state was then smoothly imposed on the Inquisition in Spain without touching the blood purity rules, in Portugal in the late 1760s and 1770s there was a direct suppression of those rules, with the abolition of both the label New Christian and the distinction between Old and New Christians, followed by an undisguised transformation of the Inquisition into a royal court controlled by the government.

New Christians were still prosecuted in the 1760s, while there was a small but steady flow of migrants from Iberia to Jewish communities in Europe and the Americas. Without the intervention of the state, the Inquisition might have been able to invent new types of denunciations to feed their trials, as had happened in various previous periods. However, the emergence of new, critical voices in the upper echelons of society brought a change of political atmosphere. It is arguable that the needs of the state were shifting away from the sort of support that religious values had supplied from medieval times to the mid-eighteenth century. The concept of the state changed with the dawn of the separation of secular and spiritual spheres. Clergymen and inquisitors aligned with Rome were placed on a defensive footing for the first time in two centuries, while the first cracks within the traditional coalition of interests between the Inquisition and the episcopate started to occur in the 1740s.[1]

The immersion of New Christians in a global society was part of a significant social and political change. The leadership of wealthy New Christian bankers and merchants petered out after decades of systematic repression and deliberate replacement by Old Christians and foreign merchants. The global assertion of their interests by competitive national merchant communities, who appropriated the policies of imperial states, left less and less space for ethnic diasporas. The ethnic identity of New Christians, which had been reinforced by inquisitorial persecution, declined irreversibly. A change in relations between the state and the Inquisition in Iberia, and the suppression of blood purity rules and the designation "New Christian" in Portugal, favoured the process of immersion that was already under way. The withdrawal of the Inquisition led to (nearly) full integration, as critical voices had always asserted it would.

Conclusion

THIS BOOK has charted the story of a minority of Jewish origin that was forced to convert to Christianity in Castile, Aragón, and Portugal in the period from 1391 to 1497. This minority was discriminated against through blood purity statutes and inquisitorial enquiries right up until the mid-eighteenth century. The creation and subsequent persecution of this minority can be defined as one of the earliest cases of institutional racism within the same religious community in Europe, and this was extended to the Iberian empires.

Most members of hitherto segregated Jewish communities in Iberia were compulsorily absorbed into the majority Christian community, only to immediately be labelled conversos, marranos, or New Christians. They were suspected of simulating their Christian faith and dissimulating a continued adherence to Jewish rituals and traditions. After three centuries and more than nine generations, their descendants were still being prosecuted as Jews. Religious antagonism was thus translated into racial hatred against converted people and their descendants, to whom the same prejudices and stereotypes produced along the centuries against Jews were applied. However, permanent labelling, discrimination, and persecution based on genealogy helped create a strong sense of ethnic identity among New Christians, with threats reinforcing solidarity and renewing common perceptions of ancestry and kinship.

I have focused on the merchant elite of the New Christian ethnicity because they played a crucial role in intercontinental trade during the sixteenth and seventeenth centuries. This section of the ethnicity drew on the significant economic power they had generated to promote resistance and ingenuity under persecution. The wider New Christian community can be observed through cases of social mobility, co-optation, and service to the most powerful, but the vast majority of New Christians were shopkeepers, peddlers, working artisans, and people without property or economic status.

This book has reconstructed the New Christian presence all over the world to better understand the historical context, main challenges, continuous prejudices, innovative activities, and long-lasting imprint of their practices, and the main changes that led to their decline and disappearance as an identifiable ethnic group. In my conclusion, I shall look again at the main threads that guided my research, starting with the crucial issue of blood purity, which set New Christians apart; then I shall summarise my main findings on the activities of the New Christian social elite, including their diaspora and the creation of Sephardic Jewish communities; and I shall highlight their cultural and religious creativity, which had an impact on contemporary art, literature, science, and spiritual quests.

Forced conversion provided the Iberian Jews with access to public office, religious orders, military orders, and ecclesiastic careers, and to positions in local government and administration, in colleges, and in the medical and legal professions. In the first two generations, in Castile, New Christians achieved high positions in the Catholic Church as bishops. Members of New Christian families became entrenched in the municipal councils of many important towns, such as Seville, Toledo, Cordoba, Ciudad Real, Segovia, and Burgos. They acquired positions at universities, mainly as lawyers and physicians, and became royal counsellors, judges, treasurers, accountants, and contractors. In the meantime, the transfer of political, financial, and trading functions from Jews to New Christians was completed by the royal decision of 1492 to expel Jewish communities from Castile and Aragón (and Sicily), a decision replicated by the Portuguese king in 1496 in a way that effectively led to a lightning forced mass conversion. Social and economic transition was facilitated and its scope was enlarged by the new institutional positions immediately accessible to New Christians.

Retribution for this fast social promotion came swiftly. From the beginning there were attempts to block New Christian access to colleges, professions, and local government, and these triggered protests and royal intervention. The anti-New Christian riot in Toledo in 1449 was the most violent of a sequence of vicious events as the first blood purity statute was issued. Excluding Jewish descendants from public office was justified by their supposed duplicitous rejection of Christianity and clandestine persistence in Jewish practices and by their alleged willingness to harm Old Christians and destroy local communities through greedy, perverse, and malicious behaviour. According to the riot leaders, who sought to dehumanise New Christians, all acts of plunder and murder were justified. The defence mounted by New Christians highlighted the unprecedented division within the Church; the absurdity of excluding the descendants of the Virgin Mary's and Jesus Christ's lineage from offices, benefices, honours, liberties, and dignities; the heretical denial of the efficacy of baptism as a sacrament; and the fact that numerous noble families and branches of the royal houses of the Iberian kingdoms had Jewish ancestors.

Violence against the basic precepts of the Christian Church prevailed. Anti-New Christians riots occurred in cities and towns across Castile and

Andalusia from the 1450s to the 1470s, until the Inquisition was established in 1478 explicitly to enquire into the real faith of New Christians. The enormous wave of prosecutions this unleashed was perceived as confirming all prejudices against New Christians. Dignitaries, clergymen, merchants, and artisans were condemned in speedy trials. The presence of New Christians in local government, religious orders, and cathedral chapters was increasingly under threat, but they managed to hang on. Nevertheless, the approval by Pope Alexandre VI in 1595 of the blood purity statute devised by the Jeronimites represented a major setback for the defenders of New Christians. New statutes were approved in Spain in the first half of the sixteenth century despite fierce opposition, but it was the statute promulgated in the cathedral of Toledo by Archbishop Silíceo in 1547 that rooted and spread the new racist norm because it was approved by both the king and the pope.

This is a telling story of the racialisation of a large group of people who had been forced to convert to Christianity. Different segments of the Old Christian population used traditional prejudices to limit and exclude competition. The former elites saw the advantage of ring-fencing their privileges, while the rural and urban middle and lower strata of the population were able to claim the higher status that blood purity bestowed. The importance of protecting the unity of the Christian Church was invoked to no avail. New Christians were targeted because they were highly competitive. In this case, racial divide and racism, understood as prejudice against ethnic descent coupled with discriminatory action, were used to create hierarchies and define barriers to protect privileges and honours. The outcome of this complex social process was not a caste society, but a distinctive society of orders in which the three estates (clergymen, nobles, and plebeians) were bisected by a virtual line of caste divide.

A gap of fifty to one hundred years separated Spain and Portugal in their imposition of forced conversion followed by discrimination. The sequence of forced conversion in Portugal in 1497 followed by the establishment of the Inquisition in 1536–1547 and the publication of blood purity statutes from the 1550s onwards (mainly during the Union of Crowns between Spain and Portugal in 1580 to 1640) looks familiar. There were, however, several differences. Forced conversion in Portugal was the result of a royal policy decision and was implemented in a fast, streamlined manner. New Christian resistance in Castile was very vocal during the first wave of inquisitorial persecution, both at the royal court and in Rome, but became relatively subdued after the 1520s. The war of the comunidades seems to have defined a turning point. New Christian resistance in Portugal articulated itself through regular political action and representation in Rome from the 1530s to the 1690s, involving, at different moments, Castilian and Aragonese relatives. The blood purity debate, which inflamed public discourse from the 1590s to the 1630s in Spain, was rekindled in the first half of the eighteenth century in Portugal in such an effective way that the new political elite of the 1750s to 1770s abolished the distinction between New Christians and Old Christians.

These divergences reveal different dynamics within the different Iberian states but do not undermine the fact that New Christians became an international ethnic group with their own shared perceptions of historical memory and relative solidarity as they faced inquisitorial prosecution—approximately 24,000 trials in Portugal and its empire, probably more than 15,000 in Spain and its empire from the late fifteenth to the mid-eighteenth century, without counting denunciations and enquiries that did not produce trials. Constant Jewish and then New Christian migration between the Iberian states in the fifteenth and sixteenth centuries because of persecution consolidated family ties across state borders. These features of the New Christians' fragile and changeable identity (within plural identities) must not be overstated, because divisions and betrayals emerged regularly within this ethnicity, partly triggered by the conflict between declared Catholic and Jewish allegiance. Changes in long-term conditions in Iberia and elsewhere contributed to the erosion of this sense of ethnic identity, an identity that would virtually disappear during the second half of the eighteenth century.

The blood purity debate needs to be placed in its political and economic context. The first period, from the 1590s to the 1630s in Madrid, coincides both with the Union of Crowns and the downturn of the economic situation into a real and perceived long-term decline. Criticism of blood purity enquiries that could stretch over four, five, or six generations became widespread. Members of different religious orders and dignitaries of the Church intervened, along with arbitristas, lawyers, inquisitors, and royal counsellors. The Dominican Agustín Salucio expressed the most cogent arguments against blood purity statutes. He insisted on the universalism of the Church and the need for new conversions; he developed the demographic argument, deriding the idea of blood purity passed down through thirty generations, which represented one million people; and he condemned the statutes as offending against good government and distributive justice, because their implementation obstructed the division of land and public offices in fair proportion and according to merit, good reason, and equity. The promotion of the interests of the state, where these necessitated the restriction of blood purity enquiries, clashed at the end of this period with the activities of those promoting a racial divide, such as Francisco de Quevedo, who used the most violent, hate-fuelled language against New Christians and was the first person to suggest a conspiracy by Jews and New Christians to ruin the Christian countries. In the end, it proved impossible to suppress or even limit blood purity enquiries, revealing the coalition of interests in favour of these procedures.

While the concept of blood purity became a rooted ideology of discrimination, its implementation was constantly manipulated, mainly through royal intervention or bribery, by those seeking to cross the barrier. We know that many New Christians, both in Spain and Portugal, became knights or hidalgos of the royal house, partly because they needed the legal powers that went with the position if they were to collect taxes, rents, or customs duties on behalf of the king. Many others became members of military orders or religious orders, successfully negotiating the enquiries into their racial background, sometimes with explicit royal help. A significant number married into the nobility or negotiated a noble title for services rendered. Evidence has been found of several cases of blood cleansing by royal fiat, as a reward for services. But it is difficult to estimate how many New Christians overcame the barriers and how many were detected and excluded. Circumvention could be temporary, because it could not guarantee automatic inclusion in the ranks of Old Christians through the succeeding generations. Many setbacks occurred at the highest level. Successful families seemed to depend on sustained local support, negotiation, and bribery.

Political criticism of the Inquisition and of blood purity ideology could sometimes go hand in hand. Blood purity was not at the forefront of political debates, neither during the papal suspension of the Inquisition in Portugal from 1674 to 1681, nor during the attempt by the Princess Orsini and the royal secretary, Macanaz, in Spain in the 1710s, to limit inquisitorial activity. In both cases, New Christians were subsequently targeted by the tribunals of the Inquisition in new waves of persecution to assert their power and undermine all opponents as promoters of apostasy.

The successful attack against the Inquisition in Portugal, which began in the 1700s but intensified from the 1740s to the 1770s, followed a different path, placing blood purity at the centre of the debate to reveal the devastating effect of the ideology on industry and trade, which drained the country of people and capital. The argument was that this ideology perverted good government through the unfair treatment of a large part of the population, who were singled out and excluded. The idea that the Inquisition fabricated Jews out of New Christians was developed in this period, while the atavistic delusion that an inclination to Judaism was passed on through blood was derided.

The decline of religion in the European values system and the jurisdictional assertion of the state over the Church in southern Europe contributed to significant changes. In Spain, in the third quarter of the eighteenth century, the Inquisition was placed under royal control through the exercise of great vigilance in recruitment. In the more centralised state of Portugal, the separate lists of New Christians used for taxation purposes were destroyed in 1768, and the distinction between New Christian and Old Christian abolished in 1773. The state took complete control of the Inquisition in 1774, with new rules for its running, long before its abolition in 1821. In Spain, however, the ideology of blood purity partly survived the final abolition of the Inquisition in 1834.

This book has analysed the rise and fall of the New Christian merchant elite against the background that shaped them and imposed a life of constant negotiation on them but at the same time stimulated their abilities and creativity. In the first period of their existence, in the fifteenth and early sixteenth century, New Christians inherited and extended Jewish business practices, which included investing and lending money, the administration of land (on behalf of noblemen, the Church, and military orders), bidding for royal contracts for rent and tax farming, and finally, participating in interregional and long-distance trade in association with foreign merchants, especially Italians and Germans. New Christians were at the forefront of the Iberian expansion to Africa, the New World, and Asia. They imported and reexported gold and silver, first from West Africa, then from the New World. They invested in the infamous and inhuman slave trade from West Africa, in the spice trade from South Asia, and in the sugar trade from Madeira, then from São Tomé and later from Brazil. During the sixteenth and seventeenth centuries, New Christians extended the scope of their trade to include gemstones from South Asia and South America, porcelain and lacquer from East Asia, textiles from South Asia, spices from Southeast Asia, indigo from Central America, cochineal from Mexico, and tobacco from the Americas.

New Christians were certainly not alone in these trades, but they did control most of the slave trade in the Atlantic until the late seventeenth century, a good part of the trade from Asia until the first quarter of the seventeenth century, and the sugar trade from Brazil until the early eighteenth century, together with part of the silver and the cochineal trade from the Americas, part of the textiles trade from South Asia, and porcelain and lacquer from East Asia. New Christians were not themselves innocent of inhuman behaviour, for example, towards the enslaved Africans who were transported to Europe and the New World in massive numbers every year. They contributed to the creation and development of a plantation system based on slavery in the New World. New Christians resisted and protested against their own inferior condition, but they did not question the status of the Black people they were transporting and selling into forced labour. Very few white Catholics contested the enslavement of Black people, and even fewer the slavery system, during the early modern period. Bartolomé de las Casas, who campaigned against the enslavement of Native Americans, never made public his opposition to the enslavement of African people.

New Christians never lost their rootedness in Iberia through their administration of land, rent, and customs contracts obtained from nobility, religious and military orders, and from local and central government; they added to these financial arrangements concessions for royal monopolies, particularly for pepper from South Asia (up to 1570), the production of salt in Spain, the collection and distribution of brazilwood from Brazil, and the processing and distribution of tobacco both in Spain and Portugal—one the most profitable concessions of the seventeenth and eighteenth centuries. Overseas trade was risky because of the dangers of shipwreck and piracy, but the margin of profit was much higher than that on trade within Iberia. Private and state-controlled trade were not strictly divided, because royal monopolies were granted through concessions and the contractors involved other subcontractors, all engaged in free trade. This was the case with the slave trade in the Atlantic, which continued to be subject to royal contract, alongside contracts for brazilwood from Brazil. Yet until the mid-eighteenth century, except for the short-lived Company of Brazil, the Portuguese Atlantic remained quite free of royal intervention concerning transport and most trade. In Spain, the carrera de Indias was under the control of a large group of merchants represented by the consulado, linked to the Casa de Contratación, the equivalent of the Casa da Índia in Lisbon, where contracts, the provisioning of ships, and the passengers and commodities carried were registered, and from where the loading and unloading of ships was supervised.

In the Portuguese case, New Christians were present as financiers who had loaned money to the king since late fifteenth century. They also traded in spices from Asia to Lisbon and then to northern Europe, until they lost control of the European trade in the last decades of the sixteenth century. In the first half of the sixteenth century, the powerful Mendes/Nasi family kept the royal trading post in Antwerp afloat, while other major financiers, such as the Nunes/Henriques, the Rodrigues, the Crasto, the Caldeira, the Pimentel, the Paz, and the Negro families invested in royal contracts in Portugal and Madeira, trading in North Africa, West Africa, and Asia. The composition of this elite group of New Christian merchants and bankers naturally changed over time, with the emergence of the Mendes de Brito family from the 1580s to the 1620s and beyond, the Solis, the Baeça, the Silveira families in the first half of the seventeenth century, the Silva, the Gama, the Penso, and the Mogadouro families from the 1630s and 1640s to the 1670s, the Paz family with long-term presence, and the Bravo, a family that surfaced in different periods of the seventeenth century, among many others. Most of these New Christian families had origins in Castile and/or Aragon.

In the case of Spain, New Christians were singled out for special taxes during the sixteenth and seventeenth centuries, which also happened in Portugal, mainly during the period of the Iberian Union of Crowns. The Coronel, the Alcázar, the Sánchez, the López, the Santa Cruz, and the Baeza families, among many other New Christian families, played a major role in holding local and central contracts for rents and customs, while those involved in trade with the Americas, such as the Illescas, the Caballero, the Jaez, the Martínez, and the Palma families, among many others, suffered from levies by Charles V, particularly the sequestration of goods traded with the Americas in 1534 to subsidize the military expedition to Tunis in 1535. While Genoese bankers had become the main lenders to the Spanish kings during the sixteenth century, the bankruptcy of Philip II in 1575 opened possibilities for Portuguese financiers, particularly the Caldeira family. The Union of Crowns in 1580 facilitated migration to, and the naturalisation of Portuguese merchants in, Seville and Madrid, which led to renewed ties with Castilian relatives. The presence of New Christian contractors in Madrid increased during the first decades of the seventeenth century, and these financiers obtained a significant share of the asientos, or royal financial contracts for borrowing money, from the 1620s onwards. Families including the Paz, the Núñez, the Silvera, the Cortizos, the Fernández, the Correa, the Monsanto, the Blandon, and the Yllán, among others, played a major role, some of them remaining influential until the last decades of the seventeenth century.

The financial asientos were negotiated among other contracts to guarantee a constant flow of money. The financiers were generally paid with silver and had trade with the Americas opened to their investment. They obtained the naturalisation of their associates and agents in Seville and Spanish America. Financial contracts for loans to the Spanish king covered payments in different parts of Europe for war and imperial administration, mainly in Antwerp, but also in Milan and Naples. These payments enhanced ties with New Christian communities in Italy and Flanders, particularly in Antwerp, and although the decline of trade with this city towards the end of the sixteenth century had an impact, war with the Netherlands until 1648 helped to maintain its status as a financial centre.

The New Christian diaspora joined the early Jewish diaspora in reaching the Ottoman Empire, North Africa, Italy, and northern Europe. Migration generally coincided with the main waves of inquisitorial persecution, from the 1480s to the 1520s in Spain, and in Portugal with the establishment of the Inquisition in 1536, followed by continuous prosecution, with property confiscation, from the late 1560s onwards. The New Christian trading elite resisted the first impact of these prosecutions in Spain, only to be confronted with growing prosecution in Portugal towards the turn of the seventeenth century. That period saw the creation of new Sephardic communities in Amsterdam and Hamburg, which developed their own economic capacity and cultural achievements. In 1640, the independence of Portugal created a divergence of interests between New Christian financiers in Spain and Portugal, but on both sides of the divide they managed to resist significant losses. The inquisitorial prosecution of New Christians reached a peak in Portugal from the late 1650s to the early 1670s, while the financial elite in Spain was also under scrutiny in the 1640s and 1650s. It was in this period that a new Sephardic community was created in London, partly prompted by the efforts of Jews from Amsterdam, particularly Menasseh ben Israel, and this developed through steady migration from Iberia.

From 1674 to 1681, the suspension of the Inquisition in Portugal brought what had been an overwhelming escalation of prosecutions to a halt. However, the backlash that followed reestablishment, complemented by the exclusion of convicted New Christians from royal privileges and contracts, followed by exile, represented a decisive blow to merchants and financiers. The War of Succession in Spain aggravated the decline of the New Christian trading elite, because the majority supported the Habsburg against the Bourbon candidate, which led to significant losses, both for Jewish financiers from Amsterdam and New Christian ones from Madrid and Lisbon.

New Christian merchants continued to be vigorously prosecuted in Spain and Portugal from the 1710s to the 1730s and 1740s. They maintained themselves through contracts for the monopoly on tobacco, the local administration of rents and customs, and the declining silk and wool industry, but the decline and virtual disappearance of New Christian asentistas in eighteenth century Iberia must be seen as resulting from their systematic persecution during the second half of the seventeenth century, which destroyed a significant section of leading families, such as the Mogadouro, the Penso and the Gama in Portugal. The reorganisation of international trade, which became based on national communities of merchants in England, France and the Netherlands, merchants who manipulated their states to their own benefit, played a further significant role. Spain favoured the emergence of French (and even English) merchants after the War of Succession, while foreign merchants in Portugal were privileged over New Christians in the late seventeenth and first half of the eighteenth century. Ethnic diasporas of which New Christians had been a thriving example in the sixteenth and seventeenth centuries—even if these had never been exclusive, having depended on partnerships with Iberian Old Christians and foreign merchants—now ceased to occupy an advantageous position in international and intercontinental trade.

The New Christian diaspora created and developed Sephardic Jewish communities, which contributed to widening the converso and Jewish commercial networks in the late sixteenth and seventeenth century. Yet there were also significant Christian communities in the Iberian empires, France, Italy, and Flanders that attracted those New Christians wishing to keep their distance from the Inquisition whilst hesitating to assume Jewish allegiance. The Spanish empire for a long time provided shelter to New Christians without systematic persecution, although significant trials did occur. New Christians became important in Lima, as the extended family of Manuel Bautista Pérez attested, and in Mexico City, around the figure of Simón Vaez Sevilla. In the end, waves of inquisitorial persecution launched in the late 1630s and early 1640s, and arguably triggered for political purposes by competitive Old Christians, ensured the disappearance of New Christians as an ethnicity in Spanish America.

New Christians who had settled in Brazil were accused very early—in the first visits by the Inquisition in the 1590s and the late 1610s—but this did not trigger a significant wave of persecution. New Christians were major sugar and tobacco merchants and were involved in the government of Bahia during the seventeenth century. They were always significant sugar producers, an activity in which they increased their presence from the 1660s to the 1700s, after which inquisitorial persecution radically reduced the community. West Africa was the initial hub for overseas New Christians involved in the slave trade with the Americas, but numbers declined in the long term, although they did contribute to the creation of mixed-race lineages. New Christians in South Asia were targeted by inquisitorial prosecution from the 1560s to the 1580s and again in the 1630s, but then they either intermarried within colonial society or managed to escape the vigilance of the tribunal of Goa. In East Asia, a significant number of New Christians lived in Manila, Macau, and Nagasaki. The long arm of the Inquisition reached them, particularly in Macau, but many escaped detection and some evaded the Iberian world by merging into Asian communities.

Withdrawal to Europe was relatively safe for the New Christian trading elite, who could keep close links either with their relatives in Iberia or with those in the Sephardic communities. Rome hosted an extraordinary number of rich New Christians, who traded with the Spanish and the Portuguese empires but also administered the properties of cardinals and nobles, lent money to the pope, and acted as brokers of the vast ecclesiastic market for nominations, benefices, and indulgences in Iberia. The families of the Fonseca, the Brandão da Costa, the Nunes Sanches, the Peres Vergueiro, the Lopes da Silva, the Gomes Homem and the Correia Bravo ended up buying land and noble titles, endowed chapels, built extraordinary palaces, and mixed into the Roman aristocracy through matrimonial alliances. The diverse branches of the Ximenes family in Lisbon, Florence, and Antwerp followed the same path of ennoblement shared by many other families, particularly the Yllán and the Silva families in Antwerp. Many of these ennobled families had Jewish relatives in the Ottoman Empire, Amsterdam, Hamburg, and London, while some of their descendants decided to return to the Jewish tradition. In France, the communities of Saint-Jean de Luz, Bayonne, Peyrehorade, Bordeaux, La Rochelle, Rouen, and Nantes continued to attract New Christians from the sixteenth century onwards, and these new arrivals benefitted from the French absence of enquiry into private religious practices. Later, after the 1720s, sections of these communities were able to publicly assume their Jewish identity.

Some of these New Christian strategies that ensured survival and economic success had a parallel in Iberia. In Lisbon and in Madrid, some of the most important families of New Christian merchants and financiers decided at different moments of the late sixteenth and seventeenth century to invest in royal interests, land, and noble alliances to escape the constant extortion of greedy agents of justice. Perseverance in trade thus had its costs, while persistence in financial investment could be penalised by changing economic and political conditions. In sum, the decline of the New Christian merchant elite was brought about slowly through a long sequence of convergent factors, which included exacerbated inquisitorial persecution, migration, ennoblement, the independence of Portugal, the War of Succession in Spain, and the changing conditions of international trade.

The impact of the New Christian merchant elite can be traced in the world economy, in legal thought, and in the development of literature, art, and natural history. New Christians did not invent intercontinental trade, but they certainly contributed to it from the very beginning of the Portuguese and Spanish maritime expansion to the New World and Asia. They helped to enlarge the circulation of bills of exchange and engaged with local merchants and bankers in Asia. They operated across frontiers in western Africa, South Asia, Southeast Asia, and East Asia, contributing to the creation of new hybrid lineages. They facilitated material cultural exchange between South Asia and East Asia, Asia and Europe, and the New World, Europe, and Africa.

New Christians participated in debates on values in the Iberian world— debates that pitched merit against noble lineage, service against supposedly pure blood, and productive activity against the nobility's traditional aversion to manual work. The sixteenth century was a period of flourishing economic and legal thought in Spain, specifically, many treatises praised the activities of merchants, who were considered to be crucial for the economy, as well as the importance of distributive justice to reward service to the royal family. It was on the back of this thought, in which Italy and northern Europe were praised for efficient integration of their merchants, that New Christians collaborating with Old Christians fuelled the debate against blood purity statutes, which loomed large from the 1590s to the 1630s.

The important painting by Bartolomé Bermejo of Jesus's descent into limbo, in which the artist reflects on the rescue of the just in a telling narrative gesture directed at Jewish ancestors, is probably the earliest contribution of New Christians to art. Pictorial creativity was at stake here, not only with the assimilation of Flemish technique but also with the innovative representation of Christ's divine and human double nature. New Christian intervention in this area was not to become relevant again until the early seventeenth century, in Seville, around the promotion of the cult of the Immaculate Conception. In this, the representation of a multiethnic and inclusive society under the protection of the Virgin Mary, and the notion of a pure milk of motherhood, arguably offered a possible alternative to the racial ideology of pure blood. Juan de Roelas and Juan de Jauregui participated in this new set of representations, in which spiritual and mystic layers from aspects of the Book of Revelation inspired the depiction of transitions between heaven and Earth and an interpretation of the Virgin Mary as the woman of the Apocalypse.

New Christian contributions to new literary genres were powerful. Interiorised religiosity was expressed in courtly love poetry by Juan Álvarez Gato, who also lamented the earthly arrogance of lineages, while the sentimental novel and the topic of love as a prison was developed by Diego de San Pedro. Radical change was introduced by Fernando de Rojas, who depicted the miseries of the manipulation and trade in love of urban life, a theme developed further by Antonio Delicado in the context of an utterly corrupt Rome. The underside of a society plagued by poverty and malign practices was further explored by the picaresque novel as a new genre, from *Lazarillo de Tormes* to Mateo Alemán.

The travails of the pilgrim and the pain of memory and continuous exile were expressed by the sentimental and pastoral novels of Alonso Núñez de Reinoso and Bernardim Ribeiro. If this literature reflected dispossession and nostalgia (or *saudade*) for a lost world, derision of the notion of pure blood was also made explicit by Cervantes and other authors. The anti-epic hybrid book written by Fernão Mendes Pinto provides a candid exposure of the plunder and greed involved in the Portuguese expansion and was visibly influenced by the picaresque novel. Francisco Rodrigues Lobo conveyed an erudite defence of the Hebrew language, praised the importance of merchants in court society, and advanced a veiled critique of the Inquisition. Antonio Enríquez Gómez, who lived in France and published some of his poems and plays there, launched an explicit and devastating critique of the Inquisition.

New Christians also shaped new understandings of natural history. Gonzalo Fernández de Oviedo, Garcia d'Orta, and Cristóbal Acosta collected information on botany, zoology, and mineralogy in the New World and Asia that radically changed the European knowledge of nature. Portuguese cartography represented new seas, new lands, and new skies through the skills of the Reinel and Homem families, while the mathematician Pedro Nunes explored spherical trigonometry, creating a new measuring device that later developed into the Vernier scale and establishing the basis for Mercator's projection of the globe. In medicine, Amatus Lusitanus played a major role with his seven volumes on diseases, each presenting a hundred clinical cases, while he also discovered blood circulation and the function of the venous valves. Rodrigo de Castro contributed to the development of gynaecology and obstetrics, while Filipe de Montalto developed his contemporaries' knowledge of mental diseases. These three physicians eventually assumed their Jewish allegiance in Salonika, Hamburg, and Florence (then Paris).

The liminal situation in which New Christians were placed encouraged their spiritual search inside the Catholic Church, a quest that sometimes moved outside both Jewish and Christian traditions. The movement of the alumbrados is a good example of the search for a direct relationship with God and was one in which women played a significant role. The mystical path developed by Teresa de Ávila within the framework of a religious order, the Carmelites, was recognised by the Catholic Church, while other New Christians, such as Luis de León and Juan de Ávila, left behind them an example of an ascetic life and a significant body of poetry and theological reflection. The spiritual movement inspired by Erasmus had a strong impact in Spain and drew the involvement of many New Christians before suspicion and enquiry by the Inquisition imposed restraint. Finally, the participation of New Christians in the first two generations (and beyond) of members of the Society of Jesus is now well known, along with these members' contribution to the blood purity debate.

New Christian intervention in political and legal thought was obviously not unconnected to their liminal condition. In the mid-seventeenth century, Manuel Fernandes Vila Real wrote in favour of freedom of conscience, defended the equality of all people before the law, and repudiated the unfair expulsion of Moriscos from Spain, an expulsion that ruined the life of many people who were in fact Christians. He was thinking about the fate of minorities targeted by racial division and permanently placed in a precarious social position. However, it was the long-lasting New Christian struggle against unfair inquisitorial trials that produced significant legal arguments against such trials, which were sent to Rome from the mid-fifteenth to the late seventeenth century. In this struggle, racial prejudices coupled with discriminatory action against a minority were exposed and condemned, and a dense critique was produced of a vicious procedure based on secrecy surrounding accusations, arbitrary property confiscations before any sentencing, the extortion of confessions and denunciations of relatives, the manipulative conditions of detention, and the systematic public humiliation of the convicted and the ruin of their families. A history of the impact New Christians had on penal and procedural law before the turn of the mid-eighteenth century remains to be written.

To sum up, New Christians were created through the forced conversion of Jewish communities in Iberia between 1391 and 1497. They lasted as a recognisable ethnic group until the mid-eighteenth century, subjected to labelling and discrimination imposed by blood purity statutes and inquisitorial prosecution. New Christian status was imposed on hundreds of thousands of people. Yet New Christian merchants circumvented the rules and achieved elevated positions through the acquisition of titles and matrimonial alliances. They also created, through migration, new Jewish communities in northern Europe and the New World. They ceased to exist as an ethnicity through the conjunction of institutional and political changes, new conditions of international trade, and the emergence of a new values system in the eighteenth century. During the three centuries of their existence, New Christians created a significant heritage of economic, financial, and cultural achievement, mainly through their contribution to intercontinental trade but also through their spiritual and religious enquiries, their scientific, literary, and artistic innovation, and their political and legal struggle against the discriminatory treatment of a minority.

NOTES

Introduction

1. Arquivo Nacional da Torre do Tombo (ANTT), Inquisição de Lisboa, Processo 10906. The analysis of this trial will guide us in these first paragraphs.

2. François-Emmanuel Guignard, *Mémoires sur l'ambassade de France en Turquie et sur le commerce des français dans le Levant*, ed. Charles Schefer (Paris: E. Leroux, 1877). Michel de Codignac was resident in Constantinople from 1553 to 1556.

3. ANTT, Inquisição de Lisboa, Processo 10906, fl. 6r.

4. ANTT, Inquisição de Lisboa, Processo 10906, fl. 7r.

5. ANTT, Inquisição de Lisboa, Processo 10906, fl. 8r and 49r.

6. ANTT, Inquisição de Lisboa, Processo 10906, fl. 9v–10r.

7. ANTT, Inquisição de Lisboa, Processo 10906, fl. 10v.

8. ANTT, Inquisição de Lisboa, Processo 10906, fl. 69r–v.

9. For estimates of the number of New Christians, see M. A. Ladero Quesada, *Judíos y conversos en Castilla en el siglo XV. Datos y comentarios* (Madrid: Dickinson, 2016); Maria José Ferro Tavares, *Os judeus em Portugal no século XV* (Lisbon: FCSH, 1982); for an estimate of the population, see Massimo Livi-Bacci, *The Population of Europe* (Oxford: Blackwell, 1999). The discussion on demography will be developed in Part I.

10. Jan de Vries, *European Urbanization, 1500–1800* (Cambridge MA: Harvard University Press, 1984) has estimated the urban population in Portugal as 3 percent of the total and in Spain 6 percent, based on a threshold of 10,000 people. In this period, towns with more than 5,000 inhabitants should be considered as significant centres of trade and crafts. This is why I calculate 8 percent of urban population in Iberia. With the estimate of de Vries, the visibility of New Christians would be even higher.

11. Robert Rowland, "New Christian, Marrano, Jew," in *The Jews and the Expansion of Europe to the West*, ed. Paolo Bernardini and Norman Fiering (New York: Berghahn, 2001), 125–148, esp. 135–136. We will return later to this important estimate.

12. Francisco Bethencourt, *Racisms: From the Crusades to the Twentieth Century* (Princeton, NJ: Princeton University Press, 2013).

13. David Nirenberg, *Anti-Judaism: The Western Tradition* (New York: Norton, 2013).

14. Jean Frédéric Schaub, *Pour une histoire politique de la race* (Paris: Seuil, 2015); Max S. Hering Torre, Maria Elena Martínez and David Nirenberg, eds., *Race and Blood in the Iberian World* (Berlin: Lit Verlag, 2012).

15. Mercedes García-Arenal and Felipe Pereda, eds., *De sangre y leche. Raza y religion en el mundo ibérico modern* (Madrid: Marcial Pons, 2021).

16. *Oxford English Dictionary*, s.v. "community," accessed December 2021, https://www.oed.com/view/Entry/37337. I have retained the definition that could be closer to this case.

17. On identity crisis and ethnicity, see David Graizbord, "A Crisis of Judeoconverso Identity and Its Echoes, 1391 to the Present," in *Religious Changes and Cultural Transformations in the Early Modern Western Sephardic Communities*, ed. Yosef Kaplan (Leiden, Brill, 2019), 3–21.

18. Nathan Wachtel, *La foi du souvernir: labyrinthes marranes* (Paris: Seuil, 2001).

19. Steve Fenton, *Ethnicity* (Cambridge: Polity Press, 2010); John Hutchinson and Anthony D. Smith, eds., *Ethnicity* (Oxford: Oxford University Press, 1996).

20. Miriam Bodian pointed out that religion was not the only factor in New Christian and then Sephardi identities: "Hebrews of the Portuguese Nation: The Ambiguous Boundaries of Self-Definition," *Sephardi Identities* 15, no. 1 (2008): 66–80; Bodian, "'Men of the Nation': The Shaping of 'Converso' Identity in Early Modern Europe," *Past and Present* 143 (1994): 48–76.

21. *Oxford English Dictionary*, online edition, December 2021, https://www.oed.com /view/Entry/60490.

22. Sebastian Conrad, *What is Global History?* (Princeton, NJ: Princeton University Press, 2016); Jürgen Osterhammel and Niels P. Petersson, *Globalization: A Short History*, trans. Dona Geyer (Princeton, NJ: Princeton University Press, 2005). The early modern global dimension still needs to be better addressed, see Serge Gruzinski, *Les quatre parties du monde: histoire d'une mondialisation* (Paris: Martinière, 2004).

23. See the discussion on notions and methods by David H. Knoke and Song Yang, *Social Network Analysis* (Los Angeles: Sage, 2019).

24. See the "Introduction" to Cátia Antunes and Francisco Bethencourt, eds., *Merchant Cultures: A Global Approach to Spaces, Representations and Worlds of Trade, 1500–1800* (Leiden: Brill, 2021).

25. For a sociological approach of the dynamic of conflict, see Norbert Elias and John L. Scotson, *The Established and the Outsiders* (1965), ed. Cas Wouters (Dublin: University College Dublin, 2008).

26. For the debate in Spain, see Albert A. Sicroff, *Los estatutos de limpieza de sangre* (orig. 1960), trans. Mauro Armiño (Madrid: Taurus, 1985), and Juan Hernández Franco, *Sangre limpia, sangre española. El debate de los estatutos de limpieza (siglos XVI–XVII)* (Madrid: Cátedra, 2011); for the implementation in Portugal, see Fernanda Olival "Rigor e interesses: os estatutos de limpeza de sangue em Portugal," *Cadernos de Estudos Sefarditas* 4 (2011): 141–170; for a comprehensive view, see João de Figueirôa-Rego, *A honra alheia por um fio: os estatutos de limpeza de sangue nos espaços de expressão ibérica (sécs. XVI–XVIII)* (Lisbon: Fundação Calouste Gulbenkian, 2011).

27. The best relational approach to social hierarchy criteria was suggested by José Antonio Maravall, "Trabajo y exclusión: el trabajador manual en el sistema social español de la primera modernidad," in *Les problèmes de l'exclusion en Espagne (XVIᵉ–XVIIᵉ siècles)*, ed. Augustin Redondo (Paris: Publications de la Sorbonne, 1983), 135–159; José Antonio Maravall, *Estado moderno y mentalidad social, siglos XV a XVII*, vol. 2 (Madrid: Alianza, 1986), 3–56. This important issue has been tackled more recently by Stuart B. Schwartz, *Blood and Boundaries: The Limits of Religion and Racial Exclusion in Early Modern Latin America* (Waltham, MA: Brandeis University Press, 2020).

28. I agree with Louis Dumond, who rejected the idea of caste society outside South Asia, *Homo Hierarchicus. The Caste System and Its Implications*, trans. Mark Sainsbury (Chicago: University of Chicago Press, 1980). But there is also criticism of Dumont's rigid vision of the caste system in India, see, for example, R. S. Khare, ed., *Caste, Hierarchy and Individualism: Indian Critiques of Louis Dumont's Contributions* (New Delhi: Oxford University Press, 2009).

29. Roberto Calasso, *Ardor* (London: Penguin, 2014). This book invalidates Gil Anidjar, *Blood: A Critique of Christianity* (New York: Columbia University Press, 2014), who argues that blood has an exclusive place in Christianity, supposedly transferred to the modern world.

30. Mary Douglas, *Purity and Danger: An Analysis of Concepts of Pollution and Taboo* (London: Routledge and Kegan Paul, 1966).

31. Pierre Bourdieu, "Les rites comme actes d'institution," *Actes de la recherché en sciences sociales* 43 (1982): 58–63.

32. Georg Simmel, "The Stranger" (1908), *On Individuality and Social Forms*, ed. Donald N. Levine (Chicago: University of Chicago Press, 1971), 143–149.

33. Arnold van Gennep, *The Rites of Passage* (1909), trans. Monika B. Vizedom and Gabrielle L. Caffee (Chicago: University of Chicago Press, 2019); Victor Turner, *The Ritual Process: Structure and Anti-Structure* (1969) (Abingdon: Routledge, 2017).

34. *Shorter Oxford English Dictionary*, 5th ed. (Oxford: Oxford University Press, 2002), 1311; Alain Rey, ed., *Dictionnaire historique de la langue française* (Paris: Le Robert, 1998), 1773–1774.

35. Claude Lévi-Strauss, ed., *L'identité* (Paris: PUF, 1983), 10–11, 15–16.

36. Michel Foucault, "Nietzsche, la généalogie, l'histoire," (1971), in *Dits et écrits*, vol. 1, *1954–1975* (Paris: Gallimard-Quarto, 2001), 1021.

37. Foucault, *Dits et écrits*, vol. 2, *1976–1988*, 36–37.

38. Judith Butler, "Subjection, Resistance, Resignification: Between Freud and Foucault," in *The Identity in Question*, ed. John Rajchman (London: Routledge, 1995), 229–249. See also the chapters by the editor and Cornel West in the same volume.

39. Henri Tajfel, ed., *Social Identity and Intergroup Relations* (Cambridge: Cambridge University Press, 1982), 2; I have synthesised the main ideas of this collective book. See also H. Tajfel, "Quantitative Judgement in Social Perception," *British Journal of Psychology* 50 (1950): 16–21; H. Tajfel and A. L. Wilkes, "Classification and Quantitative Judgement," *British Journal of Psychology* 54 (1963): 101–104; and M. Billing and H. Tajfel, "Social Categorisation and Similarity in Intergroup Behavior," *European Journal of Social Psychology* 3 (1973): 27–52.

40. Pierre Bourdieu, *La distinction. Critique sociale du jugement* (Paris: Minuit, 1979), 191, 283, 514, 562–564.

41. On the classification crisis, see David Nirenberg, "Mass Conversion and Genealogical Mentalities: Jews and Christians in Fifteenth-Century Spain," *Past and Present* 174, 1 (2002): 3–41; on what it meant to be a *converso*, see Gretchen Starr-Lebeau, *In the Shadow of the Virgin: Inquisitors, Friars, and Conversos in Guadelupe* (Princeton, NJ: Princeton University Press, 2003); on New Christian self-perceptions, see David Graizbord and Claude Stuczynski, eds., "Portuguese New Christian Identities, 1516–1700," special issue of *Jewish History* 25, no. 2 (2011).

42. Zygmunt Bauman, *Identities. Conversations with Benedetto Vecchi* (Cambridge: Polity Press, 2004); Florian Coulmas, *Identity: A Very Short Introduction* (Oxford: Oxford University Press, 2019).

43. Michael A. Hogg and Dominic Abrams, *Social Identifications: A Social Psychology of Intergroup Relations and Group Processes* (London: Routledge, 1988).

44. Wolfgang Prinz, *Open Minds: The Social Making of Agency and Intentionality* (Cambridge, MA: MIT Press, 2012).

45. Erik H. Erikson, *Life History and the Historical Moment* (New York: Norton, 1975).

46. Erving Goffman, *The Presentation of Self in Everyday Life* (1959) (London: Penguin, 1990).

47. *Diccionario de la lengua española*, 21st ed. (Madrid: Real Academia Española, 2001), 988.

48. These meanings are attested in Sebastián de Covarrubias, *Tesoro de la lengua castellana o española* (Madrid: Luis Sanchez, 1611). The same in early Portuguese dictionaries, attested by several references in Garcia de Resende, *Cancioneiro Geral*, ed. Aida Fernanda Dias (Lisbon: Imprensa Nacional, 1990). I thank João Paulo Silvestre for his help here and in the following note.

49. This is attested in Antoine Furetière, *Dictionnaire universel* (The Hague: Arnoud et Reinier Leers, 1690). One century later, Raphael Bluteau, *Vocabulario Portuguez e Latino*, tomo V (Lisbon: Pascoal e Sylva, 1716), 342, followed Furetière when he defined *marrano* as an "injurious name that some nations give to Castilians or that the same Castilians attribute to Moors or Jews who in Castile convert to the Catholic faith, with the presumption that the conversion of this kind of men is apparent and simulated" (my translation).

50. Converso is not discussed in Sebastián de Covarrubias or in Bernardo Aldrete, although it was used at the time. They indicate an Old Christian as "the clean man who has no trace of Moor or Jew; New Christian, the opposite": Bernardo Aldrete, *Del origen de la lengua castellana* (Madrid: Melchor Suarez, 1674), fl. 170r. The exact same content is accepted by Raphael Bluteau, *Vocabulario Portuguez e Latino*, tome II, 302. In the Portuguese dictionaries there is no reference to converso either.

51. Antonio de Moraes Silva, *Diccionario da lingua portugueza*, vol. 2 (Lisbon: Simão Thaddeo Ferreira, 1789), 107, indicates as *gente de nação* the New Christian descendants of Jews. Immediately after, he adds race, caste, and species as related to New Christians.

52. This is not the place to tackle the complex case of nations in Hispania in Spanish and Portuguese dictionaries. Antonio de Moraes Silva, *Diccionario da lingua portugueza*, tome 2 (Lisbon: Simão Taddheo Ferreira, 1789), 107, indicates the meaning of people from a country or region with specific laws and government, followed by "gente de nação, Jewish

descendants, New Christians; race, caste, species" (my translation). See *Shorter English Dictionary*, vol. 2 (Oxford: Oxford University Press, 2002), 1888; Alain Rey, ed., *Dictionnaire historique de la langue française*, vol. 2 (Paris: Dictionnaries Le Robert, 1998), 2345.

53. This issue is discussed by Daviken Studniki-Gizbert, *A Nation upon the Ocean Sea: Portugal's Atlantic Diaspora and the Crisis of the Spanish Empire, 1492–1640*.

54. This was taken on board by the New Christians and their allies in the debate around blood purity. I will tackle this issue especially in Part IV.

55. Yosef Kaplan, *Les nouveaux-juifs d'Amsterdam. Essais sur l'histoire sociale et intellectuelle du judaïsme séfarade au XVIIᵉ siècle* (Paris: Chandeigne, 1999).

56. Among a vast bibliography, I. S. Révah, *Uriel da Costa et les marranes de Porto*, ed. Carsten L. Wilke (Paris: Fondation Calouste Gulbenkian, 2004); Herman P. Salomon, *Portrait of a New Christian: Fernão Álvares Melo, 1569–1632* (Paris: Fundação Calouste Gulbenkian, 1982).

57. Anne Gerritsen and Giorgio Riello, eds, *Writing Material Culture History* (London: Bloomsbury, 2014); Karen Harvey, ed., *History and Material Culture* (London: Routledge, 2009); Kenneth F. Kipple, *A Movable Feast: The Millenia of Food Globalization* (Cambridge: Cambridge University Press, 2009); François Delamare and Bernard Guineau, *Colours: The Story of Dyes and Pigments* (New York: Harry N. Abrams, 2000).

58. Carmen Sanz Ayán, *Los banqueros y la crisis de la monarquia hispánica en 1640* (Madrid: Marcial Pons, 2013); James Boyajian, *Portuguese Bankers at the Court of Spain, 1626–1650* (New Brunswick, NJ: Rutgers University Press, 1983); Antonio Domínguez Ortiz, *Politica y hacienda de Felipe IV* (Madrid: Editorial de Derecho Financiero, 1960).

59. Anne Dubet and Gaetano Sabatini, "Arbitristas: acción politica y propuesta economica," in *La monarquia de Felipe III. La corte*, vol. 3, ed. José Martínez Millán and Maria Antonieta Visceglia (Madrid: Mapfre, 2008), 867–936; Sina Rauschenbach and Christian Windler, eds., *Reforming Early Modern Monarchies: The Castilian Arbitristas in Comparative European Perspectives* (Wiesbaden: Harrasowitz Verlag, 2016).

60. Juan Antonio Llorente, *Historia crítica de la Inquisición en España* (orig. French 1817–1818, Spanish 1822), int. José Jiménez Lozano, 4 vols. (Madrid: Hiperión, 1980), esp. vol. 1, ch. 5. Contrary to accusations of liberal bias by ultra-conservatives, Llorente just reproduced the main arguments of New Christians and other opponents to the Inquisition from the beginning of the tribunal in Spain. He reconstituted, in this and other books, the strand of public opinion against the Inquisition in Spain.

61. Alexandre Herculano, *History of the Origin and Establishment of the Inquisition in Portugal* (orig. 1854–59), trans. John C. Branner, prologue by Yosef H. Yerushalmi (New York: Ktav, 1972).

62. Henry Charles Lea, *A History of the Inquisition of Spain*, 4 vols. (New York: MacMillan, 1906–1907), esp. book 8, ch. 1.

63. João Lúcio de Azevedo, *História dos cristãos novos portugueses* (1921) (Lisbon: Livraria Clássica, 1975).

64. Marcel Bataillon, *Érasme et l'Espagne* 3 vols. (1937), ed. Daniel Devoto (Genève: Droz, 1991).

65. Marcel Bataillon, *Les jésuites dans l'Espagne du XVIᵉ siècle*, ed. Pierre-Antoine Fabre (Paris: Les Belles Lettres, 2009).

66. Stefania Pastore, *Una herejía española: conversos, alumbrados e Inquisición, 1449–1549*, trans. Clara Álvarez Alonso (Madrid: Marcial Pons, 2010).

67. Américo Castro, *España en su historia. Cristianos, moros y judíos* (1948) (Barcelona: Crítica, 1984); Américo Castro, *La realidad histórica de España* (1954) (Mexico: Porrúa, 1962).

68. Stephen Gilman, *The Spain of Fernando de Rojas: The Intellectual and Social Landscape of "La Celestina"* (Princeton, NJ: Princeton University Press, 1972); Francisco Márquez Villanueva, *De la España judeoconverso. Doce estudios* (Barcelona: Belaterra, 2006).

69. Antonio Domínguez Ortiz, "Los 'cristianos nuevos.' Notas para el estudio de una clase social," *Boletín de la Universidad de Granada* 21, no. 87 (1949): 249–297; Antonio Domínguez Ortiz, *La clase social de los conversos en Castilla en la edad moderna* (1955) (Granada:

Universidad, Servicio de Publicaciones, 1991); Antonio Domínguez Ortiz, *Política y hacienda de Felipe IV* (Madrid: Editorial de Derecho Financiero, 1960).

70. Julio Caro Baroja, *Los Judíos en la España Moderna y Contemporánea*, 3 vols. (1961), 3rd ed., (Madrid: Istmo, 1986).

71. Cecil Roth, *A History of the Marranos* (1932) (Philadelphia: Jewish Publication Society of America, 1959); Yitzhak Baer, *A History of the Jews in Christian Spain* (orig. 1945), trans. Louis Schoffman, vol. 2, *From the Fourteenth Century to the Expulsion* (Philadelphia: Jewish Publication Society of America, 1961); Haim Beinart, *Conversos on Trial: The Inquisition in Ciudad Real*, trans. Yael Guiladi (Jerusalem: Hebrew University, 1981); Haim Beinart, *The Expulsion of Jews From Spain*, trans. Jeffrey M. Green (Oxford: Littman Library of Jewish Civilization, 2002).

72. Jonathan Israel, *Diasporas within a Diaspora: Jews, Crypto-Jews and the World of Maritime Empires (1540–1740)* (Leiden: Brill, 2002).

73. Aron di Leone Leoni, *La nazione ebraica spagnola e portoghese negli stati estensi: per servire a una storia dell'ebraismo sefardita* (Rimini: Luisè, 1992); Aron di Leone Leoni, *La nazione ebraica spagnola e portoghese di Ferrara (1492–1559): i suoi rapporti col governo ducale e la populazione locale ed i suoi legami con le nazioni portoghesi di Ancona, Pesaro e Venezia*, 2 vols. (Florence: Olschki, 2011); Cristina Galasso, *Alle origini di una comunità: ebree ed ebrei a Livorno nel Seicento* (Florence: Olschki, 2002); Evelyne Oliel-Grausz, "Relations et réseaux intercommunautaires dans la diaspora sefarade d´Occident au XVIIIᵉ siècle," 2 vols. (thèse de doctorat, Université de Paris-I Sorbonne, 1999); Gérard Nahon, *Juifs et judaïsme à Bordeaux* (Bordeaux: Mollat, 2003); Yosef Kaplan, *Les nouveaux-juifs d'Amsterdam. Essais sur l'histoire sociale et intellectuelle du judaïsme séfarade au XVIIᵉ siècle* (Paris: Chandeigne, 1999); Miriam Bodian, *Hebrews of the Portuguese Nation: Conversos and Community in Early Modern Amsterdam* (Bloomington: Indiana University Press, 1997); Daniel M. Swetschinski, *Reluctant Cosmopolitans: The Portuguese Jews of Seventeenth-Century Amsterdam* (London: Littman Library of Jewish Civilization, 2000); Michael Studemund-Halevy, ed., *Die Sefarden in Hamburg. Zur Geschichte einer Minderheit*, 2 vols. (Hamburg: Buske, 1994–1997); Jorun Poettering, *Migrating Merchants: Trade, Nation, and Religion in Seventeenth-Century Hamburg and Portugal*, trans. Kenneth Kronenberg (Berlin: De Guyter, 2019); Edgar Samuel, *At the End of the Earth: Essays on the History of the Jews of England and Portugal* (London: The Jewish Historical Society of England, 2004); Lionel Levy, *La nation juive portugaise. Livourne, Amsterdam, Tunis, 1591–1951* (Paris: L'Harmattan, 1999); Francesca Trivellato, *The Familiarity of Strangers: The Sephardic Diaspora, Livorno, and Cross-Cultural Trade in the Early Modern Period* (New Haven, CT: Yale University Press, 2009); José Alberto Tavim, *Os judeus na expansão portuguesa em Marrocos durante o século XVI* (Braga: APPADCM, 1997); José Alberto Tavim, *Judeus e cristãos-novos de Cochim. História e memória (1500–1662)* (Braga: APPACDM, 2003); Hugo Martins, *Os judeus portugueses de Hamburgo. A história de uma comunidade mercantil no século XVII* (Florence: Firenze University Press, 2021).

74. António José Saraiva, *A Inquisição portuguesa* (Lisbon: Publicações Europa-América, 1956); António José Saraiva, *Inquisição e cristãos novos* (Porto: Inova, 1969); the 1985 edition includes the debate between Saraiva and Révah, also reproduced in *The Marrano Factory: The Portuguese Inquisition and Its New Christians, 1536–1765*, trans., rev., and augmented by H. P. Salomon and I. S. D. Sassoon (Leiden: Brill, 2001); Benzion Netanyahu, *The Marranos of Spain from the Late 14th to the Early 16th Century, According to Contemporary Hebrew Sources* (1966) (Ithaca, NY: Cornell University Press, 1999); Benzion Netanyahu, *The Origins of the Inquisition in Fifteenth Century Spain* (New York: Random House, 1995).

75. For a similar evaluation of the New Christian religious dimension, see Jaime Contreras, *Sotos contra Riquelmes: regidores, inquisidores y criptojudíos* (Madrid: Anaya & Mario Muchnik, 1992), although based on a very rich analysis of trials and local context in mid-sixteenth century Lorca and Murcia.

76. I. S. Révah left an extraordinary number of valuable studies. I highlight here *Des marranes à Spinoza*, ed. Henri Méchoulan, Pierre-François Moreau, Carsten Wilke (Paris: J. Vrin, 1995).

77. Nathan Wachtel, *The Faith of Remembrance: Marrano Labyrinths*, trans. Nikki Halpern (Philadelphia: University of Pennsylvania Press, 2013).

78. Mercedes García-Arenal and Yonatan Glazer-Eytan, eds., *Forced Conversion in Christianity, Judaism and Islam: Coercion and Faith in pre-modern Iberia and Beyond* (Leiden: Brill, 2020): Simon Ditchfield and Helen Smith, eds., *Conversions: Gender and Religious Change in Early Modern Europe* (Manchester: Manchester University Press, 2017).

79. David Graizbord, *Souls in Dispute: Converso Identities in Iberia and the Jewish Diaspora, 1580–1700* (Philadelphia: University of Pennsylvania Press, 2003).

80. Enrique Soria Mesa, *La realidad tras el espejo: ascenso social y limpieza de sangre en la España de Felipe II* (Valladolid: Universidad de Valladolid, 2016); Linda Martz, *A Network of Converso Families in Early Modern Toledo: Assimilating a Minority* (Ann Arbor: Michigan University Press, 2002); Ruth Pike, *Linajudos y conversos en Seville: Greed and Prejudice in Sixteenth- and Seventeenth-Century Spain* (Oxford: Peter Lang, 2000).

81. James Nelson Novoa, *Being the Nation in the Eternal City: New Christian Lives in Sixteenth-Century Rome* (Peterborough, ON: Baywolf Press, 2014); Miriam Bodian, "The Formation of the Portuguese Jewish Diaspora," in *The Jews in the Caribbean*, ed. Jane S. Gerber (Oxford: Oxford University Press, 2014), 17–28; Juan Gil, "El paso de los conversos a Indias," in *Los conversos y la Inquisición*, ed. Juan Gil (Seville: Fundación El Monte, 2000), 59–95; Peter Mark and José da Silva Horta, *The Forgotten Diaspora: Jewish Communities in West Africa and the Making of the Atlantic World* (Cambridge: Cambridge University Press, 2011); Lúcio de Sousa, *The Jewish Diaspora and the Perez Family Case in China, Japan, the Philippines, and the Americas (16th Century)* (Macau: Fundação de Macau, 2015); Poettering, *Migrating Merchants*; Francesca Trivellato, "Sephardic Merchants in the Early Modern Atlantic and Beyond: Towards a Historical Approach to Business Cooperation," in *Atlantic Diasporas: Jews, Conversos, and Crypto-Jews in the Age of Mercantilism, 1500–1800*, ed. Richard L. Kagan and Philip D. Morgan (Baltimore: Johns Hopkins University Press, 2009), 99–120; Daviken Studniki-Gizbert, *A Nation upon the Ocean Sea: Portugal's Atlantic Diaspora and the Crisis of the Spanish Empire, 1492–1640* (Oxford: Oxford University Press, 2007); Aliza Moreno-Goldschmidt, *Conversos de origen judío en la Cartagena colonial: vida social, cultural y economica en el siglo XVII* (Bogotá: Pontificia Universidad Javeriana, 2018).

82. Henri Lapeyre, *Une famille de marchands, les Ruiz* (Paris: Armand Colin, 1955); José Gentil da Silva, *Marchandises et finances*, 3 vols. (Paris: SEVPEN, 1956–61); Valentín Vázquez de Prada, *Lettres marchandes d'Anvers*, 4 tomes (Paris: SEVPEN, 1960); Felipe Ruiz Martín, *Lettres marchandes échangées entre Florence et Medina del Campo* (Paris: SEVPEN, 1965).

83. There is an enormous number of publications. I retain here only some books not mentioned before, Ricardo García Cárcel, *Orígenes de la Inquisición española: el tribunal de Valencia, 1478–1530* (Barcelona: Península, 1978) and the following volume; Jean Pierre Dedieu, *L'administration de la foi: l'Inquisition de Tolède, XVIᵉ–XVIIIᵉ siècles* (Madrid: Casa de Velázquez, 1989); Stephen Haliczer, *Inquisition and Society in the Kingdom of Valencia, 1478–1834* (Berkeley: University of California Press, 1990); António Borges Coelho, *Inquisição de Évora: dos primórdios a 1668*, 2 vols. (Lisbon: Caminho, 1987); Elvira de Azevedo Mea, *A Inquisição de Coimbra no século XVI: a instituição, os homens, a sociedade* (Porto: Fundação António de Almeida, 1997); Giuseppe Marcocci and José Pedro Paiva, *História da Inquisição Portuguesa, 1536–1821* (Lisbon: Esfera dos Livros, 2013); Solange Alberro, *Inquisición y sociedad en México, 1571–1700* (Mexico: Fondo de Cultura Economica, 1988); Paulino Castañeda, Pilar Hernández, and René Millar Carvacho, *La Inquisición de Lima*, 3 vols. (Madrid: Deimos, 1989–1998); Miguel Rodrigues Lourenço, *A articulação da periferia: Macau e a Inquisição de Goa (c. 1582–c. 1650)* (Macau: Fundação de Macau, 2016).

84. David Grant Smith, *The Mercantile Class of Portugal and Brazil in the Seventeenth Century: A Socio-Economic Study of the Merchants of Lisbon and Bahia, 1620–1690* (PhD dissertation, University of Texas at Austin, 1975); Leonor Freire Costa, *O transporte no Atlântico e a Companhia Geral do Comércio do Brasil (1580–1663)* (Lisbon: CNCDP, 2002).

85. James C. Boyajian, *Portuguese Trade in Asia under the Habsburgs, 1580–1640* (Baltimore: Johns Hopkins University Press, 1993).

86. Bernardo López Belinchón, *Honra, libertad y hacienda: hombres de negocio y judíos sefardíes* (Alcalá de Henares: Universidad de Alcalá, 2001); Carmen Sanz Ayán, *Los banqueros de Carlos II* (Valladolid: Universidad de Valladolid, 1988); Boyajian, *Portuguese Bankers.*

87. Cátia Antunes, *Globalisation in the Early Modern Period: The Economic Relationship between Amsterdam and Lisbon, 1640–1700* (Amsterdam: Aksant, 2004).

88. Trivellato, *Familiarity of Strangers.*

Part I

1. See the lists and maps of settlements involved in Benjamin R. Gampel, *Anti-Jewish Riots in the Crown of Aragon and the Royal Response, 1391–1392* (Cambridge: Cambridge University Press, 2016), esp. 22–25.

2. David Nirenberg, *Neighboring Faiths: Christianity, Islam and Judaism in the Middle Ages and Today* (Chicago: University of Chicago Press, 2014), mainly chapters 4 and 5, focused on issues of a constitutional and an identity crisis among Old Christians.

3. The most consistent estimates, based on fiscal documents, are from M. A. Ladero Quesada, *Judíos y conversos en Castilla en el siglo XV. Datos y comentarios* (Madrid: Dickinson, 2016), 32, 36.

4. Jonathan Ray, *After Expulsion:1492 and the Making of the Sephardic Jews* (New York: New York University Press, 2012); Joseph Perez, *History of a Tragedy: The Expulsion of the Jews from Spain,* trans. Lysa Hochroth, intr. Helen Nader (Urbana: Illinois University Press, 2007); Haim Beinart, *The Expulsion of the Jews from Spain,* trans. Jeffrey M. Green (Oxford: Littman Library of Jewish Civilization, 2002), esp. 284–290; Luis Suárez Fernández, *La expulsion de los judíos de España* (Madrid: MAPFRE, 1991); Miguel Angel Motis Dolader, *La expulsión de los judíos del Reino de Aragón* (Zaragoza: Deputación General de Aragón, 1990). Haim Beinart suggests significantly higher estimates of Jewish communities and expelled people, around 200,000.

5. Julio Caro Baroja, *Los Judíos en la España Moderna y Contemporánea,* 3rd ed., vol. 1 (Madrid: Istmo, 1986), 129–133.

6. Friedrich Nietzsche, *On the Genealogy of Morals* (1887), trans. Douglas Smith (Oxford: Oxford University Press, 1996) essay 1, §7–16. Nietzsche suggests resentment on the part of frustrated slaves and Jews against nobles. I find this problematic. Gilles Deleuze, *Nietzsche et la philosophie* (Paris: PUF, 1962) interprets Nietzsche's work as a demystification of a dialectic that uses opposition and contradiction as a theoretical principle, promoting despair, suffering, and frustration as positive developments. The philosophy of action (the praise of will and the assertion of difference) is built on a genealogy of morals and a critique of social masks; the values embodied in both the domination of the nobility and the frustration of slaves are under scrutiny. However, the choice of these social types should also be subject to criticism as assuming that resentment only concerned slaves and Jews. I believe this feeling is experienced, in different degrees and with different consequences, through all social groups. Resentment can thrive among dominant social groups fearing the loss of privileges. The New Christians were clearly targeted by the established as a new, competing group.

7. Caro Baroja, *Los Judíos en la España,* 133–147; Albert Sicroff, *Los estatutos de limpieza de sangre,* trans. Mauro Armiño (Madrid: Taurus, 1985). On the economic and social background of the riots between 1449 and 1473, not all anti-New Christian, see Angus Mackay, "Popular Movements and Pogroms in Fifteenth-Century Castile," *Past and Present* 55 (May 1972): 33–67.

8. Maria del Pilar Rábade Obradó, *Los judeoconversos en la corte y en la época de los Reyes Católicos* (Madrid: Universidad Complutense, 1990).

9. Humberto Baquero Moreno, *Marginalidade e conflitos sociais em Portugal, séculos XIV e XV* (Lisbon: Presença, 1985); Humberto Baquero Moreno, "Movimentos sociais antijudaicos no século XV," in *Jews and Conversos: Studies in Society and the Inquisition,* ed. Yosef Kaplan (Jerusalem: The Hebrew University, 1985), 62–73.

10. Maria José Ferro Tavares, *Os judeus em Portugal no século XV* (Lisbon: FCSH, 1982), 74, 256; estimates based on fiscal documents. The real numbers must have been higher.

11. The return to Castile of the New Christians who had escaped from the Inquisition was high on the list of requests included in the negotiations for the marriage of D. Manuel to Isabel of Aragon: see, among several documents, *As Gavetas da Torre do Tombo*, vol. 7, ed. A. da Silva Rego (Lisbon: Centro de Estudos Históricos Ultramarinos, 1963), 407–408. D. Manuel decided to go beyond that request and even postpone his marriage until the expulsion of the Jews (meaning mass conversion) was completed.

12. François Soyer, *The Persecution of the Jews and Muslims of Portugal: King Manuel and the End of Religious Tolerance* (Leiden: Brill, 2011); Francisco Bethencourt, "A expulsão dos judeus," in *O tempo de Vasco da Gama*, ed. Diogo Ramada Curto (Lisbon: Difel, 1998), 271–280; Elias Lipiner, *Os baptizados em pé. Estudos acerca da origem e da luta dos cristãos novos em Portugal* (Lisbon: Vega, 1998); José Alberto Tavim, *Os judeus na expansão portuguesa em Marrocos* (Braga: APPACDM, 1997), 71–87.

13. João Figueirôa-Rego, *A honra alheia por um fio: os estatutos de limpeza de sangue nos espaços de expressão ibérica (sécs. XVI–XVIII)* (Lisbon; Fundação Calouste Gulbenkian, 2011).

14. Antonio Domínguez Ortiz, *Los judeoconversos en España y America* (Madrid: Istmo, 1971), 220; Ladero Quesada, *Judeos y conversos*, 33, 217–218. In the Portuguese case, drawing on the work of Maria José Ferro Tavares, we must calculate between 60,000 and 70,000 New Christians, owing to the numerous refugees from the tribunals of Castile.

15. The figure 100,000 was suggested by Jonathan Israel, *European Jewry in the Age of Mercantilism 1550–1750*, 3rd ed. (Oxford: The Littman Library of Jewish Civilization, 1998), 5–6; it seems much too high when set against the most recent research on the numbers of Jewish and New Christian communities in Iberia and abroad. The issue is how to estimate the constant flow of emigration, even under legal constraint. For demographics, see Massimo Livi-Bacci, *The Population of Europe*, trans. Cynthia and Carl Ipsen (Oxford: Blackwell, 2000). The average size of the urban population in Spain between 1500 and 1600 varied from 6 percent to 11 percent, whereas in Portugal it varied from 3 percent to 14 percent, largely concentrated in Lisbon. But as mentioned in the Introduction, these estimates are too low, being based on towns over 10,000 inhabitants.

16. José Alberto Tavim, *Os judeus na expansão portuguesa em Marrocos durante o século XVI: origens e actividades duma comunidade* (Braga: APPACDM, 1997); José Alberto Tavim, *Judeus e Cristãos-Novos de Cochim. História e Memória (1500–1662)* (Braga: APPACDM, 2003); Jean-Frédéric Schaub, *Les juifs du roi d'Espagne: Oran 1509–1669* (Paris: Hachette, 1999).

17. See the sharp prolegomenon by Yosef Hayim Yerushalmi to Alexandre Herculano, *History of the Origin and Establishment of the Inquisition in Portugal* (1854–1859), trans. John C. Branner (New York: Ktav, 1972).

Chapter One: Background

1. Joseph Perez, *Los judíos en España* (Madrid: Marcial Pons, 2005), 62.

2. Javier Castaño González, "Social Networks in a Castilian Jewish Aljama and the Court Jews in the Fifteenth Century: A Preliminary Survey (Madrid 1440–1475)," *En la España Medieval* 20 (1997): 379–392, esp. 388.

3. Maria José Pimenta Ferro, *Os judeus em Portugal no século XIV* (Lisbon: Guimarães Editores, 1979), 105–117; Carsten L. Wilke, *Histoire des juifs portugais* (Paris: Chandeigne, 2007), 34–36. For discussion of the legal status of Jews, see David Abulafia, "The Servitude of Jews and Muslims in the Medieval Mediterranean: Origins and Diffusion," *Mélanges de l'École Française de Rome. Moyen-Age* 112, 2 (2000): 687–714.

4. More than 300 misericórdias were created in the kingdom from the late fifteenth to the eighteenth century and many dozens in Asia, Africa, and Brazil: see Isabel dos Guimarães Sá, "Managing Social Inequality. Confraternal Charity in Portugal and Its Overseas Colonies," *Social Science History* 41, 1 (Spring 2017): 121–135; Isabel dos Guimarães Sá, *Quando o rico se faz pobre: Misericórdias, caridade e poder no império português, 1500–1800* (Lisbon: CNCDP, 1997).

5. Miguel Angel Ladero Quesada, *La hacienda real de Castilla en el siglo XV* (La Laguna: Universidad de la Laguna, 1973); Iria Gonçalves, *Pedidos e empréstimos públicos em Portugal na Idade Média* (Lisbon: Centro de Estudos Fiscais, 1963); Iria Gonçalves, *As finanças municipais do Porto na segunda metade do século XV* (Porto: Arquivo Municipal do Porto, 1988); Vitorino Magalhães Godinho, "A formação do Estado e as finanças públicas" (1960), in *Ensaios e Estudos. Uma maneira de pensar* (Lisbon: Sá da Costa, 2009), 123–173.

6. Maria José Ferro Tavares, *Os judeus em Portugal no século XV* (Lisbon: FCSH, 1982), 314–327.

7. Ferro Tavares, *Os judeus em Portugal no século XV*, 313.

8. On this important counternarrative highlighting the emergence of new Jewish elites, the variety of situations, and regional differences, see Castaño González, "Social Networks," 379–392; Mark D. Meyerson, *A Jewish Renaissance in Fifteenth-Century Spain* (Princeton, NJ: Princeton University Press, 2004), based on a case study of Morvedre (nowadays Sagunto) in the kingdom of Valencia.

9. Perez, *Los judíos*, 115–116.

10. *Encyclopaedia Judaica*, 2nd ed., vol. 1 (Detroit: Macmillan/Keter, 2007), 274–275.

11. Perez, *Los judíos*, 54–55.

12. Meyerson, *Jewish Renaissance*, 17–18, 73, 106–108, 119, 149, 244–245.

13. Ladero Quesada, *La hacienda real de Castilla*.

14. Haim Beinart, *The Expulsion of Jews from Spain*, trans. Jeffrey M. Green (Oxford: The Littman Library of Jewish Civilization, 2002), 413–500, an extended chapter on the Seneor family and its immediate descendants, who inherited the tax-farming appointments of Abraham Seneor alias Fernán Núñez Coronel.

15. Ferro Tavares, *Os judeus em Portugal no século XV*, 296.

16. Isaac Abravanel, *Letters*, ed., trans., and intr. Cedric Cohen Skalli (Berlin: Walter de Gruyter, 2007); Isaac Abravanel, *La mémoire et l'espérance*, ed., trans., and intr. Jean-Christophe Attias (Paris: Cerf, 1992); Cedric Cohen Skalli, *Don Isaac Abravanel: An Intellectual Biography* (Waltham, MA: Brandeis University Press, 2021).

17. Ferro Tavares, *Os judeus em Portugal no século XV*, 287–290.

18. F. J. Martínez Medina and M. Biersack, *Fray Hernando de Talavera. Primer Arzobispo de Granada. Hombre de Iglesia, Estado y Letras* (Granada: Universidad de Granada, 2011); I. Iannuzzi, *El poder de la palabra en el siglo XV: Fray Hernando de Talavera* (Valladolid: Junta de Castilla y León, 2009); Benzion Netanyahu, *The Marranos of Spain: From the Late 14th to the Early 16th Century, According to Contemporary Hebrew Sources*, 3rd ed. (Ithaca, NY: Cornell University Press, 1999); R. Hernández Martín, "Juan de Torquemada: su doctrina socio-política," *Cuadernos Salmantinos de Filosofía* 22 (1995): 81–116; Yitzhak Baer, *A History of the Jews in Christian Spain*, vol. 2, *From the Fourteenth Century to the Expulsion* (Philadelphia: Jewish Publication Society of America, 1961).

19. Benzion Netanyahu, *Towards the Inquisition: Essays on Jewish and Converso History in Medieval Spain* (Ithaca, NY: Cornell University Press, 1997), 99–125.

20. Julio Caro Baroja, *Los judios en la España moderna y contemporanea* (1963), 3rd ed., vol. 1 (Madrid: Istmo, 1986), 130–132.

21. Antonio Domínguez Ortiz, *Los judeoconversos en España y América* (Madrid: Istmo, 1971), 37.

22. Maria Pilar Rábade Obradó, "La elite judeoconversa de la Corte de los Reyes Católicos y el negocio fiscal," *En la España Medieval* 37 (2014): 205–222.

23. Domínguez Ortiz, *Los judeoconversos en España y América*, 25–26.

24. Albert Sicroff, *Los estatutos de limpieza de sangre: controversias entre los siglos XV y XVII*, trans. Mauro Armiño (Madrid: Taurus, 1985).

25. Francisco Márquez Villanueva, *De la España judeoconversa. Doce estudios* (Barcelona: Belaterra, 2006), 137–174.

26. The importance of this historical context of forced conversion to justify genealogical obsession has been pointed out by David Nirenberg, "Mass Conversion and Genealogical Mentalities: Jews and Christians in Fifteenth-Century Spain," *Past and Present* 174 (2003): 3–41.

27. Juan Hernández Franco, *Sangre limpia, sangre española. El debate de los estatutos de limpieza (siglos XV–XVII)* (Madrid: Cátedra, 2011).

28. João Figueirôa-Rego, *A honra alheia por um fio: os estatutos de limpeza de sangue nos espaços de expressão ibérica, séculos XVI–XVIII* (Lisboa: Fundação Calouste Gulbenkian, 2011).

29. The scale of illegal exemptions was studied by Juan M. Carretero Zamora, *Gobernar es gastar. Carlos V, el servicio de las Cortes de Castilla y la deuda de la Monarquía Hispánica, 1516–1556* (Madrid: Silex, 2016), esp. 263–289.

30. Teófanes Egido, *El linaje judeo-converso de Teresa de Ávila (pleito de hidalguia de los Cepeda)* (Madrid: Editorial de Espiritualidad, 1986).

31. Systematic stigmatisation and brutal extortion preceded the expulsion of English Jews: Robert C. Stacey, "Parliamentary Negotiation and the Expulsion of the Jews from England," in *Thirteenth Century England, VI: Proceedings of the Durham Conference 1995*, ed. Michael Prestwich, R. H. Britnell, and Robin Frame (Woodbridge: Boydell, 1997), 77–101; Robert C. Stacey, "Anti-Semitism and the Medieval English State," in *The Medieval State: Essays Presented to James Campbell*, ed. J. R. Madicott and D. L. Palliser (London: Hambledon, 2000), 163–177. For the French case, see William C. Jordan, *The French Monarchy and the Jews: From Philip Augustus to the Last Capetians* (Philadelphia: University of Pennsylvania Press, 1989).

32. Kenneth R. Stow, *Alienated Minority: The Jews of Medieval Latin Europe* (Cambridge, MA: Harvard University Press, 1992).

33. Corrado Vivanti, ed., *Storia d'Italia. Gli ebrei in Italia*, vol. 1, *Dall'Alto Medioevo all'età dei ghetti* (Turin: Einaudi, 1996); for a general view, see Maurice Kriegel, *Les juifs à la fin du Moyen Age dans l'Europe méditerranéenne* (Paris: Hachette, 1994).

34. Maurice Kriegel, "Mobilisation politique et modernisation organique: les expulsions de juifs au Bas Moyen Age," *Archives de Sciences Sociales des Religions* 46 (1978): 5–20.

35. Peter Mazur, *The New Christians of Spanish Naples, 1528–1671: A Fragile Elite* (Basingstoke: Palgrave, 2013).

36. Jonathan Israel, *European Jewry in the Age of Mercantilism, 1550–1750*, 3rd ed. (Oxford: The Littman Library of Jewish Civilization, 1998), 4–18; Ana Foa, *Ebrei in Europa dalla peste nera all'emancipazione*, 2nd ed. (Roma-Bari: Laterza, 2001), 121–142, 155–173, 176–182.

37. Jean-Christophe Attias and Esther Benbassa, *Dictionnaire de civilisation juive* (Paris: Larousse, 1998), 33.

38. Jonathan Israel, *European Jewry*, 23–24.

39. Jonathan S. Ray, *After Expulsion: 1492 and the Making of Sephardic Jewry* (New York: New York University Press, 2013), suggests long-term migration and the slow creation of communities divided by origin.

40. The resurgence of Jewish historical writing in the sixteenth century is related to the expulsion from Spain: Yosef Hayim Yerushalmi, *Zakhor: Jewish History and Jewish Memory* (Seattle: University of Washington Press, 1982), esp. 55–75. I highlight the following sources: Solomon ibn Verga, *La vara de Yehuda*, trans. and ed., Maria José Cano (Barcelona: Riopiedras, 1991); Joseph ha Kohen, *Sefer 'emeq ha-bakha (the vale of tears) with the Chronicle of the Anonymous Corrector*, ed. Karim Almbladh (Upsala: Acta Universitatis Upsaliensis, 1981); Jeremy Cohen, *A Historian in Exile: Salomon ibn Verga, Shevet Yehudah, and the Jewish-Christian Encounter* (Philadelphia: University of Pennsylvania Press, 2017); Samuel Usque, *Consolação às tribulaçoes de Israel* (1553), facsimile with introductions by Yosef Hayim Yerushalmi and José V. de Pina Martins 2 vols. (Lisbon: Fundação Calouste Gulbenkian, 1989).

41. See the contemporary report, probably drawn up by Cristóbal Núñez, chaplain to the Catholic Kings, published by Fidel Fita, "Los conjurados de Sevilla contra la Inquisición en 1480," *Boletin de la Real Academia de la Historia* 16 (1890), 450–456. The impact of inquisitorial action in Seville from the 1480s to the 1510s was studied comprehensively by Juan Gil, *Los conversos y la Inquisición sevillana*, 8 vols. (Seville: Universidad de Sevilla, 2000–2003).

42. Andrés Bernaldez, "Historia de los Reyes Católicos Don Fernando y Doña Isabel," in *Crónicas de los Reyes de Castilla*, ed. C. Rosell, vol. 3 (Madrid: Biblioteca de Autores Españoles, 1953), 600–601.

43. Francisco Tomás y Valiente, "Relaciones de la Inquisición con el aparato institucional del Estado," in *Gobierno y instituciones en la España del Antiguo Régimen* (Madrid: Alianza, 1982), 13–35.

44. Gil, *Los conversos y la Inquisición sevillana*, vol. 1, 96–105, 284.

45. Fernando del Pulgar, *Crónicas de los Reyes Católicos* [1565], ed. Juan de Mata Carriazo, vol. 2 (Madrid: Espasa Calpe, 1943), 137; Juan de Mariana, *Historia General de España* [1st Latin ed. 1592, 1st Castilian ed. 1601], in *Obras*, vol. 2 (Madrid: Biblioteca de Autores Españoles, 1950), 202.

46. Albert Sicroff, *Los estatutos de limpieza de sangre*.

47. Gil, *Los conversos y la Inquisición sevillana*, vol. 2, 104.

48. Ortiz, *Los judeoconversos en España y América*, 50; Esteban Mira Ceballos, "Los prohibidos en la emigración a América (1492–1550)," *Estudios de historia social y económica de América* 12 (1995): 37–53. The ban to the Indies was reiterated since 1501 but did not prevent regular flow.

49. Gil, *Los conversos y la Inquisición sevillana*, vol. 1, 143–149, 238–254, 271–277.

50. Sicroff, *Los estatutos de limpieza de sangre*; Monique Combescure Thiry, ed., *El libro verde de Aragón*, intro., Miguel Angel Motis Dolader (Zaragoza: Certeza, 2003).

51. J. M. Carretero Zamora, "Los conversos y la hacienda de Castille en los comienzos del siglo XVI," in *La pureté de sang en Espagne. Du lignage à la race*, ed. Raphaël Carrasco, Annie Molinié, Beatrice Perez (Paris: Presses de l'université Paris-Sorbonne, 2011), 113–131; J. M. Carretero Zamora, *Gobernar es gastar. Carlos V, el servicio de las Cortes de Castilla y la deuda de la Monarquia Hispánica, 1516–1556* (Madrid: Silex, 2016); David Alonso García, *El erario del reino. Fiscalidad en Castilla a principios de la edad moderna, 1504–1525* (Valladolid: Junta de Castilla y León, 2007); David Alonso García, *Mercados y mercaderes en los siglos XVI y XVII* (Madrid: Sínytesis, 2016); J. M. Carretero Zamora and David Alonso García, *Hacienda y negocio financiero en tiempos de Isabel la Católica. El libro de hacienda de 1503* (Madrid: Universidad Complutense de Madrid, 2003); Maria del Pilar Rábade Obradó, "Los judeoconversos en la corte y en la epoca de los Reyes Catolicos" (PhD, Madrid: Universidad Complutense, 1989).

52. Domínguez Ortiz, *Los judeoconversos en España y América*, 56; Joseph Perez, *La revolución de las Comunidades de Castilla, 1520–1521* (Madrid: Siglo XXI, 1999).

53. Gil, *Los conversos y la Inquisición sevillana*, vol. 2, 37–49.

54. Gil, *Los conversos y la Inquisición sevillana*, vol. 2, 50–63.

55. Gil, *Los conversos y la Inquisición sevillana*, vol. 2, 31–34.

56. Giuseppe Marcocci and José Pedro Paiva, *História da Inquisição portuguesa, 1536–1821* (Lisbon: Esfera dos Livros, 2013), 41–47.

57. Alexandre Herculano, *Da origem e estabelecimento da Inquisição em Portugal*, 3 vols. (Lisbon: Imprensa Nacional, 1854–1859).

58. This letter was included in a book listing the privileges of the city of Goa: J. H. da Cunha Rivara, ed., *Archivo Portuguez Oriental*, fasc. 2 (1857) reprint (New Delhi: Asian Educational Services, 1992), 17. In other volumes of correspondence between the city and the king, this rule is reiterated, particularly in 1562: *Archivo Portuguez Oriental*, fasc. 1, parte I, 59. The municipality called several times for the removal of the New Christians from the Estado da Índia: *Archivo Portuguez Oriental*, fasc. 1, parte II, 13–17 (letter from 1595); 57 (letter from 1597), 77 (letter from 1600).

59. I will give plenty of examples of these policies of promotion in this and following chapters. The idea, expressed by Jonathan Israel in *European Jewry in the Age of Mercantilism, 1550–1750*, 20, and prompted by Spinoza and Vieira, that New Christians in Portugal had been excluded from all honours and offices, thus perpetuating a caste system based on resentment and separate identity, needs to be qualified in time and place. As we will see in the following chapters, the problem lies in dual royal policies combining individual promotion and collective persecution.

60. Maria José Ferro Tavares, *Judaísmo e Inquisiçao. Estudos* (Lisbon: Presença, 1987), 49.

61. Daniel Norte Giebels, *A Inquisição de Lisboa (1537–1579)* (Lisbon: Gradiva, 2018), 318–322.

62. Jaime Contreras and Gustav Henningsen, "Forty-Four Thousand Cases of the Spanish Inquisition," in *The Inquisition in Early Modern Europe: Studies on Sources and Methods*, ed. Gustav Henningsen and John Tedeschi (Dekalb: Northern Illinois University Press, 1986), 130–157. These data are based on the *relaciones de causas*, summaries of trials, which are far from complete. There are no consistent data before 1540 for the Spanish case.

63. Francisco Bethencourt, *The Inquisition: A Global History, 1478–1834*, trans. Jean Birrell (Cambridge: Cambridge University Press, 2009), 341–342.

Chapter Two: Continuities

1. Yosef Hayim Yerushalmi, *The Lisbon Massacre of 1506 and the Royal Image in the* Shebet Yehudad (Cincinnati: Hebrew Union College, 1976), which publishes the main sources, such as the anonymous German sailor's text *Von dem christenlichen streyt*, and also royal decrees and correspondence.

2. João José Alves Dias, ed., *Ordenações manuelinas, livros I–V: reprodução em facsímile da edição de Valentim Fernandes (Lisboa, 1512–1513)*, vol. 2, (Lisbon: Universidade Nova de Lisboa, 2002), fl. 65.

3. Jean Aubin, *Études inédites sur le règne de D. Manuel, 1495–1521*, ed. M. C. Flores, L. F. Thomaz and F. Aubin (Paris: Centre Culturel Calouste Gulbenkian, 2006), 58.

4. ANTT, Chancelaria de D. Manuel, Livro 16, fl. 97v.

5. ANTT, Chancelaria de D. Manuel, Livro 16, fl. 100r.

6. "Cartas de quitação del rei D. Manuel," *Arquivo Historico Portuguez* V (1907): 73.

7. "Cartas de quitação del rei D. Manuel," *Arquivo Historico Portuguez* IV (1906): 72. It seems that after his death, Rodrigues Mascarenhas was replaced in this farming of moradias by Heitor Nunes Perdigão. Before João Rodrigues, Vasco Queimado had been in charge, see "Cartas de quitação del rei D. Manuel," *Arquivo Historico Portuguez* III (1905): 158. There is another royal document dated June 6, 1501, stating that Martim Afonso, squire and buyer for the king, owed 200,000 reais to João Rodrigues Mascarenhas, contractor for the royal moradias; ANTT, Chancelaria de D. Manuel, Livro 17, fl. 45r. I follow the conversion of 1 cruzado = 385 reais suggested by Vitorino Magalhães Godinho, *Os descobrimentos e a economia mundial*, 2nd ed., vol. 1 (Lisbon: Presença, 1989), 135; the equivalence of 1 cruzado to 400 reais (or réis) was established in 1514.

8. "Cartas de quitação del rei D. Manuel," *Arquivo Historico Portuguez* IV (1906): 72.

9. "Cartas de quitação del rei D. Manuel," *Arquivo Historico Portuguez* IV (1906): 73. There is a slight discrepancy in the values given between this document, from Livro 9 da Extremadura, and those in the Chancelaria de D. Manuel, Livro 36, fl. 28r, in which we read 1,119,158 reais.

10. "Cartas de quitação del rei D. Manuel," *Arquivo Historico Portuguez* IV (1906): 73

11. "Cartas de quitação del rei D. Manuel," *Arquivo Historico Portuguez* IV (1906): 73.

12. ANTT, Corpo Cronológico, Parte II, maço 4, n. 25.

13. At the ANTT, I have checked many inventories of property taken after death as well as wills, and this form of inheritance was deeply embedded. Only with the creation of entailed property, morgados, could a set of properties be reserved with the approval of the king, to protect the noble house and guarantee the inheritance of the eldest son (or alternatives), although compensation would follow.

14. ANTT, Corpo Cronológico, Parte II, Maço 116, n. 127 and 134; Corpo Cronológico, Parte II, Maço 123, n. 155.

15. Christiano José de Senna Barcellos, *Subsídios para a história de Cabo Verde e Guiné*, Part I (Lisbon: Real Academia das Sciências, 1899), 65–67 (document dated October 23, 1510, valuable for the detail it gives of economic activity in the area).

16. Document dated December 12, 1514, quittance of Gonçalo Lopes, royal administrator of the rents of Cape Verde and Rivers of Guinea, who received 27,428,975 reais in 1511–1514,

including rents and hides, from António Rodrigues Mascarenhas; ANTT, Chancelaria de D. Manuel, Livro 11, fl. 69v–70r.

17. Document dated March 28, 1527; ANTT, Corpo Cronológico, Parte II, Maço 140, n. 27.

18. Toby Green, *The Rise of the Trans-Atlantic Trade in Western Africa, 1300–1589* (Cambridge: Cambridge University Press, 2012), 120–148. See also George E. Brooks, *Eurafricans in Western Africa: Commerce, Social Status, Gender and Religious Observance from the Sixteenth to the Eighteenth Century* (Oxford: James Currey, 2003); for a later period, Peter Mark and José da Silva Horta, *The Forgotten Diaspora: Jewish Communities in West Africa and the Making of the Atlantic World* (Cambridge: Cambridge University Press, 2011).

19. Maria José Ferro Tavares, *Judaísmo e Inquisição. Estudos* (Lisbon: Presença, 1987), 44.

20. Ferro Tavares, *Judaísmo e Inquisição. Estudos*, 42.

21. António Baião, "O comércio do pau-brasil," in *História da colonização portuguesa do Brasil*, vol. 2, ed. Carlos Malheiro Dias (Porto: Litografia Nacional, 1923), 315–347. Most of the available information on Fernão de Loronha is in this chapter.

22. José Gonçalves Salvador, *Os magnatas do tráfico negreiro (séculos XVI e XVII)* (São Paulo: Pioneira, 1981), 19.

23. ANTT, Corpo Cronológico, Parte II, Maço 102, n. 155.

24. Baião, "O comércio do pau-brasil," 324.

25. Vitorino Magalhães Godinho, *Os descobrimentos e a economia mundial*, 2nd rev. ed., vol. 3, (Lisbon: Presença, 1983), 195–196.

26. ANTT, Chancelaria de D. Manuel, Livro 41, fl. 2r–v.

27. ANTT, Corpo Cronológico, Parte I, Maço 10, n. 53.

28. ANTT, Corpo Cronológico, Parte I, Maço 9, n. 113.

29. ANTT, Corpo Cronológico, Parte I, Maço 6, n. 84.

30. ANTT, Corpo Cronológico, Parte I, Maço 6, n. 90. There are several other documents ordering deliveries of sugar from Madeira to Álvaro Pimentel between 1508 and 1512, also some that indicate subcontracting to other merchants; ANTT, Corpo Cronológico, Parte I, Maço 7, numbers 16, 89, 90, 92; also ANTT, Corpo Cronológico, Parte II, Maço 16, n. 168, Maço 22, n. 53 and Maço 36, n. 24.

31. ANTT, Corpo Cronológico, Parte I, Maço 7, n. 100 and 102; Maço 9, n. 11; Parte II, Maço 23, n. 238.

32. ANTT, Corpo Cronológico, Parte I, Maço 9, n. 10.

33. ANTT, Corpo Cronológico, Parte II, Maço 17, n. 120.

34. ANTT, Corpo Cronológico, Parte II, Maço 14, n. 21.

35. ANTT, Corpo Cronológico, Parte II, Maço 15, n. 50.

36. ANTT, Corpo Cronológico, Parte I, Maço 10, n. 85.

37. ANTT, Corpo Cronológico, Parte II, Maço 22, n. 161.

38. ANTT, Corpo Cronológico, Parte II, Maço 64, n. 120.

39. ANTT, Corpo Cronológico, Parte II, Maço 92, n. 80; Maço 129, n. 53.

40. ANTT, Corpo Cronológico, Parte I, Maço 10, n. 70 (there are more documents on this transaction).

41. Godinho, *Os descobrimentos e a economia mundial*, vol. 3, 195.

42. ANTT, Chancelaria de D. Manuel, Livro 7, fl. 36r.

43. ANTT, Corpo Cronológico, Parte I, Maço 165, n. 42.

44. ANTT, Corpo Cronológico, Parte I, Maço 29, n. 12.

45. ANTT, Corpo Cronológico, Parte II, Maço 129, n. 244.

46. ANTT, Corpo Cronológico, Parte II, Maço 65, n. 105.

47. ANTT, Corpo Cronológico, Parte I, Maço 22, n. 115; Parte I, Maço 23, n. 130; Parte I, Maço 43, n. 50.

48. Magalhães Godinho, *Os descobrimentos e a economia mundial*, vol. 3, 199.

49. ANTT, Corpo Cronológico, Parte II, Maço 80, n. 144.

50. ANTT, Chancelaria de D. Manuel, Livro 35, fl. 126v.

51. ANTT, Corpo Cronológico, Parte II, Maço 122, n. 109.

52. ANTT, Corpo Cronológico, Parte II, Maço 206, n. 88.

53. ANTT, Corpo Cronológico, Parte II, Maço 211, n. 104.

54. ANTT Corpo Cronológico, Parte II, Maço 30, n. 231; Maço 42, n. 14; Maço 45, n. 151; Maço 55, n. 152; Maço 41, n. 8; Maço 30, n. 120; Maço 33, n. 64 and 75. In 1511 the equivalence was 1 moio of wheat = 6 arrobas of sugar, but in 1512 it was 1 moio of wheat = 5 arrobas of sugar: ANTT, Corpo Cronológico, Parte II, Maço 29, n. 138; Maço 33, n. 5.

55. ANTT, Corpo Cronológico, Parte II, Maço 143, n. 139.

56. ANTT, Corpo Cronológico, Parte II, Maço 25, n. 50.

57. ANTT, Corpo Cronológico, Parte II, Maço 117, n. 16; Maço 121, n. 204.

58. ANTT, Corpo Cronológico, Parte II, Maço 143, n. 139.

59. ANTT, Colecção de Cartas, Núcleo Antigo, 889, n. 326.

60. A. A. Marques de Almeida, ed., *Dicionário histórico dos sefarditas portugueses. Mercadores e gente de trato* (Lisbon: Campo da Comunicação, 2009), 478–479.

61. ANTT, Corpo Cronológico, Parte I, Maço 25, n. 106.

62. ANTT, Chancelaria de D. Manuel, Livro 10, fl. 4r.

63. ANTT, Chancelaria de D. Manuel, Livro 22, fll. 41v–42r.

64. Marques de Almeida, ed., *Dicionário histórico dos sefarditas portugueses*, 40.

65. Magalhães Godinho, *Os descobrimentos e a economia mundial*, vol. 3, 198.

66. Magalhães Godinho, *Os descobrimentos e a economia mundial*, vol. 3, 195.

67. ANTT, Corpo Cronológico, Parte II, Maço 124, n. 26; Maço 133, n. 42; Maço 178, n. 98; Maço 127, n. 175 (this document shows that the contract reached a total value of 6 million reais for 1524 and 1525). These documents concern the period 1525–1531, but the dates of these contracts, according to Vitorino Magalhães Godinho, encompassed 1522–1523: *Os descobrimentos e a economia mundial*, vol. 4, 91.

68. ANTT, Corpo Cronológico, Parte II, Maço 31, n. 70; Parte I, Maço 18, n. 54. Yusuf Cofem must be José Cofem, identified by José Alberto Tavim, *Os judeus na expansão portuguesa em Marrocos durante o século XVI*, 288, 302, 318, and 404, in several contracts and communications with the Portuguese kings from the 1510s to the 1530s.

69. ANTT, Chancelaria de D. Manuel, Livro 10, fl. 78r.

70. ANTT, Chancelaria de D. Manuel, Livro 14, fl. 55r.

71. Carlos Manuel Valentim, *Uma família de cristãos novos do Entre-Douro e Minho, os Paz. Reprodução familiar, formas de mobilidades social, mercância e poder (1495–1598)* (MA thesis, Faculdade de Letras de Lisboa, 2007).

72. ANTT, Chancelaria de D. Manuel, Livro 36, fl. 126r.

73. Carlos Manuel Valentim, "Duarte de Paz: um líder da comunidade sefardita portuguesa em meados do século XVI. Novos elementos biográficos," in *Rumos e escrita da história. Estudos em homenagem a A. A. Marques de Almeida* (Lisbon: Colibri, 2006), 175–190.

74. ANTT, Chancelaria de D. Joao III, Livro 8, fl. 63v.

75. ANTT, Chancelaria de D. João III, Livro 48, fl. 47r.

76. ANTT, Chancelaria de D. João III, Livro 20, fl. 39v.

77. H. P. Salomon and A. Leone Leoni, "Mendes, Benveniste, De Luna, Micas, Nasci: The State of the Art (1522–1558)," *Jewish Quarterly Review* 88, 3–4 (1998): 135–211.

78. Marques de Almeida, ed., *Dicionário histórico dos sefarditas portugueses*, 419–424.

79. ANTT, Corpo Cronológico, Parte II, Maço 2, n. 107.

80. ANTT, Chancelaria de D. Manuel, Livro 2, fl. 50v.

81. ANTT, Corpo Cronológico, Parte II, Maço 49, n. 178; Maço 50, n. 49; Maço 64, n. 92.

82. Marques de Almeida, ed., *Dicionário histórico dos sefarditas portugueses*, 421.

83. ANTT, Corpo Cronológico, Parte II, Maço 192, n. 103.

84. ANTT, Corpo Cronológico, Parte II, Maço 28, n.12; Maço 29, n. 87; Maço 40, n. 1; Maço 42, n. 182; Maço 53, n. 61; Maço 54, n. 159; Maço 61, n. 179.

85. ANTT, Corpo Cronológico, Parte I, Maço 50, n. 104 (letter from Duarte Casco, royal clerk in Seville, ordering João Gomes, treasurer of the Casa da Índia, to pay 4,000 cruzados to Francisco Mendes, March 29, 1533); ANTT, Corpo Cronológico, Parte I, Maço 51, n. 49 (the same agent plus Manuel Cirne, 2,000 cruzados, June 6, 1533); ANTT, Corpo Cronológico, Parte II, Maço 178, n. 69 (another bill of exchange from Seville, June 14, 1532, with a value of 533,000 reis at 410 reais the cruzado, 1,300 cruzados).

86. ANTT, Corpo Cronológico, Parte I, Maço 10, n. 91. There was a shortfall, as usual, since the sulphur cost 520 reais the quintal, which would have meant 52,000 reais was still owed.

87. Magalhães Godinho, *Os descobrimentos e a economia mundial*, vol. 3, 198.

88. ANTT, Corpo Cronológico, Parte II, Maço 99, n. 39.

89. ANTT, Corpo Cronológico, Parte I, Maço 49, n. 87.

90. J. M. Carretero Zamora, "Los conversos y la hacienda de Castille en los comienzos del siglo XVI," in *La pureté de sang en Espagne. Du lignage à la race*, 113–131.

91. Carretero Zamora, "Los conversos y la hacienda de Castille," 114–115.

92. Juan Gil, *Los conversos y la Inquisición sevillana*, vol. 3, 134–152.

93. Carretero Zamora, "Los conversos y la hacienda de Castille," 115–116.

94. Carretero Zamora, "Los conversos y la hacienda de Castille," 117–121.

95. Gil, *Los conversos*, vol. 3, 206–211, 234–237.

96. Carretero Zamora, "Los conversos y la hacienda de Castille," 119–122.

97. Ramon Carande, *Carlos V y sus banqueros*, 3rd ed., vol. 3 (Barcelona: Crítica, 1990), 168–184.

98. Carretero Zamora, "Los conversos y la hacienda de Castille," 124–131.

99. See the significant list of itineraries and projects of New Christians seeking to escape the Iberian kingdoms to live their faith in North Africa and other destinations compiled by Silva Tavim, *Os judeus na expansão portuguesa*, 513–520.

100. Bartolomé Yun-Casalilla, *Iberian World Empires and the Globalization of Europe 1415-1668* (Singapore: Palgrave, 2019).

101. See information that backs this up in Carande, *Carlos V y sus banqueros*; also in Hermann Kellenbenz, *Los Fugger en España y Portugal hasta 1560* (1990), trans. Manuel Prieto Vilas (Valladolid: Junta de Castilla y León, 2000).

102. Magalhães Godinho, *Os descobrimentos e a economia mundial*, vol. 3, 195; Kellenbenz, *Los Fugger*, 61–63, provides more information on Markus Zimmerman, Lukas Rem, who was a factor of the Welser in Lisbon in 1504, and the brothers Diego (in Antwerp) and Cristóbal de Haro (in Lisbon), merchants from Burgos associated with the Fugger.

103. Magalhães Godinho, *Os descobrimentos e a economia mundial*, vol. 3, 198–202.

Chapter Three: Disruptions

1. Centralisation of power in different parts of Europe benefitted from the articulation between religion and state both in Protestant and Catholic areas. See Heinz Schilling, *Konfessionalisierung und staatsinteressen: internationale beziehungen, 1559-1660* (Paderborn: Ferdinand Schöningh, 2007), for a final reflection on the issue of confessionalisation, which he had started to study in the 1970s with Wolfgang Reinhard. However, I am critical of the top-down vision and simplification of history resulting from the schematic application of the notion of confessionalisation. For a sharp critique of a monolithic vision of Spain, see Stefania Pastore, *Il vangelo e la spada. L'Inquisizione di Castiglia e i suoi critici (1460-1598)* (Rome: Edizioni di Storia e Letteratura, 2003).

2. One of the best reconstructions of the debate is by Benzion Netanyahu, *The Origins of the Inquisition in Fifteenth Century Spain*, book 4 (New York: Random House, 1995). However, he accepts at face value the arguments in favour of conversos as sincere Christians, while he adopts a sharply critical attitude to Old Christians who argued that all New Christians were Jews.

3. On the Archbishop Diego de Anaya's clause, see Carlos Gilly, "The Council of Basel's 'De Neophytis' Decree as Immediate Cause of and Permanent Antidote to the Racial Purity Statutes," in *The Conversos and Moriscos in Late Medieval Spain and Beyond*, vol. 4, *Resistance and Reform*, ed. Kevin Ingram, (Leiden: Brill, 2021), 13–44, esp. 27.

4. See Tomás González Rolán, "Introducción," in *De la Sentencia-Estatuto de Pero Sarmiento a la Instrucçión del relator*, ed. Tomás González Rolán and Pilar Saquero Suárez-Somonte (Madrid: Aben Ezra, 2012), XVII–CXXXI, esp. LXVII–LXXII. This volume transcribes the main documents of the debate.

5. David Nirenberg, "Une société face à l'altérité. Juifs et chrétiens dans la péninsule ibérique, 1391–1449," *Annales HSS* 62, no. 4 (2007): 755–790.

6. I am following the compilation of documents on this riot and its consequences edited by Tomás González Rolán and Pilar Saquero Suárez-Somonte, *De la Sentencia-Estatuto de Pero Sarmiento a la Instrucçión del relator*.

7. See González Rolán, "Introducción," XVII–CXXXI; Michèle Escamilla, "La polémique autour de la pratique du 'statut de pureté de sang'," in *La pureté de sang en Espagne: du lignage à la race*, ed. Raphaël Carrasco, Annie Molinié, Beatrice Perez (Paris: Presses de l'Université Patris-Sorbonne, 2011), 49–80.

8. Pero Sarmiento, "Sentencia-Estatuto," in *De la Sentencia-Estatuto de Pero Sarmiento*, 13–31 (quote 27–28). González Rolán identified the medieval law invoked by the sentence-statute as a precedent: the fuero conceded by Alfonso VII in 1118, which excluded Jews and their descendants, including those converted to Christianity, from public offices (17–18).

9. Marcos García de Mora, "Apelaçión y suplicaçión," in *De la Sentencia-Estatuto de Pero Sarmiento*, 193–242, esp. 200, 202–203, 205, 213, 218, 231.

10. Béatrice Perez, "Une noblesse en débat au XVᵉ siècle: sang, honneur, vertu," in *La pureté de sang en Espagne*, 95–112.

11. See the resolution of the Council of Basel: https://www.papalencyclicals.net/councils/ecum17.htm; the same resolution ordered strict segregation of Jews, with whom the converts should not have contact, while it warned against the continuation of previous practices, particularly the ritual of burial. It is a clear example of the struggle for the integration of conversos, highlighting the main contentious issues.

12. Fernán Díaz de Toledo, "Instrucçión del relator para Don Lope de Barrientos, obispo de Cuenca, sobre la çiçaña de Toledo contra Pero Sarmiento y el bachiller Marcos García de Mora," in *De la Sentencia-Estatuto de Pero Sarmiento*, 95–120, esp. 96, 99, 105–106, 113–116.

13. Alonso Díaz de Montalvo, *La causa conversa*, ed. Matilde Conde Salazar, Antonio Pérez Martín, and Carlos del Valle Rodriguez (Madrid: Aben Ezra, 2008).

14. Lope de Barrientos, "Contra algunos çiçañadores de la nación de los convertidos del pueblo de Israel," and Lope de Barrientos, "Respuesta a una proposición," in *De la Sentencia-Estatuto de Pero Sarmiento*, 121–191.

15. Alfonso de Cartagena, *Defensorium Unitatis Christianæ*, trans. and ed. Guillermo Verdín-Díaz (Oviedo: Universidad de Oviedo, 1989).

16. Juan de Torquemada, *Tratado contra los madianitas e ismaelitas*, trans. and ed. Carlos del Valle Rodriguez (Madrid: Aben Ezra, 2002).

17. Alonso de Oropesa, *Luz para conocimiento de los gentiles*, ed. and trans. Luis A. Diaz y Diaz (Madrid: Fundación Universitaria Española, 1979). See the excellent study by Claude Stuczynski, "Pro-converso Apologetics and Biblical Exegesis," in *The Hebrew Bible in Fifteenth Century Spain: Exegesis, Literature, Philosophy and the Arts*, ed. Jonathan Deckter and Arturo Prats (Leiden: Brill, 2012), 151–176.

18. Rosa Vidal Doval, *Misera Hispania: Jewish and Conversos in Alonso de Espina's Fortalitium Fifei* (Oxford: Society for the Study of Medieval Languages and Literature, 2013).

19. João Figueirôa-Rego, *A honra alheia por um fio: os estatutos de limpeza de sangue nos espaços de expressão ibérica (sécs. XVI–XVIII)* (Lisbon: Fundação Calouste Gulbenkian, 2011) 66–67.

20. For two important tribunals, see Jean-Pierre Dedieu, *L'administration de la foi: l'Inquisition de Tolède, XVIᵉ–XVIIIᵉ siècles* (Madrid: Casa de Velázquez, 1989); Juan Gil, *Los conversos y la Inquisición sevillana*, 8 vols. (Seville: Universidad de Sevilla, 2000–2003); Béatrice Perez, *Inquisition, pouvoir, société: la province de Séville et ses judéoconvers sous les Rois Catholiques* (Paris: Honoré Champion, 2007).

21. Ricardo García Cárcel, *Orígenes da la Inquisición española. El tribunal de Valencia, 1478–1530* (Barcelona: Península, 1976); Stephen Haliczer, *Inquisition and Society in the Kingdom of Valencia, 1478–1834* (Berkeley: University of California Press, 1990); Patricia Banères, "Inquisition et 'pureté de sang' dans le royaume de Valence (1478–1516): aux origines d'une nouvelle forme d'exclusion," in *La pureté de sang en Espagne*, 133–161.

22. Jean-Pierre Dedieu, "Hérésie et pureté de sang: l'incapacité légale des hérétiques et de leurs descendants en Espagne aux premiers temps de l'Inquisition," in *Pouvoirs et société dans l'Espagne moderne. Hommage à Bartolomé Bennassar* (Toulouse: Presses Universitaires du Mirail, 1993), 161–177.

23. Patricia Banères, *Histoire d'une répression: les judéo-convers dans le royaume de Valence aux premiers temps de l'Inquisition: 1461–1530* (PhD thesis, Université de Paul Valéry-Montpellier III, 2012), 102, 158, 371–372.

24. Lea Sestieri, *David Reubeni. Un ebreo d'Arabia in missione segreta nell'Europa del '500* (Genova: Marietti, 1991). Sestieri provides a good analysis of Reubeni's travel log, edited and translated from the Hebrew, pointing to the plausibility of the itinerary described, against previous dismissive voices. See also Moti Benmelech, "History, Politics, and Messianism: David Ha-Reuveni's Origin and Mission," *AJS Review* 35, 1 (April 2011): 35–60, in which the influence of the contemporary messianic propagandist Abraham Halevi of Jerusalem is discussed.

25. Elkan Nathan Adler, ed., *Jewish Travellers in the Middle Ages: 19 Firsthand Accounts* (1930) (New York: Dover, 1987), 282.

26. Harris Lenowitz, *The Jewish Messiahs: From the Galilee to Crown Heights* (Oxford: Oxford University Press, 1998), 103.

27. Adler, *Jewish Travellers in the Middle Ages*, 286–320. The descriptions of the etiquette of the royal court, including the departure of Princess Isabel to be married to Charles V, are important, as well as the information on the Muslim ambassadors Reubeni met at the court.

28. Lenowitz, *Jewish Messiahs*, 93.

29. Lenowitz, *Jewish Messiahs*, 122; reproduction of the reports by Giovanni Battista Sangam, agent of the pope.

30. Lenowitz, *Jewish Messiahs*, 104–123.

31. Antonio Rodriguez Moñino, "Les judaïsants à Badajoz de 1493 à 1595," *Revue des Études Juives* CXV (1956): 73–86. This document raised a fierce polemic from Cecil Roth, since the lists of autos da fé published by António Joaquim Moreira had indicated the auto da fé of Evora in 1542 as the place of excommunication and then execution. I. S. Révah rightly accepted the document found by Rodrigues Moñino. I just need to add that Reubeni could not have been executed in Badajoz, since there was no tribunal there, but in Llerena; the sambenito was sent to the main church of Badajoz probably because many New Christians there were tried and sentenced for returning to Judaism as a result of their encounter with Reubeni. In the document, the reason given for Reubeni's execution is precisely the conversion to Judaism of many New Christians.

32. Lenowitz, *Jewish Messiahs*, 103. The Portuguese was most probably Diogo Pires (Shlomo Molkho).

33. *Memórias e alguns documentos para a história e teoria das cortes geraes que em Portugal se celebraram pelos três estados do reino* (1828), ed. Manuel Carvalhosa, viscount of Santarém, with an added study by A. Sardinha (Lisbon, 1924).

34. Fernand Braudel, *Civilisation matérielle, économie et capitalisme, XVᵉ–XVIIIᵉ sicle*, vol. 3, *Le temps du monde* (Paris: Armand Colin, 1979), chap. 2.

35. J. A. Goris, *Étude sur les colonies marchandes méridionales (portugais, espagnols, italiens) à Anvers de 1488 à 1567* (Louvain: Librairie de l'Université, 1925), 562.

36. Goris, *Étude sur les colonies marchandes méridionales*, 563–564.

37. Goris, *Étude sur les colonies marchandes méridionales*, 566–567.

38. ANTT, Núcleo Antigo, 880, n. 214.

39. ANTT, Corpo Cronológico, Parte II, Maço 228, n. 16.

40. The numbers were taken from Goris, *Étude sur les colonies marchandes méridionales*, 53–55. Goris indicates that in the 1520s there were around 20 households, and in 1570, 80 Portuguese households and 17 nonmarried people, but there are no figures in between; H. P. Salomon and A. Leone Leoni state that in the 1540s there were 900 Portuguese in Antwerp without indicating the source, but the figure is plausible due to the start of the Inquisition in

Portugal (Salomon and Leoni, "Mendes, Benveniste, De Luna, Micas, Nasci: The State of the Art (1522–1558)," *Jewish Quarterly Review* 88, nos. 3–4 (1998): 135–211, esp. 153).

41. Salomon and Leone Leoni, "Mendes, Benveniste, De Luna, Micas, Nasci," 154.

42. The laments of the papal nuncio in Portugal on the difficulty of retrieving the money promised by the New Christians due to Francisco Mendes' death is clear proof; Charles-Martial de Witte, ed., *La correspondence des premiers nonces permanents au Portugal, 1532–1553*, vol. 2 (Lisbon: Academia Portuguesa da História, 1980), 88, 100, 105, 139, 175.

43. Goris, *Étude sur les colonies marchandes méridionales*, 570.

44. A. A. Marques de Almeida, ed., *Dicionário dos sefarditas portugueses. Mercadores e gente de trato* (Lisbon: Campo da Comunicação, 2009), 385.

45. Salomon and Leone Leoni, "Mendes, Benveniste, De Luna, Micas, Nasci," 149–150.

46. Salomon and Leone Leoni, "Mendes, Benveniste, De Luna, Micas, Nasci," 152.

47. Aron di Leone Leoni, *The Hebrew Portuguese Nations in Antwerp and London at the time of Charles V and Henry VIII* (Jersey, NJ: KTAV, 2004).

48. Aron di Leone Leoni, "La diplomazia estense e l'immigrazione dei cristani nuovi a Ferrara al tempo di Ercole II," *Nuova Rivista Storica* 78, no. 2 (1994): 293–326.

49. Salomon and Leone Leoni, "Mendes, Benveniste, De Luna, Micas, Nasci," 154–165.

50. See the reconstitution of this family by Salomon and Leone Leoni, "Mendes, Benveniste, De Luna, Micas, Nasci," 210.

51. See the reconstitution of the family by Salomon and Leone Leoni, "Mendes, Benveniste, De Luna, Micas, Nasci," 211.

52. Letter from the King to João Gomes, treasurer of the *Casa da Índia*, in which he mentions a sum of 800 cruzados owed by them on contracts and forgiven, since they had paid to Fernando Álvares, royal treasurer, money to be given to the Xarife of Suz, North Africa, March 15, 1533. ANTT Corpo Cronológico, Parte I, Maço 50, n. 96. There is also a bill of exchange from Nuno Henriques received by the royal factor in Andalucia, according to a letter dated March 6, 1535; ANTT, Corpo Cronológico, Parte II, Maço 198, n. 63.

53. On September 30, 1534, D. Isabel de Brito ordered the payment of her *tença*, 30,200 reais, by the almoxarife of the customs of Lisbon to Nuno Henriques, which sum was certainly intended to pay a debt; ANTT, Corpo Cronológico, Parte II, Maço 194, n. 84.

54. ANTT, Corpo Cronológico, Parte II, Maço 191, n. 87.

55. Marques de Almeida, ed., *Dicionário histórico dos sefarditas portugueses*, 340; see *Processi del Santo Offizio di Venezia contro Ebrei e Giudaizzanti (1570–1572)*, ed. Pier Cesare Zorattini (Florence: Leo S. Olschki, 1984), 18–19, 59, 219–232.

56. ANTT, Corpo Cronológico, Parte I, Maço 72, n. 3.

57. ANTT, Gavetas, 13, Maço 8, n. 23, published in *As gavetas da Torre do Tombo*, ed. A. da Silva Rego, vol. 3 (Lisbon: Centro de Estudos Históricos Ultramarinos, 1963), 178–186.

58. ANTT, Corpo Cronológico, Parte II, Maço 237, n. 99.

59. Letter from Dr. Rodrigo Monteiro prompting King João III to write a letter to Flanders, on April 4, 1543; ANTT, Corpo Cronológico, Parte I, Maço 73, n. 68. Reply from João Rebelo, royal factor in Antwerp, on June 14, 1543; ANTT, Corpo Cronológico, Parte I, Maço 73, n. 102.

Chapter Four: Creativity

1. Kevin Ingram, *Converso Non-Conformism in Early Modern Spain: Bad Blood and Faith from Alonso de Cartagena to Diego Velázquez* (Cham: Palgrave, 2018); Kevin Ingram, ed., *The Conversos and Moriscos in Late Medieval Spain and Beyond*, 4 vols. (Leiden: Brill, 2009–2021).

2. David Martín López, "Jesuits and Conversos in Sixteenth Century Toledo," *Journal of Jesuit Studies*, 8, no. 2 (2021): 173–194.

3. They are part of a long tradition of anti-Jewish literature but directed against supposed persistent Judaism among New Christians. For the early production, see Fernando Machado, *The Mirror of the New Christians (Espelho de Cristãos Novos)* (ms. 1542), ed. Mildred Evelyn Vieira and Frank Ephraim Talmage (Toronto: Pontifical Institute of Medieval Studies,

1977); Diogo de Sá, *Inquisiçam e segredos da fee contra a obstinada perfidia dos judeus* (ms. 1550s) ANTT, Manuscritos da Livraria, 360. The most recent books on this genre are François Soyer, *Popularising Anti-Semitism in Early Modern Spain and Its Empire: Francisco de Torrejoncillo and the Centinela contra Judíos (1674)* (Leiden: Brill, 2014); Bruno Feitler, *The Imaginary Synagogue: Anti-Jewish Literature in the Portuguese Early Modern World (16th–18th centuries)* (Leiden: Brill, 2015).

4. David Theo Goldberg, *The Racial State* (Oxford: Blackwell, 2002), offers a useful theoretical reflection that needs to be adapted to the Iberian case.

5. Stephen Haliczer, *The Comuneros of Castile: The Forging of a Revolution, 1475–1521* (Madison: Wisconsin University Press, 1981); Joseph Perez, *La Revolución de las comunidades de Castilla (1520–1521)*, trans. Juan José Faci Lacasta (Barcelona: RBA, 2005).

6. Fortunato de Almeida, *História da Igreja em Portugal* (1930), vol. 2, ed. Damião Peres (Lisbon: Livraria Civilização, 1968), 383–384.

7. Alexandre Herculano, *História da origem e estabelecimento da Inquisição em Portugal* (1854–1859), vol. 1, ed. David Lopes (Lisbon: Bertrand, s.d.), 222–224, 233–236.

8. Herculano, *História da origem*, vol. 1, 248–255.

9. Francisco Bethencourt, "A Igreja," in José Mattoso, ed., *História de Portugal*, vol. 3, *No Alvorecer da Modernidade (1480–1620)*, ed. J. Romero Magalhães (Lisbon: Círculo de Leitores, 1993), 149–164.

10. See the correspondence of the nuncios in Lisbon, Charles-Martial De Witte, *La correspondence des premiers nonces permanents au Portugal, 1532–1553*, vol. 2 (Lisbon: Academia Portuguesa da História, 1986).

11. ANTT, Chancelaria de Dom João III, Próprios, Livro 46, fol. 103r; Livro 58, fols 197v–198r. More on this important family in Part II, linked much later to the Furtado de Mendonça, future viscounts of Barbacena.

12. ANTT, Chancelaria de Dom João III, Próprios, Livro 70, fol. 14v: "I have separated all those nominated, and their descendants, from the group of New Christians, as if their parents, grand-parents and great-grand-parents had been born and were beautiful Christians, and were never outside this group; I want, and it is my pleasure, that they will not be affected by any laws or statutes issued now or in the future related to New Christians" (my translation).

13. For the international culture of trade, see Cátia Antunes and Francisco Bethencourt, eds., *Merchant Cultures: A Global Approach to Spaces, Representations and Worlds of Trade, 1500–1800* (Leiden: Brill, 2022).

14. James W. Nelson Novoa, *Being the Nação in the Eternal City: New Christian Lives in Sixteenth-Century Rome* (Peterborough, ON: Baywolf Press, 2014).

15. Herculano, *História da origem*, vol. 2, 176.

16. Massimo Firpo, *La presa di potere dell'Inquisizione romana, 1550–1553* (Rome-Bari: Laterza, 2014).

17. David Norte Giebels, *A Inquisição de Lisboa (1537–1579)*, 317–371. In this initial period, the number of trials only went over 100 a year between 1558 and 1564.

18. Maria José Ferro Tavares, *Judaísmo e Inquisiçao. Estudos* (Lisbon: Presença, 1987), 155–167.

19. Alexandre Herculano and João Lúcio de Azevedo have analysed the main documents, while the correspondence of the pope with the nuncios in Lisbon, published by Charles-Martial De Witte, here quoted, reveals consistent doubts by the pope and cardinals concerning the legitimacy of forced conversion.

20. *CDP*, tome II, 430–440. The bull was not published in Portugal, being blocked by the king, as Giuseppe Marcocci and José Pedro Paiva, *História da Inquisição Portuguesa, 1536–1821* (Lisbon: Esfera dos Livros, 2013) 32, rightly point out.

21. Thomas Aquinas, *Political Writings*, ed. R. W. Dyson (Cambridge: Cambridge University Press, 2002), 233–234, 267–273; James M. Powell, "The Papacy and the Muslim Frontier," in *Muslims under Latin Rule 1100–1300*, ed. James M. Powell (Princeton: Princeton University Press, 1990), 175–203; Benjamin Z. Kedar, *Crusade and Mission: European Approaches towards the Muslims* (Princeton: Princeton University Press, 1984), 73.

22. Marcocci and Paiva, *História da Inquisição Portuguesa*, 32.

23. Carlos Manuel Valentim, "Duarte de Paz: Um líder da comunidade sefardita portuguesa em meados do século XVI. Novos elementos biográficos," in *Rumo e escrita da história. Estudos em homenagem a A. A. Marques de Almeida*, ed. Maria de Fátima Reis (Lisbon: Colibri, 2006), 175–190.

24. Shlomo Simonsohn, ed. *The Apostolic See and the Jews*, vol. 4, *Documents: 1522–1538* (Toronto: Pontifical Institute of Mediaeval Studies, 1990), 2049–2053.

25. De Witte, *La correspondence des premiers*, 100–101.

26. Aron de Leone Leoni, *The Hebrew Portuguese Nations in Antwerp and London at the Time of Charles V and Henry VIII: New Documents and Interpretations* (Jersey City, NJ: KTAV, 2005).

27. James W. Nelson Novoa, "The Vatican Secret Archive as a Source for the History of the Activities of the Agents of the Portuguese New Christians (1532–1549)," in *Dall'Archivio Segreto Vaticano. Miscellanea di testi, saggi e inventari*, vol. 3 (Città del Vaticano: Archivio Segreto Vaticano, 2009), 171–196; James W. Nelson Novoa, "The Departure of Duarte de Paz from Rome," *Cadernos de Estudos Sefarditas*, 7 (2007): 273–300. The date of death of Duarte de Paz is indicated in the trial of his son, Tomé Pegado de Paz: ANTT, Inquisição de Lisboa, Processo 10906, fl. 6v–7r.

28. ANTT, Chancelaria de D. João III, Livro 20, fl. 39v: letter of quittance from February 23, 1534, in which it is declared that Duarte de Paz made payments of 40,055,579 reis in money and 155,579 reis in silk for the collection of silk taxes imported from Castile.

29. Herculano, *História da origem*, vol. 2, 333–375, and vol. 3, 327–353, has reconstituted the main features of this significant life story.

30. Sylvie Deswarte, *Il "perfetto cotegiano" D. Miguel da Silva* (Rome: Bulzoni, 1989).

31. Ana Isabel Buescu, "D. João III e D. Miguel da Silva, bispo de Viseu: Novas razões para um ódio velho," *Revista de História da Sociedade e da Cultura* 10, no. 1 (2010): 141–168.

32. *CDP*, tome VI, 141–144, 163–170.

33. Dan Cohn-Sherbok, *The Blackwell Dictionary of Judaica* (Oxford: Blackwell, 1992), 451, 473; Jean-Christophe Attias and Esther Benbassa, *Dictionnaire de civilisation juive*, 2nd ed. (Paris: Larousse, 1998), 183–185, 235, 237, 242–243.

34. Marcel Bataillon, *Erasmo y España. Estudios sobre la historia espiritual del siglo XVI* (1937), 2nd ed., trans. Antonio Alatorre (Mexico: Fondo de Cultura Económica, 1983), 116–179. We will also be guided here by Stefania Pastore, *Una herejía española. Conversos, alumbrados e Inquisición (1449–1559)*, trans. Clara Álvarez Alonso, preface Ricardo García Cárcel and Adriano Prosperi (Madrid: Marcial Pons, 2010).

35. Thomas à Kempis, *The Imitation of Christ*, trans. with notes by Robert Jeffery, introd. Max Von Habsburg (London: Penguin, 2013), especially part IV.

36. Bataillon, *Erasmo y España*, 175–180.

37. Bataillon, *Erasmo y España*, 62–70.

38. Bataillon, *Erasmo y España*, 167–171; Angela Selke, *El Santo Oficio de la Inquisición. Proceso de fr. Francisco Ortiz (1529–1532)* (Madrid: Guadarrama, 1968). The work by Francisco de Osuna is online at http://www.documentacatholicaomnia.eu/.

39. Ángela Muñoz Fernández, *Beatas y santas neocastellanas. Ambivalencias de la religión y políticas, correctoras del poder (ss. XIV-XVI)* (Madrid: Comunidad de Madrid, 1994).

40. Javier Pérez Escohotado, *Antonio Medrano, alumbrado epicúreo: proceso inquisitorial (Toledo, 1530)* (Madrid: Verbum, 2003); M. Andrés Martin, "Alumbrados de Toledo de 1525 e Inquisición. Procesos y processados," in *Historia de la Inquisición en España y América*, ed. Joaquim Pérez Villanueva and Bartolomé Escandell Bonet, vol. 1 (Madrid: Biblioteca de Autores Cristianos, 1984), 488–520.

41. Bataillon, *Erasmo y España*, 177–179.

42. Milagros Ortega-Costa, *Proceso de la Inquisición contra Maria de Cazalla* (Madrid: Fundación Universitaria Española, 1978). There is a good section in English on the alumbrados, with material on the edict of grace and excerpts from the main trials, including that of Maria de Cazalla, in Lu Ann Homza, *The Spanish Inquisition, 1478–1614: An Anthology of Sources* (Indianapolis, IN: Hackett, 2006), 80–152.

43. Bataillon, *Erasmo y España*, 182–184.

44. Pastore, *Una herejía española*.

45. Antonio Márquez, *Los alumbrados. Orígenes y filosofía (1525–1559)* (Madrid: Taurus, 1972).

46. The text of the edict is reproduced in several books; see the English translation in Lu Ann Homza, *The Spanish Inquisition, 1478–1614*, 81–92.

47. Pastore, *Una herejía española*, 173–174.

48. Bataillon, *Erasmo y España*, 185–209, 255–278.

49. Augustin Redondo, "Luther et l'Espagne de 1520 à 1536," *Mélanges de la Casa de Velázquez* 1 (1965): 109–165; Augustin Redondo, "Les premiers 'illuminés' castillans et Luther," in *Aspects du libertinisme au XVIe siecle* (Paris: Vrin, 1974), 85–91.

50. Werner Thomas, *La represión del protestantismo en España, 1517–1648* (Leuven: Leuven University Press, 2001).

51. Valentine Zuber, *Les conflits et la tolérance: Michel Servet entre mémoire et histoire* (Paris: Honoré Champion, 2004); Miguel Servet, *Obras completas*, ed. Angel Alcalá, 7 vols. (Zaragoza: Prensas Universitárias de Zaragoza, 2003–2007); Michael Servetus, *The Restoration of Christianity*, trans. Marian Hillar and Christopher A. Hoffman, notes and introduction by Marian Hillar, preface by Alicia McNary Forsey, 5 vols. (Lewiston: Edwin Mellen, 2006).

52. Pastore, *Una herejía española*, 341–343.

53. There were very few cases in sixteenth century Portugal, in 1544 and 1568, and the involvement of New Christians is unclear; António Vítor Ribeiro, *O auto dos místicos. Alumbrados, profecias, aparições e inquisidores (séculos XVI–XVIII)* (Lisbon: Chiado, 2015).

54. Marcel Bataillon, "De Erasmo a la Compañia de Jesús," in *Erasmo y el Erasmismo*, trans. Carlos Pujol, 2nd ed. (Barcelona: Crítica, 1983), 203–244; Marcel Bataillon, *Les jésuites dans l'Espagne du XVIe siècle* ed. Pierre-Antoine Fabre (Paris: Belles Lettres, 2009); Robert A. Maryks, *The Jesuit Order as a Synagogue of Jews: Jesuits of Jewish Ancestry and Purity of Blood Laws in the Early Society of Jesus* (Leiden: Brill, 2010).

55. Juan Gil, *Los conversos y la Inquisición sevillana*, vol. 3 (Seville: Universidad de Sevilla, 2000), 120–124, 452–466.

56. Bartolomé de las Casas, *Brevissima relación de la destruición de las Indias*, ed. Trinidad Barreira (Madrid: Alianza, 2005); Bartolomé de las Casas, *Historia de las Indias*, ed. Miguel Angel Medina, 3 vols. (Madrid: Alianza, 1994); Bartolomé de las Casas, *Obra indigenista*, ed. José Alcina Franch (Madrid: Alianza, 1985). For a general approach see Anthony Pagden, *The Fall of Natural Man: The American Indian and the Origins of Comparative Ethnology* (Cambridge: Cambridge University Press, 1982).

57. Frances Ruiz y Quesada, ed., *La pintura gótica hispanoflamenca. Bartolomé Bermejo i su época* (Barcelona: Museu Nacional d'Art de Catalunya, 2003), crucial for the context; Joan Molina Figueras, ed., *Bartolomé Bermejo* (Madrid: Museo Nacional del Prado, 2018); Letizia Treves, ed., *Bartolomé Bermejo. Master of the Spanish Renaissance* (London: National Gallery, 2019).

58. Museu Nacional d'Art de Catalunya, Bartolomé Bermejo, *Davallament de Crist als Llimbs* (ca. 1474–1479), catalogue 015872.

59. Museu Nacional d'Art de Catalunya, Bartolomé Bermejo, *Ascensió* (ca. 1474–1479), catalogue 251908.

60. Grand Rapids Art Museum, Bartolomé Bermejo and Martín Bernat, *Virgin of Mercy* (1479–1484), catalogue 1965.1.1.

61. Américo Castro, *España en su historia. Cristianos, moros y judíos* (1948) (Barcelona: Crítica, 1984); Américo Castro, *La realidad histórica de España* (Mexico: Porrúa, 1962); Antonio Domínguez Ortiz, "Los 'cristianos nuevos.' Notas para el estudio de una clase social," *Boletín de la Universidad de Granada*, 21, 87 (1949): 249–297; Antonio Domínguez Ortiz, *Los judeoconversos en España y América* (Madrid: Istmo, 1971); Marcel Bataillon, "Melancolia renascentista o melancolia judía," *Estudios hispánicos: Homenage a Archer M. Huntington* (Wellesley, Mass., 1952), 39–50; Stephen Gilman, *The Spain of Fernando de Rojas: The Intellectual and Social Landscape of "La Celestina"* (Princeton: Princeton University Press, 1972);

Francisco Márquez Villanueva, *De la España judeoconverso. Doce estudios* (Barcelona: Belaterra, 2006). The openness introduced by Américo Castro and his disciples against the *castizo* vision of pure Christianity shaping Spanish culture is beneficial, although I find it problematic how the debate was narrowed down to Jewish tradition or Jewish authors, which still persists. David Nirenberg, *Neighbouring Faiths: Christianity, Islam and Judaism in the Middle Ages and Today* (Chicago: Chicago University Press, 2014), rightly defies such anachronism, mocking the obsessive identification of Jewish authors in chapter 6. He dismisses the accusations of Judaism in late medieval literature as a construct, a language of insult that had little to do with real Jews. I understand this argument, although accusations had consequences in real life.

62. Juan Álvarez Gato, *Obras completas*, ed. J. Artiles Rodriguez (Madrid: Blass, 1928); Francisco Márquez Villanueva, *Investigaciones sobre Juan Álvarez Gato* (Madrid: Real Academia Española, 1960).

63. José Francisco Ruiz Casanova, *Diccionario biográfico español online*, s.v. "Diego de San Pedro," https://dbe.rah.es/biografias/14773/diego-de-san-pedro. Accessed May 25, 2023.

64. Diego de San Pedro, *Cárcel de amor. Arnalte y Lucenda. Sermón*, ed. José Francisco Ruiz Casanova, 9th ed. (Madrid: Cátedra, 2018).

65. Francisco Márquez Villanueva, "*Cárcel de amor*, novela política." *Revista de Occidente* 41 (1966): 185–200, insists on the political meaning of the novel.

66. de San Pedro, *Cárcel de amor. Arnalte y Lucenda. Sermón*, 79–80, 89–90, 109–110; quotes from p. 110, my translation.

67. Fernando de Rojas, *La Celestina. Tragicomedia de Calisto y Melibea* (ca. 1499), intro. Stephen Gilman and ed. Dorothy S. Severin, 6th ed. (Madrid: Alianza, 1978). Nicosia Salvador Miguel doubts converso origin, but the argument that Rojas's will expresses sincere Christianity is meaningless; *Diccionario biográfico español online*, s.v. "Fernando de Rojas," https://dbe.rah.es/biografias/4856/fernando-de-rojas. Accessed May 25, 2023. This author studied and edited the 1514 Toledo edition of Fernando de Rojas, *Tragicomedia de Calisto y Melibea* (Valencia: Instituto Alfons el Magnanim, 1999).

68. de Rojas, *La Celestina*, 151–152 (I follow here the edition by Dorothy S. Severin).

69. de Rojas, *La Celestina*, 233.

70. de Rojas, *La Celestina*, 124, 151.

71. de Rojas, *La Celestina*, 125.

72. de Rojas, *La Celestina*, 146 (my translation).

73. Nicasio Salvador Miguel, "Huellas de 'La Celestina' en 'La lozana andaluza,'" in *Estudios del Siglo de Oro: Homenaje al professor Francisco Ynduráin* (Madrid: Editora Nacional, 1984), 429–460.

74. Francisco Márquez Villanueva, "El mundo converso de 'La lozana andaluza,'" in *De la España judeoconversa. Doce estudios* (Barcelona: Belaterra, 2006), 245–256.

75. Manuel da Costa Fontes, *The Art of Subversion in Inquisitiorial Spain: Rojas and Delicado* (West Lafayette, IN: Purdue University Press, 2005), 202–230.

76. Márquez Villanueva, "El mundo converso de 'La lozana andaluza,'" 245.

77. Francisco Delicado, *La lozana andaluza* (1530), ed. Ángel Chiclana (Madrid: Espasa Calpe, 1988), 135.

78. Delicado, *La lozana andaluza*, 167–168.

79. Delicado, *La lozana andaluza*, 185.

80. Delicado, *La lozana andaluza*, 206–207, 233.

81. Delicado, *La lozana andaluza*, 232.

82. Delicado, *La lozana andaluza*, 223.

Part II

1. Lúcio de Sousa, "The Jewish Presence in China and Japan in the Early Modern Period: A Social Representation," in *Global History and New Polycentric Approaches: Europe, Asia and the Americas in a World Network System*, ed. Manuel Perez Garcia and Lúcio de Sousa (Singapore: Palgrave, 2018), 183–218, esp. 201.

2. Peter Mark and José da Silva Horta, *The Forgotten Diaspora: Jewish Communities in West Africa and the Making of the Atlantic World* (Cambridge: Cambridge University press, 2011); Toby Green *The Rise of the Trans-Atlantic Slave Trade in Western Africa, 1300–1589* (Cambridge: Cambridge University Press, 2012); Isabel Castro Henriques, *São Tomé e Príncipe. A invenção de uma sociedade* (Lisbon: Vega, 2000); Luiz Felipe de Alencastro, *O Trato dos Viventes. Formação do Brasil no Atlântico Sul* (São Paulo: Companhia das Letras, 2000).

3. John H. Elliott, *Imperial Spain, 1469–1716* (1963) (London: Penguin, 2002); Henry Kamen, *Spain's Road to Empire: The Making of a World Power, 1492–1763* (London: Penguin, 2003).

4. Francisco Bethencourt, "Iberian Atlantic: Ties, Networks, and Boundaries," in *Theorising the Iberian Atlantic*, ed. Harald E. Braun and Lisa Vollendorf (Leiden: Brill, 2013), 15–36; Birgit Tremml-Werner, *Spain, China and Japan in Manila, 1571–1644* (Amsterdam: Amsterdam University Press, 2015); Charles Boxer, *The Great Ship from Amacon: Annals of Macao and the Old Japan Trade, 1555–1640* (Lisbon: Centro de Estudos Históricos Ultramarinos, 1963).

5. Julio Caro Baroja, *Los judíos en la España moderna y contemporánea*, 3rd ed., 3 vols. (Madrid: Istmo, 1986); Antonio Domínguez Ortiz, *La classe social de los conversos en Castilla en la edad moderna* (1955), reprint (Granada: Universidad de Granada, 1991).

Chapter Five: Networks

1. Francisco Bethencourt, "Contrabando: um estudo de caso," in História da Expansão Portuguesa, vol. 1, ed. Francisco Bethencourt and Kirti Chaudhuri (Lisbon: Círculo de Leitores, 1998), 387–392; Giuseppe Marcocci, "Trading with the Muslim World: Religious Limits and Proscriptions in the Portuguese Empire (c. 1480–1570)," in *Religion and Trade: Cross-Cultural Exchanges in World History, 1000–1900*, ed. Francesca Trivellato, Leor Halevi and Cátia Antunes (Oxford: Oxford University Press, 2014), 91–107; Isabel Drumond Braga, "A Inquisição portuguesa e o comércio de mercadorias defesas em meados do século XVI," offprint (Ceuta, 1998).

2. See the first set of studies on this correspondence: Henri Lapeyre, *Une famille de marchands, les Ruiz* (Paris: Armand Colin, 1955); José Gentil da Silva, *Marchandises et finances*, 3 vols. (Paris: SEVPEN, 1956–61); Valentín Vázquez de Prada, *Lettres marchandes d'Anvers*, 4 tomes (Paris, SEVPEN, 1960); Felipe Ruiz Martín, *Lettres marchandes échangées entre Florence et Medina del Campo* (Paris: SEVPEN, 1965).

3. Francesca Trivellato, "Introduction," in *Religion and Trade: Cross-Cultural Exchanges in World History, 1000–1900*, ed. Francesca Trivellato, Leor Halevi and Cátia Antunes (Oxford: Oxford University Press, 2014), 1–23, esp. 15–18; Trivellato, *The Familiarity of Strangers: The Sephardic Diapora, Livorno, and Cross-Cultural Trade in the Early Modern Period* (New Haven, CT: Yale University Press, 2009), 11–12.

4. See José Alberto Tavim, *Os judeus na expansão portuguesa em Marrocos durante o século XVI* (Braga: APPADCM, 1997).

5. For the Portuguese crisis, see Vitorino Magalhães Godinho, "A revolução dos preços e as flutuações económicas do século XVI," in *Ensaios e Estudos*, 2nd ed. (Lisbon: Sá da Costa, 2010), 293–314; for the situation in Morocco, see Daniel Rivet, *Histoire du Maroc: de Monday Idrîs â Mohammed VI* (Paris: Fayard, 2012).

6. For the political and economic background, see Robert Ricard, *Études sur l'histoire des portugais au Maroc* (Coimbra: Universidade de Coimbra, 1955); Vitorino Magalhães Godinho, *Os descobrimentos e a economia mundial*, 2nd ed., 4 vols. (Lisbon: Presença, 1989), vol. 3, 245–285, and vol. 4, 69–99.

7. For this medieval background, see Stefan Stantchev, *Spiritual rationality: Papal embargo as cultural policy* (Oxford: Oxford University Press, 2014), 45, 51.

8. Juan Luis López, *Historia legal de la bula llamada in cœna domini* (Madrid, 1768).

9. ANTT, Coleção de São Vicente, vol. 5, fl. 116r–v.

10. Virginia Rau and Jorge Borges de Macedo, *O açucar da Madeira nos fins do século XV: Problemas de produção e comércio* (Funchal: Junta Geral do Distrito Autónomo do

Funchal, 1962); Fernando Jasmins Pereira, *O açucar madeirense de 1500 a 1537: Produção e preços* (Lisbon: ISCSPU, 1969); Alberto Vieira, ed., *História do açucar: rotas e mercados* (Funchal: CEHA, 2002).

11. Henry de Castries et al., ed., *Les sources inédites sur l'histoire du Maroc de 1530 à 1845. Archives et bibliothèques d'Espagne*, tome 1 (Paris: Leroux, 1921), 214.

12. ANTT, Inquisição de Lisboa, Processo 4384, fl. 51v–52r. The accused were Damião Fernandes, Rodrigo Álvares, Pedro Cardoso, Pedro Rodrigues, Vicente Reinel, Jerónimo de Melo, and João de Gomiel.

13. ANTT, Tribunal do Santo Ofício, Inquisição de Lisboa, Livro 330, fl. 22r–v. I thank Ms. Odete Duarte Martins for giving me the equivalence from the old shelf-mark of my first notation.

14. ANTT, Inquisição de Lisboa, Processo 4384, fl. 22r–23v; Processo 5235-1, fl. 10r–11v. Royal decrees forbidding trade with Muslims, especially in time of war, and excluding New Christians and Moriscos from migrating to Muslim countries were included in the *Ordenações Manuelinas*, livro 5, títulos 81 and 82, which had successive editions in 1512–14, 1521, 1533, 1539, and 1565. There is an online edition of the latest version reprinted in 1797 (http://www.governodosoutros.ics.ul.pt/?menu).

15. ANTT, Inquisição de Lisboa, Processo 5235-1 (trial of Duarte Álvares), fl. 41v–42v. When I checked this footnote I noticed that this trial had been reorganised by the archive and a new set of page numbers added. In all the other cases I decided to keep the old folio references, still visible on the documents.

16. ANTT, Inquisição de Lisboa, Processo 12369 related to Diogo Palma, a New Christian resident of Tetouan, containing only denunciations and correspondence with the tribunal of Seville.

17. ANTT, Inquisição de Lisboa, Processos 4384, 5235, 14229, 13255.

18. ANTT, Inquisição de Lisboa, Processo 5235-1, fl. 15r–16v. Duarte Álvares also claimed private jurisdiction at the customs of Lisbon, to no avail.

19. ANTT, Inquisição de Lisboa, Processo 5235-1, fl. 17r–21r.

20. de Castries, *Sources inédites sur l'histoire du Maroc*, vol. 3, 532–533.

21. ANTT, Coleção São Vicente, vol. 8, fl. 275r–276v.

22. ANTT, Inquisição de Lisboa, Processo 5235 and 13255. One quintal corresponded to four arrobas, each weighing 14.7 kg. António de Moraes Silva, *Grande Dicionário da língua portuguesa*, 10th ed., ed. Augusto Moreno, Cardoso Júnior, and José Pedro Machado, 12 vols. (Lisbon, 1949–1959).

23. ANTT, Inquisição de Lisboa, Processos 12562 and 13255.

24. *CDP*, vol. 4, 161–165 and 465–470; vol. 7, 275–279.

25. ANTT, Inquisição de Lisboa, Processos 4384, fl. 9r and 3955, fl. 4v.

26. ANTT, Inquisição de Lisboa, Processo 5235.

27. ANTT, Inquisição de Lisboa, Processos 3855, fl. 2r, 4r and 5r; 6438, fl. 13r and 30v; 7568, fl. 5r and 11v.

28. ANTT, Processos 5234, 5235, 13255, 1278, 12562.

29. Estimates based on the excellent website, "Prices, Wages and Rents in Portugal, 1300–1910," Instituto de Ciências Sociais, http://pwr-portugal.ics.ul.pt, accessed May 5, 2021.

30. ANTT, Chancelaria de D. João III, Livro 35, fl. 93v.

31. ANTT, Chancelaria de D. João III, Livro 70, fl. 144r and Livro 54, fl. 148r–v.

32. ANTT, Chancelaria de D. João III, Livro 63, fl. 308v. Already in September 1553, King John III wrote to Rodrigo de Queñas, a member of the Financial Council in Castile, thanking him for support given to Bento Rodrigues at the fair of the previous October; ANTT, Coleção São Vicente, vol. 8, fl. 199 and 208.

33. ANTT, Corpo Cronológico, Parte I, Maço 91, n. 75.

34. ANTT, Corpo Cronológico, Parte I, Maço 87, n. 34.

35. ANTT, Corpo Cronológico, Parte I, Maço 89, n. 145.

36. ANTT, Inquisição de Lisboa, Processos 5234 and 5235.

37. ANTT, Corpo Cronológico, Parte I, Maço 90, n. 21.

38. ANTT, Chancelaria de D. João III, Livro 14, fl. 25r–v.

39. ANTT, Chancelaria de D. João III, Livro 18, fl. 65v; Livro 32, fl. 26r; Livro 24, fl. 241v, Livro 28, fl. 59r.

40. ANTT, Inquisição de Lisboa, Processo 5235-1.

41. See the study of João de Campos in Francisco Bethencourt, "Early Modern Imperialism and Cosmopolitanism," in *Cosmopolitanism in the Portuguese-Speaking World*, ed. Francisco Bethencourt (Leiden: Brill, 2018), 82–107.

42. ANTT, Inquisição de Lisboa, Processos 8722 and 12562.

43. ANTT, Inquisição de Lisboa, Processo 6438.

44. ANTT, Inquisição de Lisboa, Processo 13221.

45. J. A. Goris, *Étude sur les colonies marchandes méridionales (portugais, espagnols, italiens) à Anvers de 1488 à 1567* (Louvain: Librairie Universitaire, 1925), 615.

46. ANTT, Inquisição de Lisboa, Processos 12562, fl. 12r, 21r, 23r; 3486, fl. 3v, 4v; 5455, fl. 9v; 1278 fl. 6r.

47. There is a wealth of information on ship owners and freights in the trials of the Inquisition, see ANTT, Inquisição de Lisboa, Processos 167, fl.2v, 3r, 4v, 6r, 14v–16r, 46r, 47v–49v, 50v–51r, 65r; 14543, fl. 3r–5r; 7815, fl. 7v, 21r; 5235, fl. 35r, 40v, 67r; 12043, fl. 3r–4r; 6078, fl. 4r–5r, 27v–29v; 4384, fl. 2v, 4v–5r, 9v, 50r; 14229, fl. 2r; 3855, fl. 4v; 6438, fl. 13r, 15r, 30v; 7568, fl. 5r, 11v; 8487, fl. 6v–7r; 13255, fl. 7r; 5455, fl. 4v–5r, 9r, 12r; 6438, fl. 22r; 7567, fl. 2r–5v; 7568, fl. 2v, 4v; 5235, fl. 2v–3v, 5v.

48. ANTT, Inquisição de Lisboa, Processo 5235.

49. ANTT, Inquisição de Lisboa, Processo 12562.

50. ANTT, Inquisição de Lisboa, Processos 6438 and 13221.

51. ANTT, Inquisição de Lisboa, Processo Processos 12562 and 13221.

52. ANTT, Inquisição de Lisboa, Processo 167, fl. 68r and 70v.

53. ANTT, Inquisição de Lisboa, Processos 5455, fl. 16r–v; 7567, fl. 12r–v.

54. ANTT, Inquisição de Lisboa, Processo 6438, fl. 32r–34v.

55. ANTT, Inquisição de Lisboa, Processo1278, fl. 27r.

56. ANTT, Inquisição de Lisboa, Processo 12562, fl. 29r–v.

57. ANTT, Inquisição de Lisboa, Processo 13255, fl. 19r–v.

58. ANTT, Inquisição de Lisboa, Processo 5325, fl. 4v.

59. ANTT, Inquisição de Lisboa, Processo 8944, fl. 4v.

60. ANTT, Inquisição de Lisboa, Processo 14543, fl. 10r.

61. ANTT, Inquisição de Lisboa, Processo 8722.

62. ANTT, Inquisição de Lisboa, Processo 5235, fl. 5r–v, although expenses and profits were generally avoided.

63. ANTT, Inquisição de Lisboa, Processos 167, 4384, 13255.

64. ANTT, Inquisição de Lisboa, Processo 12562. For the Jewish community, see Tavim, *Os judeus na expansão portuguesa.* By the turn of the sixteenth to the seventeenth century, we have the famous case studied by Mercedes García-Arenal and Gerard Wiegers, *A Man of Three Worlds: Samuel Pallache, a Moroccan Jew in Catholic and Protestant Europe*, trans. Martin Beagles (Baltimore: Johns Hopkins University Press, 1999).

65. ANTT, Inquisição de Lisboa, Processo 167.

66. Cátia Antunes, "The Portuguese Maritime Empire: Global Nodes and Transnational Networks," in *Empires of the Sea. Maritime Power Networks in World History*, ed. Rolf Strootman, Floris van den Eijnde, Roy van Wijk (Leiden: Brill, 2019), 294–311; Cátia Antunes and Amélia Polónia, eds., *Beyond Empires: Self-Organising Imperial Networks, 1500-1800* (Leiden: Brill, 2016).

67. Ana Sofia Ribeiro, *Early Modern Trading Networks in Europe: Cooperation and the Case of Simón Ruiz* (London: Routledge, 2017) presents a useful analysis, but the case for a network around Simón Ruiz is disputable.

68. Lapeyre, *Une famille de marchands, les Ruiz*; Gentil da Silva, *Marchandises et finances*; Vázquez de Prada, *Lettres marchandes d'Anvers*; Ruiz Martín, *Lettres marchandes échangées*.

69. Juan Ignacio Pulido Serrano, ed., *Más que negócios: Simón Ruiz, un banquero español del siglo XVI entre las penínsulas ibérica e italiana* (Madrid: Iberoamericana, 2017).

70. ANTT, Arquivo Notarial de Lisboa, Cartório do Distribuidor, ano 1563, Livro 1, 6/22/1/1, fl. 41v. Diogo Caldeira, a knight of the king's house who was a receiver of taxes on trade in Lisbon from the 1520s to the 1540s, worth more than 7 million reais a year, might have been a relative, see ANTT, Chancelaria de D. João III, Livro 11, fl. 92r; Livro 23, fl. 89r; Livro 28, fl. 3v.

71. The chairman of the municipality and representative of Segovia at the *cortes* of Toledo in 1560 had the same name, see Diego de Colmenares, *Historia de la insigne ciudad de Segovia* (Segovia: Imprenta de la Tierra de Segovia, 1931), 116.

72. *Livro do lançamento e serviço que a cidade de Lisboa fez a El Rei nosso senhor no ano de 1565*, vol. 3 (Lisbon: Câmara Municipal de Lisboa, 1948), 41, 51. This Bento Rodrigues was probably a son of the main merchant; as a cavaleiro fidalgo, he would have been exempted without further enquiry.

73. Magalhães Godinho, *Os descobrimentos e a economia mundial*, vol. 3, 56.

74. Duarte Gomes Solis, *Discursos sobre los comercios de las dos Indias, donde se tratan materias importantes de Estado y Guerra*, s.l. 1622, fl. 110r–v.

75. Ramon Carande, *Carlos V y sus banqueros* (1967), vol. 3 (Barcelona: Crítica, 1990), 420, 494.

76. James M. Boyden, *The Courtier and the King: Ruy Gómez de Silva, Philip II and the Court of Spain* (Berkeley: University of California Press, 1995).

77. Maria da Graça Mateus Ventura, *Negreiros portugueses na rota das Índias de Castel (1541–1556)* (Lisbon: Colibri, 1999), 42–43, 47, 84. Nearly all this book focuses on Manuel Caldeira, drawing on new sources and his will.

78. Mateus Ventura, *Negreiros portugueses*, 47.

79. Magalhães Godinho, *Os descobrimentos e a economia mundial*, vol. 3, 56.

80. For information on the gift for Manuel Caldeira's daughter, see Diogo do Couto, *Da Asia. Década Décima, Parte Primeira* (Lisbon: Regia Officina Typografica, 1788), livro IV, cap. V, 423. For the relationship of Luís Mendes de Vasconcelos with New Christian contractors in the slave trade, see Luiz Felipe de Alencastro, *O trato dos viventes. Formaçao do Brasil no Atlântico Sul, séculos XVI e XVII*, 96–99, 357–359.

81. "Fue con clausula que tenia hecho cierto en la mesa de la consciencia y ordenes, tener las calidades necesarias, conforme a las leyes de aquel reyno y nueva ordenança de la orden, palabras que dichas por tal rey califican su limpieza sin admitir prueba en contrario," British Library, Egerton Ms 1133, fl. 408r.

82. Pier Cesare Ioly Zorattini, ed., *Processi del S. Uffizio di Venezia contro Ebrei e Giuddaizzanti (1548–1560)*, vol. 3 (Florence: Leo S. Olschki, 1980), 220–221. Manuel Caldeira, identified as knight of the Order of Christ, was called before the Inquisition in 1572 during the enquiry into Nuno Henriques's family, which would lead, in 1576, to the trial of the son, Henrique Nunes Righetto, finally caught in Lisbon after escaping from the Inquisition's prison in Venice. Maria Graça Ventura suggests that in the references made in 1567–1569 to Manuel Caldeira being treasurer of the "serenissima princesa de Portugal," the princess was Juana, the mother of King Sebastião, not the Infanta D. Maria: *Negreiros portugueses*, 88–89.

83. ANTT, Chancelaria de D. João III, Próprios, Livro 46, fl. 103r; Livro 58, fls. 197v–198r.

84. Luís de Albuquerque and Maria Emília Madeira Santos, eds., *História geral de Cabo Verde*, vol. 1, (Lisbon: IICT, 1991), 386.

85. Fernanda Olival, "Juristas e mercadores à conquista das honras: quatro processos de habilitação quinhentistas," *Revista de História Económica e Social* 4, 2nd series (2002): 7–53.

86. ANTT, Chancelaria de D. Sebastião, Privilégios, Livro 2, fls. 58r–59v (my translation).

87. Juan Ignacio Pulido Serrano, "La penetracion de los portugueses en la economia española durante la segunda metad del siglo XVI," in *Más que negócios. Simón Ruiz, un banquero español del siglo XVI entre las penínsulas Iberia y Italiana*, ed. Juan Ignacio Pulido Serrano (Madrid: Iberoamericana, 2017), 267–312.

88. Ioly Zorattini, ed., *Processi del Santo Uffizio*, vol. 3, 272.

89. Hans Pohl, *Die Portugiesen in Antwerpen (1567–1648): Zur Geschichte einer Minderheit* (Wiesbaden: Franz Steiner, 1977), 44, 94, 353, 366 (but the genealogical table of the Caldeira family is very limited).

90. Gentil da Silva, ed., *Marchandises et finances*.

91. Pulido Serrano, "La penetracion de los portugueses," esp. 282–295.

92. Magalhães Godinho, *Os descobrimentos e a economia mundial*, vol. 3, 65, and vol. 4, 80.

93. For the historical context, see Carlos Javier de Carlos Morales, *Felipe II: El Imperio en Bancarrota; La Hacienda Real de Castilla y los negocios del Rey Prudente* (Madrid: Dilema, 2008); Mauricio Drelichman and Hans-Joachim Voth, *Lending to the Borrower from Hell: Debt, Taxes and Default in the Age of Philip II* (Princeton, NJ: Princeton University Press, 2014).

94. Henri Lapeyre, *Simon Ruiz et les 'asientos' de Philippe II* (Paris: Armand Colin, 1953), 22–23; Luís Álvares Caldeira was a son-in-law of Jerónimo Lindo and nephew of Rodrigo Álvares Caldeira; see Ana Sofia Ribeiro, "The Evolution of Norms in Trade and Financial Networks in the First Global Age: The Case of Simon Ruiz's Network," in *Beyond Empires: Global Self-Organising, Cross-Imperial Networks, 1500–1800*, ed. Cátia Antunes and Amélia Polónia (Leiden: Brill, 2016), 12–40, esp 35.

95. Lapeyre, *Simon Ruiz*, 45.

96. Hermann Kellenbenz, "I Mendes, I Rodrigues d'Évora e I Ximenes nei loro rappori commerciali con Venezia," in Gaetano Cozzi, ed., *Gli Ebrei e Venezia, secoli XIV–XVIII* (Milan: Comunità, 1987), 154.

97. For a solid analysis of networks in a different time period, see Cátia Antunes, "Redes multiculturais de investimento no Atlântico, 1580–1776: A perspectiva da praça de Amesterdão," *Anais de história de além-mar* 14 (2013): 93–120.

Chapter Six: Migration

1. See the analysis of similar strategies by southern German merchants in Mark Häberlein, "Apprentices, Sojourners, Expatriates: Southern German Merchants in European Cities, c. 1450–1650," in *Merchant Cultures: A Global Approach to Spaces, Representations and Worlds of Trade, 1500–1800*, ed. Cátia Antunes and Francisco Bethencourt (Leiden: Brill, 2022), 231–250.

2. ANTT, Inquisição de Lisboa, Processo 10906, fl. 7r. Moses Hamon died between 1553 and 1554, shortly after Tomé's arrival; see Uriel Heyd, "Uriel Hamon, Chief Jewish Physician to Sultan Suleyman the Magnificent," *Oriens* 16 (1963): 152–170.

3. ANTT, Inquisição de Lisboa, Processo 10906, fl. 11r. See the analysis of this enquiry and the case of Jácome d'Olivares in Ana Isabel Cannas da Cunha, *A Inquisição no Estado da Índia. Origens (1539–1560)* (Lisbon: Arquivos Nacionais/Torre do Tombo, 1995), 218, 221. Jácome was born in Setubal to a New Christian mother and an Old Christian father, squire to the master of the military Order of Santiago. He emigrated to Cochin in 1540, where he became an important merchant recognised by the governors and acquired the position of notary to the fleets of India and Malacca. He was a man of letters who played the organ at the monastery of St. Anthony.

4. ANTT, Inquisição de Lisboa, Processo 10906, fl. 8r. According to Tomé, the Duke of Naxos had been alerted to the activities of Mateus Beiçudo by a letter from João Ribeiro's father in Venice. Mateus Beiçudo, who went about Aleppo dressed as a Turk, as described by Tomé Pegado de Paz, is a fascinating case. Maria José Ferro Tavares, who draws on Portuguese diplomatic correspondence, identified two Beiçudos, the uncle, Isaac, in Aleppo and the nephew, Matias (Mateus?), in Cairo, see Maria José Ferro Tavares, "Judeus, Cristaos Novos e o Oriente," *Estudos Orientais*, special issue, *O Ocidente e o Oriente através dos descobrimentos portugueses* 3, no. 3 (1992): 49–63, esp. 61. In the mid-1560s, Fr. Pantaleão de Aveiro talked to Isaac Beiçudo, then resident in Tripoli, Syria, who corresponded with the Portuguese Ambassador to Rome and offered to give information directly to the Portuguese king: see Pantaleão's *Itinerário da Terra Santa* (1592, voyage in the 1560s), ed. António Baião (Coimbra, Imprensa da Universidade, 1927), 531–532. This correspondence is mentioned by the Ambassador to Rome, Lourenço Pires de Távora, on November 30, 1560; see *CDP*, vol. 9 (Lisbon: Academia Real das Sciencias, 1884), 109.

5. ANTT, Inquisição de Lisboa, Processo 10906, fl. 70r. See the study of António da Fonseca in James Nelson Novoa, *Being the Nação in the Eternal City: New Christian Lives in Sixteenth Century Rome* (Peterborough, ON: Baywolf Press, 2014).

6. ANTT, Inquisição de Lisboa, Processo 10906, fl. 70v.

7. ANTT, Inquisição de Lisboa, Processo 10906, fl. 71v. This information is important for reconstituting the origins of the Ergas family studied by Francesca Trivellato, *The Familiarity of Strangers: The Sephardic Diaspora, Livorno, and Cross-Cultural Trade in the Early Modern Period* (New Haven, CT: Yale University Press, 2009).

8. ANTT, Inquisição de Lisboa, Processo 10906, fl. 66r.

9. See Cannas da Cunha, *A Inquisição no Estado da Índia*.

10. Cannas da Cunha, *A Inquisição no Estado da Índia*, 52–58.

11. Cannas da Cunha, *A Inquisição no Estado da Índia*, 37, 167, 215, 219–220, 224. Maria José Ferro Tavares, "Judeus, Cristãos Novos e o Oriente," also studied this case.

12. ANTT, Inquisição de Lisboa, Processo 185, fl. 144r–v.

13. ANTT, Inquisição de Lisboa, Processo 185, namely fl. 136v–137r.

14. ANTT, Inquisição de Lisboa, Processo 185, fl. 148r–151r.

15. See the list of those sentenced by the Inquisition of Goa from 1561 to 1636 in Biblioteca Nacional de Portugal (BNP), códice 203. Rogério Ribas, *Filhos de Mafoma: mouriscos, cripto-islamismo e inquisição no Portugal quinhentista* (Niterói: Eduff, 2021), studied this codex.

16. See José Alberto Rodrigues da Silva Tavim, *Judeus e cristãos-novos de Cochim. História e memória (1500–1662)* (Braga: APPACDM, 2003); Lúcio de Sousa, "The Jewish Presence in China and Japan in the Early Modern Period: A Social Representation," in *Global History and New Polycentric Approaches*, ed. M. Perez Garcia and Lúcio de Sousa (London: Palgrave, 2018), 183–218; José Pedro Paiva, "The Inquisition Tribunal of Goa: Why and for What Purpose," *Journal of Early Modern History* 21, no. 6 (2017): 565–593.

17. José Pedro Paiva, "The New Christian Divide in the Portuguese-Speaking World (Sixteenth to Eighteenth Centuries)," in *Racism and Ethnic Relations in the Portuguese-Speaking World*, ed. Francisco Bethencourt and Adrian Pearce (London/Oxford: British Academy/Oxford University Press, 2012), 260–280.

18. de Sousa, "Jewish Presence in China and Japan," 190–192, 198–204. There are other names of New Christian merchants in this article. For the case of Macau, see Miguel Rodrigues Lourenço, *A articulação da periferia: Macau e a Inquisição de Goa (c. 1582–c.1650)* (Lisbon: Centro Científico e Cultural de Macau, 2016); Miguel Rodrigues Lourenço, ed., *Macau e a Inquisição nos séculos XVI e XVII. Documentos*, 2 vols. (Lisbon: ICCM, 2012).

19. James C. Boyajian, *Portuguese Trade under the Habsburgs, 1580–1640* (Baltimore: Johns Hopkins University Press, 1993), 76–80.

20. José Alberto Tavim, "Conversos: 'A Península Desejada.' Reflexões em torno de alguns casos paradigmáticos (séculos XVI e XVII)," *Cadernos de Estudos Sefarditas* 6 (2006): 259–295.

21. José Gentil da Silva, *Stratégie des affaires à Lisbonne entre 1595 et 1607. Lettres marchandes des Rodrigues d'Évora et Veiga* (Paris: Armand Colin, 1956), 3–5, 14, 22; Hans Pohl, *Die Portugiesen in Antwerpen (1567–1648)* (Wiesbaden: Franz Steiner, 1977), 39, 66, 83–85, 358.

22. Pohl, *Die Portugiesen in Antwerpen*, mainly 356–359; see also the website created by Christine Göttler and her presentation, "Emmanuel Ximenez: A Merchant's Inventory in 1617 Antwerp," www.ximenez.unibe.ch, accessed June 15, 2020; Marcella Aglietti, "Patrizi, cavalieri e mercanti. Politiche di nobiltà tra Toscana e Spagna in età moderna," in *Istituzioni, potere e società. Le relazioni tra Spagna e Toscana per una storia mediterranea dell'Ordine dei Cavalieri di Santo Stefano*, ed. Marcella Aglietti (Pisa: ETS, 2007), 339–377.

23. Pohl, *Die Portugiesen in Antwerpen*, 80–86, 356–359.

24. Pohl, *Die Portugiesen in Antwerpen*, 36–101, 353–355.

25. ANTT, Inquisição de Lisboa, Processo 8933 (short record of seven folios).

26. ANTT, Inquisição de Lisboa, Processo 12590, particularly fls. 3r–v, 16r, 17r, 22r, 23r–25r, 27r, 37r, 56r.

27. ANTT, Inquisição de Lisboa, Processo 10377, fl. 80r–81r.

28. Archivio della Congregazzione per la Dottrina della Fede (ACDF), Codice BB5b, fl. 25r–47r and 61r. The first memorial had been compiled by Fra Zaccaria Portuguese Capuchin on July 29, 1594. This set of documents and the following ones were published by Pier Cesare Zorattini, ed., *Processi del S. Uffizio di Venezia contro ebrei e giudaizzanti. Apendice*, vol. 13 (Florence: Leo S. Olshki, 1997), 179–215.

29. ACDF, BB5b, fl. 47v–56v.

30. ACDF, BB5b, fl. 78r–83r.

31. ACDF, BB5b, fl. 78r–83r.

32. ACDF, BB5b, fl. 104r–v and 111r.

33. ANTT, Inquisição de Lisboa, Processo 10377, fl. 82r.

34. See the excellent reconstitution of these lives by James Nelson Novoa, *Being the Nation in the Eternal City*, esp. 178–226.

35. Rui Fernandes, *Descrição do terreno ao redor de Lamego duas léguas [1532–1534]*, ed. Amândio Barros (Lisbon: Caleidoscópio, 2012). This is an important example of New Christian early participation in rich local geographic and historical descriptions.

36. Novoa, *Being the Nation in the Eternal City*.

37. Arquivo do Instituto Português de Santo António in Rome (AIPSA), Actas das Congregações, 1539–1601, fl. 14r, 21v, 24r, 31r, 32v, 41v, 53v, 58r, 59r, 72r, 73r, 87r, 89v, 95v, 97v, 146r.

38. Archivio Storico Capitolino (ASC), Ms. 25449 (description of the Church of San Giacomo degli Spagnoli, ca. 1630). The movable paintings and the tombs were transferred to the Church of Monserrate in the late nineteenth century when the Church of San Giacomo degli Spagnoli was sold. My translation of the inscriptions. See James N. Novoa, "Legitimation through Art in the Rome of Gregory XIII: The Commission to Baldassare Croce in the Fonseca Chapel of San Giacomo degli Spagnoli," *RIHA Journal* 95 (2014): https://doi.org/10.11588/riha.2014.0.69951. Unfoliated, accessed August 28, 2020.

39. Gérard Nahon studied extensively the Jewish communities in France. I highlight here, Gérard Nahon, *Juifs et judaïsme à Bordeaux* (Bordeaux: Mollat, 2003); and Gérard Nahon, "D'un singulier désir à la Loi du Dieu d'Israël: les nouveaux-chrétiens portugais en France XVIᵉ–XVIIIᵉ s," in *La diaspora des "nouveaux-chrétiens,"* ed. Francisco Bethencourt, thematic issue, *Arquivos do Centro Cultural Calouste Gulbenkian* 48 (2004): 73–102.

40. Gérard Nahon, *Les "nations" juives portugaises du sud-ouest de la France (1684–1791). Documents* (Paris: Fundação Calouste Gulbenkian, 1981), 21–26.

41. Nahon, *Les "nations" juives portugaises*, 26–31.

42. Miriam Bodian, *Hebrews of the Portuguese Nation: Conversos and Community in Early Modern Amsterdam* (Bloomington: Indiana University Press, 1997), 22–25, 31–33; see also H. P. Salomon, *Os primeiros portugueses de Amesterdão: documentos do Arquivo Nacional da Torre do Tombo, 1595–1606*, offprint, *Camoniana* 8 (1983); António Borges Coelho, *Inquisição de Évora. Dos primórdios a 1668* 1 (Lisbon: Caminha, 1987), 438–448, provides an enlarged genealogy of Baruch Spinoza.

43. Miriam Bodian, "Les juifs portugais d'Amsterdam et la question identitaire," in *La diaspora des "nouveaux-chrétiens,"* ed. Francisco Bethencourt, thematic issue, *Arquivos do Centro Cultural Calouste Gulbenkian* 48 (2004): 103–116.

44. Michaël Studemund-Halévy and Jorun Poettering, "Étrangers universelles: les réseaux sépharades à Hambourg," in *La diaspora des "nouveaux-chrétiens,"* ed. Francisco Bethencourt, *Arquivos do Centro Cultural Calouste Gulbenkian* 48 (2004): 117–150, esp. 120–121.

45. ANTT, Inquisição de Lisboa, Processo 10377, fl. 91r–v.

46. Aron di Leone Leoni and Herman Princ Salomon, "La nation portugaise de Hambourg en 1617 d'après un document trouvé," in *Mémorial I.-S. Révah. Études sur le marranisme, l'hétérodoxie juive et Spinoza*, ed. Henry Méchoulan and Gérard Nahon (Paris-Louvain: E. Peeters, 2001), 263–293.

47. Jorun Poettering, *Migrant Merchants: Trade, Nation, and Religion in Seventeenth-Century Hamburg and Portugal*, trans. Kenneth Kronenberg (Berlin: De Gruyter, 2019), 21, 114.

48. Toby Green, *The Rise of the Trans-Atlantic Slave Trade in Western Africa, 1300–1589* (Cambridge: Cambridge University Press, 2012), esp. 18, 123, 145–146, 150–154, 282. See also Peter Mark and José da Silva Horta, *The Forgotten Diaspora: Jewish Communities in West Africa and the Making of the Atlantic World* (Cambridge: Cambridge University Press, 2011), particularly chap. 1.

49. António Almeida Mendes, "Le rôle de l'Inquisition en Guinée: Vicissitudes des présences juives sur la Petite Côte (XVe–XVIIe siècles)," in *Inquisição em África*, ed. Francisco Bethencourt and Philip Havik, thematic issue, *Revista Lusófona de Ciência das Religiões* 3, nos. 5–6 (2004): 137–155, esp. 146.

50. *Monumenta Missionaria Africana*, vol. 2 (Lisbon: Agência Geral do Ultramar, 1953), 475.

51. Green, *The Rise of the Trans-Atlantic Slave Trade*, 135–141.

52. Green, *The Rise of the Trans-Atlantic Slave Trade*, 155–159.

53. George E. Brooks, *Eurafricans in Western Africa: Commerce, Social Status, Gender, and Religious Observance from the Sixteenth to the Eighteenth Century* (Athens: Ohio University Press, 2003), 78.

54. António Almeida Mendes, "Le rôle de l'Inquisition en Guinée," 148.

55. Brooks, *Eurafricans in Western Africa*, 78, 81.

56. Green, *The Rise of the Trans-Atlantic Slave Trade*, 161–162.

57. Martin A. Cohen, *The Martyr: The Story of a Secret Jew and the Mexican Inquisition in the Sixteenth Century* (Philadelphia: Jewish Publication Society of America, 1973).

58. José Toribio Medina, *História del tribunal del Santo Oficio da la Inquisición en Mexico* (Santiago de Chile: Imprenta Elzeviriana, 1905), 107, 127.

59. Paulino Castañeda Delgado and Pilar Hernández Aparicio, *La Inquisición de Lima*, tomo I *(1570–1635)* (Madrid: Deimos, 1989), 423–425.

60. José Antonio Gonsalves de Mello, *Gente da nação. Cristãos-novos e judeus em Pernambuco, 1542–1654* (Recife: Fundação Joaquim Nabuco, 1996), 6.

61. Gonsalves de Mello, *Gente da nação*, vol. 9, 16–17; Bodian, *Hebrews of the Portuguese Nation*, 44–45. For a detailed analysis of the early career of João Nunes Correia, see Lúcio Manuel Rocha de Sousa and Ângelo Adriano Faria de Assis, "A diaspora Sefardita na Ásia e no Brasil e a interligação das redes comerciais na modernidade," *Revista de Cultura* 31 (2009): 101–121, esp. 111–116.

62. Gonsalves de Mello, *Gente da nação*, 8–9, 35–50.

63. José Gonçalves Salvador, *Os cristãos-novos. Povoamento e conquista do solo brasileiro (1530–1680)* (São Paulo: Pioneira, 1976).

Chapter Seven: Property

1. ANTT, Chancelaria de D. Sebastião, Privilégios, Livro 2, fl. 304v; Chancelaria de D. Sebastião, Próprios, fls. 135v–142v.

2. ANTT, Hospital de São José, escrivão Botelho, Maço 18, nº 11, cx. 548.

3. *Livro do lançamento e serviço que a cidade de Lisboa fez a El Rei nosso senhor no ano de 1565*, 4 vols. (Lisbon: Câmara Municipal de Lisboa, 1947–1948). See, for instance, vol. 1, 216, 254; but there are many other references.

4. Fernanda Olival, "Juristas e mercadores à conquista das honras: quatro processos de habilitação quinhentistas." *Revista de História Económica e Social*, 2nd series, 4 (2002): 7–53.

5. I have been adding new elements to this case since 1992; see *The Inquisition: A Global History, 1478–1834*, trans Jean Birrell (Cambridge: Cambridge University Press, 2009), 328–329.

6. ANTT, Feitos Findos, Inventários Post-Mortem, Letra L, Maço 42, nº 6.

7. *Processi del S. Uffizio di Venezia contro Ebrei e Giuddaizzanti*, vol. 3 *(1570–1572)*, ed. Pier Cesare Ioly Zorattini (Florence: Leo S. Olschki, 1984), 220–221. This precious collection of trials of Jews by the Venetian Inquisition is completed by the transcriptions of Portuguese trials concerning some of the accused. Henrique Nunes's trial in Lisbon, here impeccably presented, provides some of the best information.

8. *Processi del S. Uffizio di Venezia*, 278–281.

9. *Processi del S. Uffizio di Venezia*, 253–254.

10. *Processi del S. Uffizio di Venezia*, 255.

11. *Processi del S. Uffizio di Venezia*, 263–270.

12. *Processi del S. Uffizio di Venezia*, 213–214, Nuno Henriques' will from 1549, published by Zorattini.

13. *Processi del S. Uffizio di Venezia*, 263–264.

14. BL, Egerton, Ms 113, fl. 408v.

15. See the transcription of the will in Maria da Graça Mateus Ventura, *Negreiros Portugueses na rota das Índias de Castela (1541–1556)* (Lisbon: Colibri, 1999), 143–152.

16. See the transcription of André Caldeira's declaration of the inheritance he was due in Mateus Ventura, *Negreiros Portugueses*, 153–162.

17. Archivio di Stato di Roma (ASR), Notari del tribunale dell'auditore della camera apostolica, 1055, fl. 427r–428r.

18. ASR, Notari del tribunale dell'auditore della camera apostolica, 1055, fl. 423r–427r and 476r–481r.

19. ASR, Notari del tribunale dell'auditore della camera apostolica, 1055, fl. 465r–468v and 481r.

20. See James Nelson Nóvoa, "Unicorns and Bezoars in a Portuguese House in Rome: António da Fonseca Portuguese Inventories," *Agora. Estudos Clássicos em Debate* 14, no. 1 (2012): 91–111.

21. ASR, Notari del tribunale dell'auditore della camera apostolica, 1055, fl. 438r–455v.

22. ASR, Notari del tribunale dell'auditore della camera apostolica, 1055, fl. 428v–429r.

23. Rafael Ramis Barceló, *Doctores hispanos en leyes y canones per la Universidad de La Sapienza de Roma (1549–1774)* (Madrid: Dickinson, 2017), 237.

24. AIPSA, Actas das Congregações, 1539–1601, fl. 145v, 181r, 185r, 199v, 201r, 212v; *idem*, Actas das Congregações, 1611–1678, fl. 18r, 46v, 67v, 87r.

25. Biblioteca de la Iglesia Nacional de España (BINE), Archicofradia de la Santissima Ressurrección, A-II-71, fl. 84v.

26. BINE, Archicofradia de la Santissima Ressurrección, A-II-71, fl. 120r.

27. BINE, Archicofradia de la Santissima Ressurrección, A-II-71, fl. 120r–135v.

28. ASR, Notarile del tribunale dell'auditore della camera apostolica, 1055, fl. 476r.

29. ASR, Notarile del tribunale dell'auditore della camera apostolica, 1055, fl. Fl. 426v.

30. BINE, Archicofradia de la Santissima Resurrección, A-II-71, fl. 41r–45v. See James N. Novoa, "Between Roman Home and Portuguese Hearth: Jerónimo da Fonseca in Roma," *Historia y genealogía* 4 (2014): 341–356.

31. ACDF, BB5b, fl. 135r–137r.

32. ACDF, BB5b, fl. 322r.

33. ACDF, BB5b, fl. 326r–v

34. The best available authority on the Ximenes family is still Carlo Segrebondi, *Familie patrizie fiorentine*, vol. 1 (Florence: Carlo Cia., 1940), with copious genealogical tables and dates of birth and death of the various family members. However, the comments are outdated, and the dates need to be checked, while the wills were not explored.

35. Archivio di Stato di Firenze (ASF), Panciatichi Ximenes d'Aragona, Libro 360, fasc. I.

36. Franco Angiolini, "Rafaello de' Medici," in *Dizionario Biografico degli Italiani*, vol. 73 (Rome: Istituto della Enciclopedia Italiana, 2009).

37. ASF, Panciatichi Ximenes d'Aragona, libro 356, fl. 4. According to Segrebondi, *Familie patrizie fiorentine*, vol. 1, text and genealogical table for Fernando, the Pope later revoked the brief, but Segrebondi does not provide the source of this information. The fact is that the Ximenes never again used the name Peretti, even though the papal brief became part of their collection of documents proving their nobility.

38. ASF, Panciatichi Ximenes d'Aragona, libro 356, fl. 4–25 and 82–84.

39. The will changed several times between 1596 and 1600, but all the documents are in the ASF, Notarile Moderno, Protocolli, 7027, Francesco Quorli, 1585–1601, fl. 68r–77r. On the occasion of the burial: Archivio di Stato di Firenze, Panciatichi Ximenes d'Aragona, Libro 356, fl. 84r–85r.

40. ASF, Notarile Moderno, Protocolli, 5497, Andrea Andreini, 1593–1597, fl. 104r–111r. Codicil in ASF, Notarile Moderno, Protocolli, 7027, Francesco Quorli, 1585–1601, fl. 112r–119v.

41. ASF, Panciatichi Ximenes d'Aragona, Libro 360, fasc V. There is a copy of this will in Florence due to the litigation about inheritence of the morgado two generations later.

42. ASF, Panciatichi Ximenes d'Aragona, Libro 360, fasc V.

43. ASF, Panciatichi Ximenes d'Aragona, Libro 360, fasc. VIII. The same reference for the following paragraphs.

44. ASF, Panciatichi Ximenes d'Aragona, Libro 360, fasc. VIII.

45. ASF, Panciatichi Ximenes d'Aragona, Libro 360, fasc. XVI (the will of Sebastiano Ximenes d'Aragona, December 29, 1633).

46. ASF, Panciatichi Ximenes d'Aragona, Libro 357, fl. 35v–76r.

47. This social issue is not addressed by Paulo Drumond Braga, *D. Maria (1521–1577). Uma infanta no Portugal de Quinhentos* (Lisbon: Colibri, 2012). In the final tables, which even include the servants of the infanta, there is no evidence of New Christians, but D. Afonso de Noronha is clearly listed as the majordomo. It is no coincidence that Jerónimo Ximenes should have married one of his daughters to him. For a later period, see the importance of the social world of convents in Benjamin James, *Convents of Nuns in Lisbon (1640–1750)* (PhD, King's College London, 2022).

48. ASF, Panciatichi Ximenes d'Aragona, libro 387.

49. ASF, Panciatichi Ximenes d'Aragona, Libro 390.

Chapter Eight: Values

1. Heikki Pihlajamäki, et al., eds., *The Oxford Handbook of European Legal History* (Oxford: Oxford University Press, 2018); Serge Dauchy, et al., eds., *The Formation and Transmission of Western Legal Culture: 150 Books that Made the Law in the Age of Printing* (Switzerland: Springer, 2016); Mary Elizabeth Basile, ed., *Lex mercatoria and Legal Pluralism: A Late Thirteenth-Century Treatise and Its Afterlife* (Cambridge, MA: Ames Foundation, 1998); Manlio Bellomo, *The Common Legal Past of Europe 1000–1800*, trans. Lydia G. Cochrane (Washington DC: Catholic University of America Press, 1995).

2. Antonio Padoa-Schioppa, *A History of Law in Europe, from the early Middle Ages to the Twentieth Century*, trans. Caterina Fitzgerald (Cambridge: Cambridge University Press, 2017), 174–176.

3. The debate on *lex mercatoria* is well summarised by Francesca Trivellato, "'Usages and Customs of the Sea': Étienne Cleirac and the Making of Maritime Law in Seventeenth-Century France," *Legal History Review* 84 (2016): 193–224, esp. 195–198.

4. Padoa-Schioppa, *A History of Law*, 207–210 (on the importance of *aequitas* in canon law), 267–168, 393–294.

5. Peter John Olivi, *A Treatise on Contracts* (ms. ca. 1293–1294), ed. Sylvain Piron, trans. Ryan Thornton and Michael Cusato (St. Bonaventure, NY: Franciscan Institute Publications, 2016). For an overview of these issues see Daniel R. Coquillette, ed., *The Anglo-American Legal Heritage. Introductory Materials*, 2nd ed. (Durham, NC: Carolina Academic Press, 2004).

6. John Maynard Keynes, *The General Theory of Employment, Interest and Money* (London: Macmillan, 1936), 351–352.

7. Michael Thomas D'Emic, *Justice in the Marketplace in Early Modern Spain: Saravia, Villalón and the Religious Origins of Economic Analysis* (Lanham, Maryland: Lexington Books, 2014).

8. See Francesca Trivellato, *The Promise and Peril of Credit: What a Forgotten Legend about Jews and Finance Tells Us about the Making of European Commercial Society* (Princeton, NJ: Princeton University Press, 2019).

9. Germano Maifreda, *From Oikonomia to Political Economy: Constructing Economic Knowledge from the Renaissance to the Scientific Revolution*, trans. Loretta Valtz Mannucci (London: Routledge, 2012).

10. Sheilagh Ogilvie, *Institutions and European Trade: The Merchant Guilds, 1000–1800* (Cambridge: Cambridge University Press, 2011).

11. Regina Grafe, *Distant Tyranny: Markets, Power, and Backwardness in Spain, 1650–1800* (Princeton, NJ: Princeton University Press, 2012), 199–202, 227–230; Bartolomé Yun-Casalilla, *Iberian World Empires and the Globalization of Europe 1415–1668* (Basingstoke: Palgrave, 2018), 324, 331–335.

12. Bartolomé de Albornoz, *Arte de los contractos* (Valencia: Pedro de Huete, 1573), libro III, particularly fl. 108r.

13. Saravia de la Calle, *Instrucción de mercaderes* (1544), ed. Pablo Ruiz de Alba (Madrid: Joyas Bibliográficas, 1949).

14. de la Calle, *Instrucción de mercaderes*, 63–65.

15. de la Calle, *Instrucción de mercaderes*, 53, 99–100.

16. de la Calle, *Instrucción de mercaderes*, 177.

17. de la Calle, *Instrucción de mercaderes*, 81, 85–86.

18. de la Calle, *Instrucción de mercaderes*, 47–53.

19. Luis de Alcalá, *El tractado de los prestamos que passan entre mercaderes y tractantes y por consiguinte de los logros, cambios, compras adelantadas y ventas al fiado* (1546), ed. Elena Carpi (Pisa: Edizioni ETS, 2011), 87–88 (fl. 24v).

20. de Alcalá, *El tractado de los prestamos*, 88–89 (fl. 25v–26v).

21. de Alcalá, *El tractado de los prestamos*, 100 (fl. 33r).

22. Martín de Azpilcueta Navarro, *Comentario resolutorio de cambios* (1556), ed. Alberto Ullastres, José M. Pérez Prendes and Luciano Pereña (Madrid: CSIC, 1965).

23. de Azpilcueta Navarro, *Comentario resolutorio de cambios*, 3–12, 21–22.

24. de Azpilcueta Navarro, *Comentario resolutorio de cambios*, 23.

25. de Azpilcueta Navarro, *Comentario resolutorio de cambios*, 40.

26. de Azpilcueta Navarro, *Comentario resolutorio de cambios*, 30–31, 53, 57–58.

27. de Azpilcueta Navarro, *Comentario resolutorio de cambios*, 68–69, 74–75.

28. de Azpilcueta Navarro, *Comentario resolutorio de cambios*, 46–47.

29. This is explicitly asserted forty years later by Luís de Molina, *Tratado sobre los prestamos y la usura* (1597), ed. Francisco Gómez Camacho (Madrid: Instituto de Estudios Fiscales, 1989), 41, 62, 91–95. Molina opposed the practice, ruinous for all those involved, of farming the trade to India and selling the royal rents at interest: 122–124.

30. Tomás de Mercado, *Suma de tratos y contractos* (1569), ed. Restituto Sierra Bravo (Madrid: Editora Nacional, 1975), 111–112, 161.

31. de Mercado, *Suma de tratos y contractos*, 189.

32. de Mercado, *Suma de tratos y contractos*, 314–315.

33. de Mercado, *Suma de tratos y contractos*, 316–321.

34. de Mercado, *Suma de tratos y contractos*, 11.

35. de Mercado, *Suma de tratos y contractos*, 167

36. de Mercado, *Suma de tratos y contractos*, 168.

37. de Mercado, *Suma de tratos y contractos*, 177–184, 269–273.

38. de Mercado, *Suma de tratos y contractos*, 275–282.

39. de Mercado, *Suma de tratos y contractos*, 124–125.

40. de Albornoz, *Arte de los contratos*.

41. de Albornoz, *Arte de los contratos*, Libro III, namely fl. 108r.

42. de Albornoz, *Arte de los contratos*, fl. 110r.

43. de Albornoz, *Arte de los contratos*, fl. 116v.

44. de Albornoz, *Arte de los contratos*, fl. 130r–130v.

45. de Albornoz, *Arte de los contratos*, fl. 128r–v.

46. Martín González de Cellorigo, *Memorial de la politica necessaria y util restauración de la republica de España y estados de ella y del desempeño universal de estos reinos* (1600) ed. José Pérez de Ayala (Madrid: Antoni Bosch, 1991), 80–81, 84–87.

47. González de Cellorigo, *Memorial de la politica necessaria*, 169–172.

48. González de Cellorigo, *Memorial de la politica necessaria*, 147–152.

49. González de Cellorigo, *Memorial de la politica necessaria*, 185–188.

50. Domenico di Masi, ed., *L'emozione e la regole. I gruppi creativi in Europa dal 1850 al 1950* (Rome/Bari: Laterza, 1989), provided a comprehensive and comparative approach

including scientific organisations and informal innovative groups in sciences, technology, arts and crafts, philosophy, social sciences, and literature. New developments of research in sociology, economics, and political sciences can be found in Francesco Ramella, *Sociology of Economic Innovation* (London: Routledge, 2015), or Dan Breznitz, *Innovation in Real Places* (Oxford: Oxford University Press, 2021).

51. See Francisco Bethencourt and Forike Egmond, eds., *Correspondence and Cultural Exchange in Europe, 1400–1700* (Cambridge: Cambridge University Press, 2007; Francisco Bethencourt, "European Expansion and the New Order of Knowledge," in *The Renaissance World*, ed. John Jeffries Martin (London: Routledge, 2007), 118–139; Peter Burke wrote extensively on this subject, I highlight here *A Social History of Knowledge*, 2 vols. (Cambridge: Polity Press, 2000–2012); flourishing scholarship is well represented by Karel Davids, *Global Ocean of Knowledge, 1660–1860: Globalization and Maritime Knowledge in the Atlantic World* (London: Bloomsbury, 2020).

52. Archivio della Congregazzione per la Dottrina della Fede, BB5a Iudaizantes Lusitaniae (without foliation).

53. See the excellent study of this case by Giuseppe Marcocci, "Questioni di stile. Gastão de Abrunhosa contro l'Inquisizione Portoghese (1602–1607)," *Studi Storici* 48, no. 3 (2007): 779–815.

54. Eugenio Asensio in *El Erasmismo y las corrientes espirituales afines. Conversos, Franciscanos, Italianizantes* (Madrid: SEMYR, 2000), 73–74, used the case of Melchor Cano to invalidate the idea of modish New Christians. Although reasoned with by a wise Bataillon, who engaged in systematic correspondence with him, Asensio was aligned more with Sanchez-Albornoz than Américo Castro, since he always expressed doubts about the impact of "seudoconversos" [*sic*] (p. 54). For the case of Melchor Cano against Carranza, see José Ignacio Tellechea Idígoras, "Melchor Cano y Bartolome Carranza: dos dominicanos frente a frente," *Hispania Sacra* 15, no. 29 (1962): 5–95.

55. Melchor Cano, *De locis theologicis* (1563), ed. Juan Belda Plans and trans. into Spanish by a team of philologists (Madrid: Biblioteca de Autores Cristianos, 2006); Juan Belda Plans, *La escuela de Salamanca y la renovación de la teologia en el siglo XVI* (Madrid: Biblioteca de Autores Cristianos, 2000).

56. These connections had already been spotted by Marcel Bataillon, *Les jésuites dans l'Espagne du XVIe siècle*, ed. Pierre-Antoine Fabre (Paris: Les Belles Lettres, 2009), 235–287, 324–333.

57. Juan Hernández Franco, *Sangre limpia, sangre española. El debate de los estatutos de limpieza de sangre (siglos XVI–XVII)* (Madrid: Cátedra, 2011), 96–116 (good analysis of the conflict raised by the statutes in Toledo). On the issue of Jesuits and conversos, see Thomas M. Cohen, "Jesuits and New Christians: The Contested Legacy of St. Ignatius," *Studies in the Spirituality of Jesuits* 42, no. 3 (2010): 1–46; Claude Stuczynski, "Jesuits and Conversos as a 'Tragic Couple': Introductory Remarks," *Journal of Jesuit Studies* 8, no. 2 (2021): 159–172.

58. Hernández Franco, *Sangre limpia, sangre española.*, 169–170.

59. Giuseppe Marcocci, "Inquisição, jesuítas e cristãos novos em Portugal no século XVI," *Revista de História das Ideias* 25 (2004): 247–326.

60. Teófanes Egido, *El linaje judeoconverso de Santa Teresa (pleito de hidalguia de los Cepeda)* (Madrid: Editorial de Espiritualidad, 1986).

61. Joseph Perez, *Teresa de Ávila y la España de su tiempo* (Madrid: Algaba, 2007).

62. Teresa de Ávila, *The Interior Castle* (ms. 1577), anonymous translation revised by Benedict Zimmerman, introduction by Robert van de Weyer (London: Fount, 1995).

63. Fray Luis de León, *Poesia*, ed. Darío Fernández-Morera and Germán Bleiberg (Madrid: Alianza, 1986); Victor García de la Concha, "Fr. Luis de León," *Diccionario Biografico Español*, Real Academia de la Historia, online edition.

64. For the connection between Juan de Ávila and the Jesuits, see Bataillon, *Les jésuites dans l'Espagne*, 265–280.

65. For Juan de Ávila's spiritual influence, see Maria Jesus Fernández Cordero, *Juan de Ávila (1499?–1569): Tiempo, vida y espiritualidad* (Madrid: Biblioteca de Autores Cristianos, 2017).

66. António Baião, *Episódios dramáticos da Inquisição*, 2nd ed., vol. 1 (Lisbon: Seara Nova, 1936), 109–129; Diogo Ramada Curto, "Stranger within at the Time of Quixote," *Portuguese Studies* 13 (1997): 180–197, mainly 181–188; and the excellent analysis of this case by Miriam Bodian, *Dying in the Law of Moses: Crypto-Jewish Martyrdom in the Iberian World* (Bloomington: Indiana University Press, 2007).

67. ANTT, Inquisição de Lisboa, Processo 104, fl. 3r–20r (with the letter of denunciation and more detailed testimony given in court by D. Diogo de Sousa).

68. ANTT, Inquisição de Lisboa, Processo 104, fl. 40r–v.

69. ANTT, Inquisição de Lisboa, Processo 104, fl. 41v–44r.

70. ANTT, Inquisição de Lisboa, Processo 104, fl. 205r–213v.

71. Alonso Núñez de Reinoso, *Historia de los amores de Clareo y Florisea, y de los trabajos de Ysea* (Venice: Gabriel Giolito de Ferrara, 1552). There is a modern edition by José Jiménez Ruiz (Malaga: Universidad de Malaga, 1997).

72. Constance Hubbard Rose, *Alonso Núñez de Reinoso: The Lament of a Sixteenth-Century Exile* (Rutherford: Fairleigh Dickinson University Press, 1971).

73. Núñez de Reinoso, *Historia de los amores* (original edition), 191.

74. Helder Macedo, *Do significado oculto da Menina e Moça* (1977), rev. ed. (Lisbon: Guimarães, 1999); Bernardim Ribeiro, *Obras*, ed. Helder Macedo and Mauricio Matos (Lisbon: Presenca, 2010). The New Christian background of Bernardim was refuted by Eugenio Asensio, a position accepted by José V. de Pina Martins in his introduction to the reprint of Bernardim Ribeiro's original, *História de Menina e Moça* (Lisbon: Fundação Calouste Gulbenkian, 2002). The article by Helder Macedo, "Convergências e dissidências," in *Viagens do olhar. Retrospecção, visão e profecia no Renascimento português*, by Helder Macedo and Fernando Gil (Porto: Campo das Letras, 1998), 349–369, offers new and convincing evidence to support his original thesis.

75. Macedo, *Do significado oculto*.

76. Helder Macedo, "As obscuras transparências de Bernardim Ribeiro," in *Viagens do olhar. Retrospecção, visão e profecia no Renascimento português*, 317–347.

77. Luiz Alberto Cerqueira, "Dom Duarte e o sentido ontológico da saudade," *Revista Portuguesa de Filosofia* 47, no. 3 (1991): 455–467; Afonso Botelho and António Braz Teixeira, eds., *Filosofia da saudade* (Lisbon: Imprensa Nacional, 1986).

78. *Lazarillo de Tormes* (1554), ed. Amparo Medina-Bocos (Madrid: Cátedra, 2006).

79. Mateo Alemán, *Guzmán de Alfarache*, ed. José María Micó 2 vols. (Madrid: Cátedra, 1987).

80. Pedro Nunes, *Obras*, ed. Henrique Leitão, 6 vols. (Lisbon: Academia das Ciências and Fundação Calouste Gulbenkian, 2002–2010); Henrique Leitão, "Maritime Discoveries and the Discovery of Science: Pedro Nunes and Early Modern Science," in *Más allá de la Leyenda Negra: España y la Revolución Científica/Beyond the Black Legend: Spain and the Scientific Revolution*, ed. Victor Navarro Brotóns e William Eamon (Valencia: Instituto de Historia de la Ciencia y Documentación López Piñero, Universitat de València, C.S.I.C., 2007), 89–104.

81. António Baião, "Os netos do matemático Pedro Nunes," in *Episódios dramáticos da Inquisição Portuguesa*, 2nd ed., vol. 1 (Lisbon: Seara Nova, 1936), 163–165.

82. Armando Cortesão and Avelino Teixeira da Mota, eds., *Portugaliae Monumenta Cartographica* (1960) reprinted vol. 4 (Lisbon: Imprensa Nacional/Casa da Moeda, 1987).

83. Amato Lusitano, *Centúrias de curas medicinais*, trans. Firmino Crespo, intro. Pedro Nunes (Lisbon: CELOM, 2010); João José Alves Dias, *Amato Lusitano e a sua obra, séculos XVI e XVII* (Lisbon: Biblioteca Nacional, 2011); D. Gershon Lewental, "Amatus Lusitanus," *Encyclopedia of Jews in the Islamic World*, ed. Norman A. Stillman, vol. 1 (Leiden: Brill, 2010), 195–197.

84. Juan Pérez de Tudela y Bueso, "Gonzalo Fernández de Oviedo y Valdés," *Diccionario Biográfico Español*, Real Academia de Historia, online ed.

85. Gonzalo Fernández de Oviedo, *Sumario de la natural historia de las Indias* (1526), ed. Manuel Ballesteros (Madrid: Historia 16, 1986); Gonzalo Fernández de Oviedo, *Historia general y natural de las Indias* (1535 vol. 1; the others only printed in the nineteenth century), ed. Juan Pérez de Tudela Bueso, 5 vols. (Madrid: Atlas, 1992).

86. Garcia d'Orta, *Colóquio dos simples e drogas e coisas medicinais de India* (1563), ed. Conde de Ficalho, reprint 2 vols. (Lisbon: Imprensa Nacional, 1987); there is an English translation by C. Markham, *Colloquies on the Simples and Drugs of India* (New Delhi: Sra Sutgara, 1913). See also Charles Boxer, *Two Pioneers of Tropical Medicine: Garcia d'Orta and Nicolas Monardes* (London: The Hispanic and Luso-Brazilian Councils, 1963); and Palmira Fontes da Costa, "Geographical Expansion and the Reconfiguration of Medical Authority: Garcia de Orta and the *Colloquies of Simples and Drugs of India (1563),*" *Studies in History and Philosophy of Science* 43 (2012): 74–81.

87. Cristóbal de Acosta, *Tratado de las drogas e medicinas de las Indias Orientales* (Burgos: Martín de Victoria, 1578).

88. Carolus Clusius, *Exoticorum libri decem* (Leiden: Officina Plantiniana Raphelengii, 1605).

89. ANTT, Inquisição de Lisboa, processo 4317.

90. I. S. Révah, "La famille de Garcia de Orta," *Revista da Universidade de Coimbra* 19 (1960): 407–420. There is a signed copy, made by the inquisitors, of the proceedings of the second trial of Catarina D'Orta, in Goa. This document, which ended up in the ANTT, Inquisição de Lisboa, processo 1283, has a list of those accused in that trial, including other members of the family and Garcia d'Orta. (fl. 71v).

91. Rodrigo de Castro, *De universa mulierum medicina*, 2 vols. (Hamburg and Cologne: Officina Frobeniana, 1603) available online from the Welcome library; see Cristina Santos Pinheiro, "The Ancient Medical Sources in the Chapters about Sterility of Rodrigo de Castro *De universa mulierum medicina,*" in *The Palgrave Handbook of Infertility in History,* ed. Gayle Davis and Tracey Loughran (Basingstoke: Palgrave, 2017), consulted online without indication of pages.

92. Rodrigo de Castro, *Medicus-Politicus* (Hamburg: Frobeniana, 1614) available online; see Jon Arrizabalaga, "Medical Ideas in the Sephardic Diaspora: Rodrigo de Castro's Portrait of the Perfect Physician in Early Seventeenth Century Hamburg," *Medical History* 53, Supplement S29, *Health and Medicine in Habsburg Spain: Agents, Practices and Representations* (2009): 107–124. For a looser approach, but still useful, David B. Ruderman, *Jewish Thought and Scientific Discovery in Early Modern Europe* (New Haven, CT: Yale University Press, 1995), esp. 273–309; and Jon Arrizabalaga, "The World of Iberian Conversos Practitioners, from Lluis Alcanyis to Isaac Cardoso," in *Mas allá de la leyenda negra: España y la revolución científica,* ed. Víctor Navarro Brotóns and William Eamon (Valencia: Instituto de Historia de la Ciencia, 2007), 307–322.

93. Filipe Montalto, *Optica intra philosophiae et medicinae aream, de visu, de visus organo, et obiecto theoriam* (Florence: Cosmum Iuntam, 1606) access online via Early European Books.

94. Filipe Montalto, *Archipathologia in qua internarum capitis affectionum essentia, causae, signa, praesagia, & curatio accuratissima indagine edisseruntur* (Paris: Franciscum Iacquin, 1614), access online via Early European Books. There is a Portuguese translation and edition by Adelino Cardoso, et al. (Lisbon: Colibri, 2017).

95. Álvaro Castillo Pintado and Juan Ignácio Gutiérrez Nieto, "La hacienda real," in *Historia de España Menendez Pidal,* vol. 25, *La España de Felipe IV. El gobierno de la monarquía, la crisis de 1640 y el fracasso de la hegemonía europea,* ed. Francisco Tomás y Valiente (Madrid: Espasa-Calpe, 1982), 215–332, esp. 238.

96. Carlos Álvarez-Nogal and Leandro Prados de la Escosura, "The Decline of Spain (1500–1850): Conjectural Estimates," *European Review of Economic History* 11, no. 3 (2007): 863–894; Carlos Álvarez-Nogal and Leandro Prados de la Escosura, "The Rise and Fall of Spain (1270–1850)," *Economic History Review* 66, no. 13 (2013): 1–37.

97. João Figueirôa-Rego, *"A honra alheia por um fio." Os estatutos de limpeza de sangue nos espaços de expressão ibérica (sécs. XVI-XVIII)* (Lisbon: Fundação Calouste Gulbenkian, 2011), 66–68.

98. Enrique Soria Mesa, *La realidad tras el espejo. Ascenso social y limpieza de sangre en la España de Felipe II* (Valladolid: Universidad de Valladolid, 2016); see also Francisco de Aranda Pérez, *Poder y poderes en la ciudad de Toledo* (Cuenca: Universidad de Castilla-La

Mancha, 1999); Linda Martz, *A Network of Converso Families in Early Modern Toledo: Assimilating a Minority* (Ann Harbor: University of Michigan Press, 2002); Ruth Pike, *Linajudos and Conversos in Seville: Greed and Prejudice in Sixteenth- and Seventeenth-Century Spain* (Oxford: Peter Lang, 2000).

99. Juan Cartaya Baños, *La pasión de don Fernando de Añasco. Limpieza de sangre y conflicto social en la Sevilla de los Siglos de Oro* (Seville: Universidad de Sevilla, 2014).

100. Biblioteca Nacional de España (BNE), Ms. 18666/45: this contains the royal licence and the papal brief, in which all descendants of Pablo de Santa Maria are declared Old Christians, clean of blood, habilitated to all honours; for the blocking by the royal council, see Hernández Franco, *Sangre limpia, sangre española*, 158.

101. Francisco Bethencourt, *The Inquisition: A Global History, 1478-1834*, trans. Jean Birrell (Cambridge: Cambridge University Press, 2009), 327-329; Fernanda Olival, "Para um estudo da nobilitação no Antigo Regime: os Cristãos Novos na Ordem de Cristo (1581-1621), in *As ordens militares em Portugal. Actas do 1º Encontro sobre Ordens Militares* (Palmela: Câmara Municipal de Palmela, 1991), 233-244 (estimated 2 percent of New Christians in a total of 2,157 knights, but others passed the enquiries without royal exception).

102. Henri Mauroy, *Apologia in duas partes divisa* (Paris: V. Gaultherolt, 1553).

103. Hernández Franco, *Sangre limpia, sangre española*, 165-166.

104. Elvira Pérez Ferreiro, *El Tratado de Uceda contra los estatutos de limpieza de sangre* (with the transcription of the treatrise) (Madrid: Aben Ezra, 2000).

105. There are several manuscript copies. I consulted BNE, Mss. 18452, fl. 1–13v; BNE, Mss. 7139, fl. 1r–22v *Cautela legatur*; see also *El Tizón de la nobleza* (Madrid: Colegio Heráldico de España y de las Indias, 1992).

106. Pedro Gerónimo de Aponte (ca. 1530–ca. 1580), *Discurso sobre la limpieza de los linages de España*, in Biblioteca Nacional de España, Mss. 18452, fl. 14v–23v.

107. There are many copies of *libros verdes* at the Biblioteca Digital Hispánica. I used a good edition of a well-known text, *El libro verde de Aragón*, ed. Monique Combescure (Zaragoza: Certeza, 2003).

108. BNE, Mss. 17479, fl. 67r–115v. Agustín Salucio, *Discurso acerca de la justicia y buen gobierno de España en los estatutos de limpieça de sangre, y si conviene o no alguna limitación de ellos* (ca. 1599) (Cieza: A. Pérez y Gómez, 1975). For the biography see Alvaro Huerga Teruelo, OP, "Agustin Salucio y Adorno (Jerez de la Frontera, Cadiz, 1523-Córdoba, 29.IX.1601)", *Diccionario Biografico Español*, vol. 45 (Madrid: Real Academia de la Historia, 2013), 358-359.

109. BNE, Ms. 17479, fl. 73r–74v.

110. BNE, Ms. 17479, fl. 96v.

111. BNE, Ms. 17479, fl. 102r.

112. BNE, Ms. 17479, fl. 69r–v.

113. Giovanni Botero, *Della ragion di stato* (1589), ed. Chiara Continisio (Rome: Donzelli, 1997).

114. BNE, Ms. 3457, fl. 52r–63v.

115. BNE, Ms. 3457, fl. 52v–60r.

116. BNE, Ms. 3457, fl. 60v–63v.

117. Robert Maryks, *The Jesuit Order as a Synagogue of Jews: Jesuits of Jewish Ancestry and Purity-of-Blood Laws in the Early Society of Jesus* (Leiden: Brill, 2010).

118. Hernández Franco, *Sangre limpia, sangre española*, 173-182.

119. Yun-Casalilla, *Iberian World Empires*; Vitorino Magalhães Godinho, "1580 e 1640 – Da União Dinástica à Restauração" (1978), in *Estudos e Ensaios. Uma maneira de pensar* (Lisbon: Sá da Costa, 2009), 421-468.

120. Mauricio Drelichman and Hans-Joachim Voth, *Lending to the Borrower from Hell: Debt, Taxes and Default in the Age of Philip II* (Princeton, NJ: Princeton University Press, 2014); James Boyajian, *Portuguese Trade in Asia under the Habsburgs, 1580-1640*.

121. Punctual gestures of support for the limitation of blood purity enquiries by General Inquisitors, such as Niño de Guevara at the turn of the seventeenth century, later forced to resign, did not amount to serious political engagement with this issue; to my mind, the weight

of the Inquisition was on the side of blood purity. For a different approach see Hernández Franco, *Sangre limpia, sangre española*, 176.

122. Carlos Javier de Carlos Morales, "Los juros y el endeudamento de la Real Hacienda de Castilla, 1557–1627," in *Historia de la deuda pública en España, siglos XVI–XXI*, ed. Carlos Álvarez-Nogal and Francisco Comín Comín (Madrid: Instituto de Estudiso Fiscales, 2015), 37–66.

123. I am criticising here the view of Antonio Domínguez Ortiz, *Los judeoconversos en España y América* (Madrid: Istmo, 1971), 61–62.

124. Bethencourt, *The Inquisition*, 342.

125. António Joaquim Moreira, *História dos principais actos e procedimentos da Inquisição em Portugal* (1846), ed. João Palma-Ferreira (Lisbon: Imprensa Nacional, 1980), 145–279. The data for the early period is insufficient for my reconstitution. However, I could not disaggregate my data for periods of ten years and I needed to have a homogeneous source to compare with the seventeenth and eighteenth centuries. The increase in trials in these decades is correct.

126. Figueirôa-Rego, "*A honra alheia por um fio.*"

127. Pilar Huerga Criado, "El problema de la comunidad judeoconversa," in *Historia de la Inquisición en España y América*, ed. Joaquín Pérez Villanueva and Bartolomé Escandell Bonet, vol. 3 (Madrid: Biblioteca de Autores Cristianos, 2000), especially 489–490; Pilar Huerga Criado, *En la raya de Portugal: solidaridad y tensiones en la comunidad judeoconversa* (Salamanca: Universidad de Salamanca, 1994).

128. Ana Isabel López-Salazar, *Inquisición Portuguesa y Monarquia Hispánica en tiempos del perdón general de 1605* (Lisbon: Colibri, 2010), 42–43.

129. López-Salazar, *Inquisición Portuguesa*, 44–45. The cost of copying the record of the trial sent to Rome, 1,600 reis, was included in the bill: ANTT, Inquisição de Lisboa, Processo 14409, fl. 133r. The order of Pope Clement VII was issued on June 4, 1602, and the meek final compliance of the general council of the Inquisition of Portugal was only sent on August 13, 1604, when they knew that the general pardon was inevitable: ACDF, BB5a (not numbered, with long correspondence on this issue among many others).

130. ANTT, Inquisição de Lisboa, Processo 14409, fl. 2v.

131. ANTT, Inquisição de Lisboa, Processo 14409, fl. 5v.

132. ANTT, Inquisição de Lisboa, Processo 14409, fl. 7r–8r and 16r. Through Luzia Ferreira there are some insights into the small Japanese community in Portugal, since she was linked to another Japanese woman married in Lisbon.

133. ANTT, Inquisição de Lisboa, Processo 14409, fl. 10v, 12v

134. ANTT, Inquisição de Lisboa, Processo 14409, fl. 128r–130r. The promised groom, of Indian or Japanese origin, did not accept the 40,000 reis, or 100 cruzados, offered; he asked for a steady public job, which could not be found, and as a result he went to India.

135. ANTT, Inquisição de Lisboa, Processo 14409, fl. 131v–132r.

136. Case studied, and declarations transcribed, by Curto, "Stranger within at the Time of Quixote," 180–197.

137. António A. Marques de Almeida, "Dívida pública: Técnicas do Estado no período da União Ibérica," in *A União Ibérica e o mundo atlântico*, ed. Maria da Graça M. Ventura (Lisbon: Colibri, 1997). The sequence of actions related to the general pardon was established by Claude B. Stuczynski, "New Christian Political Leadership in Times of Crisis: The Pardon Negotiations of 1605," *Bar Ilan Studies in History* 5 (2007): 45–70.

138. López-Salazar, *Inquisición Portuguesa*, 17.

139. Memorandum on the New Christians involved in the request for a general pardon published without date by António Borges Coelho, *Inquisição de Évora—dos primórdios a 1668*, vol. 2 (Lisbon: Caminho, 1987), 203–208. As I shall explain in the text, the date is crucial; and it must be considered with caution. João Lúcio de Azevedo mentions another name in relation to this initiative, Fernão Ximenes (probably the one established in Florence), but, unusually, he does not provide the source: *História dos cristãos novos portugueses* (1921) (Lisbon: Clássica, 1975), 153.

140. Lúcio de Azevedo, *História dos cristãos novos portugueses*, 153–154.

141. Lúcio de Azevedo, *História dos cristão novos portugueses*, 155. Martim Álvares de Castro, a New Christian clerk of the customs of Lisbon, was called by the king to report on the financial situation of the kingdom, and he carried the petition presented by a group of New Christians: Juan Ignacio Pulido Serrano, "Las negociaciones de los cristianos nuevos portugueses en tiempos de Felipe III a la luz de algunos documentos inéditos (1598–1607)," *Sefarad* 66, no. 2 (July–December 2006): 345–375, esp. 351.

142. López-Salazar, *Inquisición*, 20; A. A. Marques de Almeida, "O perdão geral de 1605," in *Primeiras Jornadas de História Moderna*, vol. 2 (Lisbon: Centro de História da Universidade de Lisboa, 1989), 885–898.

143. António Borges Coelho, *Inquisição de Évora—dos primórdios a 1668*, vol. 2, 204.

144. López-Salazar, *Inquisición Portuguesa*, 72–80.

145. Stuczynski, "New Christian Political Leadership," 55.

146. López-Salazar, *Inquisición Portuguesa*, 24–25.

147. Until the late seventeenth century, the Church's hierarchy in Portugal largely resulted from previous appointments to the Holy Office, as I argued in *The Inquisition*, 147–148. This issue has been very well demonstrated by José Pedro Paiva, *Baluartes da fé e da disciplina: o enlace entre a Inquisição e os bispos em Portugal (1536–1750)* (Coimbra: Imprensa da Universidade de Coimbra, 2011).

148. Bethencourt, *The Inquisition*, 143; Giuseppe Marcocci and José Pedro Paiva, *História da Inquisição portuguesa, 1536–1821*, 139–141, in which the resistance of the general inquisitors to both reforming the tribunal and pardoning the New Christians are highlighted as motives for their forced resignation and replacement.

149. López-Salazar, *Inquisición Portuguesa*, 30–49.

150. Lúcio de Azevedo, *História dos cristão novos portugueses*, 162.

151. Marcocci, "Questioni di stile," 796.

152. Curto, "Stranger within at the Time of Quixote," 191–192, where the document is presented and extracts analysed.

153. ANTT, CGSO, Livro 314, fl. 51r–52v.

154. Boyajian, *Portuguese Trade in Asia*, 92–94. See also Stuczynski, "New Christian Political Leadership," 58; and Marques de Almeida, "O perdão geral de 1605," 885–898, esp. 890.

155. For the signs of opposition displayed, see I. S. Revah, "Le plaidoyer en faveur des 'Nouveaux-Chrétiens portugais du licence Martín González de Cellorigo [Madrid, 1619]," *Revue des Etudes Juives* 122 (1963): 279–318; and Stuczynski, "New Christian Political Leadership," 63; the long-lasting effect of this dispute is revealed by the opposition to the general pardon expressed by Melchior Gomes de Elvas and Rui Dias Angel much later, in 1622.

156. ANTT, CGSO, Livro 314, fl. 54r–v.

157. See António José Saraiva, *Inquisição e cristãos novos* (Porto: Inova, 1969), 301–302, in which he quotes Fr. Domingos de São Tomás, who denounced the fabrication of Jews by the Inquisition.

158. Borges Coelho, *Inquisição de Évora—dos primórdios a 1668*, vol. 2, 203–208.

159. Archivo Histórico Nacional (AHN), Inquisición, Legajo 171², n. 4², fl. 219r and 233r, in which Juan Núñez Sarabia declared that he was a nephew of Juan Núñez Correa (or João Nunes Correia) and would be buried in the chapel instituted by his uncle at the convent of Carmen Calzado in Madrid. See my analysis of Sarabia's trial in chapter 10.

160. ANTT, Inquisição de Lisboa, Processo 5287 and 5287-1 (detained in 1623 and again in 1627); this was the only trace I could find.

Part III

1. Teresa Sánchez Rivilla, "Inquisidores Generales y Consejeros," in *Historia de la Inquisición en España y America*, ed. Joaquín Pérez Villanjueva and Bartolomé Escandell Bonet (Madrid: Biblioteca de Autores Cristianos, 1993–2000), vol. 2, 715–30, and vol. 3, 298–437; Francisco Bethencourt, *The Inquisition*, 134–151; José Pedro Paiva, *Baluartes da fé e da disciplina: o enlace entre a Inquisição e os bispos em Portugal, 1536–1750* (Coimbra: Universidade

de Coimbra, 2011). The case of the bishop of Guarda, Afonso Furtado de Mendonça (1610–1615, then bishop of Coimbra, later archbishop of Braga, and finally archbishop of Lisbon and governor of Portugal), who regularly complained against the New Christian "infection" in his diocese and denounced many to the Inquisition, is a typical one; but it should be noted that he was the brother-in-law of a well-known New Christian, Martim de Crasto do Rio: see Giuseppe Marcocci and José Pedro Paiva, *História da Inquisição Portuguesa*, 161–163.

Chapter Nine: Conflict

1. Francisco Bethencourt, *The Inquisition: A Global History, 1478–1834*, trans. Jean Birrell (Cambridge: Cambridge University Press, 2009), 150.

2. Ana Isabel López-Salazar Cordes, *Inquisición Portuguesa y Monarquía Hispánica en tiempos del perdón general de 1605* (Lisbon: Colibri, 2010), 192. It had previously been the practice of the Inquisition of Valencia to rent out the confiscation of property from Moriscos; see Stephen Haliczer, *Inquisition and Society in the Kingdom of Valencia, 1478–1834* (Berkeley: University of California Press, 1990), 37, 43–44, 97, 263. The concordia of the Inquisition in 1555 for Aragon accepted the principle of renting out the confiscation of property from Moriscos; see Mercedes García-Arenal, "La Concordia de la Inquisición de Aragón del año 1555," in *Religion, identité et sources documentaires sur les Morisques Andalous*, ed. Abdeljelill Temimi, tome I (Tunis: Institut Supérieur de Documentation, 1984), 325–348.

3. Giuseppe Marcocci and José Pedro Paiva, *História da Inquisição Portuguesa, 1536–1821* (Lisbon: Esfera dos Livros, 2013), 146.

4. João de Figueirôa-Rego, *A honra alheia por um fio: os estatutos de limpeza de sangue nos espaços de expressão ibérica, (sécs. XVI–XVIII)* (Lisbon: Fundação Calouste Gulbenkian, 2011), 66–68.

5. Marcocci and Paiva, *História da Inquisição Portuguesa*, 173.

6. António Joaquim Moreira, *História dos principais actos e procedimentos da Inquisição em Portugal* (1846), ed. João Palma-Ferreira (Lisbon: Imprensa Nacional, 1980), 145–279.

7. Isaías da Rosa Pereira, *A Inquisição em Portugal. Séculos XVI–XVII—Período Filipino* (Lisbon: Vega, 1993), 73–83 (doc. 76, list ordered by the king in 1616, there were ten names); Marcocci and Paiva, *História da Inquisição Portuguesa*, 165–166.

8. ANTT, Conselho Geral do Santo Ofício, Papéis Avulsos, n. 2585, maço 7. The register is organised alphabetically and members of the same family appear under more than one letter, which means a significant degree of repetition.

9. ANTT, Conselho Geral do Santo Ofício, Papéis Avulsos, n. 2585, maço 7.

10. The relationship between Ana de Milão, Rodrigo de Andrade, procurator of the New Christians in Valladolid and Rome, and the Henrique Dias Milão family is clearly defined in the trial of Ana de Milão, session on genealogy; ANTT, Inquisição de Lisboa, Processo 14409, fl. 66r.

11. ANTT, Inquisição de Lisboa, Processo 6677, fl. 7v–8r (denunciation of the servant) and 94r–97r (genealogy of the accused, Henrique Dias Milão). On the convent, see *História dos mosteiros, conventos e casas religiosas de Lisboa* (ms. 1704–1708), ed. Durval Pires de Lima, tome II (Lisbon: Imprensa Municipal, 1972), 460.

12. ANTT, Inquisição de Lisboa, Processo 6677, fl. 7r–11r.

13. ANTT, Inquisição de Lisboa, Processo 6677, fl. 12r–13r.

14. ANTT, Inquisição de Lisboa, Processo 6677, fl. 192r–194r.

15. ANTT, Inquisição de Lisboa, Processos 279, 2499, 2523, 3338, 6671, 6984, 9389, and 3331.

16. ANTT, Inquisição de Lisboa, Processo 2523, fl. 226r–230r.

17. ANTT, Inquisição de Lisboa, Processo 2523, fl. 236r–v.

18. ANTT, Inquisição de Lisboa, Processo 6671, fl. 191r. The servant, Vitoria Dias, was 50 years old, born in China, but not knowing in which "kingdom or city," because she had been very little when she was enslaved, and she did not remember her parents. She was taken to Cochin and then to Goa, where Henrique Dias Milão bought her, taking her to Lisbon and there freeing her five years before the trial. She was baptised and received the chrism (or confirmation)

from the archbishop of Goa. She knew the Christian prayers, the commandments, and the mortal sins. She prepared food then considered Jewish, for instance, onions fried in olive oil with broad beans or chestnuts, and lettuce with vinegar, which in time became the defining food of people from Lisbon. Apparently, she remained loyal to the family until the end, assuming Jewish allegiance; ANTT, Inquisição de Lisboa, Processo 3331, fl. 47v–48r.

19. ANTT, Inquisição de Lisboa, Processo 6671, fl. 192r.

20. Florbela Veiga Frade, "A importância social e religiosa das famílias Milão-Dinis em Portugal e em Hamburgo," in *Portugal und das Heilige Römische Reich (16.–18. Jahrundert)*, ed. Alexandra Curvelo and Madalena Simões (Münster: Aschendorff, 2011), 181–204.

21. ANTT, Inquisição de Lisboa, Processo 6671, fl. 191r. *Gota coral* in Portuguese.

22. ANTT, Inquisição de Lisboa, Processo 2499, fl. 284r.

23. André Zysberg, *Les galériens: vies et destins de 60 000 forçats sur les galères de France, 1680–1748* (Paris: Seuil, 1991).

24. See, for example, the letter to the king on August 10, 1622: BNE, Mss. 718, fl. 249r–252r. There was an anonymous document written in 1623, which has been analysed by Ana Isabel López-Salazar Codes, *Inquisición y Política. El gobierno del Santo Oficio en el Portugal de los Austrias (1578–1653)* (Lisbon: Universidade Católica Portuguesa, 2011), 61–68, in which the general inquisitor was accused of extensive corruption and the protection of wealthy New Christians. See also Marcocci and Paiva, *História da Inquisição Portuguesa*, 152, who identified one of the New Christians allegedly under protection as Manuel Gomes de Elvas. If this is true, it would not be incompatible with harsh collective persecution; it would only raise the price for individual protection.

25. There are references in Fernanda Olival, *D. Filipe II de cognome o Pio* (Lisbon: Círculo de Leitores, 2008), 300–301, 314–315, and particularly in López-Salazar Codes, *Inquisición y Política*, 70–71.

26. BL, Egerton, Ms 1132, fl. 22r; BL, Egerton, Ms 1131, fl. 11v. These amounts, signed by viceroy Marquis of Alenquer, were forgotten in Madrid; after years of debate the royal counsellors would only recognise 70,000 cruzados received from the Inquisition and customs rents.

27. BL, Egerton, Ms 1131, fl. 11r (comment by a member of the Council of Portugal in Madrid).

28. López-Salazar Codes, *Inquisición y Política*, 71. The pressure to find money to finance the royal court was constant during the last years of the reign of Philip III, including for the king's own expenses. This led to placing the confiscation of property during the wave of persecution in Porto under the control of a judge from the tribunal of *Relação*. The pressure did not lessen in the reign of Philip IV, but was directed towards the provisioning of the fleet of the *carreira da Índia*. See the series of documents published by Rosa Pereira, *Inquisição em Portugal*, 94–110, 117–124.

29. The case of Paulo Lopes da Cunha, who denounced thirty associates, was mentioned by Christopher Ebert, *Between Empires: Brazilian Sugar in the Early Atlantic Economy, 1580–1630* (Leiden: Brill, 2008), 67.

30. ANTT, Inquisição de Coimbra, Processos 1013 (António da Fonseca), 1329 (João Baptista), 1820 (Sérgio Lopes Pinheiro), 2379 (Francisco de Almeida), 2418 (Baltasar Fernandes Mendes), 2885 (Álvaro Eanes), 3217 (Pedro Aires Vitória), 5385 (Paulo Lopes da Cunha), 6900 (Álvaro Gomes Bravo), 8970 (Manuel de Andrade), 2894 (Luís da Cunha), 3901 (António Dias da Cunha), 3925 (Inês Henriques), 5439 (Gracia do Espírito Santo), 10185 (Lopo Dias da Cunha), 2473 (Filipa da São Francisco), 2576 (Florença Dias, wife of Luis da Cunha), 4650 (Diogo de Pina), 5362 (Manuel da Fonseca), 5675 (Maria da Costa, daughter of Bento Costa Brandão and wife of Álvaro Gomes Bravo), 7437 (Gaspar da Fonseca), 8976-1 (Álvaro Velho), 5817 (Angela Cardoso, wife of Baltasar Fernandes Mendes), 640 (Francisco Machado, son of Angela Henriques and a previously deceased husband, Francisco Machado). For some reason, two of the accused were sent to Lisbon: ANTT, Inquisição de Lisboa: 1418 (Cristóvão Lopes) and 13025 (Angela Henriques). The trial of Cristóvão Lopes provides an excellent case study of a wealthy international merchant based in Viana, north of Porto, with an astonishing inventory of property and a remarkable list of local and regional debtors,

including his father-in-law, the famous Lopo Dias da Cunha, who still owed Lopes part of his daughter's dowry.

31. BNE, Ms. 718, fl. 251r–252v (the opinion of the Council of Portugal in 1618); on the royal decision of resolution of 1627 and the Inquisition's opposition to implementation, see López-Salazar Codes, *Inquisición y Política*, 346–347, 353.

32. BNE, Mss. 718, fl. 257v–260v (letter from the Council of Portugal to Fr. Luis de Aliaga, dated March 3, 1618).

33. BNE, Mss. 718, fl. 255r.

34. Olival, *Filipe II, de cognome "o Pio."* This request was repeated in different *cortes* after the restoration of independence, particularly by the ecclesiastic order.

35. Martín González de Cellorigo, *Alegación en que se funda la justicia y merced que algunos particulares del Reyno de Portugal piden a S. M.* (Madrid, 1619): only known copy available in the BL, Egerton, Ms 343, fl. 291–338. It was reprinted by I. S. Révah, "Le playdoyer en faveur des 'nouveaux-chrétiens portugais du licencié Martín González de Cellorigo (Madrid, 1619)," *Revue des Études Juives*, 4th series, 122, no. 2 (1963): 279–398.

36. Révah, "Le playdoyer," 328. It is curious to note that the ideal of happiness, included in the first article of the American Declaration of Independence, inspired by Muratori, had already been expressed by Martín González Cellorigo.

37. Révah, "Le playdoyer," 335–336.

38. Révah, "Le playdoyer," 342.

39. Révah, "Le playdoyer," 337–340.

40. Révah, "Le playdoyer," 340–341, 346–353.

41. Révah, "Le playdoyer," 357–360.

42. Révah, "Le playdoyer," 361–364.

43. Révah, "Le playdoyer," 364–367.

44. Révah, "Le playdoyer," 367–378.

45. Révah, "Le playdoyer", 386–398.

46. The full consultation is in AGS, Secretarias Provinciales, Libro 1552, fl. 555r–579r.

47. AGS, Secretarias Provinciales, Libro 1552, fl. 559r.

48. AGS, Secretarias Provinciales, Libro 1552, fl. 559r–560r.

49. AGS, Secretarias Provinciales, Libro 1552, fl. 561r–562r.

50. AGS, Secretarias Provinciales, Libro 1552, fl. 563r–565v (the most articulate opinion).

51. AGS, Secretarias Provinciales, Libro 1552, fl. 578v. In the original Portuguese: "Nao há cousa mais adequada ao entendimento que fazer a diferença de juizo onde acha diferença de razao e diferença de fundamento."

52. AGS, Secretarias Provinciales, Libro 1552, fl. 566r–578v.

53. ANTT, Manuscritos da Livraria, 1111, doc. 75.

54. ANTT, Manuscritos da Livraria, 1111, doc. 82.

55. Juan E. Gelabert, *La bolsa del rey: rey, reino y fisco en Castilia (1498-1648)* (Barcelona: Critica, 1997). I thank Ana Isabel López-Salazar for this information.

56. Hugo Ribeiro da Silva, *O Clero Catedralício Português e os Equilíbrios Soviais do Poder (1564-1670)* (Lisbon: Universidade Católica Portuguesa, 2013), 151–152.

57. Révah, "Le playdoyer"; Marcocci and Paiva, *História da Inquisição portuguesa*, 151–152.

58. António José Teixeira, *António Homem e a Inquisição* (Coimbra, 1895); António Baião, "O sábio canonista doutor António Homem (1616-1624)," in *Episódios dramáticos da Inquisição*, 2nd ed., vol. 1 (Lisbon: Seara Nova, 1936), 109–129; Joaquim Romero Magalhães, "A universidade e a Inquisição," in *História da Universidade em Portugal* (Coimbra: Universidade de Coimbra, 1997), 971–988; Marcocci and Paiva, *História da Inquisição Portuguesa*, 166–168.

59. ANTT, Inquisição de Lisboa, Processo 15421. The sentence is, unusually, in fl. 8r–17v. The trial was reorganised due to its uncommon size, but what is interesting is the precise way denunciations were patiently accumulated, how ludicrous accusations concerning ceremonies were passed on, and how enquiries on sodomy were formulated and sent to local commissioners.

60. BNP, Códice 167, fl. 54v.

61. BNP, Códice 865, fl. 69r.

62. ANTT, Inquisição de Coimbra, Processo 3901 (letter added to the trial).

63. This decision was reinforced in 1623: see João Pedro Ribeiro, *Indice chronologico remissivo da legislação portuguesa*, part 4 (Lisbon: Academia Real das Sciencias, 1807), 168, 173.

64. Elvira Cunha de Azevedo Mea, "1621–1634. Coimbra. O sagrado e o profano em choque," *Revista de História das Ideias* 9, no. 2 (1987): 229–248.

65. BNP, códice 865, fl. 71r–88v (two versions, the second with the sermon and the supplementary sentences read at the tribunal for some condemned priests).

66. António Baião, "A devassa de 1628 à Inquisição de Coimbra," in *Episódios dramáticos da Inquisição*, vol. 1, 201–240. The only Miguel Gomes I found in records of those years was sentenced in Lisbon but not excommunicated. Did the witness intend to indicate Miguel d'Almeida, executed in effigy at the auto da fé of November 26, 1623, in Coimbra? BNP, códice 865, fl. 69v–70r.

67. Baião, "A devassa de 1628"; for the career of Sebastião de Matos de Noronha, see Fortunato de Almeida, *História da Igreja em Portugal* (1930), ed. Damião Peres, vol. 2 (Porto: Livraria Civilização, 1968), 603.

68. Baião, "António Homem (1616–1624)"; Antonio Borges Coelho, *Historia de Portugal, vol. 5, Os Filipes* (Lisbon: Caminho, 2015), 170; López-Salazar Codes, *Inquisición y Política*, 65–66.

69. John H. Elliott "El programa de Olivares y los movimientos de 1640," in *La España de Felipe IV. El gobierno de la monarquia, la crisis de 1640 y el fracaso de la hegemonia europea*, ed. Francisco Tomás y Valiente, vol. 25, *Historia de España R. Menendez Pidal* (Madrid: Espasa-Calpe, 1982), 333–523. See also John H. Elliott, *The Count-Duke of Olivares: The Statesman in an Age of Decline* (New Haven, CT: Yale University Press, 1986); Antonio Feros, *Kingship and Favoritism in the Spain of Philip III, 1598–1621* (Cambridge: Cambridge University Press, 2000).

70. João Lúcio de Azevedo, *História dos cristãos novos portugueses* (1921) (Lisbon: Livraria Clássica, 1975), 182.

71. Juan Hernández Franco, *Sangre limpia, sangre española. El debate de los estatutos de limpieza (siglos XV-XVII)* (Madrid: Cátedra, 2011).

72. BL, Egerton, Ms 1133, fl. 158r.

73. João Baptista d'Este, *Dialogo entre discipulo e mestre catechizante* (Lisbon: Geraldo da Vinha, 1621), reprinted in 1674, during the process of the suspension of the Portuguese Inquisition. On anti-Jewish literature, see José Alberto Rodrigues da Silva Tavim, "Jews in the Diaspora with Sepharad in the Mirror: Ruptures, Relations and Forms of Identity: A Theme Examined through Three Cases," *Jewish History* 25 (2011): 175–205; for a global approach, see Bruno Feitler, *The Imaginary Synagogue: Anti-Jewish Literature in the Portuguese Early Modern World (15th-18th Centuries)* (Leiden: Brill, 2015).

74. Vicente da Costa Matos, *Breve discurso contra a heretica perfidia do judaismo* (Lisbon: Pedro Craesbeeck, 1622), extended in 1623 and 1625, reprinted in 1668.

75. Fernão Ximenes de Aragão, *Doutrina catholica para a instrução e confirmação dos fieis e extinção das seitas supersticiosas e em particular do judaismo* (Lisbon: Pedro Craesbeeck, 1625), reprinted in 1628 by the same publisher. The failed request of the Ximenes de Aragão family is very well analysed by Ana Isabel López-Salazar, " 'The Purity of Blood Privileges for Honors and Positions': The Spanish Crown and the Ximenes de Aragão Family," *Journal of Levantine Studies* 6 (2016): 177–201, esp. 192.

76. Fr. Luís da Apresentação, *Demonstración evangélica y destierro de ignorancias judaicas* (Lisbon: Mateus Pinheiro, 1631). See Marcocci and Paiva, *História da Inquisição Portuguesa*, 171–172.

77. See the analysis by Claude Stuczynski, "Anti-Rabbinic Texts and Converso Identities: Fernão Ximenes de Aragão's *Catholic Doctrine*," in *The Conversos and Moriscos in Late Medieval Spain and Beyond*, ed. Kevin Ingram and Juan Ignacio Pulido Serrano, vol. 3, *Displaced Persons* (Leiden: Brill, 2015), 63–94.

78. Lúcio de Azevedo, *História dos cristãos novos*, 199–200.

79. The convoluted arguments presented by the general inquisitor and general council, mixing pernicious contamination of other countries, excessive severity against innocents, loss of denunciations and testimonies, and impoverishment of the country, show where the interest lay. The general council even suggested that the expulsion was supported by New Christians themselves, and they would pay double what they had paid for the general pardon. See the set of documents published by Elkan N. Adler, "Documents sur les marranes d'Espagne et du Portugal sous Philippe IV," *Revue des Études Juives* 48 (1904), particularly 11–12, 22–26.

80. This estimate from the Inquisition, written on September 30, 1624, was published by Lúcio de Azevedo, *História dos cristãos novos*, 471–472.

81. BL, Egerton, Ms. 1131, fl. 30r–32v.

82. António Borges Coelho, *Clérigos, mercadores, judeus e fidalgos* (Lisbon: Caminho, 1994).

83. BL, Egerton, Ms 1131, fl. 32v, consultation annotated and signed by Pedro Álvares Pereira on January 7, 1622.

84. Duarte Gomes Solis, *Discursos sobre los comercios de las dos Indias* (Madrid, 1622), fl. 1v and 109r (read at BNE, R8589). This author published another text in 1628, *Alegación en favor de la compañia de la India Oriental y comercios ultramarinos que de nuevo se instituyo en el reyno de Portugal*, in which he gave advice on investing in the new company, particularly in precious stones and Indian textiles made of cotton. He also insisted on founding a university (or guild) of merchants and lamented the decline of trade visible in the lower rents at the centre of Lisbon and Antwerp, while Amsterdam had quadrupled its trade.

85. Gomes Solis, *Discursos*, fl. 2v–5v; for the quote fl. 85v.

86. Gomes Solis, *Discursos*, fl. 6r.

87. Gomes Solis, *Discursos*, fl. 11v–13v.

88. Gomes Solis, *Discursos*, fl. 136r–v and 164r.

89. Jerónimo de Ceballos, *Arte real para el buen gouierno de los reyes y principes* (Toledo, 1623) in Biblioteca Digital Hispánica. See Francisco J. Aranda, *Jerónimo de Ceballos, un hombre grave para la república: Vida y obra de un hidalgo del saber en la España del siglo de oro* (Cordoba: Universidad de Cordoba, 2001).

90. BL, Egerton, Ms 1133, fl. 408r–410r (quote fl. 408r, my translation). It is this petition that was used to reconstitute the details of the Caldeira family given in chapter 7.

Chapter Ten: Politics

1. See Antonio Domínguez Ortiz, *Política y hacienda de Felipe IV* (Madrid: Editorial de Derecho Financiero, 1960); James C. Boyajian, *Portuguese Bankers at the Court of Spain, 1626–1650*.

2. Norbert Elias and John L. Scotson, *The Established and the Outsiders: A Sociological Enquiry into Community Problems* (1965), ed. Cas Wounters (Dublin: University College Dublin Press, 2008).

3. Marcocci and Paiva, *História da Inquisição Portuguesa, 1536–1821* (Lisbon: Esfera dos Livros, 2013), 154. This decision responds to a proposal by Duarte Fernandes and Manuel Rodrigues de Elvas, representatives of the New Christians, in 1621: Marcocci and Paiva, *História da Inquisição Portuguesa*, 151.

4. António Joaquim Moreira, *História dos principais actos e procedimentos da Inquisição em Portugal* (1846), ed. João Palma-Ferreira (Lisbon: Imprensa Nacional, 1980), 145–279.

5. António de Oliveira, "O motim dos estudantes de Coimbra contra os cristãos-novos em 1630," *Biblos* 57 (1981): 597–627.

6. A record of the sentence can be found at ANTT, Feitos Findos, Diversos, Maço 17, n. 1, Caixa 17. This case and the sermons by António Vieira related to it have been very well studied by Claude Stuczynski, "Host Desecration, Conversos and 'Philosemitism': Father António Vieira's Sermons at Santa Engrácia," *Jewish Quarterly Review* 112, no. 1 (2022): 89–118.

7. ANTT, Inquisição de Lisboa, Processo 10536.

8. João Lúcio de Azevedo, *História dos cristãos novos portugueses* (1921) (Lisbon: Livraria Clássica, 1975), 202.

9. ANTT, Inquisição de Lisboa, Processo 10536, fl. 7v–8v. Duarte Nunes da Veiga, condemned in absentia, was executed in effigy at the auto da fé in Lisbon, September 5, 1638; ANTT, Inquisição de Lisboa, Processo 7193. The famous Duarte Nunes da Costa (or Jacob Curiel), settled in Hamburg and married to a niece of António Faleiro, was condemned in effigy in the same year after a similar trial (Diogo Lima, then twenty-five years old, also denounced the accused at this trial); ANTT, Inquisição de Lisboa, Processo 7192.

10. Manuscript copies of the lists of condemned were disseminated: the one consulted here is at the University of Pennsylvania, Rare Books and Manuscripts Library, Ms. Coll. 218 consulted May 25, 2019, at http://dla.library.upenn.edu/dla/medren/pageturn.html?id =MEDREN_9923641013503681&rotation=0&currentpage=6.

11. See also Juan Ignacio Pulido Serrano, *Os judeus e a Inquisição no tempo dos Filipes* (Lisbon: Campo da Comunicação, 2007), 167–170, who highlights the impact of these events on royal policies.

12. A New Christian protest concerning the massacres, which had been fuelled by preaching, was presented in Madrid to the king; see Elkan N. Adler, "Documents sur les marranes d'Espagne et du Portugal sous Philippe IV," 3. See also António de Oliveira, "O motim dos estudantes de Coimbra."

13. João Lúcio de Azevedo, *História dos cristãos novos portugueses*, 204.

14. Juan Ignacio Pulido Serrano, *Injurias a Cristo: Religión, política y anti-judaismo en el siglo XVII. Análisis de las corrientes antijudías en la edad moderna* (Alcalá de Henares: Universidad de Alcalá, 2002).

15. AHN, Leg. 171, exp. 4, and Leg. 171², exp. 4² (continuation of the trial).

16. Julio Caro Baroja, *Los judíos en la España moderna y contemporánea* (1961), 3rd ed., vol. 2 (Madrid: Istmo, 1986), 69. This remark does not challenge the extraordinary information left by Caro Baroja, but we need to overcome the predominant bias in the analysis of trials.

17. Antonio Domínguez Ortiz, "El proceso inquisitorial de Juan Núñez Sarabia, banquero de Felipe IV," *Hispania* 15 (1955): 359–381. The remark from the previous note is valid for this extraordinary historian.

18. AHN, Leg. 171, exp. 4, fl. 12r–v.

19. Teresa Sánchez Rivilla, "Inquisidores generales y consejeros de la Suprema: documentación biográfica," in *História de la Inquisición en España y América*, vol. 3, *Temas y problemas*, ed. Joaquín Pérez Villanueva and Bartolomé Escandell Bonet (Madrid: Centro de Estudios Inquisitoriales, 2000), 228–437, esp. 282–284.

20. Sánchez Rivilla, "Inquisidores generales y consejeros," 283.

21. Juan Ignacio Gutiérrez Nieto, "La limpieza de sangre," in *Dogmatismo y intolerancia*, ed. Enrique Martínez Ruiz and Magdalena de Pazzis Pi Corrales (Madrid: Actas, 1997), 33–48.

22. I agree with this thesis by Bernardo J. López Bellinchón, "Olivares contra los portugueses. Inquisición, conversos y guerra económica," in *Historia de la Inquisición en España y América*, vol. 3, 499–530.

23. AHN, Leg. 171, exp. 4, fl. 4r.

24. AHN, Leg. 171, exp. 4, fl. 142r–143v. Sarabia insisted on the case in the following years. The inquisitors even transcribed civil cases related to Sarabia, such as the case of Geronima de Sandoval, who extorted money from Sarabia during several years, and when he refused to pay more she accused him of murdering her husband: AHN, Leg. 171, exp. 4, fl. 151r–152v. This case was apparently dismissed by the civil court, as were several others against Sarabia; AHN, Leg. 171², exp. 4², fl. 209r and 277r.

25. AHN, Leg. 171, exp. 4, fl. 6r–v and 196r. The inquisitors in Coimbra managed to dig up an old denunciation from 1620 by Rodrigo Dias, then twenty-two years old, who declared he had fasted with the brothers Sarabia on his way from Madrid to the fair of Guadalupe eight years earlier, when he was fourteen years old.

26. AHN, Leg. 171, exp. 4, fl. 88r–v: Álvaro Mendes, who had settled in Pisco, in proceedings in Lima denounced his uncle, Juan Núñez Correa, and Juan Núñez Sarabia, among around fifty other people.

27. Caro Baroja, "El proceso de Bartolome Febo o Febos" (1963), in *Vidas poco paralelas* (Madrid: Turner, 1981), 13–49.

28. AHN, Leg. 171, exp. 4, fl.20r–84v, an enormous file with details of the enquiry.

29. A record of the enquiry conducted by Juan Bautista Villadiego in France was even printed, in 1636, possibly a unique case in the history of the Inquisition; BL, Egerton Ms 343, fl. 276r–288v.

30. AHN, Leg. 171², exp. 4² (fourth bundle unnumbered). The length of torture is unusual, even by inquisitorial standards.

31. AHN, Leg. 171², exp. 4² (last pages unnumbered).

32. AHN, Leg. 171², exp. 4², fl. 232r–233v, 235v–237r.

33. Angelo Adriano Faria de Assis, *João Nunes. Um rabi escatológico na Nova Lusitania. Sociedade colonial e Inquisição no nordeste quinhentista* (São Paulo: Alameda, 2011). Rodrigo de Andrade was married to Ana de Milão, and Jerónimo Henriques, son of the owner of a sugar mill in Brazil, would escape to Amsterdam in 1609 to become Joseph Cohen. See also Jesús Carrasco Vázquez, "Comercio y finanzas de una familia sefardita portuguesa: Los Núñez Correa," in *Familia, Religión y Negocio. El sefardismo en las relaciones entre el mundo ibérico y los Paeses Bajos en la Edad Moderna*, ed. Jaime Contreras, Bernardo García García, and Juan Ignacio Pulido Serrano (Madrid: Fundación Carlos de Amberes, 2003), 365–372.

34. AHN, Leg. 171², exp. 4², fl. 233r–v.

35. AHN, Leg. 171², exp. 4², fl. 375r–376r, and in another volume sewn to this one, with separate page numbers, fl 243r (the torture is in the last section, which is without page numbers).

36. AHN, Leg. 171², exp. 4² (final section, at the very end, without page numbers). Juan Núñez Sarabia could still manage a subtle irony: "punctiliously."

37. ANTT, Inquisição de Lisboa, Processo 8132, fl. 150r.

38. The attitude of the Count-Duke of Olivares concerning the Inquisition was never clear. There is the case of his informer and financier, Jacob Cansino, a Jew from Oran, who tried to convince Luis de Acosta, in 1637, to denounce the major asentista Manuel Cortizos to the Inquisition, which Luis refused to do, and was detained himself; Caro Baroja, *Los judíos en la España moderna y contemporánea*, vol. 2, 123.

39. Although Sarabia, in his defence, listed several services to the king—namely, lending money without interest for the journey to Aragon in 1626, 40,000 ducados; AHN, Leg. 171², exp. 4², fl. 235r.

40. AHN, Inquisición, Leg. 146¹, exp. 4. The trial is not well organised, the order of detention is in fl. 117r.

41. AHN, Inquisición, Leg. 146¹ exp. 4, fl. 264r and 265r.

42. AHN, Inquisición, Leg. 146¹ exp. 4, fl. 322v–323v.

43. AHN, Inquisición, Leg. 146¹ exp. 4, fl. 277r–v.

44. AHN, Inquisición, Leg. 146¹ exp. 4, fl. 324v–328r. Sentence given April 15, 1636, three years after detention.

45. AHN, Inquisición, Leg. 146¹ exp. 4, fl. 25v.

46. AHN, Inquisición, Leg. 146¹ exp. 4, fl. 123v, 130v, 138r.

47. AHN, Inquisición, Leg. 146¹ exp. 4, fl. 141r–146v.

48. AHN, Inquisición, Leg. 171, exp. 4, fl. 198v; idem, Leg. 146¹, exp. 4, fl. 122v.

49. ANTT, Inquisição de Évora, Processo 6518, particularly fl. 11r–13v (genealogy) and fl. 144r–148v (torture and sentence).

50. ANTT, Inquisição de Lisboa, Processo 11559, particularly fl. 18v–21r and 139r–140r.

51. Printed document attributed to Garcia de Yllán: BNE, VE/60/18.

52. Garcia de Yllán: BNE, VE/60/18.

53. Maurits A. Ebben, "Garcia de Yllán: A Merchant in Silver, Bread and Bullets, and a Broker in Art," in *Double Agents: Cultural and Political Brokerage in Early Modern Europe* (Leiden: Brill, 2011), 125–146.

54. Fernand Braudel, *La Méditerranée et le monde méditerranéen à l'époque de Philippe II* (1949) 6th ed., vol. 2 (Paris: Armand Colin, 1985), 68–75; the specific racialised situation of Iberia is missing in Braudel's analysis.

55. BNE, Mss. 2364, fl. 88r–93r, *Memorial sobre la nobleza*. It is inserted in *Sucesos de los años de 1632 y 1633*. This complaint has a long background; see Juan Ignacio Gutiérrez Nieto, "Los conversos y la limpieza de sangre en España del siglo XVI," *Torre de los Lujanes*, 26 (1994): 153–166.

56. BNE, Mss. 2364, fl. 88r–93r, *Memorial sobre la nobleza.*

57. Francisco de Quevedo, *Execración contra los Judios* (ms. 1633), ed. Fernando Cabo Aseguinolaza and Santiago Fernández Mosquera (Barcelona: Critica, 1996), quote on p. 29. This abject language resurfaces in the *Memorial de Francisco Quevedo contra el Conde-Duque de Olivares dado al rey Don Felipe IV*, published in *Seminario erudito que comprehende varias obras ineditas, criticas, morales, instructivas, politicas, historicas y jocosas de nuestros mejores autores antiguos y modernos*, ed. Antonio Valladares de Sottomayor, vol. 15 (Madrid: Blas Roman, 1788), 215–245, (after the publication of a paper by Agustin Salucio on the statutes of blood purity), 128–214.

58. *La isla de los monopantos* was included in *La hora de todos y la fortuna con sesos* (1650) ed. Lía Schwartz (Madrid: Castalia, 2009), 323–344; see the introduction by the editor.

59. BNE, Manuscritos, VE/35/86.

60. BNE, Manuscritos, VE/35/86.

61. António de Oliveira, *Poder e oposição política em Portugal no tempo filipino, 1580–1640* (Lisbon: Difel, 1991); Jean-Frédéric Schaub, *Le Portugal au temps du comte-duc de Olivares (1621–1640): Le conflit de juridictions comme exercice de la politique* (Madrid: Casa de Velázquez, 2001).

62. Aurélio de Oliveira, *Os motins de Vila Real em 1636* (Porto, 1973); de Oliveira, *Poder e oposição política.*

63. Vitorino Magalhães Godinho, "1580 e a Restauração," in *Ensaios II* (Lisbon: Sá da Costa, 1968), 255–291.

64. Fernando Dores Costa, *A guerra da Restauração, 1641–1668* (Lisbon: Horizonte, 2004); Rafael Valladares, *La rebelión de Portugal, 1640–1680: Guerra, conflicto y poderes en la monarquía hispánica* (Valladolid: Junta de León y Castilla, 1998).

65. It is a pity that the issue of New Christians has not been considered (nor have those of the Moriscos, Africans, and Native Americans) by Tamar Herzog, *Defining Nations. Immigrants and Citizens in Early Modern Spain and Spanish America* (New Haven, CT: Yale University Press, 2003), otherwise a very good book. For the Portuguese New Christians in Madrid, see the documents published by Juan Ignacio Pulido Serrano, "Portuguese avencindados en Madrid en la edad moderna, 1593–1646," in *Los extrangeros en la España Moderna*, ed. Maria Begoña Villar Garcia and Pilar Pezzi Cristóbal (Malaga: Universidad de Malaga, 2003), 543–554.

66. This picture is far from being black and white, because in some cases the consulado protected foreigners from enquiry, as Herzog points out in *Defining Nations*, 101. It was a matter, again, of the established versus outsiders; the latter depended on local support to overcome barriers.

67. On the specific issue of naturalizations related to trade, see Antonio Domínguez Ortiz, "La concesión de 'naturalezas para comerciar en Indias' en el siglo XVII," *Revista de Indias* 76 (1959): 227–240.

68. Archivo General de Indias (AGI), Contratación, Legajo 50A (limited page numbering, this information is in file 1).

69. AGI, Contratación, Legajo 50A, files 1, 38; AGI, Contratación, Legajo 596B (without page numbers).

70. AGI, Contratación, Legajo 596B.

71. AGI, Contratación, Legajo 50A, n. 10.

72. AGI, Contratación, Legajo 50A, n. 15.

73. AGI, Contratación, Legajo 50A, n. 19.

74. AGI, Contratación, Legajo 50A, n. 22.

75. AGI, Contratación, Legajo 50A, n. 24, and Legajo 596B

76. AGI, Contratación, Legajo 50A, n. 26.

77. AGI, Contratación, Legajo 50A, n. 28.

78. AGI, Contratación, Legajo 596B (without page numbering).

79. AGI, Contratación, Legajo 596B. The case of Domingos de Herrera seems to be the only one related to New Christians' naturalization against loans mentioned by Herzog, *Defining Nations*, 104, although she did not know his social status.

80. AGI, Contratación, Legajo 50A, n. 29 and 33.

81. AGI, Contratación, Legajo 596B.

82. AGI, Contratación, Legajo 50A, n. 30 and Legajo 596B.

83. AGI, Contratación, Legajo 50A, n. 32.

84. AGI, Contratación, Legajo 596B.

85. AGI, Contratación, Legajo 596B.

86. AGI, Contratación, Legajo 596B.

87. For all these cases, AGI, Contratación, Legajo 596B.

88. AGI, Contratación, Legajo 50B (without foliation).

89. Paulino Castañeda Delgado and Pilar Hernández Aparicio, *La Inquisición de Lima*, tome I, *(1570–1635)* (Madrid: Deimos, 1989), 421–424.

90. Castañeda Delgado and Hernández Aparicio, *La Inquisición de Lima*, tome I, 431.

91. The best analysis of Manuel Bautista Pérez's and Francisco Maldonado de Silva's trials is by Nathan Wachtel, *La foi du souvenir. Labyrinthes marranes* (Paris: Seuil, 2001), 49–101.

92. For the auto da fé and estimates of New Christians prosecuted, see Paulino Castañeda Delgado and Pilar Hernández Aparicio, *La Inquisición de Lima*, tome II, *(1635–1696)* (Madrid: Deimos, 1995), 387–415.

93. Manuel Bautista Pérez, like many other New Christians, cut his teeth as a businessman in Guinea, where in 1618 he took a significant cargo of 509 slaves to Cartagena de Indias and then to Lima, a transaction that formed the basis of his wealth; see Wachtel, *La foi du souvenir*, 81–82. For a deep analysis of Bautista Pérez's slave trade, see Linda Newson and Susin Minchin, *From Capture to Sale: The Portuguese Slave Trade to Spanish South America in the Early Seventeenth Century* (Leiden: Brill, 2007).

94. José Toribio Medina, *Historia del tribunal del Santo Oficio de la Inquisición en México* (1905) reprint (Mexico: UNAM, 1987), 181–209; Solange Alberro, *Inquisición y sociedad en México, 1571–1700* (Mexico: Fondo de Cultura Económica, 1988), 417–454, 533–585.

95. For Cartagena de Indias see José Toríbio Medina, *Historia del tribunal del Santo Oficio de la Inquisición de Cartagena de Indias* (Santiago de Chile: Universo, 1899); María Cristina Navarrete Peláez, *La diaspora judeoconversa en Colombia siglos XVI y XVII* (Santiago de Cali: Universidad del Valle, 2010).

96. Stuart Schwartz, "Panic in the Indies: The Portuguese Threat to the Spanish Empire, 1640–1650," *Colonial Latin American Review* 2, no. 1–2 (1993): 165–187.

97. Solange Alberro, *Inquisición y sociedad en México*, has one of the most penetrating analyses of the hybrid New Christian communities in the New World.

98. Caro Baroja, *Los judíos en la España moderna y contemporánea*, vol. 2, 78–81.

99. Markus Schreiber, "Cristianos nuevos de Madrid ante la Inquisición de Cuenca (1650–1670)," in *Historia de la Inquisición en España y América*, vol. 3, 531–556, esp. 545.

100. Stuart Schwartz, "The Voyage of the Vassals: Royal Power, Noble Obligations, and Merchant Capital Before the Portuguese Restoration of Independence 1624–1640," *American Historical Review* 96, no. 3 (1991): 735–762; Anita Novinsky, *Cristãos Novos na Bahia* (São Paulo: Perspectiva, 1972); Anita Novinsky, *Inquisição: prisioneiros do Brasil, séculos XVI–XIX* (São Paulo: Expressão e Cultura, 1972).

101. James Boyajian, *Portuguese Trade in Asia under the Habsburgs, 1580–1640* (Baltimore: Johns Hopkins University Press, 1993), 179.

102. Francisco Manuel de Melo, *Tácito Portuguez. Vida e Morte, Ditos e Feytos de el Rey Dom João IV*, ed. Afrânio Peixoto, et al. (Rio de Janeiro: Academia Brasileira das Letras, 1940), 87–95; Luís de Meneses, *História de Portugal Restaurado*, vol. 1, book 5 (Lisbon: João Galrão, 1679), 273–275, 287.

103. António Baião, "El-rei D. João IV e a Inquisição," *Anais da Academia Portuguesa da História*, series 1, no. 6 (1942): 6–70.

104. Enriqueta Vila Vilar, "La sublevación de Portugal y la trata de negros" *Iberoamerikanisches Archiv* 2, no. 3 (1976): 171–192, quote on 184.

105. ANTT, Inquisição de Lisboa, Processo 8132. The best study is still that of António Baião, "O banqueiro Duarte Silva," *Episódios dramáticos da Inquisição*, vol. 2, 287–401.

106. António Vieira, *Cartas Diplomáticas*, ed. Carlos Maduro (Lisbon: Círculo de Leitores, 2013), 213 (letter dated February 3, 1648).

107. António Baião, "O banqueiro Duarte Silva," 300–301.

108. ANTT, Inquisição de Lisboa, Processo 5407 (Francisco Dias da Silva), Processo 8133 (Catarina da Silva), Processo 11752 (Jorge Dias Brandão), and Processo 4107 (Rodrigo Aires Brandão).

109. For the best study on this issue, see Leonor Freire Costa, *O transporte no Atlântico e a Companhia Geral do Comércio do Brasil (1580-1663)* (Lisbon: CNCDP, 2002).

110. ANTT, Inquisição de Lisboa, Processo 8132 and 8132–1 (parallel trial on obstruction of inquisitorial action and breach of secrecy).

111. António Baião, "O banqueiro Duarte Silva," 369. Antonio de Moraes Silva, *Diccionario da lingua Portugueza*, tome II (Lisbon: Simão Thadeo Ferreira, 1789), 60 identifies *marrã* as a piglet that has just finished being suckled by its mother. The word was currently use in the seventeenth and eighteenth century.

112. ANTT, Inquisição de Lisboa, Processo 8132–1 (this was the second trial related to break of secrecy of the Inquisition).

113. ANTT, Inquisição de Lisboa, Processo 8132, fl. 387r–389r (sentence), 396r–403r (bail and petitions).

114. António Baião, "O banqueiro Duarte Silva," 389–401; the condition of son-in-law was unknown to Baião.

115. Rijksarchief Antwerpen-Beveren (RA-B), Protocollen, Staten en rekeningen, Ambrosius Sebille, 1677-1677, 3040, fl. 36r–v (presentation and opening of the will); Rijksarchief Antwerpen-Beveren (RA-B), Protocollen, Staten en rekeningen, Ambrosius Sebille, 1670-1677, 3047 (brief inventory).

Chapter Eleven: Business

1. James C. Boyajian, *Portuguese Trade under the Habsburgs, 1580-1640* (Baltimore: Johns Hopkins University Press, 1993), 81–82.

2. Isabel dos Guimarães Sá, *Quando o rico se faz pobre: misericórdias, caridade e poder no império português, 1500-1800* (Lisbon: CNCDP, 1997).

3. Boyajian, *Portuguese Trade under the Habsburgs*, 113; for an overall view, see Femme Gaastra, *The Dutch East India Company: Expansion and Decline* (Zutphen: Walburg Pers, 2003).

4. Boyajian, *Portuguese Trade under the Habsburgs*, 225, 241.

5. Francesca Trivellato, *The Familiarity of Strangers: The Sephardic Diaspora, Livorno, and Cross-Cultural Trade in the Early Modern Period* (New Haven, CT: Yale University Press, 2009), 36–37.

6. Luís Figueiredo Falcão, *Livro em que se contem toda a fazenda e real patrimonio dos reinos de Portugal, India e ilhas adjacentes* (Lisbon: Imprensa Nacional, 1859), 122; Boyajian, *Portuguese Trade under the Habsburgs*, 201.

7. Charles R. Boxer, *The Christian Century in Japan, 1549-1650* (1951), reprint (Manchester: Carcanet, 1993), 425. The suggested date of death, 1617, is disputable, because all the documents concerning the trip and the promise of a job for his grandson, Juan de Alarcon, are from 1611; see also the documents published by A. da Silva Rego in *Boletim da Filmoteca Ultramarina Portuguesa*, 44 (1971): 3–6.

8. Boyajian, *Portuguese Trade under the Habsburgs*, 44.

9. Pedro de Baeza, *Memorial y discurso de las Indias Orientales* (Madrid, 1608), read at the BL, 1324.i.9(3), fl. 1r–2v.

10. Vitorino Magalhães Godinho, *Os descobrimentos e a economia mundial*, 2nd ed., vol. 3 (Lisbon: Presença, 1983), 62.

11. Pedro de Baeza, *Memorial y discurso de las Indias Orientales* (Madrid, 1608), read at the BL, 1324.i.9(3), fl. 3r–10r. These data are not to be taken literally, they just give us an idea of the reasoning of an arbitrista who offered his services, building on trade crisis.

12. The genealogical table in Trivellato, *The Familiarity of Strangers*, 36–37, seems to sort out the confusion. Many women are missing, but this is a general problem of genealogies; concerning the Silveiras, this is the best table.

13. ANTT, Inquisição de Lisboa, Processo 11559, fl. 21v.

14. ANTT, Inquisição de Lisboa, Processo 11559, fl. 35v.

15. ANTT, Cartório do Distribuidor, 1640, livro 39, caixa 9, 6/22/1/2, fl. 37v, 38v, 42r, 45r, 46r.

16. ANTT, Inquisição de Lisboa, Processo 11559, fl. 38r. Pedro de Baeça da Silveira also claimed to have contributed to charity with staggering amounts of money. Fifty years later, these nuns at the convent of Santana still received 20,000 réis from António Correia Bravo's will, August 8, 1680; ANTT, Feitos Findos, Inventarios, Letra A, Maco 243, n. 1, Caixa 380, which indicates a long-term relation between the two families.

17. Boyajian, *Portuguese Trade under the Habsburgs*, 201 and 308.

18. Boyajian, *Portuguese Trade under the Habsburgs*, 201; James C. Boyajian, *Portuguese Bankers at the Court of Spain, 1626–1650* (New Brunswick NJ: Rutgers University Press, 1983), 154–159.

19. Boyajian, *Portuguese Trade under the Habsburgs*, 120, 310.

20. Boyajian, *Portuguese Trade under the Habsburgs*, 133.

21. Charles Ralph Boxer, "António Bocarro and the Livro do Estado da Índia Oriental. A Bio-bibliographical Note," *Garcia de Orta*, special issue (1956): 203–219; I. S. Révah, "Le retour au catholicisme d'António Bocarro," *Colóquio. Revista de Artes e Letras* 10 (1960): 58–60; António Bocarro, *O livro das plantas de todas as fortalezas, cidades e povoações do Estado da Índia Oriental*, ed. Isabel Cid (Lisbon: Imprensa Nacional, 1992), vol. 1, 27–32.

22. José Alberto Rodrigues da Silva Tavim, *Judeus e cristãos novos de Cochim. História e memória (1500–1662)* (Braga: APPACDM, 2003), 220–224.

23. Lúcio de Sousa, "The Jewish Presence in China and Japan in the Early Modern Period: A Social Representation," in *Global History and New Polycentric Approaches: Europe, Asia and the Americas in a World Network System*, ed. Manuel Perez Garcia and Lúcio de Sousa (Singapore: Palgrave, 2018), 183–218.

24. Carlos Álvarez Nogales, *Sevilla y la monarquia hispanica en el siglo XVII* (Seville: Ayuntamiento de Seville, 2000), 49; Enriqueta Vila Vilar, *Hispanoamerica y el comercio de esclavos* (Seville: Escuela de Estudios Hispano-Americanos, 1977).

25. Álvarez Nogales, *Sevilla y la monarquia hispanica*, 49–50.

26. Boyajian, *Portuguese Trade under the Habsburgs*, 312–313.

27. Álvarez Nogales, *Sevilla y la monarquia hispanica*, 140–141.

28. Álvarez Nogales, *Sevilla y la monarquia hispanica*, 142–143.

29. Enriqueta Vila Vilar, "Los asientos de portugueses y el contrabando de negros," *Anuario de Estudios Americanos* 30 (1973): 557–609; Enriqueta Vila Vilar, "La sublevación de Portugal y la trata de esclavos," *Iberoamerikanisches Archiv* 2, no. 3 (1976): 171–192.

30. Luiz Felipe de Alencastro, *O trato dos viventes. Formação do Brasil no Atlântico Sul* (São Paulo: Companhia das Letras, 2000), 80–82, 102.

31. Vila Vilar, *Hispanoamerica y el comercio de esclavos*, 26–97.

32. Archivo General de Indias, Gobierno, Indiferente General, 2796.

33. Vila Vilar, "Los asientos de portugueses," 557–609; Alice P. Canabrava, *O comércio português no Rio da Prata (1580–1640)* (1944) reprint (Belo Horizonte: Itatiaia, 1984); and de Alencastro, *O trato dos viventes*, 69, 99.

34. Vila Vilar, "Los asientos de portugueses." 557–609.

35. I follow here the brilliant reconstitution of this story by Luiz Felipe de Alencastro in the revised and translated version of his book, *The Trade of the Living: The Formation of Brazil in the South Atlantic, Sixteenth to Seventeenth Century*, trans. Gavin Adams and L. F. de Alencastro (Albany: State University of New York Press, 2018), 91–93; see also Cristina Hernández Casado, "Gonzalo Núñez de Sepúlveda: Esclavista, financiero, hidalgo. Historia de un ascenso social (1585–1655)," in *De la nobleza y la caballeria. Privilégio, poder y servicio en la articulación de la sociedad moderna, ss. XVI-XVII*, ed. Elena Maria García Guerra et al. (Palermo: New Digital Press, 2019), 361–374.

36. Daviken Studnicki-Gizbert, *A Nation upon the Ocean Sea. Portugal's Atlantic Diaspora and the Crisis of the Spanish Empire, 1492-1640* (Oxford: Oxford University Press, 2007), 117, based on Vila Vilar, *Hispano-America y el comercio de esclavos*, 209, 221–226.

37. AGI, Contaduria, 258, fls. 1r–6r, 31r.

38. Enriqueta Vila Vilar, "Los asientos de portugueses," 557–609.

39. AGI, Indiferente General, 2796.

40. AGI, Contaduria, 258, 259, 260.

41. AGI, Contaduria, 258, fl. 95r–96r.

42. Linda Newson and Susie Minchin, *From Capture to Sale: The Portuguese Slave Trade to Spanish South America in the Early Seventeenth Century* (Leiden: Brill, 2007). This is an exemplary study based on several archives, mainly the Archivo General de la Nación in Lima, Peru, where the books of accounts kept by Bautista Pérez are preserved, having been sequestrated by the Inquisition during his trial.

43. Newson and Minchin, *From Capture to Sale*, 299–300.

44. A. A. Marques de Almeida, ed., *Dicionário histórico dos sefarditas portugueses. Mercadores e gente de trato* (Lisbon: Campo da Comunicação, 2009), 373–376.

45. ANTT, Inquisição de Lisboa, Processo 4474; the sentence, checked by the General Council, the usual procedure when wealthy people were involved, extends from fl. 76r to 84r and includes the register of abjuration and the oath of secrecy; but the last fl. 85r–86r contains a copy of the verdict on Pedro de Baeça da Silveira, which is also produced in his own trial at the Inquisição de Lisboa, Processo 11559, fl. 146v. It is obvious the two trials were linked in the inquisitors' minds.

46. Studnicki-Gizbert, *A Nation upon the Ocean Sea*, 77.

47. Studnicki-Gizbert, *A Nation upon the Ocean Sea*, 62–64, 72–73, 98–99 (with an excellent diagram of relationships).

48. Francisco Bethencourt, "Iberian Atlantic: Ties, Networks, and Boundaries," in *Theorising the Iberian Atlantic*, ed. Harald E. Braun and Lisa Vollendorf (Leiden: Brill, 2013), 15–36.

49. Amy Butler Greenfield, *A Perfect Red: Empire, Espionage and the Quest for the Colour of Desire* (London: Doubleday, 2005).

50. Francisco Zamora Rodriguez, "Central American Indigo: Globalization and Socioeconomic Effects (16th–17th Centuries)," *Análise Social* 52, no. 224 (2017): 584–607.

51. Bethany Aram and Bartolomé Yun-Casilla, eds., *Global Goods and the Spanish Empire in 1492–1824: Circulation, Resistance and Diversity* (Houndmills: Palgrave, 2014), esp. chapters on cochineal and tobacco.

52. Pierre and Huguette Chaunu, *Séville et l'Atlantique (1504–1650)*, vol. 4 (Paris: A. Colin, 1959), 573–575.

53. Rafael Escobedo Romero, *El tabaco del Rey: La organizacion de un monopolio fiscal durante el Antigo Régime* (Pamplona: Universidad de Navarra, 2007); Santiago de Luxán, ed., *Política y Hacienda del tabaco en los imperios ibéricos (siglos XVII–XIX)* (Madrid: Centro de Estudios Políticos e Constitucionales, 2014).

54. Marcy Norton, *Sacred Gifts, Profane Pleasures: A History of Tobacco and Chocolate in the Atlantic World* (Ithaca, NY: Cornell University Press, 2008), 213–223; on Antonio Soria, see also João de Figueirôa-Rego, "Mobilidade dos agents do tabaco entre Portugal, Madrid e outras regiões de Castela," in *Movilidad, interacciones y espacios de oportunidad entre Castilla y Portugal en la Edad Moderna*, ed. Manuel Francisco Fernández Chaves and Rafael M. Pérez García (Seville: Universidad de Sevilla, 2019), 253–273.

55. Francisco Bethencourt, "Portuguese Empire," in *Tobacco in History and Culture: An Encyclopedia*, ed. Jordan Goodman (Farmington Hills, MI: Charles Scribner's Sons, 2004), 440–447.

56. Studnicki-Gizbert, *A Nation upon the Ocean Sea*, 109.

57. Gonçalo de Reparaz, *Os portugueses no vice-reinado do Peru (séculos XVI e XVII)* (Lisbon: Instituto de Alta Cultura, 1976), 139.

58. Alfonso W. Quiroz, "The Expropriation of Portuguese New Christians in Spanish America, 1635–1649," *Ibero-Amerikanishes Archiv* 11, no. 4 (1985): 407–465, esp. 459.

59. Gonçalo de Reparaz, *Os portugueses no vice-reinado do Peru*, 138–140; Rene Millar Corbacho, "Las confiscaciones de la Inquisición de Lima a los comerciantes de origen judío-portugués en la 'Gran Complicidad' de 1635," *Revista de Indias* 43 (1983): 27–58; Stanley

Hordes, "The Inquisition as Economic and Political Agent: The Campaigns of the Mexican Holy Office against the Crypto-Jews in the Mid-Seventeenth Century," *The Americas* 39 (1982): 23–38; Boyajian, *Portuguese Bankers*, 124, indicates the value of Manuel Bautista Pérez's estate as 650,000 ducados (893,750 pesos).

60. Quiroz, "Expropriation of Portuguese New Christians," esp. 426–27.

61. Gonçalo de Reparaz, *Os portugueses no vice-reinado do Peru*, 83; Maria da Graça Ventura, *Portugueses no Peru no tempo da União Ibérica: Mobilidade, cumplicidade e vivências*, vol. 1 (Lisbon: Imprensa Nacional, 2005), 347–457, 535–536; we know that the fortune had been much bigger, perhaps 200,000 pesos was the amount confiscated. In any case, the vast amount invested in trade would have been extremely difficult to recover after the execution of Manuel Bautista Pérez.

62. Gleydi Sullón Barreto, *Extrangeros integrados. Portugueses en la Lima Virreinal, 1570–1680* (Madrid: Consejho Superior de Investigaciones Científicas, 2016), 205–206.

63. Archivo General de la Nación (AGN), Lima, Peru, SO-CO 83-563.

64. AGN, Lima, Peru, SO-CO, 32-333. The claims by Francisco Fernández de Solis are in fl. 199r-201v, Manuel Mendes de Acuña in fl. 243r-245v, Afonso and Gaspar Rodrigues Passarinho in fl. 281r-282v and 310r-311v, Manuel López de Noronha fl. 293r-v.

65. Solange Alberro, *Inquisición y sociedad en México, 1571–1700* (México: Fondo de Cultura Economica, 1988), 444–452.

66. Stuart Schwartz, "Panic in the Indies: The Portuguese Threat to the Spanish Empire, 1640–1650," *Colonial Latin American Review* 2, nos. 1–2 (1993): 165–187.

67. Anita Novinsky, *Cristãos Novos na Bahia* (São Paulo: Perspectiva, 1972).

68. Anita Novinsky, *Inquisição: Prisioneiros do Brasil, séculos XVI-XIX* (Rio de Janeiro: Expressão e Cultura, 2002), 35. Anita Novinsky, *Inquisição. Rol dos culpados. Fontes para a história do Brasil, século XVIII* (Rio de Janeiro: Expressão e Cultura, 1992), listed 1819 denounced from Brazil in the eighteenth century.

69. Thiago Krause, *A Formação de uma Nobreza Ultramarina: Coroa e Elites locais na Bahia Seiscentista* (PhD thesis, Universidade Federal do Rio de Janeiro, 2015), 96–103. The significant differences in New and Old Christian intermarriage over time and place still needs to be researched. For Pernambuco, see Evaldo Cabral de Mello, *O nome e o sangue. Uma fraude genealógica no Pernambuco colonial* (São Paulo: Companhia das Letras, 1989), 104–110; for Rio, see Lina Gorenstein Silva, *Heréticos e impuros: A Inquisição e os cristãos novos no Rio de Janeiro, século XVIII* (Rio de Janeiro: Prefeitura do Rio de Janeiro, 1995), 50–109.

70. Ambrósio Fernandes Brandão, *Diálogo das grandezas do Brasil*, ed. José Antonio Gonsalves de Melo, 2nd ed. (Recife: Imprensa Universitária, 1966); English trans. Frederick Holden Hall (Albuquerque: University of New Mexico Press, 1987).

71. Alencastro, *O trato dos viventes*.

72. José Gonçalves Salvador, *Os magnatas do tráfico negreiro* (São Paulo: Pioneira, 1981), 43–44; Marques de Almeida, ed., *Dicionário histórico dos sefarditas portugueses*, 328–329.

73. Leonor Freire Costa, *O transporte no Atlântico e a Companhia Geral do Comércio do Brasil (1580–1663)*, vol. 1 (Lisbon: CNCDP, 2002), 65, 138.

74. Frédéric Mauro, *Le Portugal et l'Atlantique au XVIIᵉ siècle, 1570–1670* (Paris: SEVPEN, 1960), 449.

75. Mauro, *Le Portugal et l'Atlantique*, 468–469; Costa, *O transporte no Atlântico*, vol. 1, 100.

76. Costa, *O transporte no Atlântico*, vol. 1, 16–21, 64.

77. Costa, *O transporte no Atlântico*, vol. 1, 108.

78. Charles R. Boxer, *Salvador Correia de Sá and the Struggle for Brazil and Angola, 1602–1686* (London: Athlone, 1952).

79. Costa, *O transporte no Atlântico*, vol. 1, 516; David Grant Smith, *The Mercantile Class of Portugal and Brazil in the Seventeenth Century: A Socio-Economic Study of the Merchants of Lisbon and Bahia, 1620–1690* (UMI reproductions, PhD thesis, University of Texas at Austin, 1975); David Grant Smith, "Old Christian Merchants and the Foundation of the Brazil Company," *Hispanic American Historical Review* 2 (1974): 233–259.

80. Virginia Rau, "Subsídios para o estudo do movimento dos portos de Faro e Lisboa durante o século XVII," *Anais da Academia Portuguesa de História* 5, no. 2 (1954): 199–277; Costa, *O transporte no Atlântico*, vol. 1, 140–162, 539–540.

81. Maria Valentina Cotta do Amaral, *Privilégios de mercadores estrangeiros no reinado de D. João III* (Lisbon: Instituto de Alta Cultura, 1965).

82. Novinsky, *Cristãos Novos na Bahia*, 76.

83. ANTT, Inquisição de Lisboa, Processo 5391, fl. 8r–10r (inventory of property), 11v and 13r (denouncers), 43r–v (genealogy).

84. ANTT, Manuscritos da Livraria, 1111, doc. 82.

85. ANTT, Inquisição de Lisboa, Processo 5391, fl. 35r (copy of the first confession in Brazil, September 1618), 99r and 103r (sentence and register of release).

86. Novinsky, *Os cristãos novos na Bahia*, 80–82; Krause, *Formação de uma Nobreza Ultramarina*, 97.

87. ANTT, Mesa da Consciência e Ordens, Habilitações para a Ordem de Santiago, Letra A, maço 6, n. 65.

88. ANTT, Registo Geral de Mercês, Mercê das Ordens Militares, liv. 12, fl. 171v–172r.

89. ANTT, Mesa da Consciência e Ordens, Habilitações para a Ordem de Cristo, Letra D, Maço 12, n. 57; the letter of habilitation was dispatched on October 10, 1663, Registo Geral de Mercês, Mercês das Ordens Militares, Liv. 5, fl. 221r.

90. ANTT, Registo Geral de Mercês, Marcês de D. Afonso VI, Liv. 5, fl. 324v; privilige renewed on November 8, 1667; ANTT, Registo Geral de Mercês, Marcês de D. Afonso VI, Liv. 10, fl. 163v.

91. ANTT, Registo Geral de Mercês, Mercês das Ordens Militares, Liv. 14, fl. 70v (António's *tença*) Registo Geral de Mercês, Mercês de D. Afonso VI, Liv. 16, fl. 176r (*tenças* for the daughters); Registo Geral de Mercês, Mercês de D. Afonso VI, Liv. 28, fl. 167v (transmission of the job).

92. ANTT, Registo Geral de Mercês, Mercês de D. João V, Liv. 3, fl. 291r.

93. Bruno Feitler, *Inquisition, juifs et nouveaux-chrétiens au Brésil: le Nordeste, XVIᵉ et XVIIᵉ siècles* (Leuven: Leuven University Press, 2003).

94. Elias Lipiner, *Izaque de Castro. O mancebo que veio preso do Brasil* (Recife: Fundação Joaquim Nabuco, 1992).

95. Novinsky, *Inquisição: Prisioneiros do Brasil*, 109, 153, 162.

96. Boyajian, *Portuguese Bankers*, Appendix B.

97. Álvaro Castillo Pintado and Juan Ignacio Gutiérrez Nieto, "La hacienda real," in *La España de Felipe IV. El gobierno de la monarquia, la crisis de 1640 y el fracaso de la hegemonia europea*, ed. Francisco Tomás y Valiente, *Historia de España R. Menendez Pidal*, vol. 25 (Madrid: Espasa-Calpe, 1982), 215–333, esp. 238–240.

98. Ana Paula Lloyd, whose brilliant PhD on the suspension of the Portuguese Inquisition will be mentioned in part IV, is now preparing to tackle this crucial issue.

99. Darlene Abreu-Ferreira, "A status of her own: Women and family identities in seventeenth century Aveiro, Portugal," *Journal of Family Studies* 34, no. 1 (2009) 3–24; Darlene Abreu-Ferreira, *Women, Crime and Forgiveness in Early Modern Portugal* (Farnham: Ashgate, 2015); see also Ana Maria Rodrigues, Abreu-Ferreira, Isabel Sá, and Amélia Polónia/ Rosa Capelão's contributions to *Gendering the Portuguese-Speaking World*, ed. Francisco Bethencourt (Leiden: Brill, 2021).

100. Boyajian, *Portuguese Bankers*, 53. The best source of information on New Christian women is Studnicki-Gizbert, *A Nation upon the Ocean Sea*, 81–84. There is also an article by Isabel M. R. Mendes Drumond Braga, "Do trabalho e dos patrimônios das cristãs novas nos século XVII e XVIII," *Revista Digital NIEJ* 4, no. 7 (2013): 10–23.

101. Boyajian, *Portuguese Bankers*, Appendix D.

102. Studnicki-Gizbert, *A Nation upon the Ocean Sea*, 83.

103. Antonio Domínguez Ortiz, "Marcos Fernández Monsanto y los Almojarifazgos de Sevilla," in *Los extranjeros en la vida española en el siglo XVII*, ed. León Carlos Alvarez Santaló (Seville: Diputación de Sevilla, 1996), 275–288.

104. Boyajian, *Portuguese Bankers*, namely, Appendixes C and D.

105. José Gonçalves Salvador, *Os cristãos novos e o comércio no Atlântico meridional* (São Paulo: Pioneira, 1978), 214.

106. Boyajian, *Portuguese Bankers*, Appendix D.

107. Archivo General de Simancas (AGS), Secretarias Provinciales, Libro 1536, fl. 196v.

108. AGS, Secretarias Provinciales, Libro 1536, fl. 198r–v.

109. AGS, Secretarias Provinciales, Libro 1536, fl. 210r.

110. AGS, Secretarias Provinciales, Libro 1536, fl.213r–v. On these issues, see Rafael Valladares, "De ignorancia y lealtad: Portugueses en Madrid, 1640–1670," *Torre de los Lujanes* 37 (1998): 133–150.

111. AGS, Secretarias Provinciales, Libro 1536, fl. 228v–229r.

112. AGS, Secretarias Provinciales, Libro 1536, fl. 205v–206r.

113. AGS, Secretarias Provinciales, Libro 1536, fl.269r–v.

114. AGS, Secretarias Provinciales, Libro 1536, fl. 233r.

115. AGS, Secretarias Provinciales, Libro 1536, fl. 248v–249v.

116. AGS, Secretarias Provinciales, Libro 1536, fl. 254v.

117. AGS, Secretarias Provinciales, Libro 1472, fl. 43r.

118. AGS, Secretarias Provinciales, Libro 1472, fl. 14r–15r.

119. AGS, Secretarias Provinciales, Libro 1472, fl. 22r–27r.

120. AGS, Secretarias Provinciales, Libro 1472, fl. 30r–31r.

121. AGS, Secretarias Provinciales, Libro 1472, fl. 206r–207r (there was a discount of 2 million réis to pay officials).

122. AGS, Secretarias Provinciales, Libro 1472, fl. 32r–34r.

123. AGS, Secretarias Provinciales, Libro 1472, fl. 49r and 133r–134r.

124. AGS, Secretarias Provinciales, Libro 1472, fl. 52r.

125. AGS, Secretarias Provinciales, Libro 1472, fl. 120r.

126. AGS, Secretarias Provinciales, Libro 1472, fl. 208r.

127. AGS, Secretarias Provinciales, Libro 1472, fl. 278r–283r. The petitioners quantified their losses.

128. AGS, Secretarias Provinciales, Libro 1472, fl. 136r.

129. AGS, Secretarias Provinciales, Libro 1472, fl. 164r.

130. AGS, Secretarias Provinciales, Libro 1472, fl. 343r–344r.

131. AGS, Secretarias Provinciales, Libro 1552, fl. 7r–12r. The terms of negotiation after the initial bids could be changed several times.

132. AGS, Secretarias Provinciales, Libro 1552, fl. 15r–16r.

133. AGS, Secretarias Provinciales, Libro 1552, fl. 22v.

134. AGS, Secretarias Provinciales, Libro 1552, fl. 56r–57r.

135. AGS, Secretarias Provinciales, Libro 1552, fl. 104r.

136. AGS, Secretarias Provinciales, Libro 1552, fl. 382r–388r.

137. AGS, Secretarias Provinciales, Libro 1552, fl. 233r, 238r, 239v, 241v.

138. ANTT, Miscelâneas Manuscritas do Convento da Graça, Pecúlio tomo 8F, 94.

139. ANTT, Miscelâmeas Manuscritas do Convento da Graça, Pecúlio tomo 8F, 193.

140. ANTT, Miscelâneas Manuscritas do Convento da Graça, Pecúlio tomo 8F, 183, 193, 226–227.

141. ANTT, Miscelâneas Manuscritas do Convento da Graça, Pecúlio tomo 3, 210.

142. ANTT, Inquisição de Lisboa, Processo 8132, fl. 139r–176r (inventory of property).

143. ANTT, Inquisição de Lisboa, Processo 8132, fl. 139r–176r.

144. Costa, *O transporte no Atlântico*, vol. 1, 418–419.

145. Costa, *O transporte no Atlântico*, vol. 1, 509, 516–517.

146. Virgínia Rau, "Fortunas ultramarinas e nobreza portuguesa no século XVII," *Revista Portuguesa de História* 8 (1961): 1–29.

147. Novinsky, *Cristãos novos na Bahia*, 72–73.

148. ASF, Deputazione sopra la nobiltà e citadinanza. Processi di nobiltà, Libro 17 (without page numbers). The will of the Marquis Sebastian Ximenes, December 29, 1633, established the succession of Tommaso to the title, fief, and property, entailed according to the law of primogeniture, while it left legacies to the other children—namely, the Jesuit Ferdinando,

the nun of the Santo Spirito in Florence, Maria Celestiale, and the other daughter, Costanza, who was married to Giovanni Bardi, Count of Vernio; ASF, Panciatichi Ximenes d'Aragona, Libro 360, fasc. XVI.

149. ASF, Notarile Moderno, Protocolli, 8627, Graziadio Squadrini, fl. 21v–24, will of Catarina Ximenes, born Medici, widow of Sebastião Ximenes, March 3, 1638, in which she leaves half of her inheritance to her son, Rafaello, and the other half to the other children. ASF, NM, Prot., 9323, Giuseppe Bardi, will of Maria Serguidi, born Ximenes, widow of Francesco Serguidi, knight of Santo Stefano, September 9, 1627, who had a daughter in a convent, leaves many small bequests to convents, confraternities, and friends, and divides the main sum, held at the Monte di Pietà, between her son, Francesco Maria Serguidi, knight of Santo Stefano, and her daughter-in-law, Selvaggia.

150. ASF, Panciatichi Ximenes d'Aragona, Libro 360, fasc. XI, Niccolò Ximenes, October 2, 1610, and fasc. XII, codicilo from June 9, 1611. There was litigation in Seville concerning the inheritance of Diogo Henriques Leão: Niccolò claimed the one-sixth due to his mother, Gracia Rodrigues de Évora, who had been married to Rui Nunes Ximenes.

151. The couple was represented in a sumptuous painting: Otto van Veen's *The Adoration of the Shepherds* (1601), a triptych, with the patrons Simão Rodrigues de Évora and Ana Ximenes, oil on wood, 230.5×204.5 cm (central panel), 238.5×94.5 cm (right panel), 237.7×95 cm (left panel). Maagdenhuis Museum, Antwerp inv. nr. 95. The painting was commissioned by Simão Rodrigues de Évora for the women's chapel of St. Anne's Almshouse he founded in Antwerp for twelve women.

152. See the website http://ximenez.unibe.ch/ on "The Possessions of the Portuguese Merchant-Banker Emmanuel Ximenez (1564–1632) in Antwerp," organised by Christine Göttler, accessed several times in 2018 and 2019.

153. Hans Pohl, *Die Portugiesen in Antwerp (1567–1648)* (Wiesbaden: Franz Steiner, 1977), 334–335.

154. Pohl, *Die Portugiesen in Antwerp (1567–1648)*, 69–71, also the genealogical tables, 357–371.

155. The portraits of Filipe Godines (ca. 1630, oil on canvas, 211.5×137.5 cm) and Sebilla van den Berghe (ca. 1630, oil on canvas, 210.5×136.7 cm) by Anthonis van Dyck are in Munich, Alte Pinakothek, inv. nr. 995 and 201; the anonymous portrait of António Gomes da Mata, postmaster general, has been dated ca. 1630–1640, oil on canvas, 70×53 cm, MNAA, inv. 1639 Pint.

156. Miriam Bodian, *Hebrews of the Portuguese Nation: Conversos and Community in Early Modern Amsterdam* (Bloomington: Indiana University Press, 1997), 28.

157. Jonathan Israel, "The Jews in Venice and Their Links with Holland and with Dutch Jewry (1600–1710)," in *Gli ebrei a Venezia, secoli XIV–XVIII*, ed. Gaetano Cozzi (Milan: Comunità, 1987), 95–116, esp. 99–100.

158. Bodian, *Hebrews of the Portuguese Nation*, 23–24.

159. H. P. Salomon, *Portrait of a New Christian: Fernão Álvares Melo, 1569–1632* (Paris: Fundação Calouste Gulbenkian, 1982).

160. Christopher Ebert, *Between Empires: Brazilian Sugar in the Early Atlantic Economy, 1580–1630* (Leiden: Brill, 2008), 72.

161. Bodian, *Hebrews of the Portuguese Nation*, 36–37.

162. Daniel M. Swetschinski, *Reluctant Cosmopolitans: The Portuguese Jews of Seventeenth-century Amsterdam* (London: Littman Library of Jewish Civilization, 2000), 91–92.

163. Yosef Kaplan, *Les nouveaux-juifs d'Amsterdam. Essais sur l'histoire sociale et intellectuelle du judaïsme séfarade au XVIIᵉ siècle* (Paris: Chandeigne, 1999).

164. Feitler, *Inquisition, juifs et nouveaux-chrétiens au Brésil*.

165. Jonathan Israel and Stuart Schwartz, eds., *The Expansion of Tolerance: Religion in Dutch Brazil (1624–1654)* (Amsterdam: Amsterdam University Press, 2007).

166. Ebert, *Between Empires*, 72–73.

167. Michaël Studemund Halévy and Jorun Poettering, "Étrangers universels: les reseaux séfarades à Hambourg," *Arquivos do Centro Cultural Calouste Gulbenkian* 48 (2004): 117–150, esp. 122, 127, 135.

168. The Vaz family is the main subject of the study by Peter Mazur, *The New Christians of Spanish Naples, 1528-1671: A Fragile Elite* (Basingstoke: Palgrave, 2013).

169. Gaetano Sabatini, "The Influence of Portuguese Economic Thought on the *Breve Trattato*; Antonio Serra and Miguel Vaaz in Spanish Naples," in *Antonio Serra and the Economics of Good Government*, ed. R. Patalano and S. A. Reinert (Basingstoke: Palgrave, 2016), 81–111.

170. Gaetano Sabatini, "The Vaaz: The Rise and Fall of a Family of Portuguese Bankers in Spanish Naples," *Journal of European Economic History* 29, no. 3 (2010): 627–659; Benedetta Crivelli and Gaetano Sabatini, "La carrera de un mercader judeoconverso en el Nápoles español. Negocios y relaciones políticas de Miguel Vaaz (1590–1616), *Hispania* 76, no. 253 (2016): 323–354; Mazur, *New Christians of Spanish Naples*.

171. Pilar Huerga Criado, "Cristianos nuevos de origen ibérico en el Reino de Nápoles en el siglo XVII," *Sefarad* 72, no. 2 (2012): 351–387.

172. Archivio Storico della Banca d'Italia (ASBI), Banco di Santo Spirito, Contabilità, regg. 1, *Libro mastro dei depositi per l'anno 1610*, fl. 203; regg. 4, *Libro Mastro dei depositi per l'anno 1612*, regg. 4, *Libro mastro dei depositi per l'anno 1612*, fl. 440, 603, 707 and 729; regg. 8 and 9, *Libro mastro dei depositi per l'anno 1615*, fl. 474, 671 and 901; regg. 14, *Libro mastro dei depositi per l'anno 1618*, fl. 369; regg. 17 and 18, *Libro mastro dei depositi per l'anno 1620*, fl. 452 and 603; regg. 32, *Libro mastro dei depositi per l'anno 1629*, fl. 414.

173. BINE, Archicofradia de la Ssma. Resurrección, H-III-583, Registro de matriculas de cofrades, 1603–1679 (without page numbers).

174. BINE, Archicofradia de la Ssma. Resurrección, N-II-1117, Libro de registro de actas, 1613–1632, fl. 9v–10r, 15v, 23v–24v, 30r, 31v–32r, 54r–55r, 64r, 83r, 101r, 118v, 119v, 122v, 124v, 126r, 127r, 159v, 175v, 176r–v, 211r, 213v, 224v.

175. AIPSA, Actas de Congregações, 1611–1678, fl. 1r, 14r, 18r–v, 30v, 67v, 74r, 87r, 90r, 112r.

Chapter Twelve: Identities

1. *Shorter Oxford English Dictionary*, 5th ed. (Oxford: Oxford University Press, 2002), 1311.

2. Henri Tajfel, ed. *Social Identity and Intergroup Relations* (Cambridge: Cambridge University Press, 1982); John Rajchman, *The Identity in Question* (London: Routledge, 1995); Florian Coulmas, *Identity: A Very Short Introduction* (Oxford: Oxford University Press, 2019).

3. The idea of New Jews was developed by Yosef Kaplan, *Les nouveaux-juifs d'Amsterdam. Essais sur l'histoire sociale et intellectuelle du judaïsme séfarade au XVIIe siècle* (Paris: Chandeigne, 1999), to underline the necessary (and sometimes uncomfortable) re-adaptation of New Christians to Jewish norms.

4. ANTT, Inquisição de Lisboa, Processo 8132.

5. ANTT, Inquisição de Lisboa, Processo 6677.

6. *Diccionario de la lengua Española*, 22nd ed. (Madrid: Real Academia Española, 2001), 967; *Dicionário Houaiss da língua portuguesa* (Rio de Janeiro: Objetiva, 2001), 526.

7. This issue was raised by Robert Rowland, "New Christian, Marrano, Jew," in *The Jews and the Expansion of Europe to the West*, ed. Paolo Bernardini and Norman Fiering (New York: Berghahn, 2001), 125–148.

8. The detachment of southern inquisitors from witch hunting was well analysed by Gustav Henningsen, *The Witches' Advocate: Basque Witchcraft and the Spanish Inquisition, 1609-1614* (Reno: University of Nevada Press, 1980).

9. Francisco Bethencourt, *Racisms: From the Crusades to the Twentieth Century* (Princeton, NJ: Princeton University Press, 2013), 144–154.

10. David L. Graizbord, *Souls in Dispute: Converso Identities in Iberia and the Jewish Diaspora, 1580-1700* (Philadelphia: University of Pennsylvania Press, 2003); David L. Graizbord, "Commercial practices by New Christians/Jewish Groups and Their Sense of 'Cultural Identity,' 'Loyalties' and 'Belongings,'" in *Merchant Cultures: A Global Approach to Spaces, Representations and Worlds of Trade, 1500-1800*, ed. Cátia Antunes and Francisco Bethencourt (Leiden: Brill, 2021), 41–51.

11. Claude B. Stuczynski, "Not Hybridity but Counterculture: Portuguese New Christian Judaizers Confronting Christianity (and Islam) (Bragança, 16th Century)," in *Conversos, marrani e nuove comunità ebraiche in età moderna*, ed. Myriam Silvera (Florence: Giuntina, 2015), 61–71; and Kevin Ingram, *Converso Non-Conformism in Early Modern Spain: Bad Blood and Faith from Alonso de Cartagena to Diego Velázquez* (Cham: Palgrave, 2018), a stimulating book, even if open to discussion.

12. Nathan Wachtel, *The Faith of Remembrance: Marrano Labyrinths* (Philadelphia: University of Pennsylvania Press, 2013), 28–68.

13. Graizbord, *Souls in Dispute*, 1.

14. Ben Kaplan, Robert Moore, Henk van Nierop, and Judith Pollman, eds. *Catholic Communities in Protestant States: Britain and the Netherlands, 1580–1720* (Manchester: Manchester University Press, 2009).

15. Gérard Nahon, *Juifs et judaïsme à Bordeaux* (Bordeaux: Mollat, 2003).

16. The notion of religious frontiers that were persistently trespassed was tackled by Francisco Bethencourt and Denis Crouzet, eds., *Frontières religieuses à l'époque moderne* (Paris: Presses de l'Université de Paris-Sorbonne, 2013).

17. Stuart B. Schwartz, *All Can Be Saved: Religious Tolerance and Salvation in the Iberian World* (New Haven, CT: Yale University Press, 2008).

18. Jonathan Israel, *Radical Enlightenment: Philosophy and the Making of Modernity, 1650–1750* (Oxford: Oxford University Press, 2001).

19. Jonathan Israel and Stuart B. Schwartz, *The Expansion of Tolerance: Religion in Dutch Brazil (1624–1654)* (Amsterdam: Amsterdam University Press, 2007).

20. On the complex presence of New Christians and Jews in early modern Brazil, see Bruno Feitler, *Inquisition, juifs et nouveaux-chrétiens au Brésil: le Nordeste, XVIe et XVIIe siècles* (Leuven: Leuven University Press, 2003).

21. On portfolio capitalists see Sanjay Subrahmanyam and Christopher Bayly, "Portfolio Capitalists and the Political Economy or Early Modern India," *Indian Economic and Social History Review* 25, no. 4 (1988): 401–424.

22. Tirtsah Levie-Bernfeld, *Poverty and Welfare among the Portuguese Jews in Early Modern Amsterdam* (Oxford: Littman Library of Jewish Civilization, 2012).

23. Antonio Domínguez Ortiz, *Los judeoconversos en la España moderna* (Madrid: Istmo, 1971), 6; Juan Hernández Franco, *Sangre limpia, sangre española: el debate sobre los estatutos de limpieza (siglos XV–XVII)* (Madrid, Cátedra, 2011), 161.

24. See the chapters on New Christians by Pilar Huerga Criado, Bernardo López Belinchón, Markus Schreiber, José Martínez Millan, and M. Torres Arce in *Historia de la Inquisición en España y América*, ed. Joaquín Pérez Villanueva and Bartolomé Escandell Bonet, vol. 3, *Temas y problemas* (Madrid: Biblioteca de Autores Cristianos, 2000), 441–693; Pilar Huerga Criado, *En la raya de Portugal: solidaridad y tensiones en la comunidad judeo-conversa* (Salamanca: Universidad de Salamanca, 1994).

25. Paulino Castañeda Delgado and Pilar Hernandez Aparicio, *La Inquisición de Lima*, tome II *(1635–1696)* (Madrid: Deimos, 1995), 387–478; Solange Alberro, *Inquisición y sociedad en México, 1571–1700* (México: Fondo de Cultura Económica, 1988), 417–454, 533–585; Daviken Studniki-Gizbert, *A Nation upon the Ocean Sea: Portugal's Atlantic Diaspora and the Crisis of the Spanish Empire, 1492–1640* (Oxford: Oxford University Press, 2007), 48–49; Gleydi Sullón Barreto, *Extrangeros integrados. Portugueses en la Lima Virreinal, 1570–1680* (Madrid: Consejho Superior de Investigaciones Cientificas, 2016), 61–64.

26. See Francisco Bethencourt and Diogo Ramada Curto, eds., *A memória da nação* (Lisbon: Sá da Costa, 1991); the tense relationship between Castile and Spain was addressed by José Ortega y Gasset, *La España invertebrada* (1921) (Madrid: Espasa-Calpe, 2006).

27. Raphael Bluteau, *Vocabulario Portuguez e Latino*, vol. 5 (Lisbon: Pascoal da Sylva, 1726), 658–659. This includes mythical people from legends and folk history.

28. Antonio de Moraes Silva, *Diccionario da lingua portuguesa* vol. 2 (Lisbon: Simão Thaddeo Ferreira, 1789), 107 (my translation here and the following quotes).

29. Moraes Silva, *Diccionario da lingua portuguesa*, vol. 2, 60.

30. Moraes Silva, *Diccionario da lingua portuguesa*, vol. 2, 25.

31. For the travails of Morais Silva at the Inquisition, see António Baião, "O dicionarista e gramático Morais e Silva," in *Episódios dramáticos da Inquisição*, vol. 2 (Lisbon: Seara Nova, 1938), 123–146.

32. Sebastián de Covarrubias Orozco, *Tesoro de la lengua castellana, o española*, vol. 1 (Madrid: Luis Sanchez, 1611), fl. 560r.

33. de Covarrubias Orozco, *Tesoro de la lengua castellana, o española*, vol. 2, fl. 3r.

34. de Covarrubias Orozco, *Tesoro de la lengua castellana, o española*, vol. 1, fl. 540v.

35. See Ingram, *Converso Non-Conformism in Early Modern Spain*, 7, 245.

36. *El ingenioso hidalgo Don Quijote de la Mancha* (1605–1615), ed. Luis Andrés Murillo, vol. 1 (Madrid: Clásicos Castalia, 1987), 77 (my translation).

37. Francisco López de Ubeda, *Libro de entretenimiento de la pícara Justina* (1st ed. 1605), ed. David Mañero Lozano (Madrid: Cátedra, 2012), 331 (the quote), 334. David Mañero suggests that the real author might have been Jeronimo Patón, from the circle of Lope de Vega. Justina is the third case of a female protagonist, after Celestina and Lozana Andalusa, within a recently renewed tradition of picaresque novels by *Guzmán de Alfarache*.

38. *Don Quijote de la Mancha*, vol. 1, 263 (part 1, ch. 21), my translation.

39. *Don Quijote de la Mancha*, vol. 2, 390 (part 2, ch. 47), my translation.

40. *Don Quijote de la Mancha*, vol. 2, 525–531 (part 2, ch. 53).

41. Jorge Santos Alves, ed., *Fernão Mendes Pinto and the Peregrinação: Studies, Restored Portuguese Text, Notes and Indexes*, 4 vols. (Lisbon: Fundação Oriente, 2010); for an English translation see Fernão Mendes Pinto, *The Travels*, ed. and trans. Rebecca D. Catz (Chicago: The University of Chicago Press, 1989).

42. Francisco Rodrigues Lobo, *Corte na aldeia* (1619), ed. Afonso Lopes Vieira (Lisbon: Sá da Costa, 1972).

43. ANTT, Inquisição de Lisboa, Processo 3003. The order of detention (fl. 5r) clearly identified him as brother of Francisco Rodrigues Lobo, poet, already deceased. Miguel Lobo admitted to having three-quarters New Christian blood, mostly from his father's side, while he declared himself the possessor of eighty books on the humanities, including manuscripts from his brother still to be printed (fl. 7v). He was married to Luísa Cunha de Moura, an Old Christian (fl. 331r).

44. Rodrigues Lobo, *Corte na aldeia*, 26.

45. Daniel O'Callaghan, ed., trans., *The Preservation of Jewish Religious Books in Sixteenth-Century Germany: Johann Reuchlin's Augenspiegel* (Leiden: Brill, 2012).

46. Rodrigues Lobo, *Corte na aldeia*, 273.

47. Rodrigues Lobo, *Corte na aldeia*, 286.

48. Rodrigues Lobo, *Corte na aldeia*, 288.

49. Rodrigues Lobo, *Corte na aldeia*, 324 (my translations).

50. Among many other authors the following should be noted: I. S. Révah, *Antonio Enríquez Gómez. Un écrivain marrane (v. 1600–1663)*, ed. Karsten Wilke (Paris: Chandeigne, 2003); Karsten Wilke, *Jüdisch-Christliches Doppelleben im Barock. Zur Biographie des Kaufsmanns und Dichters Antonio Enríquez Gómez* (Frankfurt: Peter Lang, 1994); Constance H. Rose, "The Marranos of the Seventeenth Century and the Case of the Merchant Writer Antonio Enríquez Gómez," in *The Spanish Inquisition and the Inquisitorial Mind*, ed. Angel Alcalá (New York: Columbia University Press, 1987), 53–71.

51. Antonio Enríquez Gómez, *Academias Morales de la Musas* (Madrid: Ioseph Fernandez de Buendia, 1668), 41 and 66.

52. Enríquez Gómez, *Academias Morales de la Musas*, 364 (my translation).

53. Révah, *Antonio Enríquez Gómez*, esp. 285.

54. Sarah Raup Johnson, *Historical Fictions and Jewish Hellenistic Identity: Third Maccabees in Its Cultural Context* (Berkeley: University of California Press, 2004); Elias J. Bickerman, *The God of the Maccabees: Studies on the Meaning and Origin of the Maccabean Revolt* (Leiden: Brill, 1979).

55. Miguel de Silveira, *El Macabeo: poema heroico* (Naples: Egidio Longo, 1638).

56. Révah, *Antonio Enríquez Gómez*, 295–299. See the editions of these texts by Révah, "Un pamphlet contre l'Inquisition d'Antonio Enríquez Gómez: la deuxième partie de la

Politica Angelica," *Revue d'Etudes Juives* 121 (1962): 81–168, and Antonio Enríquez Gómez, *El siglo pitagórico y vida de don Gregorio Guadaña*, ed. Teresa de Santos (Madrid: Cátedra, 1991).

57. Antonio Enríquez Gómez, *La Inquisición de Lucifer y visita de todos los diablos*, critical ed. Constance Hubbard Rose and Maxim. P. A. M. Kerkhof (Amsterdam: Atlanta, 1992), 34–35

58. Enríquez Gómez, *Inquisición de Lucifer*, 39.

59. Enríquez Gómez, *Inquisición de Lucifer*, 41, 44.

60. Enríquez Gómez, *Inquisición de Lucifer*, 46, 50.

61. Enríquez Gómez, *Inquisición de Lucifer*, 62–63.

62. Alain Rey, *Le Robert. Dictionnaire historique de la langue français* (Paris: Le Robert, 1998), 2013.

63. Ramos Coelho, *Manuel Fernandes Vila Real e o seu processo na Inquisição da Lisboa* (Lisboa: Ocidente, 1894); Manuel Fernandes de Vila Real, *Epítome Genealógico do Eminentíssimo Cardeal Duque de Richelieu e Discursos Políticos sobre Algumas Acções de Sua Vida* (1641), ed. Antonio Borges Coelho (Lisboa: Caminho, 2005).

64. de Vila Real, *Epítome Genealógico do Eminentíssimo Cardeal*, esp. 79, 129, 141, 142, 149–153, 194.

65. de Vila Real, *Epítome Genealógico do Eminentíssimo Cardeal*, 126–128.

66. de Vila Real, *Epítome Genealógico do Eminentíssimo Cardeal*, 127 (my translation).

67. Israel, *Radical Enlightenment*, esp. 167–170.

68. Israel, *Radical Enlightenment*, provides the best intellectual context. I have used the *Collected Works of Spinoza*, ed. and trans. Edwin Curley, 2 vols. (Princeton, NJ: Princeton University Press, 1985–2016). Among a vast bibliography I would note here Yitzhak Y. Melamed, ed., *Spinoza's Ethics: A Critical Guide* (Cambridge: Cambridge University Press, 2017), esp. the chapters by Beth Lord and Michael LeBuffe; and Yitzhak Y. Melamed and Hasana Sharp, eds., *Spinoza's Political Treatise: A Critical Guide* (Cambridge: Cambridge University Press, 2018), esp. the chapters by Justin Steinberg and Filipo del Lucchese.

69. Ingram, *Converso Non-Conformism*, 194–197, 206–209.

70. Although Franciscans, Jesuits, and other religious orders argued for an Immaculate Conception defined even before the creation of the world, the Dominicans stuck to Thomas Aquinas's reasoning that the conception of the Virgin Mary was carnal and could not have preceded the original sin. For the medieval background and the Catholic Reformation, see Miri Rubin, *The Mother of God: A History of the Virgin Mary* (London: Penguin, 2010), 303–304, 408–412. For the visual expression of the Immaculate Conception, see the excellent article by Felipe Pereda, "Vox Populi: Carnal Blood, Spiritual Milk, and the Debate Surrounding the Immaculate Conception, ca. 1600," *Medieval Encounters* 24 (2018): 286–334, which will guide me here.

71. See "Ineffabilis Deus: The Immaculate Conception," Papal Encyclicals Online, https://www.papalencyclicals.net/pius09/p9ineff.htm (accessed December 14, 2020).

72. Juan de Roelas, *Allegory of the Immaculate Conception*, 1616. Museo Nacional de la Escultura, Valladolid.

73. Juan de Jauregui, *The Woman of the Apocaplypse*, in Luis de Alcázar, *Vestigatio arcani sensus in Apocalypsi* (Seville, 1614); I consulted the edition from Lugduni: Antonij Pilehotte, 1618.

74. See the introduction to Juan de Jauregui, *Poesia*, ed. Juan Matas Caballero (Madrid: Catedra, 1993).

75. José Javier Ruiz Ibánez and Gaetano Sabatini, eds., *La Immaculada Concepción y la Monarquia Hispánica* (Madrid: Fondo de Cultura Económica, 2019).

Part IV

1. Julio Caro Baroja, *Los Judíos en la España Moderna y Contemporánea*, 3rd ed., vol. 3 (Madrid: Istmo, 1986), 190.

Chapter Thirteen: Persecution

1. António Joaquim Moreira, *História dos principais actos e procedimentos da Inquisição em Portugal* (1846), ed. João Palma-Ferreira (Lisbon: Imprensa Nacional, 1980), 145–269; a bit more consistent but without annual estimates is José Veiga Torres, "Uma longa guerra social. Os ritmos da repressão inquisitorial em Portugal," *Revista de História Económica e Social* 1 (1978): 55–68.

2. Francisco Bethencourt, *The Inquisition: A Global History, 1478–1834*, trans. Jean Birrell (Cambridge: Cambridge University Press, 2009), 345–346, although we have no precise data for the full period of the different tribunals. The percentage of New Christians under trial increased in the second half of the seventeenth century.

3. João Lúcio de Azevedo, *História dos cristãos novos portugueses* (1921) (Lisbon: Livraria Clássica, 1975), 250–264.

4. Giuseppe Marcocci and José Pedro Paiva, *História da Inquisição Portuguesa, 1536–1821* (Lisbon: Esfera dos Livros, 2013), 185–192.

5. For the decline and integration of the Companhia do Brasil, see Leonor Freire Costa, *O transporte no Atlântico e a Companhia Geral do Comércio do Brasil (1580–1663)*, vol. 1 (Lisbon: CNCDP, 2002), 597–599.

6. Jaime Contreras and Gustav Henningsen, "Forty-Four Thousand Cases of the Spanish Inquisition (1540–1700): Analysis of a Historical Data Bank," in *The Inquisition in Early Modern Europe: Studies in Sources and Methods*, ed. Gustav Henningsen and John Tedeschi (Dekalb: Northern Illinois University Press, 1986), 100–129, esp. 119.

7. Caro Baroja, *Los judíos en la España moderna y contemporánea* (1961), 3rd ed., vol 2 (Madrid: Istmo, 1986), 83.

8. Bernardo López Belinchón, *Honra, libertad y hacienda (Hombres de negocio y judíos sefardíes)* (Alcalá de Henares: Universidad de Alcalá, 2001); Carmen Sanz Ayán, *Los banqueros de Carlos II* (Valladolid: Universidad de Valladolid, 1988), 336–337.

9. Sanz Ayán, *Los banqueros de Carlos II*, 166.

10. Caro Baroja, *Los judíos en la España moderna*, vol. 2, 84–88.

11. Caro Baroja, *Los judíos en la España moderna*, vol. 2, 93–101.

12. AHN, Inquisición, Legajo 161, exp. 6, fl. 4r–v.

13. AHN, Inquisición, Legajo 161, exp. 6, fl. 189r–190r.

14. ANTT, Inquisição de Coimbra, Processo 6790, fl. 31r and following (confession) and 62r–63r (sentence). At the beginning of the confession, April 1, 1651, he declared himself to be thirty-four years old. The existence of this trial was drawn to my attention by João de Figueirôa-Rego, "Mobilidade dos agentes do tabaco entre Portugal, Madrid e outras regiões de Castela (século XVII)," in *Movilidad, interacciones y espacios de oportunidad entre Castela y Portugal en la Edad Moderna*, ed. Manuel F. Fernández Chaves and Rafael M. Pérez Garcia (Seville: Universidad de Sevilla, 2019), 253–273.

15. AHN, Inquisición, Legajo 161, exp. 6, fl. 110r.

16. AHN, Inquisición, Legajo 161, exp. 6, fl. 235v–240r and 249r–259v.

17. AHN, Inquisición, Legajo 161, exp. 6, fl. 265r–272r.

18. AHN, Inquisición, Legajo 161, exp. 6, fl. 102r.

19. AHN, Inquisición, Legajo 161, exp. 6, fl. 105r–v.

20. AHN, Inquisición, Legajo 161, exp. 6, fl. 106r–110v.

21. AHN, Inquisición, Legajo 161, exp. 6, fl. 110v–113r.

22. AHN, Inquisición, Legajo 161, exp. 6, fl. 96r. For the importance of peddlers, see Laurence Fontaine, *History of Pedlars in Europe*, trans. Vicki Whittaker (Cambridge: Polity, 1996).

23. Carmen Sanz Ayán, *Los banqueros de Carlos II*, 362–363. The genealogy of the Baron of Aguilar needs to be better researched.

24. Caro Baroja, *Los judíos en la España moderna y contemporanea*, vol. 2, 115–127.

25. Sanz Ayán, *Los banqueros de Carlos II*, 358.

26. Sanz Ayán, *Los banqueros de Carlos II*, 191, 454.

27. Sanz Ayán, *Los banqueros de Carlos II*, 166–167, 190–191.

28. Sanz Ayán, *Los banqueros de Carlos II*, 337–341.

29. Sanz Ayán, *Los banqueros de Carlos II*, 342–345.

30. Sanz Ayán, *Los banqueros de Carlos II*, 346–351.

31. Sanz Ayán, *Los banqueros de Carlos II*, 351–352.

32. Sanz Ayán, *Los banqueros de Carlos II*, 353–354.

33. ANTT, Inq. Coimbra, Proc. 8237 (badly foliated, around 600 fl.), fl. 12r. This case was briefly mentioned by several authors, namely, Freire Costa, *O transporte no Atlântico*, 517–519, 594–596, but it deserves a proper study, because it is a crucial episode of inquisitorial persecution.

34. ANTT, Inq. Coimbra, Proc. 8237, fl. 11r.

35. ANTT, Inq. Coimbra, Proc. 8237, fl. 21v.

36. ANTT, Inq. Coimbra, Proc. 8237, fl. 18v. See also the trial of Henrique Fernandes Mendes, ANTT, Inq. Coimbra, Proc. 1447, fl. 4r (with the date of prison).

37. ANTT, Inq. Coimbra, Proc. 8237, fl. 19r. Filipa Nunes de Tovar is mentioned by Veigão as "mother-in-law." She was then forty-five years old; see her trial ANTT, Inq. Coimbra, Proc. 535. Filipa's daughter Violante was then around ten, because when she was detained two years later in Aveiro, where she had taken refuge, she declared herself to be twelve or thirteen years old; see her trial ANTT, Inq. Coimbra, Proc. 3853.

38. ANTT, Inq. Coimbra, Proc. 8237, fl. 19v.

39. ANTT, Inq. Coimbra, Proc. 8237, fl. 19r–v.

40. ANTT, Inq. Coimbra, Proc. 8237, fl. 4r–v.

41. ANTT, Inq. Coimbra, Proc. 8237, fl. 26v.

42. ANTT, Inq. Coimbra, Proc. 8237, fl. 24r.

43. Jaime Contreras, *Sotos contra Riquelmes: regidores, inquisidores y criptojudíos* (Madrid: Anaya & Mario Muchnik, 1992).

44. ANTT, Inq. Coimbra, Proc. 2718, fl. 10r–v.

45. Freira Costa, *O transporte no Atlântico*, 477–598; see 517, 564, 583, 593–594, and 597 for references to Henrique Fernandes Mendes.

46. Leonor Freire Costa, *Império e grupos mercantis entre o Oriente e o Atlântico (século XVII)* (Lisbon: Horizonte, 2002), 100.

47. ANTT, Inq. Coimbra, Proc. 8237, fl. 11r and 20r (second foliation): Veigão mentioned that Policarpo was a nephew of Manuel Fernandes, but it seems that his sister Leonor had married into that family in Rouen.

48. ANTT, Inq. Coimbra, Proc. 8237, fl. 8or (second foliation).

49. ANTT, Inq. Coimbra, Proc. 8237, fl. 20r–21v (second foliation).

50. ANTT, Inq. Coimbra, Proc. 8237, fl. 1r–3r (second foliation). I thank Conceição Borges de Sousa for clarifying the meaning of "Moscow Chairs."

51. ANTT, Inq. Coimbra, Proc. 8237, fl. 3v–16v (second foliation).

52. ANTT, Inq. Coimbra, Proc. 535, fl. 25r–26r.

53. ANTT, Inq. Coimbra, Proc. 535, fl. 27r.

54. ANTT, Inq. Coimbra, Proc. 535, fl. 27v–28v.

55. ANTT, Inq. Coimbra, Proc. 8237, fl. 5r–6v.

56. ANTT, Inq. Coimbra, Proc. 8237, fl. 7r. I could not find some of these trials, such as the one of António Rodrigues Pinhel, whose wife Ana Henriques Tovar was detained and reconciled with formal abjuration; ANTT, Inq. Coimbra, Proc. 1095.

57. ANTT, Inq. Coimbra, Proc. 8237, fl. 7r–v.

58. ANTT, Inq. Coimbra, Proc. 8237, fl. 6r (folio between the first and second).

59. ANTT, Inq. Coimbra, Proc. 8237 (the last folii), Proc. 2718 (Nicolau de Oliveira) Proc. 3853 (Violante Henriques Tovar, who proved extremely competent at the age of 13, contributing to the reduction of the penalties of her husband and mother).

60. ANTT, Inq. Coimbra, Proc. 535, fl. 91r–92r (with a medical certificate).

61. ANTT, https://digitarq.arquivos.pt/results?t=Processo+Inquisicao+Coimbra&di=1658&df=1658, accessed and searched October 6, 2019. But a significant number of people were detained pending trial who do not show up in this digital catalogue in the National Archives of Portugal.

62. ANTT, Inq. Lisboa, Proc. 6707.

63. António Júlio de Andrade and Maria Fernanda Guimarães, *Os Isidros. A epopeia de uma família de cristãos-novos de Torre de Moncorvo* (s.l.: Lema de Origem, 2012), 55–67.

64. ANTT, Inq. Coimbra, Proc. 2257.

65. ANTT, Inq. Coimbra, Processo 1447, fl. 34r–38r.

66. ANTT, Inq. Coimbra, Proc. 1447, fl. 38v–41v.

67. There were detentions in Lisbon linked to the wave in Porto. Besides Manuel Rodrigues Isidro, I would point to the case of Baltasar Fernandes Mendes, son of Henrique Fernandes Mendes; ANTT, Inq. Lisboa, Proc. 11158.

68. BINE, Archicofradia de la Ssma. Ressurrección, X-III-2195, Actas y varios de congregaciones, 1604–1698; AIPSA, Actas de congregações, 1611–1678.

69. Fabrizio Nuñez, *Disaggregazione di un patrimonio fidecommissario romano* (tesi di laurea, Roma: Università degli Studi di Roma La Spienza, 1997), 28–38.

70. Roberto Valeriano, *Palazzo Torlonia* (Rome: De Luca, 2017), 30–31.

71. ASBI, Banco di Santo Spirito, Contabilità, regg. 71, c. 118, Libro Mastro dei depositi per l'anno 1665, fl. 394 (38 payments including Fernão and Manuel da Costa Brandão, total 19,203.45 scudi, and entries 23,872.10, particularly from Baltasar Gomes Homem); regg. 77, Libro Mastro dei depositi per l'anno 1671, fl. 299 with payments of 9,021.62 and 2,733.74 scudi, entries of 20,580.57; regg. 95, c. 945, Libro Mastro dei depositi per l'anno 1685, fl. 945 (42 payments including Francisco Correia Bravo, total 21,698.26 and entries 34,672.90 scudi).

72. Roberto Valeriano, *Palazzo Torlonia*. Part of this wealthy block at the center of Rome is now the flagship of the fashion house Max Mara.

73. James C. Boyajian, *Portuguese Trade in Asia under the Habsburgs,1580–1640* (Baltimore: Johns Hopkins University Press, 1993), 164, 181, 183, 206, 215, 225, 238.

74. Ana Paula Lloyd, "The Suspension of the Portuguese Inquisition, 1674–1681: Trade, Religion and Cross-Cultural Political Networks in Early Modern Europe" (PhD thesis, King's College London, 2018), 174.

75. See James W. Nelson Novoa, *Humanismo e Ciência: Antiguidade e Renascimento* (Aveiro: Universidade de Aveiro, 2015), 227–248.

76. AIPSA, Actas de congregações, 1611–1678; ANTT, Inq. Lisboa, Proc. 310, fl. 53r.

77. ANTT, Inq. Lisboa, Proc. 310, fl. 5r–30r.

78. ANTT, Inq. Lisboa, Proc. 310, fl. 32r–47v (for the shares in fortresses, with detailed buying and selling, see fl. 34v and 35v).

79. ANTT, Inq. Lisboa, Proc. 310, fl. 53r–v.

80. ANTT, Inq. Lisboa, Proc. 310, fl. 300r–v.

81. ANTT, Inq. Lisboa, Processo 8132, fl. 141r and 152v.

82. ANTT, Inq. Lisboa, Processo 8132, fl. 376r.

83. ANTT, Inq. Lisboa, Processo 8132, fl. 180r–183r.

84. ANTT, Inq. Lisboa, Processo 8132, fl. Fl. 182r.

85. Boyajian, *Portuguese Trade*, 215.

86. António Baião, *Episódios dramáticos da Inquisição*, 2nd ed., vol. 2 (Lisbon: Seara Nova, 1938), 400.

87. Baião, *Episódios dramáticos da Inquisição*, vol. 2, 401.

88. ASF, Deputazione sopra la nobiltà e citadinanza, Processi di Nobiltà, Libro 17, fasc. 19 (without foliation).

89. ASF, Panciatichi Ximenes de Aragona, fasc. XXI. The will and codicils have dates ranging from July 25, 1654, to June 25, 1663. The documentation was sent from Lisbon at the request of Tomás Ximenes de Aragão, who wanted to challenge the right to inheritance of Afonso Jorge de Melo Ximenes.

90. Micol Ferrara, *Dentro e fuori del ghetto: i luoghi della presenza ebraica a Roma tra XVI e XIX secolo* (Milan: Mondadori, 2015), 9; Francesca Trivellato, *The Familiarity of Strangers: The Sephardic Diapora, Livorno, and Cross-Cultural Trade in the Early Modern Period* (New Haven, CT: Yale University Press, 2009), 54–55; Marina Caffiero, *Storia degli ebrei nell'Italia moderna* (Roma: Carroci, 2014), 53–54, 58.

91. Cristina Galasso, "Il ritorno all'ebraismo dei cristiani nuovi e delle cristiane nuove di Livorno e Pisa," in *Donne nella storia degli ebrei d'Italia*, ed. Michele Luzzati and Cristina Galasso (Florence: Giuntina, 2007), 233–262; see also Cristina Galasso, *Alle origine di una communità: ebree e ebrei a Livorno nel Seicento* (Florence: Olshki, 2002).

92. Trivellato, *Familiarity of Strangers*.

93. Hans Pohl, *Die Portugiesen in Antwerpen (1567–1648)* (Wiesbaden: Franz Steiner, 1977), 354–355.

94. Pohl, *Die Portugiesen in Antwerpen*, 95.

95. Pohl, *Die Portugiesen in Antwerpen*, 97–98, 100–101, 354–355.

96. Jorun Poettering, *Migrating Merchants. Trade, Nation, and Religion in Seventeenth-Century Hamburg and Portugal*, trans. Kenneth Kronenberg (Berlin: De Guyter, 2019), 16.

97. Jon Arrizabalaga, "Medical Ideas in the Sephardic Diaspora: Rodrigo de Castro's Portrait of the Perfect Physician in Early Seventeenth Century Hamburg," *Medical History Supplement* 29 (2009): 107–124.

98. I.-S. Révah, *Uriel da Costa et les marranes de Porto. Cours au Collège de France, 1966–1972* ed. Carsten L. Wilke (Paris: Fondation Calouste Gulbenkian, 2004).

99. Aron di Leone Leoni and Herman Prins Salomon, "La nation portugaise de Hambourg en 1617 d'après un document inédit," in *Mémorial I.-S. Révah. Études sur le marranisme, l'hétérodoxie juive et Spinoza*, ed. Henri Méchoulan and Gérard Nahon (Paris-Louvain: E. Peeters, 2001), 263–293.

100. Poettering, *Migrating Merchants*, 110.

101. Numbers are still in dispute, see the assessment by Poettering, *Migrating Merchants*, 114–115.

102. Michael Studemund-Halévy and Jorun Poettering, "Étrangers universels: les réseaux sépharades à Hambourg," *Arquivos do Centro Cultural Calouste Gulbenkian* 48 (2004): 117–150; Jonathan Israel, "An Amsterdam Jewish Merchant of the Golden Age: Jerónimo Nunes da Costa (1620–1697) Agent of Portugal in the Dutch Republic," *Studia Rosenthaliana* 18, no. 1 (1984): 12–40; Jonathan Israel, "Duarte Nunes da Costa (Jacob Curiel), of Hamburg, Sephardi Nobleman and Communal Leader (1585–1664)," *Studia Rosenthaliana* 21, no. 1 (1987): 14–44.

103. There is a certain gap between the first estimates of 2,500 people in 1674–1675 by Yosef Kaplan and the 3,300 suggested by Hubert P. H. Nustelling, "The Jews in the Republic of the United Provinces: Origins, Numbers and Dispersion," in *Dutch Jewry: Its History and Secular Culture (1500–2000)*, ed. Jonathan Israel and Reinier Salverda (Leiden: Brill, 2002), 43–62. See also Daniel M. Swetschinski, *Reluctant Cosmopolitans: The Portuguese Jews of Seventeenth Century Amsterdam* (London: Littman Library of Jewish Civilization, 2000), 61–62, 90.

104. Swetschinski, *Reluctant Cosmopolitans*, 117, 119, 122–129, 133.

105. Swetschinski, *Reluctant Cosmopolitans*, 135–138.

106. Odette Vlessing, "The Portuguese-Jewish Merchant Community in Seventeenth-Century Amsterdam," in *Entrepreneurs and Entrepreneurship in Early Modern Times: Merchants and Industrialists within the Orbit of the Dutch Staple Market*, ed. C. Lesger and L. Noordegraaf (The Hague: Stichting Hollandse Historische Reeks, 1995), 225–243, esp. 228.

107. Swetschinski, *Reluctant Cosmopolitans*, 141–142.

108. ANTT, Inquisição de Lisboa, Processo 2332, fl. 106v and 126v. Penso had spread the false information that he had cut off trade with his father-in-law when the latter became Jewish in Amsterdam. More difficult to find information about is Sara Penso, who married Moses Pessoa, the youngest son of Jerónimo Gomes Pessoa, in 1664.

109. Edgar Samuel, *At the End of the Earth: Essays on the History of the Jews in England and Portugal* (London: Jewish Historical Society of England, 2004), 194, 197.

110. Arnold Wiznitzer, *Jews in Colonial Brazil* (New York: Columbia University Press, 1960), ch. 7.

111. Samuel, *At the End of the Earth*, 194–197.

112. Jonathan Israel, "The Jews of Dutch America," in *The Jews and the Expansion of Europe to the West*, ed. Paolo Bernardini and Norman Fiering (New York: Berghahn, 2001),

333–349; Wim Klooster, "Jews in Suriname and Curaçao," in *The Jews and the Expansion of Europe to the West*, 350–368.

113. National Archives of the United Kingdom (NA), PROB 11/358/140.

114. NA, PROB 11/358/140.

115. NA, PROB 11/358/140.

116. NA, PROB 11/394/66.

117. Jonathan Israel and Stuart B. Schwartz, *The Expansion of Tolerance: Religion in Dutch Brazil (1624-1654)* (Amsterdam: Amsterdam University Press, 2007).

118. Bruno Feitler, "Jews and New Christians in Dutch Brazil, 1630–1654," in *Atlantic Diasporas: Jews Conversos, and Crypto-Jews in the Age of Mercantilism, 1500-1800*, ed. Richard L. Kagan and Philip D. Morgan (Baltimore: Johns Hopkins University Press, 2009), 123–151.

119. Wiznitzer, *Jews in Colonial Brazil*, chapter 6, in which the list of 117 members of the congregations Zur Israel and Magen Abraham from 1648 to 1654 is published. The peak numbers were corrected by Swetschinski, *Reluctant Cosmopolitans*, 115. See also Ronaldo Vainfas, "Tipologia do desengano: Cristãos-novos portugueses entre Amesterdão e o Brasil holandês," *Cadernos de Estudos Sefarditas* 7 (2008), 9–29; and Ronaldo Vainfas, *Jerusalém colonial: Judeus portugueses no Brasil holandês* (Rio de Janeiro: Civilização Brasileira, 2010).

120. Wiznitzer, *Jews in Colonial Brazil*, chapters 4 and 7.

121. Anita Novinsky, *Inquisição: prisioneiros do Brasil*; Daviken Studnicki-Gizbert, *A Nation upon the Ocean Sea: Portugal's Atlantic Diaspora and the Crisis of the Spanish Empire, 1492-1640* (Oxford: Oxford University Press, 2007).

122. Elias Lipiner, *Izaque de Castro, o mancebo que veio preso do Brasil* (Recife: Fundação Joaquim Nabuco, 1992), esp. 149–157.

123. Gérard Nahon, *Les "nations" juives portugaises du Sud-Ouest de la France (1684-1791). Documents* (Paris: Fundação Calouste Gulbenkian, 1981); Gérard Nahon, "The Portuguese Jewish Nation of Saint-Esprit-lès-Bayonne: the American Dimension," in *The Jews and the Expansion of Europe to the West*, 255–267; Silvia Marzagalli, "Atlantic Trade and Sephardim Merchants in Eighteenth Century France: The Case of Bordeaux," in *The Jews and the Expansion of Europe to the West*, 268–286.

Chapter Fourteen: Suspension

1. The best study of the suspension, seen for the first time from multiple angles, including from Rome, is by Ana Paula Lloyd, *The Suspension of the Portuguese Inquisition, 1674-1681: Trade, Religion and Cross-Cultural Political Networks in Early Modern Europe* (PhD thesis, King's College London, 2018).

2. Angela Xavier and Pedro Cardim, *D. Afonso VI* (Lisbon: Círculo de Leitores, 2006); Paula Lourenço, *D. Pedro II* (Lisbon: Círculo de Leitores, 2007).

3. Data collected in António Joaquim Moreira, *História dos principais actos e procedimentos da Inquisição em Portugal* (1846), ed. João Palma-Ferreira (Lisbon: Imprensa Nacional, 1980), 145–269.

4. Luís de Bivar Guerra, *Inventário dos processos da Inquisição de Coimbra (1541-1820)*, vol. 1 (Paris: Fundação Calouste Gulbenkian, 1972), 174–195.

5. ANTT, Inquisição de Lisboa, Processo 9948, fl. 38r–74r.

6. The inheritance was valued at 20,000 cruzados; ANTT, Inq. Lx, Proc. 9948, fl. 44v–45r. For the relationship with Manuel da Gama de Pádua, which is not clear in Rodrigues da Costa's trial, see ANTT, Inquisição de Lisboa, Processo 8071, fl. 18r-19v, where Manuel da Gama mentions, in 1636, his young sister, Guiomar Soeiro.

7. ANTT, Inq. Lx, Proc. 9948, fl. 38v.

8. ANTT, Inq. Lx, Proc. 9948, fl. 39r–40r.

9. ANTT, Inq. Lx, Proc. 9948, fl.40v–44r.

10. ANTT, Inq. Lx, Proc. 9948, fl. 172r–175v (torture), 186r–v (sentence).

11. ANTT, Inq. Lx, Proc. 9948, fl. 78r.

12. ANTT, Inquisição de Lisboa, Processo 81.

13. ANTT, Inq. Lx, Proc. 81, fl. 27r–29r.

14. ANTT, Inq. Lx, Proc. 81, fl. 35r–73r.

15. ANTT, Inq. Lx, Proc. 81, fl. 82r–83r, 87r–88r.

16. ANTT, Inq. Lx, Proc. 81, fl. 90r.

17. ANTT, Inquisição de Lisboa, Processo 5412, fl. 187r.

18. ANTT, Inquisição de Lisboa, Processos 1716 (Francisco Carlos ended up with abjuration of mildly suspected heresy on May 13, 1682), 4426 (Diogo de Chaves, who died in jail and was absolved on April 24, 1682), 9792 (Simão Rodrigues Chaves, who also died in jail and was absolved on May 10, 1682). I shall concentrate on the other trials.

19. ANTT, Inquisição de Lisboa, Processo 5412, fl. 14r–24v.

20. ANTT, Inq. Lx, Proc. 5412, fl. 25r–36v.

21. Declarations copied into the father's trial, ANTT, Inq. Lx, Proc. 5412, fl. 40v–42r; Brites' trial includes a record of many of the prayers she uttered; ANTT, Inquisição de Lisboa, Processo 4427, fl. 114r–119r.

22. ANTT, Inq. Lx, Proc. 5412, fl. 49v; Pantaleão's trial is in ANTT, Inquisição de Lisboa, Processo 7100.

23. ANTT, Inquisição de Lisboa, Processo 1747.

24. ANTT, Inquisição de Lisboa, Processo 11262.

25. ANTT, Inq. Lx, Proc. 5412, fl. 55r.

26. ANTT, Inq. Lx, Proc. 5412, fl. 59v.

27. ANTT, Inq. Lx, Proc. 5412, fl. 61v–62r.

28. ANTT, Inq. Lx, Proc. 5412, fl. 65r–69v.

29. ANTT, Inq. Lx, Proc. 5412, fl. 147r–152v.

30. ANTT, Inq. Lx, Proc. 5412, fl. fl. 143r–v.

31. ANTT, Inq. Lx, Proc. 5412, fl. 214r–217v. The list of this auto da fé was printed; BNP, Códice 863, fl. 299v. The trial of Branca Henriques is also interesting; ANTT, Inquisição de Lisboa, Processo 8447, particularly the sentence, fl. 147r–150.

32. ANTT, Inq. Lx, Proc. 8447, fl. 97r–103r, 147r–150r; Proc. 8408, fl. 24r, 82r–83r.

33. ANTT, Inq. Lx, Proc. 5412, fl. 93v and 94v.

34. ANTT, Inquisition of Lisbon, Processo 2332 and 2332–1 (a second trial). The case of Fernão Rodrigues Penso is briefly mentioned by João de Figueirôa-Rego, "Mobilidade dos agentes do tabaco entre Portugal, Madrid e outras regiões de Castela (século XVII)," in *Movilidad, interacciones y espacios de oportunidad entre Castilla y Portugal en la Edad Moderna*, ed. Manuel Francisco Fernández Chaves, Rafael M. Pérez García (Seville: Universidad de Sevilla, 2019), 253–273.

35. ANTT, Inq. Lx, Proc. 2332, fl. 106r–v and 66v.

36. ANTT, Inq. Lx, Proc. 2332, fl.73r–103r, related to this and the following paragraphs.

37. ANTT, Inq. Lx, Proc. 2332, fl. 66r–66v.

38. ANTT, Inq. Lx, Proc. 2332, fl. 86r–v.

39. ANTT, Inq. Lx, Proc. 2332, fl. 221v.

40. ANTT, Inq. Lx, Proc. 2332, fl. 193r.

41. ANTT, Inq. Lx, Proc. 2332, fl. 210r.

42. ANTT, Inq. Lx, Proc. 2332, fl. 244r.

43. ANTT, Inq. Lx, Proc. 2332, fl. 252r–256v.

44. ANTT, Inq. Lx, Proc. 2332, fl. 8r.

45. ANTT, Inq. Lx, Proc. 2332, fl. 213v.

46. ANTT, Inq. Lx, Proc. 2332, fl. 62v.

47. António Baião, *Episódios dramáticos da Inquisição*, 2nd ed., vol. 2 (Lisbon: Seara Nova, 1938), 400–401; the brief is reproduced in *CDP*, tome XIV (Lisbon: Real Academia das Sciencias, 1910), 26–27.

48. João Lúcio de Azevedo, *História dos cristãos novos portugueses* (1921) (Lisbon: Livraria Clássica, 1975), 289.

49. Lúcio de Azevedo, *História dos cristãos novos portugueses*, 293.

50. Lúcio de Azevedo, *História dos cristãos novos portugueses*, 291.

51. Lúcio de Azevedo, *História dos cristãos novos portugueses*, 293, quoting a well-known newsletter of the time, *Monstruosidades do tempo e da fortuna*.

52. Marcocci and Paiva, *História da Inquisição Portuguesa, 1536-1821* (Lisbon: Esfera dos Livros, 2013), 174, 202, 488 (footnote 50) and 491 (footnote 88).

53. I did not find any trace of this law in any compilation of Portuguese legislation.

54. Francisco Bethencourt, "Sumptuary Laws in Portugal and its Empire from the Fourteenth to the Eighteenth Century," in *The Right to Dress: Sumptuary Laws in a Global Perspective, c. 1200-1800*, ed. Giorgio Riello and Ulinka Rublack (Cambridge: Cambridge University Press, 2019), 273-298.

55. Lúcio de Azevedo, *História dos cristãos novos portugueses*, 294-295.

56. ANTT, Armário Jesuítico, Maço 29, doc. 14.

57. ANTT, Armário Jesuítico, Maço 29, doc. 18.

58. ANTT, Armário Jesuítico, Maço 29, docs 31 and 33.

59. ANTT, Armário Jesuítico, Maço 29, doc. 35.

60. ANTT, Armário Jesuítico, Maço 29, doc. 50 (this document has a date, August 28, 1673).

61. Lúcio de Azevedo, *História dos cristãos novos portugueses*, 295.

62. ANTT, Armário Jesuítico, Maço 29, doc. 40.

63. ANTT, Armário Jesuítico, Maço 29, doc. 46.

64. José Pedro Paiva, *Baluartes da fé e da disciplina: o enlace entre a Inquisição e os bispos em Portugal (1536-1750)* (Coimbra: Imprensa da Universidade de Coimbra, 2011), 242-258.

65. ANTT, Armário Jesuítico, Maço 29, docs 21, 47, 53.

66. ANTT, Armário Jesuítico, Maço 29, docs 55, 56, 60 (this last one an extraordinary testimony of fear from a Jesuit of the University of Évora, who reflects on the tense atmosphere among theologians, especially in Coimbra); ANTT, Armário Jesuítico, Maço 30, doc. 29 (letter from Manuel Pereira de Melo, governor of the University of Coimbra, to Manuel Fernandes, Jesuit confessor of the regent, in which he apologises for not being able to obtain support for the appeal, "*empenho da Companhia*," from the Professors of Theology and Canon Law).

67. ANTT, Armário Jesuítico, Maço 30, docs 2-4, 12.

68. ANTT, Armário Jesuítico, Maço 30, doc. 19.

69. ANTT, Mesa da Consciência e Ordens, Habilitações para a Ordem de Cristo, Letra D, Maço 2, n. 2.

70. ANTT, Inquisição de Lisboa, Processo 1716, fl. 57r-59v (genealogy of Francisco Carlos).

71. ANTT, Mesa da Consciência e Ordens, Habilitações para a Ordem de Cristo, Letra A, Maço 52, n. 80.

72. Edgar Samuel, *At the End of the Earth: Essays on the History of the Jews in England and Portugal* (London: Jewish Historical Society of England, 2004), 198.

73. ANTT, Inquisição de Lisboa, Processo 8071, fl. 18r-20r, 188r-191v.

74. The appointment as treasurer is dated June 20, 1654; ANTT, Registo Geral das Mercês, Mercês da Torre do Tombo, Livro 22, fl. 493v.

75. ANTT, Mesa da Consciência e Ordens, Habilitações para a Ordem de Cristo, Letra M, maço 42, n. 30.

76. ANTT, Inquisição de Évora, Processo 1022.

77. ANTT, Inquisição de Évora, Processos 6502 and 9433.

78. ANTT, Registo Geral das Mercês, Mercês de D. Afonso VI, Livro 10, fl. 163r and Mercês de Vários Reis, Livro 1, fl. 167v.

79. ANTT, Inquisição de Lisboa, Processo 2833.

80. ANTT, Inquisição de Lisboa, Processo 2835.

81. ANTT, Registo Geral de Mercês, Mercês das Ordens Militares, Livro 34, fl. 35v.

82. ANTT, Armário Jesuítico, Maço 30, doc. 32.

83. ANTT Armário Jesuítico, Maço 29, n. 33, especially fl. 50v and 54r.

84. Samuel, *At the End of the Earth*, 198. I have applied the equivalence of 1 pound = 7.5 cruzados within the range 7.3-8.0 reconstituted for the 1680s by Markus A. Denzel, *Handbook*

of World Exchange Rates, 1590–1914 (London: Routledge, 2016), 30. There are no reliable figures for the previous period. The purchasing power of £36,000 in 1675 could be estimated at around 8 million pounds today, see https://www.statista.com/statistics/1031884/value-pound -sterling-since/, accessed May 20, 2019. See my analysis of this case in chapter 13.

85. Lloyd, *Suspension of the Portuguese Inquisition*, 77–83.

86. ANTT, Armário Jesuítico, Maço 30, doc. 24 (letter dated May 5, 1674).

87. See the reconstitution of this divergence in José Pedro Paiva, "Revisitar o processo inquisitorial do Padre António Vieira," *Lusitania Sacra*, 2nd series, 23 (2011): 151–168. On the importance of sermons in this period, see João Marques, *A parenética portuguesa e a Restauração, 1640–1668: a revolta e a mentalidade* (Porto: INIC, 1989).

88. Maria del Carmen Sáenz Berceo, *Confesionario y poder en la España del siglo XVII: Juan Everardo Nithard* (Logroño: Universidad de la Rioja, 2014).

89. ANTT, Armário Jesuítico, Maço 30, doc. 55.

90. See Paiva, *Baluartes da fé e da disciplina.*

91. I agree with the notion of the Catholic Church as a legalistic institution suggested by Kenneth Stow, "Papal Power, the Portuguese Inquisition and a Consilium of Cardinal Pier Paolo Pariseo," *Journal of Levantine Studies* 6 (2016): 89–105.

92. I use here the copy published in *CDP*, tomo XIV, 238–260. The General Council of the Inquisition in Portugal was well aware of this document, duly transcribed; ANTT, CGSO, Livro 158 (I thank José Pedro Paiva for this information).

93. *CDP*, tomo XIV, 238–239.

94. *CDP*, tomo XIV, 239–240.

95. *CDP*, tomo XIV, 241. We have seen in other chapters how officials of the Inquisition's exchequer and inquisitors, among them future bishops, ended up with a good portion of confiscated property, including the houses of condemned people.

96. *CDP*, tomo XIV, 239–242.

97. *CDP*, tomo XIV, 245–247.

98. *CDP*, tomo XIV, 239–240.

99. *CDP*, tomo XIV, 242–244.

100. *CDP*, tomo XIV, 244. The case of António Homem, discussed in part III, centred on a professor of the University of Coimbra accused of performing Jewish rituals as a high priest. He was excommunicated without ever confessing, and the case must have inspired this exposure of the absence of corpus delicti. In this case, the corruption of the Inquisition in the confiscation of his property was blatant.

101. *CDP*, tomo XIV, 247.

102. *CDP*, tomo XIV, 248–249.

103. *CDP*, tomo XIV, 250–251.

104. *CDP*, tomo XIV, 253–254.

105. *CDP*, tomo XIV, 255–256.

106. *CDP*, tomo XIV, 256–257.

107. *CDP*, tomo XIV, 257–259.

108. Cesare Beccaria, *Dei delitti e delle penne* (1764), ed. Franco Venturi (Turin: Einaudi, 1973); Cesare Beccaria, *On Crimes and Punishments and Other Writings*, ed. and trans. Richard Bellamy (Cambridge: Cambridge University Press, 1995); Edward Peters, *Torture* (Philadelphia: University of Pennsylvania Press, 1996).

109. See Adriano Prosperi, *Tribunali della coscienza: inquisitori, confessori, missionary* (1996), rev. ed. (Turin: Einaudi, 2009).

110. Archivio della Congregazzione per la Dottrina della Fede (ACDF), BB5a (without foliation).

111. ACDF, BB5a (without foliation).

112. ACDF, mainly codices BB5a, BB5b, BB5c, BB5d, BB5e, BB5f, CC5b, CC5d, CC5e, I3h. The series BB5 has the common title "Iudaizantes Lusitaniae," but the dates indicated in each codex do not correspond to the content, being generally more comprehensive.

113. ACDF, BB5a, without foliation (my translation).

114. ACDF, BB5d, from the initial folios up to fl. 49r; there is no other major issue.

115. *CDP*, tomo XIV, 155 (letter from June 3, 1673) and 162.

116. ACDF, BB5d, fl. 48r–49r.

117. ACDF, BB5d, fl. 81r.

118. *CDP*, tomo XIV, 162 (letter from September 9, 1673).

119. ANTT, CGSO, Maço 21, doc. 27, letter by Jerónimo Soares, March 9, 1675 (I thank José Pedro Paiva for this information).

120. BINE, Archicofradia de la Ssma. Ressurrección A-II-71, fl. 91v; X-III-2195 (the marquis was still active in the early 1680s); AIPSA, Actas das Congregações, 1611–1678 (there is a gap before the next book 1696–1732, but the continued presence of Nunes Sanches is attested).

121. Fabrizio Nuñez, *Disaggregazione di un patrimonio fidecommissario romano* (tesi di laurea, Rome: Università degli Studi di Roma La Spienza, 1997), 34, 40–41; Lloyd, *Suspension of the Portuguese Inquisition*, 177.

122. Roberto Valeriani, *Palazzo Torlonia* (Roma: De Luca, 2017).

123. A copy of the will of Gonçalo Nunes Sanches, dated 1682, exists at the AIPSA, Testamentos 006 (1644–1828). It lists nine benefices in different parts of Portugal plus one benefice and one pension in the parish of Santa Justa, Lisbon.

124. Nuñez, *Disaggregazione di un patrimonio fidecommissario romano*, 22–25.

125. ASR, Notai Auditori della Camera, vol. 843, Belletus, fl. 297r–308v.

126. ASBI, Banco di Santo Spirito, Contabilità, regg. 77, Libro Mastro dei depositi par l'anno 1671, fl. 645, payments 3,154.50 scudi; regg. 95, Libro Mastro dei depositi par l'anno 1685, fl. 308, payments 5.051.80, entries 4,590.73 scudi.

127. BINE, Archicofradia de la Ssma. Ressurrección, X-III-2195 Actas y varios de congregaciones, 1604–1698 (without foliation); H-III-583, Registro de matriculas de cofrades, 1603–1679 (without foliation), Baltasar Gomes Homem registered in 1653, Francisco de Azevedo registered in 1675.

128. AIPSA, Actas das Congregações, 1611–1678, fl. 328v–329r and 334v.

129. *CDP*, tome XV, letters from the ambassador in 1677, 366, 431, 436, 440.

130. AIPSA, Actas das Congregações, 1696–1732, fl. 6r.

131. Velázquez, Portrait of Ferdinando Brandani, ca. 1650, oil on canvas, 50.5×47 cm, Madrid, Museo Nacional del Prado, inv. nr. P-7858.

132. Francesca Curti, "Il ritratto svelato di Ferdinando Brandani. Carreira e interessi artistici di un banchiere amico di Diego Velázquez e di Juan de Córdoba," *Boletín del Museo del Prado* 29, no. 47 (2011): 54–67 (very accurate research with a valuable genealogical table on 64).

133. Lloyd, *Suspension of the Portuguese Inquisition*, 169.

134. Antonio J. Díaz Rodríguez, "Mercaderes de la gracia: las compañias de negocios curiales entre Roma y Portugal en la edad moderna," *Ler História* 72 (2018): 55–76

135. ASR, Trenta Notai, Capitolino, Ufficio 1, Testamenti, vol. 850, Franciscus Floridus 1699–1723, fl. 31v (Francisco Nicolau died on November 13, 1699, and the will was read the day after).

136. This is the main thesis of in Lloyd, *Suspension of the Portuguese Inquisition*.

137. Maria Antonietta Visceglia, *La Roma dei Papi: La corte e la politica internazionale (secoli XV-XVII)*, ed. Elena Valeri and Paola Volpini (Rome: Viella, 2018); Gianvittorio Signorotto and Maria Antonietta Visceglia, eds., *Court and Politics in Papal Rome, 1492–1700* (Cambridge: Cambridge University Press, 2002); Richard Bösel, Antonio Menniti Ippolito, Andrea Spiriti, Claudio Strinato, Maria Antonietta Visceglia, eds., *Innocenzo XI Odescalchi: papa, politico, commitente* (Rome: Viella, 2014); Irene Fosi, *Papal Justice: Subjects and Courts in the Papal State, 1500-1750*, trans. Thomas V. Cohen (Washington, DC: Catholic University of America Press, 2011).

138. *CDP*, tome XIV, 221–224.

139. Lúcio de Azevedo, *História dos cristãos novos portugueses*, 310–311.

140. Lloyd, *Suspension of the Portuguese Inquisition*, 177.

141. ACDF, BB5e, fl. 428r–429r (votes of cardinals concerning different issues of the Portuguese Inquisition).

142. Marcocci and Paiva, *História da Inquisição Portuguesa*, 205–206.

143. ACDF, BB5a (without foliation).

144. ACDF, BB5e, fl. 191r–197r.

145. *CDP*, tome XIV, 311–313 (December 12, 1676, letter from the Portuguese ambassador). This became a regular request, reported by the ambassador in the following years.

146. *CDP*, tome XV, 1st part, 71, letter from the Portuguese ambassador, Luís de Sousa, on October 18, 1678, in which he reports an outburst of anger from Pope Innocent XI when the latter was talking to Jerónimo Soares, representative of the Portuguese Inquisition. See José Pedro Paiva, "Representar e negociar em favor da Inquisição. A missão em Roma de Jerónimo Soares (1674–1682)," in *Estudos em Homenagen de Joaquim Romero Magalhães. Economia, Instituições e Império*, eds L. Freire Costa, L. Miguel Duarte, and A. Garrido (Coimbra: Almedina, 2012), 157–177.

147. Marcocci and Paiva, *História da Inquisição Portuguesa*, 206–208.

148. Ronaldo Vainfas, *Antônio Vieira* (São Paulo: Companhia das Letras, 2011).

149. RA-B, Protocollen, Staten en rekeningen, Ambrosius Sebille, 1677–1677, 3040, fl. 36r–v. The reference to the elevation of Francisco da Silva to the position of Marquis of Monfort is in Julio Caro Baroja, *Los judíos en la España moderna y contemporánea* (1961), 3rd ed., vol. 2 (Madrid: Istmo, 1986), 138.

150. Eric Duverger, *Antwerpse Kunstinventarissen*, vol. 10 (Brussels: Fontes Historiae Artis Neerlandicae, 1999), 220–223.

151. Ana Paula Lloyd, "Manuel da Gama de Pádua's Political Networks: Service, Subversion and the Disruption of the Portuguese Inquisition," *Journal of Levantine Studies* 6 (2016): 251–275.

152. See the abundant references in Lloyd, *Suspension of the Portuguese Inquisition*, in which it is clear that Cardinal Barberini was pushing for the assertion of papal powers but at the same time left the door open for a negotiated solution.

153. Norbert Elias, *The Court Society* (1969), trans. Edmund Jephcott, revised (Dublin: University College Dublin Press, 2006).

154. *CDP*, tome XV, 1st part, 265, 273, 274.

155. *CDP*, tome XV, 1st part, 376, 379.

156. *CDP*, tome XV, 2nd part, 61 (letter from September 17, 1678).

157. *CDP*, tome XV, 2nd part, 72 (letter from October 18, 1678).

158. *CDP*, tome XV, 2nd part, 234 and 238 (letter from June 21, 1679).

159. *CDP*, tome XV, 2nd part, 188–190.

160. Paiva, "Representar e negociar em favor da Inquisição"; and Lloyd, *Suspension of the Portuguese Inquisition*.

161. *CDP*, tome XV, 2nd part, 352.

162. *CDP*, tome XV, 2nd part, 388–189 (the initial idea all the inquisitors), 507–508 (specified Manuel de Moura and Bento de Beja as offensive to the pope).

163. *CDP*, tome XV, 2nd part, 129.

164. The issue of royal patronage of the Church overseas in relation to the *Propaganda Fide* is the second major problem dealt by Ambassador Luís de Sousa, see *CDP*, tome XV, 1st part, 11, 17, 22–23, 120, 159, 217–220, 234–235, 321–322. For the context of the Portuguese royal patronage see Ângela Barreto Xavier and Fernanda Olival, "O padroado da coroa de Portugal: Fundamentos e práticas," in *Monarquias Ibéricas em Perspectiva Comparada (séculos XVI–XVIII): Dinâmicas imperiais e circulação de modelos administrativos*, ed. Ângela Xavier, Federico Palomo and Roberta Stumpf (Lisbon: Imprensa de Ciências Sociais, 2018), 123–160.

165. Marco Cavina, *La giustizia criminale nell'Italia moderna (XVI–XVIII sec.)* (Bologna: Pàtron, 2012).

Chapter Fifteen: Breakdown

1. Azevedo, *História dos cristãos novos portugueses* (1921) (Lisbon: Livraria Clássica, 1975), 321–322; Marcocci and Paiva, *História da Inquisição Portuguesa, 1536–1821* (Lisbon: Esfera dos Livros, 2013), 239–240, although here more nuanced.

2. Marcocci and Paiva, *História da Inquisição Portuguesa*, 242–243, where the slowing down of activity is acknowledged.

3. *An Account on the Rise and Present State of the Inquisitions Showing that Those of Spain and Portugal Are Contrary to the Divine and Political Laws, and More Cruel and Tyrannical in Their Proceedings than That in Italy* (London: J. Brotherton, 1730), 29. The book's author appears to have been in Rome, but it could have been a compilation from various sources.

4. For the original papal brief, ACDF, BB5a (without foliation) and BB5b (printed brief at the beginning); *An Account of the Rise and Present State of the Inquisitions*, 29–31.

5. ACDF, BB5a and BB5b; *An Account on the Rise and Present State of the Inquisitions*, 31–34. On the issue of proof, see Ana Caldeira Cabral Santiago de Faria, "O Regimento de 1640 e a justiça inquisitorial portuguesa" (MA dissertation in History, Universidade de Coimbra, 2016), 88–94.

6. I am inspired here by David Theo Goldberg, *The Racial State* (Oxford: Blackwell, 2002), although reflection on the early modern state needs a specific approach.

7. This is a complex issue, because papal authority concerning canonization was expressed as infallible by the late Middle Ages. See Donald Prudlo, *Certain Sainthood: Canonization and Origins of Papal Infallibility in the Medieval Church* (Ithaca, NY: Cornell University Press, 2015). I thank Simon Ditchfield for calling my attention for this issue.

8. Maria Antonietta Visceglia, ed., *Papato e politica internazionale nella prima età moderna* (Rome: Viella, 2013); Gianvittorio Signorotto and Maria Antonietta Visceglia, eds, *Courts and Politics in Papal Rome, 1492–1700* (Cambridge: Cambridge University Press, 2002).

9. José Pedro Paiva, *Os bispos de Portugal e do império, 1495–1777* (Coimbra: Imprensa da Universidade de Coimbra, 2006).

10. Richard Bösel, Antonio Menniti Ippolito, Andrea Spiriti, Claudio Strinato, Maria Antonietta Visceglia, eds., *Innocenzo XI Odescalchi: Papa, politico, committente* (Rome: Viella, 2014).

11. Marina Caffiero, *Battesimi forzati: Storie di ebrei e cristiani convertiti nella Roma dei Papi* (Rome: Viella, 2004), 82. Among several good studies on this cardinal, I would highlight that of Agostino Lauro, *Il cardinale Giovan Battista de Luca: diritto e riforma nello stato della Chiesa (1676-1683)* (Naples: Jovene, 1991); Rafaelle Coppola and Ezio M. Lavoràno, eds., *Alla riscoperta del Cardinale Giovanni Battista de Luca, giureconsulto* (Potenza: Osanna, 2016).

12. Irene Fosi, *Papal Justice: Subjects and Courts in the Papal State*, trans. Thomas V. Cohen (Washington, DC: Catholic University of America Press, 2011).

13. ACDF, BB5, without foliation.

14. António Joaquim Moreira, *História dos principais actos e procedimentos da Inquisição em Portugal* (1846), ed. João Palma-Ferreira (Lisbon: Imprensa Nacional, 1980), 249.

15. BNP, Códice 167, fl. 224r.

16. BNP, Códice 167, fl. 231r.

17. BNP, Códice 167, fl. 242v.

18. ANTT, Inquisição de Lisboa, Processo 5412, fl. 161v–205r, 210r–217v.

19. ANTT, Armário Jesuítico, Maço 30, doc. 87.

20. ACDF, BB5a without foliation.

21. ANTT, Armário Jesuítico, Maço 30, doc. 89 (letter from Manuel Dias).

22. Marcocci and Paiva, *História da Inquisição Portuguesa*, 239–240.

23. Moreira, *História dos principais actos e procedimentos da Inquisição em Portugal*.

24. Azevedo, *História dos cristãos novos portugueses*, 325–327.

25. ANTT, Armário Jesuítico, Maço 30, docs 91, 92, and 93.

26. BNP, Códice 13168 (this must have been the book organised by the Marquis of Gouveia for the implementation of the extermination law).

27. Azevedo, *História dos cristãos novos portugueses*, 330.

28. ANTT, Armário Jesuítico, Maço 30, doc. 87 (in 1682, among the complaints against the Inquisition).

29. ANTT, 2° cartório notarial de Lisboa, Livro 266, caixa 53, 22/4/5, Livro do Tabelião Francisco de Pina e Sá, fl. 73r–73v.

30. ANTT, Inquisição de Lisboa, Processo 2332–1, fl. 33r.

31. ANTT, Registo Geral de Mercês, Mercês de D. Pedro II, Livro 1, n. 37, fl. 374.

32. A crucial finding by Fernanda Olival, *As ordens militares e o Estado moderno. Honra, mercê e venalidade em Portugal (1641–1789)* (Lisbon: Estar, 2001), 306, although the usual ability to negotiate blood purity barriers, this time without reference to any "defect," leaves a question mark.

33. ANTT, Inquisição de Lisboa, Processo 6307, fl. 166r–170v.

34. ANTT, Inq. Lx, Proc. 2332–1, fl. 33r–v.

35. ANTT, Inq. Lx, Proc. 2332–1, fl. 41v, 47r–49r.

36. ANTT, Inq. Lx, Proc. 2332–1, fl. 34r. So worn out was he by the torture that he was unable to sign the declaration of secrecy imposed by the inquisitors: fl. 50r.

37. ANTT, Inq. Lx, Proc. 2332, 2332–1, 6307, cross-reading of dates of detention and release.

38. ANTT, Inq. Lx, Proc. 6307, fl. 178r, handwritten on top, "delivered by Manuel Ferreira from the Company of Jesus, 6 de Janeiro de 1684" (my translation).

39. ANTT, Inq. Lx, Procs 5414 and 8413.

40. António had been received into the Order of Christ in 1664–1665, when he was still a child of seven years; ANTT, Mesa da Consciência e Ordens, Habilitações para a Ordem de Cristo, Letra A, Maço 49, n. 68. He was received into the order on February 26, 1665; ANTT, Registo Geral das Mercês, Mercês de Ordens Militares, Livro 5, fl. 345r. He had also received a guarantee that he would inherit from his father the comenda of São Francisco de Ponte de Sor of the Order of Christ on December 26, 1664; ANTT, Registo Geral das Mercês, Mercês de Ordens Militares, Livro 5, fl. 326v. The inheritance of the comenda was confirmed after his father died; ANTT, Registo Geral das Mercês, Mercês de Ordens Militares, Livro 14, fl. 237v (February 9, 1680) and Livro 5, fl. 326v (March 3, 1680).

41. ACDF, BB5f, fl. 180r–212v (the case ended up in the folders of the New Christians at the Roman Congregation). I did not find any record of the trial of Manuel Sequeira at the Inquisition. There were other trials traces of which have disappeared. However, the pope and the nuncio might have intervened.

42. ANTT, Registo Geral das Mercês, Mercês de D. João V, Livro 10, fl. 5r.

43. ANTT, Viscondes de Vila Nova de Cerveira, Caixa 25, n. 6, 7, 8, and 9: October 12, 1707, bill for the granting of a papal bull ceding the gains from the canonry of Évora's cathedral to Tomás da Silva Teles, signed in Rome by António Ranuntio Filipe da Gama de Pádua, Manuel de Andrade, Pascoal da Paz e Silva, Francisco Soeiro de Azevedo, and Gaspar Peres Vergueiro. The total sum is 2,418 scudi, a very high bill, corresponding to the quality of the benefice.

44. This genealogy was obtained from the record of the trial of André Correia Bravo; ANTT, Inquisição de Lisboa, Processo 5418, fl. 25r and following.

45. Surviving records show padrões de tença for the conventual dowries of the daughters Maria da Cruz da Saudade and Laura do Sacramento, both at 30,000 réis a year; ANTT, Registo Geral das Mercês, Mercês de D. Afonso VI, Livro 5, fl. 192r (February 27, 1661) and Livro 10, fl. 268v (June 10, 1669).

46. ANTT, Registo Geral das Mercês, Mercês de Ordens Militares, Livro 7, fl. 45r.

47. ANTT, Registo Geral das Mercês, Mercês de D. Afonso VI, Livro 19, fl. 8r.

48. I could not find Bento's trial at the Inquisition. There is an almost homonymous Bento Bravo da Silva, nephew of Bento da Silva Bravo, who also accused André; ANTT, Inquisição de Lisboa, Processo 11267. However, I found our Bento da Silva Bravo on one of the lists for autos da fé. This indicated he was presented on the same date as André, November 29, 1684, in a private auto da fé at the tribunal, then a rare courtesy of the inquisitors, in which he abjured *de levi*, being identified as a knight of a "certain military order" (it was the Order of Christ); BNP, Códice 167, fl. 247r. The accusation is transcribed in the trial of André Correia Bravo, ANTT, Inq. Lx, Proc. 5418, fl. 7r–10v (denunciations).

49. ANTT, Inq. Lx, Proc. 5418, fl. 25r and following.

50. ANTT, Inq. Lx, Proc. 5418, fl. 7r–10v.

51. ANTT, Inq. Lx, Proc. 5418, fl. 17r–22r (inventory of property).

52. ANTT, Inq. Lx, Proc. 5418, fl. 83r–v.

53. ANTT, Inq. Lx, Proc. 5418, fl. 53r–v.

54. ANTT, Inq. Lx, Proc. 5418, fl. 90r–v. On the absence of autos da fé under the Roman Inquisition, see Francisco Bethencourt, *The Inquisition. A Global History, 1478–1834*, trans. Jesn Birrell (Cambridge: Cambridge University Press, 2009), 310–315.

55. ANTT, Feitos Findos, Inventários, Letra A, Maço 243, n. 1, Caixa 380.

56. ANTT, Feitos Findos, Inventários, Letra A, Maço 243, n. 1, Caixa 380, fl. 102e–106r.

57. ANTT, Feitos Findos, Inventários, Letra A, Maço 243, n. 1, Caixa 380, fl. 112r–113v and 116r–v. The large investment with this familiar of the Inquisition apparently brought some return.

58. ANTT, Feitos Findos, Inventários, Letra A, Maço 243, n. 1, Caixa 380, fl. 124r–v. Witnesses of the certificate the beneficiary Pascoal da Paz e Silva and João Francisco Arnaldo.

59. See Ana Paula Lloyd, *The Suspension of the Portuguese Inquisition, 1674–81: Trade, Religion and Cross-Cultural Political Networks in Early Modern Europe* (PhD thesis, King's College London, 2018), 43, 115–117, 141–144.

60. AIPSA, Actas de Congregações, 1611–1678, fl. 350r and 351r.

61. Matilde de Angelis d'Ossat, "Il marchese Correa e il mausoleu de Augusto," in *Illuminismo e ilustración: le antichità e i loro protagonisti in Spagna e in Italia*, ed. José Beltran Fortes, et al. (Rome: L'Erma di Bretschneider, 2003), 121–142.

62. ASR, Trenta Notai, Capitolini, Testamenti, Ufficio 19, 1700–1702, vol. 26 (Senepa Noris), Testamento de Benedictus de Silva Bravo, fl. 451–473 (new foliation, does not correspond to the old index).

63. ASR, Trenta Notai, Capitolini, Testamenti, Ufficio 19, 1700–1702, vol. 26 (Senepa Noris), Testamento de Benedictus de Silva Bravo, fl. 452v–467v.

64. ANTT, Feitos Findos, Inventários, Letra A, Maço 243, n. 1, Caixa 380, fl. 130r–v and 146r.

65. ANTT, Feitos Findos, Inventários, Letra A, Maço 243, n. 1, Caixa 380, fl. 138r and 139v–140v.

66. ANTT, Feitos Findos, Inventários, Letra A, Maço 243, n. 1, Caixa 380, fl. 150v, 159v–160r, 166r.

67. ANTT, Feitos Findos, Inventários, Letra A, Maço 243, n. 1, Caixa 380, fl. 208r, 212r–213v.

68. Jonathan Israel, *Diasporas within a Diaspora: Jews, Crypto-Jews and the World of Maritime Empires, 1540–1740* (Leiden: Brill, 2002), ch. 17.

69. Maria Valentina Cotta do Amaral, *Privilégios de mercadores estrangeiros no reinado de D. João III* (Lisbon: Instituto de Alta Cultura, 1965).

70. Leonor Freire Costa, Pedro Lains, and Susana Münch Miranda, *An Economic History of Portugal, 1143–2010* (Cambridge: Cambridge University Press, 2016), 82–83, 92–93.

71. Adrian Pearce, *British Trade with Spanish America, 1763–1808* (Liverpool: Liverpool University Press, 2007).

72. M. B. Vilar García and P. Pezzi Cristóbal, eds., *Los extranjeros en la España moderna*, 2 vols. (Malaga: Universidad de Malaga, 2003).

73. J. R. Jones, *The Anglo-Dutch Wars of the Seventeenth Century* (London: Longman, 1996).

74. Gregory Hanlon, *European Military Rivalry, 1500–1750: Fierce pageant* (London: Routledge, 2020).

75. David Hancock, *Oceans of Wine: Madeira and the Emergence of American Trade and Taste* (New Haven, CT: Yale University Press, 2009).

76. Lucien Bély, *Les relations internationales en Europe, XVII*ᵉ*–XVIII*ᵉ *siècles*, 4th ed. (Paris: PUF, 2007).

77. Nunziatella Alessandrini, ed., *Con gran mare e fortuna: Circulação de mercadorias, pessoas e ideias entre Portugal e Itália na época moderna* (Lisboa: Cátedra Alberto Benveniste, 2015); Nunziatella Alessandrini, *Os italianos na Lisboa de 1500 a 1680: das hegemonias florentinas às genovesas*, 2 vols. (PhD thesis, Lisbon: Universidade Aberta, 2009).

78. Jean-François Labourdette, *La nation française à Lisbonne de 1669 à 1790. Entre Colbertisme et Libéralisme* (Paris: Fondation Calouste Gulbenkian, 1988), 416–417, who reworked data from Joaquim Veríssimo Serrão, *História de Portugal*, vol. 5 (Lisbon: Verbo, 1980), 79–80. I have further aggregated data based on political allegiance, Irish with English and Riga with Swedish, at the time. The data collected from Virgínia Rau in Costa, Lains, and Münch Miranda, *An Economic History of Portugal, 1143–2010*, 151, related to the period 1641–1688, confirms the predominance of Northern powers: Dutch 477 ships, English 398, Hanseatic 145, Swedish 31, Danish 22, French 20; but there is no reference to ships from Italy.

79. L. M. E. Shaw, *Trade, Inquisition and the English Nation in Portugal, 1650–1690* (Manchester: Carcanet, 1989), 205, 210.

80. Jorun Poettering, *Migrant Merchants: Trade, Nation, and Religion in Seventeenth-Century Hamburg and Portugal*, transl. Kenneth Kronenberg (Berlin: De Guyter, 2019), 116.

81. Labourdette, *La nation française à Lisbonne de 1669 à 1790*, 457–458.

82. There are exceptions, such as the temporary detention of the English consul Maynard and his chaplain Michael Geddes by the Inquisition in 1686, see Shaw, *Trade, Inquisition and the British Nation in Portugal, 1650–1690*, 105–106.

83. José Ferreira Borges de Castro, ed., *Colecção dos tratados, convenções, contratos e actos públicos celebrados entre a coroa de Portugal e as mais potências desde 1640 até ao presente*, tome I (Lisbon: Imprensa Nacional, 1856), 44–45 (art. XXVI), my translation.

84. Poettering, *Migrant Merchants*, 117; Paulo Drumond Braga, *Portugueses no estrangeiro, estrangeiros em Portugal* (Lisbon: Hugin, 2005); Isabel Drumond Braga, *Os estrangeiros e a Inquisição portuguesa, séculos XVI e XVII* (Lisbon: Hugin, 2002).

85. There is an interesting consultation on record related to the granting of a secular title to a foreign Lutheran, probably someone involved in a military function. The theologians considered that the king could give such a person juros, tenças, or a secular military job; but could not give him a position of civil authority, nor naturalise him, if he were a Protestant, nor make him a vassal, nor give him a comenda in a military order. They clearly invoked the absence of freedom of conscience in Portugal to explain these restrictions; ANTT, Armário Jesuítico, Livro 20, Maço, nᵒ 7, dated December 23, 1663.

86. Poettering, *Migrant Merchants*, 99–100, 203, 212.

87. Poettering, *Migrant Merchants*, 133–134, 255–259. In the second set of pages, Poettering underlines the importance of relatives who had entered the religious life, another feature shared with the New Christians.

88. Labourdette, *La nation française à Lisbonne de 1669 à 1790*, 579, 591–606.

89. Carmen Sanz Ayán, "La burguesía financiera en le reinado de Carlos II. Comportamientos económicos y actiutudes sociales," in *La burguesía española en la Edad Moderna*, ed. Luis Miguel Enciso Recio, vol. 2 (Valladolid: Universidad de Valladolid, 1996), 577–704, esp. 579, 590.

90. Manuel Bustos Rodriguez, "La burguesía mercantil en el Cádiz del siglo XVII: Proceso de formación y estructura," in *La burguesía española en la Edad Moderna*, ed. Luis Miguel Enciso Recio, vol. 3 (Valladolid: Universidad de Valladolid, 1996), 1233–1265, esp. 1253.

91. Bustos Rodriguez, "La burguesía mercantil en el Cádiz del siglo XVII," 1259–1264.

92. Regina Grafe, *Distant Tyranny. Markets, Power, and Backwardness in Spain, 1650–1800* (Princeton, NJ: Princeton University Press, 2012), 58–60.

93. AGI, Gobierno, Indiferente General, 2778, which gives the information for this and the next paragraph. There was a fiscal trial related to 73 gold bars sequestered on the detention of Gaspar de Andrade, who died in prison; AGI, Pleitos de la Gobernación de Cartagena, Escribania, 581A.

94. ANTT, Inquisição de Lisboa, Processo 11267. Bento Bravo da Silva was detained on May 2, 1682, and presented at the auto da fé on August 8, 1683.

95. Henry Kamen, *The War of Succession of Spain, 1700–1715* (London: Weidenfeld and Nicolson, 1969); Stanley J. Stein and Barbara H. Stein, *Silver, Trade and War: Spain and America in the Making of Early Modern Europe* (Baltimore: Johns Hopkins University Press, 2000);

Joaquim Albareda Salvadó, *La Guerra de Sucesión de España (1700–1710)* (Barcelona: Crítica, 2010), 67–71, 97.

96. Carlos Malamud, *Cádiz y Saint Malo en el comercio colonial peruano (1689–1725)* (Cadiz: Diputación Provincial, 1986); Albareda Salvadó, *La Guerra de Sucesión de España,* 70, 244.

97. Kamen, *War of Succession in Spain,* 81–90.

98. Albareda Salvadó, *La Guerra de Sucesión de España,* 245–246.

99. Aurelio García López, *Don Juan de Goyeneche, un hombre de negocios y financiero al servicio de la monarquia en los reinados de Carlos II y Filipe V* (Madrid: Asociación del Patrimonio Histórico de Nuevo Baztán, 2014).

100. Israel, *Diasporas within a Diaspora,* 535–536, 544–545.

101. Israel, *Diasporas within a Diaspora,* 545–548, 551, 558.

102. Albareda Salvadó, *La Guerra de Sucesión de España,* 168–170, 218, 260–262, 315–329.

103. Albareda Salvadó, *La Guerra de Sucesión de·España,* 330, 336–344.

104. Israel, *Diasporas within a Diaspora,* 566.

105. University of Southampton Library, Ms. 155; NA, SP 35/40/77 and SP 35/40/771.

106. David Chandler, *Marlborough as Military Commander* (London: Batsford, 1973), 302. I have corrected the last figure using the printed report at Cambridge University Library, Ch(H), Political Papers 4, after n. 11, 22–23.

107. Cambridge University Library, Ch(H), Political Papers, 4, n. 11 (Deposition of Solomon de Medina about payments for provisions in the Low Countries, December 6, 1711). The printed report included in this folder contains an edited version of Solomon's deposition and the depositions of two other contractors, John Montgomery and William Preston.

108. NA, C8/375/2, C8/496/20, C8/496/17, C7/666/35, C8500/9, SP 41/5/128, C8/496/5, C11/1727/4. See also West Sussex Record Office PHA/8361, 8362.

109. NA, PROB 11/640/106.

110. John A. Hobson, *Imperialism: A Study* (1902) (London: Routledge, 2016).

Chapter Sixteen: Immersion

1. Julio Caro Baroja, *Los Judíos en La España Moderna y Contemporánea* (1961), 3rd ed., vol. 3 (Madrid: Istmo, 1986); Joaquin Pérez Villanueva and Bartolome Escandell Bonet, eds., *Historia de la Inquisición en España y América,* vol. 1 (Madrid: Biblioteca de Autores Cristianos, 1984), contributions by Teófanes Egido under different titles, 1204–1211, 1227–1247, 1380–1404.

2. Evelyne Oliel-Grausz, *Relations et réseaux intercommunautaires dans la diaspora sefarade d´Occident au XVIIIe siècle,* 2 vols. (thèse de doctorat, Université de Paris-I Sorbonne, 1999).

3. M. Torres Arce, "Judaizantes y el Santo Oficio de Logroño en el reinado de Felipe V," in *Historia de la Inquisición en España y América,* ed. Joaquín Pérez Villanueva and Bartolomé Escandell Bonet, vol. 3, *Temas y problemas* (Madrid: Biblioteca de Autores Cristianos, 2000), 657–693, esp. 660–661 (tables); José Martínez Millán, "La persecución inquisitorial contra los criptojudaicos en el siglo XVIII. El tribunal de Llerena (1700–1730)," in *Historia de la Inquisición en España y América,* vol. 3, 557–656.

4. Stephen Haliczer, *Inquisition and Society in the Kingdom of Valencia, 1478–1834* (Berkeley: University of California Press, 1990), 233.

5. Martínez Millán, "La persecución inquisitorial," 603–611.

6. Teófanes Egido, "Las modificaciones de la tipología. Nueva estructura delictiva," in *Historia de la Inquisición en España y América,* vol. 1, 1380–1404, esp. tables in 1395 and 1398.

7. Real Academia de la Historia, "Melchor Rafael de Macanaz," http://dbe.rah.es /biografias/12503/melchor-rafael-de-macanaz, accessed June 25, 2020. For Macanaz's trial, see Carmen Martín Gaite, *El proceso de Macanaz. Historia de un empapelamiento* (Madrid: Editorial Moneda y Credito, 1970); for the context, see Francisco Precioso Izquierdo, *Melchor*

Macanaz, la derrota de un "heróe": poder político y mobilidad familiar en la España moderna (Madrid: Cátedra, 2017), 201–232.

8. Data collected from António Joaquim Moreira, *História dos principais actos e procedimentos da Inquisição em Portugal* (1846), ed. João Palma-Ferreira (Lisbon: Imprensa Nacional, 1980), tables 146–249, based on manuscript and printed lists from autos da fé, much more reliable than the *relaciones de causas* in Spain, but still not complete. More precise data for the tribunal of Évora was compiled by Michèle Janin-Thivos Tailland, *Inquisition et société au Portugal. Le cas du tribunal d´Évora, 1660-1821* (Paris: Centre Culturel Calouste Gulbenkian, 2001), 46–54; she confirmed the main trends, although there is a slight increase in trials in the 1740s and 1750s compared to the previous two decades, followed by a general decline.

9. Janin-Thivos Tailland, *Inquisition et société au Portugal*, 134.

10. Caro Baroja, *Los judíos en la España moderna y contemporánea*, vol. 3, 24, 58–59, 77.

11. AHN, Inquisición, leg. 3722, exp. 182 (lawyer's accusation, here translated). Francisco de Torres had been reconciled on November 22, 1717, and this accusation was formulated in 1718. The main trial is at AHN, Inquisición, leg. 186, exp. 3. I could not find the trial of Francisco de Miranda; the catalogue held by PARES, the portal of the Spanish archives, does not indicate other sources for this figure. In fact, I found very few references in PARES to the various names collected by Caro Baroja from the *relaciones de Autos de Fe*.

12. Caro Baroja, *Los judíos en la España moderna y contemporánea*, vol. 3, 24, 57, 67, 77.

13. Caro Baroja, *Los judíos en la España moderna y contemporánea*, vol. 3, 71, 74–76.

14. Caro Baroja, *Los judíos en la España moderna y contemporánea*, vol. 3, 55, 61, 73, 78–80. AHN, Inquisición, leg. 160, exp. 11.

15. Caro Baroja, *Los judíos en la España moderna y contemporánea*, vol. 3, 59, 67–8.

16. Caro Baroja, *Los judíos en la España moderna y contemporánea*, vol. 3, 26–7. There was also a civil action brought by Francisco Silveira concerning the debts of Diego de Ávila and the transfer of a contract to Antonio Carrillo: AHN, Inquisición, leg. 1912, exp. 33.

17. Caro Baroja, *Los judíos en la España moderna y contemporánea*, vol. 3, 58. For the civil action, see AHN, Inquisición, leg. 2339, exp. 1–11; AHN, Inquisición, leg. 4524, exp. 1, 2 and 5; and AHN, Inquisición, leg. 508, exp. 2.

18. Caro Baroja, *Los judíos en la España moderna y contemporánea*, vol. 3, 97, 102, 109, 123

19. Martínez Millán, "La persecución inquisitorial," 585, 589, 591.

20. Caro Baroja, *Los judíos en la España moderna y contemporánea*, vol. 3, 25; Archivo General de Índias, Consulados, doc. 465; AGI, Contaduria, 406; AGI, Escribania, 960.

21. Caro Baroja, *Los judíos en la España moderna y contemporánea*, vol. 3, 27, 92–93, 95, 102.

22. Caro Baroja, *Los judíos en la España moderna y contemporánea*, vol. 3, 108, 114–115, 122, 124.

23. Haliczer, *Inquisition and Society*, 233–234.

24. Caro Baroja, *Los judíos en la España moderna y contemporánea*, vol. 3, 97.

25. Martínez Millán, "La persecución inquisitorial," 563–565.

26. Torres Arce, "Judaizantes y el Santo Oficio."

27. Anita Novinsky, *Inquisição. Prisioneiros do Brasil (séculos XVI-XIX)* (Rio de Janeiro: Expressão e Cultura, 2002).

28. For this analysis I have used the series of original lists of autos da fé compiled by António Joaquim Moreira at the BNP, códices 166, 167, 168, 863, 864, 865.

29. ANTT, Inquisição de Lisboa, Processo 511.

30. ANTT, Inquisição de Lisboa, Processo 511, fl. 51r–63r.

31. ANTT, Inquisição de Lisboa, Processo 511, fl. 51r–63r.

32. ANTT, Inquisição de Lisboa, Processo 511, fl. 51r–63r.

33. ANTT, Inquisição de Lisboa, Processo 511, fl. 63r–82r.

34. ANTT, Inquisição de Lisboa, Processo 511, fl. 483r–487v, 495r–504r.

35. ANTT, Inquisição de Lisboa, Processo 9344.

36. ANTT, Inquisição de Lisboa, Processo 1571, fl. 29r–82v.

37. ANTT, Inquisição de Lisboa, Processo 1571, fl. 29r–82v.

38. ANTT, Inquisição de Lisboa, Processo 1571, fl. 29r–82v. The inventory of the inheritance left by Diogo Mendes de Crasto, the father, is at ANTT, Feitos Findos, Inventários post mortem, letra D, maço 45, n. 6.

39. ANTT, Inquisição de Lisboa, Processo 1571, fl. 88r–90r.

40. ANTT, Inquisição de Lisboa, Processo 1571, fl. 2v–12r.

41. ANTT, Inquisição de Lisboa, Processo 1571, fl. 453r–457r.

42. ANTT, Inquisição de Lisboa, Processo 1571, fl. 485r–489r.

43. ANTT, Inquisição de Lisboa, Processo 6515; the inventory of property for this trial was published by Anita Novinsky, *Inquisição. Inventários de bens confiscados a Cristãos Novos* (Lisbon: Imprensa Nacional, 1976), 223–224.

44. ANTT, Inquisição de Lisboa, Processo 9103. I could not find records of the trials of several women relatives who also denounced Mendes de Crasto.

45. ANTT, Inquisição de Lisboa, Processo 7454, fl. 6r–14v.

46. ANTT, Inquisição de Lisboa, Processo 7454, fl. 22r–24r (inventory of property).

47. ANTT, Inquisição de Lisboa, Processo 7454, fl. 25r–29v (genealogy).

48. ANTT, Inquisição de Lisboa, Processo 7454, fl. 289r–262v.

49. ANTT, Inquisição de Lisboa, Processo 7454, fl. 264r–269r.

50. ANTT, Inquisição de Lisboa, Processo 7454, fl. 273r.

51. ANTT, Inquisição de Coimbra, Processo 1781. Gaspar Rodrigues Nabo's registration as a legal practitioner is at ANTT, Desembargo do Paço, Leitura de Bacharéis, Letra G, maço 6, n. 40.

52. Anonymous, Portrait of Diogo de Brito do Rio, fidalgo of the royal house, and Aldonça da Mota, founders of the Jesuit College of Santiago in Elvas, Portugal, ca. 1700, oil on canvas, 159×120.5 cm. Private collection [auction Cabral Moncada, catalogue 176, February 29, 2016]; photo of the marble tomb of Diogo de Brito do Rio and Aldonça da Mota, founders of the College of Santiago, Society of Jesus, in Elvas, Portugal, 1702 by Rui Jesuíno. I thank José Mantas for the information on the painting, Rui Jesuíno and Cabral Moncada Leilões for the authorization to reproduce the photos.

53. ANTT, Inquisição de Lisboa, Processo 4151, fl. 27r–28v and 29r–31r (Ana do Vale); ANTT, Inquisição de Lisboa, Processo 11492, fl. 32r–34r (son, Simão Rodrigues de Andrade); ANTT, Inquisição de Lisboa, Processo 4166, fl. 4r–14r (son, Manuel do Vale da Silveira, who had powers of administration delegated by his mother); ANTT, Inquisição de Lisboa, Processo 8138, fl. 6r–v (another son, José Ramires do Vale); ANTT, Inquisição de Lisboa, Processo 6517, fl. 8r–13r (another son, Domingos Rodrigues Ramires). The inventories are, in general, well transcribed by Anita Novinsky, *Inquisição. Inventários de bens confiscados a Cristãos Novos.*

54. ANTT, Inquisição de Lisboa, Processo 1191, fl. 6r–8v.

55. ANTT, Inquisição de Lisboa, Processo 11475 (Angela de Mesquita, married to Domingos Rodrigues Ramires, daughter of António do Vale de Mesquita and Helena do Vale), Processo 11480 (João Soares de Mesquita, married to Isabel Gomes de Andrade), Processo 11784 (Isabel Gomes de Andrade), Processo 6678 (Alexandre Soares Pereira, brother of Isabel Gomes de Andrade and married to Leonor Mendes de Paz), Processo 7212 (Isabel Mendes de Paz). I could not find any record of the trial of António do Vale da Silveira (or de Mesquita), who testified against his sister-in-law, Ana do Vale, and other members of the family.

56. ANTT, Inquisição de Lisboa, Processo 7201, fl. 11r–12r.

57. ANTT, Inquisição de Lisboa, Processo 7201, fl. 13r–16v.

58. ANTT, Inquisição de Lisboa, Processo 7201, fl. 17r–20v.

59. ANTT, Inquisição de Lisboa, Processo 7201, fl. 102r–107v.

60. ANTT, Inquisição de Lisboa, Processo 8772, fl. 7r, 9r–v.

61. ANTT, Inquisição de Coimbra, Processo 7237 (António Lopes Henriques); ANTT, Inquisição de Lisboa, Processo 7732, fl. 5r–37v (sixteen denunciations), 42r–45r (genealogy) and 253r–269r (sentence João Henriques Ferreira); ANTT, Inquisição de Coimbra, Processo 3689 (Diogo Henriques Ferreira); ANTT, Inquisição de Coimbra, Processo 5334 (Alvaro Henriques Ferreira). Luiz Fernando de Carvalho Dias, "Os lanifícios na política económica do conde da Ericeira," *Lanifícios. Boletim Mensal da Federação Nacional dos Industriais de Lan-*

ifícios 47–48 (Nov.–Dec. 1953): 339–398, esp. 382–395, mentioned the contracts held by these brothers, first in Alhandra in 1698, then in Fundão in 1700, and finally in Covilhã in 1702.

62. ANTT, Inquisição de Lisboa, Processo 3689, fl. 39r–41r; ANTT, Inquisição de Lisboa, Processo 5334, fl 26r–28r; ANTT, Inquisição de Lisboa, Processo 7732, fl. 38r–41v.

63. Inquisição de Lisboa, Processo 7732, fl. 39v–40v. For a background to woollen cloth production in Covilhã, see Leonor Freire Costa, Pedro Lains, and Susana Münch Ferreira, *An Economic History of Portugal, 1143–2010* (Cambridge: Cambridge University Press, 2016), 140–143, for the 1670s and 1680s, 189–190, for the 1780s. The first contracts for woollen cloth production in Covilhã were studied by Luís Fernando Carvalho Dias, "Os lanifícios na política económica do Conde de Ericeira," *Lanifícios. Boletim da Federação Nacional dos Industriais de Lanifícios* 44 (Agosto 1953): 199–239; 47–48 (Nov.–Dec. 1953): 339–398; and 49 (Jan. 1954): 3–22. He highlighted frequent local riots against the monopoly on this trade, commented on how the Inquisition was used by different interest groups, which included New and Old Christians, and pointed out the economic consequences of inquisitorial activity.

64. ANTT, Inquisição de Lisboa, Processo 7732, fl. 253r–269r (sentence registered with the master of the galleys, João Oliveira; declaration by the guarantor, the goldsmith Francisco Ribeiro).

65. Unfortunately, the extensive research by Claude Stuczynski for the sixteenth century exists only in Hebrew. From 1701 to 1753, the Inquisition of Coimbra sentenced 184 New Christian textile producers, nearly all from Bragança, mainly weavers and squeezers, but also dyers and carders, and producers of taffeta, velvet, and stockings. In the same period, the Inquisition of Lisbon sentenced 59 New Christian textile workers, including several dyers from Covilhã, but the majority were again from Bragança, some of them having migrated to work at silk production in Lisbon long before the creation of the royal factory. This information was collected at the BNP, Códices 865 and 863. For the Inquisition of Évora, the data compiled by Janin-Thivos Tailland, *Inquisition et société au Portugal*, 187–189, includes shearers, dyers, and silk workers. It is in line with the numbers from Lisbon, but much lower than the figures presented for the sixteenth and seventeenth centuries by António Borges Coelho, *Inquisição de Évora. Dos primórdios a 1668*, vol. 1 (Lisbon: Caminha, 1987), 382–384.

66. This issue has not been systematically researched, although there is a remark concerning the economic impact of the Inquisition in Costa, Lains, and Miranda, *An Economic History of Portugal*, 142–143.

67. BNP, códices 863 and 865: Manuel Dias Pereira, resident in Torres Novas, sentenced 1703; António de Leão, Salvaterra, 1703; Miguel Rodrigues, Benavente, 1703; Luís Álvares Nunes, Porto, 1711; António da Costa, Soure, 1713; Diogo José Ramos, Beja, 1723; Manuel de Leão, Lisbon, 1726 (father of a sentenced person); António Gomes, Bragança, 1726 (father of another sentenced detainee); Luís Ferreira da Costa, Torres Vedras, 1726; Gaspar Furtado Ferro, Guarda, 1726; Luís de Miranda e Crasto, Porto, 1726; Bento Correia, Lamego, 1726; Diogo Soares da Fonseca, Peso da Régua, 1727; Duarte Pereira d´Eça, Lisbon, 1728; António Gomes, Bragança, 1728; Francisco da Silva, Moimenta da Beira, 1731; Manuel da Silva Cardoso, Bragança, 1737; Diogo Soares, Lisbon, 1747 (father of another sentenced detainee); António Mendes Pereira, Tomar, 1756. Six of them had been born in Castile.

68. ANTT, Inquisição de Coimbra, Processo 5861.

69. ANTT, Inquisição de Coimbra, Livros 758, 759, 760, and 762. A significant number of account books retained by the Inquisition of Coimbra following sequestration of property need to be researched.

70. ANTT, Inquisição de Lisboa, Processo 8881, fl. 21r–26r (genealogy of Diogo do Vale Cordeiro).

71. ANTT, Inquisição de Lisboa, Processo 8881, fl. 10r–19r.

72. ANTT, Inquisição de Coimbra, Processo 5861 (Luís do Vale); Inquisição de Lisboa, Processo 8881, fl. 71r–73v.

73. ANTT, Inquisição de Lisboa, Processo 1898, fl. 32r–34r, 100r–101v.

74. ANTT, Inquisição de Lisboa, Processo 11727, fl. 4r and 38r–42v; ANTT, Inquisição de Lisboa, Processo 11731.

75. ANTT, Inquisição de Lisboa, Processo 9689, fl. 185r–189v.

76. Maria Fernanda Bicalho, *A cidade e o império: o Rio de Janeiro no século XVIII* (Rio de Janeiro: Civilização Brasileira, 2003).

77. ANTT, Inquisição de Lisboa, Processo 11683, fl. 29r–35r.

78. ANTT, Inquisição de Lisboa, Processo 11683, fl. 4r–27r (denunciations), 37r–42v (genealogy).

79. ANTT, Inquisição de Lisboa, Processo 11683, fl. 278r–279r (torture), 284r–285r (sentence October, 24, 1717).

80. ANTT, Inquisição de Lisboa, Processo 11683, fl. 289r–290r (petition and authorisation). Anita Novinsky has transcribed his inventory of property but excluded him from the list of New Christian prisoners. I would not be so sure about that. His strategy of denying inquisitorial classification proved a winner. But I have doubts about José Pacheco's claim of having pure Old Christian blood. In his younger days he had visited Évora and Montemor-o-Novo, so he may well have had relatives there whom he chose not to mention.

81. ANTT, Inquisição de Lisboa, 8887, fl. 31r–37r.

82. ANTT, Inquisição de Lisboa, 8887, fl, 5v–30v (denunciations and enquiry); 378r–382r (sentence).

83. ANTT, Inquisição de Lisboa, Processo 6268, fl. 11r–28r (inventory), 86r–87v (sentence).

84. ANTT, Inquisição de Lisboa, Processo 6268, fl. 8r.

85. ANTT, Inquisição de Lisboa, Processo 8912, fl. 3v, 7r–9v, 53r–54r (José Pinto Ferreira); ANTT, Inquisição de Lisboa, Processo 8659, fl. 3v, 7v–10r, 31r–32v (Tomás Pinto Ferreira).

86. Anita Novinsky, *Inquisição. Inventário de bens confiscados a cristãos novos*, 181–183. The best study on the diamond trade is by Tijl Vanneste, *Global Trade and Commercial Networks: Eighteenth Century Diamond Merchants* (London: Pickering and Chatto, 2011), but he concentrates his research on the period after the first contract of exploration in Brazil in 1739. See Daniela Tonello Levy, "O papel dos judeus convertidos no desenvolvimento de Minas, 1700–1750" (PhD thesis, São Paulo: Universidade de São Paulo, 2019), 150–152, where this case is discussed. Júnia Ferreira Furtado, *Chica da Silva e o contratador de diamantes* (São Paulo: Companhia das Letras, 2003), includes a study of two generations of diamond contractors, the Fernandes de Oliveira family.

87. ANTT, Inquisição de Lisboa, Processo 14407.

88. ANTT, Códice 863, fl. 447v (my translation).

89. ANTT, Inquisição de Lisboa, Processo 14407, fl. 41r.

90. ANTT, Inquisição de Lisboa, Processo 14407, fl. 41r.

91. ANTT, Inquisição de Lisboa, Processo 14407, fl. 42r–v.

92. ANTT, Inquisição de Lisboa, Processo 14407, fl. 45r–46v.

93. ANTT, Inquisição de Lisboa, Processo 14407, fl. 47r–52v. The initial costs of the enquiry are included in the trial, 24,412 réis, fl. 114v, with a second tranche of 5,235 réis fl. 145v. There was a first deposit of 40,000 réis made by the petitioners, fl. 121r.

94. ANTT, Inquisição de Lisboa, Processo 14407, fl. 57r–110r. The marginal comments on the record of the enquiry are interesting (I translate): sem raça (without race); sem fama (without reputation); infamado (defamed); sem infâmia dos ascendentes (without defamed ascendants); murmurado de Cristão Novo (rumoured to be New Christian).

95. ANTT, Inquisição de Lisboa, Processo 14407, fl. 110v–112r.

96. ANTT, Inquisição de Lisboa, Processo 14407, fl. 119r, 132r, 149r–151r (there are several requests from the candidate). This part, added to the trial, was not incorporated in a chronological way.

97. ANTT, Inquisição de Lisboa, Processo 14407, fl. 127r–146r, 151v–152v. They also ordered that the case of Father Manuel de Aguilar Macedo should be included in the enquiry and discovered that, in the place where he lived in 1686, in the diocese of Viseu, one Franciscan had expressed doubts about the blood purity of his grandfather, doubts which had been rebuked as biased.

98. ANTT, Inquisição de Lisboa, Processo 14407, fl. 153r–154v (August 21, 1752).

99. ANTT, Inquisição de Lisboa, Processo 14407, fl. 4r (first declarations), 9r–11v (genealogy), 13v–30r (confessions and denunciations).

100. This manuscript was presented by João Lúcio de Azevedo, *História dos cristãos novos portugueses* (1921) (Lisbon: Livraria Clássica, 1975), 339, 490–491 (summary). Maria Luísa Braga notes that the copy in Évora has the name of the author: *A Inquisição em Portugal na primeira metade do século XVIII* (Lisbon: INIC, 1992), 62, but the manuscript has not been studied. I accept here the authorship, but with reservations; it needs further research, since the manuscript identifies the author on the front page but indicates "para mandar a Nuno da Cunha, Primeiro Ministro del Rey de Purtugal, e Inquizidor Geral no mesmo Reyno." The notion of Prime Minister did not exist in the early eighteenth century. Manuel Correia died in Rome on July 30, 1708; Josephus Fejér, *Defuncti secundi secoli Societatis Iesu, 1641–1740*, vol. 1, A–C (Rome: Institutum Historicum S. J., 1989). Here I draw on the copy at the BNP, Coleção Pombalina, códice 484, fl. 282v–313v and compare it with the copy at the Biblioteca Pública e Arquivo Distrital de Évora, códice CXIIId, fl. 166r–216v. The author mentions the "new dignity" of Nuno da Cunha, which could only be his elevation to General Inquisitor in 1707 (fl. 296v), an indication that is valuable for dating the document.

101. BNP, cod. 484, fl. 282v–286r.

102. BNP, cod. 484, fl. 287r–294r.

103. BNP, cod. 484, fl. 294v–302v.

104. BNP, cod. 484, fl. 304v–305r.

105. BNP, cod. 484, fl. 305v–313r.

106. BNP, cod. 484, fl. 313v.

107. See the short biography in Charles E. O'Neill and Joaquín M. Dominguez, eds., *Diccionario historico de la Compañía de Jesus* (Rome: Institutum Historicum S. I., 2001), 965.

108. Maximiano Lemos, *Ribeiro Sanches: a sua vida e a sua obra* (Porto: E. Tavares Martins, 1911) is still the best reference. For a modern approach to the political period of Pombal, see Antonio Rosa Mendes, *Ribeiro Sanches e o marquês de Pombal: intelectuais e poder no absolutismo esclarecido* (Cascais: Patrimonia, 1998).

109. António Nunes Ribeiro Sanches, *Cristãos Novos e Cristãos Velhos em Portugal*, ed. Raúl Rego, 2nd ed. (Porto: Paisagem, 1973), 44–47, 50–55, 57–58, 60, 63.

110. Ribeiro Sanches, *Cristãos Novos e Cristãos Velhos*, 64–65 (quote from this last page, my translation).

111. Ribeiro Sanches, *Cristãos Novos e Cristãos Velhos*, 41–43.

112. Ribeiro Sanches, *Cristãos Novos e Cristãos Velhos*, 70–71, 73–74.

113. Ribeiro Sanches, *Cristãos Novos e Cristãos Velhos*, 77–81.

114. Isabel Cluny, *D. Luís da Cunha e a ideia de diplomacia em Portugal* (Lisbon: Livros Horizonte, 1999).

115. Luís da Cunha, *Testamento político ou Carta de conselhos ao Senhor D. José sendo Príncipe*, ed. Abílio Diniz Silva (Lisbon: Biblioteca Nacional de Portugal, 2013), 88.

116. da Cunha, *Testamento político*, 107.

117. da Cunha, *Testamento político*, 114. This story had already been used by Ribeiro Sanches.

118. da Cunha, *Testamento político*, 115–116.

119. da Cunha, *Testamento político*, 116.

120. da Cunha, *Testamento político*, 117.

121. da Cunha, *Testamento político*, 119.

122. da Cunha, *Testamento político*, 118.

123. da Cunha, *Testamento político*, 119.

124. da Cunha, *Testamento político*, 120. I could not find this law, supposedly from 1728, previously referred to by Ribeiro Sanches.

125. da Cunha, *Testamento político*, 121–122.

126. Luís da Cunha, *Instruções inéditas a Marco António de Azevedo Coutinho*, ed. Pedro de Azevedo and António Baião (Coimbra: Imprensa da Universidade, 1929), 81.

127. da Cunha, *Instruções inéditas*, 90–92.

128. da Cunha, *Instruções inéditas*, 83–84.

129. da Cunha, *Instruções inéditas*, 74–76.

130. da Cunha, *Instruções inéditas*, 77–78.

131. da Cunha, *Instruções inéditas*, 89–90.

132. Caro Baroja, *Los judíos en la España moderna y contemporánea*, vol. 3, 189–190.

133. For the historical background, especially the two massive waves of repression in 1677–1679 and 1688–1691, see Angela Selke, *The Conversos of Mallorca: Life and Death in a Crypto-Jewish Community in XVII Century Spain* (Jerusalem: The Hebrew University, 1986); Baltasar Porcel, *Els Xuetes mallorquins: quinze segles de racisme* (Barcelona: Edicions 62, 2002).

134. Francisco Marti Gilabert, *La abolicion de la Inquisicion en España* (Pamplona: Universidad de Navarra, 1975), chap. 1, esp. 30–34, 37–49.

135. Giuseppe Marcocci and José Pedro Paiva, *História da Inquisição Portuguesa, 1536–1821* (Lisbon: Esfera dos Livros, 2013), 341–360, for an extensive analysis.

136. BNP, códices 863, 864, and 865.

137. António Delgado da Silva, *Colecção de Legislação Portugueza*, tome II, *1763–1774* (Lisbon: Typografia Migrense, 1829), 339–341.

138. Delgado da Silva, *Colecção de Legislação Portugueza*, 672–678.

139. Delgado da Silva, *Colecção de Legislação Portugueza*, 849–852.

140. *Regimento do Santo Officio da Inquisição dos reinos de Portugal. Ordenado com o Real Beneplácito e Régio Auxílio pelo Eminentíssimo e Reverendíssimo Cardeal da Cunha, do Conselho de Estado e Gabinete de Sua Magestade e Inquisidor Geral neste Reinos e em Todos os Domínios* (Lisbon: Manescal da Costa, 1774). Royal approval was explicitly indicated in the title of this crucial set of rules, while it was not indicated in the previous rules printed in 1613 and 1640.

Conclusions to Part IV

1. José Pedro Paiva, *Baluartes da fé e da disciplina: o enlace entre a Inquisição e os bispos em Portugal, 1536-1700* (Coimbra: Universidade de Coimbra, 2011), 394–418.

GLOSSARY

Alcabala—a regular tax based on transactions in Spain; equivalent to *sisa* in Portugal.

Alumbrado—meaning "enlightened"; member of a spiritual movement that searched for a direct connection to God.

Arbitrista—a person who provided suggestions and advice to the king concerning fiscal, financial, and political issues.

Asentista—the person responsible for the *asiento* (contract).

Asiento—a contract or obligation to provide money, equipment, weapons, or food to the government or dependent institutions.

Auto da fé—ritual of public presentation of the sentenced accused of heresy and apostasy by the Inquisition.

Bill of exchange—a letter by which one merchant ordered his correspondent in some other city to make a payment to another merchant in that city. It was an instrument of cashless payment and a means of providing credit. It avoided the risky physical transport of money.

Brazilwood—wood used for dyeing cloth, which gave its name to Brazil; called in Portuguese *pau-brasil*.

Carreira da Índia—the convoy of ships dedicated to annual trade with the *Estado da Índia*.

Carrera de Indias—the convoy of ships organised for trade with Spanish America.

Casa da Índia—the royal institution that managed contracts of trade with the *Estado da Índia* related to concessions of royal monopolies. It also managed shipbuilding and provision of the *carreira da Índia*. It stored commodities from India and supervised the loading and unloading of ships.

Casa da Mina—the royal institution that managed contracts and imports of gold from the region of Mina, Gulf of Guinea.

Casa de Contratación—an institution created in Seville for the management of contracts of trade with Spanish America.

Comenda—benefice attributed to knights of the military orders. In Spanish, *encomienda*. The receiver of this benefice was called *comendador*.

Consulado—the guild of merchants in several ports of Spain that also functioned as a tribunal to decide the validity of contracts and resolve trade conflicts.

Contradictas—legal objection to testimonies considered biased or false.

Conversos—Jews forced to convert to Catholicism from 1391 to 1497 in Iberia, whose descendants were subject to the discriminatory blood purity statutes. See *New Christians*.

Estado da Índia—the Portuguese set of forts and enclaves from East Africa to Macau under the direct or indirect authority of the governor (or viceroy) nominated by the king.

Fidalgo—the son of someone important in Portugal; a nobleman. See *hidalgo*.

Fidalgo de solar—a nobleman with a manor.

Fidecommesso—an entailed property inherited by a designated successor of a family, which could not be sold or partitioned (in Italy); the same as *morgado* and *mayorazgo*.

Hidalgo—literally, the son of someone important in Spain; a nobleman. See *fidalgo*.

Jurado—a citizen responsible for the administration of justice or the exercise of a public job in Spain.

Lacre—see *sealing wax*.

Malagueta—a small fiery red pepper from West Africa.

Mayorazgo—an entailed property inherited by a designated successor of a family, which could not be sold or partitioned (in Spain); the same as *morgado* and *fidecommesso*.

Merchant—"a person whose occupation was to purchase and sell goods or commodities for profit; from the sixteenth century chiefly, it was restricted to wholesale traders, especially

those having dealings with foreign countries" (*Oxford English Dictionary*, https://www
.oed.com/view/Entry/116651, accessed March 15, 2021). In this book, this term is used
for those dealing in exchanges, tax farming, and financial investments. The term "trading
elite" is used interchangeably for stylistic purposes.

Millones—Spanish tax on consumption, particularly wine, vinegar, meat, olive oil, soap, and
candles.

Moradia—the salary for noblemen registered in the royal books as receiving rewards for
services to the king, and these were transformed into interest for the recipients' heirs.

Morgado—an entailed property inherited by a designated successor of a family, which could
not be sold or partitioned. In Spain, *mayorazgo*; in Italy, *fidecommesso*.

New Christians—Jews forced to convert to Catholicism from 1391 to 1497 in Iberia, whose
descendants were subject to the discriminatory blood purity statutes. See *converso*.

Quintal—a measure of weight in Portugal; 1 quintal = 4 arrobas, each weighing 14.7 kg =
58.8 kg.

Sealing wax—a composition containing shellac, rosin, turpentine, and vermillion that was
used to receive the impression of seals. It could be used on pottery. In Portuguese, *lacre*.

Sephardi (or Sephardic)—comes from *Sepharad*, meaning "Spain" in medieval Hebrew. It
refers to Jews of Iberian background who lived in Europe and the New World (Kaplan,
Israel, Trivellato).

Sisa—a regular tax based on transactions; equivalent to *alcabala* in Spain.

Tença—a regular payment as a reward for royal service.

Vintena—taxation of one twentieth or 5 percent of value applied to trade with the rivers of
Guinea.

CURRENCIES: EXCHANGE RATES

THERE IS A SIGNIFICANT variation of exchange rates between currencies in time and place. This list merely provides schematic orientation for the reader. The period of reference is the second half of the seventeenth century unless indicated otherwise.

Amsterdam

1 gulden or guilder/florin = 20 stuivers
1 guilder = 1.2 mark (Hamburg)
1 guilder = 1.01 guilder (Brabant)
1 guilder = 1.2 livres tournois (Paris)

Antwerp [1567–1648, Pohl]

1 pond (pound, livre, Pfund) Vlaams = 20 schellingen (sous, schillings) =
    240 groten (deniers, gros)
1 gulden/florin or carolus gulden = 1/6 pond Vlaams = 20 patards
    (stuivers) = 40 groten (gros)
1 pond Vlaams = 6 gulden = 1.5 pond Brabant
1 ducado = 375 maravedis = 120 groten (vlaams) = 1/2 pond Vlaams
1 escudo = 400 maravedis (ca. 1609) = 440 maravedis (after 1609) =
    550 maravedis (after 1642)
1 cruzado = 400 réis = 120 groten
1 écu Philippe = 6 sous = 72 groten
[in line with Goris, who equates ponds with livres of Flanders: in 1546
    43,200 livres of Flandres = 259,000 florins carolus, 1:6]

England

1 pound sterling = 20 shillings = 240 pence (1 shilling = 12 pence)
1 pound sterling = 4.55 ducati (Venice)
1 pound sterling = 10.6 guilders Flemish (Amsterdam)
1 pound sterling = 7.3–8.0 cruzados (Portugal) in the 1680s [Denzel];
    8.3–9.3 in the 18th century [Fisher]
1 pound sterling = 4.7 pesos (Spain)
1 pound sterling = 10.7 guilders (Brabant)

Flanders [1560s–1590s, Parker]

1 florin = 20 patards (1566–1576)

1 ducado = 37 patards (1574)

1 escudo de 10 reales = 40 patards (1574)

10 florins = 1 pound sterling (1570s)

1 scudo d'Italia = 57 patards (1580s)

1 escudo = 59 patards (1580s)

1 écu de France = 60 patards (1580s)

Livorno

1 pezza de otto = 1.1. ducati (Venice) = 1 scudo (Genoa) = 60–75 sous of
   French livre tournois = 2.5 guilders (Dutch) = 600–850 réis = 50–60
   pence (ca. 0.25 pound sterling) [early 18th century, Trivellato]

Portugal

Cruzado: gold coin used as unit of account during the early modern
   period in Portugal.

1 cruzado = 385 reais (later réis) before 1514

   = 400 réis after 1514 [Godinho]

1 cruzado = 1.2–1.7 guilders (Amsterdam) [Denzel indicates
   1 cruzado = 1.75 guilders for 1661; his series starts in 1680]

1 cruzado = 0.8 soldi (Genoa)

1 cruzado = 0.8 scudi di marche (in the 1590s)

1 cruzado = 0.59 ducati (Venice; late 17th century)

1 cruzado = 0.33 scudi d'oro (Rome; late 17th century)

Spain

Doblón: gold coin with the value of 2 escudos or 6.75 grams of gold;
   doblón de a quatro = 32 reales, 13.5 grams of gold; doblón de a
   ocho = 8 escudos, 27 grams of gold

Ducados: gold coin (3.6 grams) used as one of the units of account in
   the sixteenth and seventeenth centuries in Spain.

1 ducado = 11 reales = 375 maravedís = 1 (Portuguese) cruzado (1.1 cruzado after the devaluation of 1631)

1 real = 34 maravedís

Escudo: another gold coin of less value (3.4 grams) than the ducado
   used as a unit of account in the late sixteenth and seventeenth
   century Spain.

1 escudo = 10 reales = 340 maravedís = 1 (Portuguese) cruzado (after
   the devaluation of 1631)

Peso: known as *real de a ocho* or Spanish dollar, began to be coined in sixteenth century Mexico and Peru; it had a significant diffusion in colonial Americas; in the 18th century, it became a currency standard for
the international economy [Irigoin].

1 ducado = 1.375 pesos (or reales de a ocho) [Boyajian]

1 peso = 0.9 cruzados [Boyajian]

Venice

1 ducato = 200 soldi

1 ducato = 0.22 pound sterling (England)

1 ducato = 1 écu d'or (Lyon)

1 ducato = 1 pezza da otto reali (Livorno)

1 ducato = 0.56 scudi d'oro (Roma)

1 ducato = 2.4 guilders Flemish (Amsterdam)

1 ducato = 2.9 marks (Hamburg)

Bibliography for Currencies

Boyajian, James C. *Portuguese Trade in Asia under the Habsburgs, 1580–1640*. Baltimore:
    Johns Hopkins University Press, 1993, esp. p. xvii; not all exchange rates are acceptable.
Denzel, Markus A. *Handbook of World Exchange Rates, 1590–1914*. London: Routledge, 2016.
    This is the main source for my estimates.
Fisher, H. E. S. *The Portugal Trade. A Study of Anglo-Portuguese Commerce 1700–1770*. London:
    Methuen, 1971.
Godinho, Vitorino Magalhães. *Os descobrimentos e a economia mundial*, 2nd ed., 4 vols.
    Lisbon: Presença, 1989.
Goris, J. A. *Étude sur les colonies marchandes méridionales (portugais, espagnols, italiens) à
    Anvers de 1488 à 1567*. Louvain: Librairie Universitaire, 1925, esp. p. 381.
Irigoin, Alejandra. "Rise and Demise of the Global Silver Standard." In *Handbook of the His-
    tory of Money and Currency*, edited by Stefano Battilossi, Youssef Cassis, Kazuhiko Yago,
    383–410. Singapore: Springer, 2020.
Parker, Geoffrey. *The Army of Flanders and the Spanish Road 1567–1659*. Cambridge:
    Cambridge University Press, 1972.
Pohl, Hans. *Die Portugiesen in Antwerpen (1567–1648)*. Wiesbaden: Franz Steiner, 1977,
    esp. p. 372.
Trivellato, Francesca, *The Familiarity of Strangers. The Sephardic Diapora, Livorno, and
    Cross-Cultural Trade in the Early Modern Period*. New Haven, CT: Yale University Press,
    2009, esp. p. xi.

ACKNOWLEDGMENTS

THIS BOOK would not have been possible without the award of a Leverhulme Major Fellowship for 2017–2019, which created the conditions for sustained research in different countries, and without the sabbatical leave granted by King's College London in 2020–2021, which allowed me to complete the manuscript. I should like to highlight the support I received from my colleagues at King's College London. King's also provided financial support for manuscript revision, illustrations copyrights, and index creation.

I am extremely grateful to Cátia Antunes, Ana Isabel López-Salazar Codes, José Pedro Paiva, Claude Stuczynski, and Francesca Trivellato, who generously agreed to read and comment on parts of the manuscript. I also benefitted from the comments of the anonymous readers who reviewed the manuscript for the publisher, particularly Stuart Schwartz and Simon Ditchfield, who disclosed their contribution. Any remaining mistakes are certainly mine, but the readers' comments were invaluable in making the book coherent. Ben Tate, senior editor at Princeton University Press, has been extremely supportive; his vision played a role in this project. Dimitri Karetnikov guaranteed the drawing of maps and genealogies, which are so important in this book.

The symposium *Of Blood and Milk. Race and Religion in the Late Medieval and Early Modern Iberian Worlds*, organised by Mercedes García-Arenal in February 2019 in Madrid, was crucial to testing the main argument of this book. I enjoyed a very good exchanges of ideas with her, Fernando Bouza, Fernando Marías, David Nirenberg, Stefania Pastore, Felipe Pereda, Jean-Frédéric Schaub, among other colleagues and friends. The conference of the Society for Sephardic Studies, *Sephardi Jews between the Mediterranean Sea and the Atlantic Ocean*, organised by José Alberto Tavim in June 2019 in Lisbon, allowed me to meet young colleagues and renew old connections. The symposium on *Purity of Blood. The Iberian World in Comparative Perspective* that I organised in London in December 2019 also created a stimulating reflection on these issues. I remember exchanges with Miriam Bodian, the late and much missed Trevor Dadson, John Edwards, João Figueirôa-Rego, Chloe Ireton, Giuseppe Marcocci, and Fernanda Olival. In Rome, I had the support of Ana Paula Lloyd, who knows well the intricacies of local archives, and I was very well received by Maria Antonietta Visceglia. I recall excellent conversations with her, Irene Fosi, and Marina Caffiero. I also benefitted from student feedback in my modules on World History: Power and Inequality; The Inquisition in the World: Racism and Minorities; and on European Expansion: Civil Rights and Ethnic Prejudices, at King's College London. Unfortunately, several lectures and seminar sessions in London, Oxford, Madrid, and Rome were cancelled as a result of the COVID-19 pandemic.

I received excellent support in the eighteen archives and libraries' manuscript sections I consulted for this work. I wish especially to thank rector Dr. Mariano Sanz González at the Biblioteca de la Iglesia Nacional Española in Rome; rector Agostinho da Costa Borges and Francisco de Almeida Dias at the Biblioteca do Instituto de Santo António dos Portugueses in Rome; Danielle Ponzioni at the Archivio della Congregazione per la Dottrina della Fede; Daniella Ronzitti at the Archivio Storico Capitolino; Riccardo Gandolfi at the Archivio di Stato di Roma; Eleanora Costantino at the Archivio Storico della Banca d'Italia; Michel Oosterbosch at the Rijksarchief Antwerpen-Beveren; and director João Silvestre and Odete Martins at the Arquivo Nacional da Torre do Tombo. The generous and efficient digitalization service at the national archives of Portugal and at the Biblioteca Nacional de Portugal has been invaluable. I revised the manuscript at the Wissenschaftskolleg zu Berlin. I thank the extraordinary support of the librarians, particularly Anja Brockmann.

My research began with two long and very useful conversations with José Alberto Tavim and Leonor Freire Costa in Lisbon. They put me on the right track. My reflections on literature were improved by conversations with Helder Macedo. Susana Münch Miranda and João Paulo Salvado helped me to better understand currencies. Luiz Felipe de Alencastro, Liam Brockey, Joaquim Caetano, Nuno Camarinhas, Isabel Cluny, Denis Crouzet, Diogo Ramada Curto, Ramiro Gonçalves, Thiago Krause, José Mantas, Margarida Marques, Peter Mason, the late and much missed Joe McDermott, Federico Palomo, Helen Pfeifer, Daniel Strum, Maria de Lurdes Rosa, Walter Rossa, the late and much-missed Robert Rowland, João Paulo Silvestre, Conceição Borges de Sousa, Vítor Serrão, and Bartolomé Yun-Casalilla gave me good bibliographical indications and information. José Manuel Díaz Blanco generously offered to photograph several paintings and sculptures at the Cathedral of Seville. I am grateful to Helen Hancock for providing a reliable, competent, and involved revision of my manuscript.

This book was mostly written during lockdown. I would have been unable to continue without the love and support of my family. My wife, Ulinka, as usual, asked me the most challenging questions. The fact that we were simultaneously completing our new books helped a great deal. Our children, João and Sophie, are now at the university and finding their own way. They have a strong sense of the importance of human rights, and it is to them that I dedicate this book about historical forms of oppression and the resistance of a minority.

INDEX

Page numbers in *italics* indicate illustrations.

Maynard (English consul), 543n82
mayorazgo, 171, 174, 221, 551
Medeiros, Domingos de, 256
Medeiros, Manuel de, 125
medical, scientific, and scholarly contributions, 184–87, 468
Medici, Caterina de', 160, 164
Medici, Cosimo I de', 128
Medici, Ferdinando I de, 161
Medici, Rafaello, 160
Medici family, 142, 166, 525n149
Medicis, Marie de, 187
Medicus-Politicus (Rodrigo de Castro), 187
Medina, Bartolomé de, 189
Medina, David de, 354
Medina, Domingos Baltanás, 189
Medina, Gabriel de, 353, 354, 364, 365–66, 427
Medina, Gabriel Luis de, 432
Medina, Joseph de, 353
Medina, Manuel Martim, 339
Medina, Rafael Luis de, 432
Medina, Solomon, 353
Medina, Solomon de, 418, 544n107
Medina d'Azevedo, Ester de, 418
Medina del Campo fair, 45, 55, 172
Medina family, 55
Medrano, Antonio de, 87
Fr. Melchor, 87
Mello, Evaldo Cabral de, 272–73
Melo, David Abenatia, 293
Melo, Fernão Álvares (David Abenatar Melo), 290–91, 303, 474n56
Melo, Francisco Manuel de, 234
Melo, Henrique de, 54
Melo, Manuel Pereira de, 536n66
Melo, Martim Afonso de, 347, 360
Memorial sobre la nobleza (1632), 242–43
Mena, Francisco de, 56
Menasseh ben Israel, 251
Mendes, Álvaro, 125–28, 133, 515n26
Mendes, Ana (later Reina), 53, 71–72
Mendes, André, 388
Mendes, António Vaz, 261–62
Mendes, Beatriz (Beatriz de Luna; later Gracia Nasi), 53, 70–72
Mendes, Beatriz (daughter of Diogo Mendes and Brianda de Luna), 71
Mendes, Bendana, 133
Mendes, Clara, 404
Mendes, Diogo, 54, 68, 69, 71, 72, 73

Mendes, Fernando, 354
Mendes, Fernando (Daniel Ferro), 132
Mendes, Filipa, 72
Mendes, Francisco, 47, 52, 53–55, 70–72, 284, 484n85, 488n42
Mendes, Francisco Lopes, 388
Mendes, Gabriel, 277
Mendes, Gonçalo, 47, 71
Mendes, Gregório, 286
Mendes, Heitor, 119, 130–31, 133, 134, 135, 153, 202, 339
Mendes, Isabel, 339
Mendes, Jorge Francisco, 131, 133
Mendes, Luís, 130
Mendes, Mateus, 337
Mendes Bravo, Heitor, 138
Mendes Brito, Francisco Dias, 328–29
Mendes da Costa, Diogo, 432
Mendes de Almeida, António, 284, 337, 353
Mendes de Almeida, Simão, 284, 353
Mendes de Brito, Ana, 328
Mendes de Brito, Diogo, 256
Mendes de Brito, Fernão Dias (Abraham Abendana), 138
Mendes de Brito, Fernão Dias (David Abendana), 349
Mendes de Brito, Francisco Dias, 256
Mendes de Brito, Heitor (*see also* Heitor Mendes), 118–19, 138, 198, 220, 229, 328, 349
Mendes de Crasto, Francisco, 431–32
Mendes de Vasconcelos, Álvaro, 150
Mendes de Vasconcelos, Luís, 116, 150
Mendes family, 53, 68–72, 75
Mendes Henriques family, 341
Mendez de Acuña, Manuel, 272
Mendez Enríquez, Luis, 270
Mendonça, Afonso Furtado de, 510n1
Mendonça, Isabel de, 347
Mendonça, Isabel Noronha de, 160
Mendonça, Maria de, 347
Mendoza Dukes of Infantado, 88
Mendoza y Bobadilla, Francisco de (cardinal), 190
Menéndez Pelayo, 95
Meneses, Cristóvão Pereira de, 442
Meneses, Diogo de, 282
Meneses, Francisco de, 224
Meneses, Francisco de Sá de, 220
Meneses, Manuel de Magalhães de, 388
Meneses, Rodrigo de, 360, 373

A NOTE ON THE TYPE

THIS BOOK has been composed in Miller, a Scotch Roman typeface designed by Matthew Carter and first released by Font Bureau in 1997. It resembles Monticello, the typeface developed for The Papers of Thomas Jefferson in the 1940s by C. H. Griffith and P. J. Conkwright and reinterpreted in digital form by Carter in 2003.

Pleasant Jefferson ("P. J.") Conkwright (1905–1986) was Typographer at Princeton University Press from 1939 to 1970. He was an acclaimed book designer and AIGA Medalist.

The ornament used throughout this book was designed by Pierre Simon Fournier (1712–1768) and was a favorite of Conkwright's, used in his design of the *Princeton University Library Chronicle*.